T0348570

COMPUTER-GRAPHIC FACIAL RECONSTRUCTION

COMPUTER-GRAPHIC FACIAL RECONSTRUCTION

John G. Clement
Centre for Human Identification, Victorian Institute of Forensic Medicine, and School of Dental Science, University of Melbourne, Australia

and

Murray K. Marks
Department of Anthropology, University of Tennessee, and Department of Pathology, University of Tennessee Medical Center, USA

ELSEVIER
ACADEMIC PRESS

Amsterdam • Boston • Heidelberg • London • New York • Oxford
Paris • San Diego • San Francisco • Singapore • Sydney • Tokyo

This book is printed on acid-free paper

Elsevier Academic Press
30 Corporate Drive, Suite 400, Burlington, MA 01803, USA
http://www.elsevier.com

Elsevier Academic Press
84 Theobald's Road, London WC1X 8RR, UK
http://www.elsevier.com

Library of Congress Catalog Number: 2005921118

British Library Cataloguing in Publication Data
A catalogue record for this book is available from the British Library

ISBN 0-12-473051-5

Acquisitions Editor: *Mark Listewnik*
Associate Acquisitions Editor: *Jennifer Soucy*
Developmental Editor: *Pamela Chester*
Marketing Manager: *Christian Nolin*
Cover Designer: *Eric DeCicco*

CONTENTS

FOREWORD

> It is the common wonder of all men, how among so many millions of faces, there should be none alike
>
> Thomas Browne, *Religio Medici*

The Roman philosopher Cicero said that "everything is in the face", and truly the human face is a complex, multifunctional part of our anatomy which tells the world, who we are and what we are feeling both emotionally and physically, as well as performing a number of essential physiological functions. We all have to live with our own face and with how others perceive us through its appearance. It can effect our self esteem and if we are unhappy with it we may try to alter it.

Its physical appearance and its perception by others act together powerfully to set us a real challenge in identifying an individual. This is particularly so when we try to reconstruct a face from a skull of unknown provenance. We start with the not insignificant difficulty of trying to achieve a recognition from an acquaintance of the deceased, when we have no idea who the person was to begin with or how they were remembered during life – were they happy and smiling, sad or angry? Did they have a condition which in some way characterized their facial appearance – we know that chronic pain or severe mental disorders such as schizophrenia can significantly alter facial affect in a person. Nevertheless, despite these obstacles, identifying an individual from their facial appearance remains a fascinating challenge for us worthy of serious academic study and development.

I am also mindful that facial identification, in this day and age, is an important tool to be considered both as a primary and secondary characteristic of identity, especially with the need to identify victims of conflicts around the globe that are found in mass graves and also those who have perished from apparently ever increasing natural mass disasters. There has never at any time been a problem of such magnitude needing to be resolved, and the application of different facial identification techniques may in many instances be of significant assistance.

I am delighted that John Clement and Murray Marks have assembled a text covering all the important elements of the field and with such a distinguished group of contributors, thus bringing this complex subject into the 21st century.

Together with all the high tech electronic advances which are indeed an essential cornerstone to important developments in the field, the authors are always mindful of the basic principles that underpin good science and high quality work. They remind us that there is no substitute for knowing how to accurately assess the anthropology and morphology of the face and the psychological parameters which inform our understanding of how we recognize each other. It is gratifying to see therefore that the need for the continuing use of traditional techniques is recognized.

Those of us involved in facial identification through reconstruction, should always be mindful of what is meant by "a successful reconstruction". It is not just about whether the new face is recognized. Indeed, there are many factors which can act together to make recognition difficult, if not impossible. Hence the most physically accurate reconstruction may be deemed a "failure". Conversely, some of the crudest attempts at reconstruction may succeed, even though the final reconstructed image does not resemble the identified person. This may be the case if the population is small and well defined with only a small number of known missing persons.

In spite of these inherent difficulties, it is essential that we always strive through scientific endeavour to improve the accuracy of the reconstructed face to achieve a good "likeness" with the person during life. I am delighted to see that this text is aiming precisely to achieve just that.

Peter Vanezis
Head of Forensic Medical Services
Forensic Science Service
UK

PREFACE

This book grew out of the FBI's 2000 International Association for Craniofacial Identification meeting, held in Washington, DC. The editors agreed to cooperate on a project that would gather the research results presented there. Four years later, as this book goes to press, research in the field of computer-graphic facial reconstruction and related areas has progressed considerably, as the variety of contributions included here testifies.

The volume is organized in four sections that discuss the current state of forensic reconstructive facial anatomy, conceptual modeling of computer-based reconstruction and their practical applications, psychological perception of facial recognition, and practical applications of facial morphometric comparisons for proof of identity.

Clement and Marks introduce the scope of the work in Chapter 1 by underscoring the anatomical and anthropological issues requiring attention by those striving to develop and employ modern computer-based methods to augment, improve, or supplant the more traditional methods for restoring a likeness upon skeletal remains in a legal or medical context.

Chapter 2, by Quatrehomme and Subsol, covers the classical approach to facial reconstruction, setting up the historical context for the material that follows.

Taylor and Craig in Chapter 3 describe the pre-reconstructive techniques necessary for the anatomical and anthropological interpretation of the skull. They demonstrate a traditional clay-based reconstruction method that provides the baseline for computer enhancement by a police artist and a comparative reference for other recent advances described in other chapters.

In Chapter 4 Thomas's "3D quantification of facial shape" critically emphasizes the need for landmark definitions and how to discern biological distance between skulls or faces or the morphological differences between reconstructions. This chapter stresses measurement and underscores the necessity in selecting the most appropriate method for the specific research question posed.

Subsol describes in Chapter 5 an automated system for 3D facial reconstruction using feature-based registration of a reference head and provides practical examples that promise to make this reconstruction process faster, more flexible, and less subjective.

Stephan and co-workers in Chapter 6 describe "average" 2D computer-generated human facial morphology and how information gleaned from these approximations should relax reliance upon the subjective information routinely used in many forensic reconstructions/approximations.

Vargas and his co-author Sucar describe in Chapter 7 their ongoing research that applies Bayesian "artificial intelligence" networks and computer graphics to forensics and anthropometry of the head and face. Their system attempts to predict facial features from skeletal. This technique is also highly relevant to corrective plastic surgery.

Tu and co-workers detail in Chapter 8 a computer graphic morphing technique using principal components analysis for generating a 3D model of a head/face from clinical CT scans of flesh depth data. This statistical treatment allows appreciation for the inherent soft tissue variation from subject to subject.

Subke describes the application of CAD/CAM engineering tools in Chapter 9 to reconstruct fragmented skulls by rearticulating images of the scanned fragments in an electronic environment. This provides an entry point for other programs predicting shape and form of overlaying facial tissues.

Davy and co-workers describe in Chapter 10 a computer-based method that faithfully emulates manual forensic sculpting. It emphasizes that such reconstructions can be attained more easily than using craft-based techniques with options for deconstruction, backtracking, and then reconstruction, while saving previous versions. Their methods aim to provide the most reliable, expeditious, and accurate reconstructions as possible without all the steps currently used in clay modeling.

In Chapter 11 Stephan and co-workers explore the recognition limits of 2D facial approximations constructed using averages. Recognition tests, based upon warping average facial color and texture on the exact face shape of specific individuals resulted in low success rates. These conditions provided observers with a more accurate representation of the individual than was possible to infer from the skull and such recognition rates for traditional clay-based reconstructions were much lower.

In Chapter 12 Kusnoto and co-workers have developed a non-invasive, economical and reliable method for measuring facial soft tissue thickness using 3D finite-element modeling from photographic and radiographic data using radio-opaque markers situated on anatomical landmarks.

Senn and Brumit describe in Chapter 13 a computer-aided dental identification method for use in a forensic setting. This system attempts to move from unverifiable subjective observations to more objective techniques for establishing identity from orofacial characteristics.

In Chapter 14 Rakover explores two methodologies in memory research entitled "explanation-testing" and "reconstruction" which critiques face recognition research and anatomical reconstruction of appearance in a forensic context that incorporate cognitive and computational models applied to facial perception.

Hill in Chapter 15 uses laser scans of faces to address perception issues. This chapter specifically describes how topography and the role of shape can be separated from the effects of other cues used in recognition. Important findings emphasize the role of the average face and movement in discriminating identity.

Shaweesh and co-workers use comparative non-contact surface measurements of young Japanese and Australian adults in Chapter 16 to create average 3D faces. Different measurement methods are illustrated and electronic hybrids with differing proportions from each ethnic group are created that could form the basis for threshold testing in series recognition experiments.

Kuratate in Chapter 17 describes the creation of perceptibly accurate 3D talking head animations from only profile and frontal photographs. This is achieved by transferring face motion from one subject to another and by extracting a small set of feature points common to both photographs and using a small set of principal components to build the facial image on which movements are displayed.

Yoshino describes in Chapter 18 a Japanese system for the morphological comparison between 3D facial scans and potential 2D image matches obtained from surveillance videos during commission of a crime. Comparison of facial outlines and anatomical landmarks are both employed and threshold values for positive identification are established.

In Chapter 19 Yoshino further develops the system described in Chapter 18 as a new retrieval system for a 3D facial image database. The system automatically adjusts orientation of all 3D images in a database for comparison with the 2D image of the suspect. It then explores the closeness of fit between the two images using graph matching.

As this summary of the contents demonstrates, this book offers a snapshot of the current state of the field. We hope that it will serve as a stimulus to further research and discussion of the rich complexities of facial reconstruction in all its facets.

John G. Clement
Murray K. Marks
October 2004

In addition to thanking all the contributors for their patience and fortitude during the gestation of this book, I should like to acknowledge the contributions of David Thomas, Sherie Blackwell and Diana Zeppieri, all of the Oral Anatomy, Medicine and Surgery Unit in the School of Dental Science at the University of Melbourne, who made extraordinary additional and unacknowledged efforts to see this work come to fruition.

J.G.C.

I would like to thank the contributors for so eloquently putting their research interests into words and images. I would also like to thank Academic Press/Elsevier, especially Nick Fallon, who originally allowed the notion of a volume on this topic to materialize, Mark Listewnik and Pam Chester for incredible patience and tolerance and Renata Corbani for systematically tidying up the loose ends.

M.K.M.

ABOUT THE EDITORS

John G. Clement is Professor and Inaugural Chair in Forensic Odontology, School of Dental Science, University of Melbourne, Australia. He is also Director of the Victorian Institute's newly formed Centre for Human Identification, a multidisciplinary core group with overarching responsibilities for mitigating the impact of crime and terrorism throughout the region of the Western Pacific rim and SE Asia. He is past President of both the UK and Australian societies of forensic odontology (BAFO and ASFD) and a founder member of the International Dental Ethics and Law Society (IDEALS) and the International Association for Craniofacial Identification (IACI). He has assisted in identification of remains after the tsunami of December 2004, has served on an expert advisory panel to the International Committee of the Red Cross's "The Missing" project dealing with such situations as Iraq and former Yugoslavia, and is a member of the Scientific Steering Committee on Forensic Science Programs to the International Commission on Missing Persons (ICMP).

Murray K. Marks is an Associate Professor, Department of Anthropology, University of Tennessee (USA), Associate Director of the Forensic Anthropology Center, and Associate Professor, Department of Pathology, University of Tennessee Medical Center. He is a Diplomate and Board Member of the American Board of Forensic Anthropology and Special Consultant to the Tennessee Bureau of Investigation. He is course director of the Forensic Anthropology Center's annual Human Remains Recovery School for the Federal Bureau of Investigation and on faculty in the university's National Forensic Academy, a training program designed for law enforcement agencies.

Abdalmajeid Alyassin
GE Global Research Center, 1 Research Circle, Niskayuna, New York 12309, USA

Paula Brumit
Center for Education and Research in Forensics, University of Texas Health Science Center at San Antonio Dental School, 7703 Floyd Curl Drive – Mail Code 7919, San Antonio, Texas 78229-3900, USA

John G. Clement (co-Editor)
Centre for Human Identification, Victorian Institute of Forensic Medicine, and School of Dental Science, University of Melbourne, Victoria 3010, Australia

Pamela Craig
School of Dental Science, University of Melbourne, Victoria 3010, Australia

Stephanie L. Davy
Research Centre for Human Identification, School of Medicine, University of Sheffield, Beech Hill Rd, Sheffield S10 2RX, UK

C. A. Evans
Department of Orthodontics, University of Illinois at Chicago, Chicago, Illinois 60612, USA

Martin P. Evison
Research Centre for Human Identification, School of Medicine, University of Sheffield, Beech Hill Rd, Sheffield S10 2RX, UK

Timothy Gilbert
Aims Solutions Ltd., Unit 3, Stoney Rd, Nottingham NG1 1LG, UK

Rajiv Gupta
GE Global Research Center, 1 Research Circle, Niskayuna, New York 12309, USA

Richard I. Hartley
GE Global Research Center, 1 Research Circle, Niskayuna, New York 12309, USA

Linda Heier
Department of Radiology, Weill Medical College, Cornell University, Ithaca, New York 14853, USA

Maciej Henneberg
Department of Anatomical Sciences, University of Adelaide, Australia, 5005

Harold Hill
ATR Human Information Science Labs, Keihanna Science City, Kyoto 619-0288, Japan

Takaaki Kuratate
ATR Human Information Science Labs, Keihanna Science City, Kyoto 619-0288, Japan

B. Kusnoto
Department of Orthodontics, University of Illinois at Chicago, Chicago, Illinois 60612, USA

William E. Lorensen
GE Global Research Center, 1 Research Circle, Niskayuna, New York 12309, USA

Murray K. Marks (co-Editor)
Department of Anthropology, University of Tennessee, and Department of Pathology, University of Tennessee Medical Center, USA

Ian S. Penton-Voak
Department of Experimental Psychology, University of Bristol BS8 1TN, UK

David I. Perrett
School of Psychology, University of St. Andrews, Scotland KY16 9JU

S. Poernomo
Department of Forensic Science, Medical and Dental Division of Bhayangkara Police Headquarters, Ujung Pandang, Indonesia

Gérald Quatrehomme
Laboratoire de Médecine Légale et Anthropologie médico-légale, Faculté de Médecine, Avenue de Valombrose, 06107 Nice cedex 2, France

Sam S. Rakover
Department of Psychology, Haifa University, Haifa 31905, Israel

P. Sahelangi
Department of Forensic Science, Medical and Dental Division of Bhayangkara Police Headquarters, Ujung Pandang, Indonesia

Damian Schofield
School of Computer Science and IT, University of Nottingham, University Park, Nottingham NG7 2RD, UK

David R. Senn
Center for Education and Research in Forensics, University of Texas Health Science Center at San Antonio Dental School, 7703 Floyd Curl Drive – Mail Code 7919, San Antonio, Texas 78229-3900, USA

Ashraf I. Shaweesh
School of Dental Science, University of Melbourne, Victoria 3010, Australia and Jordan University of Science and Technology, Jordan

Carl N. Stephan
Department of Anatomical Sciences, University of Adelaide, Australia, 5005 and School of Dental Science, University of Melbourne, Victoria 3010, Australia

Joerg Subke
Department of Clinical and Medical Engineering, Environmental Engineering, and Biotechnology, University of Applied Sciences Giessen-Friedberg, Wiesenstr. 14, D-35390 Giessen, Germany

Gérard Subsol
FOVEA Project* and Intrasense, Cap Oméga – CS 39521 Rond Point Benjamin Franklin, 34960 Montpellier cedex 2, France

Luis Enrique Sucar
ITESM Campus Morelos, Paseo de la Reforma 182-A, Cuernavaca, Morelos, Mexico

Ronn Taylor
School of Dental Science, University of Melbourne, Victoria 3010, Australia

C. David L. Thomas
School of Dental Science, University of Melbourne, Victoria 3010, Australia

Bernard P. Tiddeman
School of Computer Science, University of St. Andrews, Scotland KY16 9SS

Peter Tu
GE Global Research Center, 1 Research Circle, Niskayuna, New York 12309, USA

---

*http://foveaproject.free.fr

Juan E. Vargas
Department of Computer Science and Engineering, University of South Carolina, Columbia, South Carolina, USA

Eric Vatikiotis-Bateson
Department of Linguistics, University of British Columbia, Vancouver, BC, Canada and ATR Human Information Science Labs, Keihanna Science City, Kyoto 619-0288, Japan

Hani Camille Yehia
Department of Electronic Engineering, Universidade Federal de Minas Gerais, Belo Horizonte, Brazil

Mineo Yoshino
First Forensic Science Division, National Research Institute of Police Science, 6-3-1, Kashiwanoha, Kashiwa, Chiba 277-0882, Japan

PART I

HISTORY AND BACKGROUND

CHAPTER 1

INTRODUCTION TO FACIAL RECONSTRUCTION

John G. Clement

Centre for Human Identification, Victorian Institute of Forensic Medicine, and School of Dental Science, University of Melbourne, Victoria 3010, Australia

Murray K. Marks

Department of Anthropology, University of Tennessee, and Department of Pathology, University of Tennessee Medical Center, USA

1.1 BACKGROUND

Facial reconstruction or approximation has evolved from different origins, some not scientific. Within the scientific arena, however, the main stimuli for research design have sprung from the forensic need to identify victims or suspects and in other fields, such as craniofacial orthopedics, from the need to improve pre-operative surgical planning substantially. The theoretical underpinning for both trajectories is derived from academic human anatomy. While each trajectory has disparate, though equally rich, histories, both fields have similar end-points; they both require precision and accuracy in the final predictive result. This is essential for success, especially given the burgeoning advancement in research where expression of genotype can be compared with the phenotype—a topic discussed in more detail below.

At the 2000 International Association for Craniofacial Identification meeting in Washington, DC, hosted by the Federal Bureau of Investigation, the authors were impressed not only by the breadth of the clinical, academic, and forensic interests of the participants, but also by the quality of their research. Consequently, we have been encouraged to produce a single volume that would encapsulate the current state-of-the-art research in the computer-graphic approximation of faces and in highly pertinent closely related subjects which need to be taken into consideration for the results of approximations to be interpreted appropriately and in the correct context.

1.2 UNITING MICRO- AND MACROMORPHOLOGICAL THEMES

The new millennium has witnessed a renewed interest in the scientific description of human shape and form. During the second half of the preceding century, purely descriptive anatomy was thought to have already passed its zenith and was considered to be in a slow but inexorable decline. The previous emphasis on macromorphology was unfashionably redundant in the face of newer immunohistochemical developments that permitted the precise localization of active enzymes, specific proteins, and cellular end-products within tissues. Additionally, this "scientific" revolution was, in part, fueled by the development and equally rapid deployment of electron microscopy as a clinical and academic research tool. The traditional emphasis on macromorphology became a casualty of the new opportunities presented by the latest ultrastructural analyses. These advances have in turn recently been overshadowed by an even larger explosion in the newly discovered techniques in molecular biology. In concert, these technical and theoretical discoveries have allowed the precise mapping of the genes within the DNA molecule which control the internal cellular processes that had previously been revealed by histochemistry.

However, after a period of scientific fervor probably unparalleled in human history epitomized by the mapping of the human genome, there came a growing realization that, while knowledge at the genotypic molecular level was growing exponentially, studies of equivalent sophistication (and relevance) of the resulting phenotype were subsequently lagging. This intellectual and applied "asymmetry" was so severe that it began to impede a thorough interpretation of many molecular discoveries and even threatened the conceptualization of future strategies within the molecular disciplines. In short, if one could not qualify or quantify the effects of genetic discoveries at the organ and animal level, the real potential of any such discoveries would never be fully understood or exploited. Fortunately, the conjunction of several emerging technologies, all heavily reliant upon the greatly increased capacity of ever-cheaper and more ubiquitous computers, permitted a re-evaluation of the place of macromorphological studies in modern biology and medicine. In the last decade the result has been little short of a renaissance, as evidenced by some new academic perspectives reuniting these two recently diverging conceptual frameworks and signaling that the possibilities for conducting macromorphometric analyses using genotypic guidelines are not inconceivable (see O'Higgins and Cohn 2000).

While most medical schools in prosperous, modern, urbanized societies today devote less curriculum time to gross, regional, or topographical anatomy (particularly dissection), there has been a corresponding and compensatory increased reliance upon modern, noninvasive diagnostic imaging to provide students with a realistic three-dimensional (3D) representation of the patient's anatomy. Imaging modalities range from sonography, through computerized x-ray tomography and magnetic resonance imaging, to positron-emission tomography. Each technology has its own strengths and weaknesses for imaging particular substrates, defined by the fundamental physics employed in each technique. The 3D appreciation of structure has also been accompanied by a capacity to measure in 3D space. This advance has not been restricted to simple euclidean distances between arbitrary anatomical landmarks; but by the use of thresholding and other image-processing techniques, surface-area and volume measurements of organs and tissues are now routine procedures.

Another major advance in recent times, also dependent upon advances in computer technology, has been greatly increased capacity for noncontact surface measurements. This can be achieved using a variety of methods, for example, laser scanning, stereophotogrammetry, or optical scanning using grating systems that reveal topography. Laser scanning of faces is rapidly becoming redundant because of the reluctance of ethics committees to sanction the use of lasers near the eyes of participants and because laser scanners, using monochromatic coherent light, can only record surface topography and not texture or color information from the skin. Furthermore, other optical techniques are usually faster, which is important when subject compliance is poor, as with some children and the intellectually compromised.

Capitalizing on recent technical advances in 3D facial mapping the groundbreaking work of Shaweesh *et al.* (2004) (see also Chapter 16 in this volume) clearly demonstrates that quantitative 3D analyses of human faces hold the potential to discriminate between populations with differing average morphologies. Each ethnic group can be considered analogous to a facial "syndrome". Hammond *et al.* (2004) studying children with craniofacial dysmorphic syndromes have aptly demonstrated that automated, quantitative, 3D morphological screening can provide a reliable initial diagnosis in many cases. In the future such screening can then be used as a precursor to further biochemical or molecular testing to confirm the diagnosis. This will be of great assistance to less experienced clinicians who currently struggle to make a gestalt diagnosis. Such a nexus between genetic and quantitative morphological research has enormous power, each approach having the potential to inform and amplify the value of the other.

Perhaps the most exciting possibility for the future in identification science is to consider such recent advances in our ability to check phenotype against genotype and the reverse. At the beginning of this volume we need to ask whether it will ever be possible to infer sufficient features from a person's DNA to predict their physical appearance; and, if so, to what degree and with how much certainty. Such ideas are obviously contentious, particularly where societies are often guilty of "demonizing" particular ethnic groups within their midst, frequently attributing the bulk of street crime and petty theft to persons with a certain type of appearance, often despite factual evidence to the contrary.

1.3 FORENSIC IMPERATIVES

The success of medico-legal investigations of death in the past decade result, in part, from methodological developments within many research domains of forensic science. However, the recent marked increase in the popularity of all things "forensic" is also peripherally responsible for an active media feeding the public's fixation on a "mystery" and society's innate morbid curiosity. A symbiotic relationship flourishes between the media, science, the medico-legal community, and the public that synergistically promotes research progress on many fronts. Add to this mixture a recent burgeoning influx of funding from many governments around the world in attempts to combat a heightened vulnerability to terrorism, and there exists a fertile environment for development and deployment of many cutting-edge techniques in the forensic sciences.

Determination of cause and manner of death and estimation of time since death are the main duties of forensic pathology. Additionally, exhaustive attempts often have to be made to identify the deceased. In many criminal cases identification of the victim is often a mandatory prerequisite to any attempt to build a case for the prosecution. Even when the legal case doesn't mandate this procedure, it is still a very important part of the overall investigative process. When identification becomes impossible (or improbable) because the traditional means of visual, dermatoglyphic, or radiographic analyses cannot be applied, reliance on facial approximation techniques may be the only remaining option for the investigator. This exercise has a long history, originating outside the forensic area where it now finds frequent application through a variety of similar and overlapping methods (see İşcan and Helmer 1993, Prag and Neave 1998, Taylor 2001, Miyasaka 1999, Wilkinson 2004, and Taylor and Craig in this volume).

The editors of this volume both come from anatomical and anthropological backgrounds steeped in the forensic sciences, where the techniques of facial approximation remain controversial and where, even for insiders, hard factual information has been hard to find. It was actually the long-standing, but still urgent, need to understand the relationship of the bone surface to the overlying skin that provided the stimulus for, and some initially naive assumptions about, the scope and content of this work. Consequently, it was initially envisaged that this volume's principal focus would explore this relationship between skull and face in rather concrete terms describing how advances in 3D scanning, computer graphics, and medical imaging would facilitate or recover an accurate reconstruction of the lost anatomical soft tissue features. The assumption was that if only we could reconstruct in a more informed and more accurate manner then recognition rates of the resulting facial reconstructions would also improve from the present lamentably low levels. Of course, as always, the devil lurks in the detail. The "detail" in this case is, of course, the role of "psychological factors" in face recognition.

It quickly became apparent that issues of recognition and perception were special problems where faces were concerned, and so these topics needed to be granted greater emphasis if the predictive models for facial morphology, also included in this book, were to be fully understood and appreciated in the forensic context in which they were to be employed. Psychological factors have a crucial role to play in facial recognition and this cannot be overemphasized at a time when automated search engines are being developed to retrieve plausible matches of surveillance images with known "persons of interest" from 3D databases, to assist investigators and security agencies. Proof of identity is a difficult endeavor, fraught with problems, and needs to be performed rigorously, in a manner enabling audit and review by others (see Yoshino 2004 and Chapter 18 in this volume).

For the identification of the living, we quote Wells *et al.* (1994, p. 229):

> There is no threshold number below which the dangers of false identification are significant and above which they are not.

Moreover, there is the added complex disparity between scientific proof and proof in the legal sense. People other than expert witnesses are typically restricted in their evidence to relating only matters of fact. They are not permitted to express opinions. Paradoxically, this sits rather uneasily with a requirement to "tell the truth, the whole truth, and nothing but the truth"; for when it comes to eyewitness testimony relating to the identification of suspects, they can only offer opinion evidence, and yet the basis of the opinion is not challenged. Witnesses can, and are, accused of having poor eyesight, defective memory, or malicious intentions, but at the same time there is a general acceptance by the courts about their opinions relating to the identity of others and justification for those opinions is not required. This situation has probably arisen for purely pragmatic reasons. If we exclude a handful of unfortunate people with rare types of brain damage, all of us can easily and rapidly recognize and identify family, friends, and workmates by face alone. However, it is much harder for us to describe the faces of the same people in sufficient detail to ensure individuation, unless they have a special unique peculiarity such as a characteristic scar or birthmark.

Some years ago, during a graduate forensic program at the University of Melbourne, four students spent about 2 hours having a tutorial with a well-known emeritus professor. One month later the students were asked to make a facial composite of the professor from memory using the quite advanced computer-based, full-color, facial component system of the local police force. The students found this task most difficult, either singly or together, and by objective criteria the resulting composite compared poorly with the subject whom it purported to describe. Nevertheless, when the composite was shown to other students and staff in the large department where the professor had worked in the recent past, many people still recognized the target individual. Perhaps more importantly, everyone agreed that the composite image could not possibly be anyone else in the building if it were not the target individual. This simple example illustrates several important points: recall of facial characteristics is far from perfect even when exposure to the target individual is conducted under comfortable and nonthreatening conditions over an extended period of time, albeit removed from the immediate past. It also demonstrates that facial reconstructions do not have to be perfect to provoke recollections. Further, as all four students never had any difficulty recognizing the professor since their first meeting in the original tutorial, it also shows that the ability to recognize a person with whom one is familiar usually transcends the ability to describe or visualize them.

Victims or witnesses able to provide accurate descriptions about attackers, robbers, and other criminals are often invited to pick the suspect from a line-up. Ironically, the better the initial verbal description, the narrower the range of choices in the ensuing line-up for the investigators who are required to choose participants that have characteristics in common with the suspect. Actually, this means that the better the witness, the more rigorously they may be challenged. There is the additional concern that asking the witness to verbally describe a suspect may adversely affect their ability to recognize the subject later. If this really is the case, and some of the research is still somewhat contradictory (Schooler and Engst-Schooler 1990, Schooler *et al.* 1996), then those witnesses who can initially clearly verbalize a description of the suspect may later be put at a double disadvantage. The consequences in the reverse situation are obviously potentially equally very serious. Witnesses who can only offer poor descriptions are given wider choices during line-ups and may also make mistakes. There are many cases where suspects have been found guilty on the testimony of a single witness and in a worrying number of those cases the opinions of the witnesses have later shown to be incorrect. Ainsworth (1998) deals very comprehensively with psychology, law, and eyewitness testimony in adversarial legal systems. He cites that almost 30 years ago miscarriages of justice and a number of high-profile wrongful convictions in Britain persuaded the British Home Office to appoint a senior judicial figure to assemble a committee to examine the problem. A milestone report was published almost 30 years ago (Devlin Report 1976) and yet despite its insights into the conflicts between the concrete (and unrealistic) requirements of the courts, the imperfections of the human witness, and the psychological evidence relating to memory and recognition, the most important recommendations have been largely ignored. For this reason, the issues covered in Rakover's chapter here (based in part on his and Cahlon's 2001 book *Face Recognition: Cognitive and Computational Processes*) have become so crucial in issues of recognition and identity.

Of course, it would be quite wrong for morphologists trying to improve methods for reconstruction to take refuge in our uncertainty about just how faces are perceived in order to explain our own current results. Many reconstructive anatomists have looked upon recent opportunities for access to MRI and CT data derived from routine clinical examinations as a golden opportunity to redress the previous dearth of information related to soft-tissue depths at specific anatomic sites of the face. However, it has to be admitted that, despite this additional information, the success rates of facial reconstructions derived from such data are not much better than previously. The problem may lie in the fact that all faces are remarkably similar, and so updating average data for a population does little to help with individualization. We all have a nose in the middle of our faces with an eye on either side and the mouth beneath. Bruce (1988) realized that, no matter how these relationships are studied, the measurable differences still remain small. In turn, she inferred that human beings must be astute at perceiving remarkably subtle differences from face to face. Hence, we may reasonably assert that, if our reconstructions of faces upon skulls are not all to look the same, we need to base our reconstructions upon a meticulous anthropological and anatomical analysis of the particular skeletal remains in order to record any information that is unique or individualizing. Craig and Taylor's chapter in this volume describes how the sites of origin and insertion of muscles can be interpreted to give some understanding of the loads applied at these sites, and from these observations the importance of fine-tuning average anthropological values of soft-tissue thickness appropriate for that region of the face for that particular set of remains can be assessed.

It is difficult to discover the success rates of forensic artists and sculptors judged on the criterion of successful outcomes from appeals to the public to come forward if they recognize the image produced by the artist. There also is a tendency for forensic artists and sculptors to become competitive because past success develops a reputation for their expertise and they are then asked to undertake future work. Unfortunately, this rivalry can obscure the facts where success in casework is concerned. This important area of uncertainty has spawned experiments to explore the "recognizability" of facial reconstructions in laboratory settings. Stefan and Henneberg (2001) have demonstrated that recognition rates for some reconstructions are little better than chance under what must be optimal conditions. This confirms the earlier conclusion of Logie *et al.* (1987) that the chance of the public correctly identifying a person from a facial reconstruction is indeed low, but noting that police persist in using this approach as a tactic of last resort in the identification of otherwise completely unidentifiable remains.

Despite clichés about police ineptitude, homicide-squad detectives are invariably an elite. Generally, they know exactly what tactics they may need to employ to give direction to a stalled investigation. For their purposes (i.e., the public's purpose) reconstructions do not have to be perfect, just similar enough to provoke the possibility of a recollection. This notion, validated by recent research, has been hard learned for many forensic reconstructionists with "failure to identify" seemingly attributed to certain anatomies "not polished enough". Furthermore, it must be borne in mind that success rates cited by successful forensic artists need to be examined in the context of the additional information circulated about the deceased. The skeleton may be that of a victim from the nonmajority ethnic group, of an age not typically targeted, perhaps having been found with specific clothing or jewelry, or the remains may carry evidence of past medical interventions such as treated fractures, orthopedic prostheses, or unusual dental treatment. Haglund (1998) has demonstrated that the timing, style, and choreography of publicity also has an important reinforcing or detracting role to play depending upon the precision with which it is undertaken. For example, it may well be worthless releasing a request for information about an unknown missing person on a day when the public is being confronted by what it processes as much more urgent news such as an attack on the World Trade Center.

From the forensic artist's and reconstructive anatomist's point of view there lurks another danger. In our quest for the most faithful reconstructions of lost soft-tissue features we run the danger of producing a close, but not perfect, likeness. The danger arises because, should the reconstruction, without supporting collateral information, be the only medium available, then a psychological barrier to the graphic representation arises: it is "not quite right" and therefore "wrong", and so we deem it truly unrecognizable (Mori 1982). It may be argued that, perhaps fortuitously, while 3D images or solid "bust" reconstructions are the output of the artist or sculptor, the television monitor is still 2D and newspapers are mostly monochrome, and as these are the most reliable conduits for mass communication, inaccurate and potentially confusing detail is actually reduced or excluded, which may perhaps enhance the chances of success.

A conflicting, though highly convincing, view argues that it has been long appreciated and accepted that movement, preferably horizontal axis rotation, will enhance the observer's understanding of the 3D structure of an object and aid recognition (O'Toole *et al.* 2002). So reconstructions, real or virtual, require display in a format permitting them to be seen in this manner.

The current literature reveals the technical difficulty in accommodating the overlapping roles of motion and facial expression *per se* away from perception of spatial information. These important criteria are dealt with in Hill and Kuratate's chapters in this volume. Obviously, issues of illumination, surface reflectance, and skin color and texture are critical cues to enhancing perceptions of topography. These are explored in the chapter by Davey *et al.*, along with their contribution to perception of age.

It just remains to remind the reader that controversy has dogged any technique of facial reconstruction from skeletal remains for almost a century. von Eggeling (1913) was an early critic of the methods available in that day, and in more recent times many have expressed skepticism about the capability of any methods to reconstruct an "accurate" reproduction of the lost face upon a skull. Yet, as mentioned, many practitioners (e.g., Prag and Neave 1997) continue to claim success in practical police cases. In fact, the ongoing popularity of hands-on courses by experienced forensic artists and sculptors who teach methods for clay facial reconstruction underscore that the method can be successful in the identification process. Artists and sculptors who routinely employ their skills are continually striving to accommodate new clinical findings (e.g., CT, MRI, and ultrasound) that may reflect changes in soft tissue anatomy with age and sex and by population (Wilkinson 2004). If nothing more, the popularity and continuity of study and implementation of the traditional clay bust creation is a testament to the lack of anything better that is currently routinely accessible in a computer-based environment.

Furthermore, on the computational front, this volume is not intended to replace previous established methods or escort patrons from one realm of the identification process to another, but merely represents recent attempts to appreciate first and then automate the anatomical precision and accuracy long developed by those traditional artistic methods of identification. On the contrary, a volume of this caliber will hopefully enable the traditional facial reconstructionists to perceive grounds for improvement and collaboration in the computational or computer-graphic process. In fact, success in developing any computer-graphic method will depend on collaboration from the artistic community. One of our main purposes with this book is to introduce the quality and diversity of research to all in the field and to instigate some standardization that will require collaboration. Moreover, we are not advocating or predicting that the continued development of computer-graphic approaches will make the traditional 3D clay sculpting of facial approximation obsolete. The astute anatomical prowess of the artist or sculptor has much to offer the software development stage in everything from shape and form to color, texture, and, most importantly, believability.

We remain confident that the controversies of the last century will persist until more scientifically rigorous thinking is applied to the mechanical and perceptual problems in facial reconstruction. We do not advocate moving all that has been done in the past to an electronic environment merely to throw a veneer of scientific respectability over what is still a challenging area that requires a truly dispassionate and rigorous re-evaluation. This book is a timely collection of work from some of the most well-informed scholars currently working on these challenges. While the immediate focus of the challenge is the forensic arena of victim or suspect identification, opportunities for beneficial spin-off into other disciplines, particularly reconstructive plastic surgery, telecommunications and computer gaming, and biometrics for security applications, can be anticipated to bring much greater economic and social benefits in the future.

Overall, computer facial modeling presents an exciting and multifaceted field of scientific inquiry, with the potential for even more far-reaching future developments. Our hope is that the current volume will serve to stimulate future research in the areas of facial recognition and reconstruction.

REFERENCES

Ainsworth P. B. (1998) *Psychology, Law and Eyewitness Testimony.* Wiley, Chichester.

Bruce V. (1988) *Recognising Faces.* Lawrence Erlbaum, London.

Devlin Report (1976) *Report to the Secretary of State for the Home Department of the Departmental Committee on Evidence of Identification in Criminal Cases.* HMSO, London.

Haglund W. (1998) "Forensic 'Art' in Human Identification", in: *Craniofacial Identification in Forensic Medicine* (J. G. Clement and D. L. Ranson, eds.). Arnold, London, pp. 235–244.

Hammond P., Hutton T. J., Allanson J. E., Campbell L. E., Hennekam R. C. M., Holden S., Patton M. A., Shaw A., Temple I. K., Trotter M., Murphy K. C. and Winter R. M. (2004) "3D Analysis of Facial Morphology", *Am. J. Med. Gen.* 126A, 339–348.

İşcan M. Y. and Helmer R. P. (eds.) (1993) *Forensic Analysis of the Skull.* Wiley-Liss, New York.

Logie R. H., Baddeley A. D. and Woodhead M. M. (1987) "Face Recognition: Pose and Ecological Validity", *Appl. Cog. Psychol.* 1, 53–69.

Miyasaka S. (1999) "Progress in Facial Reconstruction Technology", *Forensic Science Review* 11(1), 51–90. Central Police University Press, NRIPS, Kashiwanoha, Japan.

Mori M. (1982) *The Buddah in the Robot.* Charles E. Tuttle Co.

O'Higgins P. and Cohn M. (eds.) (2000) *Development, Growth and Evolution: Implications for the Study of the Hominid Skeleton.* Linnean Society Symposium Series No. 20. Academic Press, San Diego.

O'Toole A. J., Roark D. and Abdi H. (2002) "Recognizing Moving Faces: A Psychological and Neural Synthesis", *Trends in Cognitive Sciences* 6, 261–266.

Prag J. and Neave R. (1997) *Making Faces: Using Forensic and Archaeological Evidence.* Butler and Tanner Ltd, London.

Rakover S. S. and Cahlon B. (2001) *Face Recognition: Cognitive and Computational Processes*. John Benjamins, Amsterdam, Philadelphia.

Schooler J. W. and Engst-Schooler T. Y. (1990) "Verbal Overshadowing of Visual Memories; Some Things Are Better Left Unsaid", *Cog. Psychol.* 22, 36–71.

Schooler J. W., Ryan R. S. and Reder L. (1996) "The Cost and Benefits of Verbally Rehearsing Memory for Faces", in: *Basic and Applied Memory Research: Practical Applications*, Vol. 2. Lawrence Erlbaum, London.

Shaweesh A. I., Thomas C. D. L. and Clement J. G. (2004) "Delineation of Facial Archetypes by 3D Averaging", *Ann. Royal Australasian College of Dental Surgeons* 17.

Stefan C. N. and Henneberg M. (2001) "Building Faces from Dried Skulls: Are They Recognised Above Chance Rates?", *J. Forensic Sci.* 46, 432–440.

Taylor K. T. (2001) *Forensic Art and Illustration*. CRC Press, Boca Raton.

von Eggeling H. (1913) *Archiv Für Anthropologie* 12, 44–47.

Wells G. L., Seelau E. P., Rydell S. M. and Luus C. A. E. (1994) "Recommendations for Properly Conducted Line-up Identification Tasks", in: *Adult Eyewitness Testimony: Current Trends and Developments* (D. F. Ross, J. D. Read and M. P. Toglia, eds.). Cambridge University Press, Cambridge, p. 229.

Wilkinson C. (2004) *Forensic Facial Reconstruction.* Cambridge University Press, Cambridge.

Yoshino M. (2004) "Conventional and Novel Methods for Facial-Image Identification", *Forensic Science Review* 16(2), 92–102. Central Police University Press, NRIPS, Kashiwanoha, Japan.

CLASSICAL NON-COMPUTER-ASSISTED CRANIOFACIAL RECONSTRUCTION

Gérald Quatrehomme
Laboratoire de Médecine Légale et Anthropologie médico-légale, Faculté de Médecine, Avenue de Valombrose, 06107 Nice cedex 2, France
Gérard Subsol
FOVEA Project[*] and Intrasense, Cap Oméga – CS 39521 Rond Point Benjamin Franklin, 34960 Montpellier cedex 2, France
[*] *http://foveaproject.free.fr*

2.1 INTRODUCTION

Identification (ID) is of the utmost importance in any democratic society: every corpse must be positively identified. There has been significant scientific and technical progress in this field over the last several decades. Numerous circumstances may cause an individual to lose his or her identity: loss, theft, or destruction of identity papers, neurological and psychiatric disease, age, emigration, and so on. These factors may apply to living subjects as well as to the deceased. In the latter case, however, the loss of identity may also be explained by additional factors such as traumatic mutilation, submersion and decomposition, skeletonized remains, and even criminal acts such as dismemberment or cremation, essentially to conceal the body or bodily fragments in order to delay the identification process.

Identification must be positive or precluded. Society should not be satisfied with possible or likely ID (Quatrehomme *et al.* 1999). See Table 2.1. There are only four reliable scientific methods of comparison for determining positive ID or precluding ID: fingerprint comparison, radiological comparison, odontological comparison, and DNA comparison. Any other method gives only a probability, or what we have called a likely or possible ID. Probability is not determined scientifically but inferred from frequency: the discovery of identity papers in the pocket of a deceased person represents, in terms of frequency, likely ID but does not have any scientific value. In such cases, the possibility of substitution of identity cannot be excluded.

Any comparative method adopted demands elements of comparison. At the beginning of an investigation there is often no clue, and it is necessary

Computer-Graphic Facial Reconstruction
John G. Clement and Murray K. Marks, Editors

Table 2.1

The four possibilities met in forensic ID[a].

Quality of ID	Examples
Positive ID	Radiological comparisons Odontological comparisons Fingerprints DNA
Likely ID	Identity cards Tattoo[b] Dental chart[c]
Possible ID	Scar[b] Background of diseases
Exclusion of ID	Incompatible dental chart Incompatible fracture background

[a] After Quatrehomme *et al.* (1999), modified.
[b] In some cases, positive ID is possible from these elements.
[c] Radiological odontological comparisons result in positive ID, dental charts allow likely ID and sometimes positive ID, if sufficient elements of comparison remain.

to use methods that are called "reconstructive" in order to narrow down the field of possibilities and then gradually focus on one missing individual. These reconstructive methods are often traditional and simple, such as the description of the body, or more specialized, such as the use of forensic anthropology for the estimation of stature, sex, age, and race, or even sophisticated, such as so-called "facial reconstruction" or "facial reconstitution", which require considerable skill.

The terminology is sometimes ambiguous: facial or craniofacial reconstitution, restitution, restoration, and reconstruction are used with different meanings by different authors (Quatrehomme 2000, Quatrehomme and İşcan 2000). Facial superimposition is the comparison of the craniofacial skeleton with a portrait (historically) or a photograph (currently) of the missing person. Facial restoration deals with skulls that have a sufficient amount of soft tissue, even if the quality of this soft tissue is poor. Photographs, sketches, or casts of the restored face can be published in the media, which is often helpful in identifying John or Jane Doe. Craniofacial reconstruction deals with a smooth totally skeletonized skull, or is used when the soft tissue is insufficient or when the restoration is not conclusive. Comparison of photographs or video images has proved to be an important tool, given the increasing availability of images obtained by video surveillance. Artificial ageing of the photograph of a missing person is a relatively new technique. This process, made possible by the computer, takes into account the face of the missing child and the faces of both parents.

All these methods require a precise knowledge of the anatomy of the face, the thickness of soft tissue at salient anthropological points, and the relationship between various "key features" (eyes, nose, lips, chin, ears) in terms of proportion. However, facial recognition is an amazingly complex process. Children develop the ability to recognize people at a very early age. Our brain displays an astonishing capacity to distinguish between thousands of known and unknown faces with amazing speed. This ability seems to be more highly developed in women, and recognition is more successful among people of the same race, especially when some salient features are visible. The context of memorization and recognition ("contextualization") is also important: sometimes one identifies a person by the context more than by the face itself (making mistakes is not rare under these circumstances). Conversely, one can have great trouble recognizing a perfectly familiar face merely because the person is seen out of his or her usual context. Every feature of the face has a different threshold for recognition. For this reason, the difficulty in recognizing a photograph increases from front view to oblique to profile view. Strange things happen, for example, when one presents a photograph upside down. Although the objective structure of the stimulus is not affected, recognition of the face is considerably disrupted. In the same way, recognition of a face from a negative film is very difficult even though complete information is transmitted to the brain. Many levels of information processing exist and different strategies of recognition are adopted according to the level chosen. Training improves performance.

2.2 CRANIOFACIAL RECONSTRUCTION

As noted above, craniofacial reconstruction (CFR) deals with a totally skeletonized skull or with those cases where restoration was impossible or inconclusive. This method is used as a last resort when all other techniques of reconstructive ID have failed. Facial reconstruction is justified by the fact that, to a certain extent, the skull can be considered as a matrix of the living head supporting the soft tissue. In other words, the bony skull is a hard core that supports, and is linked to, the soft face. The goal is to attempt an approximation of the shape of the face using the skull as a starting point (Rathbun 1984). Various methods exist which can be two- or three-dimensional, computer-assisted or not. Of course, the relationship between any point of the craniofacial skeleton and the soft tissue will never be known with precision, and the bony skull cannot tell us everything about the soft face. Because the face is made up of many details and subtle nuances, it is very difficult to obtain a completely accurate CFR. However, if one admits that the skull supports the soft tissue, one can attempt to reconstitute the approximate shape of the face and hope for sufficient resemblance. Furthermore, in forensic anthropology the goal is not perfect resemblance but, rather, sufficient likeness to be a help, a stimulus, or a lead towards ID by the next of kin if some resemblance does indeed exist. One must be aware that the result of CFR will be only an approximation of the face (Rathbun 1984) since the statistical average of soft tissue thicknesses that is used only allows the reconstruction of the general features of the face. In addition, certain features cannot be ascertained from the bony matrix, for example, physiological features (weight), chromatic features (color of eyes and hair), and social features (hairstyle, eyeglasses). Unfortunately, these features are often considered by the next of kin as vital clues for identification. Sometimes these elements can partly be known if an autopsy of the remains is still possible, as with decomposed bodies. More often, however, the reconstitution of anatomical features raises difficult questions (e.g., the precise positioning of the nasal tip), so that certain subtle details of the face will never be known. It is evident that the impossibility of obtaining an exact resemblance between the actual face of the missing person and the CFR often renders ID by the family very difficult. Even if CFR has met with some success (often highly mediatized), the linking of a skull and a CFR to a face does not prove that the CFR achieved exact resemblance. For science, the important issue is to determine the percentage of cases in which one obtains a resemblance, at least fairly good (and, if possible, excellent) between the CFR and the actual face of the deceased subject. A significant percentage of success would justify the pursuing of research in this field. It is necessary, therefore, to develop programs of scientific validation of CFR methods and to increase our understanding of the difficulties encountered in reconstituting certain parts of the face. Finally, we must improve our way of presenting results (linked to the neuropsychological process of facial recognition) in order to make CFR a more effective tool in the identification process.

2.3 HISTORY OF CFR

Paul Broca, a French anthropologist (quoted by Fedosyutkin and Nainys 1993), studied the relationship between the skull and the soft tissue of the face. He underlined the difficulty of establishing a link between the bone and the soft face, due especially to differing soft tissue thicknesses in each individual. The first facial CFRs were developed by German anatomists at the end of the nineteenth century for identifying famous people, including Dante (Caldwell 1981, Krogman and İşcan1986), and also Bach, Kant, and Haydn (Fedosyutkin and Nainys 1993). Wilder (1912) attempted to reconstruct faces of American Indians. These first attempts are interesting because the researchers tried to understand the complex relationship between the bony frame and the soft tissue. Later, they experimented with the use of information derived from x-rays and death masks.

At the beginning of the twentieth century, CFRs were realized for museums. Gerasimov (1971) reconstructed the faces of Neanderthal and Cro-Magnon skulls. Gerasimov (1949) developed a manual three-dimensional (3D) method and used it on paleontological specimens and then on forensic cases. He described his "anatomical method" as the placing of "muscles, fat, salivary glands", then the "skin", made of specific materials.

Some scientists were very skeptical about the usefulness of this research, questioning the possibility of obtaining actual resemblance (Brues 1958, Kerley 1977, Stewart 1954), but the work continued. Krogman (1946) thought it would be possible to use the method in forensic ID and, indeed, success in actual forensic cases gave a boost to research (Ilan 1964, Suzuki 1973). In 1979, İşcan used a sketch made by an artist following his instructions. After the subject had been identified by other methods, comparison between the sketch and the actual face of the missing person was possible. İşcan concluded that the resemblance was interesting (Krogman and İşcan 1986). A manual 3D CFR of the same subject (made by Charney) permitted further comparison and İşcan and Charney concluded that there were resemblances between the sketch and the CFR (Krogman and İşcan 1986). Maples *et al.* (1989) reconstructed the face of Francisco Pizarro, murdered in 1541.

Many researchers have objected that CFR, which is based on average soft-tissue thickness calculated from some biological groups, can only lead to an "average face". Research in the field of soft-tissue depth has been very active in the last 30 years. But even if we knew the soft-tissue depths at some salient anthropological points, there are an infinity of them. Most researchers recognize the difficulty of reconstructing certain features (e.g., the tip of the nose) and the necessity of understanding the influence of the position of the jaws, teeth, chin, etc., not only to understand the position of the correlated soft points (of the cheeks, lips, or chin), but also to understand the relationship existing between several key parts of the face, which, in the end, would permit the reconstruction of an exact likeness in terms of balance or harmony of the features (Caldwell 1981, Cherry and Angel 1977, Gatliff 1984, Rathbun 1984, Rhine *et al.* 1982).

Even if the current trend is to develop computer-assisted methods (justified by their rapidity and the decrease in subjectivity), manual methods of CFR remain of great interest for forensic ID. They continue to be used worldwide by forensic scientists (pathologists, anthropologists, and odontologists) as well as by artists, and various 2D and 3D manual methods have been proposed by forensic researchers (see particularly Aulsebrook *et al.* 1995 and Quatrehomme and İşcan 2000).

2.4 ANTHROPOLOGICAL ANALYSIS OF THE SKULL

Whatever the technique adopted, CFR demands a thorough anthropological analysis. After precise observation of the skull, the classical measurements—horizontal, vertical, and sagittal—must be made. Index and angles are calculated, giving the race (caucasoid, negroid, or mongoloid) and the general shape of the skull and face. For example, the glabella–pogonion (or nasion–pogonion)/bizygomatic breadth index gives the more or less elongated or rounded contour of the face. Therefore, the cranial, facial, and craniofacial indices are very useful in this analysis.

Skull angles can be measured directly on skull or on x-rays, and some of them can be calculated from simple measurements performed on the skull (Paysant and Quatrehomme 2002). They are useful in giving some clues to the shape of the skull and in assessing orthognathism or prognathism. Three main angles are measured or calculated on the profile, namely, those between the Frankfort horizontal and the nasion–prosthion (Figure 2.1), nasion–subspinale, and subspinale–prosthion line. The gnathic index (basion-prosthion/basion-nasion, Figure 2.2) also indicates the presence of prognathism. The facial angle (nasion–pogonion/Frankfort, Figure 2.3) indicates the position of the chin. From profile x-rays, the SNA angle (mean value 81°) determines the antero-posterior position of point A (the deepest point between the anterior nasal spine and prosthion) relative to the anterior cranial base (Rakosi 1982), and therefore the degree of prognathism from the maxilla. The SNB angle (Rakosi 1982) determines the anteroposterior position of the mandible in relation to the anterior cranial base and hence the prognathism for the mandible (mean

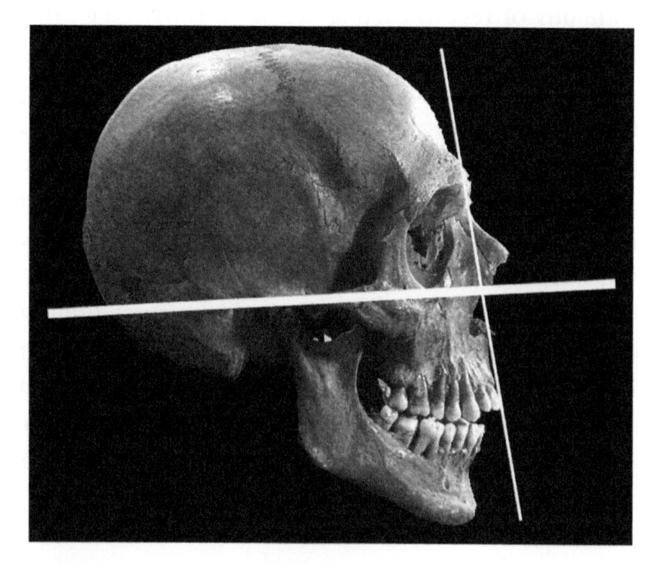

Figure 2.1

Angle between the nasion–prosthion line and the Frankfort horizontal.

value 79°, Figure 2.4). The ANB angle represents the difference between the SNA and SNB angles and explains the relationship, in the sagittal line, of the maxillary and mandibular bases (Rakosi 1982).

Skeletal facial types are defined from the vertical and horizontal balances of the skull and face. This analysis is made by numerous methods (Delaire 1978, George 1987, 1993), particularly on profile x-rays, using the Frankfort horizontal, and avoiding any radiologic distortion. The skull can be classified as (vertical balance) deep-bite (the anterior lower facial height is too small in reference to the upper facial height; and the posterior facial height is too

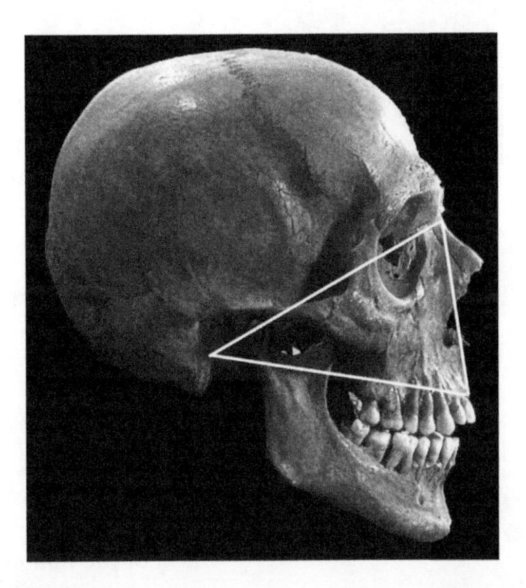

Figure 2.2

The gnathic index.

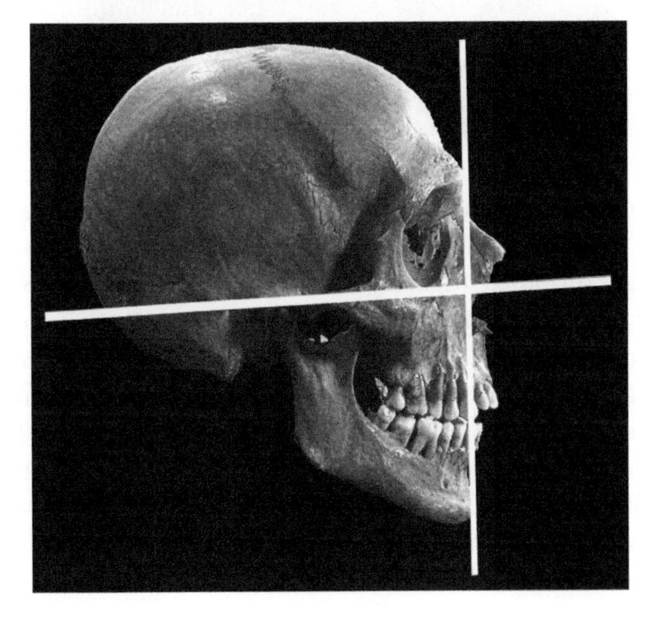

Figure 2.3

The facial angle, between the nasion–pogonion line and the Frankfort horizontal.

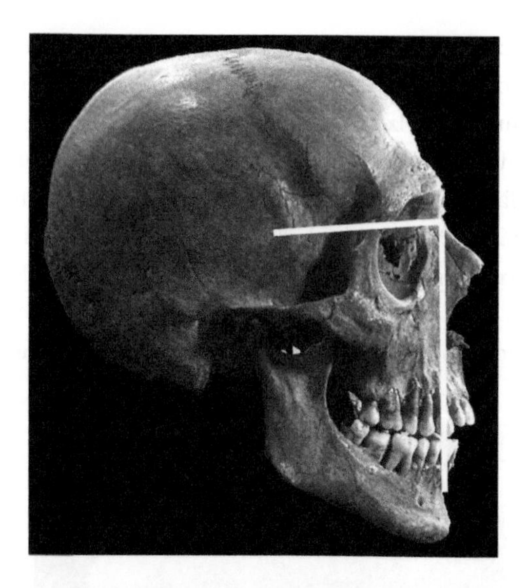

Figure 2.4
The SNB angle.

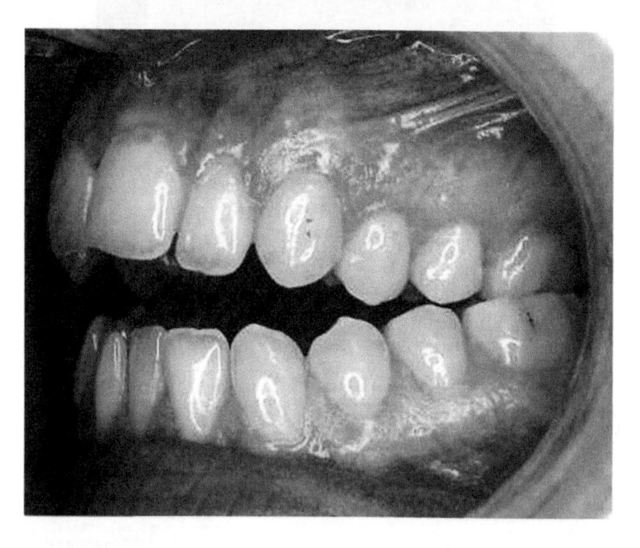

Figure 2.5
Open-bite (vertical balance).

large in reference to the total facial height), and open-bite (the converse, Figure 2.5). The skull is classified as (horizontal or anteroposterior balance) skeletal class II (mandible backwards in reference to the skull base) and class III (the converse). The orthognathic face (skeletal class I) shows normal relationship between the maxillary and mandibular bases and the anterior cranial base (SN plane) (Rakosi 1982): the SNA and SNB angles are normal.

Dentoalveolar analysis studies the angulation of the upper and lower incisors, the interincisal angle, the relation of the upper incisors to the nasion–pogonion plane, the relation of the lower incisors to the nasion–pogonion plane, the spaces between teeth, and the presence of crowding. Class II malocclusion is usually a distocclusion, which can be a dentoalveolar class II occlusion (with balanced skeletal structure of the face), or a dental distal translocation in occlusion (whereas there is a normal relationship between the jaws in rest position), or a class II2 malocclusion (incisal distal translocation). In class III malocclusion, the mandible seems to move forward, occlusion is reversed, but again there is a normal relationship between the mandibular bases and the anterior cranial base. Therefore one should remember that malocclusion can exist with or without bone shift in reference to the base of the skull.

2.5 SOFT-TISSUE DEPTH

Numerous works have given soft tissue thicknesses related to various anthropological points and various biological groups of both sexes, based on the idea that the bony matrix supports the soft tissue and that it is possible to estimate the average soft-tissue depth for some salient points. Most of these measurements were made on cadavers. This approach has met with criticism, for the anthropological points are not pinpointed by filling in the whole face of the cadaver, and the methods of measurement are very crude (a needle put through the skin until the bone is encountered by the tip of the needle). Furthermore, there are inevitable postmortem alterations (dehydration, beginning of decomposition). Therefore, the current trend is to measure the soft-tissue depths in living individuals by lateral x-rays (Dumont 1986), the ultrasonic method (Hodson *et al.* 1985), tomodensitometry, or any similar method. Some authors have suggested measuring soft-tissue depth in a vertical (and not lying) position (Aulsebrook 2000).

Obviously there is a wide range of variation depending on the sex, body build, biological group, and age of the subject, but also simply on individual differences (Lebedinskaya *et al.* 1993, Moore 1981, Rhine and Campbell 1980, Rhine *et al.* 1982). Nowadays there exist several reference tables which take into account these various factors. The weight of the subject cannot be ascertained from his bones alone, but sometimes sufficient remains are present to determine weight.

2.6 MANUAL 2D CFR

2.6.1 SKETCHES

Sketches can be made by a "forensic artist" working under the direction of a scientist (a forensic anthropologist, pathologist, or odontologist) who first performs classical ID analysis to determine the age, sex, stature, and race of the subject and then identifies specific individual details that will help the artist with his or her realization. Artists work from a photograph of the skull, usually enlarged to 1:1, which they mark at salient anthropological points, the length of the marks indicating the average soft-tissue depth for each point. The main objection to this method is that it is subjective, the final result being more artistic than scientific essentially because the artist goes beyond the scientifically verifiable indication in order to interpret the face and "humanize" it. However, some successful experiences with this method have been cited in the literature (Taylor 2001).

2.6.2 GEORGE'S METHOD

This method is based on average soft-tissue thicknesses placed in relation to profile x-rays of the face. George (1987) worked on a sample of white Americans of both sexes (males: 14 to 36 years of age, $N = 17$; and females: 14 to 34 years of age, $N = 37$). From this sample, George measured the soft-tissue depths in relation to some radiological points (namely, supraglabella, glabella, nasion, nasale, subspinale, supramentale, supraprogonion, pogonion, gnathion, and menton). Then the soft-tissue points were reconstructed by drawing a slope perpendicular to the radiological point (e.g., supraglabella, glabella), or oblique to it, with a known angle (e.g., the bony nasion, sella, and soft-tissue nasion form an average 4° angle), setting up the appropriate length on this slope, representing the average soft-tissue depth at this point. Some reconstructions were more complex, such as the reconstruction of the subnasal plane, the nasal angle (between the inferior part of the nose and the Frankfort horizontal), and the location of the nasal tip.

It should be pointed out that George's method gives only a stylized profile and probably will not permit direct recognition by the family. But it does avoid important mistakes in the reconstruction of the profile of the subject and is very useful for the CFR process.

2.7 MANUAL 3D CFR

A distinction is made between the anatomical (morphological, morphoscopic) method and the morphometric (sculptural) method. In the anatomical method, the "muscles", "salivary glands", and "fat" are positioned and then covered over by a layer of "skin". The morphometric method "sculpts" the face following indications of the average thickness of certain salient anthropological points. Most researchers choose this method as it is probably easier and it has not been demonstrated scientifically that one method is better than the other.

In any event, the scientist has to perform a thorough analysis of the skull from an anthropological and odontological standpoint. In light of what we have said above, a lateral craniographic George's method is highly recommended before starting a manual 3D reconstruction. The CFR is based on the analysis of the skull and of soft-tissue depths at certain anthropological points in order to understand the relationship between various parts of the face. Numerous guides for reconstruction have been published in the literature (e.g., İşcan and Helmer 1993, Krogman and İşcan 1986). The process starts by placing markers of accurate average soft-tissue depth at some anthropological points and then filling in between these points. But numerous questions arise during the CFR.

The *general shape* of the face can be divided into the upper contour of the skull in norma frontalis (half-sphere, pentagon, oval, or rectangle) and the lower contour (either wide – round or square – or narrow – oval or triangular) (Fedosyutkin and Nainys 1993). The forehead and the parietal and occipital regions follow the bone. The temporal regions are built by adding 12 to 14 mm for temporal muscle, and the vertex 2 to 3 mm (Krogman and İşcan 1986). Some things must be taken into account, such as the prominence of the arcades or local convexities of the body of the mandible, which must be "translated" in terms of soft tissue.

The reconstruction of the *nose* is particularly difficult (Quatrehomme and İşcan 2000), because the distal part of the nose is not supported by a bony frame. The upper part of the nasal bridge follows more or less the bone whose convexity, straightness, or concavity, along with the width, have to be "translated" in terms of soft tissue. The cartilage (under the rhinion) has often disappeared in actual forensic situations and the ideal proportions of the nasal dorsum (i.e., 2/5, 2/5, and 1/5) are only theoretical.

The tip of the nose is called the "pronasal". This important point is very difficult to reconstruct. Various data have been published. Most scientists consider that the pronasal can be built at the intersection of the tangent to the lower part of the nasal bones and the tangent to the nasal spine. Macho (1986), working on a sample of 154 male and 199 female lateral x-rays from Vienna (Austria), suggested several equations for helping to locate the pronasal. Generally speaking, the projection of the nasal–pronasal vertical distance is less than 2 times the horizontal distance. The oblique nasion–pronasal distance is 1.5 to 2 times the distance nasion–rhinion (Macho 1986) or 50% to 60% (Manera and Subtelny 1961), and on average the proportion is 2/5 (nasion–rhinion) : 2/5 (rhinion-lower part of the cartilage) : 1/5 (free part of the nose), respectively (Legent *et al.* 1981).

The subnasale–pronasal distance has been estimated as 3 times the length of the nasal spine on average (Gatliff and Snow 1979, Macho 1986). The nasolabial angle defines the slope of the "horizontal" part of the nose and is 90° on average (Legent *et al.* 1981), varying from 80° to 100° (Bennaceur and Couly 1995).

Furthermore the tip of the nose displays a wide range of morphological aspects (Macho 1989), which are often unpredictable from the bones. There are variations with sex (the tip is often wider in men) and race (wider in mongoloids, and even more so in negroids). Probably a narrow nasal tip will be associated with a narrow nasal spine, and a narrow piriform aperture, and vice versa (Fedosyutkin and Nainys 1993). The bialar width has been estimated as 28 to 45 mm in caucasoids (Krogman and İşcan 1986) and equal to the distance between the endocanthi. Most authors add 8 to 12 mm to the piriform aperture.

Ocular reconstruction requires placing the globe in the three dimensions of space. In the sagittal direction, the cornea is tangent to a line drawn between the upper and lower orbital rims. The vertical position of the globe is determined by the vertical position of the pupilla, placed either in the middle of the orbit considered from bottom to top (Fedosyutkin and Nainys 1993) or in the upper three-fifths of it, or just above a line joining the ectocanthus to the endocanthus (Quatrehomme 2000). The horizontal position is determined by the interpupillar distance, which is difficult to calculate accurately. Anthropological analysis of the telorism index and the equation of Eisenfeld *et al.* (1975) are used. The palpebral slit is defined by the position of both canthi (ecto- and endocanthus). The line joining both canthi is located in the lower third of the orbit, considered from bottom to top, and not in the middle (Yoshino and Seta 2000), and it slants downward and inward. The endocanthus must be placed at the point of attachment of the internal palpabral ligament (Aulsebrook 2000), and the ectocanthus at the malar tubercle of Whitnall, which is about 2 mm higher than the endocanthus. The upper lid covers the upper third of the iris, and the lower lid is tangent to the lower part of the iris (Krogman and İşcan 1986).

The *reconstruction of the mouth and lips* is also a difficult challenge. For some authors, the exact shape of the lips cannot be determined from the skull (Taylor and Brown 1998), though there is a definite relationship between the lips and the underlying bone (Subtelny 1959). There are variations according to sex, age, and race. The skeletal class and occlusion play a large role in the shape of the mouth and lips (Burstone 1958). For example, in cases of open-bite, the closure of the lips is not possible, so that the subject strains his or her orbicular muscles and one observes an increase in lip thickness. Obviously, alveolar prognathism has an impact on the location, shape, and thickness of the lips (Ricketts 1968).

The bicheilion distance determines the width of the labial slit and is equal, or very nearly equal, to the interpupillar width, the cheilion point projecting into the canine-first premolar region (Krogman and İşcan 1986, Rogers 1987). This labial slit is horizontal or slightly convex (upwards or downwards). The stomion is located in the lower quarter of the upper incisor in males and the lower third in females (George 1987). The thickness of the lips varies a great deal and is particularly influenced by race and by skeletal and occlusion abnormalities. Seen in profile, the lips are usually within a line drawn between pronasal and progonion for Caucasians and a little forward of this line for Negroes.

The *chin* is classified as round, oblong, oval, or triangular (Fedosyutkin and Nainys 1993). It is square and more robust in males, and more gracile, rounded, or even pointed in females. Though the soft chin tends to follow the bony chin, including the local convexities of the body of the mandible, there are some unexpected variations, due, for example, to fat accumulation (Lévignac 1988), as in the witch's chin. Prognathism of the chin must be translated by the shape of the soft tissues. Supraprogonion is the thickest point of the chin (George 1987). The chin must not be reconstructed as an isolated part, but rather within a "mouth–lips–chin complex", depending largely upon the skeletal and occlusion classes of the particular individual.

Ear reconstruction is hazardous because there is no bony frame and the ear exhibits a wide range of variations. The general axis of the ear is more or less parallel to the nasal bones (Broadbent and Matthews 1957) between 15° and 30° in reference to a vertical line (Gatliff and Snow 1979). The height of the ear should be close to the nasion-pronasal distance (Fedosyutkin and Nainys 1993) or the width of the mouth (Rogers 1987). The top of the ear is near the level of the eyebrows, or the glabella, the lower extremity near the level of the nasal tip, and the upper attachment of the ear near the line of the eyes (Broadbent and Matthews 1957). The width of the ear should be about 50% to 65% of its height (Rogers 1987, Tolleth 1978).

The final stage of CFR is the adding of *chromatic and social characteristics*: eye and hair color, hairstyle, beard, spectacles, clothes, and so on. Some of this information is sometimes partly known from autopsy when it is still possible, depending on the extent of decomposition or mutilation of the body. If no information is available, classical short hair in men and shoulder-length hair in women may be added.

2.8 DISCUSSION

CFR is difficult because knowledge of soft-tissue thicknesses is only one aspect of the problem. Caricatures are easily recognized, though soft-tissue depths are totally altered in these pictures. The whole balance of the face, the relation and balance between certain salient key structures that we call the "noble parts of the face", must be well understood if we are to hope to respect the proportions of the face and therefore to obtain slight, or good, resemblance between the CFR and the actual face of the deceased person. Furthermore, certain features (such as weight) cannot be determined from the bones and other features (what we have called chromatic and social characteristics) are usually unknown. Unfortunately, the latter (e.g., hairstyle, spectacles, etc.) are often of the greatest importance to the next of kin for identification of a missing person.

The "artistic canons" of beauty are not of great help in CFR because they are only general tendencies which are rarely applicable to specific cases (George 1993). They are, at best, crude approximations and not scientific truths. For example, soft-tissue facial height can be artistically divided into two (vertex–nasion; nasion–menton), three (trichion–nasion; nasion–subnasale; subnasale–menton), or four (vertex–trichion; trichion–glabella; glabella–subnasale; subnasale–menton) equal parts. But this theoretical division into two parts corresponds to only 10% of real cases, and the other proportions have never been obtained (Farkas and Munro 1987). The same result is observed with other artistic horizontal or oblique proportions.

In the authors' opinion, the main issue today is the lack of scientific validation of international data. We have to be aware that, even if a CFR leads to identification, this does not necessarily mean that the CFR was a likeness and, therefore, scientifically successful. It might have been a stimulus to the family despite the lack of resemblance, or ID might have been established by chance. Sometimes the deceased person is identified by other means and there is no link at all between the CFR and the identification process.

There is little research today attempting to validate the methods of CFR. Sadler (1991) performed a blind CFR on a skull and compared the result with a death mask: the resemblance was obvious. A frequent criticism is that from the same skull two scientists may obtain different results, sometimes bearing no resemblance to each other. But Helmer *et al.* (1993) stated that two independent teams are able to come up with similar results (in terms of resemblance) from the same skull. Quatrehomme (2000) studied 24 controlled observations, comparing the blind CFR with either a photograph or a death mask of the deceased person. The results in terms of resemblance were considered to be poor in over 62% of the cases.

Above all, an understanding of the neuropsychological processes of face recognition will probably stimulate new research in the forensic field. The ability to recognize a face, despite physiological (ageing, disease) or more subtle (mimics) modifications, is impressive. The manner in which the results of CFR are released to the media might increase the possibility of recognition (e.g., the full face is said to be better recognized, but the oblique view decreases the margin of error in reconstruction). Different social features and weights should be given to the media for each reconstructed face. This is very difficult unless a computer-assisted method has been adopted.

It cannot be concluded that successful identification, cited by several authors in the literature, confirms the accuracy of CFR in terms of resemblance. What can be said, however, is that research is very active in this field and that CFR is emerging as a potentially interesting tool in forensic identification.

ACKNOWLEDGEMENTS

The authors are grateful to Amy Laborde for critically editing the manuscript.

REFERENCES

Aulsebrook W. A., İşcan M. Y., Slabbert J. H. and Becker P. (1995) "Superimposition and Reconstruction in Forensic Facial Identification: a Survey", *Forensic Sci. Int.* 75(2–3), 101–120.

Aulsebrook W. A. (2000) "Facial Tissue Thickness in Facial Reconstruction", in: *Encyclopedia of Forensic Sciences* (J. A. Siegel, P. J. Saukko and G. C. Knupfer, eds.). Academic Press, San Diego, pp. 779–788.

Bennaceur S. and Couly G. (1995) "Morphologie Céphalique Humaine. Données Anthropométriques du Vivant", *Encyclopédie Médico-Chirurgicale* (Paris). Stomatologie-Odontologie, 22 001 D^{10}, pp. 1–12.

Broadbent T. R. and Matthews V. L. (1957) "Artistic Relationships in Surface Anatomy of the Face: Application to Reconstructive Surgery", *Plastic and Reconstructive Surgery* 20(1), 1–17.

Brues A. M. (1958) "Identification of Skeletal Remains", *J. Criminal Law, Criminology, and Police Science* 48, 551–563.

Burstone C. J. (1958) "The Integumental Profile", *Am. J. Orthodontics* 44(1), 1–25.

Caldwell M. C. (1981) "The Relationship of the Details of the Human Face to the Skull and Its Application in Forensic Anthropology". *Master's Thesis*, Arizona State University, Tempe, AZ.

Cherry D. G. and Angel J. L. (1977) "Personality Reconstruction From Unidentified Remains", *FBI Law Enforcement Bull.* 46(8), 12–15.

Delaire J. (1978) "L'analyse Architecturale et Structurale Crânio-Faciale (de Profil)", *Rev. Stomatol.* 79(1), 1–33.

Dumont E. R. (1986) "Mid-facial Tissue Depths of White Children: an Aid in Facial Feature Reconstruction", *J. Forensic Sci.* 31(4), 1463–1469.

Eisenfeld J., Mishelevich D. J., Dann J. J. and Bell W. H. (1975) "Soft–Hard Tissue Correlations and Computer Drawings for the Frontal View", *The Angle Orthodontist* 45(4), 267–272.

Farkas L. G. and Munro I. R. (1987) *Anthropometric Facial Proportions in Medicine.* Charles C. Thomas, Springfield, IL.

Fedosyutkin B. A. and Nainys J. V. (1993) "The Relationship of Skull Morphology to Facial Features", in: *Forensic Analysis of the Skull* (M. Y. İşcan and R. P. Helmer, eds.). Wiley-Liss, New York, pp. 199–213.

Gatliff B. P. (1984) "Facial Sculpture on the Skull for Identification", *Am. J. Forensic Med. Pathol.* 5(4), 327–332.

Gatliff B. P. and Snow C. C. (1979) "From Skull to Visage", *J. Biocommunic.* 6(2), 27–30.

George R. M. (1987) "The Lateral Craniographic Method of Facial Reconstruction", *J. Forensic Sci.* 32(2), 1305–1330.

George R. M. (1993) "Anatomical and Artistic Guidelines for Forensic Facial Reconstruction", in: *Forensic Analysis of the Skull* (M. Y. İşcan and R. P. Helmer, eds.). Wiley-Liss, New York, pp. 215–227.

Gerasimov M. M. (1949) *Principles of Reconstruction of the Face on the Skull.* Moscow, Nauka [en langue russe]. Cited by: Fedosyutkin B. A., Nainys J. V. (1993) "The Relationship of Skull Morphology to Facial Features", in: *Forensic Analysis of the Skull* (M. Y. İşcan and R. P. Helmer, eds.). Wiley-Liss, New York, pp. 199–213.

Gerasimov M. M. (1971) *The Face Finder.* Philadelphia, Lippincott.

Helmer R. P., Röhricht S., Petersen D. and Möhr F. (1993) "Assessment of the Reliability of Facial Reconstruction", in: *Forensic Analysis of the Skull* (M. Y. İşcan and R. P. Helmer, eds.). Wiley-Liss, New York, pp. 229–246.

Hodson G., Liebermann S. and Wright P. (1985) "In Vivo Measurements of Facial Tissue Thickness in American Caucasoid Children", *J. Forensic Sci.* 30(4), 1100–1112.

Ilan E. (1964) "Identifying Skeletal Remains", *International Criminal Police* (175), 42–45.

İşcan M. Y. and Helmer R. P. (eds.) (1993) *Forensic Analysis of the Skull: Craniofacial Analysis, Reconstruction, and Identification.* Wiley-Liss, New York.

Kerley E. R. (1977) "Forensic Anthropology", in: *Forensic Medicine* (C. D. Tedeschi, W. G. Eckert and L. G. Tedeschi, eds.). Vol. II, Physical Trauma. WB Saunders Co, Philadelphia, pp. 1101–1115.

Krogman W. M. (1946) "The Reconstruction of the Living Head From the Skull", *FBI Law Enforcement Bull.* 15(7), 11–18.

Krogman W. M. and İşcan M. Y. (1986) *The Human Skeleton in Forensic Medicine*. Charles C. Thomas, Springfield, IL.

Lebedinskaya G. V., Balueva T. S. and Veselovskaya E. V. (1993) "Principles of Facial Reconstruction", in: *Forensic Analysis of the Skull* (M. Y. İşcan and R. P. Helmer, eds.). Wiley-Liss, New York, pp. 183–198.

Legent F., Perlemuter L. and Vandenbrouck C. L. (1981) *Cahiers d'Anatomie ORL*. Masson (ed.), Paris, 3ème édition.

Lévignac J. (1988) *Le Menton (Monographies de Chirurgie Réparatrice)*. Masson (ed.), Paris.

Macho G. A. (1986) "An Appraisal of Plastic Reconstruction of the External Nose", *J. Forensic Sci.* 31(4), 1391–1403.

Macho G. A. (1989) "Descriptive Morphological Features of the Nose: an Assessment of Their Importance for Plastic Reconstruction", *J. Forensic Sci.* 34(4), 902–911.

Manera J. F. and Subtelny J. D. (1961) "A Cephalometric Study of the Growth of the Nose", *Am. J. Orthodontics* 47(9), 703–705.

Maples W. R., Gatliff B. P., Ludena H., Benfer R. and Goza W. (1989) "The Death and Mortal Remains of Francisco Pizarro", *J. Forensic Sci.* 34(4), 1021–1036.

Moore C. E. (1981) *"A Problem in Human Variation: the Facial Tissue Thicknesses of Caucasoids, Negroids, and Mongoloids"*. PhD Dissertation, The University of New Mexico, Albuquerque, New Mexico.

Paysant A. and Quatrehomme G. (2002) "Nouvelle Méthode de Calcul d'Angles Crâniens en Anthropologie Médico-Légale", *Journal de Médecine Légale Droit Médical* 45(1), 43–51.

Quatrehomme G. (2000) *"La Reconstruction Faciale: Intérêts Anthropologique et Médico-Légal"*. Ph.D.Thesis, Bordeaux, France.

Quatrehomme G., Cotin S., Alunni V., Garidel Y., Grévin G., Bailet P., Ollier A. and Ayache N. (1999) "La Superposition, la Restauration et la Reconstruction Faciales: Une Aide à L'identification Médico-légale", *Journal de Médecine Légale Droit Médical* 42(1), 11–22.

Quatrehomme G. and İşcan M. Y. (2000) "Computerized Facial Reconstruction", in: *Encyclopedia of Forensic Sciences* (J. A. Siegel, P. J. Saukko and G. C. Knupfer, eds.). Academic Press, San Diego, pp. 773–779.

Rakosi T. (1982) *An Atlas and Manual of Cephalometric Radiography.* London, Wolfe Medical Publications.

Rathbun T. A. (1984) "Personal Identification: Facial Reproductions", in: *Human Identification: Case Studies in Forensic Anthropology* (T. A. Rathbun and J. E. Buikstra, eds.). Charles C. Thomas, Springfield, pp. 347–356.

Rhine J. S. and Campbell H. R. (1980) "Thickness of Facial Tissues in American Blacks", *J. Forensic Sci.* 25(4), 847–858.

Rhine J. S., Moore C. E. and Weston J. T. (eds.) (1982) *Facial Reproduction: Tables of Facial Tissue Thicknesses of American Caucasoids in Forensic Anthropology.* Maxwell Museum Technical Series 1, Albuquerque, New Mexico.

Ricketts R. M. (1968) "Esthetics, Environment, and the Law of the Lip Relation", *Am. J. Orthodontics* 49(11), 826–850.

Rogers S. L. (1987) *Personal Identification from Human Remains.* Charles C. Thomas, Springfield, IL.

Sadler (1991) Cited by Ubelaker D. H. (1991) *"Human skeletal remains", Manuals of Archaeology, Library of Congress,* 2nd edition, Taraxacum Washington, p. 124.

Stewart T. D. (1954) "Evaluation of Evidence from the Skeleton", in: *Legal Medicine* (R. B. H. Gradwohl, ed.). Mosby, St. Louis.

Subtelny J. D. (1959) "A Longitudinal Study of Soft Tissue Facial Structures and Their Profile Characteristics, Defined in Relation to Underlying Skeletal Structures", *Am. J. Orthodontics* 45(7), 481–507.

Suzuki T. (1973) "Reconstruction of a Skull", *Int. Criminal Police Review* (264), 76–80.

Taylor K. T. (2001) *Forensic Art and Illustration.* CRC Press, Boca Raton, Fl.

Taylor J. A. and Brown K. A. (1998) "Superimposition Techniques", in: *Craniofacial Identification in Forensic Medicine* (J. G. Clement and D. L. Ranson, eds.). Arnold, London, pp. 151–164.

Tolleth H. (1978) "Artistic Anatomy, Dimensions, and Proportions of the External Ear", *Clinics in Plastic Surgery* (5), 337–345.

Wilder H. (1912) "The Physiognomy of the Indians of Southern New England", *Am. Anthropol.* (14), 415–436.

Yoshino M. and Seta S. (2000) "Skull-photo Superimposition", in: *Encyclopedia of Forensic Sciences* (J. A. Siegel, P. J. Saukko and G. C. Knupfer, eds.). Academic Press, San Diego, pp. 807–815.

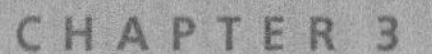

CHAPTER 3

THE WISDOM OF BONES: FACIAL APPROXIMATION ON THE SKULL

Ronn Taylor and Pamela Craig
School of Dental Science, University of Melbourne, Victoria 3010, Australia

3.1 INTRODUCTION

The discovery of the largely intact 1.5 million year old skeleton of the Nariokotome boy by Walker and Leakey in 1984 had a profound effect on the study of human evolution. The information contained in the bones gave the paleoanthropologists not only the expected information regarding the age

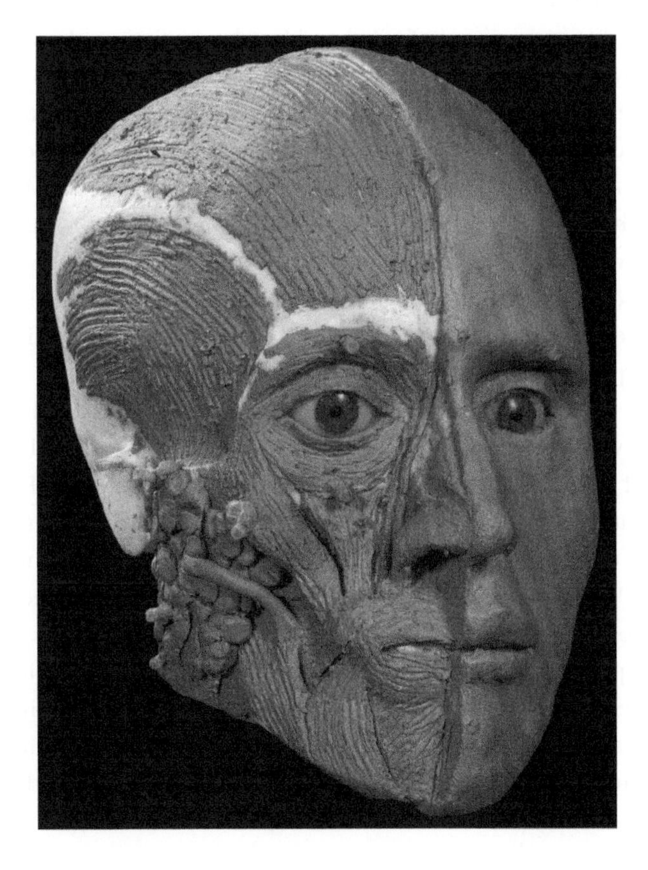

Figure 3.1
Three-dimensional clay approximation overlaid on the skull following the method of Neave (Prag and Neave 1997).

Computer-Graphic Facial Reconstruction
John G. Clement and Murray K. Marks, Editors

at death, stature, and sex, but also details about muscle and brain development, as well as breathing and walking patterns, that enabled them to further our understanding of the antiquity of human anatomy, physiology, and behavior.

Bone, while being one of the most durable tissues in the body after death, is also one of the most plastic, having the ability to reflect the activity of the soft tissues that it supports. Muscle and tendon attachments reveal the placement and strength of the musculature; cortical thickness and bony morphology relate to the weight bearing and muscular movements of the body part. In addition the skull will give information about sex, age, diet, and occasionally pathological processes involving the teeth and jaws. It is therefore not surprising that the evidence borne by the skull should be used in a forensic investigation in an effort to establish the identity of unknown human remains.

3.2 THE PURPOSE OF FACIAL APPROXIMATION

A trait that is innate among human beings is an ability to recognize faces, particularly those with whom they are familiar. This fascination with the facial form long predates written human history and may well be hardwired into the brain as an aid to recognition of tribal and family associations. From a forensic point of view, recognition of an unknown body relies heavily on this visual aspect of identification. When no soft tissue remains, attempts can be made to reconstruct the soft tissues on the remaining bony framework of the skull, hopefully to the extent that will make facial recognition possible. When examined carefully, the skull can deliver a surprising amount of information about its former owner. When interpreted by a skilled anthropologist together with an artist or sculptor, the story the bones tell can result in a resemblance that, when handled properly, may lead to the recollection of an individual face and a subsequent identification.

From a reconstructive point of view, the skull may be related to the soft tissues in a variety of ways. Whichever method is being used, be it a two-dimensional drawing, a three-dimensional clay approximation (Figure 3.1), or a computerized overlay of soft features against an image of the skull, it depends on the accurate interpretation of a series of anthropometric measurements. These measurements can be obtained from established databases that relate to an individual's sex and ethnic origin.

Such an approximation is at best an attempt to create a resemblance of the facial features of the deceased. Hopefully it will stimulate interest in the wider population, and somebody will recognize a similarity to the features of their missing friend or relative. The clay technique as described in this chapter is merely a starting point in the following forensic investigation. Modern technology has enabled the completed clay approximation to be scanned into a computer and appropriate features added or changed digitally.

General information such as age, height, weight, sex, and ethnic grouping are paramount in the success or otherwise of a facial approximation. Depending upon evidence being available, hair color, length, and texture, male facial hair, skin coloring, jewelry, and clothing will enhance the approximation.

The success of the technique of clay approximation depends upon the accuracy of the available data, the skill of the sculptor involved in the approximation, and the ability of the media to disseminate the resulting image as widely as possible.

3.3 A HISTORIC PERSPECTIVE

Facial approximation has a long history. Plaster faces superimposed on skulls found in Jericho dating to 5500 BCE are thought to have been an attempt to reconstruct the features of the deceased (Prag and Neave 1997a).

During the nineteenth century a more "scientific" method was developed. It was thought that, if the thickness of the muscle and skin overlying the bones were known, the face could be represented accurately. The German anatomist Welkler was the first to measure the thickness of the soft tissue of cadaver specimens at various anthropometric points on the face and subsequently used the measurements to recreate the face of the playwright Schiller (Welcker 1883). Soon afterwards, fellow German anatomist, His, used another set of soft-tissue measurements obtained from cadavers to construct a three-dimensional clay model on the skull to confirm the identity of the composer J. S. Bach (His 1895, Gruner 1993).

More recently facial approximation has been used to enhance museum exhibits of archaeological remains. As these are constructed for interest only, the degree of accuracy need not be as high as that which is sought in a forensic investigation (Prag and Neave 1997b).

In 1946 the anthropologist W. M. Krogman tested the technique for possible use in a forensic investigation. Working with a sculptor, he attempted to "restore" the face of a cadaver whose face was known to him but not to the artist. He found the resulting resemblance to the original face sufficiently successful to warrant its use in a genuine forensic investigation (Krogman *et al.* 1948).

Collaborative pairing of the skills of the forensic sculptor and the forensic anthropologist lay behind the most successful early attempts (Stewart 1979). This is because the method is founded on the anatomical relationship of the skull to the overlying soft tissues. It is the thickness of these soft tissues, the muscles, the fascia, and the fat pads in the skin which give the face its

Investigator	His		Kollman & Büchly		Helmer	Rhine & Moore		Rhine & Campbell		Suzuki		Ogawa	Miyasaka *et al.*	
Method	Puncturing		Puncturing		Sonography	Puncturing		Puncturing		Puncturing		Puncturing	Radiography	
Subjects	Europ. White cadav.		Europ. White cadav.		Europ. White live subjects	Amer. Cauca. unemb'ed cadav.		Amer. Black cadav.		Japanese cadav.		Japanese emb'ed cadav.	Japanese live subjects	
Sample Size	M:24	F:4	M:21	F:4	M:13	M:37	F:19	M:44	F:15	M:48	F:7	M:44	M:56	F:12
Trichion	4.08	4.16	3.07	3.02	4.30	—	—	—	—	2.30	2.20	2.69	4.78	4.31
Metopion (Supra Glabella)	—	—	—	—	5.00	4.25	3.50	4.75	4.50	2.60	2.00	3.12	5.17	4.91
Glabella	5.17	4.75	4.29	3.90	5.70	5.25	4.75	6.25	6.25	3.40	3.20	3.61	5.94	5.06
Nasion	5.45	5.00	4.31	4.10	8.20	6.50	5.50	6.00	5.75	3.70	3.40	3.87	6.91	5.55
Sellion	—	—	—	—	3.00	—	—	—	—	3.70	3.40	—	6.24	4.43
Rhinion (End of Nasal Bone)	—	—	2.12	2.07	2.30	3.00	2.75	3.75	3.75	2.00	1.60	2.01	2.41	1.99
Subnasale (Mid-Philtrum)	11.25	9.75	11.65	10.10	15.5	10.00	8.50	12.25	11.25	9.90	9.40	10.18	13.50	11.89
Prosthion (Upper lip margin)	9.37	8.26	9.46	8.10	14.00	9.75	8.50	14.00	13.00	—	—	—	12.62	11.44
Infradentale (Lower lip margin)	—	—	—	—	14.20	11.00	10.00	15.00	15.50	—	—	—	14.58	13.28
Labiomentale (Chin-lip fold)	10.00	9.75	9.84	10.95	12.00	10.75	9.50	12.00	12.00	9.20	8.50	8.72	13.12	12.71
Pogonion (Mental eminence)	11.05	10.75	9.02	9.37	9.70	11.25	10.00	12.25	12.25	6.40	5.30	10.84	12.91	11.96
Gnathion (Beneath chin)	6.16	6.50	5.98	5.85	7.50	7.25	5.75	8.00	7.75	3.50	2.80	4.50	7.51	6.56
Frontotemporale	—	—	—	—	—	—	—	—	—	R2.80	R2.00	R3.85	—	—
Supraorbitale	5.80	5.50	L5.41	L5.15	7.30	8.25	6.75	L4.75	L4.50	R4.10	R3.60	R4.68	—	—
Orbitale (Suborbital)	4.90	5.25	L3.51	L3.65	5.20	5.75	5.75	L7.50	L8.50	R3.70	R3.00	R5.72	—	—
Ala	—	—	—	—	—	—	—	—	—	R8.50	R8.00	R11.18	—	—
Lateral orbit	—	—	L6.62	L7.73	—	9.75	10.50	L13.00	L14.25	R4.40	R4.70	R6.48	—	—
Zygion (Zygomatic arch.Mid)	—	—	L4.33	L5.32	—	7.00	7.00	L8.75	L9.25	R3.30	R2.90	R5.28	7.48	7.18
Auriculare (Supraglenoid)	6.05	6.75	L7.42	L7.10	—	8.25	7.75	L11.75	L12.00	—	—	—	—	—
Occlusal line	—	—	—	—	—	17.75	17.00	L19.50	L18.25	R12.20	R10.40	R16.10	—	—
Gonion	—	—	—	—	11.00	11.00	9.75	L14.25	L14.25	R6.00	R4.90	R8.78	13.57	13.25
m1 (Sub-M2)	—	—	—	—	—	15.25	15.25	L15.75	L16.75	R8.80	R9.70	R11.83	—	—
m1 (Supra-M2)	—	—	—	—	—	18.50	17.75	L22.25	L20.75	R11.90	R12.30	R18.02	—	—

Reproduced from Miyasaka, S. *Forensic Science Review* 11(1), June 1999, p. 54.

individual character. Early measurements in Europe in the nineteenth century were obtained manually on cadaver specimens using a puncturing instrument fitted with a measurement guide. The instrument was inserted through the soft tissues at specified anthropological points on the face (Gerasimov 1971). Recent work involving living individuals has been made possible with the development of ultrasound and radiological techniques. These latter techniques are more reliable as the ability to match the anthropological landmark on the skin to the underlying bone can be more readily checked (Helmer *et al.* 1993).

Many ethnic groups have been studied, predominantly Caucasian, Negroid, and Mongoloid individuals (El-Mehallawi 2001, Rhine 1980, Rhine 1982, Suzuki 1948, Wilkinson *et al.* 2002). Several studies have measured the soft tissue thickness of children (Dumont 1986, Manhein 2000, Wilkinson 2002, Williamson *et al.* 2002). There are great variations between authors depending on whether their subjects were cadavers, unembalmed cadavers, or live subjects, and whether the measurements were obtained by needle puncturing, ultrasonography, or radiography.

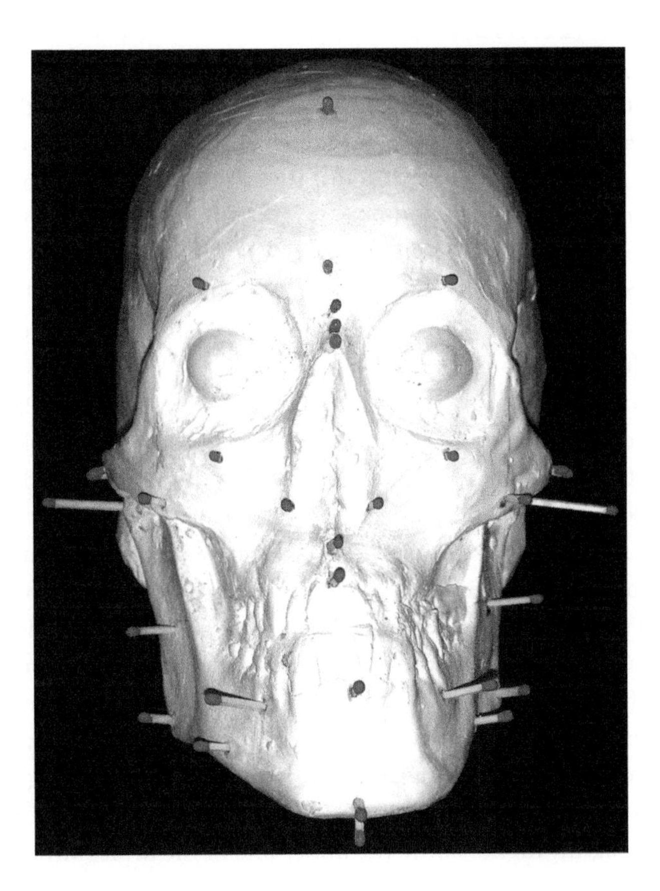

Figure 3.2

The depth markers placed at right angles to specified anatomical landmarks allow the build-up of clay to the predetermined depth.

Individual variations exist in relation to the degree of fat on the face as a reflection of nutritional status. There is also a problem as to the age of the individual as the facial tissue thickness measurements vary with age, particularly after the age of 60 (Simpson and Henneberg 2002). Information as to the approximate age of the individual can frequently be obtained from further examination of the postcranial skeleton.

3.4 WHAT THE SKULL CAN TELL US: POSITIONAL RELATIONSHIPS BETWEEN THE SKULL AND THE FACIAL FEATURES

Facial features such as eyebrows, eyes, and eyelids, and to a lesser extent the ears, nose, and lips form the recognizable features of the face. As they are variable from individual to individual, only general information can be gleaned from a study of a population, particularly that of mixed ethnicity. The published literature has focused on single ethnic groups and some of the following generalizations need to be varied to account for differing populations.

3.4.1 THE RELATIONSHIP BETWEEN THE ORBIT AND THE EYE

In general it is agreed that the eyeball is centered in the orbit with the apex of the cornea lying at the junction of the line connecting the midpoint of the medial and lateral orbital margins and the superior and inferior margins. The position of the lateral canthus is variable, being reported by differing investigators as on or medial to the lateral wall of the orbit to varying degrees (Angel 1978, Caldwell 1986, Yoshino 2000). The size of the adult eyeball varies little. In lateral view the protrusion of the eyeball from the orbit varies with the ethnic origins of the individual (Stephan 2003). Some Caucasian males with a thickened supra-orbital ridge appear to have more deeply set eyes as the upper part of the orbit protrudes relative to the lower (Wilkinson and Mautner 2003). In the case of Japanese subjects the upper eyelid is located more anteriorly (Miyasaka 1999).

Eyebrow formation is variable both between and within ethnic groups. Krogman and İşcan (1986) found that, in a Caucasian population, the eyebrows are 3 to 5 mm above the upper orbital margin and in profile view projecting 2 to 3 mm in front of the lower forehead contour. The prediction of shape is difficult, although Fedosyutkin and Nainys (1993) related it to the degree of development of the supra-orbital ridges. However, several Japanese authors have found that it is far more variable than this, having identified three different types in the Japanese with the midline of the eyebrow in the female lying slightly higher above the upper line of the orbit (Miyasaka 1999).

3.4.2 THE RELATIONSHIP BETWEEN THE BONY NASAL APERTURE AND THE NOSE

While the appearance of the bony nasal aperture and nasal bones gives some guide to the morphology of the nose, it is composed largely of soft tissue and cartilage. Nasal shape and size vary between individuals and population groups (Rogers 1987). Nasal width is particularly variable. In Caucasian individuals, the general width of the bony nasal aperture is approximately three-fifths of the total nasal width including the alai. Negroid individuals have a wider and more fleshy alai than Caucasians (Aulsebrook *et al.* 1996). Gatliff and Snow (1979) recommended that the position of the alai should be 5 mm in Caucasians and 8 mm in Negroids lateral to the lateral margin of the nasal aperture. Japanese, on the other hand, are more of the order of 5 to 6 mm (Miyasaka 1999).

It is in a profile perspective that difficulties arise in the approximation of the nose. The projection of the nasal bones as suggested by Gerasimov (1971) is a popular method of establishing nose profile. The relationship between the position and forward projection of the nasal bones and the anterior nasal spine may be used as suggested by Krogman and İşcan (1986). By extending a line forward parallel to the Frankfort plane 2 mm below the anterior nasal spine, the lateral projection will be 15 to 18 mm in Caucasians and 10 to 12 mm in Negro populations. This method will account for the different elevations of the nasal bones themselves, so that if they are higher than 45° and the distance from the nasion to the rhinion is small, an aquiline nose shape will result.

Several investigators have correlated the profile of the nose with the general facial profile, so that a convex nasal shape can be correlated with a convex face and a concave nose with concave facial profile. Aquiline humps appear more frequently in those individuals with a Class 2 occlusion (associated with a prognathic upper jaw) (Clements 1969, Krogman and İşcan 1986).

The position of the nasal tip can sometimes be suggested by the direction of the protrusion of the anterior nasal spine, an upward direction suggesting a higher tip. Miyasaka found that these directions did not accurately apply to Japanese faces, the noses being shorter and the protrusion of the nasal bones less (Miyasaka *et al.* 1998).

A lateral radiographic study of Caucasian faces led Macho to demonstrate statistically that the profile line does not follow the underlying bony structure. She found that, while the nasal bridge could be related to the direction of the nasal bones, the nasal tip was determined by the degree of subcutaneous fat deposition and age of the individual (Macho 1986, 1989). The nose has been found to increase in length throughout life, the tip becoming more downturned and the bridge becoming wider (Neave 1998).

3.4.3 THE RELATIONSHIP BETWEEN THE SKULL, THE TEETH, AND THE MOUTH

The mouth is a variable and extremely mobile part of the face and contributes to facial expression. It appears to have an important role to play in recognition in certain population groups (Haig 1984). Of the muscles that surround it, the orbicularis oris and platysma have no origin or insertion into the bone, and thus no information can be gleaned from the skull. Other muscles of facial expression such as the levator and depressor muscles of the mouth arise from the bone, and markings can be seen on the skull.

It is generally agreed that the width of the mouth is approximately equal to the interpupillary distance (Caldwell 1986, Krogman and İşcan 1986). However, the position of the canines and premolars have been used by American investigators in cases where teeth are present, commissures (chelion) being positioned at a point on a line normal to the interproximal contact points distal to the canines (Angel 1978, Gatliff 1984, Krogman and İşcan 1986). Others, however, have positioned it more posteriorly toward the premolars, and even the first molars (Fedosyutkin and Nainys 1993). Stephan and Henneberg's (2003) investigations in this area using two-dimensional photographic data found the mouth width to be approximately 133% of the intercanine width. The width between the most prominent buccal bulges of the canine teeth is easy to measure with calipers and is a straight-line measurement. They found that if interpupillary width is used, the mouth will be too wide for most Caucasians and Asians.

The horizontal center of the mouth is placed symmetrically over the teeth at a height either at the inferior border of (Fedosyutkin and Nainys 1993) or one-quarter to one-third of the distance up the central incisor teeth (George 1987). This placement controls the height of the upper lip, and this appears to be an important contributor to facial recognition (Haig 1984).

The thickness of the lips is highly variable and cannot be determined from the skull (Caldwell 1986, Stewart 1979). Using radiographic data, George (1987) found that the upper and lower vermilion borders were usually a height within the gingival quarter of the central incisors for Caucasian subjects, Negroids having fuller lips. George (1987) and Miyasaka (1999) found that Japanese Asian lips were slightly narrower. The lips are supported by the incisor teeth. Therefore the position of the teeth will influence the amount of support the lips receive. This is determined by the dental occlusion, whether the teeth are biting approximately edge to edge (normal), or the upper teeth protrude, or the lower teeth protrude (Miyasaka 1999).

Using lateral radiographs, Roberts *et al.* (2001) measured the vertical angle of the upper incisor teeth and attempted to relate this to lip shape. From two baselines, longitudinal axis of maxillary incisor and hard palate, measurements were taken to specific points on the soft tissue outline of the upper lip. Neither horizontal nor vertical measurements were found to have any significant correlation with the incisal angle. However, it was proved statistically that the most anterior point of the upper lip had strong correlation with the point corresponding to three-quarters of the distance of the lip from the base of the nose, both in vertical and horizontal directions. A similar correlation was found between the most posterior point of the upper lip and a quarter of the lip length from the base of the nose, approximately 0.78 and 0.45 in the vertical and horizontal measurements, respectively.

3.4.4 THE RELATIONSHIP BETWEEN THE SKULL AND THE EARS

The shape and projection of the ear is another feature that is impossible to glean from the skull. The soft-tissue ear hole lies in close approximation and about 10 mm laterally to the external auditory meatus. Most investigators use a rule-of-thumb approach, the ear being approximately the same length as the nose, with one-third being above the external auditory meatus and two thirds below (Fedosyutkin and Nainys 1993, Gatliff 1984).

3.4.5 SEXUAL DIMORPHISM IN THE FACE

Sexual dimorphism exists in many animals including humans. Skeletal evidence of sexual dimorphism appears during puberty, and it is therefore rarely difficult for a physical anthropologist to be able to assign the sex of an adult body provided that enough material is available for examination. Dimorphism in the skull is found in the supraorbital ridges, antegonial notching of the mandible and the generally more heavily marked muscle and tendon attachments in male skulls. The female skull is generally lighter and smaller with smoother muscle markings (Penton-Voak *et al.* 2001, Williams 1995). However, skulls exist in which the sexual characteristics are so indistinct that it is difficult to assign a sex in the absence of any postcranial information.

3.5 BUILDING THE FACE FROM THE SKULL

3.5.1 PRELIMINARY COLLECTION OF DATA

Specialists such as crime-scene investigators, police, pathologists, anthropologists, and odontologists provide important information for the sculptor. It is necessary to collect as much data as possible from the scene. Clothing and jewelry may be found on the body or in its vicinity. Details such as race, sex, age, build, and whether teeth are natural or artificial, should be obtained where possible by thorough investigation of the skeletal remains.

3.5.2 CLEANING AND PREPARATION OF THE SKULL

The remains must be properly cleaned prior to any reassembly being attempted. Any remaining soft tissue may be removed carefully with surgical hand tools and brushes followed by gentle heating in water to complete removal. If available, an insect colony will clean fragile weak bony parts extremely efficiently. Russell (1947) describes an insect colony as used in the Museum of Vertebrate Zoology in Berkeley, California. Hide beetles (*Dermestes maculatus*) may be bred in a warm environment of approximately 30°C and established using a diet of fresh meat until maximum insect population is attained. The moisture content of the colony and its diet (the fat content in particular) must be right, and hiding places for deposition of eggs are essential, for the establishment of a good colony. He also recommends adding dried sheep heads to the insect colony in addition to the skeletal material to be cleaned. In a well-maintained insect colony a skull can be cleaned in 12 hours or less.

3.5.3 REPAIRING THE DAMAGED SKULL

When skeletal remains are presented in a fragmented condition, this poses a challenge for the reconstructive sculptor. The skull may have been damaged by trauma, burning, or environmental or animal activity. The bones of the cranium and mandible may be fragmented in many places, and portions of either may be lost. The bones may also be in an extremely friable condition requiring great care if further damage is to be avoided. Such fragmented skulls can be rebuilt and held together with the aid of dental modeling waxes. Initially a sticky wax may be used sparingly. A strong yet brittle wax, it allows the sculptor to maintain the larger connecting pieces in their correct anatomical position temporarily. However, sticky wax leaves an undesirable residue which will impede further processes. In an emergency situation, when small pieces need to be held together, a cyanoacrylate resin or even proprietary hairspray may be used.

Burnt bone is extremely fragile and requires particular care. Support can be added to these structures by infusing the porous cancellous bone with liquid dental modeling wax. The wax is melted on the blade of a small knife and flowed onto the damaged bony surface, which is then gently heated with a gas torch. The molten wax will flow freely into the cancellous spaces, solidifying and thereby supporting them and providing a matrix for the further process of joining adjacent pieces together. Dental modeling wax has sufficient inherent strength to support these structures to the extent that an impression of the bone may be taken.

Once the fractured pieces of bone have been restored and placed together in the appropriate anatomical relationships, any missing portions can be sculpted to shape in the modeling wax. Restoration of missing parts requires a sound

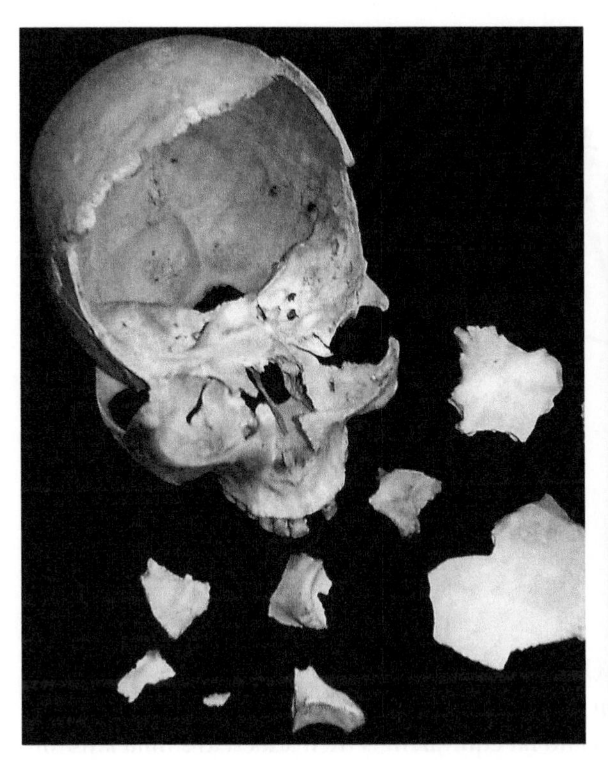

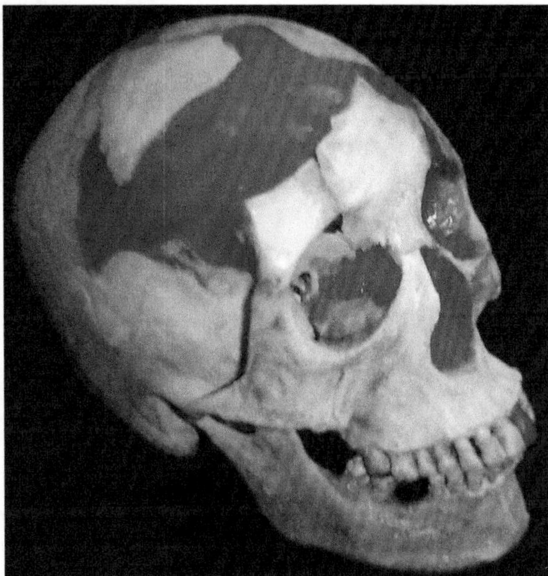

Figures 3.3 and 3.4 Repair of fragmented skull with dental modeling wax.

knowledge of the osteology of the skull, but if there is a contralateral part, the missing pieces can be sculpted to match. The undamaged side is measured with anthropomorphic and divided calipers and the missing side remodeled to match with the aid of a mirror. Once the skull is completely restored and checked for uniformity, it can be reproduced in plaster and a facial approximation constructed in the usual way.

It is the practice in most jurisdictions to return human remains to the coroner or medical examiner. The wax must be removed from the skull and the bones returned as they were received. After completion and checking of the plaster casting, boiling water can be gently sprayed on the damaged bone and this will remove all of the wax without residue.

3.5.4 THE CLAY MODELING PROCEDURE

Facial approximation in clay is an artistic endeavor and, as such, relies heavily on the individual skill of the sculptor. To be scientifically relevant, however, certain procedures need to be followed based on the established data. There are two approaches to this. The philosophy of the so-called "Russian method",

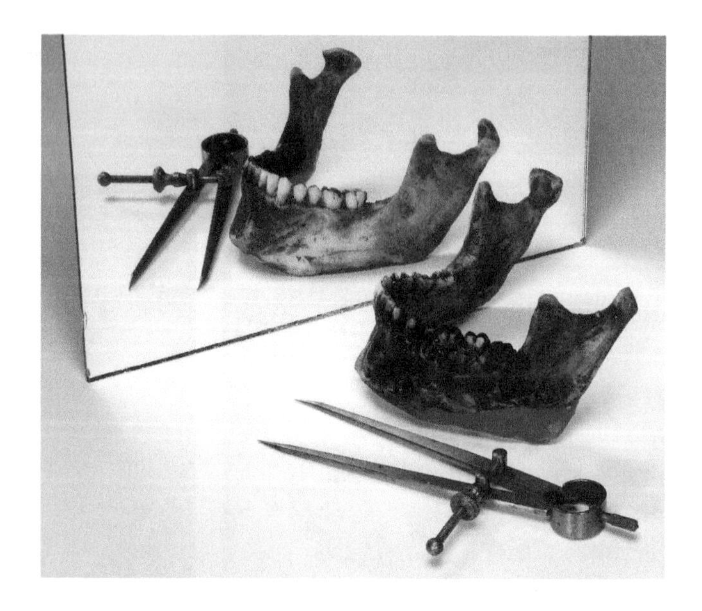

Figure 3.5
The contralateral undamaged side is used to assist in the repair process.

developed by Gerasimov (1971), is to work close to the skull itself, noting the placement and definition of muscle markings on the skull and rebuilding these muscles in clay. Skin and fat equivalent is then added as a final layer on this. In contrast, the "American method", developed by Gatliff and Snow (1979), relies totally on the tissue thicknesses at various anthropometric points and an artistic ability to interpret these to produce a likeness. Recently, a composite approach, such as that used by Prag and Neave (1997b) and Taylor and Angel (1998), in which muscles are laid out and the skin applied using soft-tissue thickness measurements, has become popular among many sculptors.

A casting of the skull is prepared and the soft-tissue markers placed at the appropriate anthropometric points. The muscles of the neck, the muscles of mastication in the cheeks, and those of facial expression are applied according to the position and development of the markings on the skull. The muscles of facial expression, such as the orbicularis oris and orbicularis oculi, do not have an origin on the bone, but arise and are inserted into the facial soft tissue. These must be placed according to known anatomic relationships. Covering the muscles is a layer of fat and skin that will vary according to sex, age, and nutritional status. The tissue thickness measurements used therefore need to reflect these variations.

The problem areas of nose and mouth in which most variation is likely to be found constitute the greatest challenge to the sculptor. A conservative approach based as closely as possible on the bones and a resistance to the temptation to artistically enhance the project is to be considered at all times. The completed model is then cast in resin or plaster. It can be displayed as is, painted, or, more commonly today, scanned and enhanced digitally with additions of hair, eyebrows, clothing, etc., prior to release to the media.

3.6 HOW SUCCESSFUL IS FACIAL APPROXIMATION?

If the bones of the skull and the soft tissues of the face are interrelated, it stands to reason that the anatomy of the former will predict that of the latter, but is it predictable? There have been many successes reported in the literature, and forensic sculptural approximation remains a popular if last-ditch attempt to identify unknown remains (Prag and Neave 1997b).

Given all the problems associated with the reproduction of soft-tissue structures, it is perhaps not surprising that facial approximation has had many critics, as it became obvious that different artists would interpret the bones differently and thus produce different faces. von Eggeling's (1913) early experiments confirmed this when the same skull for which a face was known was given to two sculptors. Each produced a different face and neither resembled the original. Although there have been many criticisms in the intervening years as to the ultimate usefulness of the technique (Stephan 2001, Vanezis *et al.* 1989), many successes have been reported (Gatliff and Snow 1979, Gatliff and Taylor 2001).

Stephan and Henneberg (2001) attempted to apply a statistical method for the identification of individuals from approximations and found that only 1 in 16 was identified at a statistical level above chance.

It may be that the skill of the sculptor has a bearing on the success rate. Helmer *et al.* (1993) asked two experienced forensic sculptors to render a likeness on 12 pairs of identical casts of skulls of known individuals. In this tightly controlled study the resulting approximations were sufficiently accurate for independent observers to identify the photograph of the original to rate the resemblance overall at between 33% and 42%.

Given the relative unimportance of features such as mouth and cheeks, a bland interpretation of features is just as likely to be successful and perhaps in some cases more so than a highly artistic and lifelike approximation (Helmer *et al.* 1993). Such an approximation can prompt the viewer to imaginatively add personal details if the overall proportions are correct. It is these proportions that are gleaned from the careful examination of the skull and a sympathetic approach to the task of facial approximation. The success may therefore lie in what artist Karen Taylor calls "the gestalt of the face"; in other words, the whole is more than the sum of the component parts (Taylor 2001). The proportions of the features rather than the details themselves appear to trigger the recognition (George 1993). Of the details, the features in the

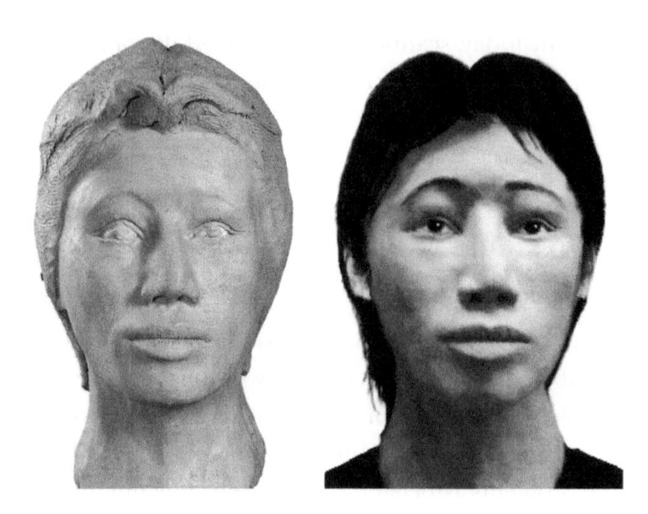

Figure 3.6
Computer enhancement of an approximation of an Asian face.

upper part of the face are considered first. Details of hair appear most important, followed by eyes and eyebrows (Davies *et al.* 1981).

This was borne out by a recent study by one of the present authors of a longitudinal series of frontal photographs of the same individuals from birth to 20 years of age. It established statistically that most individuals could be correctly identified from the age of about 5 years by an independent observer, even though the growth of the lower part of the face has not taken place. The ultimate proportions of the face are indeterminate until the prepubertal growth spurt, after which the probability of recognition increases with age until adulthood (Craig *et al.* 2004).

3.7 COMPUTER ENHANCEMENT OF THE APPROXIMATION

To photograph and scan the result into a computer will allow details to be added that humanize the face and make it more lifelike. Full-frontal and profile photographs will allow features such as hairstyles, moustaches, and beards to be displayed. Any jewelry, eyeglasses, or other personal adornments found with the body can be added to personalize the image. Image processing software such as Adobe Photoshop® is used to apply features from an image database. Adobe Illustrator® or Corel Draw® will enable drawings to be done directly on the image. Such a process is easily and quickly achieved and the features can be changed at short notice if further evidence comes to hand. A copy of the original scanned image is always kept and can be referred to at all times. Photoshop® has an inbuilt history which allows all changes to be recorded. The importance of collaboration between the sculptor and the computer artist cannot be overemphasized. It is important that changes are

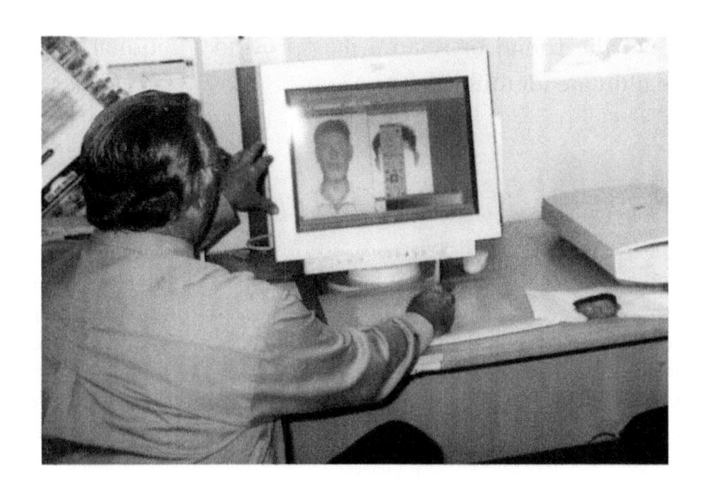

Figure 3.7

Computer enhancement of Case 2 by Det. Sgt. Adrian Paterson of the Victoria (Australia) Police.

restricted to the added details in the areas of eyebrows, lashes, hairstyle, and eyes, and the temptation to reshape or tidy up features on the original clay approximation is resisted.

A three-dimensional scan can be achieved using 3D imaging equipment such as the Fiore Physiognomic Range Finder. The clay approximation then becomes a virtual model which can be delivered electronically and allows remote investigators the opportunity to examine it from all aspects through rotation on the computer screen or the construction of a duplicate through CAD/CAM technology. It is also possible to compare the approximation with a photograph of a possible match by superimposition following the technique developed by Yoshino *et al.* (2000). The 3D image is rotated about three dimensions and matched to the photograph at seven selected anatomical landmarks using Rugle® software. The landmarks used by Yoshino are the pupils, nasion, pronasale, stomion, and subaurale. Of these, the pupils, nasion and pronasale are the most likely to be correctly positioned on the clay approximation.

3.8 PUBLICIZING THE RESULTS

Since the aim of facial approximation in a forensic setting is to establish the identity of the deceased, the final likeness must be publicized in a manner that will ensure the greatest exposure to the general public, and therefore the greatest possibility that someone will recognize a missing friend or relative. Prominent photographs in black and white of the face together with a brief description of the discovery of the body will stimulate interest, particularly on a day when there is no other newsworthy event to divert attention (Haglund and Reay 1991). There may be more than one tentative identification, but each of these can be investigated further at that point. Additional information obtained from the friend or relative may provide additional evidence that leads to the ultimate identification.

3.9 CASE REPORTS

CASE 1

On the 26 April 1988 skeletonized human remains (Figure 3.8a) were found in a shallow grave in secluded bushland west of Melbourne in Australia. The pathology and odontology report showed that the deceased was a 174-cm-tall Caucasian male aged between 50 and 55 years at death. There were no teeth, and the dental ridges were well resorbed, indicating that the teeth had been extracted many years earlier. No clothing was found at the scene, but several strands of hair of gray and brown color were recovered.

In 1990, after all avenues to establish the identification of the deceased had been exhausted, the coroner requested that a facial approximation be attempted to try and resolve the case. Key points in the facial approximation:

- It was unfortunate that no dentures were found with the body, but this did not concern us unduly. We have a good health system in Australia and it is unusual to see people without dentures, but it is common for animals to take them especially when the body is dumped in bushland.
- It was agreed in consultation with the odontologist to re-establish the height of the jaws of the deceased to that which it was presumed the dentures occupied (Figure 3.8b). Registration rims constructed in dental modeling wax were fitted to the maxillary and mandibular arches following the standard measurements set out by Basker *et al.* (1979) of 20–22 mm for the upper and 15–17 mm for the lower rims. Consideration was then given to lip support. The amount of resorption of the gums indicated to us that the man would have had thin lips and fine creases around the mouth due to age and the lack of properly placed teeth.
- A plaster cast was made of the skull with the registration rims in place. This was used to build the clay facial approximation, leaving the original skull free to use as a reference guide. Muscle markings and other bony landmarks were noted.
- Soft-tissue depth markers were placed in the correct anatomical position and soft tissue buildup completed.
- A digital photograph of the finished clay model (Figure 3.8c) was imported into the computer to enhance the image as described above. In this case we had 17 strands of hair—2 silver and 15 brown (reddish)—that were wavy; hence we gave him a brush-backed "rock'n roll" style (Figures 3.8c, d).
- Media release is as important as any other part of the investigation and needs to be conducted in such a way as to gain the best possible coverage. First publicized on 30 November 1990, the newspaper story coincided with a hotly contested Federal Election campaign and no replies were received. The following Easter 1991, the story was run again on a television channel. This resulted in the daughter coming forward, and the identity was finally confirmed with DNA (Figure 3.8e).

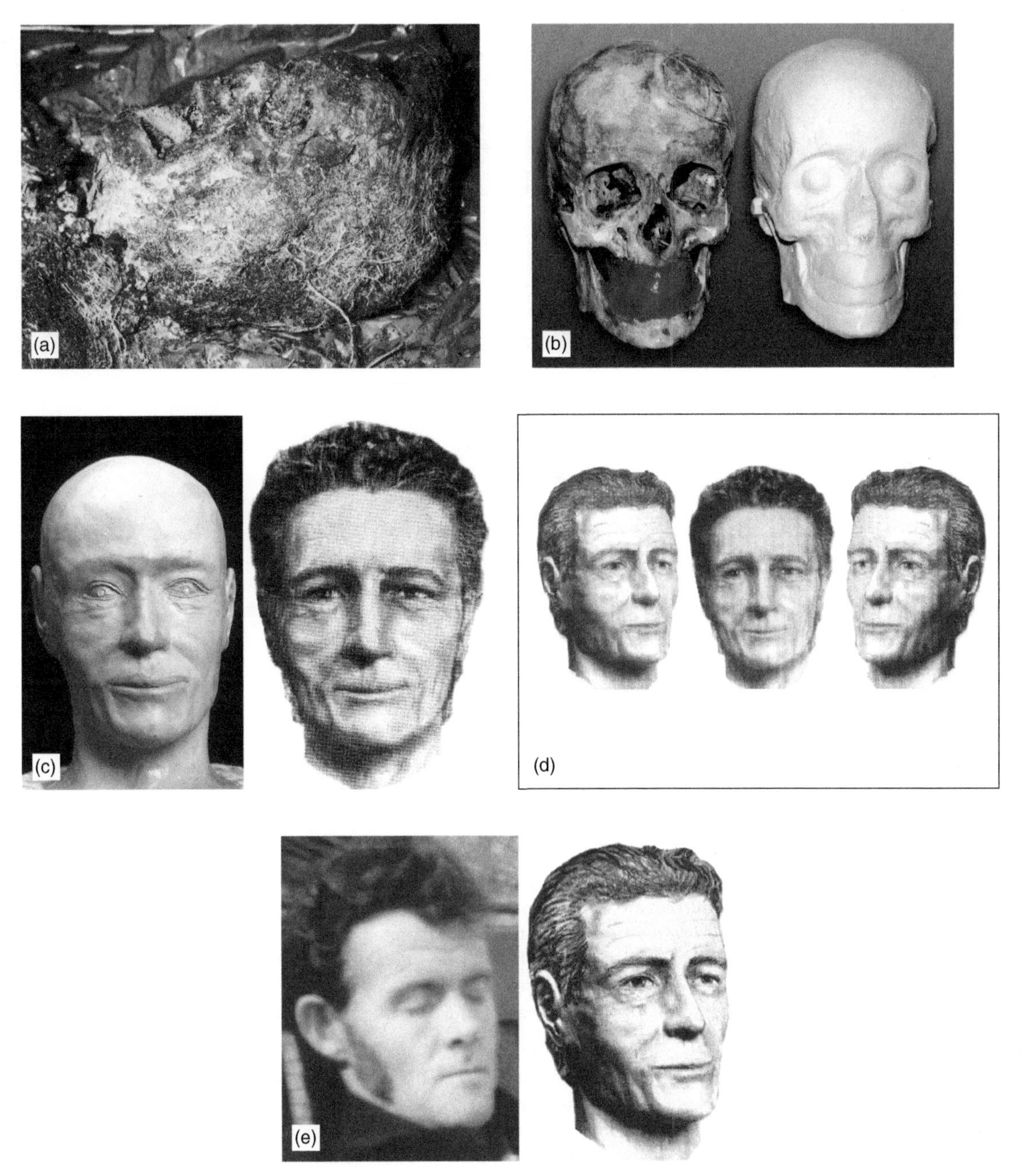

Figure 3.8(a–e) Case 1

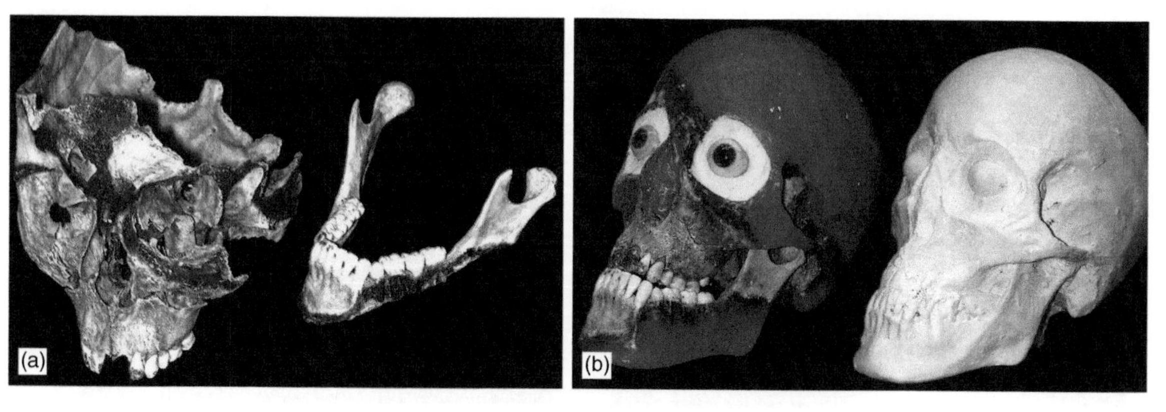

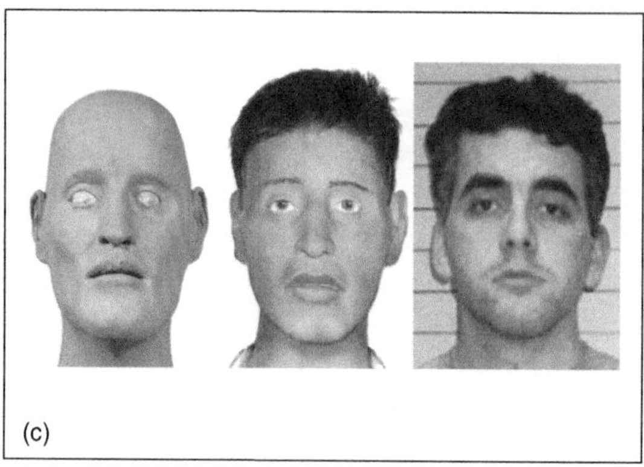

Figure 3.9(a–c) Case 2

CASE 2

In January 2002 a badly charred body was retrieved from a stolen car in a bay-side suburban area of Melbourne, Australia. It had been involved in a high-speed collision with a tree, where the car had ignited on impact. No documentation to assist with identification was found with the body. The pathology and odontology report showed that the deceased was a brown-haired male in his mid-twenties with a height of 182 cm and weight of 62 kg. Large sections of the skull and soft tissue were destroyed by fire (Figure 3.9a).

The teeth were burnt, especially on the left side of the face. Dental x-rays were taken and published in the newsletter of the Australian Dental Association in Australia and New Zealand in an effort to identify any dental work, but without success. The coroner requested that a facial approximation be attempted after the deceased had remained unidentified for seven months. Key points in the facial approximation:

- Dermestes (hide) beetles were used to clean the extremely brittle skull. Missing and damaged sections of the skull were recreated with dental modeling wax (Figure 3.9b).
- Interpretation of individual muscle markings and the bony structural shapes were noted, and the approximation rebuilt on a plaster cast. Finally, computer enhancement of the clay approximation provided a humanized image as well as alternate

likenesses. This was especially important in this case since it was impossible to determine hairstyle (Figure 3.9c).

- Media release needs to concentrate on the image produced and not on the artist that created it. The enhanced approximation was released to the media, and, noting the initial failure previously, we asked the reporter to wait until there was a slow news day before publicizing it in the national press. This was done, and the following day the police received a telephone call from the boy's mother in Cairns in northern Queensland. The identity was subsequently confirmed by DNA.

3.10 CONCLUSION

Facial approximation is a controversial, time-consuming, and limited technique, but may offer the one avenue open to investigators when the only clues to identification of the victim are contained within his bones. A badly damaged skull can only be scanned with a computer with difficulty and the authors believe that more accuracy can be achieved through manual restoration, leaving the computer to enhance the finished reconstruction. Whether a clay approximation is attempted on the skull, or it is merely restored and then scanned, the skills of the anthropologically trained forensic sculptor are necessary if one attempts to use the clues contained within the bones in order to attempt an identification of an unknown body.

REFERENCES

Angel J. L. (1978) *"Restoration of Head and Face for Identification", 30th Meeting of the American Academy of Forensic Sciences,* St Louis, Missouri.

Aulsebrook W. A. and Becker P. J. *et al.* (1996) "Facial Soft-tissue Thicknesses in the Adult Male Zulu", *Forensic Sci. Int.* 79(2), 83–102.

Basker R. M., Devenport J. C. and Tomlin H. R. (1979) *Prosthetic Treatment of the Edentulous Patient.* McMillan, London.

Caldwell P. C. (1986) "New Questions (and some Answers) on the Facial Reproduction Techniques", in: *Forensic Osteology* (K. J. Reichs, ed.). Charles C. Thomas, Springfield, IL, pp. 229–254.

Clements B. S. (1969) "Nasal imbalance and the orthodontic patient", *Am. J. Orthod.* 55, 244–264.

Craig P. J. G. *et al.* (2004) A Longitudinal Study of Facial Morphometrics from Birth to Adulthood Using the Fiore Morphometric Range Finder. *Proceedings of the A.N.Z.F.S.S. Conference, Wellington, New Zealand.*

Davies G., Ellis H. and Shepherd J. (1981) *Perceiving and Remembering Faces.* Academic Press, London.

Dumont E. R. (1986) "Mid-facial Tissue Depths of White Children: An Aid in Facial Feature Reconstruction", *J. Forensic Sci.* 31, 1463.

El-Mehallawi I. H. and Soliman E. M. (2001) "Ultrasonic Assessment of Facial Soft Tissue Thickness in Adult Egyptians", *Forensic Sci. Int.* 117, 99–107.

Fedosyutkin B. A. and Nainys I. V. (1993) "The relationship of Skull Morphology to Facial Features", *Forensic Analysis of the Skull* (M. Y. İşcan, ed.). Wiley-Liss, New York, pp. 199–213.

Gatliff B. P. (1984) "Facial sculpture on the skull for identification", *Am. J. Forensic Med. Path.* 5, 327.

Gatliff B. P. and Snow C. C. (1979) "From Skull to Visage", *J. Biocomm.* 6, 27.

Gatliff B. P. and Taylor K. T. (2001) "Three-Dimensional Facial Reconstruction on the Skull", *Forensic Art and Illustration* (K. T. Taylor, ed.). CRC Press, Boca Raton, pp. 419–475.

George R. M. (1987) "The Lateral Craniographic Method Of Facial Reconstruction", *J. Forensic Sci.* 32, 1305–1330.

George R. M. (1993) "Anatomical and Artistic Guidelines for Forensic Facial Reconstruction", *Forensic Analysis of the Skull* (M. Y. İşcan, ed.). Wiley-Liss, New York, pp. 215–227.

Gerasimov M. (1971) *The Face Finder.*

Gruner O. (1993) "Identification of Skulls: an Historical Review and Practical Applications", *Forensic Analysis of the Skull* (M. Y. İşcan, ed.). Wiley-Liss, New York.

Haglund W. I. and Reay D. T. (1991) "Use of Facial Approximation Techniques in Identification of Green River Serial Murder Victims", *Am. J. Forensic Med. Pathol.* 12(2), 132–142.

Haig N. D. (1984) "The Effect of Feature Displacement on Face Recognition", *Perception* 13, 505–512.

Helmer R. P., Rohricht S., Petersen D. and Mohr F. (1993) "Assessment of the Reliability of Facial Reconstruction", *Forensic Analysis of the Skull* (M. Y. İşcan, ed.). Wiley-Liss, New York, pp. 229–246.

His W. (1895) "Anatomische Forschungen uber Johann Sebastian Bach's Gebeine und Antlitz Nebst Bemerkungen uber Dessen Bilder", *Abh. MathPhysikal. Kl. Kgl. Sachs. Ges. Wiss.*

Krogman W. M. (1946) "The Reconstruction of the Living Head from the Skull", *FBI Law Enforcement Bull.* 11–18.

Krogman W. M., McGregor J. and Frost B. (1948) "A Problem in Human Skeletal Remains", *FBI Law Enforcement Bull.* 17.

Krogman W. M. and İşcan M. Y. (1986) "Restoration of Physiognomy", *The Human Skeleton in Forensic Medicine.* Charles C. Thomas, Springfield, IL, pp. 13–457.

Macho G. A. (1986) "An Appraisal of Plastic Reconstruction of the External Nose", *J. Forensic Sci.* 31, 31.

Macho G. A. (1989) "Descriptive Morphological Features of the Nose. An Assessment of their Importance for Plastic Reconstruction", *J. Forensic Sci.* 34, 902.

Manhein M. H. L. G., Barsley R. E., Musselman R., Barrow N. E., and Ubelaker D. H. (2000) "In Vivo Facial Tissue Depth Measurements for Children and Adults", *J. Forensic Sci.* 45, 48–60.

Miyasaka S. (1999) "Progress in Facial Reconstruction Technology", *Forensic Sci. Rev.* 11(1), 52–90.

Miyasaka S., Kubota S., Matsuda H., Imaizumi I. K. and Yoshino M. (1998) "Anatomical Relations of Skull Morphology to Facial Features by Cephalometrics", *Proceeding – 7th Meeting of International Association of Craniofacial Identification*, Melbourne, Australia.

Neave R. (1998) "Age Changes to the Face in Adulthood", in: *Craniofacial Identification in Forensic Medicine* (J. G. Clement and D. L. Ranson, eds.). Oxford University Press, New York, pp. 225–231.

Penton-Voak I. S., Jones B. C., Little A. C., Baker S., Tiddeman B., Burt D. M. and Perrett D. I. (2001) "Symmetry, Sexual Dimorphism in Facial Proportions and Male Facial Attractiveness", *Proceedings of the Royal Society* 268, 1617–1625.

Prag J. and Neave R. (1997a) *Making Faces: Using Forensic and Archaeological Evidence.* British Museum Press, London.

Prag J. and Neave R. (1997b) "Techniques and the Forensic Evidence", *Making Faces* (J. Prag and R. Neave, eds.). The British Museum Press, London, pp. 20–40.

Rhine J. S. and Campbell C. H. (1980) "Thickness of Facial Tissues in American Blacks", *J. Forensic Sci.* 25, 847–858.

Rhine J. S. and Moore C. E. (1982) "Facial Reproduction: Tables of Facial tissue Thicknesses of American Caucasoids in Forensic Anthropology", *Maxwell Museum Technical Ser. 1*; Albuquerque, NM, 1982. Cited by D. H. Ubelaker.

Roberts V., Vaskoski K. and Craig P. J. G. (2001) "The Association of Lip Shape with Incisal Angle in Facial Profile", *International Association of Craniofacial Identification*, Bari, Italy.

Rogers S. L. (1987) "Reconstructing the Face", *Personal Identification from Human Remains* (S. L. Rogers, ed.). Charles C. Thomas, Springfield, IL.

Russell W. C. (1947) "Biology of the Dermestid Beetle with Reference to Skull Cleaning", *J. Mammology* 28(3), 284–287.

Simpson E. and Henneberg M. (2002) "Variation in Soft Tissue Thicknesses on the Human Face and Their Relation to Craniometric Dimensions", *Am. J. Phys. Anthropol.* 118, 121–133.

Stephan C. N. and Henneberg M. (2001) "Building Faces from Dry Skulls: Are They Recognized above Chance Rates?", *J. Forensic Sci.* 46(3), 432–440.

Stephan C. N. (2003) "Commentary on Facial Approximation: Globe Projection Guideline Falsified by Exophthalmometry Literature", *J. Forensic Sci.* 47(4), 730–735.

Stephan C. N. and Henneberg M. (2003) "Predicting Mouth Width from Intercanine Width: A 75% Rule", *J. Forensic Sci.* 48(4), 725–727.

Stewart T. D. (1979) "Reconstruction of the Facial Soft Parts", *Essentials of Forensic Anthropology* (T. D. Stewart, ed.). Charles C. Thomas, Springfield, IL, pp. 255–274.

Suzuki K. (1948) "On the Thickness of the Soft Parts of the Japanese Face", *J. Anthropol. Soc. Nippon* 60, 7–11.

Taylor K. T. (2001) "Holistic Encoding", *Forensic Art and Illustration.* CRC Press, Boca Raton, pp. 143–145.

Taylor R. G. and Angel C. (1998) "Facial Reconstruction and Approximation", *Craniofacial Identification in Forensic Medicine* (J. G. Clement and D. Dawson, eds.). Arnold, London, pp. 177–186.

Vanezis P., Blowes R. W., Linney A. D., Tan A. C., Richards R. and Neave R. (1989) "Application of 3-D Computer Graphics for Facial Reconstruction and Comparison with Sculpting Techniques", *Forensic Sci. Int.* 42(1–2), 69–84.

von Eggeling H. (1913) "Die Leistungsfahigkeit Physiognomischer Rekonbstruktionsversuche aufGrundlage des Schadels", *Archiv fur Anthropologie* 12, 44–47.

Welcker H. (1883) *Schiller's Schhdel und Todenmaske, nebst Mittheilungen uber Schildel und Todenmaske Kants.* Fr. Vieweg und Sohn, Germany.

Wilkinson C. M. (2002) "In Vivo Facial Tissue Depth Measurements for White British Children", *J. Forensic Sci.* 47(3), 459–465.

Wilkinson C. M. and Mautner S. A. (2003) "Measurement of Eyeball Protrusion and Its Application in Facial Reconstruction (Technical Note)", *J. Forensic Sci.* 48, 12–16.

Wilkinson C. M., Neave R. A. H. and Smith D. (2002) "How Important to Facial Reconstruction Are the Correct Ethnic Group Tissue Depths?", *10th Biennial Scientific Meeting of the International Association for Craniofacial Identification,* Bari, Italy.

Williams P. L. (1995) *Gray's Anatomy.* Churchill Livingstone, New York.

Williamson M. A., Nawrocki S. P. and Rathbun T. A. (2002) "Variation in Midfacial Tissue Thickness of African-American Children", *J. Forensic Sci.* 47, 25.

Yoshino M., Matsuda H., Kubota S., Imaizumi K. and Miyasaka S. (2000) "Computer-assisted Facial Image Identification System using a 3D Physiognomic Range Finder", *Forensic Sci. Int.* 109, 225–237.

Yoshino M. and Seta S. (2000) "Skull-photo Superimposition", *Encyclopaedia of Forensic Sciences* (J. A. Seigel, P. J. Saukko and G. C. Knupfer, eds.). Academic Press, San Diego, pp. 807–815.

CHAPTER 4

THREE-DIMENSIONAL QUANTIFICATION OF FACIAL SHAPE

C. David L. Thomas
School of Dental Science, University of Melbourne, Victoria 3010, Australia

4.1 INTRODUCTION

Anatomy is a subject that is going through a transition from being entirely descriptive to being a quantitative science based on measurement. The delay in transferring methods that are common in the physical sciences to biology is partly due to the innate complexity of biological systems and partly to the difficulties inherent in making sufficiently accurate measurements on the very complex objects created by biological systems (Alexander 2003, Lestrel 2000: Chap. 6, Smye and Clayton 2002). With these inherent difficulties in mind, this chapter will introduce the reader to some of the current approaches to the quantitative analysis of facial form. The rationale for measuring and describing faces and some of the context of the field will be described. Methods for the acquisition of three-dimensional (3D) surface data will be reviewed; this is a rapidly changing subject and detailed information will soon be out of date, but the principles and requirements described here will remain relevant. Some of the methods of analysis that are discussed will be described in detail and explained by the use of an example.

4.2 BACKGROUND: WHY MEASURE FACES?

The reasons for attempting to quantify aspects of the human face influence very strongly the methods adopted for measurement and analysis. All facial analyses make some assumptions regarding the nature of a face, that is, they assume some underlying model of the characteristics of a face and a model of the context in which information from that face is to be used. Different models of facial form capture different characteristics of the face; different applications require different classes of information.

Computer-Graphic Facial Reconstruction
John G. Clement and Murray K. Marks, Editors

Faces may need to be measured and modeled in order to:

- quantify the differences between faces, to predict change in the face;
- diagnose medical conditions;
- predict one set of facial characteristics from another.

Comparisons between faces may be made:

- for identification of offenders;
- to identify missing persons;
- to confirm or refute claims of identity;
- to study the relationship between the skull and the overlying soft tissue;
- to develop diagnostic methods for facial syndromes.

Applications of facial models include the comparison of faces in photographs (2D–2D superimposition), comparison of security camera images with 3D scans of faces (2D–3D comparison), 3D studies of growth or asymmetry, and studies of the relationships between soft and hard issue (pure 3D studies). Each area requires specialized methods and it is unlikely that any one model of a face will be suitable for all applications. Models relating soft tissue to skeletal structure may provide guidelines for forensic facial reconstruction or be of use to orthodontists and oral surgeons for predicting the changes in facial appearance resulting from the changes they make to the skull and jaws.

The group in which the present author works is principally interested in methods for describing the difference between faces or, in the forensic context, for deciding which of a group of faces most closely resembles a test face. Other projects have looked at the relationship between soft- and hard-tissue surfaces (Rose *et al.* 2003), genetic effects in the shape of faces of twins (Darwis *et al.* 2003, Loo *et al.* 2004, Tangchaitrong *et al.* 2000), and the development of methods for the matching of faces in 2D images with 3D surface scans (Fraser *et al.* 2003, Yoshino *et al.* 2002).

4.3 BACKGROUND: WHAT IS A FACE?

The human face is a feature that is so familiar that, for everyday purposes, it does not require a definition. Except for people with very specific neurological deficits, we all think we know what constitutes a face. The *Pocket Oxford Dictionary* provides the definition “front of head from forehead to chin”. Other definitions (collected from the Internet) include:

> the front of the human head, where the eyes, nose, mouth, chin, cheeks, and forehead are

and

> that part of the head, esp. of man, in which the eyes, cheeks, nose, and mouth are situated.

In the facial modeling literature, Waters (1992) defines a face as

> the frontal view of the head from the base of the chin to the hairline, and the frontal half of the head from the lateral view.

This corresponds to the dictionary definitions but the inclusion of the hairline may limit the value of this definition in the case of middle-aged and older males.

For quantitative facial analysis, the use of a repeatable and reproducible definition of the face is vital and the anthropological and orthodontic literature provides some examples. Ferrario *et al.* (1992) defined the facial profile as a line "between the submental soft tissue profile and the prolongation of the mandibular edge, and at the intersection of the forehead profile with a line joining the first point and the lateral eye canthus". Vanco *et al.* (1995) defined the profile to be the soft-tissue outline anterior to a line perpendicular to Camper's plane and passing 5 mm posterior to soft tissue nasion. Camper's plane is defined as a line joining the trageal notch to the lower border of the ala of the nose. These two definitions are useful as a basis for measurement, but both are dependent on the identification of soft-tissue anatomical points, which are not always easy to locate in a repeatable way. Vanco's definition (Figure 4.1) has been used successfully for facial profile analysis by groups associated with the author in the School of Dental Science, University of Melbourne (Darwis *et al.* 2003, Rose *et al.* 2003, Tangchaitrong *et al.* 2000), but has required modification for faces with more extreme characteristics (e.g., excessive retrognathism). This definition is extended to three dimensions by using it to create a cutting plane rather than a line.

Kapur *et al.* (1990) used a complex definition of the profile based on cephalometric hard-tissue landmarks which has the advantage of providing a much more repeatable definition of a face but at the expense of requiring a lateral head radiograph. The portion of the profile used is very restricted with its upper limit on the nose somewhere below nasion and its lower limit near the point of the chin. In the work of Lu (1965), which pioneered the use of Fourier shape analysis of faces, a similar definition was used, but the face was defined to be that portion of the profile between the points menton and nasion and was thus slightly larger. These latter definitions provide much less ambiguity but they exclude the brow-ridges and forehead and thus are restricted in their application. Definitions that refer to profiles are inherently two-dimensional and for many purposes the human face can be considered as two-dimensional. This is possible because the main features of a face lie close to a plane passing through the eyes and a point at the center of the commissure of the mouth. Current face recognition technology relies on this

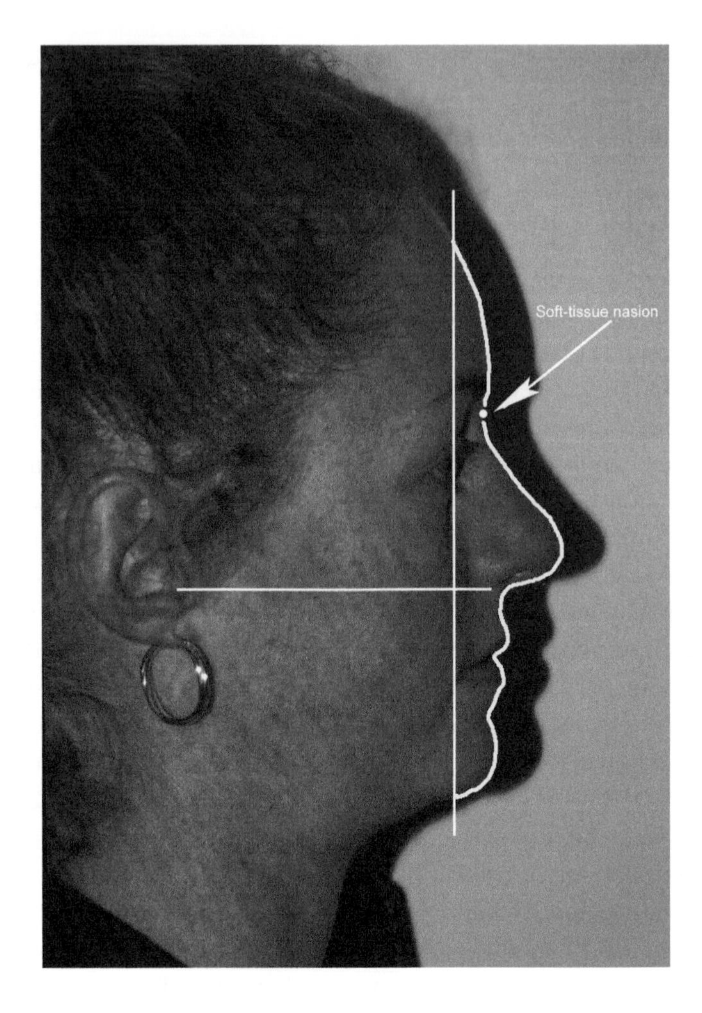

Figure 4.1

Illustrating the definition of a face from Vanco et al. *(1995). This definition can be converted to three dimensions by extending this vertical line into a plane.*

assumption (usually implicit) that the face is two-dimensional, and many of the problems met when attempting to apply face recognition systems in unfavorable conditions of lighting and pose stem from this underlying problem.

This section has attempted to describe some of the properties of the face. What faces do not have are clearly defined edges or vertices and the absence of these introduces some difficult measurement issues into the study of facial differences.

4.4 DATA ACQUISITION METHODS

The development of noncontact methods for acquiring 3D images of faces has made many previously impossible research projects practicable. The absence of any need to make contact with the face removes the difficulties of discomfort and distortion that limit the accuracy and usefulness of measurements made with anthropometric calipers, rulers, or tape measures. Current 3D scanners resolve to around 0.2 mm or better in each dimension and can be calibrated to the same level. This degree of detail is almost certain to be adequate for any studies of entire faces. Acquisition times of two seconds or faster are possible with both structured light systems (e.g., NEC Fiore, Breuckmann faceSCAN II) and laser stripe scanners (e.g., Minolta Vivid 910; the Cyberware 3030 is high quality but somewhat slower). In the author's experience a scanning time of two seconds allows successful, if not entirely trouble-free, scanning of children as young as three years old.

Once acquired, 3D scan images have the considerable advantage of allowing repeated measurements on a subject without the need to recall the individual. One possible drawback is that anatomical points that can only be located accurately by palpation can only be found with limited accuracy. If accurate location of such points is vital to a project, then it is possible, with some inconvenience to the subject, to locate and mark them prior to scanning.

In a clinical setting an alternative path to 3D data from the head is via reconstruction from CT or MRI scans. The resolution is a little lower from CT and noticeably so from MRI, but these imaging modalities give access to internal structures and are particularly valuable for any study that seeks to relate soft tissue features to the underlying skeleton.

The information in this section will be out of date almost as soon as it is written, but some background information is necessary for completeness and is particularly important for those just starting out. At the time of writing there were about 100 manufacturers of 3D scanners around the world, so it should be possible to find a machine to suit most projects. The major problem is still that the costs are very high, particularly when essential software packages are included.

4.5 SOFTWARE TOOLS FOR DATA EXTRACTION AND ANALYSIS

Finding software for the measurement of faces is much more of a problem than finding suitable scanners. Special needs make special demands on the software that may not easily be met, and for many projects, researchers will have to be able to write their own programs. To date the author has only found two commercial packages specifically designed for the 3D measurement and analysis of faces: 3DRugle3 (Medic Engineering, Kyoto, Japan; http://www.rugle.co.jp) and DigiSize (Cyberware, Monterey, California; http://www.cyberware.com), which is part of a whole-body scanning package. Commercial reverse engineering software such as PolyWorks (Innovmetric Software, Quebec, Canada; http://www.innovmetric.com/) and Rapidform

(INUS Technology, Seoul, Korea; http://www.inustech.com) deal very well with the point cloud data produced by many scanners. In particular they are invaluable for composing multiple 3D scans of a single object into a composite model. With many scanners this process is necessary for the creation of full head (or even ear-to-ear) surfaces.

Statistical analysis of landmark data can be carried out in any of the many commercial statistical programs, but one freeware package that has been specifically developed for this purpose is PAST (PAlaeontological STatistics; http://folk.uio.no/ohammer/past/). The shareware package MorphoStudio (http://www.morphostudio.com/) is specifically intended for the analysis of facial data. This software provides advanced morphometric tools for analysis and predictive modeling. Forecasting algorithms are available for modeling the effects of surgical implants.

Researchers with the need to develop their own analysis methods have a wide range of options available to them but for ease of use and comprehensive mathematical and plotting capabilities Matlab (The Mathworks, Natick, Massachusetts, USA; http://www.mathworks.com) is hard to beat. Most of the illustrations in the following section have been created using Matlab for both analysis and plotting.

4.6 QUANTITATIVE DIFFERENCES BETWEEN FACES

The morphometric descriptions of faces that are presented in this chapter are derived empirically from measurement and observation; they do not pretend to represent the underlying biological processes that drive the growth and development of a face. As such they do not constitute *models* of the face in the sense of having any predictive power. Lestrel (2000: p. 102) asks a basic question regarding morphometrics:

> ... whether biological processes can even be derived, in some sense, from an analysis of size and shape. It [is] precisely this question that remains a challenge for morphometrics.

Again from the writing of Lestrel (2000: p. 109), we have:

> Related ... is the need for an adequate numerical characterization of form which becomes, in one way or another, the *raw data* for model building.

In the studies of facial form described here, we are collecting the data needed for quantitative descriptions of faces that will be useful for the calculation of inter- and intraface differences.

Faces have a very complex structure and the differences between individual faces are subtle. However, the general conformation of a face is always the

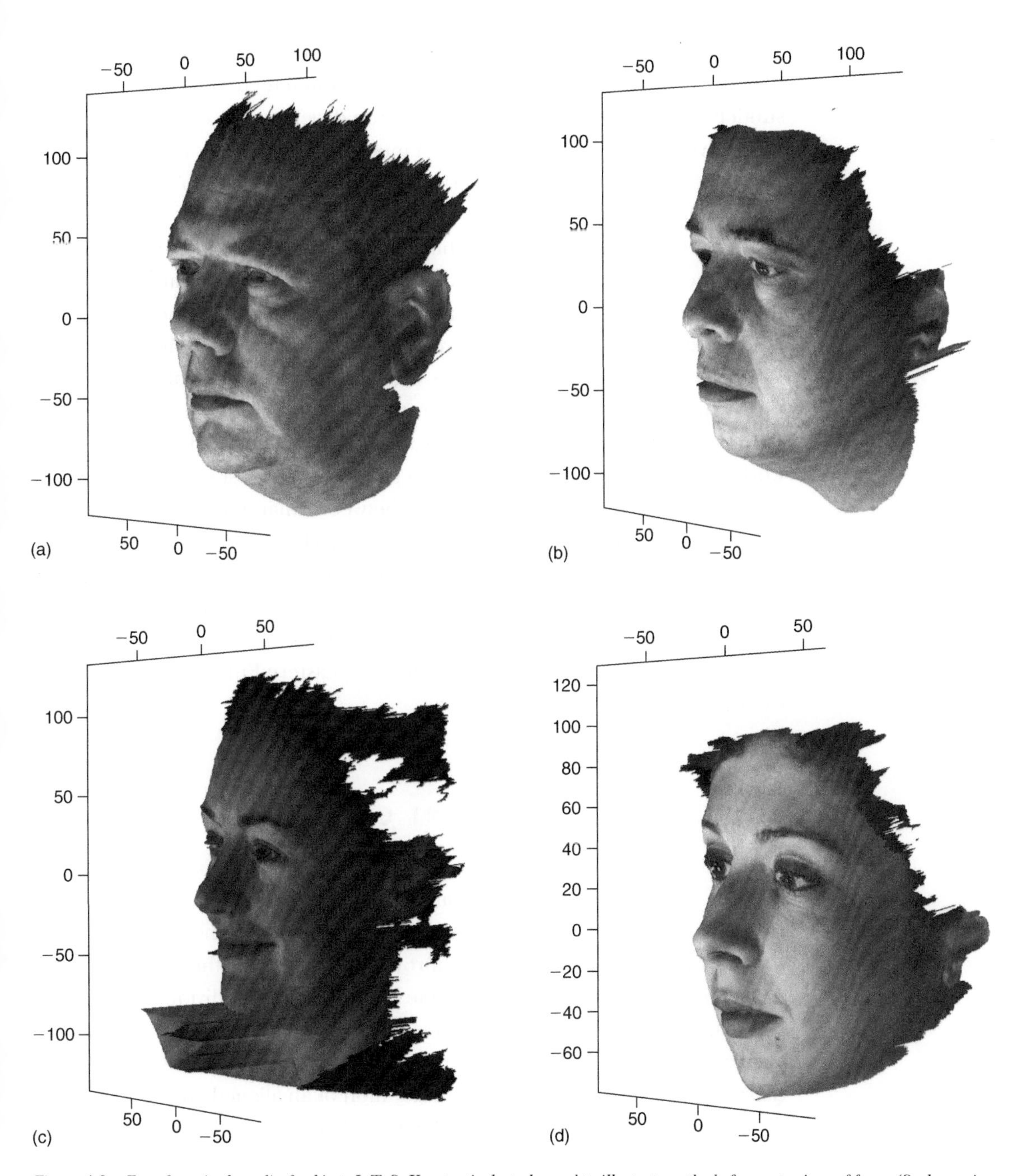

Figure 4.2 Four faces (a, b, c, d) of subjects J, T, S, K respectively, to be used to illustrate methods for comparison of faces. (Scales are in millimeters.)

same: the eyes are above the nose and spaced more or less evenly each side of the midline, the mouth is below the nose and (baring normal asymmetry or deformity) centered on the midline. It is probable that no two faces are identical, even in monozygotic twins (Loo 2004, Tangchaitrong 2000), and it must be recognized that the differences discussed here are second-order and are likely to be measured in small numbers of millimeters. The complexity and subtlety of faces is a major problem for the development of more complete predictive (as opposed to descriptive) models of facial form. It is to be hoped that the current quantitative descriptive studies will lead on to the creation of more biologically meaningful models of the human face.

If we restrict ourselves to describing faces, then the methods of description chosen need to be appropriate for the problem. Landmarks cannot give outline information, outlines lack a global location relative to other outlines or landmarks, and volumetric measurements are best done on point cloud data. Whatever morphometric method is used, it should be possible to calculate with it, and its statistical properties must be manageable. Three general classes of morphometric method are applicable to 3D analysis of faces: those that work directly with the point cloud data generated by most scanners, methods that use the location of, and distances between, anatomical landmarks, and methods that analyze boundary (outline) data. These various methods will be illustrated with a simple experiment to measure the differences between four faces; subject J is a heavily built Anglo-Celtic male in his mid-50s, subject T is a heavily built Eastern European male of 45 years, subjects S and K are slightly built females in their mid- to late-20s, K being Eastern European and S Anglo-Celtic in origin (Figure 4.2(a–d)).

4.7 DATA TYPES: POINT CLOUDS

Many 3D scanning systems produce data in the form of point clouds, either as random x, y, z locations or as rectangular arrays of z values. The addition of color information for each location turns the point cloud into a complete 3D surface image of a face. As well as improving the realism of the facial scans, the availability of the color image makes the identification of individual anatomical landmarks very much easier and more accurate. Scanning systems based on triangulation or structured light patterns usually provide the color data automatically; laser stripe scanners require the addition of an aligned and synchronized digital camera. Typically, point-cloud data sets that represent faces contain a few hundred thousand points; the NEC Fiore system in the author's laboratory produces surface images of 640×640 ($=409\,600$) points, each with x, y, z measurements and RGB color data. With such high-resolution data available, the calculation of intersurface distances and volume differences between pairs of faces (or successive images from a time series of a single face) becomes possible.

Intersurface and volume differences have formed the basis of projects designed to measure the differences between faces over time. For example,

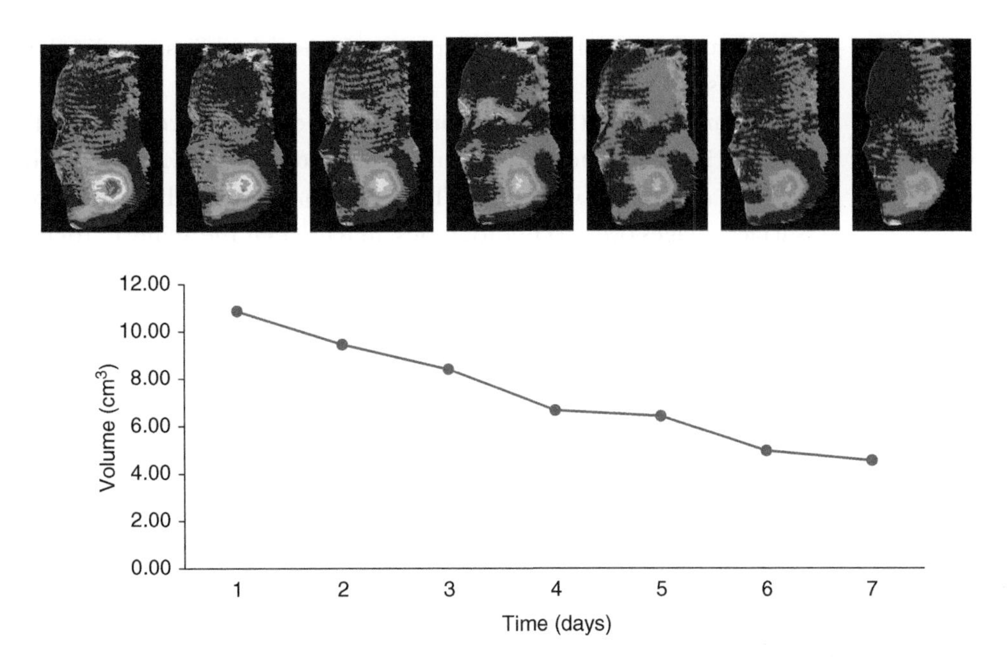

Figure 4.3 Measurement of the resolution of a facial swelling: "before and after" comparison on the same face.

Yip *et al.* (2004) assessed the usefulness of a range-camera system for the measurement of facial swelling (Figure 4.3) and concluded that

> the ... imaging system is an accurate, reproducible and rapid method for the volumetric evaluation of facial swelling.

They simulated post-operative facial swelling using silicone inserts and were able to measure the resulting facial surface deformation to an accuracy of around 2% or better. Liu and Palmer (2003) studied facial asymmetry using 3D point cloud surface scans of faces that were reduced from 200 000 points to a network of 15 625 grid points, the reduction process taking account of the amount of detail in different parts of the face. In their data analysis, they calculated two measures of asymmetry: the height difference between corresponding grid points each side of the midline of the face, and the difference in the orientation of the surface normals at the same set of corresponding points. They concluded that the technique could detect bilateral facial asymmetry and was sensitive enough to show the greater degree of asymmetry in male faces than in female ones. They also state that

> ... many current research efforts are showing promising gains towards the ultimate goal of constructing a completely autonomous 3D human identification system,

an opinion with which the present author agrees. The goal is still some way in the future but there is no doubt that completely autonomous human identification that accounts for all possible variations in pose and lighting will rely on 3D methods.

Hammond *et al.* (2001) explored the use of 3D surface scans for the diagnosis of Noonan syndrome, a congenital syndrome that includes mild abnormalities of facial morphology. They point out some of the advantages of 3D surface images over 2D photographs, in particular the ability to rotate the 3D images to obtain different views of the face, something that is not possible with a photograph, where the viewpoint is permanently fixed. This flexibility in selection of new viewpoints is a powerful argument for the use of 3D scanning for any study of facial morphology. This argument is particularly compelling in studies of growth in children, where the very growth that is being studied makes later repeats of a measurement impossible. Hammond goes on to describe the creation and display of thin-plate spline surfaces from their models and illustrates that these can display the visual characteristics of Noonan syndrome.

A simple application of point-cloud data is the calculation of "average faces", and the author has developed software to find the mean and standard deviation of faces acquired using an NEC "Fiore" range-finding scanner. Figure 4.4(a, b) show the results of carrying out this procedure on 24 Japanese male faces. These faces were scanned by Dr. Mineo Yoshino and his staff at the National Research Institute of Police Science of Japan and registered to each other by Dr. Ashraf Shaweesh. The choice of landmarks for registration is a major problem in that we need to align one face with another in a reproducible manner. The faces used to create Figure 4.4 were collocated using the point subnasal and aligned in rotation by registering the outer canthi of the eyes.

Figure 4.4

(a) The average of 24 Japanese male faces; (b) the associated standard deviation image.

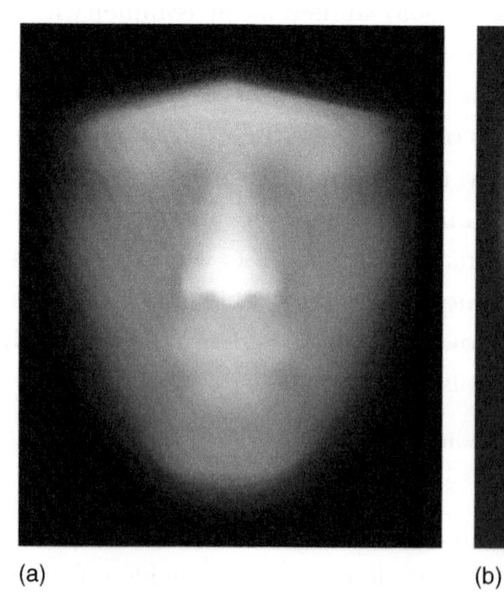

(a)

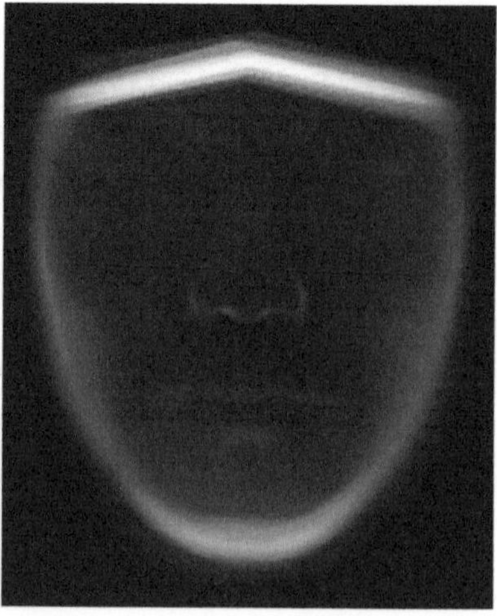

(b)

The results of measurements will vary depending on this alignment; in particular the maximum variation between faces is zero at the point used for registration (subnasal in Figure 4.4). Facial averages, surface–surface distances, and volume difference calculations all vary with the alignment of the faces being compared. This dependence on landmarks for alignment makes the distinction between methods of analysis that use point-cloud data and those that are purely landmark-based somewhat arbitrary. However, there are methods that make use of landmarks alone, and these will be described in the next section.

4.8 DATA TYPES: LANDMARKS

If a number of faces are to be compared quantitatively, then a coordinate system must be established on each individual face in such a way as to allow the relative location and alignment of the faces to be standardized. Such a coordinate system can be defined by identifying a set of anatomical landmarks on each of the faces being compared, and Figure 4.5 shows 15 landmarks that are, with the possible exception of numbers 5, 14, and 15, reasonably easy to identify and locate on all faces. Landmarks are either anatomical features defined on the soft-tissue surface (e.g., the canthi of the eye) or on a radiograph (e.g., sutures between bones of the skull), or points defined as extremes of location or curvature (e.g., the tip of the nose) and hence referred to as extremal points.

Analysis of the relative locations of landmarks may also be used as the major method for comparisons between faces. Descriptions of a method for

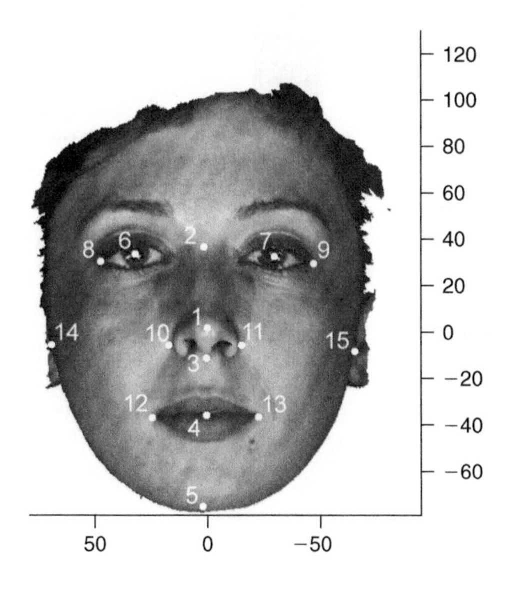

Figure 4.5

The fifteen landmarks used in the examples. (Scales are in millimeters.)

the matching of 3D models to 2D images can be found in the work of Yoshino and co-workers (Fraser *et al.* 2003, Yoshino *et al.* 2000, Yoshino *et al.* 2002). In this work the 3D model is rendered to a monitor screen in a pose controlled by the operator and the pose is adjusted to match that apparent in the 2D image (Figure 4.6). After alignment the 2D distances apart of up to 15 corresponding landmarks (some landmarks may be obscured in some cases) are summed to give an estimate of how well the faces match. Yoshino demonstrated that summed distance values less than 2.8 mm for 15 landmarks give a high probability that the images are of the same person.

When comparing faces, the choice of landmarks for alignment will have a significant impact on the observed location of differences. For example, in the work on average faces described in the previous section, faces are aligned using the two outer canthi of the eyes and a subnasal point. These points were chosen for the ease with which they can be located repeatedly and for being well spaced on the face, which maximizes the accuracy of alignment. However, this choice of alignment landmarks inevitably results in the maximum differences between faces being observed to occur in the lower portion, particularly around the chin, of the face. In work where it is the overall difference between faces that is of interest, this biasing in location of the shape differences doesn't matter; in studies that attempt to quantify the magnitude and direction of facial growth, for example, it is critical, so critical in fact as to make use of this method inappropriate for studies of growth (Bookstein 1978, O'Higgins 1997). This effect will occur whatever landmarks are chosen, as

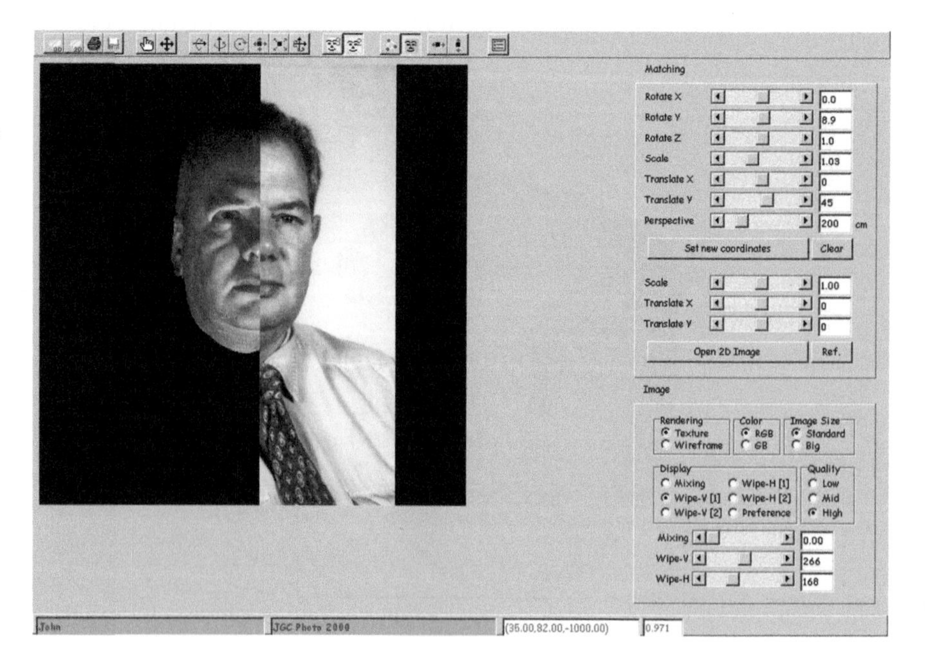

Figure 4.6

The 2D–3D face matching process in 3D Rugle. Here a 2D image is being matched to a 3D scan using corresponding landmarks.

both reference points and non-reference points will appear to move away from them.

One useful way to avoid problems with the registration of multiple faces is to use a method such as euclidean-distance matrix analysis (EDMA), with which the distances between landmarks, rather than the coordinates of their locations, are compared. As with the methods of Yoshino *et al.* (2000, 2002), the differences between corresponding interlandmark distances can be summed to generate a measure of the similarity between two faces. Some results from carrying out an EDMA on the four test subjects are summarized in Tables 4.1 and 4.2. The values in the upper part of Table 4.1 are millimeter distances between the labeled points for Subject J. In the lower half of Table 4.1 are the differences (again in millimeters) between corresponding measurements for Subject J and Subject T, along with the total difference calculated using the magnitudes of the differences only. Column 2 of Table 4.2 summarizes the results of carrying out the same procedure for all pairs of the four subjects. These results confound differences in facial shape with differences in size,

Table 4.1

Examples of euclidean distance matrices: see Figure 4.5 for definitions of points 1–15. Upper table contains millimeter distances between points; the lower table has the differences (again in mm) between the measurements for two subjects.

Point	2	3	4	5	6	7	8	9	10	11	12	13	14	15
1	40.8	16.7	45.2	77.7	47.5	48.3	58.1	57.0	25.1	26.3	54.4	53.1	78.2	72.9
2		57.5	86.0	118.5	37.2	36.5	51.8	49.8	60.1	61.1	92.2	91.0	86.0	81.6
3			28.5	61.0	59.7	60.8	67.9	67.2	19.3	20.4	40.7	39.4	80.9	75.7
4				32.5	84.3	85.5	89.7	89.2	35.0	34.8	27.1	25.5	92.8	87.6
5					114.5	115.9	117.9	117.9	64.5	64.2	40.4	40.5	113.5	109.4
6						71.5	14.6	84.5	50.0	73.8	79.0	99.0	49.7	112.0
7							86.1	13.3	73.4	51.7	101.4	79.7	117.0	47.0
8								99.0	54.7	84.2	79.9	107.1	36.8	125.7
9									81.9	54.4	107.8	79.6	129.1	35.4
10										39.6	32.2	54.3	62.3	94.2
11											56.2	30.2	100.7	56.4
12												52.5	73.1	112.0
13													115.7	68.9
14														150.9

Point	2	3	4	5	6	7	8	9	10	11	12	13	14	15	Row
1	3.3	4.7	6.1	3.7	0.7	0.6	2.2	1.2	3.9	6.9	4.6	3.4	1.8	3.2	46.3
2		8.0	9.5	7.0	6.0	0.8	8.1	2.6	10.4	11.1	9.0	6.3	1.3	2.3	82.2
3			1.5	1.0	4.1	3.7	4.7	3.2	0.4	2.1	0.7	0.8	0.1	2.9	25.1
4				2.5	5.5	4.7	5.6	3.6	0.2	0.9	1.0	1.3	3.0	1.8	30.1
5					2.5	2.9	2.2	1.7	2.9	3.6	1.5	0.0	1.9	1.4	20.5
6						5.0	2.1	6.5	5.4	8.3	3.8	3.3	5.5	0.1	40.1
7							7.1	1.8	5.3	6.3	4.4	2.7	0.3	3.5	31.4
8								8.5	5.4	9.0	3.4	3.8	7.9	1.6	39.5
9									5.1	4.6	3.9	1.3	0.9	5.4	21.1
10										3.0	1.4	1.4	0.1	2.0	7.9
11											0.5	4.9	2.5	3.9	11.8
12												0.0	3.1	1.7	4.9
13													0.5	1.5	1.9
14														5.0	5.0
														Total	367.7

Table 4.2

A set of differences between euclidean distance matrices. Values are sums of the square roots of the squares of all differences between EDMs. Units are millimeters.

Subjects	Difference value	Normalized difference
J to T	368	3.34
K to S	462	3.30
K to T	618	2.98
J to K	813	2.43
S to T	1015	5.83
J to S	1235	4.07

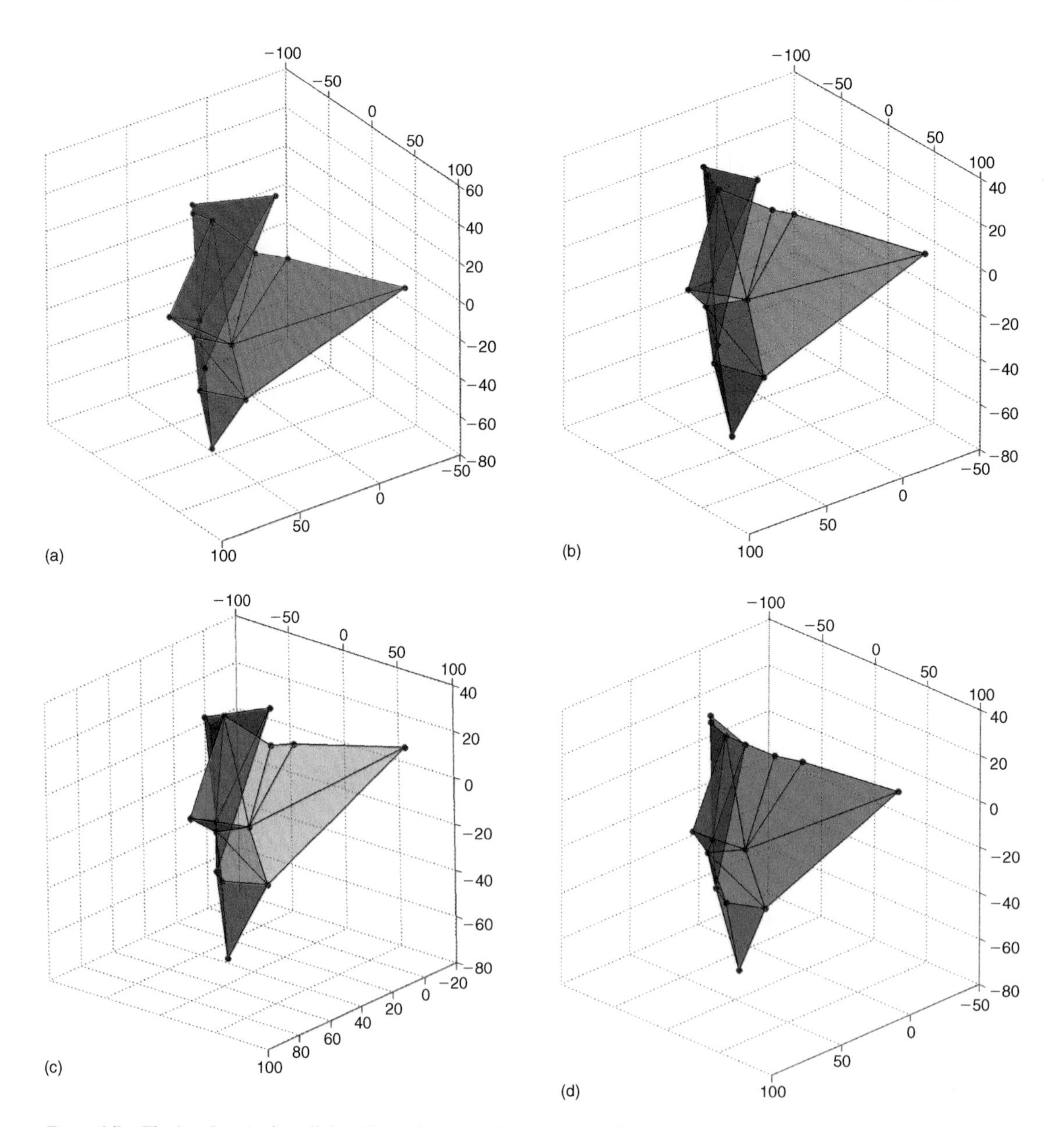

Figure 4.7 The four faces (a, b, c, d) from Figure 4.2 rendered as triangular planes connecting the landmarks shown in Figure 4.5. This illustrates the maximum information contained in a set of landmarks. (Scales are in millimeters.)

and for purposes of identification from facial images this is what is required. However, if the aim is to study differences in facial shape, independent of size, then column 3 of Table 4.2 shows a set of values derived from an EDMA procedure carried out using distances normalized for a measure of facial height. The main problem with such attempts to separate the size and shape components of facial forms is the choice of a size measure. No single linear dimension is going to serve for all purposes and, in any case, normalization to a linear measurement is only really appropriate for one-dimensional distance measurements. For 2D normalization an area should be used as the standard, but for 3D a volume would be more appropriate.

The most significant limitation to studies using landmarks is that they are incapable of recording any information at all regarding the form of the surfaces between the landmark points. For example, with the faces derived from the 3D surface scans of the four test subjects shown in Figure 4.7, it is not possible to distinguish between faces with full cheeks (*a* and *b*) or flat ones (*c* and *d*). Thus landmark-based methods ignore a very significant proportion of the information available for discriminating between faces.

4.9 DATA TYPES: OUTLINES

For the purposes of this chapter, 2D (or perhaps they should be called $2\frac{1}{2}$ D) outlines are extracted from sets of 3D data by defining a set of planes having one of the three dimensions held constant, probably at the value for an anatomical landmark. Values in the other two dimensions vary to describe the outline. Facial profiles (Figure 4.8) can provide a very much richer method for the description of a set of faces than can be obtained from landmark data alone. Analysis of multiple outlines is a useful and practical intermediate step between landmark analysis and yet-to-be-developed methods for the detailed quantitative description of 3D surfaces. This analysis can generate sets of numbers that are able to capture most of the shape information available in individual faces and that will allow comparisons to be made with maximum effectiveness.

The rest of this section will concentrate on describing in detail one method, elliptical Fourier functions (EFFs), for the analysis of outline data. This is a widely accepted and very general method for the analysis of any outline shape. For more extensive treatments of boundary morphometrics, the reader could start with the work of Lestrel (1997, 2000) or O'Higgins (1997), both of which discuss the topic in detail and have extensive bibliographies.

Fourier series analysis is named after Joseph Fourier (1768–1830), an amateur mathematician and professional colonial administrator under Napoleon. The basic idea of Fourier analysis is that any smooth and continuous periodic

Figure 4.8

A representation of a face using thirteen profiles.

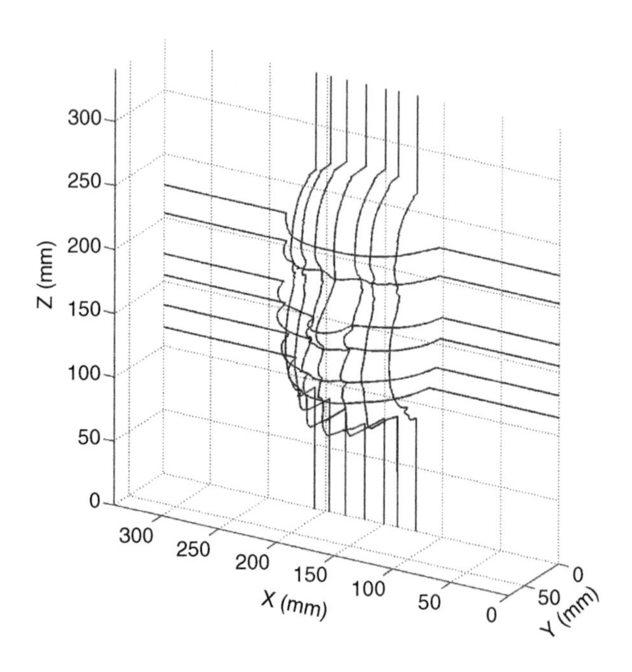

function, including completely arbitrary ones described by a table of data points, can be represented as the sum of a series of sine and cosine terms. The idea of applying Fourier analysis to biological shapes originated with Thompson (1917) in connection with leaf outlines, but the severe limitation imposed by hand calculation probably made the method impractical. Kuhl and Giardina (1982) introduced EFFs and early on they were proposed as a method for identification by pattern recognition of military targets such as aircraft. The method fell out of fashion for pattern recognition but has proved to be a useful technique for shape analysis of biological forms. The outline under study is analyzed as two series, one of each of its projections onto two orthogonal planes. Each term in the Fourier series has a magnitude, and these coefficients can be considered as a frequency spectrum of the function; in shape analysis this can be called a "shape spectrum", and higher-order terms should be interpreted as describing finer detail. The desired precision determines how many terms are needed in the series: for facial profiles, 20 to 30 terms will give a very accurate analysis. The process is reversible, and the Fourier series can be truncated and the inverse transform performed in order to recover an approximation of the original shape. Figure 4.9 is a transverse profile of Subject J at the level of the tip of the nose.

Figure 4.10 shows plots of the magnitudes of the coefficients of the first 30 terms in the EFF of the profile from Figure 4.9. As is typical of facial profiles the projection (labeled "Y projection" in the figure) that represents the

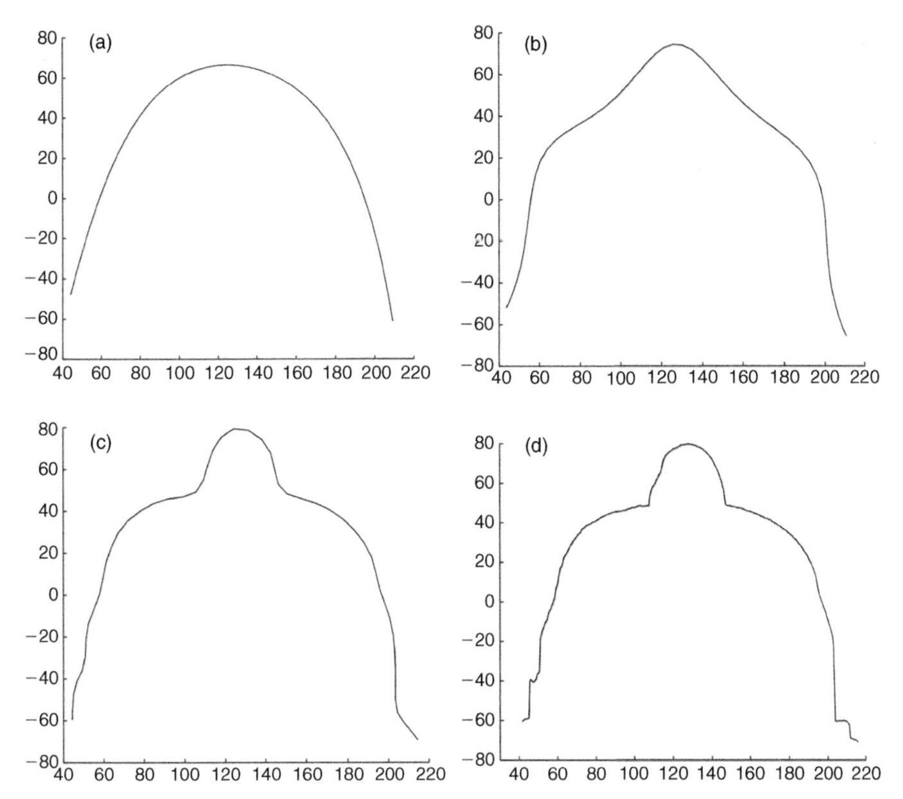

Figure 4.9

Illustrating Fourier shape reconstruction of a facial profile. Increasing the number of terms of the Fourier series (a two terms, b five, c 20, d 30) that are used in the reconstruction increases the amount of detail provided. The scales are in millimeters.

anterior–posterior direction has more information (i.e., shows a more detailed and extended shape spectrum). A characteristic of EFFs used for the analysis of open outlines is that the nth term in the series represents the contribution of details at a scale of the overall size of the outline divided by $n/2$. In the case of a facial profile 150 mm high, the 30th term represents features of around 10 mm in size. Unfortunately a single number represents the contributions of all features at this scale, and it is not often possible to ascribe anatomical meaning to any given term in the Fourier series.

EFFs may be better for describing the difference between faces than for analyzing the anatomical features statistically. The method preserves the starting point of the outline being studied (O'Higgins 1997), which may be chosen to be an anatomical landmark. Thus, if we analyze faces in several anatomically meaningful sections, this will at least partly overcome the objection that the coefficients of a Fourier shape spectrum do not give information about the location of features. The difficulties with shape analysis of the boundaries of biological objects are due to the complexity of the problem and will continue to make analysis of facial shape difficult and incomplete.

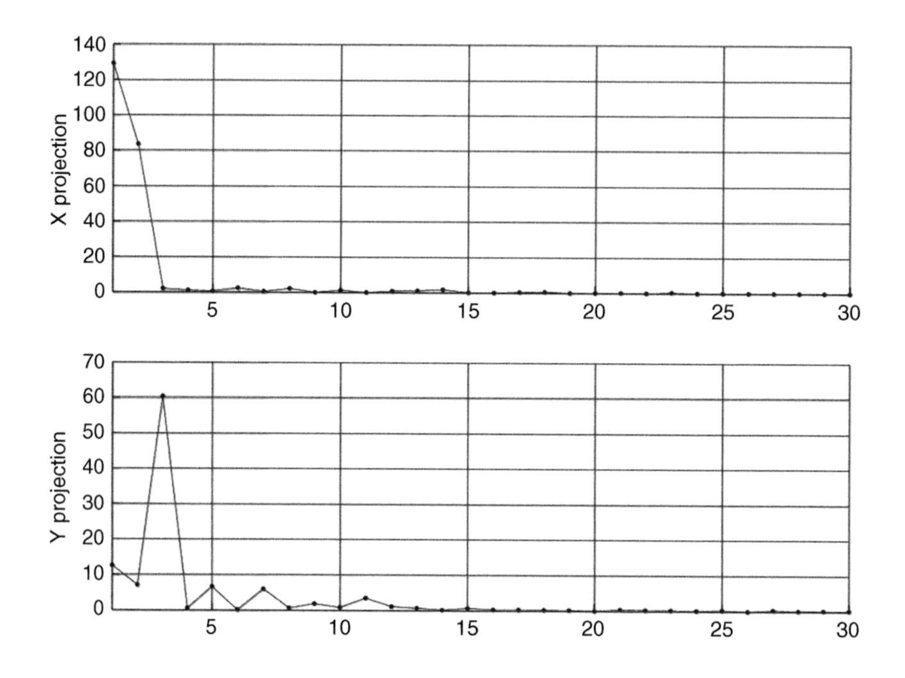

Figure 4.10

Shape spectrum of the profile shown in Figure 4.9.

4.10 CALCULATION OF DIFFERENCES BETWEEN FACES

Table 4.1 shows an example of a simple calculation of the difference between the EDMs of two faces.

When this process is carried out for all possible pairs of the test subjects, the final result is as Table 4.2. The results in Table 4.2 indicate that the differences bear out the intuitive assessment that the heavily built males and slightly built females should form pairs that are the most similar.

At the least similar end of the table the greatest differences are found between one of the females (subject S) and both males. The differences between subject K and the two males are less pronounced. One way to find the difference between two EFFs is to take the sum of the absolute differences between corresponding pairs of coefficients. Table 4.3 presents the results of doing this for all possible pairs of the subjects and for five parasagittal and three transverse profiles.

Here the order of similarity is less easily explained, but the two people of Eastern European origin form the most similar pair of subjects. The least similar are the two thin females. Clearly this method is capturing a different type of similarity. In the absence of serious statistical analysis, and with a very small sample, no real conclusion can be drawn from this little example other than that the choice of method for the comparison of facial shape in 3D can be critical to the outcome.

Parasagittal		Transverse	
K to T	7.70	K to T	3.88
J to T	18.19	J to K	10.93
J to S	20.79	J to S	13.09
J to K	24.44	J to T	13.74
S to T	26.53	K to S	18.27
K to S	31.80	S to T	20.17

Table 4.3

Sets of differences between EFFs of both parasagittal and transverse sets of facial profiles. Sorted with the most similar pairs of subjects at the top.

4.11 CONCLUSION

This chapter has presented some of the issues to be considered in the analysis and comparison of human faces using 3D measurements. A brief review of the available commercial scanning equipment and software has been provided. Methods for the description of faces have been discussed and contrasted and two methods for the calculation of the difference between faces introduced. Only recently has 3D data been available at reasonable cost, and methods for its analysis are still under development. The difficulties with shape analysis of faces indicate that the problem is complex and will continue to make analysis of facial shape difficult and incomplete. Nevertheless, the developments in 3D data acquisition and analysis provide the promise of great progress in the understanding of the myriad differences between human faces and this subject looks set for strong growth.

ACKNOWLEDGEMENTS

The author and his colleagues are particularly grateful to NEC Japan for the ongoing loan of the Fiore facial rangefinder and associated software, without which their work on the 3D morphometrics of faces would not have been possible. Mr. Toyohisa Tanajiri of Medic Engineering, Kyoto, Japan, made his 3DRugle software available and has been very generous in assisting with its modification and use.

Dr. Mineo Yoshino, Director of the First Forensic Science Division of the National Research Institute for Police Science of Japan has been helping, guiding, and encouraging the author for a long time and his continued support is very gratefully acknowledged.

Among the author's colleagues, Dr. Tim Bakerov provided technical help and permission to use images of his face. Ms. Sherie Blackwell, Professor John Clement, and Dr. Kornelija Sfera gave permission for the use of images of their faces. John Clement inspired the work described in this chapter when he asked the author if it was possible to find a number that would describe a human face.

That single number is likely to prove elusive, but with John's support and encouragement the search for meaningful sets of numbers to describe a face continues.

Some of the work on which this chapter is based was supported by the Australian Research Council via Discovery-Projects Grant No. DP0208510.

REFERENCES

Alexander R. McN. (2003) "Modelling Approaches in Biomechanics", *Philosophical Transactions of the Royal Society of London* 358, 1429–1435.

Atsuchi M., Noguchi K., Kubota S., Imaizumi K., Sakurada K., Yoshino M., Fraser N. L., Thomas C. D. L. and Clement J. G. (2002) "Evaluation of Morphometric Matching for the Identification of Caucasian Faces from Blurred Images", *Japanese Journal of Science and Technology in Identification* 6(2).

Bookstein F. L. (1978) "The Measurement of Biological Shape and Shape Change", *Lecture Notes in Biomathematics Vol 24*. Springer, Berlin.

Darwis W. E., Messer L. B. and Thomas C. D. (2003) "Assessing Growth and Development of the Facial Profile", *Pediatric Dentistry* 25(2), 103–108.

Ferrario V. F., Sforza C., Miani A., Poggio C. E. and Schmitz J. (1992) "Harmonic Analysis and Clustering of Facial Profiles", *Int. J. Adult Orthodontics and Orthognathic Surgery* 7(3), 171–179.

Fraser N. L., Yoshino M., Imaizumi K., Blackwell S. A., Thomas C. D. L. and Clement J. G. (2003) "A Japanese Computer-Assisted Facial Identification System Successfully Identifies Non-Japanese Faces", *Forensic Sci. Int.* 135, 122–128.

Hammond P., Hutton T. J., Patton M. A. and Allanson J. E. (2001) "Delineation and Visualisation of Congenital Abnormality Using 3D Facial Images", presented at the *Intelligent Data Analysis in Medicine and Pharmacology* workshop, MEDINFO 2001, London.

Kapur K. K., Lestrel P. E. *et al.* (1990) "The Use of Fourier Analysis to Determine Age-Related Changes in the Facial Profile", *Int. J. Prosthodontics* 3(3), 266–273.

Kuhl F. P. and Giardina C. R. (1982) "Elliptic Features of a Closed Contour", *Computer Graphics and Image Processing* 18, 236–258.

Lestrel P. (ed.) (1997) *Fourier Descriptors and Their Applications in Biology.* Cambridge University Press.

Lestrel P. (2000) *Morphometrics for the Life Sciences.* World Scientific Publishing Co.

Liu Y. and Palmer J. (2003) "A Quantified Study of Facial Asymmetry in 3D Faces", in: *Proceedings of the 2003 IEEE International Workshop on Analysis and Modelling of Faces and Gestures*, in conjunction with the 2003 International Conference of Computer Vision (ICCV'03), October 2003.

Loo S. M., Messer L. B., Thomas C. D. L. and Townsend G. C. (2004) "Frontal Facial Features in Young Twins: Assessment by Fourier Shape Analysis", submitted to *The Angle Orthodontist*, 27th February 2004.

Lu K. H. (1965) "Harmonic Analysis of the Human Face", *Biometrics* (June 1995), 491–505.

O'Higgins P. (1997) "Methodological Issues in the Description of Forms", in: *Fourier Descriptors and Their Applications in Biology* (Pete E. Lestrel, ed.). Cambridge University Press, Cambridge, pp. 74–105.

O'Higgins P. and Jones N. (1998) "Facial Growth in *Cercocebus Torquatus*: an Application of Three-Dimensional Geometric Techniques to the Study of Morphological Variation", *J. Anatomy* 193, 251–272.

O'Higgins P. (2000) "The Study of Morphological Variation in the Hominid Fossil Record: Biology, Landmarks and Geometry", *J. Anatomy* 197, 103–120.

Rose A. D., Woods M. G., Clement J. G. and Thomas C. D. L. (2003) "Lateral Facial Soft-Tissue Prediction Model: Analysis Using Fourier Shape Descriptors and Traditional Cephalometric Methods", *Am. J. Phys. Anthropol.* 121(2), 172–180.

Sheridan C. S., Thomas C. D. L. and Clement J. G. (1997) "Quantification of Ethnic Differences in Facial Profile", *Australian Orthodontic J.* 14(4), 218–224, March.

Smye S. W. and Clayton R. H. (2002) "Mathematical Modelling for the New Millennium: Medicine by Numbers", *Medical Engineering and Physics* 24, 565–574.

Tangchaitrong K., Messer L. B., Thomas C. D. L. and Townsend G. C. (2000) "Fourier Analysis of Facial Profiles of Young Twins", *Am. J. Phys. Anthropol.* 113, 369–379.

Thompson D. W. (1917) *On Growth and Form*. Cambridge University Press.

Vanco C., Kasai K. *et al.* (1995) "Genetic and Environmental Influences on Facial Profile", *Australian Dental Journal* 40(2), 104–109.

Waters K. (1992) "Modelling Three-Dimensional Facial Expressions", in: *Processing Images of Faces* (V. Bruce and M. Burton, eds.). Norwood, NJ, Ablex, pp. 202–227.

Yip E., Smith A. and Yoshino M. (2004) "Volumetric Evaluation of Facial Swelling Utilizing a 3-D Range Camera", *Int. J. Oral and Maxillofacial Surgery* 33, 179–182.

Yoshino M., Matsuda H., Kubota S., Imaizumi K. and Miyasaka S. (2000) "Computer-Assisted Facial Image Identification System Using a 3-D Physiognomic Range Finder", *Forensic Sci. Int.* 109, 225–237.

Yoshino M., Noguchi K., Atsuchi M., Kubota S., Imaizumi K., Thomas C. D. L. and Clement J. G. (2002) "Individual Identification of Disguised Faces by Morphometrical Matching", *Forensic Sci. Int.* 127, 97–103.

CHAPTER 5

AUTOMATIC 3D FACIAL RECONSTRUCTION BY FEATURE-BASED REGISTRATION OF A REFERENCE HEAD

Gérard Subsol
FOVEA Project and Intrasense, Cap Oméga – CS 39521*
Rond Point Benjamin Franklin, 34960 Montpellier cedex 2, France

*http://foveaproject.free.fr

Gérald Quatrehomme
Laboratoire de Médecine Légale et Anthropologie médico-légale,
Faculté de Médecine, Avenue de Valombrose, 06107 Nice cedex 2, France

5.1 INTRODUCTION

As emphasized by Bramble *et al.* (2001), "two and three-dimensional computer-based reconstruction systems have been developed to make the reconstruction process faster, more flexible and to remove some of the subjectivity and inconsistencies associated with the traditional approaches (illustrative identikit and 3D clay based reconstruction)". We can attempt to classify the 3D computer-based methods that have been presented in the last fifteen years into the three following categories.

MORPHOMETRY-BASED METHODS

The user chooses some sites on the skull surface where he defines the facial thickness. A facial surface is then adjusted (or "warped") to fit with the selected sites by applying some 3D transformations. The main difficulty is in determining a class of transformations that are both complex and regular enough to deform precisely and consistently the face surface. Vanezis *et al.* (1989), who made one of the first attempts to use a 3D computer-graphic method, applied transformations that are nonuniform scalings. Since then, more complex transformations such as bilinear interpolation (Plasencia 1999), spline functions (Archer *et al.* 1998, Vignal 1999), radial basis functions (Vanezis *et al.* 2000), and hierarchical volume deformation (Petrick 2000) have been introduced.

Computer-Graphic Facial Reconstruction
John G. Clement and Murray K. Marks, Editors

MORPHOLOGY-BASED METHODS

The user sets up the morphology of the face by including the muscles and the fat, before ending the reconstruction by putting on the skin layer. Wilhelms and Van Gelder (1997) presented computer-graphics algorithms to model the bones, muscles, and underlying skin. Kähler *et al.* (2003) fitted a precise reference anatomical model of the head on the unidentified skull by using the correspondences between some skull and skin landmarks. A similar procedure was also developed to simulate or plan facial surgery by Koch *et al.* (1996).

In fact, these two classes of methods combine an automatization and an extension of traditional reconstruction processes that are described by Quatrehomme and Subsol (2005). The first one is easier to implement as it does not require any anatomical model; rather it relies on data—some tens of landmarks and the corresponding facial thicknesses—that are very sparse.

REGISTRATION-BASED METHODS

This class of methods requires first to design a reference head model, consisting of a skull and a face model that can be extracted from 3D images acquired by computer tomography (Shaham *et al.* 2000) or 3D laser scanning (Tyrrell *et al.* 1997). The reference skull is then registered with the model of the unknown skull in order to compute a 3D deformation. This deformation can then be applied to the reference face in order to infer the unknown face (see Figure 5.1). In Nelson and Michael's (1998) paper, some structures called "discs" that define the 3D deformation are manually placed on key features around the unknown and the reference skulls. Seibert (1997) used simulated

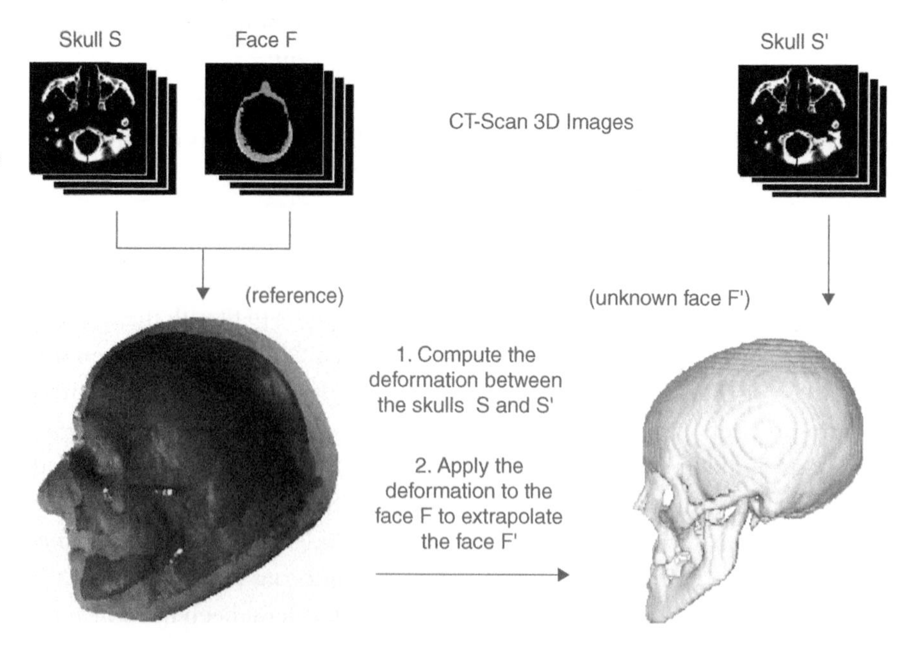

Figure 5.1

In registration-based methods, the reference and the unidentified skulls are registered and the resulting 3D deformation is applied to the reference face to infer the unknown face.

annealing to support a manual identification of corresponding features. The method of Attardi *et al.* (1999) is in two steps: some anthropological points are manually identified on the two skulls and define a first deformation that allows them to track and register new feature points in order to obtain a refined deformation. Jones (2001) proposes an algorithm based on intensity correlation between the two 3D images of the skulls to extract the feature points automatically. Tu *et al.* (2004) transform the 3D skull model into a 2.5D representation by using cylindrical coordinates. This allows the performance of a 2D registration algorithm that is based on the intensity.

Notice that the different classes of method can be also mixed. For example, Jones (2001) uses the registration result to map the facial thickness of all the points of the reference head on the unidentified skull in order to define the underlying face.

The registration-based methods appear to us as the most promising as they do not require any anthropological measurements or complex anatomical knowledge and can be based on the whole surface data of the skull and the face. Moreover, a lot of progress has been made in 3D image processing in recent years (see e.g., Ayache 2003) and many registration algorithms have been developed and tested. In the next section, we will describe the method we have investigated for several years (Quatrehomme *et al.* 1997). We will then present some results before discussing some difficulties raised by this class of methods.

5.2 DESCRIPTION OF THE METHOD

5.2.1 DATA ACQUISITION

THE ACQUISITION PROCESS

Computer-tomographic (CT) scanning of the head of a cadaver may lead to many problems. For ethical reasons, it becomes quite impossible to use a regular medical CT scanner that is used for living persons. Moreover, some technical problems can occur, for example, caused by the presence of metallic material in teeth (Spoor *et al.* 2000). A solution can be to take a cast of the face and to digitize it separately from the dry skull (Quatrehomme *et al.* 1997).

The skull and the face cast are then placed into the CT device (see Figure 5.2) which gives, in a few minutes, a series of several tens of digital images representing the successive slices of the anatomical structure. These images are, in general, of a resolution of 512 by 512 pixels which are coded in several thousands of gray levels. They are then "stacked" in order to build up a three-dimensional image. CT scanners that are routinely used in medical radiology have a resolution of one millimeter, whereas special industrial microscanners can reach up to a resolution of 100 microns (Thompson and Ilerhaus 1998).

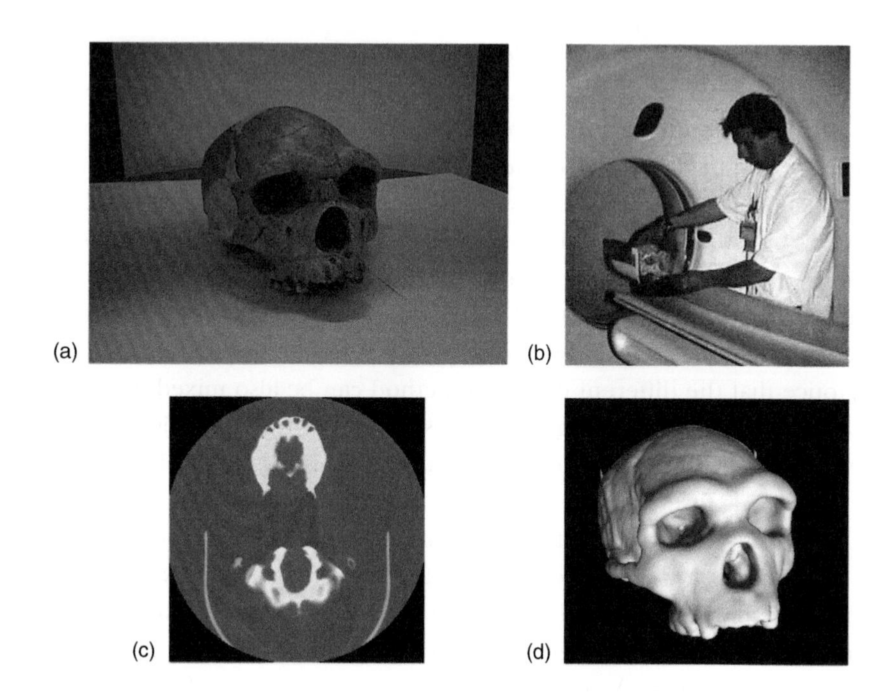

Figure 5.2

Obtaining a 3D representation of the head. The anatomical structure (or its cast) (a) is placed in the CT scanner (b). We obtain then a series of several tens of digital images of 512 by 512 pixels in gray levels that correspond to slices (c). It is then possible to "stack" the slices, extract the surface of the anatomical structure, and visualize it in 3D on a computer screen (d).

Some 3D image-processing algorithms developed for medical imaging or computer-assisted design (CAD) are applied to extract the surface of the structure from the 3D image and to display it, from any point of view, on the screen of a computer.

THE REFERENCE HEAD

As reference-head data, we used the CT scan of the cast of the face and of the dry skull of a man who died in his seventies (see Figure 5.3). The 3D images consist in 62 slices with a thickness of 3 mm, composed of 512 by 512 pixels of 0.6 by 0.6 mm. The face and the skull were aligned manually by fitting some anatomical landmarks—a difficulty being that the opening angle of the mandible must be exactly the same on the cadaver as on the skeletonized skull, and a special device had to be developed. For this reason, in the following experiment number 2, we have "deleted" the mandible in order to focus only on the upper part.

EXPERIMENT 1: UNKNOWN CONTEMPORARY SKULL

We applied the same procedure as described for experiment 2 (see Figure 5.4).

EXPERIMENT 2: PREHISTORIC SKULL OF THE MAN OF TAUTAVEL

In the second experiment, we use a CT scan of a cast of the reconstruction of the skull of an ante-Neandertalian, known as the "man of Tautavel", estimated

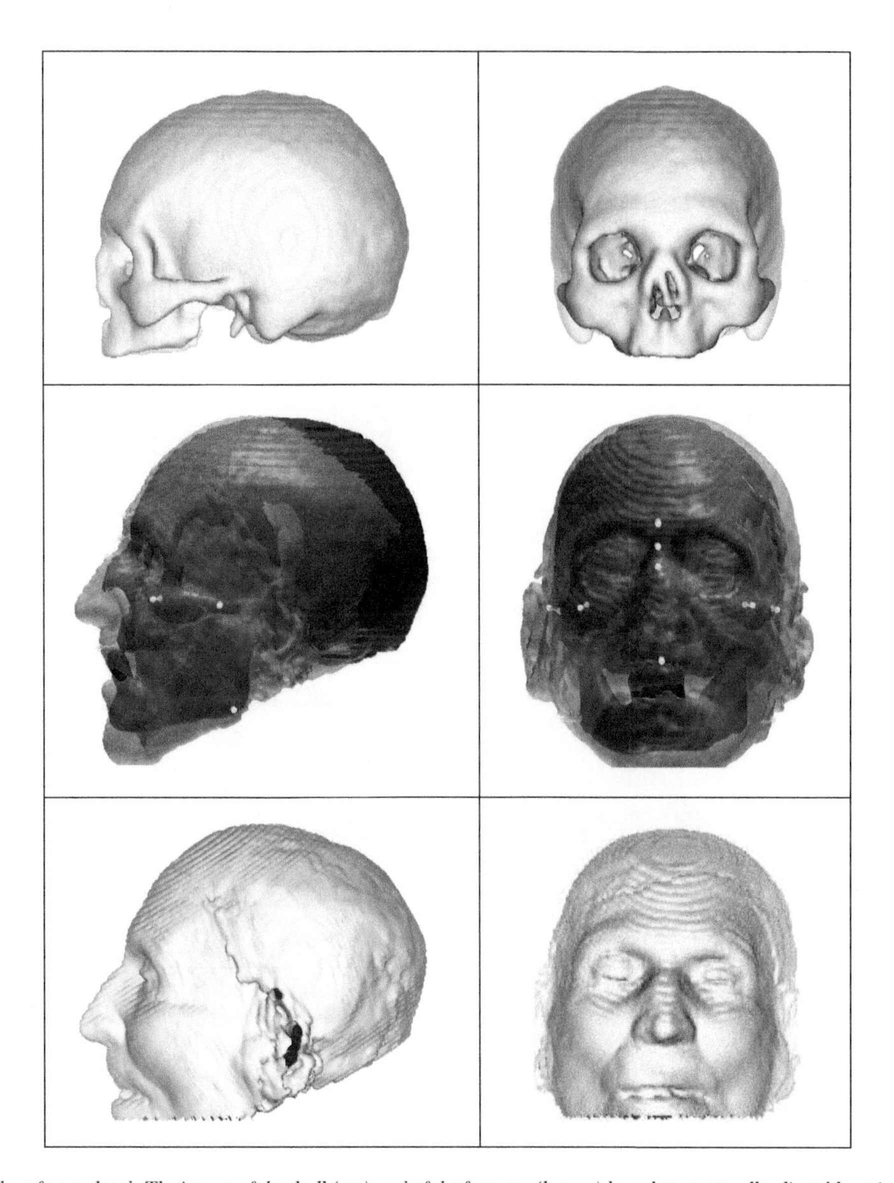

Figure 5.3 The reference head. The images of the skull (top) and of the face cast (bottom) have been manually aligned by using some anatomical landmarks (middle).

to be 450 000 years old (see Figure 5.5). The prehistoric reconstitution is based on the face (Arago XXI) and on the right parietal (Arago XLVII) that were found in the Arago cave at Tautavel, France, in 1971, and on the left parietal being obtained by symmetry, on a mold of the Swanscombe occipital, and on the temporal bone and its symmetric of Sangiran 17 (Pithecanthropus VIII) (de Lumley *et al.* 1982). The 3D image consists of 154 slices with a thickness of 1 mm, composed of 512 by 512 pixels of 0.5 by 0.5 mm.

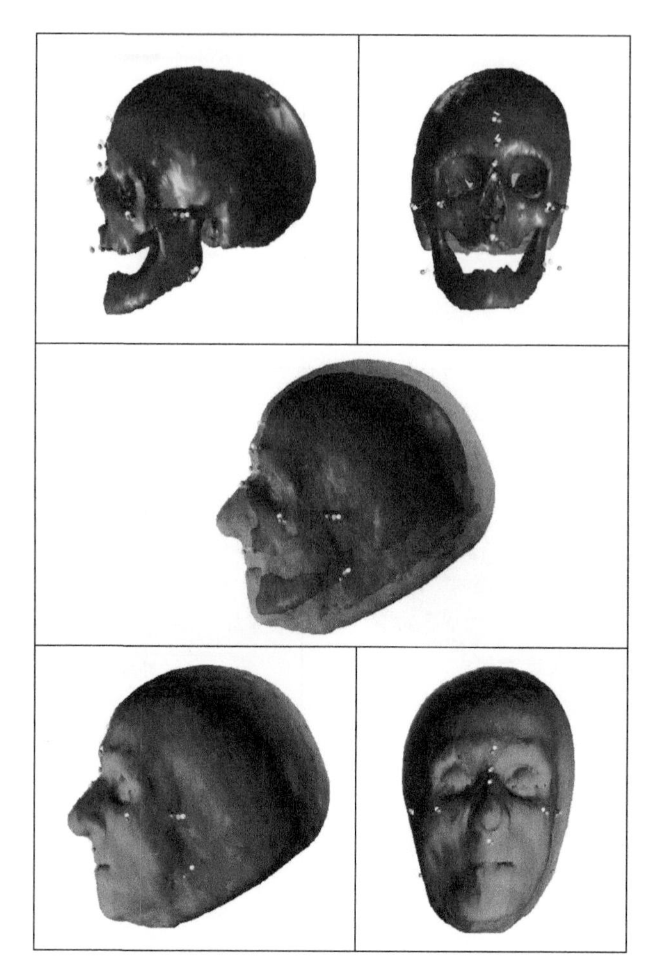

Figure 5.4 Experiment 1: as for the reference head, the images of the skull (top) and of the face cast (bottom) have been manually aligned by using some anatomical landmarks (middle).

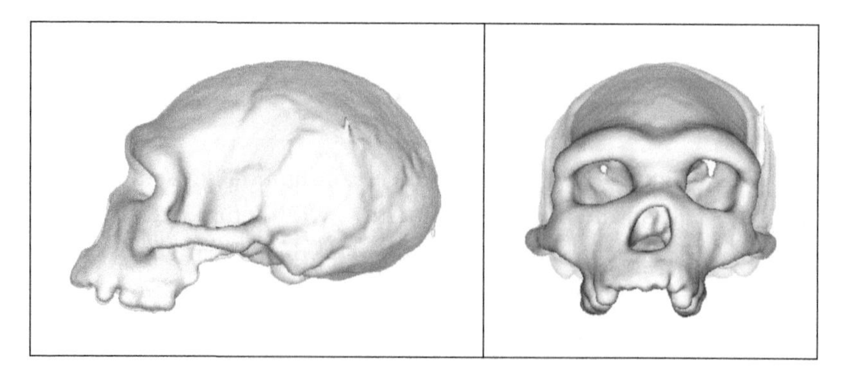

Figure 5.5 Experiment 2: the aim is to infer the prehistoric face of the Man of Tautavel from the fossil skull that is estimated to be 450 000 years old.

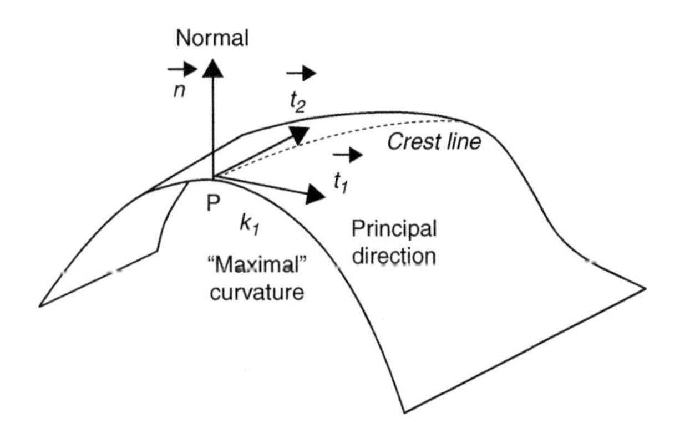

Figure 5.6

Mathematical definition of crest lines:
k_1: maximal principal curvature in absolute value,
t_1: associated principal direction.
grad $k_1 \cdot t_1 = 0 \Leftrightarrow P$ *is a crest point and belongs to a crest line.*
Reprinted from Medical Image Analysis (Subsol et al. *1998), with permission from Elsevier.*

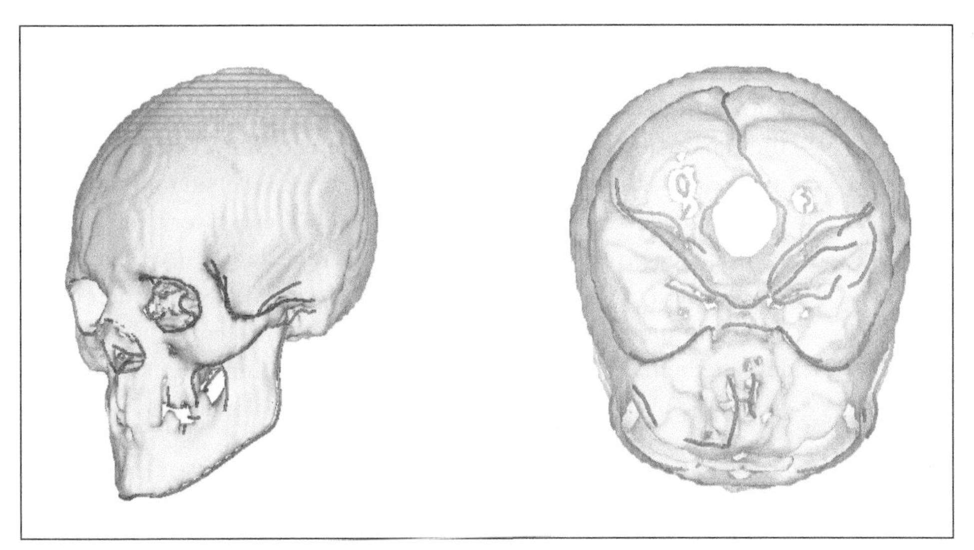

Figure 5.7 Crest lines automatically extracted in a CT scan of a skull. Notice how crest lines emphasize the mandible, the orbits, the cheekbones, or the temples and also, inside the cranium, the sphenoid and temporal bones as well as the foramen magnum. Reprinted from Medical Image Analysis (Subsol et al. *1998), with permission from Elsevier.*

5.2.2 EXTRACTION OF FEATURE POINTS AND LINES

To compute the 3D transformation, we have to find some landmarks on the surface of the skull. They must be defined by an unambiguous mathematical formula to be automatically computed and be anatomically relevant to characterize the structure. We chose "crest lines" (Thirion and Gourdon 1996) which are defined by the extrema of the principal curvature, where it has the largest absolute magnitude, along its associated principal direction (see Figure 5.6). By their definition, these lines follow the salient lines of a surface. We can check this in Figure 5.7 where the crest lines, automatically extracted in a CT scan of a skull, emphasize the mandible, the orbits, the cheekbones, or the temples and also, inside the cranium, the sphenoid and temporal bones as well as the foramen magnum.

Salient structures are also used by doctors as anatomical landmarks. For example, the crest-line definition is very close to the "ridge-line" one given by Cutting *et al.* (1993) (see Figure 5.8), which corresponds to the type II landmark in Bookstein's typology (Bookstein 1991). In Figure 5.9, we display on the same skull the crest lines (in gray) which were automatically extracted and the ridge lines (in black) which were extracted semimanually under the supervision of an anatomist. The two sets of lines are visually very close, showing that crest lines would have a strong anatomical significance.

5.2.3 REGISTRATION OF FEATURE LINES

We extracted several hundred crest lines composed of several thousand points on the skulls and then needed to find the correspondences between these features (see Figure 5.10). Usually this is done manually by an anatomist who knows the biological homology: two features are put into correspondence if they characterize the same biological functionality. In our case, there are so many points that this becomes impossible, and we had to design an algorithm to find the correspondences automatically. This is a very well known problem in 3D image processing called "automatic registration" (Ayache 2003). We have developed a method described by Subsol *et al.* (1998) that deforms iteratively and continuously the first set of lines towards the second one in order to superimpose them. At the end of the process, each point P_i of the first set is matched with the point Q_i of the second set that is the closest, and some inconsistent

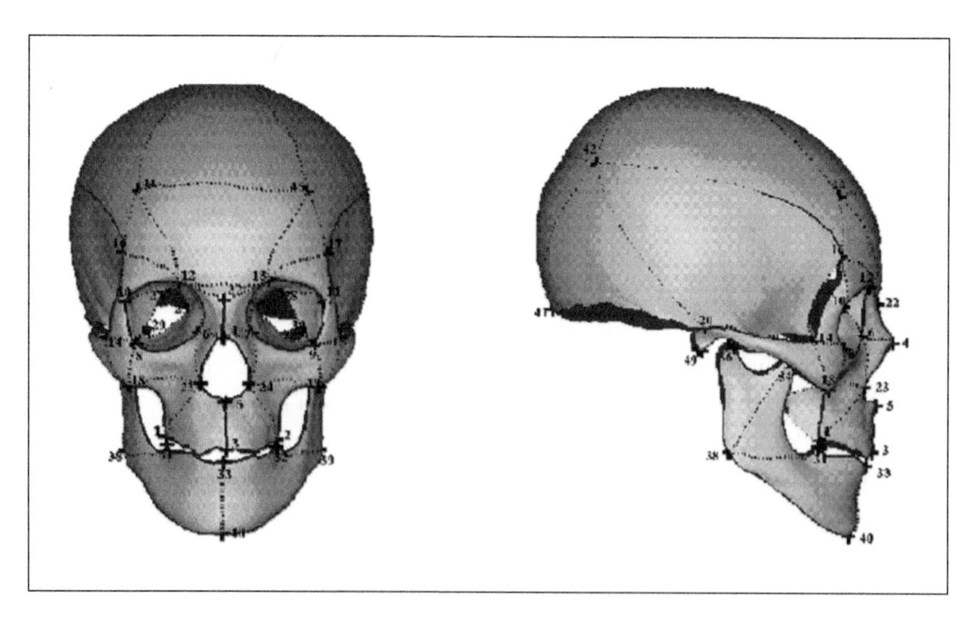

Figure 5.8 "Ridge lines" are extracted semimanually under the supervision of an anatomist and are used for applications in craniofacial surgery and paleontology (Dean et al. *1998). By permission of the Journal of Craniofacial Surgery.*

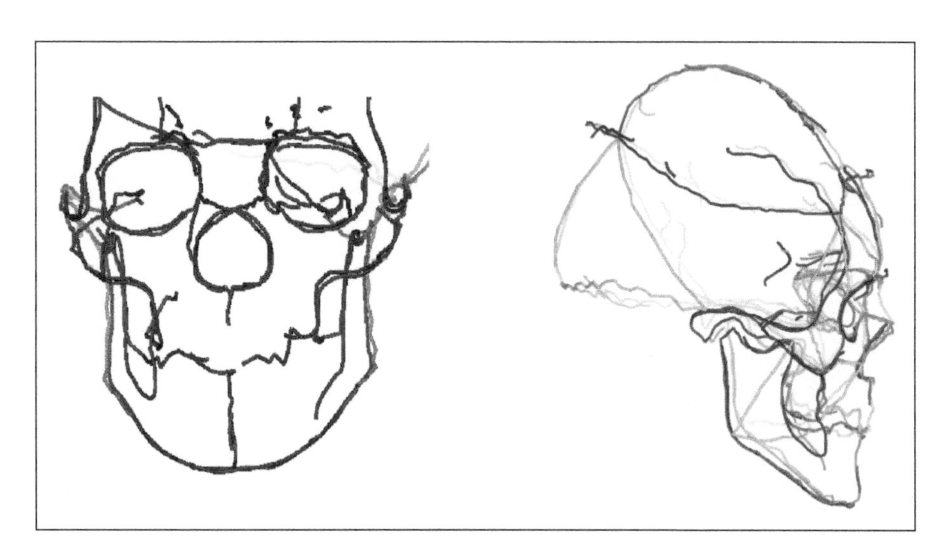

Figure 5.9 Comparison of "ridge" lines and "crest" lines. The precise superimposition of crest (in red) and ridge lines (in blue) shows that crest lines would have a strong anatomical significance, even if they are based on a mathematical definition. Reprinted from Medical Image Analysis (Subsol et al. *1998), with permission from Elsevier.*

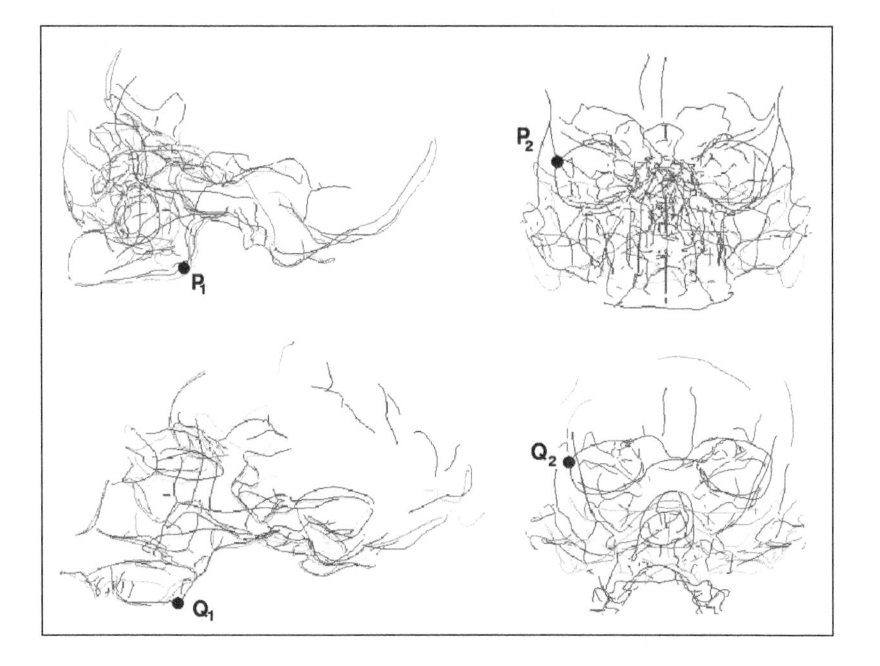

Figure 5.10

The registration problem in experiment 2. The difficulty is to find the correspondences between the features as for example, the pairings (P_1, Q_1) or (P_2, Q_2).
Top: crest lines on the reference skull (536 lines and 5,756 points).
Bottom: crest lines on the skull of the Man of Tautavel (337 lines and 5,417 points).

correspondences are discarded. In our experiments, the algorithm finds in some minutes, on a standard personal computer, around 1,500 points pairings (P_i, Q_i), located all around the inside and outside surfaces of the skull.

Thirion *et al.* (1996) checked on the data of several skulls that these registration results are consistent with those obtained by another automatic method

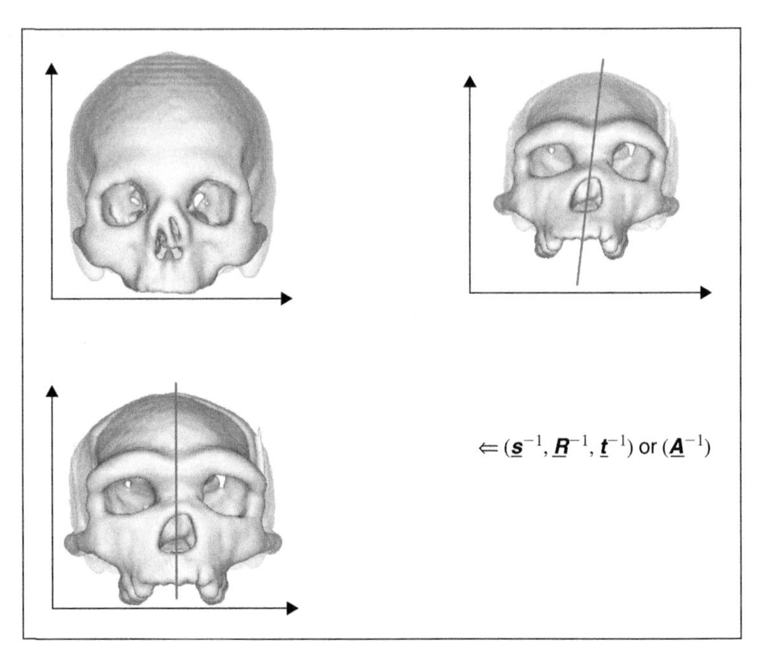

Figure 5.11 The complex geometrical normalization in experiment 2. First, the rotation $\underline{\boldsymbol{R}}$*, the translation* $\underline{\boldsymbol{T}}$*, and the scaling* $\underline{\boldsymbol{s}}$ *are automatically computed based on pairs of homologous points* (P_i, Q_i) *in order to align the two skulls in the same position and orientation and to compensate for the difference of global size. Moreover, we can notice that the skull of the Man of Tautavel is bent (top, right). This is due to the fact that it had lain on its side and was compressed by gravity. We have modeled this taphonomic deformation by applying an affine transformation* $\underline{\boldsymbol{A}}^{-1}$*: the two skulls are now normalized and comparable (bottom, left).*

and by a semimanual method where an anatomist supervises the detection of homologous points.

5.2.4 GEOMETRICAL NORMALIZATION

Before computing the deformation between the reference and the unknown skulls, we have to align them in the same position and orientation and to compensate for the difference of global size (see Figure 5.11). This requires the computation of the three following transformations: the rotation $\underline{\boldsymbol{R}}$, the translation $\underline{\boldsymbol{T}}$, and the scaling $\underline{\boldsymbol{s}}$. Several methods exist to compute $(\underline{s}, \underline{R}, \underline{t})$ based on pairs of homologous points (P_i, Q_i), as the "Procrustes superimposition" (Boostein 1991) or the "least-square distance" minimization that leads to:

$$(\underline{s}, \underline{R}, \underline{t}) = \text{Argmin}\ (s, R, t) \sum_i \| sRP_i + t - Q_i \|^2.$$

Sometimes, the shape of the unknown skull was altered either at the moment of the death (e.g., local deformation in the case of a traumatism or an assault) or postmortem (e.g., compression due to the weight of earth in the case of burying). It then becomes necessary to model this alteration in order to recover the original shape of the skull. Such a task is extremely difficult, as the alterations can be geometrically very complex.

Thus, in the case of experiment 2, we can notice that the skull of the Man of Tautavel is bent (see Figure 5.11, top, right). This is due to the fact that it had lain on its side and was compressed by the gravity and the weight of sediments. We have modeled this taphonomic deformation by computing an affine transformation $\underline{\boldsymbol{A}}$ between the reference and the unknown skulls. The degrees of freedom corresponding to the coefficients in the matrix representing $\underline{\boldsymbol{A}}$ allow to model the bending alteration. After applying $\underline{\boldsymbol{A}}^{-1}$, the reference and the unknown skulls are really comparable (see Figure 5.11, bottom, left).

Another way to recover the bending of the skull would be to extract automatically the midsagittal plane (Thirion *et al.* 2000) and to realign it with the vertical plane. Nevertheless, the knowledge of the in situ orientation of the fossil is indispensable, since similar deformations might be the result of many different taphonomic events (Ponce de León and Zollikofer 1999).

5.2.5 COMPUTING THE 3D TRANSFORMATION

Now, we have to compute the 3D transformation between the reference and the unknown skulls that have been both normalized. The "thin-plate spline" method (Bookstein 1991), widely used in morphometry, allows the computation of such a function that interpolates the displacements of the normalized homologous points (P'_i, Q'_i) with some mathematical properties of regularity. Nevertheless, interpolation is relevant when the matched points are totally reliable and distributed regularly (for example, a few points being located manually). In our case, these points are not totally reliable, due to possible mismatches of the registration algorithm, and are sparse in a few compact areas as they belong to lines. So, we have developed a spline approximation function that is regular enough to minimize the influence of an erroneous matched point (Subsol *et al.* 1998). The coordinate functions are then computed by a 3D tensor product of B-spline basis functions. To compute this 3D transformation $\underline{T}$, we maximize the weighted sum of an approximation criterion (quadratic distance between $\boldsymbol{T}(P'_i)$ and Q'_i) and a regularization criterion (minimization of the sum of the second-order derivatives that correspond to the "curvature" of the function):

$$\underline{T} = \mathrm{Argmin}_{(T)} \left(\sum_i \| \boldsymbol{T}(P'_i) - Q'_i \|^2 + \rho \iiint_V [(\partial^2 \boldsymbol{T}/\partial x^2) + (\partial^2 \boldsymbol{T}/\partial x \partial y) + \cdots] \mathrm{d}V \right).$$

The parameter ρ balances the approximation accuracy and the smoothness of the transformation.

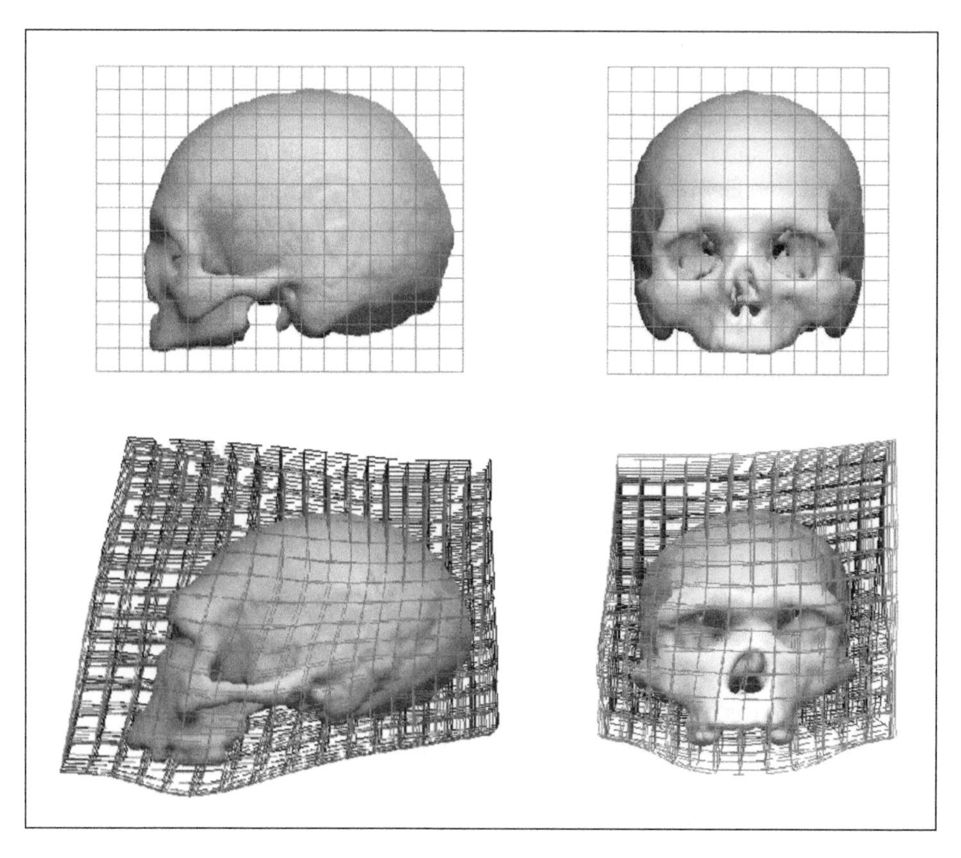

Figure 5.12 Experiment 2: the 3D transformation between the reference skull (top) and the skull of the Man of Tautavel (bottom) is automatically computed based on the registered crest lines. Notice how the deformed mesh emphasizes the main features of the skull of the Man of Tautavel: low cranium, receding forehead, and protuberant face as well as an important frontal dissymmetry due to the taphonomic deformations.

By applying $\underline{\boldsymbol{T}}$ to a 3D regular mesh, it becomes possible to display the transformation. In particular, we can notice in Figure 5.12 that the deformed mesh emphasizes the main features of the skull of the Man of Tautavel: low cranium, receding forehead, and protuberant face as well as an important frontal dissymmetry due to the taphonomic deformations (Mafart *et al.* 1999).

5.3 RESULTS AND DISCUSSION

5.3.1 *THE PROBLEM OF THE VALIDATION*

EXPERIMENT 1

As for all the methods of facial reconstruction, the main concern is the validity of the reconstruction result. In the first case presented, we are able to compare the automatic facial reconstruction with the real face (see Figure 5.13). Even if the reference and the actual faces have such different morphology that it is no

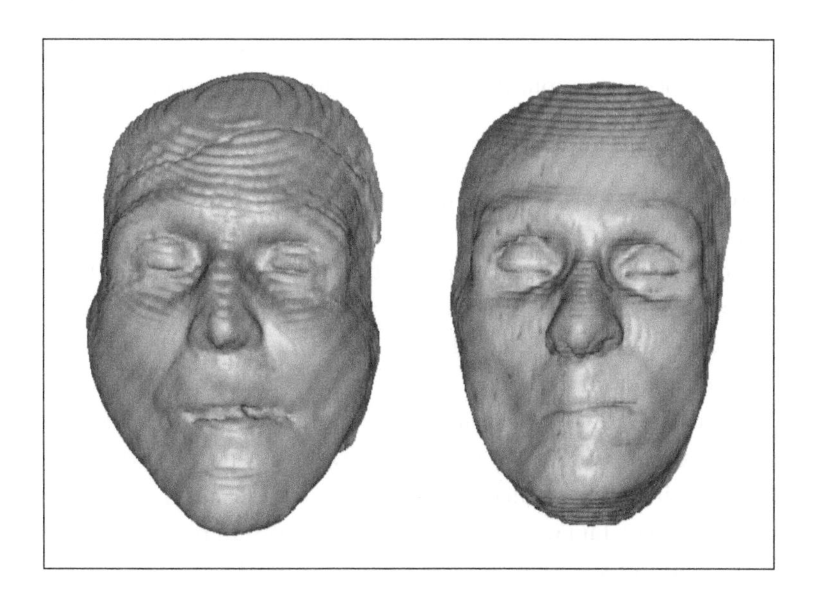

Figure 5.13

Experiment 1: comparison of the deformed reference face and of the actual "unknown" face (Quatrehomme et al. *1997). The overall proportions of the face are correctly inferred. By permission of the Journal of Forensic Sciences.*

more valid to assume the hypotheses of similarity of age or corpulence, the result looks fairly interesting. In particular, the overall proportions of the face such as the width, the interocular distance, or the eyebrow thickness are correctly inferred. The low part is less resembling, but this may be due to the difference of the opening of the mandible between the reference and the "unidentified" skulls. The soft parts as the nose or the cheeks are also not very significant.

In fact, it is very difficult to quantify the resemblances between two faces. We could compute an objective distance, based for example on the squared sum of distances between some feature points of the deformed reference and the actual faces, or even between the whole surfaces if we use dense meshes. As the distance will be never strictly equal to zero, it would require defining a threshold to decide if two faces really resemble each other. This value should be under the average distance corresponding to the intravariability of different human faces. But such a parameter, which must be computed on a very large database of representative faces, is not known yet. Moreover, some features such as hair, skin complexion, or the color of the eyes are totally absent in our virtual reconstructions, whereas they are most important for recognition. At last, when we deal with 3D models, the problem becomes much more complex: a slight shift of orientation of the representation of the reconstructed head can induce large differences in the perception of the face shape due to differences of shading or lighting.

As emphasized in (Quatrehomme and Subsol 2005), very few studies have been performed on the validation of 3D reconstruction methods on a "significant" scale, whether it is automated or not.

In conclusion, there is a strong need to define a clear and reproducible protocol to evaluate the quality of a 3D computer-assisted facial reconstruction with respect to the real face. This will allow the performance of a retrospective study to compare and validate the different methods as has been done for other image processing applications such as rigid registration (West *et al.* 1999).

EXPERIMENT 2

In the case of the Man of Tautavel, the problem is much more difficult as we do not know the actual face! Nevertheless, we can compare our reconstruction with the ones obtained with different methods (see Figure 5.14): 2D drawings and manual 3D facial reconstructions performed by an artist and by forensic medical doctors. All these methods emphasize the same morphological features of ante-Neandertalians.

The global similarity of the results are encouraging and indicate that our automatic method can give a consistent overall appearance of the face. This is all the more interesting since the reference head was not, a priori, consistent with the Man of Tautavel; the morphology is very different, as 450 000 years of human evolution separate the two men, and the Man of Tautavel is estimated to be 20–30 years old, whereas the reference man was in his seventies.

To refine the reconstruction, we could test several hypotheses on age or corpulence, based on different reference heads. This is clearly the main advantage of an entirely automatic method that allows the performance of a reconstruction in a few minutes. The problem is then to set up a significant reference head.

5.3.2 DEFINING A REFERENCE HEAD

The variation of the shape of the head is so huge that, even if we restrict a population group based on sex, corpulence, or ethnicity criteria, it is impossible to find a subject with the perfect "average" head, that could be scanned in 3D. So, very often, reference heads are taken among the models that are available to the user as the Visible Human Data Set (Koch *et al.* 1996). Nevertheless, we can describe two ways to build a significant reference head.

The first idea consists in using anthropometric or cephalometric measurements to model a virtual reference head with computer-graphic tools. DeCarlo *et al.* (1998) synthesized 3D face models of a North American Caucasian young adult male and female based on data presented by Farkas (1994).

The second idea is to infer an average model directly from a database of 3D images of different heads (see Figure 5.15). Cutting *et al.* (1993) and Subsol *et al.* (1998) extract and register line landmarks in the 3D images of a skull. The positions of the corresponding landmarks are then averaged to define the reference model. Blanz and Vetter (2004) generate 3D face models based on 200 heads of young adults (100 male and 100 female). As the images were obtained by a laser scan, it was possible to model not only the 3D geometry of the face but also the texture. The second method appears more precise, as the averaging process will take into account all data available

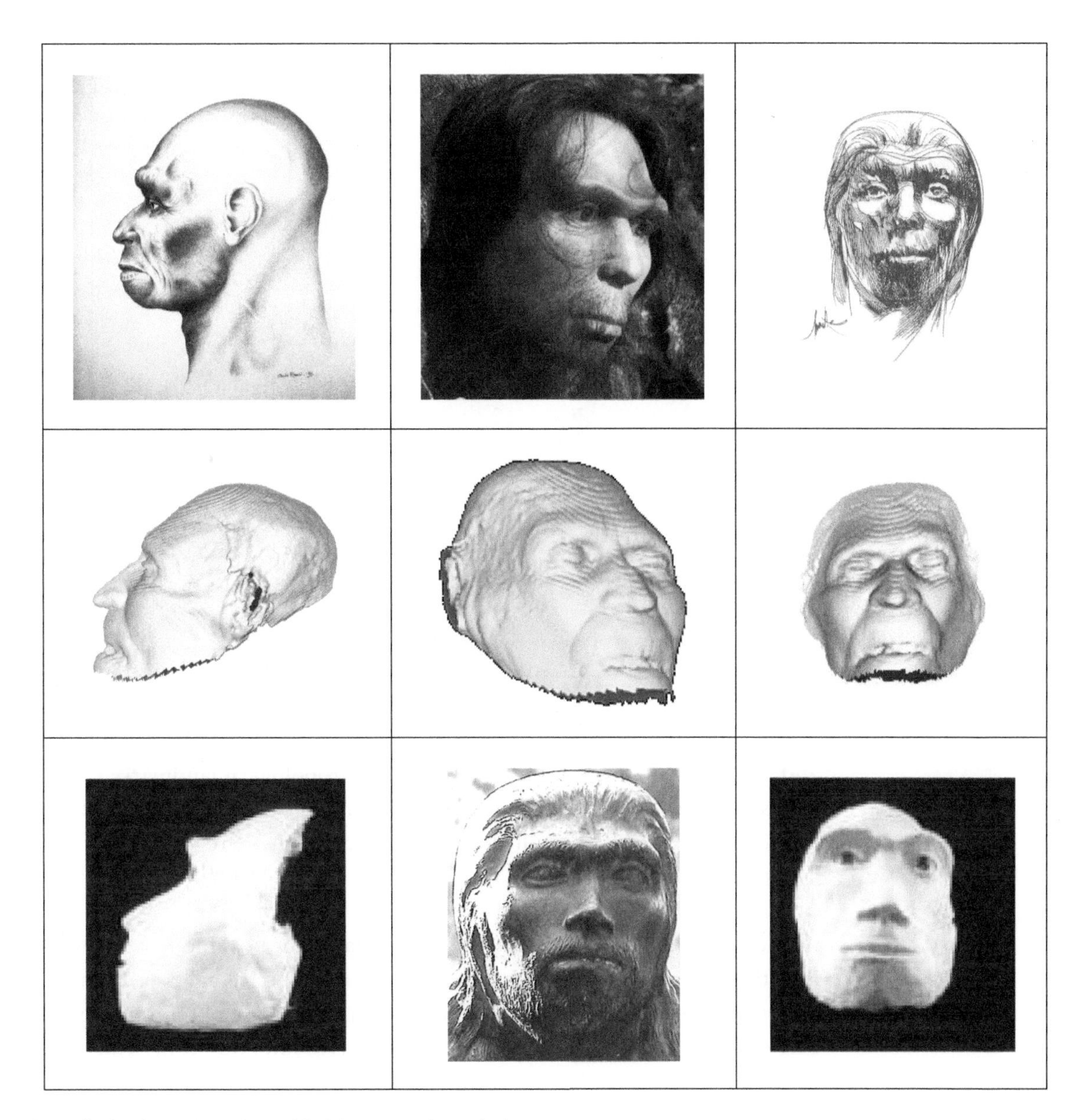

Figure 5.14 Comparison of several facial reconstruction methods.

- *Upper line, from left to right: a 2D artistic drawing by Carlos Ranzi; a 3D manual facial reconstruction performed by an artist, Elisabeth Daynes under the scientific direction of a paleontologist, Marie-Antoinette de Lumley; a 2D artistic drawing by Carlo Moretti. All these images by permission of the Centre Européen de Recherches Préhistoriques de Tautavel and its president Henry de Lumley (Tautavel, Web).*
- *Middle line: different views of our 3D computerized facial reconstruction.*
- *Bottom line:*

Left & right: a 3D manual facial reconstruction performed by forensic medical doctors (Odin et al. *2002). By permission of the authors.*

Middle: a 3D manual facial reconstruction performed by an artist, André Bordes, under the scientific direction of a paleontologist, Marie-Antoinette de Lumley. By permission of the Centre Européen de Recherches Préhistoriques de Tautavel and its president Henry de Lumley.

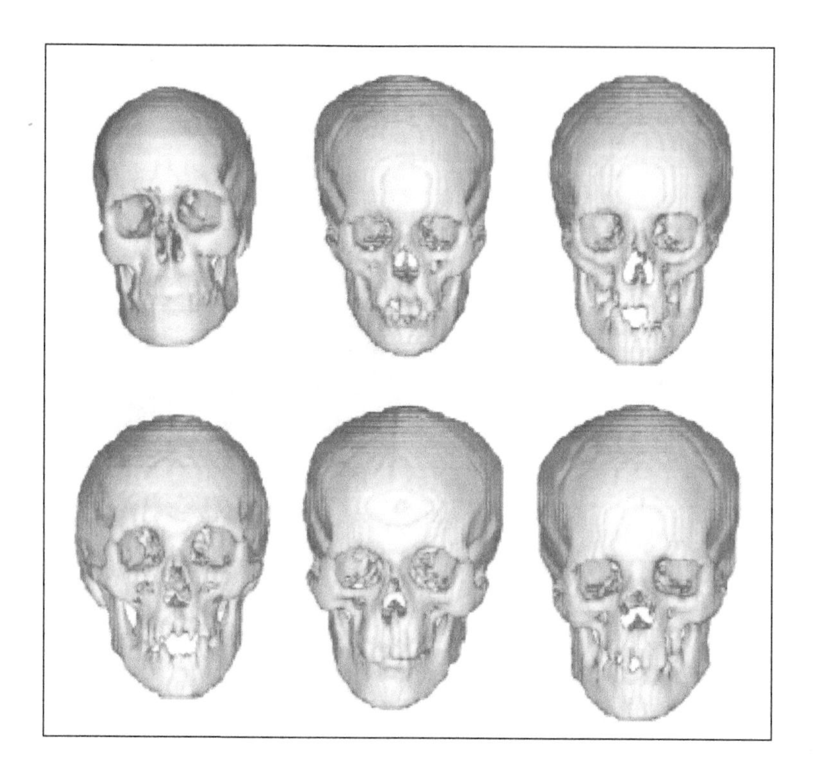

Figure 5.15
A dataset of 6 different skulls segmented from CT scans. Notice how the shapes are different. Reprinted from Medical Image Analysis (Subsol et al. *1998), with permission from Elsevier.*

in the images—up to several thousand points if the surface meshes are dense—and not only the position of some tens of anthropological landmarks. Nevertheless, no one has yet designed a complete average model of the head that includes both an average skull and a face model which are registered.

5.3.3 MODELING THE HUMAN VARIABILITY

As the presented method is automatic and fast, it is possible to test several hypotheses of reconstruction based on different criteria as age, sex, ethnicity, or corpulence. As it seems impossible to set up a database of reference heads corresponding to all the categories, a solution is to infer different heads from a reference one.

AGE

Milner *et al.* (2001) alter the 2D profile of a skull according to some cephalometric measurements and perform a manual face reconstruction to infer a face that is 50 years older. The authors caution that their work is more an exercise than a real methodology as there is no other result against which to compare it. Evison (2001) interpolates between a young and an old 3D facial reconstruction of a male, leading to intermediately aged faces. But the method is based on the hypothesis that the points of the face move linearly between the two extremes, which could be considered simplistic. Hutton *et al.* (2003) build a more complex model of facial growth based on a training set of 3D surface scans of 199 male and 201 female subjects with ages between 0 and 50. Coughlan (1997) decomposes craniofacial growth into two processes called remodeling and displacement. This model is combined with a 3D computer-based facial reconstruction method by Archer *et al.* (1998).

ETHNICITY

Dean *et al.* (1998) build average skull models using a database of skull CT-scan images of Caucasian Americans and African Americans, male and female. It allows emphasis on the anatomical differences between the ethnicities and the sexes. A range of variation that corresponds to individuals of mixed African and European ancestry could be obtained by using 3D interpolation (Evison 2001).

CORPULENCE

Archer *et al.* (1998) tune the length of the virtual "dowels" that link the face and skull models to allow the user to modify the corpulence. A 3D interpolation (Evison 2001) process can then synthesize a potential range of obesity.

EXPRESSIVITY

Kähler *et al.* (2003) build the reference head model on an anatomical basis which comprises the underlying muscles and the bone layers. Once the model is fitted to the unknown skull, it becomes possible to animate the face and obtain different expressions by setting muscle contractions. If the generic reconstruction is based on a neutral pose, it can be helpful to present several expressions for identification purposes.

5.3.4 INFERRING ILL-DEFINED FACIAL PARTS OR FEATURES

Many soft parts of the face are difficult to infer, in particular the nose, chin, eyes, lips, or ears (Quatrehomme and Subsol 2005). Kähler *et al.* (2003) express some empirical rules that are used in traditional facial reconstruction, by automatically placing vertical and horizontal guides in a frontal view. The user can then move or update some landmarks in order to refine the reconstruction. Tu *et al.* (2005) extracted a collection of eye, nose, and lip models from 3D scans of various individuals. The user can then place manually a model that will be blended on the 3D reconstruction.

More generally, a facial editing tool described by Archer *et al.* (1998) enables the user to modify locally the shape of the reconstruction. Vanezis *et al.* (2000) show how a frontal 2D view of the 3D reconstruction can be imported into a police identikit system which allows the addition of features as opened eyes, hair, or glasses.

Another way to make the reconstruction more realistic is to map a reference texture of the head on the 3D reconstruction. Attardi *et al.* (1999) and Tu *et al.* (2005) generate a cylindrical texture either from a set 2D of views or from a 2.5D laser scan of an individual whose face is assumed to resemble the face to reconstruct. The texture is then fitted and projected on the 3D reconstruction.

Notice that much research has also been performed to synthesize wrinkles (e.g., Wu *et al.* 1995) that could be added to the 3D reconstruction.

5.4 CONCLUSION

Facial reconstruction is used more and more for museum presentations (Prag and Neave 1997), but still only for human beings. With the advent of 3D computer-graphic methods, which are more flexible and require less effort and time, we can imagine performing facial reconstructions on animals. For example, the appearance of a prehistoric felid (Antón and García-Perea 1998) could be inferred from a fossil skull by using as a reference head one of a modern felid. This is completely feasible with the method presented in this chapter, as it does not depend on soft-tissue thickness measurements that we are not aware of in the case of animals. Moreover, some data are available as several fossil animals have been already CT-scanned, for example in the CT-Lab of the University of Texas at Austin, USA. Such facial reconstructions would be of the most interest for museums and could be presented either in real exhibition rooms with special graphic devices (Bimber *et al.* 2002) or on virtual Web sites (Yasuda *et al.* 2002).

ACKNOWLEDGEMENTS

The work described in this chapter is currently part of research carried out in the FOVEA Project funded by the Program “Société de l’Information” of the French Center of Scientific Research, CNRS. Part of this work was done when Gérard Subsol was with EPIDAURE Project, INRIA Sophia Antipolis, France and with the Laboratory of Computer Science of the University of Avignon, France. The authors would like to thank Bertrand Mafart for his valuable help and Marie-Antoinette and Henry de Lumley for making the Man of Tautavel’s material available.

REFERENCES

The links to the electronic versions were checked at the beginning of 2005. Since this date, some of them may have been moved or deleted.

Antón M. and García-Perea R. (1998) "Reconstructed Facial Appearance of the Sabretoothed Felid Smilodon", *Zoological Journal of the Linnean Society* 124, 369–386.

Archer K., Coughlan K., Forsey D. and Struben S. (1998) Software Tools for Craniofacial Growth and Reconstruction. Graphics Interface, Vancouver (Canada), June 1998. Electronic version: http://www.graphicsinterface.org/proceedings/1998/120/.

Attardi G., Betrò M., Forte M., Gori R., Guidazzoli A., Imboden S. and Mallegni F. (1999) "3D Facial Reconstruction and Visualization of Ancient Egyptian Mummies Using Sprial CT Data – Soft Tissues Reconstruction and Textures Application", *SIGGRAPH. Sketches and Applications Los Angeles (U.S.A.), August 1999.* Electronic version: http://medialab.di.unipi.it/Project/Mummia/.

Ayache N. (2003) "Epidaure: a Research Project in Medical Image Analysis, Simulation and Robotics at INRIA", *IEEE Transactions on Medical Imaging* 22(10), 1185–1201. Electronic version: http://www-sop.inria.fr/epidaure/BIBLIO/.

Bimber O., Gatesy S., Witmer L., Raskar R. and Encarnação L. (2002) "Merging Fossil Specimens with Computer-Generated Information", *Computer*, September, 45–50. Electronic version: http://citeseer.nj.nec.com/ bimber02merging.html.

Blanz V. and Vetter T. (1995) "A Morphable Model for the Synthesis of 3D Faces", *ACM SIGGRAPH Conference Proceedings, Los Angeles, USA*. Electronic version: citeseer.ist.psu.edu/blanz99morphable.html.

Bookstein F. (1991) *Morphometric Tools for Landmark Data*. Cambridge University Press.

Bramble S., Compton D. and Klasén L. (2001) "Forensic Image Analysis", *13th INTERPOL Forensic Science Symposium, Lyon, France, October 2001*. Electronic version: http://www.interpol.int/Public/Forensic/IFSS/meeting13/Reviews/Image.pdf.

Coughlan K. (1997) "Simulating Craniofacial Growth". Master's Thesis, University of British Columbia, April 1997. Electronic version: http://www.cs.ubc.ca/labs/imager/th/coughlan.msc.1997.html.

CTLab, Web http://www.ctlab.geo.utexas.edu/.

Cutting C., Bookstein F., Haddad B., Dean D. and Kim D. (1993) A spline-based approach for averaging three-dimensional curves and surfaces, in: *SPIE Conference on Mathematical Methods in Medical Imaging II*, Vol. 2035, pp. 29–43.

Dean D., Bookstein F. L., Koneru S., Lee J. H., Kamath J., Cutting C. B., Hans M. and Goldberg J. (1998) "Average African American Three-Dimensional Computed Tomography Skull Images: The Potential Clinical Importance of Ethnicity and Sex", *J. Craniofacial Surgery* 9(4), July.

DeCarlo D., Metaxas D. and Stone M. (1998) "An Anthropometric Face Model Using Variational Techniques", *SIGGRAPH* pp. 67–74, Orlando (U.S.A.), July 1998. Electronic version: http://athos.rutgers.edu/~decarlo/anthface.html.

Evison M. (2001) "Modeling Age, Obesity, and Ethnicity in a Computerized 3-D Facial Reconstruction", *Forensic Science Communications*, 3(1). Electronic version: http://www.fbi.gov/hq/lab/fsc/backissu/april2001/evison.htm.

Farkas L. (ed.) (1994) *Anthropometry of the Head and Face*. Raven Press.

Hutton T., Buxton B. and Hammond P. (2002) "Estimating Average Growth Trajectories in Shape-Space using Kernel Smoothing", *IEEE Transactions on Medical Imaging* 22(6), 747–753.

Jones M. (2001) "Facial Reconstruction Using Volumetric Data", in: *Vision, Modeling, and Visualization 2001* (T. Ertl, B. Girod, G. Greiner, H. Niemann and H. Seidel, eds.). IOS Press, Stuttgart (Germany), pp. 135–142. Electronic version: http://citeseer.nj.nec.com/482378.html.

Kähler K., Haber J. and Seidel H. (2003) "Reanimating the Dead: Reconstruction of Expressive Faces from Skull Data", *ACM SIGGRAPH Conference Proceedings,* San Diego, USA. Electronic version http://www.mpi-sb.mpg.de/resources/FAM/demos.html.

Koch R., Gross M., Carls F., von Büren D., Fankhauser G. and Parish Y. (1996) "Simulating Facial Surgery Using Finite Element Models", *Computer Graphics* Vol. 30, Annual Conference Series, pp. 421–428. Electronic version: http://citeseer.nj.nec.com/koch96simulating.html.

de Lumley H., de Lumley M. and David R. (1982) "Découverte et reconstruction de l'Homme de Tautavel", *1er Congrès de Paléontologie Humaine, Tome 1, Nice (France), 1982.*

Mafart B., Méline D., Silvestre A. and Subsol G. (1999) *3D Imagery and Paleontology: Shape differences between the Skull of Modern Man and that of Tautavel Man.* B. Hidoine, A. Paouri, designers and directors, video 451–452, Department of Scientific Multimedia Communication, INRIA. Electronic version: http://www.inria.fr/multimedia/Videotheque/0-Fiches-Videos/451-fra.html.

Mafart B. and Delingette H. with the collaboration of Subsol G. (eds.) (2002) "Colloquium on Three-Dimensional Imaging in Paleoanthropology and Prehistoric Archaeology", Liège (Belgium), September 2001. Published in *British Archaeological Reports International Series*, No. 1049, Archaeopress.

Milner C., Neave R. and Wilkinson C. (2001) "Predicting Growth in the Aging Craniofacial Skeleton", *Forensic Science Communications* Vol. 3, (3). Electronic version: http://www.fbi.gov/hq/lab/fsc/backissu/july2001/milner.htm.

Nelson L. and Michael S. (1998) "The Application of Volume Deformation to Three-Dimensional Facial Reconstruction: A Comparison with Previous Techniques", *Forensic Sci. Int.* 94, 167–181.

Odin G., Quatrehomme G., Subsol G., Delingette H., Mafart B. and de Lumley M. A. (2002) "Comparison of a Three-Dimensional and a Computerized-Assisted Method for

Cranio-Facial Reconstruction: Application to the Tautavel Man", *XIV International Congress of Prehistoric and Protohistoric Science, Liège (Belgium), September 2001*. Abstract page 23 in preprints. For the full text, see Mafart and Delingette (2002) in the references above (pp. 67–69).

Petrick M. (2000) "Volumetric Facial Reconstruction for Forensic Identification", *Seminar Computergraphik*, Universität Koblenz Landau (Germany), October 2000. Text in German. Electronic version: http://www.uni-koblenz.de/~cg/veranst/ws0001/4.1.26_Seminar_Computergraphik.html.

Plasencia J. (1999) International Conference in Central Europe on Computer Graphics, Visualization and Interactive Digital Media'99, Plzen-Bory, Czech Republic, February 1999. Electronic version: http://citeseer.nj.nec.com/490826.html.

Ponce de León M. and Zollikofer C. (1999) "New Evidence from Le Moustier 1: Computer-Assisted Reconstruction and Morphometry of the Skull", *The Anatomical Record* 254, 474–489.

Prag J. and Neave R. (1997) *Making Faces – Using Forensic and Archaeological Evidence*. British Museum Press.

Quatrehomme G., Cotin S., Subsol G., Delingette H., Garidel Y., Grévin G., Fidrich M., Bailet P. and Ollier A. (1997) "A Fully Three-Dimensional Method for Facial Reconstruction Based on Deformable Models", *J. Forensic Sci.* 42(4), 649–652.

Quatrehomme G. and Subsol G. (2005) "Classical Non Computer-Assisted Craniofacial Reconstruction", *Computer-Graphic Facial Reconstruction*, Chapter 2. Academic Press.

Seibert F. (1997) "Model-Based 3D-Reconstruction of Human Faces", *Computer Graphik Topics*, No. 3, 8–9. Electronic version: http://www.inigraphics.net/press/topics/index.html.

Shaham D., Sosna J., Makori A., Slasky B., Bar-Ziv J. and Donchin Y. (2000) "Post Mortem CT-Scan: An Alternative Method in Forensic Medicine and Trauma Research", *The Internet Journal of Rescue and Disaster Medicine* 2(1). Electronic version: http://www.ispub.com/ostia/index.php?xmlFilePath = journals/ijrdm/archives.xml.

Spoor F., Jeffery N. and Zonneveld F. (2000) "Imaging Skeletal Growth and Evolution". Chapter 6 in: *Development, Growth and Evolution.* The Linnean Society of London. Electronic version: http://evolution.anat.ucl.ac.uk/people/spoor/spmain.htm.

Subsol G., Thirion J. and Ayache N. (1998) "A General Scheme for Automatically Building 3D Morphometric Anatomical Atlases: Application to a Skull Atlas", *Medical Image Analysis* 2(1), 37–60.

Tautavel, http://www.tautavel.culture.gouv.fr/.

Thirion J. and Gourdon A. (1996) "The 3D Marching Lines Algorithm", *Graphical Models and Image Processing* 58(6), 503–509. Electronic version: http://www.inria.fr/rrrt/rr-1881.html.

Thirion J., Subsol G. and Dean D. (1996) "Cross Validation of Three Inter-Patients Matching Methods", in: *Visualization in Biomedical Computing, Hamburg (Germany), Lecture Notes in Computer Science* (K. H. Höhne and R. Kikinis, eds.). Vol. 1131. Springer, pp. 327–336.

Thirion J., Prima S., Subsol G. and Roberts N. (2000) "Statistical Analysis of Normal and Abnormal Dissymmetry in Volumetric Medical Images", *Medical Image Analysis* 4(2), 111–121. Electronic version: http://citeseer.nj.nec.com/thirion97statistical.html.

Thompson J. and Illerhaus B. (1998) "A New Reconstruction of the Le Moustier 1 Skull and Investigation of Internal Structures Using 3-D-μCT data", *J. Human Evolution* 35, 647–665.

Tu P., Hartley R., Lorensen W., Allyassin A., Gupta R. and Heier L. (2005) "Face Reconstructions using Flesh Deformation Modes", *Computer-Graphic Facial Reconstruction*, Chapter 8. Academic Press.

Tyrrell A., Evison M., Chamberlain A. and Green M. (1997) "Forensic Three-Dimensional Facial Reconstruction: Historical Review and Contemporary Developments", *J. Forensic Sci.* 42(4), 653–661.

Vanezis P., Blowes R., Linney A., Tan A., Richards R. and Neave R. (1989) "Application of 3D Computer Graphics for Facial Reconstruction and Comparison with Sculpting Techniques", *Forensic Sci. Int.* 42, 69–84.

Vanezis P., Vanezis M., McCombe G. and Niblett T. (2000) "Facial Reconstruction using 3-D Computer Graphics", *Forensic Sci. Int.* 108, 81–95. Electronic version: http://citeseer.nj.nec.com/vanezis00facial.html.

Vignal J. (1999) "Les Reconstitutions faciales assistées par ordinateur: données tomodensitométriques, déformation d'image ou 'warping'", Éditions Artcom.

West J., Fitzpatrick J., Wang M., Dawant B., Maurer C., Kessler R., Maciunas Barillot C., Lemoine D., Collignon A., Maes F., Suetens P., Vandermeulen D., van den Elsen P., Hemler P., Napel S., Sumanaweera T., Harkness B., Hill D., Studholme C., Malandain G., Pennec X., Noz M., Maguire G., Pollack M., Pellizzari C., Robb R., Hanson D. and Woods R. (1996) "Comparison and Evaluation of Retrospective Intermodality Image Registration Techniques", *SPIE Conference on Medical Imaging* 2710, 332–347, Newport Beach, USA. Electronic version: http://citeseer.nj.nec.com/west98comparison.html.

Wilhelms J. and Van Gelder A. (1997) "Anatomically Based Modeling", *Computer Graphics*, 31, Annual Conference Series, pp.173–180. Electronic version: http://citeseer.nj.nec.com/wilhelms97anatomically.html.

Wu Y., Magnenat Thalmann N. and Thalmann D. (1995) "A Dynamic Wrinkle Model in Facial Animation and Skin Ageing", *Journal of Visualization and Computer Animation* 6(4), 195–206. Electronic version: http://citeseer.nj.nec.com/wu95dynamic.html.

Yasuda T., Yokoi S., Yoshida S. and Endo M. (2002) "A Method for Restoration and Exhibition of Relics in the Virtual Museum". *Museums and the Web*, Boston, USA. Electronic version: http://www.archimuse.com/mw2002/abstracts/prg_170000684.html.

PART II

CONCEPTS AND CREATION OF FACIAL RECONSTRUCTION MODELS

TWO-DIMENSIONAL COMPUTER-GENERATED AVERAGE HUMAN FACE MORPHOLOGY AND FACIAL APPROXIMATION

Carl N. Stephan
Department of Anatomical Sciences, University of Adelaide, Australia, 5005, and School of Dental Science, University of Melbourne, Victoria 3010, Australia

Ian S. Penton-Voak
Department of Experimental Psychology, University of Bristol BS8 1TN, UK

David I. Perrett
School of Psychology, University of St. Andrews, Scotland KY16 9JU

Bernard P. Tiddeman
School of Computer Science, University of St. Andrews, Scotland KY16 9SS

John G. Clement
School of Dental Science, University of Melbourne, Victoria 3010, Australia

Maciej Henneberg
Department of Anatomical Sciences, University of Adelaide, Australia, 5005

6.1 INTRODUCTION

The arithmetic mean is the first of the moment statistics and is one of the most common mathematical tools used to describe data sets. Means are useful because they indicate the central tendency of a sample without the need to present all individual data. This is especially the case when the sampled data are distributed symmetrically (e.g., tend to a normal distribution) since the mean will approximate most of the sample well (Figure 6.1). For nonsymmetrical distributions, other variables may be more appropriate, for example, distributions with high skewness (statistical moment 3) are likely to be more appropriately described by a median (50% quantile), which minimizes the

Computer-Graphic Facial Reconstruction
John G. Clement and Murray K. Marks, Editors

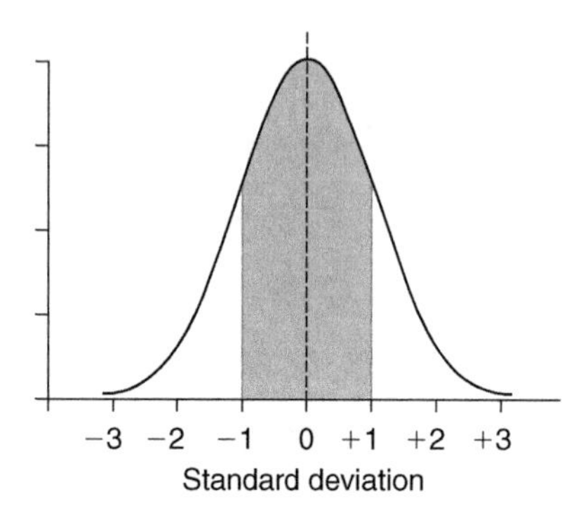

Figure 6.1

A sample displaying a normal distribution. The dashed line indicates the mean. Note that about 68% of the sample is included in the range spanning one standard deviation either side of the mean (gray area), and values in this range lie "close" to the mean.

sum of the absolute differences between itself and each datum point in the sample.

Since many anthropometric characters of the body, including those of the face, display distributions that approximate the normal distribution, means appear to be useful for describing these characters. Farkas and colleagues, for example, use means to describe various groups and subgroups of particular face features (e.g., mouth width) measured using traditional anthropometric methods (e.g., sliding calipers); see Farkas *et al.* (1994a,b). While means calculated from measurements of traits displayed by an individual are useful for describing faces, they are of limited value, since they describe highly specific traits and are numerical. For example, the mean value for mouth width specifically indicates how wide mouths typically are, but gives little or no indication of the shape or color of these lips or how a face with average values, including those of the mouth, may appear. Furthermore, when presented with many numerical averages relating to face dimensions, it is difficult to imagine how they relate to each other morphologically. These limitations can be avoided by averaging whole face images, rather than quantitative measures of specific face traits, by using a more holistic approach to calculating averages from faces.

Many attempts have been made in the past to create images of the average human face. This began with Galton in 1878 (Benson and Perrett 1992) and has continued through to the present time, with studies by Perrett and colleagues being some of the more recent (see, for example, Penton-Voak *et al.* 1999). The most interest in average face composites has been in psychology, where two-dimensional (2D) average faces have been generated from photographs and used in face perception studies assessing an array of issues including facial attractiveness (Alley and Cunningham 1991, Grammer and Thornhill 1994, Kujawa and Strzalko 1998, Langlois and Roggman 1990, Langlois *et al.* 1994, Perrett *et al.* 1998, Perrett *et al.* 1994, Rhodes *et al.* 1999, Rhodes and Tremewan 1996), and facial preference for mates (Little *et al.* 2001,

Penton-Voak *et al.* 1999). However, it is worth noting that facial averages have also been generated from 2D outlines (Rabey 1977–8) and in three dimensions using laser-scanned images of faces (McCance *et al.* 1997a, Tiddeman *et al.* 2000, Tiddeman *et al.* 1999).

Although the visualization of average features seems applicable to many disciplines for various purposes, average faces appear to be useful to the technique of facial approximation: the building of a face from a skull. Facial approximation is a "last-resort" forensic technique used to help identify skeletal remains (Caldwell 1986). It requires the face to be constructed from a skull and the advertisement of the built face to try and obtain a correct recognition from the public (Caldwell 1986, Gatliff 1984, Prag and Neave 1997, Taylor 2001). Many other terms have been used to describe this technique, however, facial approximation will be used in this chapter since it is reported to be the most appropriate (see for discussion: George 1987, Haglund 1998, Stephan and Henneberg 2001, Stephan 2003, Taylor 2001).

Facial-approximation practitioners rely heavily upon averaging methods to build individuals' faces from their skulls, since few facial relationships between hard and soft tissue are actually known and can be predicted at the level of individuals. The standard use of average soft-tissue depths in facial approximation (Prag and Neave 1997, Taylor 2001) is a prime example of this. Average soft-tissue depths play a fundamental role in most facial approximation methods, namely both the American and combination methods which appear to be the most commonly used techniques at this time (Prag and Neave 1997, Taylor 2001). However, almost all methods of soft-tissue prediction presently used in facial approximation rely on some kind of central tendency or average; see, for example, guidelines used to estimate eyeball projection (Stephan 2002a), mouth width (George 1987, Haglund 1998, Stephan and Henneberg 2001, Stephan 2003, Taylor 2001), superciliare position (Stephan 2002b), and ear height (Farkas *et al.* 1987).

Since similar averaging methods are applied in every facial approximation irrespective of skull morphology, all facial approximations, at least those of the same age and sex, should look fairly similar and average (Brues 1958, Maat 1998–9). That is, all facial approximations should look like an average face that has been "stretched" to fit an individual's skull. Yet it is clearly evident that this is not the case, since few facial approximations of the same age, sex, and population group look alike or similarly average. This is probably due to facial-approximation practitioners using subjective interpretation to establish how features that are not determinable from the skull actually look, rather than using empirically derived, whole average face information as described in many other papers (see above). Using such average faces as guides in the facial-approximation process seems useful because it may help to restrict subjective judgements of the practitioner, maintaining at least to some degree of objectivity and repeatability in the facial-approximation process.

"Whole-face" average information, in contrast to average values of specific facial traits, have recently been employed in some facial-approximation attempts, for example, the facial approximation of Tutankhamen by R. Richards and colleagues (Antenna 2002). Evenhouse and colleagues (1990) also report a method for generating something similar to average faces for use in facial approximation as discussed in the following paragraphs. The disadvantage of using averaging techniques is that few people, if any, are average in all characters and therefore the use of such averaging methods may result in a face that is not representative of the actual target individual (person to whom the skull belongs) and may not be recognized (Brues 1958). This effect seems especially pronounced for target faces that are distinctive (Bruce and Young 1998). Such an effect may not be so problematic for less distinctive target faces since they already approach the population average (Bruce and Young 1998).

Here we discuss methods previously used to produce 2D average human faces and present new high quality 2D images of average human face morphologies using improved techniques. These images may serve as guides to, or the basis for, 2D facial approximation.

6.2 AVERAGING FACES

In order to generate reliable average faces, adequate methods and samples must be used. Early attempts at generating average images consisted of superimposing facial images at various picture opacities (Grammer and Thornhill 1994, Kujawa and Strzalko 1998, Langlois and Roggman 1990, Langlois *et al.* 1994) (see Figure 6.2). However, this method did not generate average faces well; rather it displayed the variability within the facial set, with the more "solid" parts of the face representing standard deviations more than averages (Figure 6.2). Also, the color information displayed in these faces was not average, since corresponding points on the faces were not blended together. For example, the color information of the lips of one facial image may be blended with the color information of part of the cheeks of another facial image. Such superimposition methods also often involved the manipulation of individual facial images to make the interpupillary distance and the height of stomion the same across individuals so that the clarity of the average image was improved (Grammer and Thornhill 1994, Langlois and Roggman 1990); see Figure 6.2. However, this image manipulation changes the size, proportions and individual features of the face (see Figure 6.2), so can only be valid if they

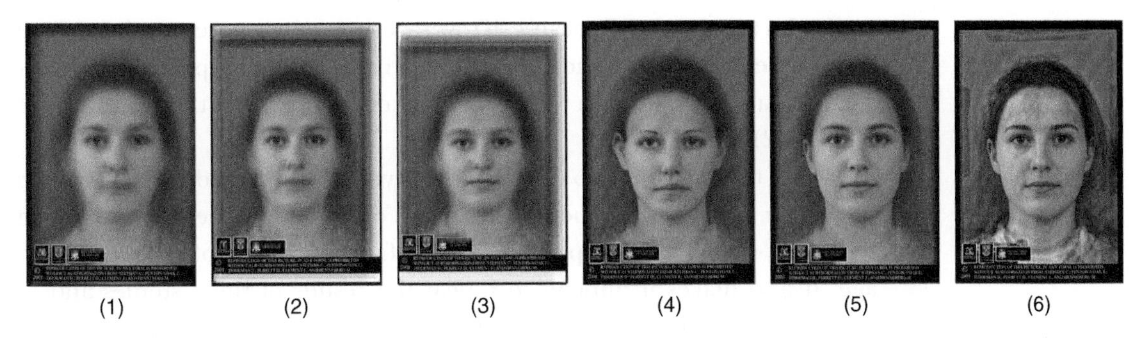

Figure 6.2 Examples of "average faces" made from the same 32 female Europeans using different techniques. (1) The "average face" resulting from superimposing images after aligning at nasion; (2) The "average face" resulting from superimposing images after normalizing faces based on pupil width (not average) and aligning on pupils; (3) The "average face" resulting from superimposing images after normalizing faces on pupil width and stomion position (not average) and aligning images based on these points; (4) The "average face" resulting from methods similar to those used by Evenhouse and colleagues (1990) employing the "average face template" of Farkas (1981); (5) The calculated average face using a linear averaging method; (6) The calculated average face made using additional algorithms to preserve texture information.

replicate the true average dimensions of these faces (Alley and Cunningham 1991, Rowland and Perrett 1995).

Evenhouse *et al.* (1990) used an average-face template described by Farkas (1981) to generate their average faces rather than using the shape information from their data set to calculate the average (see Figure 6.2). Thus, their average face was generated by warping and blending (five) faces to the "average" template described by Farkas (1981). Facial approximations were then created by warping this average face to fit skulls. However, the approach of Evenhouse *et al.* (1990) appears to be less than optimal, since average feature shapes were not represented in the average faces. The average-face templates used were based on the main facial proportions and feature dimensions described by Farkas (1981), which excluded other facial characteristics like shape. Rather than using a small sample and the average proportional face template presented by Farkas (1981), average faces can be better generated by using larger samples and directly calculating the average facial shape, color, and texture information for these samples.

Since these earlier attempts, methods of generating average faces have improved. The approach taken now is to calculate the average facial shape from (x, y) coordinates of individual images before warping the individual images to the average shape and blending the color information together. This method was pioneered by D. Perrett and colleagues (Benson and Perrett 1992, Penton-Voak *et al.* 1999, Perrett *et al.* 1998, Perrett *et al.* 1994, Rowland and Perrett 1995, Tiddeman *et al.* 2001) and others have employed similar approaches (Kujawa and Strzalko 1998, Rhodes *et al.* 1999, Rhodes and Tremewan 1996). Here this method will be referred to as the calculated-average technique (see paragraphs following for details of the technique). This method is advantageous because 2D average facial shapes are calculated from the sample under study, and the color information at corresponding points is averaged across all faces in the sample (for comparison to other methods see Figure 6.2).

One of the limitations to the calculated averages presented in the literature is that the photographic methods used are often not well described, making it difficult to know how representative the face images are of the actual average. It also makes it difficult to repeat the results of these studies and to compare images between studies. Many papers, for example, simply state that frontal photographs, with neutral expression, were digitized (e.g., Langlois *et al.* 1994, Perrett *et al.* 1994, Rhodes and Tremewan 1996), while others go as far as saying that faces were also photographed under the same/standard lighting conditions (Kujawa and Strzalko 1998, Perrett *et al.* 1998, Rowland and Perrett 1995) and at standard distances (Langlois and Roggman 1990), but do not specify what the standard conditions actually were.

Although it has been suggested that standardization for lighting, view, facial expression, and makeup, is not necessary when making average faces from samples larger than 30 individuals (Rowland and Perrett 1995), this does not argue against using standardized images. While it is true that a small number of images that deviate from standardized conditions have little power to affect averages made from large numbers of highly standardized photographs, the case seems to be different for small samples of poorly standardized images. Poorly standardized photographs are likely to include variations between many images increasing their power to affect the mean. Such variations are unlikely to be random, particularly in smaller samples ($n < 50$), resulting in different means in comparison to highly standardized images. Even when methods and equipment designed for repeatable and highly standardized craniofacial photography are used, some variation between the images usually remains (Stephan *et al.* 2004), so it seems favorable for the images to be as highly standardized as possible using constant lighting, equipment set up, subject camera distances, and head position.

In the following paragraphs we present new average human faces generated from strictly standardized craniofacial photographs of individuals in the natural head position using improved computerized averaging techniques that retain texture information according to methods of Tiddeman *et al.* (2001). The averages are of Australian individuals grouped into 4 categories according to self-perceived ancestry: (a) Male Central/South-East Asians; (b) Female Central/South-East Asians; (c) Male Europeans; (d) Female Europeans. The averages are not intended to be standards of East-Asian or European face anatomies, but rather an illustration of socially perceived population specific morphotypes.

6.3 GENERATING THE NEW AVERAGE FACES

6.3.1 SAMPLE

The sample consists of 170 individuals, aged between 18 and 34 years, living in Melbourne, Australia. Participants were grouped according to sex (n = 97 females and n = 73 males) and according to their main perceived ancestral background. Four groups were established to classify the sample according to self-reported population ancestry: Female European (n = 57 at rest, n = 56 smiling), Male European (n = 29 at rest, n = 27 smiling), Female Central/South-East Asian (n = 28 at rest, n = 27 smiling) and Male Central/South-East Asian (n = 31 at rest, n = 30 smiling). Some sample numbers differ between smiling and nonsmiling scenarios, since several subjects failed to smile and/or stay correctly positioned during photography of the smiling pose. Seven individuals reported mixed socially perceived ancestries and so were not included in the socially perceived subcategories. Additionally, eighteen individuals reported socially perceived population groups other than those above and so were not included here.

6.3.2 PHOTOGRAPHY

Participants were photographed, in smiling and neutral expressions, in both frontal and right side profile, on a specially designed craniofacial photography rig that is similar to that described by Dobrostanski and Owen (1998). The rig is a permanent structure that enables frontal and profile photographs to be taken simultaneously (see for images: Stephan 2003, Stephan *et al.* 2004). The rig uses two cameras that are fitted with 105 mm 1: 2.8 Macro Nikor lenses, and the camera shutters are simultaneously activated using a remote infrared unit. The rig also uses two self-contained flash units (Elinchrom Prolinca 2500) to illuminate the subject. These units are placed above the subject with the flash unit right of the subject being positioned slightly closer, so that a three-dimensional effect is seen on the subjects' faces in the photographs (Dobrostanski and Owen 1998). This rig enables precise and repeatable photography of a subject using an optical and projected-light range-finding system (Stephan *et al.* 2004).

Subject head rotation was controlled by placement of each subject's head in the natural head position (the position of the head "when a person is standing with his visual axis horizontal" (Broca 1862)) since individuals were then represented as they naturally appear in life (Cooke and Wei 1988b, Moorees and Kean 1958, Moorees *et al.* 1976). There are many other reference lines that can be used to standardize head position, the Frankfort horizontal being one that has previously been used for generating facial averages (McCance *et al.* 1997b, Rabey 1977–8, Tiddeman *et al.* 1999). However, these reference lines are not optimal because they do not represent the typical position in which the head is normally held, and they assume stability of reference points that are, in reality, subject to biological variability (Cavallaro *et al.* 1974, Garn 1961, Moorees *et al.* 1976). Benefits of using the Frankfort horizontal also appear to be somewhat overstated, as this plane was derived for the purpose of orienting skeletal remains that could no longer assume an upright posture (Moorees *et al.* 1976), and in the living, a natural head posture can be directly obtained (Moorees *et al.* 1976). The natural head position also has the advantage that it is fairly repeatable—even after 15 years (Peng 1999)—having an error of about 2° (Cooke 1990, Peng 1999, Siersbaek-Nielsen and Solow 1982), whereas other reference planes like the Frankfort horizontal and the nasion–sella line have an error of about 5° (Cooke and Wei 1988a,b, Moorees and Kean 1958, Solow and Tallgren 1971).

The faces of subjects were centrally positioned in the camera viewfinder at a distance of 1204 mm from the film plane of the frontal camera using a light range-finding system. Subject–camera distance was approximately 1204 mm from the film plane in profile but varied slightly according to width of the participant's head, since the position of the profile camera was fixed. The positioning of subjects at 1204 mm from the film plane of the cameras reduced distortions due to perspective, and lens aberrations, to levels similar to those present during "normal" social contact (Dobrostanski and Owen 1998). Positioning at these subject–camera distances was achieved by use of two lecture-theatre-style light pointers (light range-finding system). One pointer lamp is placed on each side of the frontal camera and tilted so that the projected beams of light converged at the precise focal plane of the frontal camera lens (at glabella). The left pointer (from the subject) projects a <-shaped image, and the right pointer projects a >-shaped image. The two pointers are calibrated so that the V-shaped images form an X at the point of sharpest focus (indicating the position at which the subject is positioned using a reference point, in this case glabella). If the subject is too close to the lens, the two V-shaped images overlap, and if the subject is too far away, the two V-shaped images are spread apart (for images see Stephan *et al.* 2004). When the camera shutters are activated, the light emitted from the flash units overpowers the pointer lights so the Vs are not seen on the face.

Photographs were taken using E200 ISO Ektachrome reversal slide film. Each subject had a total of 4 photographs taken (simultaneous profile and frontal photograph in a relaxed neutral expression and a simultaneous profile and frontal photograph in a smiling position). Film development was standardized as much as possible by having the same qualified photographer develop the photographs in-house. Once the slides were processed, they were scanned into a computer using a Nikon® SF-2000 slide scanner. Several preferences in

Nikon® Scan were selected (e.g., clean-image function was set to normal, bit depth was set to 8, multisample was set to 4× (fine), interpolation was default, color space was RBG Adobe 1998, and autofocus and autoexposure were turned on) during image scanning. These preferences were held constant during the scanning of the slides. The resultant pictures were 1200 pixels in width and 1803 pixels in height, and were originally saved in TIFF format before being converted to JPEG format for easier file management. Since the images were very large natural images, conversion to JPEG format did not appear to affect their visual appearance.

6.4 AVERAGING PROCEDURE

This procedure involved two steps: delineation and averaging. Both were done using software developed by Perrett and colleagues (Benson and Perrett 1992, Rowland and Perrett 1995, Tiddeman *et al.* 2001) at the Perception Laboratory, University of St. Andrews, Scotland. Since highly standardized photographs were used, we did not have to "normalize" our images to compensate for any differences in size and/or orientation as has been done in other average-face studies (Langlois and Roggman 1990, Penton-Voak *et al.* 2001, Penton-Voak and Perrett 2000, Perrett *et al.* 1994, Rowland and Perrett 1995). This is advantageous because normalization techniques assume that the registration points being used (often the pupil centers) are stationary, or fixed, across faces, which is not necessarily the case (Garn 1961, Moorees *et al.* 1976). Our images were, therefore, registered about a single midsagittal point at glabella, with two direction vectors (the vector of the individual facing the camera and the downwards vector of gravity), reducing the number of assumptions made about stationary landmarks.

6.4.1 DELINEATION

Once scanned into the computer, all the faces in the sample were delineated, by hand, before averaging took place. The delineation process involved placing landmarks at certain locations on the face, some being standard anthropometric points (Figure 6.3). Many of the landmarks were joined together by contour lines that gave the outline shape of the face or a "delineation map" (Figure 6.3). Although automated delineation methods are possible (Vetter *et al.* 1997), they are not always exact, and so a manual approach was taken here to ensure that anthropometric landmarks were correctly placed at specific anatomical locations.

The delineation maps were originally adapted from Brennan (Rowland and Perrett 1995). In the past these delineation maps, have included 174

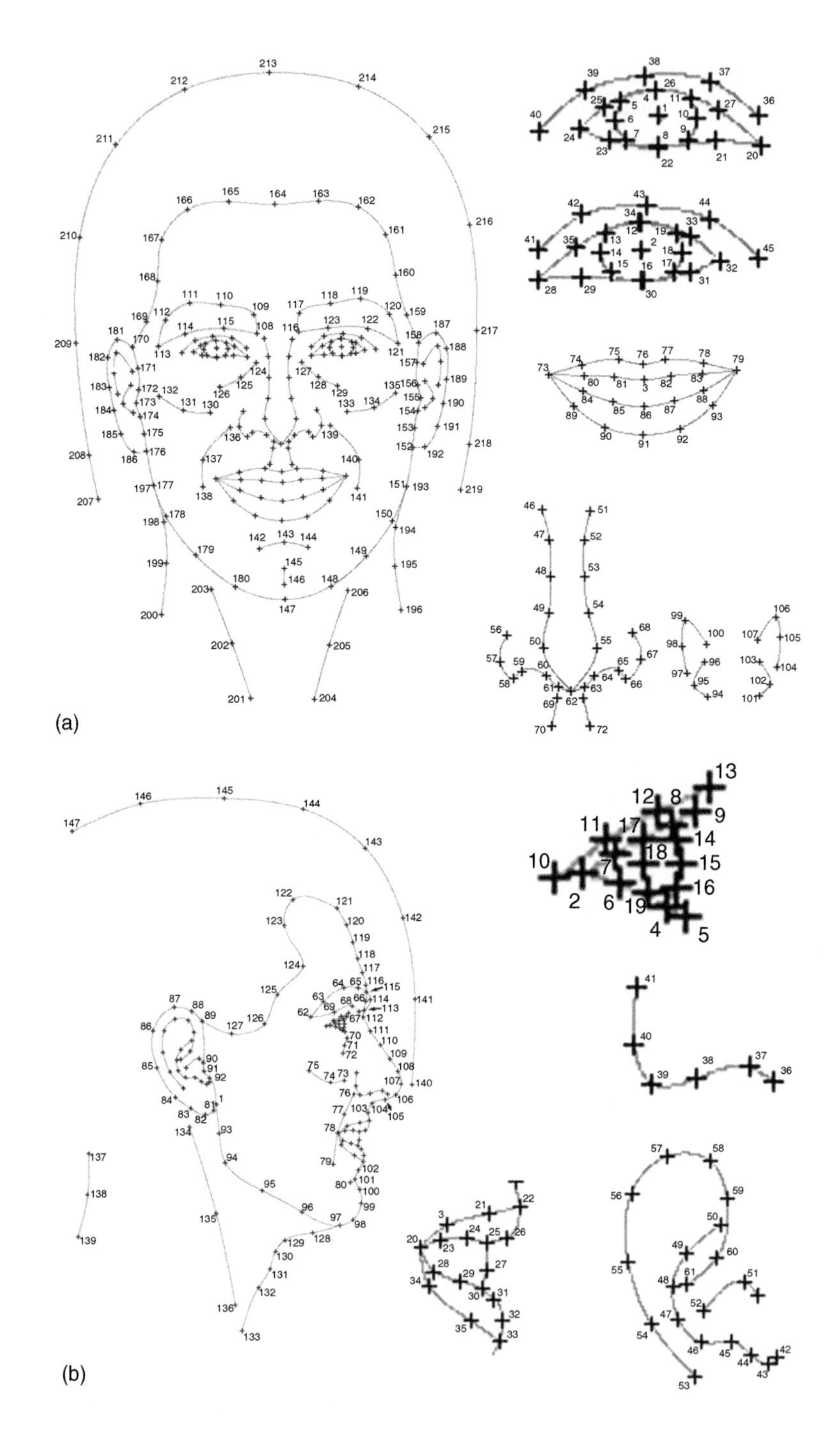

Figure 6.3

Delineation maps. (a) The frontal delineation map including 219 points (see Appendix 1 for landmark descriptions). (b) The profile delineation map including 147 points (see Appendix 2 for landmark descriptions).

landmarks in frontal. For this study, we modified an existing frontal delineation map and created a new profile map. The new frontal delineation map included 219 points (Figure 6.3) placed at strategic anatomical locations, many of which are standard anthropometric landmarks. The inclusion of

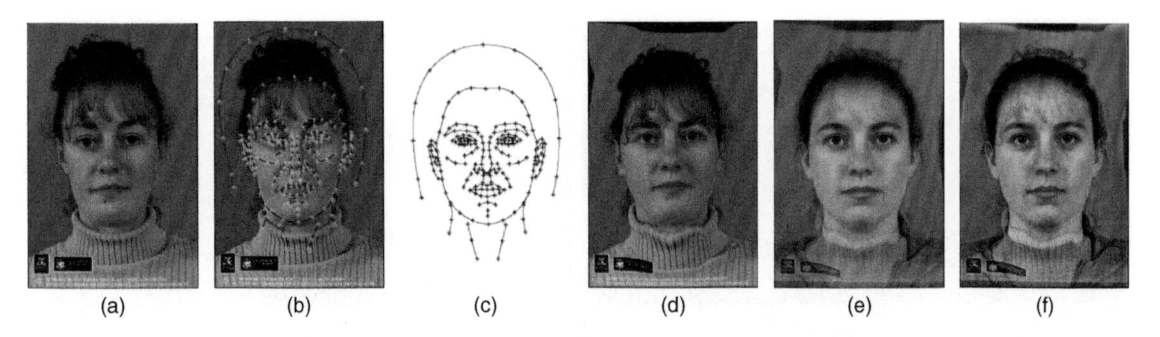

Figure 6.4 Example of face averaging. (a) A standardized face photograph. (b) Delineation of the standardized face photograph. (c) The average of the face delineations for each photograph in the sample. (d) Warping of an individual's face to the average shape. (e) Faces warped to the average face shape are then blended together to generate the average face. (f) The average face with the "texture-preserving" algorithm applied.

more landmarks in the new delineation map enabled the shape of many more morphological features to be included. The new profile delineation map included 147 landmarks (Figure 6.3) and outlined similar features as described by the frontal delineation map, again using many standard anthropometric landmarks.

6.4.2 AVERAGING

The averaging procedure had several steps, as illustrated in Figure 6.4. First the computer generated an average delineation map from the individual delineation maps by calculating the average x and y coordinate for every point along the contour lines. The computer then warped each individual's face into the average template using a multiscale algorithm (Tiddeman 1998). The average color (with red, green, and blue components) of each pixel was calculated to produce the initial average face image. To preserve textural detail in the blends an additional algorithm was applied to amplify the edges (at different positions, spatial scales and orientations) to the appropriate amount for the sample (Tiddeman *et al.* 2001). This improved the quality of the average-face images since less texture information was lost reducing the "smooth" appearance of the faces (Tiddeman *et al.* 2001) (see Figure 6.2 for example). The resultant average faces had the same resolution as the original input faces, being 1200 by 1803 pixels. Figure 6.5 shows the frontal averages generated for each population of origin. Figure 6.6 shows the average faces for each population of origin in profile view. These pictures demonstrate high quality because the photographs were highly standardized, participants were photographed in the natural head position, postphotographic normalization was not used in the averaging process, and texture detail was retained.

The superiority of these average images is evident from the single flash unit reflections seen on the eyes, and the distinctiveness of facial characteristics;

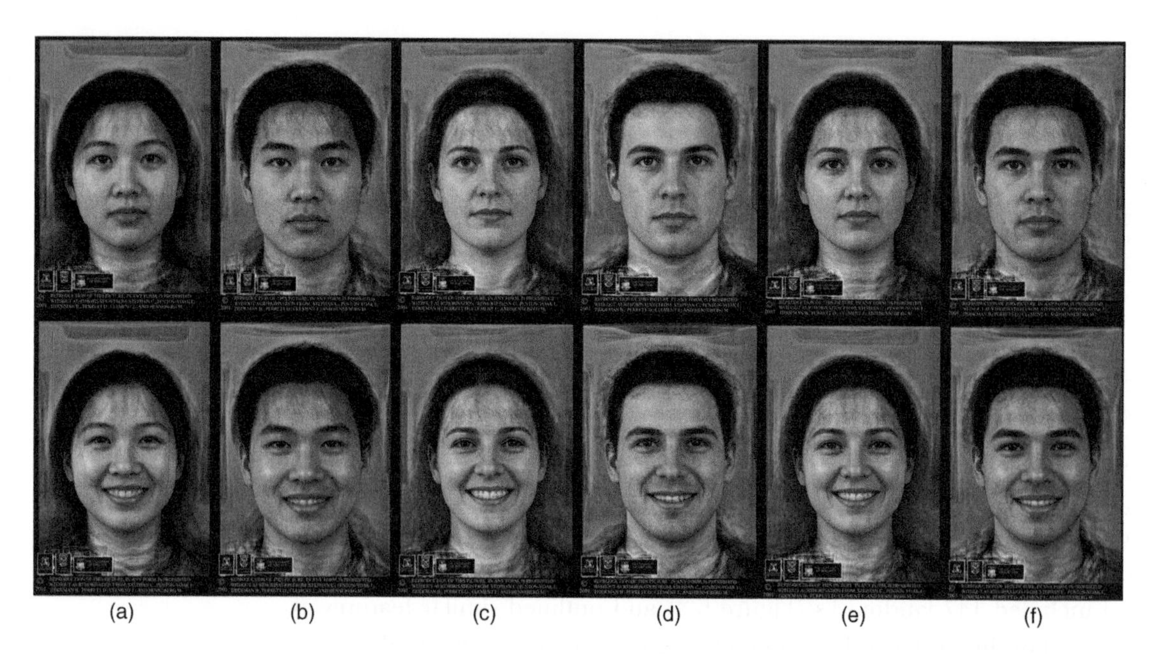

Figure 6.5 Average frontal faces generated for each socially perceived group. Top row shows the average with neutral expression, lower row shows smiling expression. (a) Female Central/South-East Asian: top n = *28 (aged 20 ± 2 years); bottom* n = *27. (b) Male Central/South-East Asian: top* n = *31 (aged 20 ± 3 years); bottom* n = *30. (c) Female European: top* n = *57 (aged 23 ± 4 years); bottom* n = *56. (d) Male European: top* n = *29 (aged 22 ± 4 years); bottom* n = *27. (e) Female total: top* n = *97 (aged 22 ± 4 years); bottom* n = *95. (f) Male total: top* n = *73 (aged 21 ± 3 years); bottom* n = *70.*

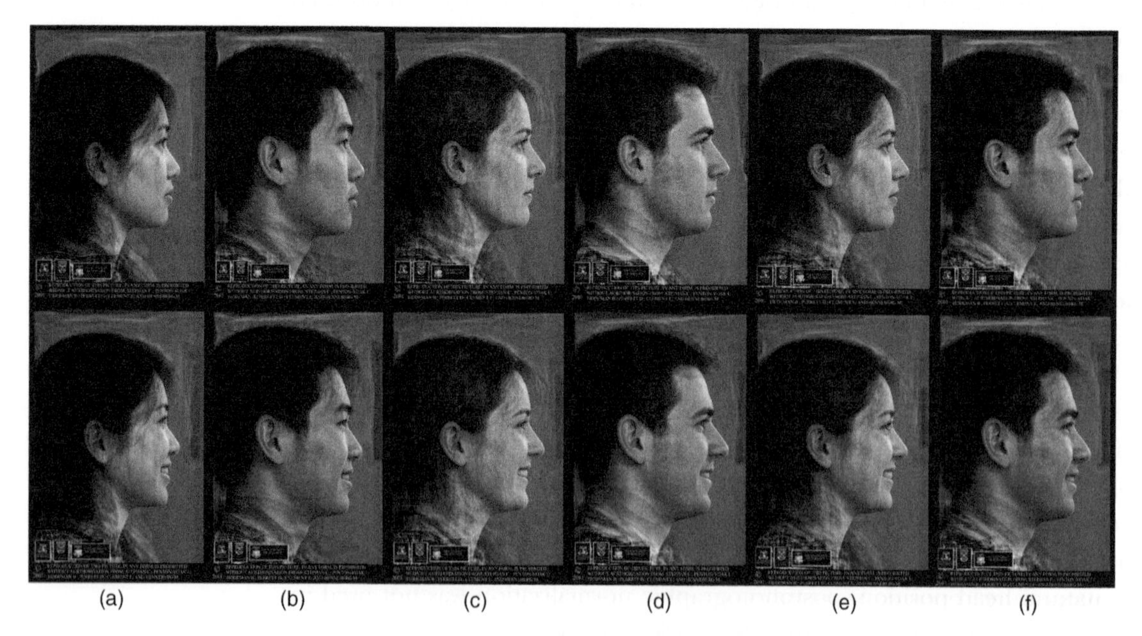

Figure 6.6 Average profile faces generated for each socially perceived group. Top row shows the average with neutral expression; lower row shows smiling expression. Sample sizes are identical to frontal images displayed in Fig. 6.5. (a) Female Central/South-East Asian. (b) Male Central/South-East Asian. (c) Female European. (d) Male European. (e) Female total. (f) Male total.

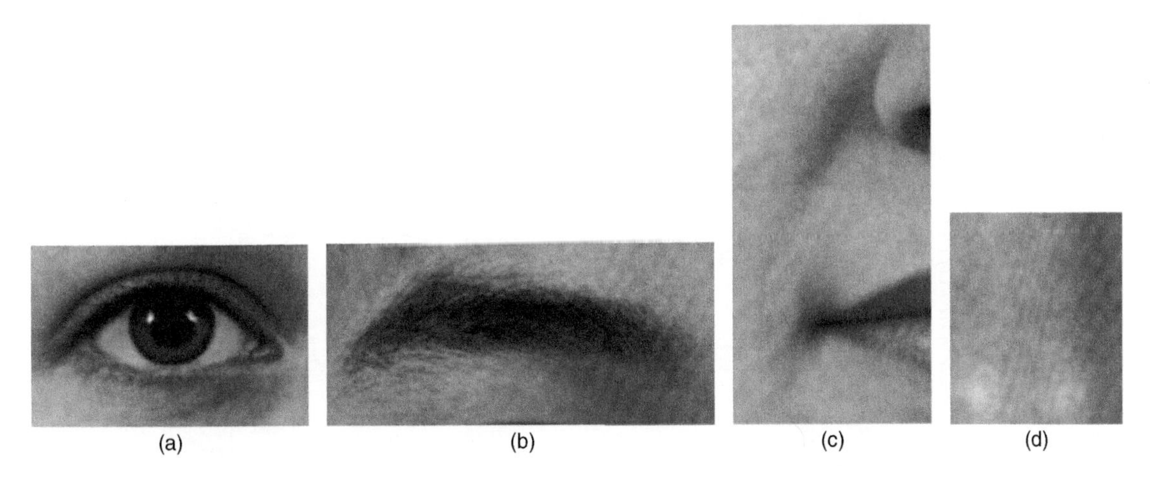

Figure 6.7 Enlarged average face features to show detail. (a) Enlarged eye (female European) showing flash reflections, medial canthal ligament and maybe even individual eyelashes. (b) Enlarged eyebrow (male Asian) showing well defined hairs. (c) Enlarged nasolabial fold (female European). (d) Enlarged tip of nose (male European) illustrating skin pigmentation.

for example, medial canthal ligaments can easily be seen, and perhaps individual hairs in the eyelashes and eyebrows are evident. Figure 6.7 shows enlarged facial features that demonstrate the high resolution of these pictures.

Since direct anthropometric measurements have not been taken for the sample used here, we measured the final average images and compared them to direct anthropometric measures made by Farkas and colleagues (1994a,b) on similar ancestral groups but from North America, in an attempt to check for accuracy. Since profile and frontal images were taken simultaneously, feature distances from the focal plane could be determined. Since we knew the magnification effects of placing an object of known size (100 mm) at known distances about the point of sharpest focus, we could roughly correct feature measurements for scale (Stephan *et al.* 2004). Measurements taken from the scanned photographic images (in millimeters) were first scaled to life size by a factor of 4.98 and then adjusted by 1% (up or down) to compensate for every 10 mm that the site being measured fell behind or in front of point of sharpest focus (Stephan *et al.* 2004).

Since it has been found that only eye and mouth measurements made photogrammetricly compare to direct anthropometric measures (Farkas 1994, Farkas *et al.* 1980), we expected only these to be similar if the average faces were to be representative of reality, however, other measures we made, like ear height, were also found to be accurate, falling close to the expected population range reported by Farkas (i.e., 1.96 standard errors about the sample mean, see Table 6.1).

It is worth emphasizing that categorical average faces made here based on socially perceived population groupings do not indicate differences between

Table 6.1 Comparison of average face measures (adjusted) to those taken on similar populations by Farkas et al. *(1994a,b): 95% confidence intervals of Farkas* et al. *of population means are represented by the 1.96 SEM; measurements en-en to sa-sba (l) are taken from frontal images; measurements n-gn to sn-sto are taken from profile images.*

Measurements	Male European			Female European			Male Asian			Female Asian		
Frontal	Farkas *et al.*	1.96 SEM	Av. Face	Farkas *et al.*	1.96 SEM	Av. Face	Farkas *et al.*	1.96 SEM	Av. Face	Farkas *et al.*	1.96 SEM	Av. Face
en-en	33.3	0.5	33.1	31.8	0.3	31.0	37.6	1.2	37.0	36.5	1.1	35.8
ex-ex	91.2	0.6	88.5	87.8	0.4	85.8	91.7	1.4	92.2	87.3	1.9	86.8
en-ex	31.3	0.2	28.0	30.7	0.2	27.9	29.4	0.5	27.9	28.5	0.6	26.2
ps-pi	10.8	0.2	11.1	10.9	0.2	11.1	9.4	3.4	10.0	9.5	0.4	11.0
al-al	34.9	0.4	37.8	31.4	0.3	33.8	39.2	1.0	41.8	37.2	0.8	38.3
ch-ch	54.5	0.6	51.7	50.2	0.5	48.8	48.3	2.4	49.5	47.3	1.2	48.0
ls-sto	8.0	0.3	6.0	8.7	0.2	5.5	11.2	0.4	8.4	10.1	0.5	7.4
sto-li	9.3	0.3	9.4	9.4	0.2	8.5	10.8	0.5	10.9	10.5	0.5	10.4
sa-sba [r]	62.7	0.7	61.4	59.6	0.5	56.1	61.0	1.3	61.4	58.8	1.3	54.3
sa-sba [l]	62.9	0.7	62.5	59.9	0.5	56.7	60.7	1.4	63.0	57.6	1.4	57.5
Profile												
n-gn	124.7	1.1	125.7	111.4	0.7	116.4	123.6	1.9	124.0	114.9	1.8	113.4
n-sto	76.6	0.8	75.6	69.4	0.4	70.2	78.2	1.4	75.0	71.8	2.0	69.7
sn-gn	72.6	0.8	72.0	64.3	0.6	66.5	72.7	1.9	72.4	66.4	2.0	65.0
sto-gn	50.7	0.8	50.1	43.4	0.4	46.3	53.4	1.5	49.0	47.2	1.2	43.7
prn-gn	91.7	1.1	85.0	81.4	0.6	78.0	88.8	1.8	84.4	81.2	1.5	76.4
g-sn	67.2	0.9	68.8	63.1	0.6	68.1	66.5	1.3	74.0	62.3	1.6	71.8
t-ex	85.3	0.6	78.0	78.9	0.5	76.5	87.3	1.4	81.9	82.5	1.1	77.4
n-sn	54.8	0.6	53.7	50.6	0.4	50.4	53.5	1.0	51.6	51.7	1.2	48.4
sn-sto	22.3	0.4	21.9	20.1	0.3	19.8	23.5	0.8	23.4	21.6	0.8	21.3

"races", nor are they standards of European and Asian facial anatomy since the faces were not segregated into groups based on *real* categorical genetic ancestries (Brace 1996, Cavalli-Sforza *et al.* 1996, Livingstone 1962). Categories were established based on subjects' *self-perceived* ancestry, excluding those who reported mixed perceived ancestry. For this reason, these faces represent arbitrary socially perceived facial morphotypes that may be indicative of population stereotypes. Figures 6.5(e, f) and 6.6(e, f) represent the means for the whole sample, separated by sex, so these faces are probably the most biologically valid as fewer abstract and arbitrary assumptions have been made.

It can be seen from Figures 6.2 and 6.3 that the teeth are distorted in average images of the smiling faces. This results from the warping of individual faces to the average shape without delineation of the teeth. The hair also appears to have a wavy appearance and again, this is due to a lack of delineation and the averaging process. These artifacts may be reduced by inclusion of more delineation points; however, these features have large variability between individuals and are not easily delineated (not all persons smile showing the same number of teeth, nor do they all have similar haircuts). These artifacts need to be addressed in future work so current techniques can be further improved. Additionally the new average faces presented here are limited because they have been generated from a rather specific sample, which predominantly comprises individuals from the University of Melbourne, Australia, and are unlikely to closely represent the average face morphologies of other samples worldwide, perhaps not even those of other Australian Universities. It is worth noting, however, that some tables of average soft-tissue depths have been constructed using even smaller samples than those reported here.

The faces presented here display high-quality average face morphology that can be used as a basis for facial-approximation modeling rather than relying on subjective practitioner interpretations of how the "average" human face appears. This should see facial approximations become more objective in the future. The application of average face anatomy to three-dimensional computer modeling would seem advantageous since objectivity and repeatability could be further increased in facial-approximation methods. This approach appears to be especially useful for representing face shapes (e.g., eye commissures, alars, lips, ears, etc.), face colors, and face textures that remain unpredictable from the skull. Attempts are currently being made to pursue this avenue.

6.5 SUMMARY

Average faces appear to be useful reference guides for facial-approximation practitioners who use techniques relying on general trends because these faces provide objective average information that has previously been subjectively determined. The new 2D average faces presented here hold advantages because they are made from highly standardized photographs and improved computerized averaging techniques, allowing fine anatomical detail to be retained. This process produces very lifelike images which appear to approximate true sample averages more closely than ever before. The use of these average faces as reference guides in traditional manual methods of facial approximation should see the faces built become more objective and more repeatable, but also more similar to each other. Subjectivity in facial-approximation methods could be further reduced by directly using these faces in facial-approximation methods, for example, by warping sex and age specific average faces to fit skulls (see Evenhouse *et al.* 1990, and Chapter 11). Production of average face anatomy in three dimensions would also seem to be useful in future work.

ACKNOWLEDGEMENTS

Thanks to the Prince Alfred Hotel, Melbourne, for their support towards time reimbursement of participants who were photographed for generation of the average faces. Thanks also to those participants who consented to the display of their photographs here.

REFERENCES

Alley T. R. and Cunningham M. R. (1991) "Averaged Faces are Attractive, But Very Attractive Faces are Not Average", *Psychol. Sci.* 2, 123–125.

Antenna. (2002) "Tutankhamun: beneath the mask", *Science Museum* http://www.sciencemuseum.org.uk/antenna/tutankhamun/115.asp.

Benson P. and Perrett D. (1992) "Face to Face with the Perfect Image", *New Scientist* 22nd February, 26–29.

Brace C. L. (1996) In *Race and Other Misadventures: Essays in Honor of Ashley Montagu in His Ninetieth Year* (T. Reynolds and L. Lieberman, eds.). General Hall, New York, pp. 106–141.

Broca M. (1862) "Sur les Projections de la Tete, et sur un Nouvean Procede de Cephalometrie", *Bull. de la Societe d'Anthropologie de Paris* 3, 514–544.

Bruce V. and Young A. (1998) *In the Eye of the Beholder.* Oxford University Press, New York.

Brues A. M. (1958) "Identification of Skeletal Remains", *J. Criminal Law and Criminology and Police Science* 48, 551–556.

Caldwell P. C. (1986) "New Questions (and Some Answers) on the Facial Reproduction Techniques", in: *Forensic Osteology* (K. J. Reichs, ed.). Charles C. Thomas, Springfield, IL, pp. 229–254.

Cavallaro A., Winzar C. F. and Kruger B. J. (1974) "The Reproducibility of Two Methods of Lateral Skull Radiography for Cephalometric Analysis", *Aust. Dent. J.* 19, 122–126.

Cavalli-Sforza L. L., Menozzi P. and Piazza A. (1996) *The History and Geography of Human Genes.* Princeton University Press, New York.

Cooke M. S. (1990) "Five-year Reproducibility of Natural Head Posture: A Longitudinal Study", *Am. J. Orthod. Dentofacial Orthop*. 97, 489–494.

Cooke M. S. and Wei S. H. Y. (1988a) "An Improved Method for the Assessment of the Sagittal Skeletal Pattern and its Correlation to Previous Methods", *Eur. J. Orthod.* 10, 122–127.

Cooke M. S. and Wei S. H. Y. (1988b) "The Reproducibility of Natural Head Posture: A Methodological Study", *Am. J. Orthod. Dentofacial Orthop.* 93, 280–288.

Dobrostanski T. and Owen C. D. (1998) "Craniofacial Photography in the Living", in: *Craniofacial Identification in Forensic Medicine* (J. G. Clement and D. L. Ranson, eds.). Oxford University Press, New York, pp. 137–149.

Evenhouse R., Rasmussen M. and Sadler L. (1990) "Computer Aided Forensic Facial Approximation", *Biostereometric Technology and Applications* 1380, 147–156.

Farkas L. G. (1981) *Anthropometry of the Head and Face in Medicine*. Elsevier, Oxford.

Farkas L. G. (1994) In *Anthropometry of the Head and Face* (L. G. Farkas, ed.). Raven Press, New York, pp. 79–88.

Farkas L. G., Bryson W. and Klotz J. (1980) "Is Photogrammetry of the Face Reliable?" *Plast. Reconstr. Surg*. 66, 346–355.

Farkas L. G., Hreczko T. M. and Katic M. (1994a) "Craniofacial Norms in North American Caucasians from Birth (One Year) to Young Adulthood", in: *Anthropometry of the Head and Face* (L. G. Farkas, ed.). Raven Press, New York, pp. 241–336.

Farkas L. G., Munro I. R. and Kolar J. C. (1987) "The Validity of Neoclassical Facial Proportion Canons", in: *Anthropometric Facial Proportions in Medicine* (L. G. Farkas and I. R. Munro, eds.). Charles C. Thomas, Springfield, IL, pp. 57–66.

Farkas L. G., Ngim R. C. K. and Lee S. T. (1994b) "Craniofacial Norms in 6-, 12-, and 18-year-old Chinese Subjects", in: *Anthropometry of the Head and Face* (L. G. Farkas, ed.). Raven Press, New York, pp. 337–346.

Garn S. M. (1961) In *Roentgenographic Cephalometrics.* J.B. Lippincott & Co., Philadelphia.

Gatliff B. P. (1984) "Facial Sculpture on the Skull for Identification", *Am. J. Forensic Med. Pathol.* 5, 327–332.

George R. M. (1987) "The Lateral Craniographic Method of Facial Reconstruction", *J. Forensic Sci.* 32, 1305–1330.

Grammer K. and Thornhill R. (1994) "Human (Homo Sapiens) Facial Attractiveness and Sexual Selection: The Role of Symmetry and Averageness", *J. Comp. Psychol.* 108, 233–242.

Haglund W. D. (1998) "Forensic 'Art' in Human Identification", in: *Craniofacial Identification in Forensic Medicine* (J. G. Clement and D. L. Ranson, eds.). Arnold, London, pp. 235–243.

Kujawa B. and Strzalko J. (1998) "Standard of Physical Attractiveness", *Anthropol. Rev.* 61, 31–48.

Langlois J. H. and Roggman L. A. (1990) "Attractive Faces are Only Average", *Psychol. Sci.* 1, 115–121.

Langlois J. H., Roggman L. A. and Musselman L. (1994) "What is Average and What is Not Average About Attractive Faces?", *Psychol. Sci.* 5, 214–220.

Little A. C., Burt D. M., Penton-Voak I. and Perrett D. I. (2001) "Self-Perceived Attractiveness Influences Human Female Preferences for Sexual Dimorphism and Symmetry in Male Faces", *Proc. R. Soc. Lond. B Biol. Sci.* 268, 1–6.

Livingstone F. B. (1962) "On the Non-existence of Human Races", *Curr. Anthropol.* 3, 279–281.

Maat G. J. R. (1998–1999) "Facial Reconstruction: A Review and Comment", *TALANTA* 30–31, 247–253.

McCance A. M., Moss J. P., Fright W. R., Linney A. D. and James D. R. (1997a) "Three-Dimensional Analysis Techniques – Part 1: Three-Dimensional Soft-Tissue Analysis of 24 Adult Cleft Palate Patients Following Le Fort I Maxillary Advancement: A Preliminary Report", *Cleft Palate-Craniofacial J.* 34, 36–45.

McCance A. M., Moss J. P., Fright W. R., Linney A. D. and James D. R. (1997b) "Three-Dimensional Analysis Techniques – Part 2: Laser Scanning: A Quantitative Three-Dimensional Soft-Tissue Analysis Using a Color-Coding System", *Cleft Palate-Craniofacial J.* 34, 46–51.

Moorees C. F. A. and Kean M. R. (1958) "Natural Head Position: A Basic Consideration in the Interpretation of Cephalometric Radiographs", *Am. J. Phys. Anthropol.* 16, 213–234.

Moorees C. F. A., van Venrooij M. E., Lebret L. M. L., Glatky C. B., Kent R. L. J. and Reed R. B. (1976) "New Norms for the Mesh Diagram Analysis", *Am. J. Orthod.* 69, 57–71.

Peng L. (1999) "Fifteen-year Reproducibility of Natural Head Posture: a Longitudinal Study", *Am. J. Dentofacial Orthop*. 116, 82–85.

Penton-Voak I. S., Jones B. C., Little A. C., Baker S., Tiddeman B., Burt D. M. and Perrett D. I. (2001) "Symmetry, Sexual Dimorphism in Facial Proportions and Male Facial Attractiveness", *Proc. R. Soc.* B 268, 1617–1625.

Penton-Voak I. S. and Perrett D. I. (2000) "Female Preference for Male Faces Changes Cyclically – Further Evidence", *Evolution and Human Behavior* 21, 39–48.

Penton-Voak I. S., Perrett D. I., Castles D. L., Kobayashi T., Burt D. M., Murray L. K. and Minamisawa R. (1999) "Menstral Cycle Alters Face Preference", *Nature* 399, 741–742.

Perrett D. I., Lee K. J., Penton-Voak I., Rowland D., Yoshikawa S., Burt D. M., Henzill S. P., Castles D. L. and Akamatsu S. (1998) "Effects of Sexual Dimorphism on Facial Attractiveness", *Nature* 394, 884–887.

Perrett D. I., May K. A. and Yoshikawa S. (1994) "Facial Shape and Judgements of Female Attractiveness", *Nature* 368, 239–242.

Prag J. and Neave R. (1997) *Making Faces: Using Forensic and Archaeological Evidence.* British Museum Press, London.

Rabey G. P. (1977–78) "Current Principles of Morphanalysis and their Implications in Oral Surgical Practice", *Br. J. Oral Surgery* 15, 97–109.

Rhodes G., Sumich A. and Byatt G. (1999) "Are Average Facial Configurations Attractive Only Because of their Symmetry", *Psychol. Sci.* 10, 52–58.

Rhodes G. and Tremewan T. (1996) "Averageness, Exaggeration, and Facial Attractiveness", *Psychol. Sci.* 7, 105–109.

Rowland D. A. and Perrett D. I. (1995) "Manipulating Facial Appearance Through Shape and Color", *IEEE.* 15, 70–76.

Siersbaek-Nielsen S. and Solow B. (1982) "Intra- and Interexaminer Variability in Head Posture Recorded by Dental Auxiliaries", *Am. J. Orthod.* 82, 50–57.

Solow B. and Tallgren A. (1971) "Natural Head Position in Standing Subjects", *Acta Odontoloiga Scandinavia* 29, 591–607.

Stephan C. and Henneberg M. (2001) "Building Faces from Dry Skulls: Are They Recognized Above Chance Rates?", *J. Forensic Sci.* 46, 432–440.

Stephan C. N. (2002a) "Facial Approximation: Falsification of Globe Projection Guideline by Exophthalmometry Literature", *J. Forensic Sci.* 47, 1–6.

Stephan C. N. (2002b) "Position of Superciliare in Relation to the Lateral Iris: Testing a Suggested Facial Approximation Guideline", *Forensic Sci. Int.* 130, 29–33.

Stephan C. N. (2003) "Facial Approximation: An Evaluation of Mouth-Width Determination", *Am. J. Phys. Anthropol.* 121, 48–57.

Stephan C. N., Clement J. G., Owen C. D., Dobrostanski T. and Owen A. (2004) "A New Rig for Craniofacial Photography Put to the Test", *Plast. Reconstr. Surg.* 113, 827–833.

Taylor K. T. (2001) *Forensic Art and Illustration*. CRC Press, Boca Raton.

Tiddeman B., Burt M. and Perrett D. (2001) "Prototyping and Transforming Facial Textures for Perception Research", *IEEE Computer Graphics and Applications* 21, 42–50.

Tiddeman B., Duffy N. and Rabey G. (2000) "Construction and Visualisation of Three-Dimensional Facial Statistics", *Computer Methods and Programs in Biomedicine* 63, 9–20.

Tiddeman B., Rabey G. and Duffy N. (1999) "Synthesis and Transformation of Three-Dimensional Facial Images: Extending the principles of Face-Space Transformations by Using Texture-Mapped Laser-Scanned Surface Data", *IEEE Engineering in Medicine and Biology* 64–69.

Tiddeman B. P. (1998) Unpublished PhD, Heriot-Watt University, Edinburgh.

Vetter T., Jones M. J. and Poggio T. (1997) A Bootstrapping Algorithm for Learning Linear Models of Object Classes. Paper presented at the *IEEE, Computer Vision and Pattern Recognition*, Puerto Rico.

APPENDIX 1

Table of landmarks for the frontal delineation map (Figure 6.3(a)). Left-side bilateral landmarks and landmarks falling midway between two other landmarks are not shown. Standard anthropological landmarks are shown in bold type.

Label	Soft Tissue Landmark
1	**Right center of pupil (p)**
3	**midline point of inferior border of upper lip (in rest point 3 & 86 form the stomion (sto))**
4	most superior point on iris border
6	most lateral point on iris border
8	most inferior point on iris border
10	most medial point on iris border
20	**endocanthion (en)**
21	point at flexion of medial lower lid
22	**palpebrale inferius (pi)**
24	**exocanthion (ex)**
26	**palpebrale superius (ps)**
36	most medial point on epicanthal fold
38	most superior point on epicanthal fold
40	most lateral point on epicanthal fold
46	most superior point on bridge of nose
49	point of flexion of nose bridge and bulb
50	lateral point encompassing bulb of nose
56	most superior point of alare insertion to the face
57	**alare (al)**
58	**subalare (sbal)**
59	point at most superior flexion of nostril
60	base of visible nostril
62	base of bulb of nose
69	point at upper level of right philtrum ridge
70	**crista philtri landmark (cph)**
73	**cheilion (ch)**
75	point on vermillion border below pt. 70
76	**labriale superius (ls)**
81	point at flexion of the right lower border of upper lip near the tubercule
86	**midline point of superior border of lower lip (in rest point 3 & 86 form stomion (sto))**
91	**labriale inferius (li)**
94	point at flexion of antitragus
95	point at flexion of concha
96	point at the superior visible end of the concha
97	point at the visible inferior end of the proximal helix border
99	point of flexion of proximal helix border
100	point at the most inferior proximal aspect of helix border
108	point at most medioinferior aspect of brow
109	point at most mediosuperior aspect of brow
111	**superciliare (sci)**
113	most lateral point of brow
124	upper point following nasal bridge line
126	lower point following nasal bridge line
130	medial point following cheek prominence
132	lateral point following cheek prominence
136	upper point of nasolabial line
137	midpoint of nasolabial line
138	lower point of nasolabial line
142	right lateral point on mental labial ridge
143	**sublabiale (sl)**

145	superior sagittal point on mental cleft
146	inferior sagittal point on mental cleft
147	**gnathion approximation (gn)**
164	**trichion (tr)**
170	**otobasion superius (obs)**
172	superior junction of tragus and face
173	lateral most edge of tragus
174	inferior junction of tragus and face
176	**otobasion inferius (obi)**
177	**gonion approximation (go)**
181	**superaurale (sa)**
184	point opposite 95 on free border of ear
186	**subaurale (sba)**
197	point opposite 177 on free border of neck
198	point opposite, but just inferior to 178, on neck
200	point at inferior region of visible neck
201	point on inferior sternocleidomastoid line
203	point on superior sternocleidomastoid line
207	point opposite 197
208	point opposite 186
209	point opposite 181
213	mid sagittal point above 164

APPENDIX 2

Table of landmarks for the profile delineation map (Figure 6.3(b)). Left-side bilateral landmarks and landmarks falling midway between two other landmarks are not shown. Standard anthropological landmarks are shown in bold type.

1	**Otobasion inferius (obi)**
2	**Exocanthion (ex)**
4	point at corneal junction with lower lid
5	**palpebrale inferius (pi)**
8	point at corneal junction with upper lid
9	**palpebrale superius (ps)**
10	most lateral point of epicanthal fold
13	most anterior point of epicanthal fold
15	most anterior point of corneum
17	point at superior margin of iris
18	point at mid margin of iris
19	point at inferior margin of iris
20	**right chelion (ch)**
22	most anterior point on upper vermillion border = **labriale superius approximation (ls)**
25	point at junction of upper incisors and upper lip or **stomion (sto) when relaxed**
26	point at flexion of upper lip curve
27	lower point of anterior incisor or **stomion (sto) when relaxed**
30	point at junction of lower incisors and lower lip or **stomion (sto) when relaxed**
33	most anterior point on lower vermillion border = labriale inferius approximation (li)
36	most anterior point of visible nostril
37	point at most superior flexion of nostril
38	most posterior point of visible nostril
39	**subalare (sbal)**
40	**alar curvature point (ac)**
41	most superior point of alar insertion to the face
42	point on intertragal notch near the junction of the inferior tragus with the face
43	deepest point of intertragal notch
45	point of flexion on antitragus
46	point at flexion between antitragus and antihelix

(Continued)

50	superior point on concha border near the anterior antihelix
51	point on helix-tragal junction directly above the external auditory meatus
52	visible point at the outer helix near concha junction
53	most inferior visible point on inner helix border
54	point on inner helix border opposite 47
56	point on inner helix border opposite 86
57	point on inner helix border directly below pt. 87
59	point near the proximal anterior border of helix
60	point at flexion of inner helix border near helix-tragal junction
61	visible point at the inner helix near concha junction
62	lateral point of brow
64	point just lateral to superciliare
65	point just medial to superciliare
67	inferior-anterior point of brow
68	**approximation of orbital superios (os)**
70	superior point on nasal bridge line
71	midpoint on nasal bridge line
72	inferior point on nasal bridge line
73	anterior point following cheek prominence
74	midpoint following cheek prominence
75	posterior point following cheek prominence
76	point on upper nasolabial line, near pt. 39
78	point on nasolabial line, near pt. 20
79	inferior point on nasolabial line
80	posterior point on mental labial ridge
82	**subaurale (sba)**
83	point at tip of ear lobe
85	point on free margin of ear opposite pt. 47
86	point near postaurale (pa) so that contour follows free margin of ear
87	**superaurale (sa)**
89	**otobasion superius (obs)**
90	**tragion (t)**
91	point at posterior flexion of tragus
92	point at junction of the lower tragus with the face
94	**gonion approximation (go)**
97	**gnathion approximation (ga)**
99	**pogonion (pg)**
101	**sublabiale (sl)**
104	**subnasale (sn)**
107	**pronasale (prn)**
109	point of flexion of nose bridge and bulb
112	**sellion (se)**
113	point at junction of lower brow and profile of face
114	anterior point of eyebrow
115	point at junction of upper brow and profile of face
116	**approximation of glabella (g)**
121	**trichion (tr)**
122	point at flexion of receding hairline (if present)
123	point at flexion of hairline near temple
129	point at flexion of the neck and jaw
130	point at flexion of the neck and Adam's apple
131	point at most projecting point of Adam's apple
132	point at lower border of Adam's apple
133	approximation of suprestenale
134	point on upper sternocleidomastoid line
135	mid point on sternocleidomastoid line
136	point on inferior sternocleidomastoid line
137	upper point on posterior neck line
138	midpoint on posterior neck line
139	inferior point on posterior neck line
140	hair point just anterior to 107
147	posterior point of hair in profile

CHAPTER 7

PREDICTING THE MOST PROBABLE FACIAL FEATURES USING BAYESIAN NETWORKS, MATHEMATICAL MORPHOLOGY, AND COMPUTER GRAPHICS

Juan E. Vargas
Department of Computer Science and Engineering, University of South Carolina, Columbia, South Carolina, USA

Luis Enrique Sucar
ITESM Campus Morelos, Paseo de la Reforma 182-A, Cuernavaca, Morelos, Mexico

7.1 INTRODUCTION

For years, anthropologists and facial surgeons have tried to identify the most important features defining the cranial-facial geometry of humans (Farkas 1981). The problem is not simple, considering that a small part of a human face can express millions of different shapes (Altobelli 1994).

Facial surgeons use sets of landmarks (Figure 7.1) in the skull and the face to perform reconstructive or corrective surgery. Forensic artists use similar sets of landmarks when they sculpt facial clay models to identify the remains of individuals, or when they compose age-adjusted photographs of missing

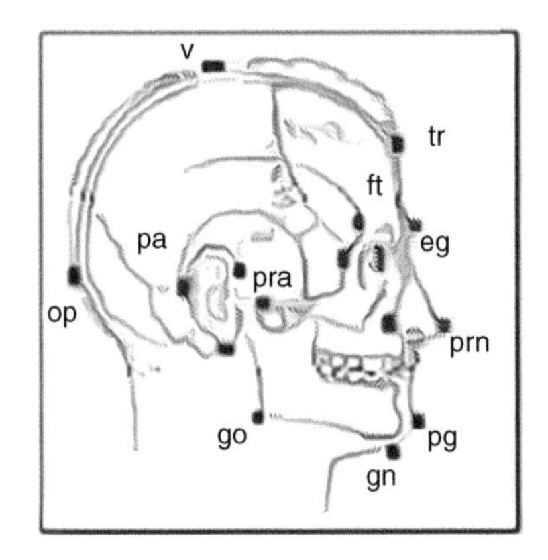

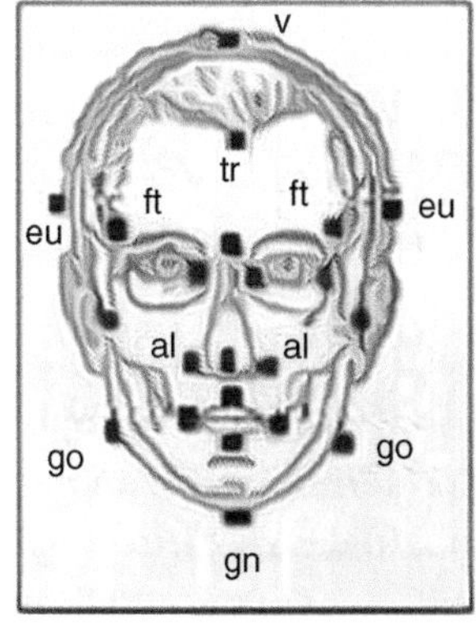

Figure 7.1
Facial landmarks can be used to establish points of reference for digital analysis. Using these landmarks, specific regions in a sample's face could be located and matched against regions stored in databases. From Farkas (1981).

Computer-Graphic Facial Reconstruction
John G. Clement and Murray K. Marks, Editors

children. Landmarks are anatomical locations in the skull or the face where identifiable concavities or convexities exist to accommodate facial features such as lips or eyes, or to provide supporting points for the insertion of muscular tissue into bony tissue. Research has been conducted to identify the location and shape of the most appropriate landmarks for forensic analysis and plastic surgery. Tables have been published describing distances and arcs between facial landmarks in the head, face, eye orbits, nose, mouth, and ears, which use sex and age as predicting variables (Farkas 1981). Tables of cranial landmarks that use sex and age as predicting variables are also available (Saksena 1987).

Forensic experts know that strong anatomical relationships exist between certain facial and cranial landmarks. For example, Farkas' facial glabella (g) corresponds to İşcan's bony glabella. Farkas' facial gonion (go) is identical to İşcan's bony gonion, while Farkas' facial endocanthion (en) corresponds to the bony landmark (mo) used in cephalometry (Farkas 1981, İşcan 1993). However, no statistical studies have been conducted to validate or characterize the relationships between facial and cranial landmarks. Likewise, a statistical correlation between the bony-tissue and soft-tissue landmarks around eye orbits, nose, mouth, ear, and head has yet to be made. Research into assessing the most probable landmark values and interlandmark proportions, given conditioning sets richer than those used by Farkas (sex and age), requires significant effort. Studies relating facial or cranial features given anthropometric information, such as ethnicity, race, height, or combinations of these gathered from parents, are also not available. The importance of these assessments is clear when considered within the context of current methods used for forensic reconstruction of faces from skulls, or for composition of age-adjusted photographs.

Forensic artists create facial models by superimposing clay at specific locations of the skull, aligned around cranial and facial landmarks. The amount and shape of clay is for the most part decided by the artists on the basis of experience and the available information about the victim, such as sex, race, ethnicity, estimated age, skeletal type, bone constitution, hair, etc. However it is well known that most of the information needed to recognize a face is captured in less than 10 per cent of the tissue, particularly around the eyes, nose, lips, and ears. Nonetheless, most forensic artists decide the amount of clay and facial traits at these regions on a subjective basis, using heuristic rules such as "Vietnamese are thinner than Caucasians", "blacks have wider noses than Caucasians", and so on. Since the number of facial traits is large, and the number of interlandmark proportions is even larger, it is not rare to find traces of "preferred" traits among the faces reconstructed by the same artist. Clearly, a method for selecting the most probable facial features, given anthropometric information, would be a tremendous asset.

Our research uses Bayesian networks to narrow down the set of most probable features given anthropometric information. The premise is that a set of Bayesian networks may assist humans to reconstruct faces from skulls or to compose age-adjusted photographs. Not having normative studies relating facial landmarks to other parameters, Bayesian networks can provide the basis for assessing the correspondences between facial landmarks to other parameters, including cranial landmarks, race, ethnicity, age, skeletal frame, etc.

For the estimation of the most probable face of a missing child, given early photographs, three-dimensional (3D) models can be created from photographs or from artist-composed sketches. Facial features can be extracted from these models and given to a morphing program, which could adjust the features against facial norms modeled by a Bayesian network matching the characteristics of the child. The Bayesian network could also estimate the most probable age-induced changes in the facial features of the child, given the known parameters. The estimated features could be given to the morphing program to adjust them in order to blend the estimated age-caused facial growth into the original face.

A Bayesian network is shown near the end of this chapter, in Figure 7.11. In this context a Bayesian network is a graph created from the anthropometric data and expert knowledge. The network can explain how a set of variables, in this case the most probable features of a person, can be obtained given known values of sex and age. In the network of Figure 7.11, each outer node represents a variable associated to a facial index and related to some specific landmarks.

Information about the shape of a skull can be obtained from a set of cranial images containing transversal slices. These images can be processed to extract the information of the cranial contours in order to build a 3D model. Once that model is created, a matching template process can locate discrete landmarks in the model. The skull model can be updated each time new evidences are fed to the Bayesian networks. Figure 7.2 shows the main stages of this process.

A related problem is the estimation of indices associated with the facial landmarks given the shape of the skull. A series of transversal cuts of a human skull can be processed in order to get a 3D model of the skull. The landmarks can be automatically located from the 3D model, and the thickness of the tissue and the relation between the landmarks can be displayed.

This chapter outlines a method to model a human skull (by building its graphic model) and a method to locate templates of facial regions (such as nasal fissures, ocular fissures, etc.). The chapter also discusses how a set of cranial landmarks' locations are deduced from the spatial position of the located templates. This method will permit automatic updates of the results given by a Bayesian network. Section 2 of this paper briefly describes the techniques

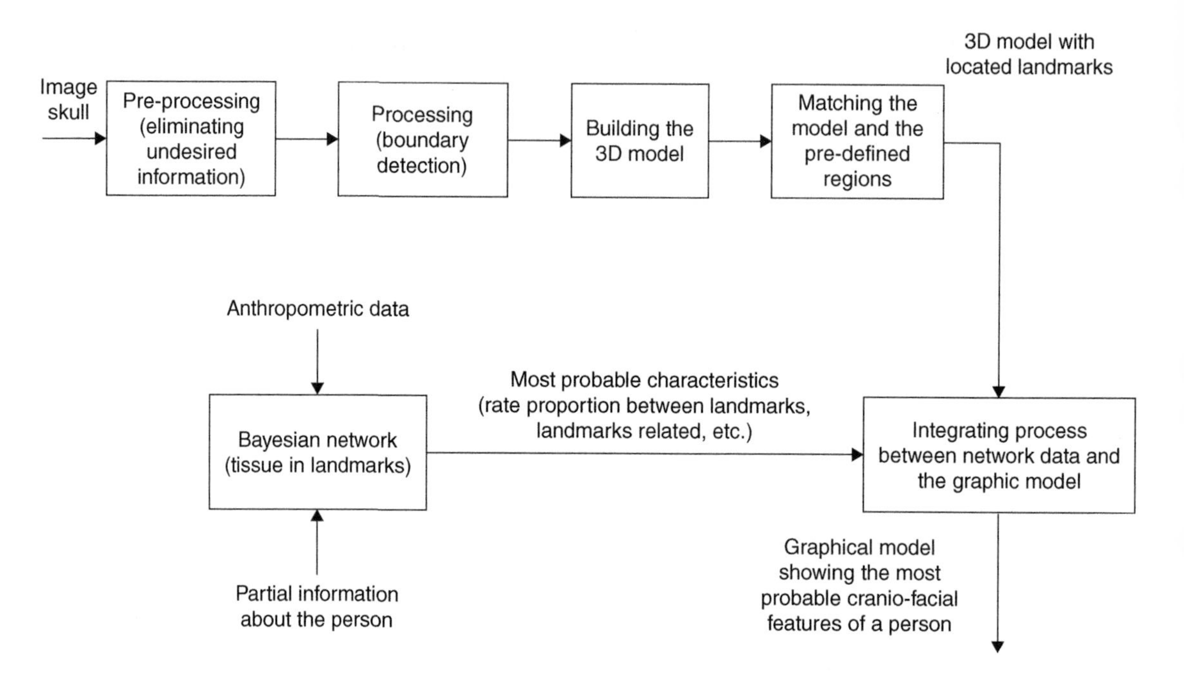

Figure 7.2 Main stages involved in obtaining a graphical model with the most probable features of a face.

used to process the initial images. Section 3 shows how a 3D model of the skull is built. Section 4 presents a technique to locate discrete landmarks on the model. Section 5 discusses a method used to estimate indices using a Bayesian network. Section 6 gives the conclusions derived from this work.

7.2 IMAGE PROCESSING

The first step towards the construction of the graphic model of the skull is to process a set of input images containing transversal slices of a human skull, as showed in Figure 7.3. It is necessary to eliminate the undesired information of the image and detect the area of the image where the boundary of the skull is located. Techniques of mathematical morphology were used to get the desired results.

Mathematical morphology, as originally developed by Matheron and Serra, is a theory of set mappings, modeling binary image transformations, which are invariants under the group of euclidean translations (Serra 1988). The initial step in this process is to convert the image into binary form. This is done as follows: given a threshold intensity value, all the points (*pixels*) with intensities lower than the threshold are changed to the minimum level of intensity. All points equal to or above the threshold are set to the maximum intensity.

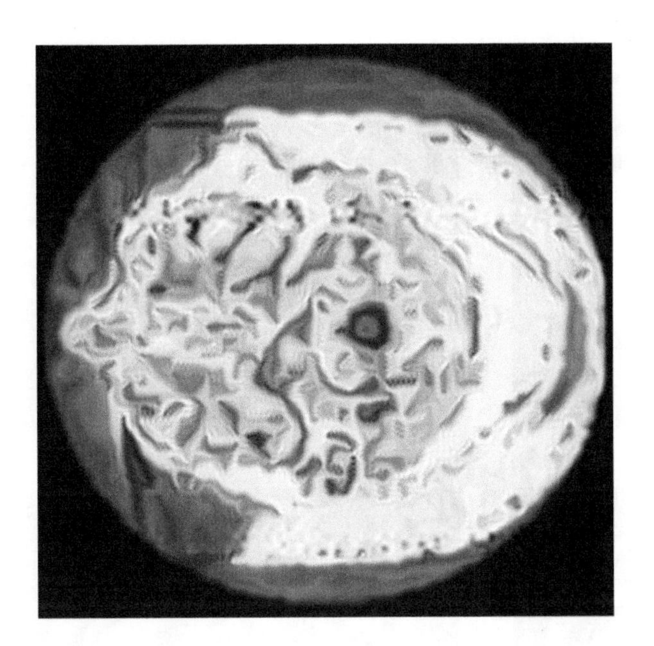

Figure 7.3

Digital image obtained from a magnetic resonance device. The image is a single slide. Using digital filtering, the various type of tissues (bone, facial, etc.) can be identified from the image.

Morphological operators such as erosion and dilation are applied to the binary image (Gonzalez 1992, Haralick 1987). These operators are used to emphasize specific parts of the image, and to engross or attenuate interest regions. Formally, these operations are defined as follows:

Dilation: With *A* and *B* sets in Z^2 and Ø denoting the empty set, the dilation of *A* by *B*, denoted $A \oplus B$, is defined as:

$$A \oplus B = \{x | (\hat{B})_x \cap A \neq \varnothing\}$$

This is the set of all displacements such that $\hat{B}$ and *A* overlap by at least one nonzero element.

Erosion: For sets *A* and *B* in Z^2, the erosion of *A* by *B*, denoted $A \Theta B$, is defined as:

$$A \Theta B = \{x | (B)_x \subseteq A\}$$

Dilation and erosion are duals of each other with respect to set complement and reflection. These techniques are used to eliminate undesired information (noise), as shown in Figure 7.4.

After the noise is removed, the areas inside the region of the cranial border (pixels in black) are filled to normalize the region. The contour can be determined by using a set-difference operation involving the original binary image and the image formed by setting the bordering pixels as white pixels (derived from the same image).

The result of this process is an image that defines the contour of the cranial region. The white pixels in this image form a level curve which is used as an input to the graphical module.

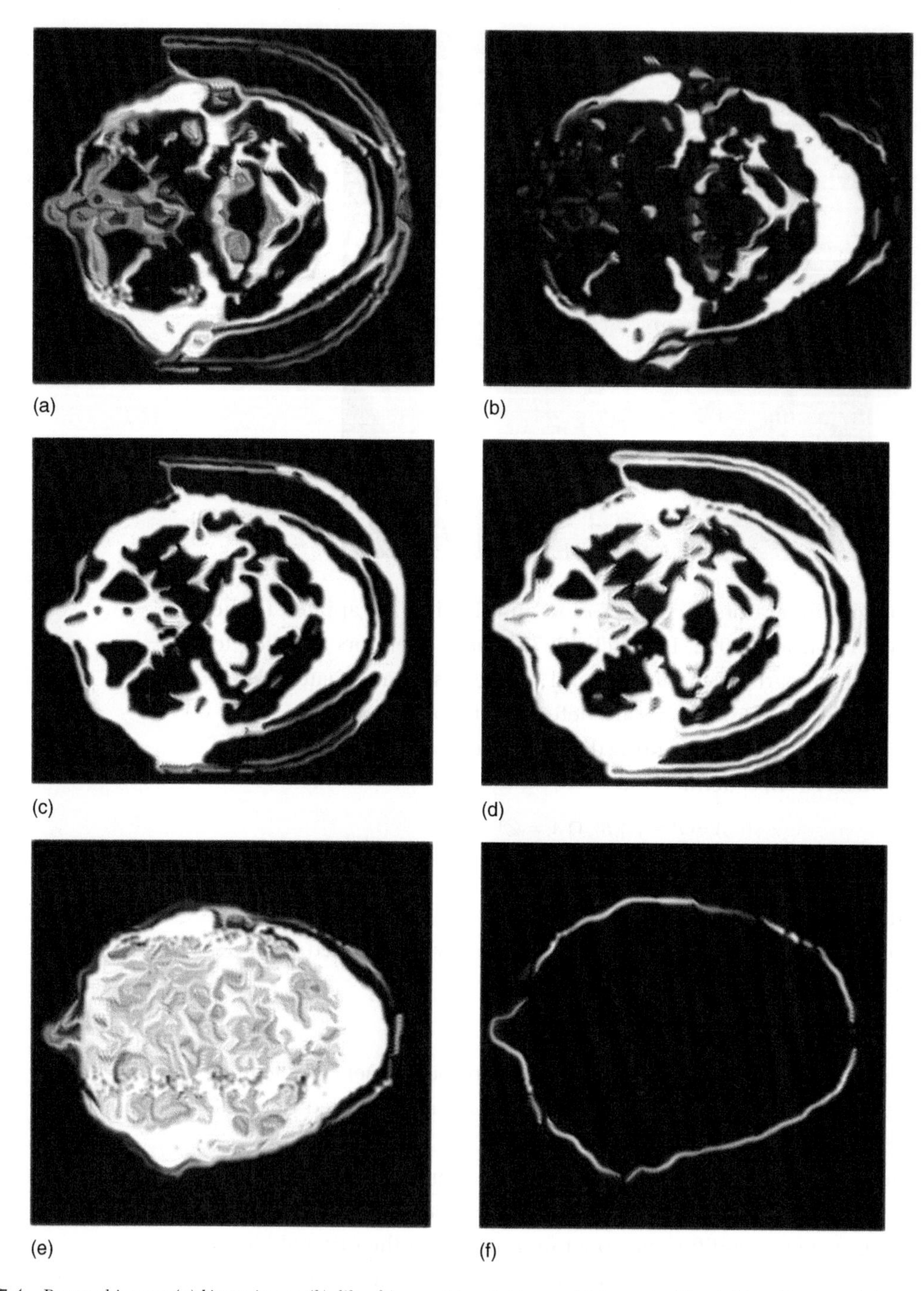

Figure 7.4 Processed images: (a) binary image; (b) dilated image; (c) eroded image; (d) image in dilated; (e) uniform cranial area; (f) closed boundary obtained.

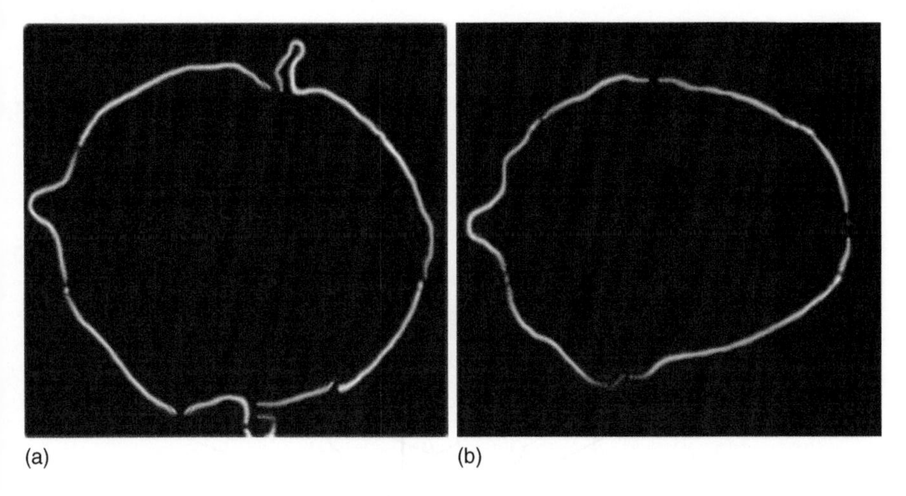

Figure 7.5

Detected closed boundaries identified using dilation and erosion. In the figure, the contour of the bony tissue has been identified.

7.3 GRAPHICAL MODEL

The boundary points obtained from the previous process are represented as level curves in a parametric way:

$$x = X(t), \qquad y = Y(t), \qquad z = Z(t)$$

After this, a sampling process is applied to each curve to get the set of points with which a bivariate interpolation is done. The sampled points are obtained by using a reference point (located in the center of the cranial contour) and by taking points of the curve each n degree angles in areas with low changes in its derivative. In regions where the curve exhibits larger variations in its derivative, the process of sampling consists of taking points each a certain number of points in the curve (see Figure 7.6).

The boundaries obtained from the processed images are used to build the graphical model. Thus, each resulting image (containing information about one slice of skull) is used as a level curve at different heights of the cranial surface (Figure 7.7).

The model surface consists of a set of Bézier patches defined with a set of control points. The Bézier patches were chosen due to their flexibility. A Bézier patch is a parametric representation which is used to represent complex areas on the skull with a relative low number of control points. One advantage of using Bézier patches is that it is possible to make local changes to a control point without affecting the rest of the points. Each of these patches is defined in a way that its control points are adjusted so that the defined surface interpolates the points in the level curves (Rogers 1990). A Bézier patch has the form

$$b^{m,n}(u,v) = \sum_{i=0}^{m}\sum_{j=0}^{n} b_{i,j} B_i^m(u) B_j^n(v),$$

where B_i^m are the unidimensional parameters of a Bézier curve (Farin 1990).

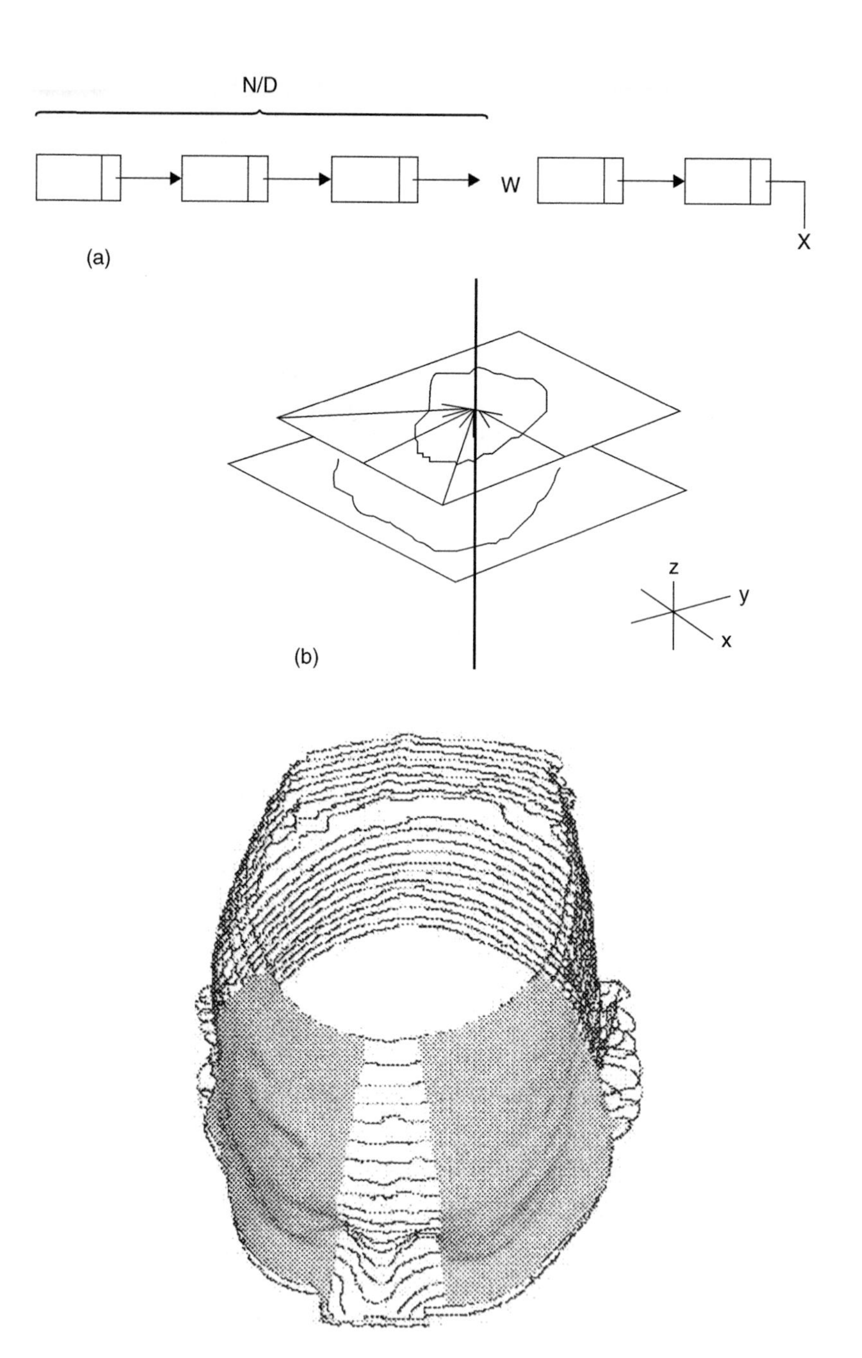

Figure 7.6

Sampling Process. (a) When the derivatives of the curve have a significant variation, the sampling process is implemented taking points at a certain rate from the curve. (b) In regions with low changes in the curve derivative, points are selected each n degrees taking as reference the center of the contour.

Figure 7.7

Graphic model of a human face using wire frames and Bézier surfaces. The model was obtained from a set of slices obtained from images similar to the ones shown in Figure 7.5.

7.4 DISCRETE LANDMARK LOCATION

One of the most difficult problems is to develop efficient methods of identifying the precise location of interest points (discrete landmarks) on the surface of the model. The method proposed here is based on defining templates of the most distinctive zones of the head and human face, such as eye fissures,

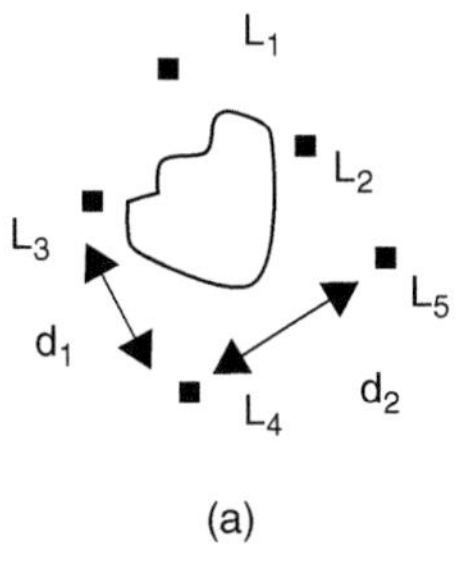

(a)

Slice of a predefined model (template) and its relation with some landmarks

L_k = Position of the landmark with respect to the predefined model

d_k = Distance relationship between landmarks

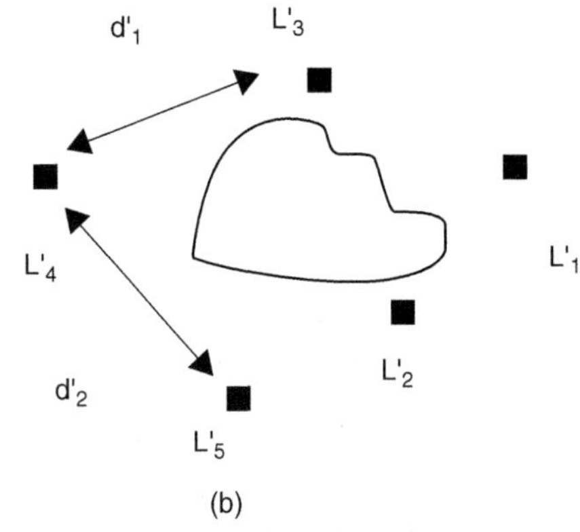

(b)

Transversal cut of an object (graphic model of a skull)

Figure 7.8

(a) Transversal slice obtained from a predefined template and its relation with the landmarks in its neighborhood, (b) transversal slice obtained from the tridimensional model built and the intersection between a search plane. With these two curves the matching process is done. When the correspondence between their points is found, the position of each landmark is automatically located.

nasal fissures, etc., and then identifying on them spatial relationships with respect to sets of landmarks associated in their neighborhood.

Given a set of templates together with their landmarks, the method searches each template in the skull and locates an area similar to that described by the template (using a parametric representation). Due to the representation used, the search space can be drastically reduced since the matching process is done considering only the control points of the surface. When one potential matching surface is found, the template adjusted to this surface is also located and the transformation parameters used to approximate the real piece are found. The parameters of this transformation can then be used to determine automatically the precise position of the landmarks associated with the template.

We selected the generalized Hough transform (Ballard 1981) as the algorithm used to locate the templates in the surface of the cranial model. The algorithm works as follows: the template is defined with a set of level curves that represent the shape of the template at different depths (depending on the degree of detail required). This set of curves is associated with the positions of a set of discrete landmarks related to the curves' neighborhood (Figure 7.8). Thus, the set of curves becomes a 3D surface. A set of bi-dimensional curves can be obtained by intersecting the skull model with many search planes.

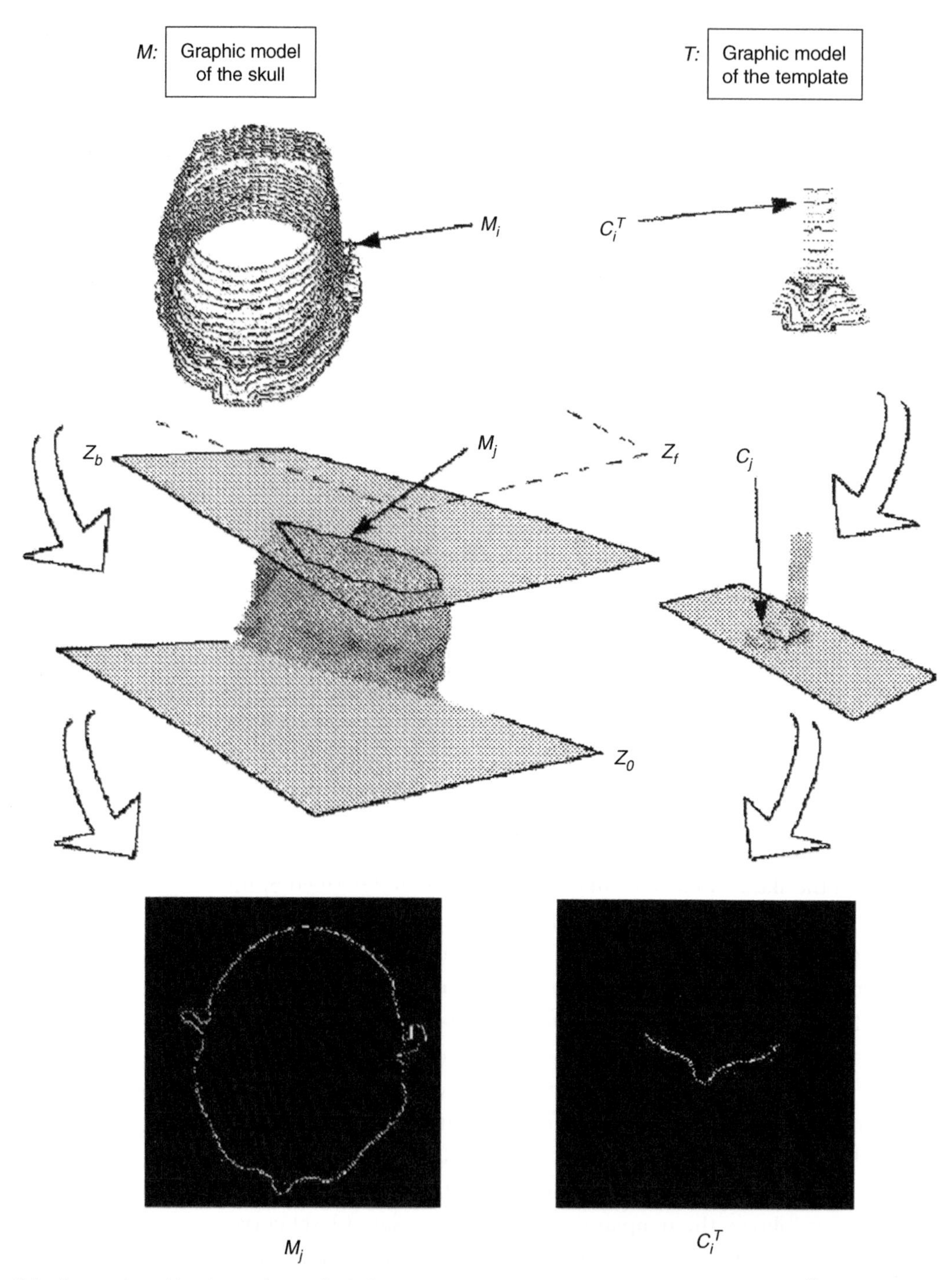

Figure 7.9 Process of searching the template on the skull surface. M_i represents the ith level curve of the model M; C_i^T is the ith level curve of the template T; M_j is the ith intersection of the search plane Z_b and the skull model M; C_j is the ith slice of the template T; Z_o and Z_f are two parallel planes defining the search space (given by the user). The problem of template matching is transformed to an image-matching problem between the images formed by M_j and C_j.

If we think about these bidimensional curves as images and the points in each intersection with a cutting plane as white pixels of a binary image, the method now is transformed to locate a segment of curve over an image containing another curve (the traversal slice of the skull). Figure 7.9 shows these ideas in a graphical way.

The Hough transform is a method employed to detect curves in an image, exploiting the duality between the points in the curve and its parameters. The problem to solve here is similar to the one solved by Ballard *et al.* with this technique for binary images (Ballard 1981). In other words, we are interested in finding the boundaries of the template (a curve defined using parametric methods) on the boundaries of the skull. Points at the boundary of the template can be transformed into a parametric space and then located in the image formed by the bidimensional projection of the graphical model.

7.4.1 OBTAINING THE MOST PROBABLE FEATURES OF A FACE

Anthropometric techniques are used to obtain the most probable features of a human face. The information used to complete the reconstruction is stored in tables containing anthropometric information such as facial measures, proportional ratios and angular relations between different parts of the human face (Figure 7.10). Bayesian networks (Pearl 1988) are used to capture the

Table 1: Eye fissure inclination (en_ex index) right

Age years	Masculine right side N	Mean	Variance	Female right side N	Mean	Variance
0–5 months	8	5.9	0.5	6	7.4	2.1
0–12 months	20	5.3	2.2	8	4.7	1.6
1	18	5.2	2.5	22	6.3	2.2
18	50	2.1	1.3	58	4.1	2.2
17	48	2.3	1.6	51	6.0	2.8
11	50	2.7	1.6	50	3.5	2.1
16	48	2.7	1.5	51	4.0	2.5
12	52	2.8	2.0	53	3.4	1.8
6	50	2.8	1.7	53	4.1	2.1
14	50	3.0	2.2	61	3.0	2.2
16	48	3.0	2.0	61	4.7	2.2
13	60	3.1	2.0	48	3.8	2.0
7	60	3.2	2.1	58	4.7	2.4
9	60	3.3	1.7	49	3.7	2.1
10	50	3.3	2.0	48	3.8	1.9
3	58	3.4	1.6	30	4.3	1.7
8	80	3.5	2.9	51	3.4	8.3
2	31	3.8	1.9	34	4.3	1.4
4	30	5.3	2.2	10	6.9	2.1
5	30	5.3	2.3	10	6.6	2.0

Figure 7.10

Example of an anthropometric table. From Farkas (1981).

variables that experts know are crucial in determining the anatomic features of a facial model. The Bayesian networks capture the most probable relationships between facial features, given anthropometric parameters, and with this information and the information about the shape of the skull, the most probable values for the indices determining the face of the person can be obtained. Due to the fact that propagation in Bayesian networks can be made from evidence to hypothesis or from hypothesis to evidence, both predictive and diagnostic reasoning is possible. Thus a Bayesian network can do inverse inferencing and estimate the set of parameters to determine the cranial-facial reconstruction (because Bayesian networks can estimate the missing parameters in both sets given partial information).

The set of Bayesian networks takes the estimation of the facial features as input. This information and the information given by the skull will be integrated to show the results in a 3D graphic model. There is no other current study that utilizes statistically robust methods to validate or characterize the relations between the landmarks of the skull and the human face. Our work uses probabilistic models to represent the relations between facial characteristics and the anthropometric parameters such as sex, age, weight, etc. The final objective will be to discover new relations. Anthropometric tables are a rich source of information for this purpose.

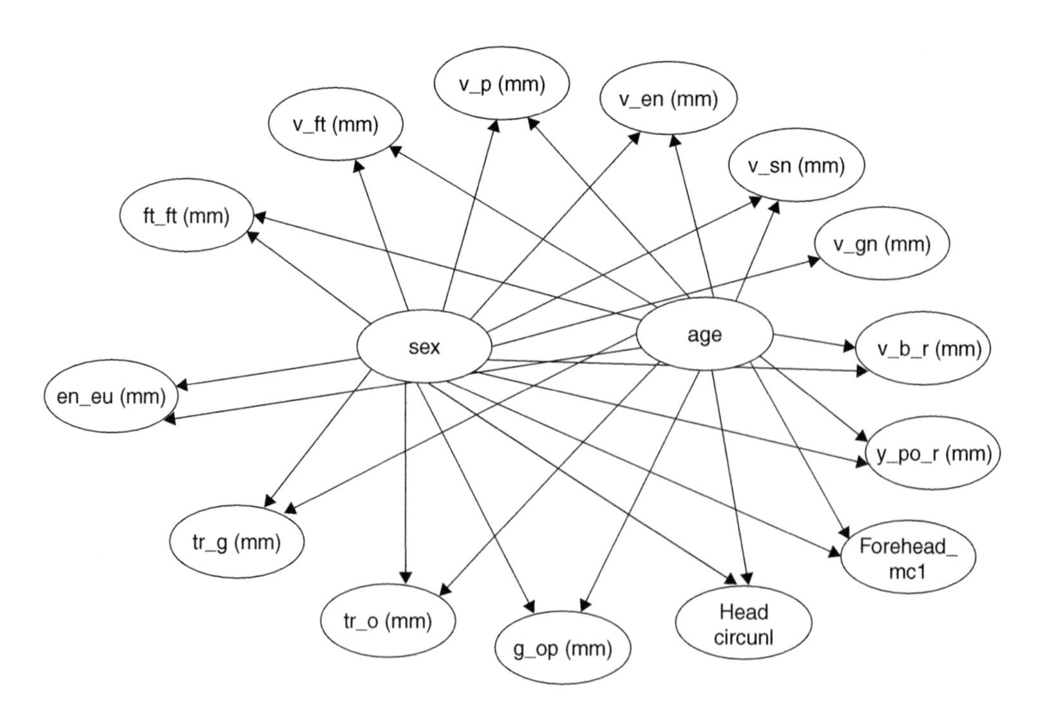

Figure 7.11 A Bayesian network that conditions 14 features of head and face over the variables sex and age.

Bayesian propagation will be used to predict the most probable features given a set of incomplete or uncertain data. The majority of the tables of cranial landmarks use sex and age as predictors. It is necessary to do normative studies to correlate the cranial-facial landmarks with a larger set of data that could be used to obtain better predictions. Currently, we use five Bayesian networks (Vargas 1996) which were built from the anthropometric tables of Dr. Leslie Farkas (Farkas 1981), relating only sex and age with five anatomic regions. These networks have a topology similar to that shown in Figure 7.11.

The predictions obtained with this initial structure always give the desired results, but this is a weak result because we have used only two conditioning variables (sex and age) to predict anthropometric landmarks. More interesting results will be obtained as more conditioning variables are added to the current network topologies.

7.5 CONCLUSIONS

Currently, methods to reconstruct the most probable face of a person are done by handmade clay models. Discrete landmarks are located in these models and then used for the reconstruction facial process. Heuristics are used to determine how the artist should sculpt the model. Since there are no normative studies relating facial landmarks and other parameters, this work proposes a platform to assess and display correspondences between facial landmarks to

N	DX	Angle	SX	SY	Votes	Points	%
1	15	2.50	0.90	0.90	96	261	36.7
2	15	2.50	0.90	0.90	109	232	46.9
3	20	0.00	1.00	1.00	136	248	54.8
4	15	−2.50	1.10	1.10	80	241	33.2
5	5	0.00	1.10	1.10	82	231	35.5
6	−10	−2.50	1.10	1.10	84	206	40.7
7	0	−2.50	1.20	1.20	70	200	35.0
8	10	0.00	1.20	1.20	59	64	35.9
9	−5	−2.50	1.10	1.10	82	135	60.7
10	20	0.00	1.20	1.20	114	109	100.0
11	20	−2.50	1.20	1.20	106	100	100.0
12	20	−2.50	1.20	1.20	95	85	100.0
13	0	−2.50	1.10	1.10	70	84	100.0
14	15	−2.50	1.20	1.20	72	61	100.0
15	10	0.00	1.20	1.20	70	64	100.0
16	−10	−2.50	1.10	1.10	67	54	100.0
17	−15	2.50	1.10	1.10	44	69	63.7
18	5	2.50	1.20	1.20	53	58	91.3
19	5	−2.50	1.20	1.20	66	56	100.0
20	15	−2.50	1.20	1.20	68	58	100.0
21	25	−2.50	1.20	1.20	67	59	100.0

Table 7.1

Results of the searching process of a template (that corresponds to the nasal area) and a graphic model of a skull. This table shows the transformation parameters that must be applied to each curve in the template. These parameters are displacements, scalings and rotations. N is the slice number. The percentages in the last column give an idea of the similarity between the slices.

other parameters. An advantage of this scheme is that updates in the model could be made automatically. To support this work, a graphic tool was developed using the topics presented in this paper. This tool consists of two main modules: one focused on the processing and analysis of the input images and the other in building and displaying the graphic model of the skull.

The morphological operations of dilation and erosion were implemented to manipulate the input images. Other filtering operations were implemented (such as the median filter) to improve the quality of the image and to get the desired boundaries.

In the graphics part, this tool provides a mechanism to display a 3D model of the skull given the results of the image module. The model is built using level curves obtained by a processed set of input images. A graphic editor is used to manipulate the displayed graphical model, using translation, scaling, and rotation operations. The location of the interest parts can be found by using the Hough transform scheme. Research conducted elsewhere has shown that searches can be done efficiently using this method. Table 7.1 shows the result of the searching process applied to the template of a nose on a skull.

7.6 FUTURE WORK

The main aspects to consider for future work are as follows: Analyze the existing anthropometric data to propose new topologies for the Bayesian networks. Learning algorithms for Bayesian networks can be used to asses new relations between anthropometric data and the variables that define the features of a face.

- Automate the image processing module to detect the skull contours. Currently, work is being done on this topic.
- Automate the process of template location by adding spatial relations between templates and some constraints to orient the search process.
- The integration of the parameter estimation module and the 3D display module.
- Realize more tests using different templates and evaluate the results.

REFERENCES

Altobelli E. D. and Farkas L. G. (1994) *Anthropometry of the Head and Face.* Raven Press, New York.

Ballard D. H. (1981) "Generalization of the Hough Transform to Detect Arbitrary Shapes", *Pattern Recognition* 13(2), 111–122.

Farin G. (1990) *Curves and Surfaces for Computer Aided Geometric Design, A Practical Guide.* Second edition, Academic Press.

Farkas L. G. (1981) *Anthropometry of the Head and Face in Medicine.* Elsevier.

González C. R. and Woods E. R. (1992) *Digital Image Processing.* Addison Wesley, U.S.A.

Hall V. (1992) PhD. Thesis: *Facial Animation and Speech,* Curtin University of Technology.

Haralick M. R., Stanley R. S. and Xinhua Z. (1987) "Image Analysis Using Mathematical Morphology", *IEEE Transactions on Pattern Analysis and Machine Intelligence* 9(4).

İşcan M. Y. and Helmer R. P. (1993) *Forensic Analysis of the Skull.* Wesley-Liss, New York.

Pearl J. (1988) *Probabilistic Reasoning in Intelligent Systems: Networks of Plausible Inference.* Morgan Kaufmann, San Mateo, CA.

Rogers A. (1990) *Mathematical Elements for Computer Graphics.* Second Edition, McGraw Hill, U.S.A.

Saksena B. (1987) *A Clinical Atlas of Roentgenphalometry in Normal Lateralis.* Wiley-Liss, New York.

Scheepers F. (1996) PhD. Thesis: Anatomic Representation of the Human Figure, Ohio University.

Serra J. (1988) *Image Analysis and Mathematical Morphology, Vol. 2: Theoretical Advances.* Academic Press, New York.

Vargas J. E. (1996) *Prediction Facial Features using Bayesian Networks.* Internal Report, Dept of Electrical and Computer Engineering, University of South Carolina.

CHAPTER 8

FACE RECONSTRUCTIONS USING FLESH DEFORMATION MODES

Peter Tu, Richard I. Hartley, William E. Lorensen, Abdalmajeid Alyassin, and Rajiv Gupta
GE Global Research Center, 1 Research Circle, Niskayuna, New York 12309, USA

Linda Heier
Department of Radiology, Weill Medical College, Cornell University, Ithaca, New York 14853, USA

8.1 INTRODUCTION

In this paper, a database of x-ray computer tomography (CT) head scans is used to reconstruct the face of an unknown subject given its skeletal remains. Skull and face surfaces can be extracted from each CT head scan. By establishing point correspondences between the CT skull and the subject's skull, the CT face can be morphed to coincide with the subject's skull. The morphing process removes differences that are caused by deviation in skull structure. Any remaining discrepancies can be attributed to variation in soft tissue.

By morphing each head scan in the CT database, a collection of estimates of the subject's face is generated. These estimates can be viewed as samples from a *face space* that is tuned to the subject's skull. Given these estimates, principal-component analysis is applied to determine the main modes of deformation. Initially the operator is provided with the average estimate of the subject's face. The operator can then explore face space by applying the dominant deformations in a convenient manner.

The face-space approach provides methods for estimating the overall structure of the subject's face. A set of postprocessing tools allows the operator to define specific details. A face editing process is used to change the shape of features such as the nose, eyes, and lips. Texture maps are tailored to the subject creating a lifelike appearance.

This paper is divided into three main parts. In section 1, details regarding development of the CT head-scan database are provided. In section 2, the method used to create an estimate of the subject's face from a CT head scan is described. Finally, in section 3, various postprocessing tools are demonstrated.

8.2 COLLECTION AND PROCESSING OF CT DATABASE

A problem of basic forensic importance is to determine the identity of human skeletal remains. For this purpose, the skull often gives the best available information. One approach to the identification problem is to superimpose images of a person's face onto a given skull (Aulsebrook *et al.* 1995, Shahrom *et al.* 1996, Yoshino *et al.* 1997). This is essentially a method of verifying a hypothesized identification by determining the goodness of fit of a photographic image of a person with a correctly oriented image of the skull.

In the absence of a specific hypothesized identity, a commonly used practice is to build a model of the face using all available evidence, but essentially based on the skull shape. Traditional manual methods of reconstructing a face from a skull are based on tissue-depth tables (İşcan and Helmer 1993). Depth markers are placed on the skull at strategic locations and are used to guide the depth of modeling clay that is used to build up a face over the top of the skull. An example of such a reconstruction process is shown in Figure 8.1.

Instead of relying on tissue-depth tables, our approach is to acquire tissue-depth information from a set of CT scans. Philips and Smuts (1993) used CT scans to make specific flesh depth measurements. We utilize the entire dataset. Conceptually, this is a simple idea. The surface of the skull and the face are extracted from a CT data set, and from these tissue thickness may be measured. For useful statistics to be gathered from this data, it is necessary to align the scans to each other, and most of the description of the data-gathering phase of this project will be concerned with this alignment process.

The output of a complete head scan is a 3D block of intensity values (known as voxel data), which is usually viewed slice by slice by radiologists in clinical medical applications. Figure 8.2 shows some typical CT slices of a head. For

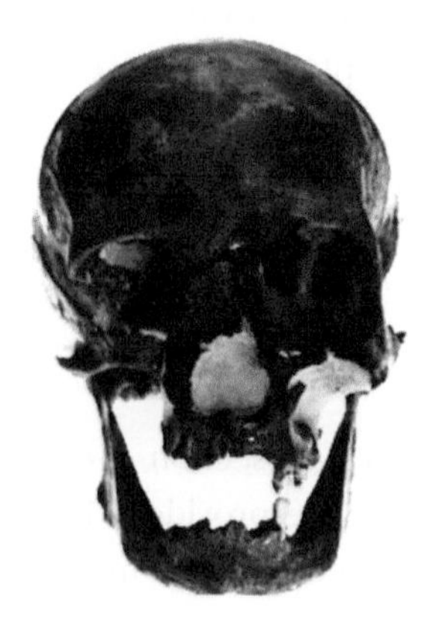

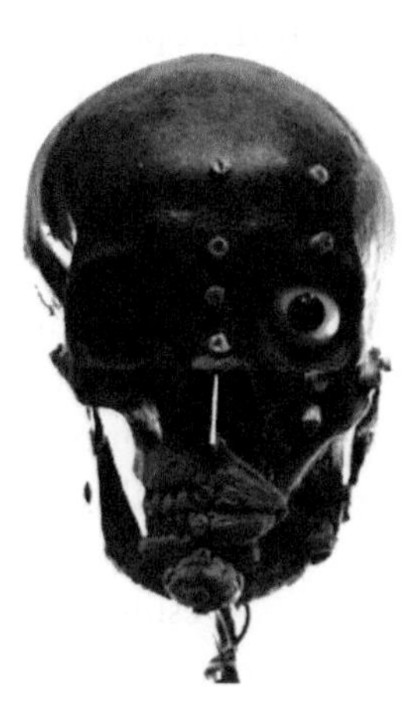

Figure 8.1

Method of reconstruction of a face model from a skull, using depth markers and modeling clay. The image shown here is of a 200-year old female skull found in Albany, NY. Thanks to Gay Malin and the New York State Museum for permission to use this image.

the present application, however, a 3D model needs to be built. Based on calibrated intensity values for flesh and bone, the surface of the bone and the air–flesh interface is extracted from the voxel data. A well-known algorithm that gives excellent results is the "Marching Cubes" algorithm (Lorensen and Cline 1987). Subsequently, the surface is triangulated to give a polyhedral model, and each triangle is shaded according to a lighting model and view direction to give a realistic image of the skull or skin surface. The model may be viewed from any direction. Figure 8.3 shows a rendered skull overlaid with the triangulated skin surface.

The complete process of data collection is composed of several steps, which will be explained more clearly later. The reader may refer back to these steps in reading the following sections.

- Obtain a CT scan of the head.
- Apply a 3D reconstruction algorithm (Marching Cubes) to extract skull and face (to be more exact, skin) surfaces.
- Select alignment points on the skull surface.
- Use these alignment points to align the skull with a canonic skull via a scaled rigid transformation. Apply the same transformation to the face model. The canonic

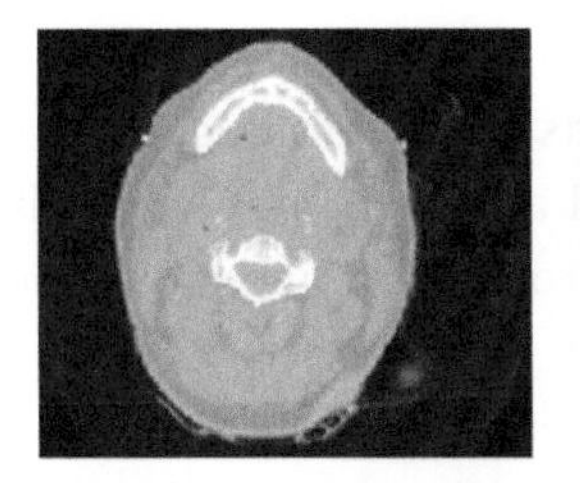
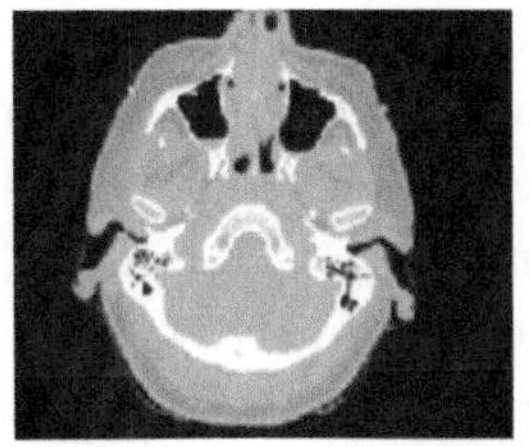
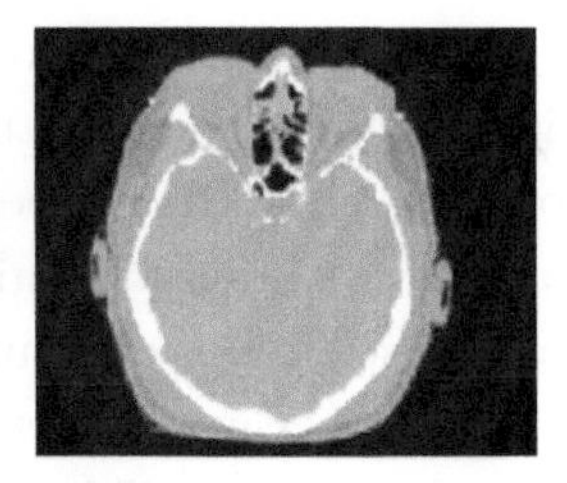

Figure 8.2

Slices from a CT data set of a head.

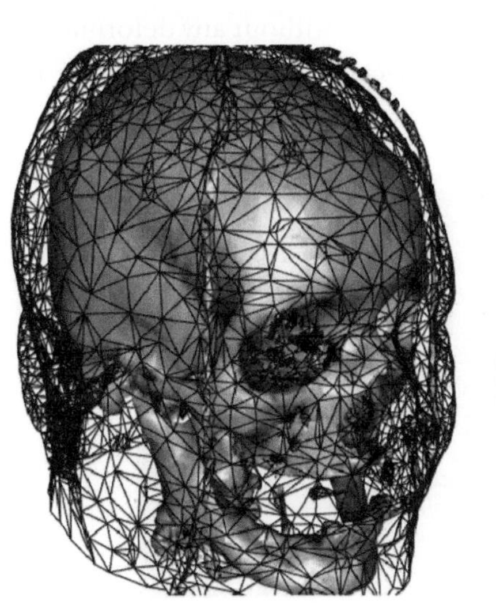
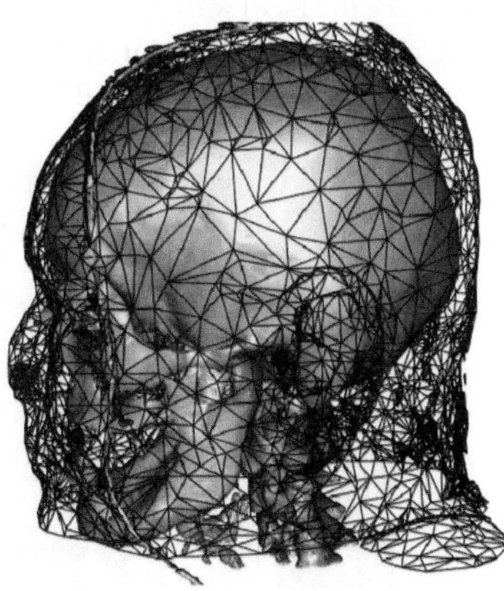

Figure 8.3

Reconstructed skull surface and overlaid triangulation of the skin surface obtained from a CT data set. The model is 3D and may be viewed from any direction.

skull can be chosen arbitrarily. Its function is to make sure that all head scans are in the same relative position, orientation, and scale.

- Project both face and skull models into a cylindrical coordinate system, and produce an image-like representation of skull and face in which the radius coordinate represents image intensity. This will be referred to as the 2.5D skull or face model, namely a 2D image in which intensity represents radial depth of the surface. See Figure 8.3.
- Pick new fiducial points on the 2.5D skull model (see Figure 8.5) to enable alignment with other models.

The fiducial points are used to align each database head scan to a target model, working with the 2.5D skull image model. The alignment takes place in two steps as follows.

- Fiducial points are used to align the head scan to the target model by 2D warping of the 2.5D image model. This 2D feature-based alignment is based on a concept of *saliency*, aligning sections of high variability in the skull images.
- The second stage of morphing is depth adjustment, in which a depth offset δ_r is added at each pixel, based on fitting an interpolating surface.

This method of alignment through morphing is described in detail later.

8.2.1 RIGID ALIGNMENT OF SKULL

In order to standardize the database, each set of skull and face surfaces is aligned with a canonical model. This process starts by establishing a set of point correspondences between the scanned skull and the canonical skull. Once this is done an optimal metric transform (rotation, translation, and uniform scaling) is computed (Horn 1987).

This processing step is performed on all scanned data. Figure 8.4 illustrates this process. This operation defines an overall alignment of the skull (and hence the face) with the canonical model, but without any deformation taking place. This alignment allows a cylindrical coordinate system to be aligned to the skull model, as will be seen later.

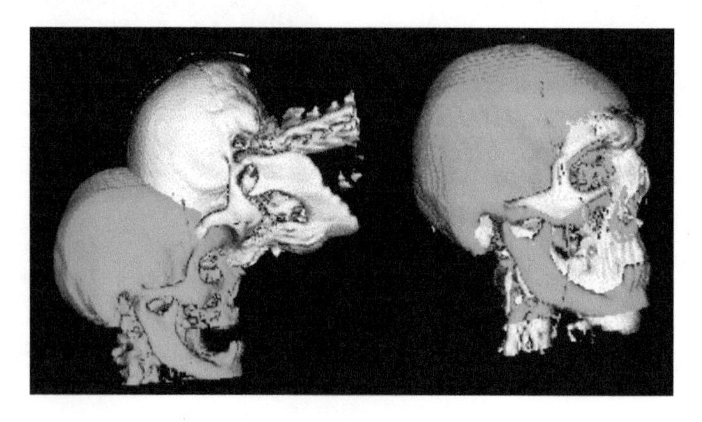

Figure 8.4

The green skull is the canonical model and the white skull is the subject. Left shows initial misalignment. Once the operator specifies a few point correspondences, the two skulls can be aligned. Right image shows the two skulls after alignment.

8.2.2 NONRIGID MORPHING OF SKULL TO MODEL

Next the mechanism for morphing a single CT head scan onto a model skull is described. The main idea is to apply a transformation to the CT head scan so that its skull assumes the shape of the target skull. The same transformation is applied to the face of the head scan resulting in an estimate of the model's face. This estimate will be reasonably accurate for areas with little soft-tissue variation such as around the eyes, the forehead, and the cheekbones. In Section 2.1, methods for modeling the remaining areas will be described.

Both 2D and 3D morphing rely on a set of point correspondences between a source (the skull of the head scan) and the target (the subject's skull). These correspondences are used to create a *warping field* where any point in the source space can be transformed into the target space (Wolberg 1988). Vanezis *et al.* (1989) added face surfaces to digitized skulls using adjustments based on conventional flesh depth tables. Nelson and Michael showed that 3D volumetric morphing can be used to transform one skull into another. In this paper, it is argued that the morphing mechanism should be divided into two steps: a 2D surface morph, where each point on the surface becomes registered, and a depth adjustment process. Both steps require a set of point correspondences to create a warping field. However, different criteria are used for selecting these control points. As shown by Blanz and Vetter (1999), a so-called 2.5D image-like representation of the data based on cylindrical coordinates provides a convenient framework for the morphing process. The PCA and postprocessing methods described in Sections 2.1 and 3 can also take advantage of this representation.

8.2.3 CYLINDRICAL COORDINATE SYSTEM

Blanz and Vetter (1999) showed that it is useful to have an image-like representation of a 3D face surface. We have found that this is also true for a skull surface. Let the origin of a cartesian coordinate system be placed at the center of the base of the head. The z-axis points toward the top of the head. The x-axis points toward the left side of the head, and the y-axis points toward the front of the head. A point can be defined by its cartesian coordinates (x, y, z) or by its cylindrical coordinates

$$\theta = \tan^{-1}\frac{y}{x}, \qquad h = z, \qquad r = \sqrt{x^2 + y^2}.$$

A 2D image is defined such that the horizontal axis corresponds to the angular coordinate θ, the vertical axis corresponds to the height coordinate h and the intensity of each pixel is set to the radial coordinate r. A surface defined by a polygonal mesh can be transformed into this image representation in the

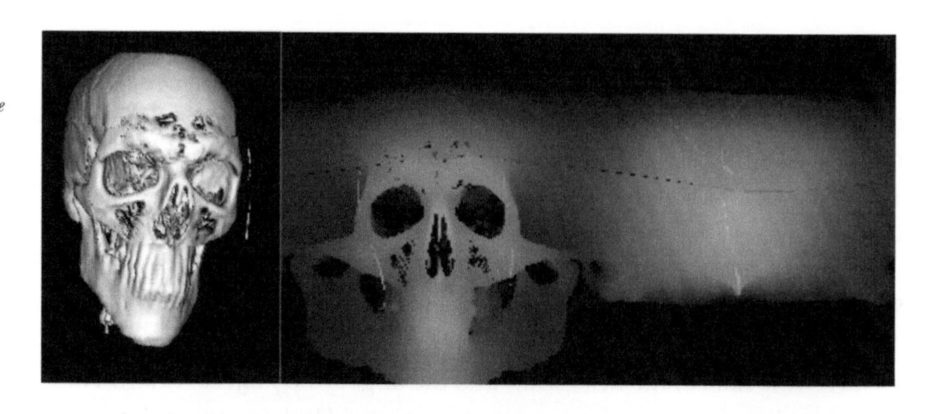

Figure 8.5

The left image shows a 3D polygonal mesh of a skull. The right is a 2.5D representation of the skull. The horizontal axis, vertical axis, and pixel intensity are associated with the cylindrical coordinates.

Figure 8.6

The left image shows a 3D polygonal mesh of a face. The right is a 2.5D representation of the face. The vertical axis, horizontal axis, and pixel intensity are associated with the cylindrical coordinates.

following way: a ray in space is defined for each pixel i with coordinates (θ_i, h_i). The point of intersection between the ray and the polygonal mesh is found. This establishes the value of r_i. The intensity of pixel i is set to r_i. In Figures 8.5 and 8.6, a face and a skull are shown in this format. One advantage of this approach is that many 2D image-processing operations can be performed on the data in this format.

8.2.4 2D MORPHING

Given image representations of the head scan and subject skulls, a two-step morphing process can be implemented. First, the image representation of the head-scan skull is morphed in a 2D sense. That is, a warping field is used to align each pixel in the head-scan image with a pixel in the subject's skull image. Second, an intensity alignment is performed so that the two images become almost indistinguishable. These operations are also performed on the face of the head scan. Figure 8.7 illustrates this process.

Figure 8.7 illustrates the two phases of the morphing process. A cross section of the two skulls is shown to illustrate the method better. The face of the

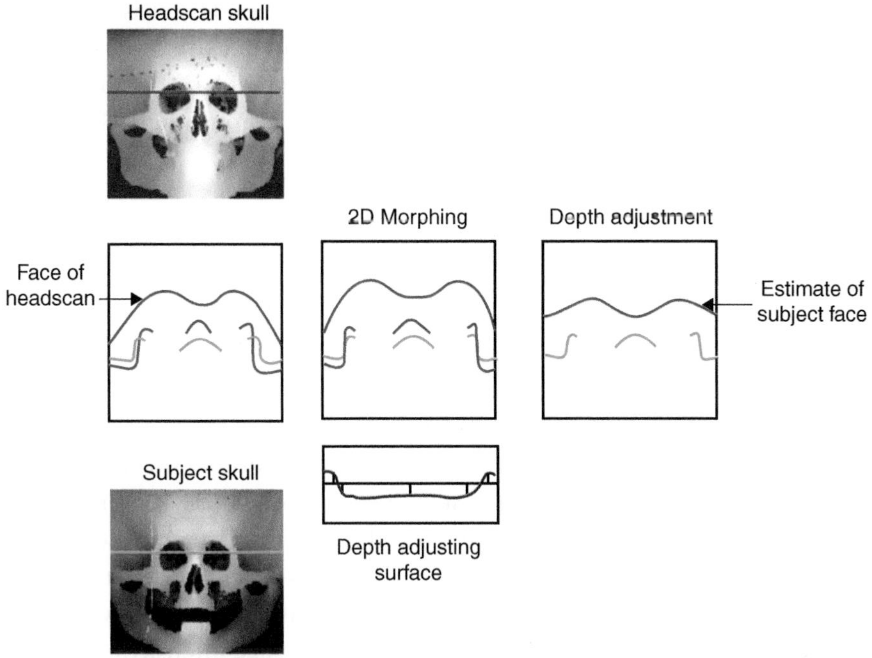

Headscan skull
2D Morphing
Depth adjustment
Face of headscan
Estimate of subject face
Subject skull
Depth adjusting surface

Figure 8.7

The morphing process.

head scan (from the database) is also shown in the cross section. In the first phase, the head scan undergoes a 2D morph so that each pixel becomes registered to the subject skull. This aligns the cross sections in the image plane. In the second phase, depth or intensity adjustment is performed. This aligns the cross sections in the radial direction. The processing steps applied to the head scan skull are also applied to its face. The modified face becomes the estimate of the subject's face.

The first 2D morphing step is now described. A 2D warping field is defined so that pixels $(\hat{\theta}, \hat{h})$ in the source image are mapped to pixels (θ, h) in the target image. The warping field is defined as:

$$\theta = F_\theta(\hat{\theta}, \hat{h}), \qquad h = F_h(\hat{\theta}, \hat{h}),$$

where F_θ and F_h are 2D surfaces defined parametrically. Given a set of P point correspondences $(\hat{\theta}, \hat{h})$ to (θ, h), two cost functions C_θ and C_h are defined as

$$C_\theta = \sum_{i=1}^{P}(\theta_i - F_\theta(\hat{\theta}_i, \hat{h}_i))^2, \qquad C_h = \sum_{i=1}^{P}(\theta_i - F_h(\hat{\theta}_i, \hat{h}_i))^2.$$

The parameters for F_θ and F_h are determined such that C_θ and C_h are minimized in a least-squares sense. There are various sorts of surface that can be used to define F_θ and F_h. In this system a set of continuous bicubic finite elements are used.

The criterion for selecting the initial point correspondences is based on saliency. This method favors points on the two images that are easily identifiable such as the region around the eye socket and boundaries of the cheek and jawbone. In terms of image features, these are regions where there are large discontinuities in pixel intensity.

8.2.5 SKULL DEPTH ALIGNMENT

Once the head-scan pixels have been aligned with the subject pixels, an adjustment must be made on the r intensity values. The approach taken in this paper is to define an adjusting surface $\delta_r\,(\theta, h)$. Each head-scan pixel i with coordinates (θ_i, h_i) will have its pixel intensity adjusted by adding the value of $\delta_r\,(\theta_i, h_i)$. Once again the relationship between the head-scan skull and the subject skull will be used. The value of the adjusting surface cannot be measured for all points, since the skull surfaces have holes. Therefore, the adjusting surface must be interpolated based on a set of Q points where skull depths can be accurately measured. Since the pixels are registered, the criterion for selecting the Q control points shifts from saliency to stability.

Measurements should be taken where the bone image intensity values are changing slowly and continuously. Note that this is the exact opposite of the criterion taken for selecting points that define the 2D morph.

A least-squares criterion for generating $\delta_r\,(\theta, h)$ is used:

$$\sum_{i=1}^{Q}\left[(r_{\text{skull}}(\theta_i, h_i) - \hat{r}_{\text{skull}}(\theta_i, h_i)) - \delta_r(\theta_i, h_i)\right]^2$$

where $r_{\text{skull}}(\theta_i, h_i)$ and $\hat{r}_{\text{skull}}(\theta_i, h_i)$ are the pixel intensity values for the subject and the head-scan skulls at the Q measurement points. As in the previous section, $\delta_r\,(\theta, h)$ is a bicubic finite-element surface defined parametrically.

Taking two head scans from the database and using the skull of the first head scan as the subject skull, we demonstrate this process. Figure 8.8 shows the faces of these two head scans. Figure 8.9 shows a tool used to perform the morph. The estimated face and the true face of the subject will be different. It can be argued that variation due to skeletal structure has been removed and that remaining differences are the result of nonuniform soft-tissue structures. In Section 2.1, principal-component analysis will be used to model these soft-tissue or flesh depth variations.

Figure 8.9 shows a tool used to transform the right face of Figure 8.8 into the left face. The left images are the cylindrical representations of the two skulls. The connected green points are used to control the 2D image morphing. The red lines show regions used to control the depth adjustment. The right figure shows the result of morphing. Color is used to depict the difference between the true subject face and the morphed face, where green is

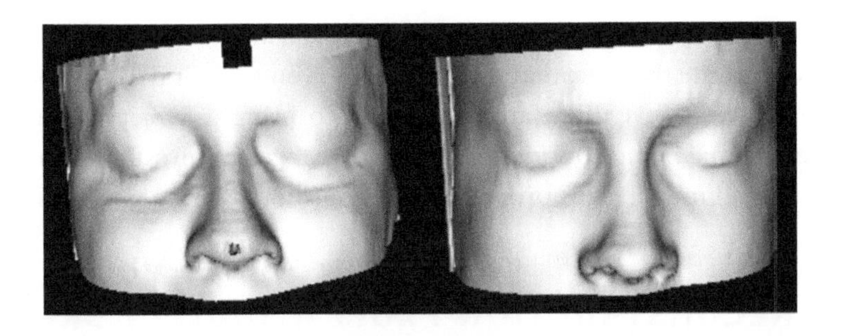

Figure 8.8

The morphing process is demonstrated with two scanned heads taken from the CT database. The left face is that of the subject. The right face will be morphed so as to approximate the left face.

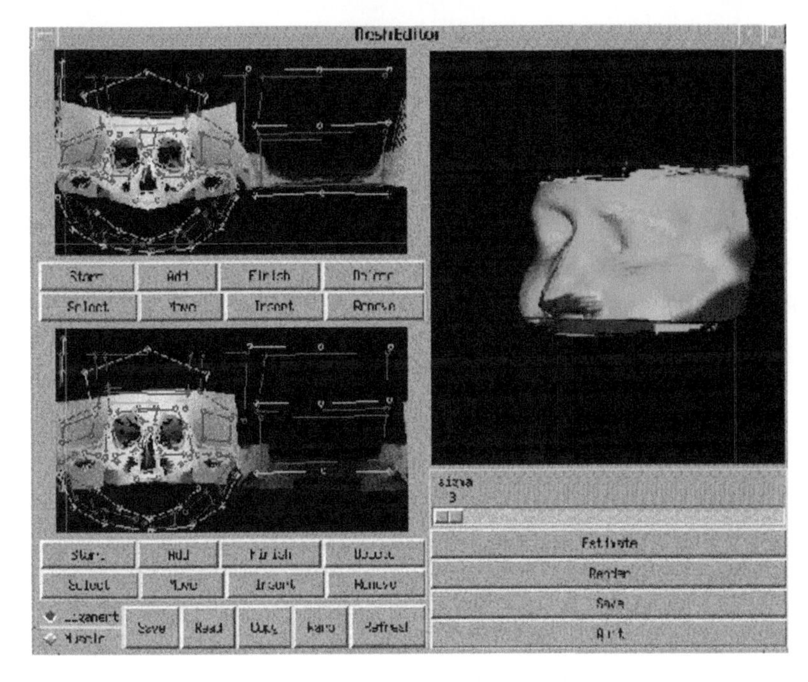

Figure 8.9

A morphing tool.

small error, blue is positive error, and red is negative error. As can be seen most of the error occurs where soft tissue is most prominent.

8.2.6 EXTRACTION OF STATISTICS

In the previous sections, we have described how the skull and face models generated from a CT scan may be aligned with a canonical skull model. Once this has been done for several data sets, it is possible to derive statistical data about the depth and variance of soft tissue at any chosen point on the skull model. More generally it is possible to compute the correlation of tissue depths at different points on the model, and in fact at every pixel in the 2.5D cylindrical representation of the skull. By carrying out principal-component analysis (to be described below) on the set of face and skull models it is possible to compute the principal modes of variation of the face or of tissue depth.

In doing this, one may choose any skull as the canonical skull model. This may be one of the skulls from the database, or even a general CAD model. In practice, we find that there are advantages to using a subject's skull (for instance, the one being considered in a specific forensic investigation) as the canonical skull model. This process will be considered in the next section.

8.3 RECONSTRUCTION FROM A SUBJECT SKULL

The sequence of steps that are used to process a subject skull and from it to reconstruct a face model will be described in this section. The first step in this process is to obtain a computer model of the skull. The recommended method is to use a CT scan, though other methods are possible, for instance, laser scanning. Figure 8.10 shows a model generated from a CT scan of (a plaster cast of) the skull shown in Figure 8.1. Once a 3D model is obtained, each of the database skull models is aligned with it, and statistics are gathered. The steps of the complete process are as follows:

- Scan the subject skull.
- Perform the Marching Cubes algorithm to get a skull model.
- As in the data-collection phase, select reference points to be used to align it with the head scan skulls from the database.
- Create a cylindrical-coordinate image model and pick fiducial points to be used for morphing the database head scans.
- Morph each of the database skulls in turn to align them to the subject skull model, as described previously.
- PCA: Carry out a principal-component analysis on the aligned *face* images to obtain an average face and the principal deformation modes of the face.

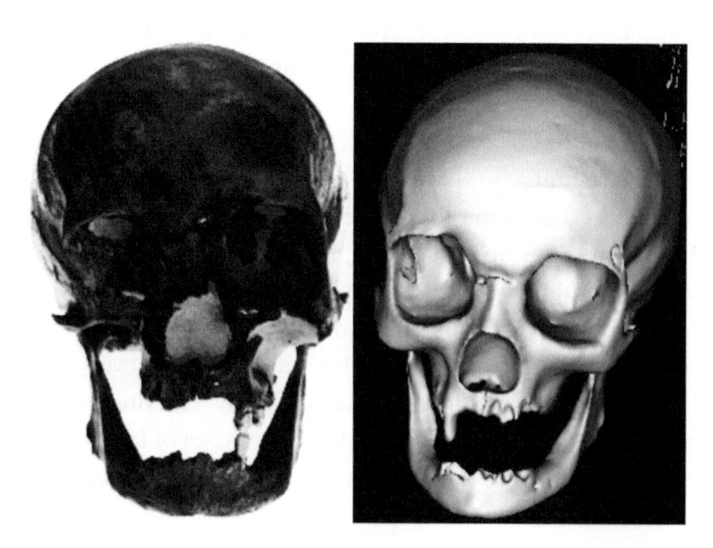

Figure 8.10

The right image shows the CT scan of the skull shown in the left.

- Modify the appearance of the face by varying the principal deformation modes using control-bar sliders.
- Postprocessing: Substitute features from a feature library to obtain the desired appearance.
- Texture-map the reconstructed face to give a more realistic appearance, add hair, etc.

Note that the average face and principal deformation modes of the face obtained by this method are computed after database models are morphed to the actual shape of the subject skull. Thus, the average face and its variants are in fact average faces *subject to* the restrictions imposed by the subject skull's shape. The remaining details of this procedure will now be given.

8.3.1 PRINCIPAL-COMPONENT ANALYSIS

In the previous section, a method for morphing a specific head scan on to the subject's skull was described. By repeating this process for all of the N heads in the CT database, a collection of estimates of the subject's face is generated. Each estimate is represented by an image structure, which can be viewed as a vector X of length L, where L is the number of pixels in the image. Each element of X is equal to a particular pixel intensity in a one to one fashion. The vector X_i corresponds to the estimate generated from the ith head scan.

The idea of principal-component analysis is to model a complex set of data in as simple a manner as possible. In this case the data are the set of subject face estimate vectors X_i. One can compute the average data vector, and then express any particular data vector as the average vector plus a deviation from the average. One wants to approximate any possible face vector in terms of an average, plus a linear combination of a small number of fixed representative (or basis) vectors representing deviations from the average. This represents a face-space continuum. In general, it is not possible to model a complex data set precisely with a small number of basis vectors. However it is desirable to choose the basis vectors so that the expected error is as small as possible. In terms of linear algebra, one desires that the span of the basis vectors approximates the full data set as closely as possible. The solution to this problem is based on the eigenvector decomposition of a covariance matrix (Press *et al.*, 1992).

8.3.2 DEFORMATION MODES

The first step is to compute the mean face

$$\hat{X} = \frac{1}{N}\sum_{i=1}^{N} X_i.$$

Consider the matrix

$$M = [X_1 - \hat{X}, X_2 - \hat{X}, \ldots, X_N - \hat{X}].$$

The matrix M has L rows and N columns. The covariance matrix C is defined as

$$C = MM^{\mathsf{T}}.$$

The eigenvectors E of C are a set of independent basis vectors and are defined by

$$CE = E\Lambda,$$

where E is identified with a matrix E whose columns are the elements of E, and where Λ is a diagonal matrix of eigenvalues. In principle, E and Λ can be computed directly from C. The matrix C is an L by L matrix where L is the number of pixels in each image. Since L is very large, the required computational cost would be overwhelming. However, it was shown by Turk and Pentland (1999) that the number of independent eigenvectors is limited to $N - 1$, where N is the number of head scans in the database. This leads to the following formulation: compute V and Φ such that

$$M^{\mathsf{T}}MV = V\Phi.$$

This is a cheap computation since $M^{\mathsf{T}}M$ is an N by N matrix. Multiply both sides of the equation by M, resulting in

$$CMV = MV\Phi.$$

Therefore

$$E = MV, \qquad \Lambda = \Phi.$$

Given the mean face $\hat{X}$ and the eigensystem E and Λ, reconstruction based on a continuum of faces can now be performed.

8.3.3 RECONSTRUCTION

A particular reconstruction can be defined as the mean estimate $\hat{X}$ plus a linear combination of the eigenvectors in E. The eigenvalues define the dominance of each mode. Large eigenvalues are associated with large global deformations. Low eigenvalues correspond to specific aspects of a particular face. Since we are only interested in the overall shape of the face, only the major eigenvectors need be considered. Figures 8.11 and 8.12 illustrate how the face-space models are used to create an initial reconstruction. The user starts off with the average estimated face, and then slider bars are used to define the contribution of the various deformation modes. Figure 8.13 shows a face that is generated by this process. Figure 8.14 shows a tool used for the reconstruction process. As shown in Figure 8.15, the transparency of the reconstruction can be set so that the relationship between bone and flesh can be scrutinized.

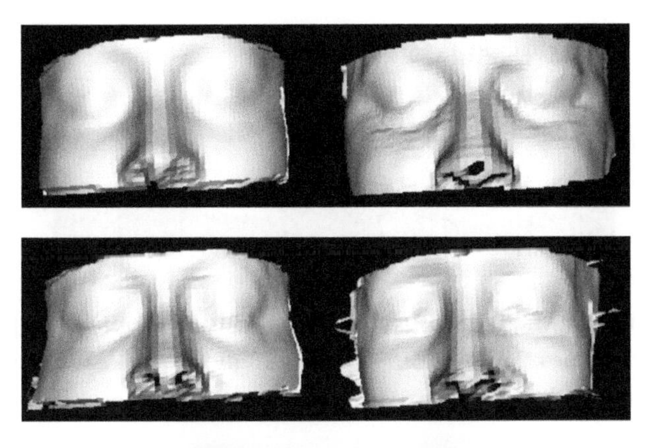

Figure 8.11

The left image shows the true face of the subject. The right face shows the average morphed face.

Figure 8.12

A deformation mode.

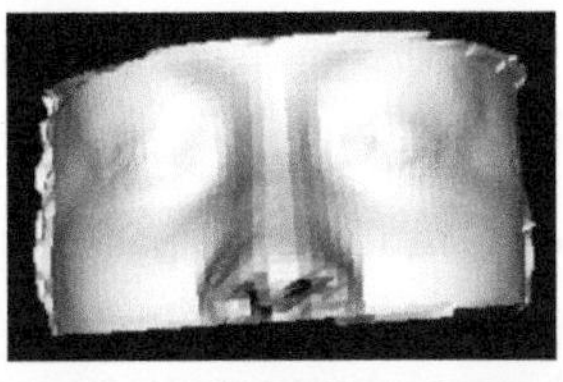

Figure 8.13

This figure shows a particular reconstruction after adjusting various deformation modes.

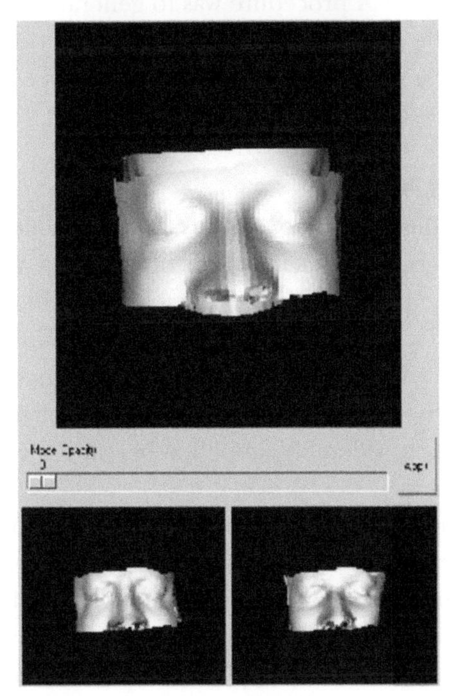

Figure 8.14

A reconstruction tool. The main image shows the current reconstruction. The lower images show the extremes of a deformation mode. By selecting a deformation mode, the reconstruction is modified by varying the degree of deformation.

Once the operator is satisfied with the estimated face, a set of postprocessing tools are used to make local alterations and to generate a texture map resulting in a lifelike reconstruction.

Figure 8.12 shows the range of deformations associated with a single deformation mode. This deformation mode corresponds approximately to

Figure 8.15

The user can also specify the transparency of the reconstruction so that the relationship between bone and flesh can be scrutinized.

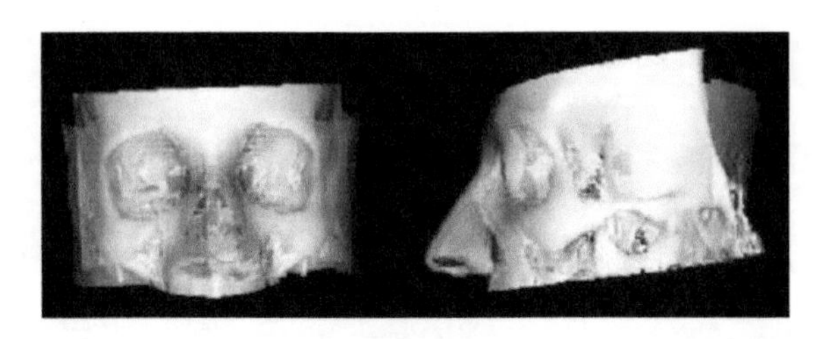

fatness/thinness of the face. By varying this mode, one obtains a spectrum of different facial types. Varying other principal modes will cause the shape of the face to vary in different ways.

8.4 POSTPROCESSING

A reconstruction generated from the face-space continuum represents a linear combination of all the estimated faces generated from the CT head scans. The motivation of the PCA procedure was to generate an initial estimate of the basic shape of the subject's face. Based on prior evidence, heuristics or intuition, the operator may decide to change certain aspects of the face. A set of tools for this process has been provided.

8.4.1 FACE EDITING

The face editing facility is based on a parts library. A collection of eye, nose, and lip models has been extracted from 3D scans of various individuals. Figure 8.16 shows the part gathering process. By defining a few point correspondences, the part can be placed directly onto the model, replacing what was previously there. A blending operation is performed so that a smooth transition occurs between the model and the transplanted part. Many of these operations are considerably simplified by using the image representation of the face.

Over the years, a number of heuristics or rules of thumb regarding the relationship between bone and flesh have been developed. For example there are various structures in the nasal cavity that can be used to predict where the tip of the nose should be placed. In order to utilize this knowledge, a *scaffolding* mechanism has been implemented. The user can place various linear structures into the reconstruction so as to guide the positioning of parts. Figure 8.17 illustrates this mechanism.

8.4.2 TEXTURE MAPPING

The final geometric face model can be rendered as a polygonal mesh. The model will appear more lifelike if it is viewed with a real texture map. There

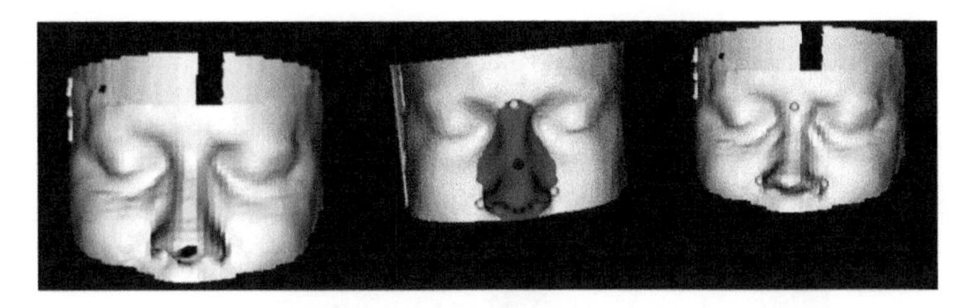

Figure 8.16 Face editing. The left image is the original face. The middle image shows a part from a donor face. The right image shows the combined face. The spheres show the point correspondences. Merging algorithms are used to create a smooth border.

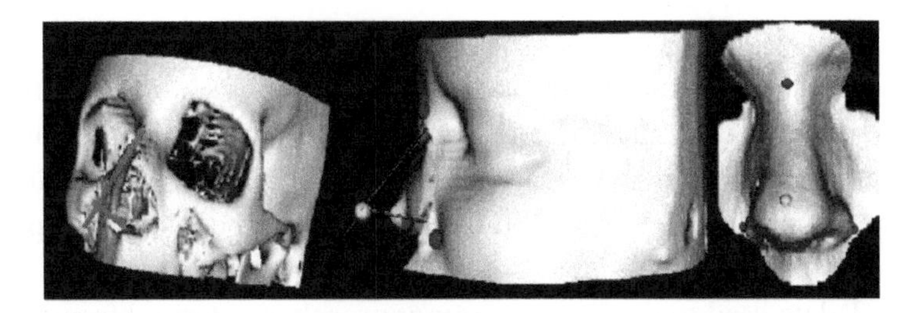

Figure 8.17

The user can place linear structures into the reconstruction so as to guide the placement of soft-tissue parts such as the tip of the nose.

Figure 8.18

Transferring texture maps. The top left image is the donor face. The bottom left image is the subject face. The middle image is a texture map of the donor face. The right image is the subject face with the donor texture map.

are a number of devices that can be used to capture a texture map from an individual. These maps can be tailored to the face model by specifying a few fiducial points on the source texture map and the geometric model. Figure 8.18 shows an example of this process. Since the source texture map comes from a particular individual, too much fine detail may be introduced. Another approach is to create an average texture map and use this to render the model. In this way specific features that can lead the eye are removed, however, the overall lifelike appearance still remains.

An alternative technique is to take 3D reconstruction and turn it into a sketch. Figure 8.19 illustrates this technique.

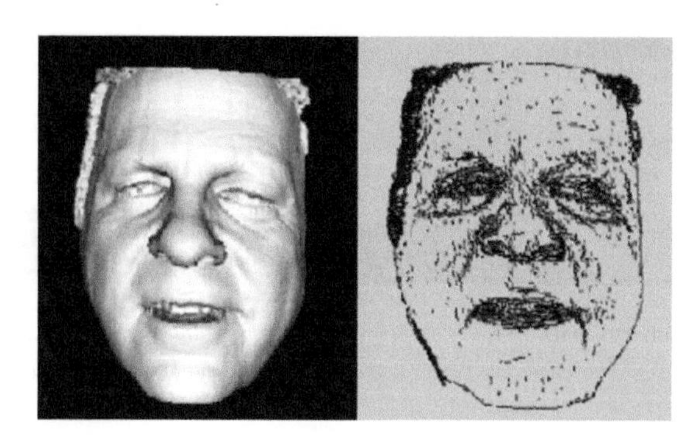

Figure 8.19

An alternative to texture mapping is to generate a sketch-like representation.

8.5 DISCUSSION

In this paper, we have described a system for creating a set of face estimates based on the skeletal remains of an unknown individual. These estimates are viewed as samples of a face space tailored to a specific skull. Principal-component analysis is performed so that operators can explore this space in a convenient manner.

The CT data used to demonstrate our approach was derived from a set of sinus studies. The initial results have been encouraging. We are now in the process of collecting a set of complete head scans so that full reconstructions can be performed. The utility of this system will be determined by measuring human recognition rates on this new data.

It can be argued that a major obstacle in facial reconstruction is the inability to predict the shape of features such as the nose and the eyes based on skeletal information. One path may be to take a more anatomical approach where muscle models are used to build up the face. An alternative solution is to partition the face space into regions that contain distinct facial features. Based on CT head-scan data, it may be possible to correlate these regions with various measurable features derived directly from the skull. If successful, this would result in a major improvement in face reconstruction capability.

8.5.1 FUTURE WORK

The work discussed in this chapter is the result of a preliminary study. Based on these initial accomplishments, the FBI is sponsoring a continuation of this work. There are several areas that will be addressed. One of the drawbacks of this initial study is that we were limited to the use of partial facial scans. We are planning to collect 300 full head scans divided evenly across gender and race. From an algorithmic point of view, automatic deformable registration methods will be developed. The new approach will match the surfaces of the skulls instead of a set of landmarks. This may have the advantage of generating more accurate transformations for the flesh. By the end of the next study, we hope to be in a position to access the validity of this approach, with the possibility of generating automatic recognition algorithms that can be applied to databases of missing persons.

ACKNOWLEDGEMENTS

This work has been funded by a research grant from the Federal Bureau of Investigation under the guidance of Myke Taister. We would also like to thank Gay Malin and Chuck Fisher from the New York State Museum for their many contributions.

REFERENCES

Aulsebrook W. A., İşcan M. Y. and Slabbert J. H. (1995) "Superimposition and Reconstruction in Forensic Facial Identification: a Survey", *Forensic Sci. Int.* 75, 101–120.

Blanz V. and Vetter T. (1999) "A Morphable Model for the Synthesis of 3D Faces", *SIGGRAPH,* 187–194.

Horn B. K. (1987) "Closed-Form Solution of Absolute Orientation Using Unit Quaternions", *J. Opt. Soc. Am. A.* 4(4), 629–642.

İşcan M. Y. and Helmer R. P. (1993) *Forensic Analysis of the Skull.* Wiley-Liss.

Lorensen W. E. and Cline H. E. (1987) "Marching Cubes: a High Resolution 3D Surface Construction Algorithm", *Computer Graphics* 21(3), 163–169.

Nelson L. A. and Michael S. D. (1998) "The Application of Volume Deformation to Three-Dimensional Facial Reconstruction: A Comparison with Previous Techniques", *Forensic Sci. Int.* 94, 167–181.

Phillips V. M. and Smuts N. A. (1996) "Facial Reconstruction: Utilization of Computerized Tomography to Measure Facial Tissue Thickness in Mixed Racial Population", *Forensic Sci. Int.* 83, 51–59.

Press W. H., Flannery B. P., Teukolsky S. A. and Vetterling W. T. (1992) "Numerical Recipes in C the Art of Scientific Computing", University of Cambridge Press, Syndicate.

Shahrom A. W., Vanezis P., Chapman R. C., Gonzales A., Blenkinsop C. and Rossi M. L. (1996) "Techniques in Facial Identification: Computer-Aided Facial Reconstruction Using a Laser Scanner and Video Superimposition", *Int. Journal of Legal Medicine* 108, 194–200.

Turk M. A. and Pentland A. P. (1999) "Face Recognition Using Eigenfaces", *Proc. Computer Vision and Pattern Recognition,* 598–603.

Vanezis P., Blowes R. W., Linney A. D., Tan A. C., Richards R. and Neave. (1989) "Application of 3D Computer Graphics for Facial Reconstruction and Comparison with Sculpting Techniques", *Forensic Sci. Int.* 42, 69–84.

Wolberg G. (1988) *Digital Image Warping*. IEEE Computer Society Press.

Yoshino M., Matsuda H., Kubota S., Imaizumi K., Miyasaka S. and Seta S. (1997) "Computer-Assisted Skull Identification System Using Video Superimposition", *Forensic Sci. Int.* 90, 231–244.

CHAPTER 9

DIGITAL 3D RECONSTRUCTION OF SKULLS FROM FRAGMENTS USING SLT AND CAD/CAM TOOLS

Joerg Subke

Department of Clinical and Medical Engineering, Environmental Engineering, and Biotechnology, University of Applied Sciences Giessen-Friedberg, Wiesenstr. 14, D-35390 Giessen, Germany

9.1 INTRODUCTION

The goal of this paper is to present a method that can be used to digitally reconstruct fragmented skulls for the identification of unknown dead persons. This method—as compared to other commonly used ones—makes it possible to quickly reconstruct a destroyed skull and represents at the same time an additional digital component to reconstruct facial features of unidentified persons by using computer-aided three-dimensional (3D) methods. The basis of this method is a 3D measuring technique to document the bone fragments. It also employs CAD processes to digitally reconstruct the fragmented skull.

Based on these digitally reconstructed skulls, other 3D programs can be used to model the facial features of the unidentified dead persons and show facial variants within a short amount of time. The necessity for facial variants is due to the lack of information about certain cranial areas, which prohibits an unambiguous reconstruction of the face. Such missing cranial areas can be decomposed cartilage or missing bone fragments. Depending on which parts of the skull are missing, these gaps can be filled either by interpolation or, if that is not possible, by establishing a number of fragment variants for missing parts (e.g., front teeth, chin, and nose). This approach can, however, strongly influence the result of the reconstruction. Based on the number of variants in some cases, it might prove necessary to reconstruct more than one version of the face. Once the skull has been fully assembled, one can choose from two procedures to reconstruct the facial features:

- classic sculpting and modeling with clay or Plasticine
- computer-aided 2D and 3D techniques.

Using classic sculpting, the anatomical features are constructed layer by layer, from the muscle to the skin, paying special attention to the thickness of the soft tissue. The face is modeled with an intended facial expression. Another variant of classic sculpting consists in applying strips of modeling clay with the required soft-tissue thickness to the surface of the skull, and filling the gaps in between, respecting the soft-tissue thickness and modeling the facial features. The computerized methods of facial reconstructions are classified either as 2D or 3D techniques (Sharom *et al.* 1996).

The 2D techniques are based on the superimposition of images of the skull on photographs of suitable persons. The skull is photographed in a way simulating the conditions in which the photographs have been taken (e.g., same distance, same position). The alignment is based on visual control and aims at an optimum correspondence between skull and face (Helmer 1984, İşcan and Helmer 1993).

The 3D techniques are based on the superimposition of a three-dimensional skin surface onto a three-dimensional skull surface, according to the thickness of the soft tissue. A number of methods can be applied to superimpose the skin surface onto the skull surface, adopting different strategies and techniques of adjustment. The common denominator of these methods are the digitized 3D surfaces of the skull and face. The digitalization of the surfaces is done either by using radiological methods—computer tomography (CT) or magnetic-resonance imaging (MRI)—or optical surface measuring methods: Streifenlichttopometrie (SLT: Subke 2000)—i.e., light-stripe topometry—or laser scanner. The strategies to adjust the skin surface to the skull differ with respect to the degree of automatization and the selection of the anatomical features.

Vanezis (1989) uses soft-tissue thickness as a criterion and positions the soft-tissue markers on the skull surface as well as on the skin surface. The skin surface is then adjusted to the soft-tissue markers like a flexible mask. An appropriate average skin surface is chosen from a 3D database, based on the criteria of race, gender, and build, to speed up the process of reconstruction.

Nelson (1998) makes use of mathematical methods in his procedures, drawing on the similarity of human facial features. The mathematical transformations utilized by Nelson describe the geometrical transformation of a chosen skull to the skull of the unidentified dead person. In order to simplify the transformational calculations, he accesses a database containing a multitude of geometrical data of heads (facial and cranial data) and chooses a set of data for a specific head as a reference to be manipulated by the transformation. As a criterion for selection, he uses the smallest possible difference between the skull of reference and the skull of the unidentified dead person. He then calculates the geometrical transformation between the geometries of the two skulls. Under the premise that the established transformation between the two skulls can also be applied to the facial surface, the skin surface of the unidentified dead person is generated by mathematical transformation of the skin surface of the reference head. Using this procedure, it is possible to adjust the skin surface in a short amount of time, resulting in the reconstruction of the face of the unidentified dead person.

No matter whether the reconstruction has followed a classical or digital method, the forensic artist decides how to reconstruct hair, nose, ears, lips, and eyes, not being restricted by guidelines based on the anatomy of the skull, and thus increasing the number of facial variants. We asked if it is possible to reconstruct not only the surface of the skin, but also the fragmented skull applying computerized methods. If so, this would be the hitherto missing component in a completely digitized reconstruction, starting with the bone fragments and resulting in the restoration of a face.

9.2 METHOD

Highly efficient hardware and software tools (ABW Gmbh 3D measurement equiment, NTSI workstation, CAD software Surfacer)[1, 2, 3] are required for a computerized reconstruction method in order to digitize the bone fragments three-dimensionally and to assemble the single components to fit as precisely as possible. Crucial elements of this method are the 3D measuring or digitalization of the surface of the fracture with a local resolution better than one millimeter, and controlling the precision of the fit of the joint bone fragments as well as a numerical presentation regarding the precision of the fit by means of a distance measurement (locally and averaged over the fracture area).

[1] *ABW Gmbh, Siemensstr. 3, D-72636 Frickenhausen, Germany, www.abw-3d.de*

[2] *NTSI New Technology Solutions GmbH, Einhornstrasse 9, D-72138 Kirchentellinsfurt, Germany, www.ntsi.com, www.ntsi-europe.de*

[3] *Imageware, Unigraphics Solutions Gmbh, Hohenstaufenring 48-54, D-50674 Koeln, Germany, www.ugsolutions.de*

Three steps are necessary to apply this reconstruction method. In a first step, the bone fragments are digitized using SLT (Subke 2000), a surface measuring process in which digital true-to-scale three-dimensional copies of the fragments are produced. In a second step, the digitized bone fragments are assembled. The correlation between the bone fragments is done morphologically on the basis of the geometry of the fracture and the anatomical features. In a third step, the assembly quality is controlled. To do so, the distance between the surface fracture of the two fragments is measured and evaluated. The last two steps are repeated until all fragments for the digital skull reconstruction are used.

Having completed these steps, the reconstruction of the facial soft tissue begins following Vanezis' or Nelson's method as applied to the digitally reconstructed skull (Nelson 1998, Vanezis 1989).

9.2.1 DIGITALIZATION OF THE BONE FRAGMENTS

The goal of this first step in the working process is to produce a true-to-scale 3D digital copy of the bone fragments. The following requirements have to

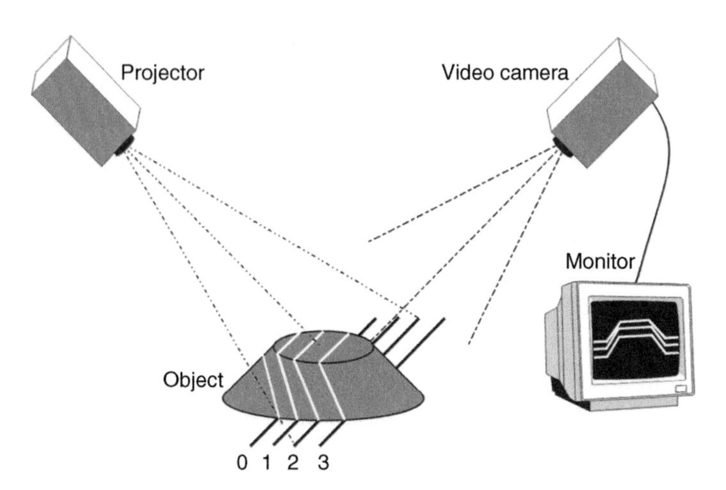

Figure 9.1
Triangulation method.

be met by the measuring system in order to assemble the digitized bone fragments using a CAD program:

- High local resolution of the bone fragments to capture the precise shape of the fractured surface as well as the anatomical features (e.g., slightly rough surface structures, suturae)
- Detailed documentation of the surface color
- Short times of exposure
- Multiple task measuring components for quick adaptation to varying geometrical measuring conditions.

For the digitalization of the bone fragments, we use SLT, a noncontact optical surface measuring process. In order to measure the 3D geometry of an object based on a 2D picture, a pattern of stripes is projected onto the object. Because of the elevated parts of the skull, the stripes are distorted in their straightness. The deviation of the straightness of the stripes is a measure for the height or depth of the object in question.

These distortions can only be observed if the camera, the projector, and the object to be measured form a triangle (Figure 9.1). This is known as the triangulation method (Wolf 1998). Another indication is the discontinuity of the stripes. The course of stripes stops at an elevation or a ridge and continues again in a different place (Figure 9.1). In order to determine the exact depth of this point it is necessary to know exactly where the individual stripe continues. Therefore, the stripes are differentiated from one another. This differentiation is achieved by the superimposition of a sequence of six different patterns of stripes of light—from the finest to the coarsest—resulting in the allocation of an individual light-to-dark value to each of the stripes and their consequent codification (see line numbers in Figure 9.1).

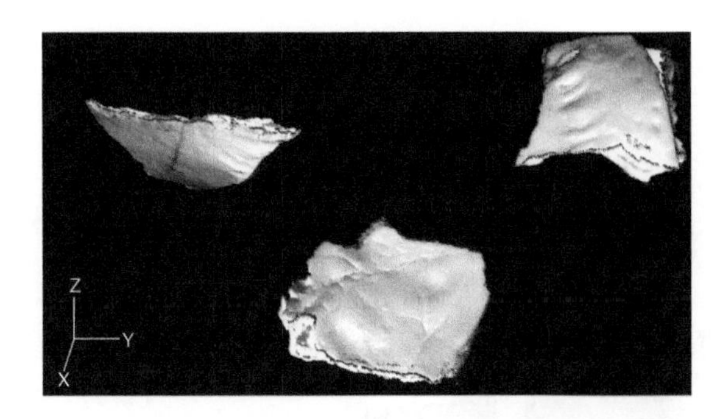

Figure 9.2

Digital 3D copies of three skull fragments.

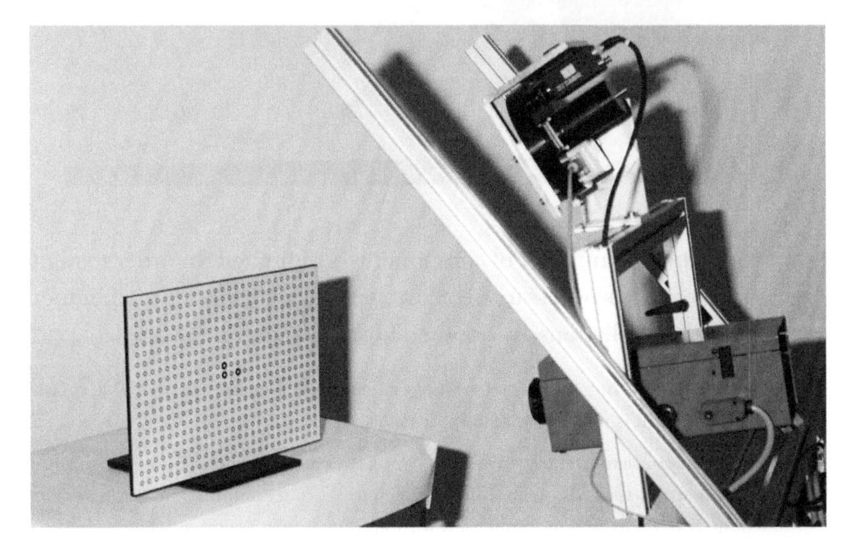

Figure 9.3

The basic SLT system.

In the next step, the natural color is assigned to every measured point. The object measured according to the procedure described above is recorded by a video camera using red, green, and blue optical filters. The color information of each pixel of the three pictures is then assigned to the accompanying measured points, thus creating a six-dimensional vector $(x_i, y_i, z_i, r_i, g_i, b_i)$ for every point p_i.

Thus SLT is based on the projection of stripes of light, the recording of the distortion of the stripes of light due to the fragment's topography, and the recording of the surface color in order to obtain a three-dimensional, colored, and photographically realistic documentation of the skull fragments (Figure 9.2).

The measuring system is conceived as a module, corresponding to a unit construction system. The advantage of this modular conception is that a measuring system for complex measuring constellations can be built. Integrating additional projectors and cameras can enhance the basic system, consisting of a projector and a camera (Figure 9.3). The entire measuring process consists of a series of pictures taken with a specific camera–projector pair for each

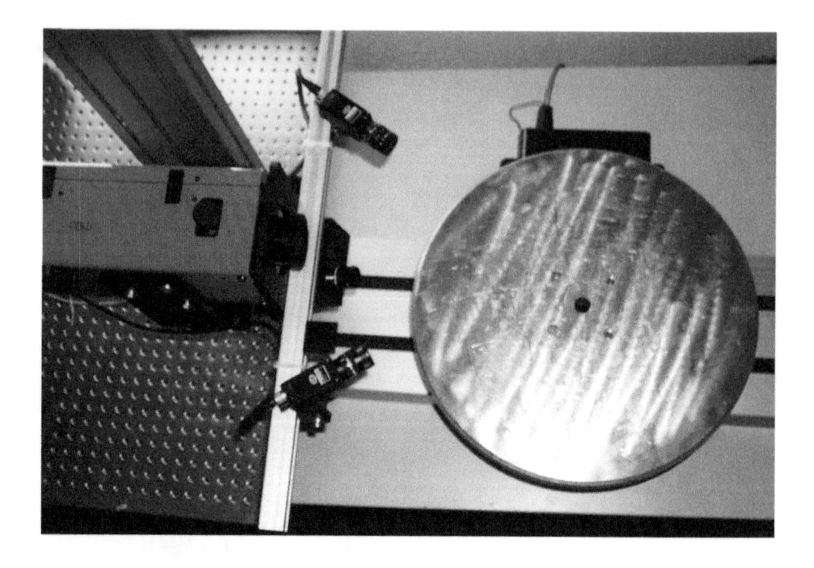

Figure 9.4

Measuring system and turntable (from ABW with permission).

picture. In general, the number of components is unlimited. In order to digitize the bone fragments, it is necessary to record the entire surface of the fragments. Two measuring constellations are adapted for this kind of recording:

- a system consisting of a projector, two cameras and a controlled turntable on which the fragment is positioned (Figure 9.4)
- a system consisting of four projectors and four cameras, each of them positioned tetrahedrally towards one another and allowing for a complete measuring of the bone fragments in panoramic view without moving the fragment (Figure 9.5).

The difference between the two systems is the measuring procedure. Both systems have in common that they try to capture the entire surface of the bone fragments.

Using the turntable system, the cameras record only a part of the surface of the bone fracture, so that the bone fragments are positioned step by step, by moving the turntable towards the cameras in order to record the entire surface. Using the tetrahedral system, it is not necessary to move and position the bone fragments, since the cameras capture the entire bone-fragment surface in one position. The turntable system, as compared to the static tetrahedral system, requires an additional working process to obtain the entire surface of the object to be measured. It is part of the process to assemble the partial surface structures that have been recorded from different positions of the turntable for creating the whole surface.

Due to the repositioning of the bone fragments on the turntable, each measurement record of the fragment edges presents a different spatial orientation and makes it necessary to geometrically join the surface parts, thus creating a closed surface. In order to join two surface parts in a geometrically precise way,

Figure 9.5
Tetrahedral measuring system (from ABW with permission).

the two parts have to adhere to a shared coordinate system that, in addition, is fixed with respect to a body. Using the terminology of measuring technique, the points defining such a shared coordinate system are called "points of minor control". These points of minor control are realized during measuring by creating an area of overlap for each and every single recording of the surface parts and by using this area of overlap for their identification. Using SLT, the program module ABW-FIT[4] performs the matching process.

The tetrahedral system, as compared to the turntable system, is convenient in that the recording area between the projectors and the cameras is unambiguously defined by calibration and that the single measurement records taken from different directions are geometrically orientated. One working step, that is, the matching of the measurement records taken from different angles, can be spared this way.

[4] ABW Gmbh, Siemensstr. 3, D-72636 Frickenhausen, Germany, www.abw-3d.de

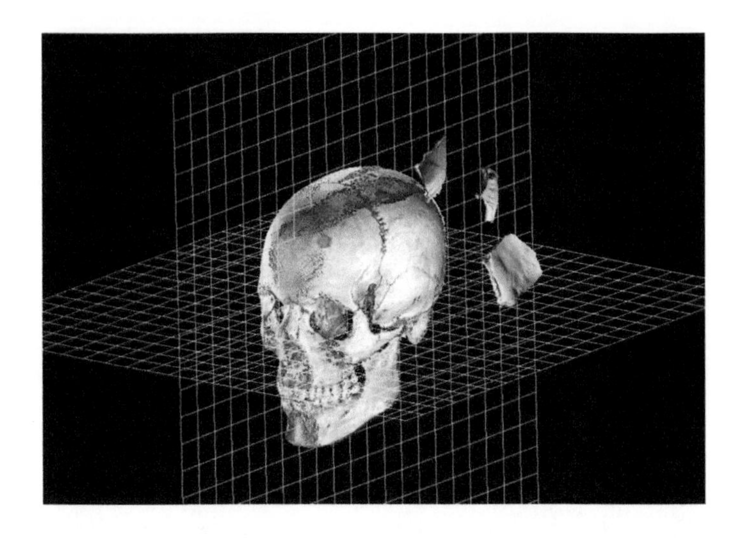

Figure 9.6
Skull and fragments from front, diagonally.

9.2.2 SKULL RECONSTRUCTION

After having digitized the fragments as well as having matched them morphologically, the digitized copies of the fragments are assembled using the CAD software Surfacer. The assembly of the digital fragments in the CAD system requires specific techniques, since no mechanical contacts can be used and the fragments cannot be touched.

Compensating for these disadvantages is the fact that no support structures are necessary for the assembly, since there is no gravity within the CAD system. Also, the time necessary for the glued parts to dry can be deducted. Furthermore, the CAD system offers an array of tools to measure the digital fragments while not causing damage to the parts.

Similar to the strategies employed to solve jigsaw puzzles, a template can be used to orientate the fragments and facilitate their assembly. An intact skull is chosen as a template, not exactly copying the geometry of the fragmented skull, but showing anatomical similarities and thereby allowing for a rough and preliminary positioning of the fragments (Figure 9.6). This reference skull serves only to demonstrate the position of the bone fragments and has no direct influence on the result of the reconstructed shape of the skull. By comparing characteristic anatomical features of the fragments to the skull of reference (also called landmarks), an approximate position of the fragments within the correct anatomical area is located so that the fragments can be positioned there (Figure 9.7). Using the adjacent fragments, the new fragment is orientated.

It is a prerequisite for this procedure to use a high local resolution to digitize the skull in order to make the exact structure of the fracture and the anatomical features of the skull surface easy to recognize. The SLT method is also used here.

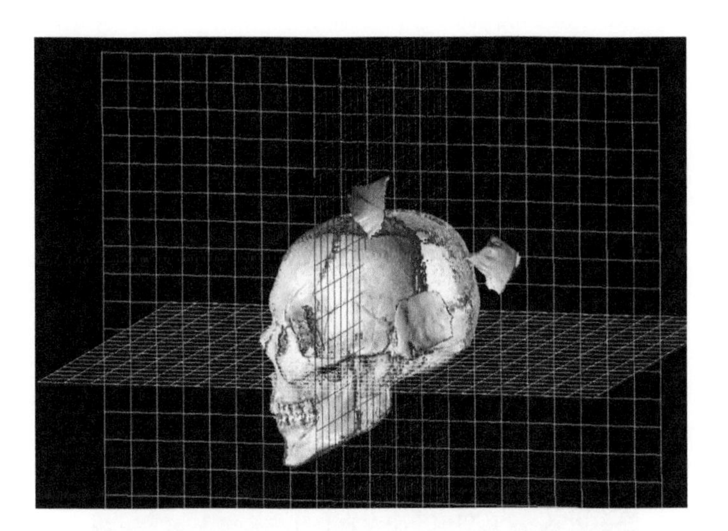

Figure 9.7
Skull and fragments from side.

A property of digital 3D objects in a CAD program is that they can overlay and penetrate each other without resistance. This means that, when the user moves a digital object with a mouse, there is no mechanical resistance if it collides with another digital object, nor is it possible for the user's sense of touch to capture the shape of the surface of a digital object. It is for these reasons that specific working techniques are necessary for the digital joining of two fragments, guided by visual control, metrical tests, and geometrical calculations.

Visual control, for the selection of adjacent fractured edges or fragments marked by the same landmarks, is similar to the method used by anthropologists. A detailed representation and high resolution, especially as far as the fracture edges are concerned, are essential to manipulate the digital copies on the screen effectively. Properties of the fragments (representation of the fragments via colored 3D surface points) and properties of the geometrical and visualization functions of the CAD software are therefore used.

To further facilitate visual control of the contacts, it is possible to isolate the important areas on the screen—that is to say, the fractured areas. The areas interfering with visual control are therefore made transparent, reducing the number of visualized 3D points belonging to the interfering area through elimination (see Figure 9.8 and Figure 9.9). In extreme cases, it is possible to remove these areas completely. This way, the analyst can easily see the fractured areas while joining the parts and visually control distance and penetration.

The two fragments are joined either manually or semiautomatically, using the CAD functions. The digitized bone fragments are thereby moved and rotated in a virtual 3D space. If joined manually, the direction of displacement and axis of rotation are freely selected and then rotated using visual control. The resulting distance between the two fractures can be measured selecting two manually chosen points from the two areas or by using an algorithm applied to the

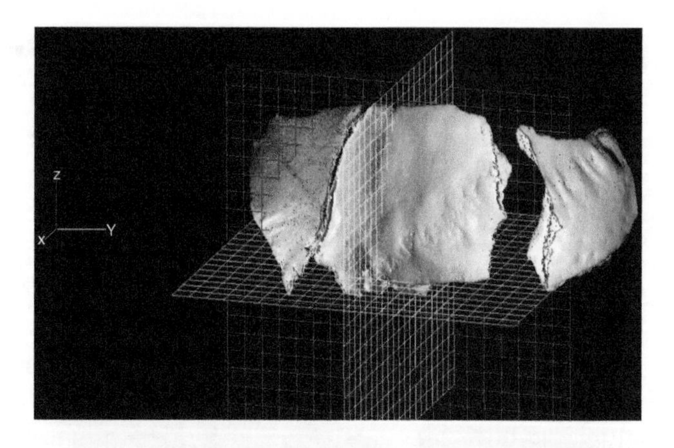

Figure 9.8

Three fragments, illustration with all points.

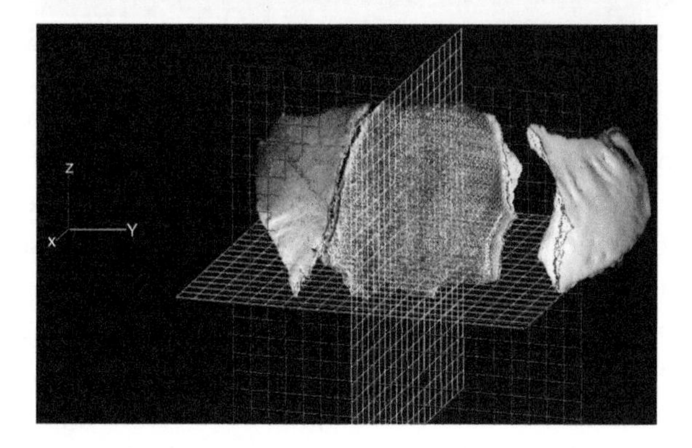

Figure 9.9

Three fragments, fragment in middle transparent.

entire fracture surfaces. If the fragments are joined semiautomatically, a geometrical matching algorithm is employed. This algorithm allows the connecting of the two fracture surfaces, to calculate the single distances per surface area and to thus determine the average distance. This procedure, following a process of optimization implemented in the algorithm, is repeated until the average distance has reached a minimum.

The quality of the result is strongly influenced by the shape of the two fracture surfaces. The more specific the shapes of the two surfaces, the better the chances for a precise fit. If, for example, little pieces of the fracture surface of one fragment are missing, it is possible that during the optimization process the two fracture surfaces don't match exactly. In this case, either the position of the rotated fragment is corrected manually or partial views of the fracture surfaces are selected manually. These views would have to be roughly congruent, thus allowing for a better match.

9.2.3 CONTROLLING THE PRECISION OF THE FIT

The control of the precision of a fit of two digitally adjoining surfaces is the crucial procedure in the process of the digital reconstruction. On the one

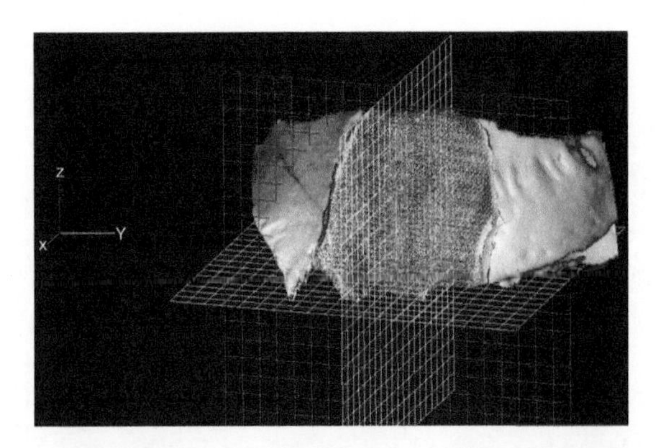

Figure 9.10

Three fragments, with joined right fragment.

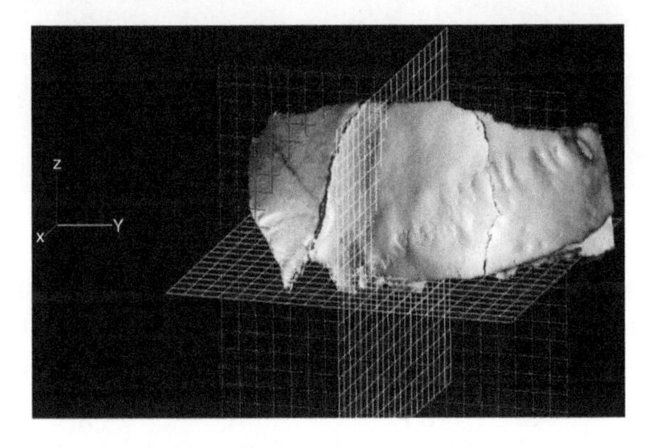

Figure 9.11

Visualization of the three joined fragments; illustrated with all points to control the anatomical structures.

hand, the digital copies of the bone fragments being merely clouds of points, forming a closed surface and enclosing a certain volume in a virtual space, there is no mechanical contact to prevent the interference or overlapping of two neighboring surfaces. On the other hand, visualization techniques and metric properties of the CAD software allow an exact determination of the precision of the match. To this end, the irregular surfaces of the fractured areas have to be digitized with a high local resolution in the submillimeter range.

After matching two digital bone fragments there are three possible ways to control the quality of the match:

- purely visual control
- measurement of the distance between two surface points
- measurement of the distance of two neighboring surfaces.

Visual control of a match of two fragment areas is carried out with the help of a number of visualization properties of the CAD program.

It is, for example, possible to change the transparency of the surface area so that the otherwise hidden structures of the fragmented areas are made visible (see Figures 9.10 and 9.11). The joined bone fragments can be rotated in their virtual space and viewed from different angles. With the zoom function,

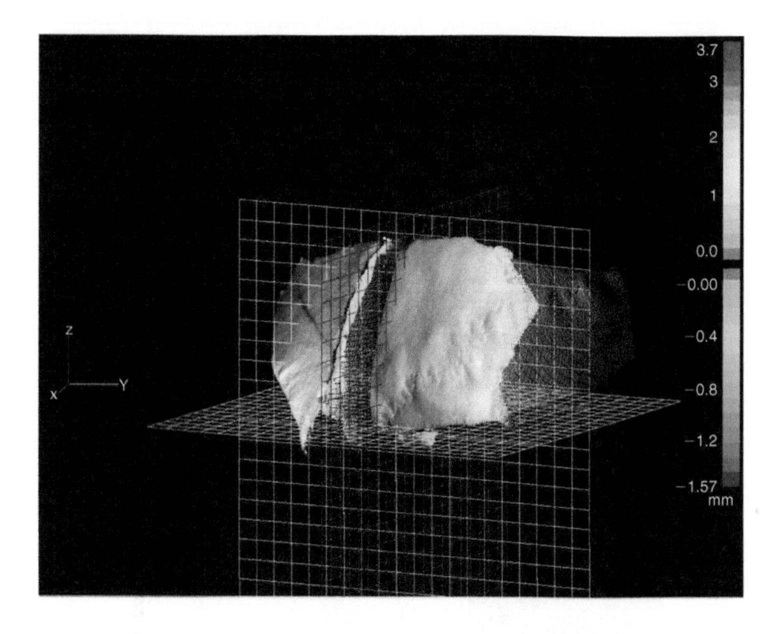

Figure 9.12

Controlling the precision of the fit by making some parts of the fragments transparent.

the distance between the observer's eye and the object can be adjusted from a microscopic range to a complete overview of the position of all joined bone fragments. Therefore the zoom function allows the visualization of the microscopic structure of neighboring points as well as an oversight of the continuous anatomical structure—for example, of suturae (Figure 9.12) and of the fragment pattern.

In order to assign significant points to the respective surfaces more easily in an overview, it is possible to use a digital process to vary the representation of the points regarding color, form, and size. The points can be visualized as spheres or cubes. Their natural color can be changed into primary colors (red, green, blue, yellow, etc.) or any user-defined color. These facilities contribute to the clarity of the representation and the determination by purely visual control if a match of two fragments was found or if it was merely established by the overlapping of surfaces.

To determine how precisely two fragment surfaces fit, we need recourse to metric properties of the CAD software. The metric properties allow measurements of the distance between neighboring points or between sectors of surfaces. To measure the distance between single points, the points of neighboring surfaces are manually chosen with the cursor of the mouse. A numerical value representing the distance between the points is automatically displayed. This method can be applied to instantly determine the distance between the fractured surfaces at single prominent points. To determine how well the surface pair (or a sector of it) fits, the neighboring surfaces, consisting of single digital points, have to be selected and marked. The overall distance between the

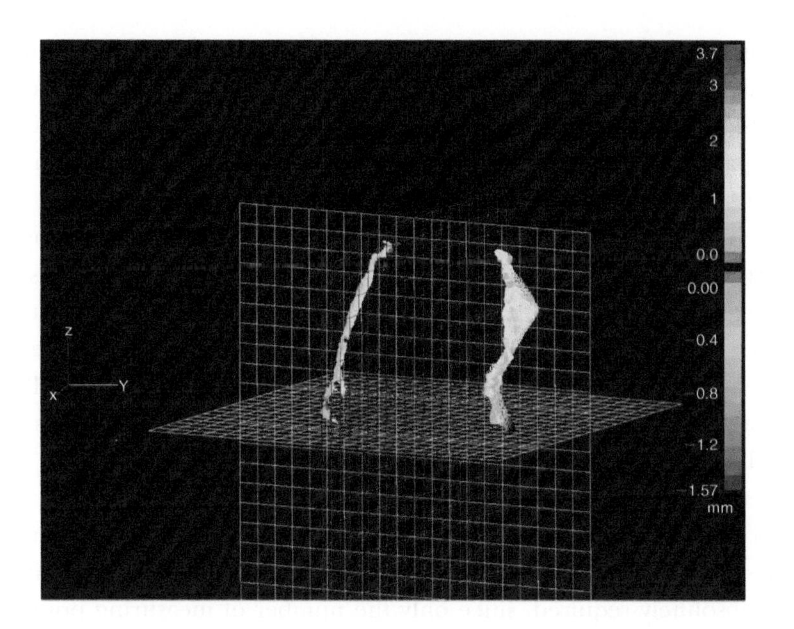

Figure 9.13

Controlling the precision of the fit by visualization of only the fragment surfaces with color scale.

selected surfaces is determined by means of a metric function, and the result is automatically presented graphically as a color scale indicating the distance between neighboring points of the adjoining surfaces and by visualizing the depth of the gaps by means of vectors (Figure 9.12).

With the help of the metric values and the color-coded representation of the distances, how closely the fragment surfaces fit can be determined instantly and with numerical precision. The measurements represent a quantitative quality control of the match (Figure 9.13).

9.3 DISCUSSION

The necessary steps for the reconstruction of the skull include the duplication of the bone fragments (allowing for a DNA analysis of the original fragments), the construction of the skull with the existing fragments, and the metric control of the joint fragments with regard to the precision of the fit.

9.3.1 DUPLICATION OF BONE FRAGMENTS

The first step of the skull reconstruction requires the duplication of the bone fragments. In the classical method, this is only required if a DNA analysis has to be performed in order to gain more information (e.g., individual, gender, family relations) about the unknown dead person. During this process, the analyst makes a mold of the bone fragment and uses it for the duplication of the fragment. Since the mold consists of at least two parts and has an opening for pouring the material, another working step is required in order to prepare the cast, taking off the edges and seams that were created during the moulding process. It is important not to take off too much material from the cast. A comparison with the original is imperative, either by touch or by using a noncontact 3D procedure.

The digital copying is done by using SLT system, a surface measuring procedure that makes the 3D coordinates of the surface available in spot shape, showing their natural color. In addition, this procedure works without contact, not causing deterioration of the material (Subke 2000). Once the bone fragments are three-dimensionally digitized, one can technically use all original fragments for DNA analysis in order to determine other factors (e.g., individual, gender, family relations).

After the fragments have been three-dimensionally recorded and the partial surfaces have been joined to form a coherent surface, the only thing left to do is to work on the areas of overlap between the partial surfaces. This step is not absolutely required, since only the number of measuring points per unit area is increased in the overlap areas, which does not change the surface geometry. This step is only done in order to obtain a homogeneous distribution of points with regard to the entire volume.

If, for some reason, more copies of the fragment are required, one has to repeat the same steps for each copy when using the classical method. Applying the digitized process, though, the analyst only needs to repeat the copying process; no other working step is required. Since digital copying is quick, much time is saved.

9.3.2 CONSTRUCTION OF THE SKULL

After the bone fragments are copied, they are joined in the next step. During the process in which the fractured pieces are joined, the classical process allows for mechanical contact in addition to visual control. This contact is helpful in joining the fragments but interferes with visual control. In joining the pieces mechanically, it is impossible to see the entire surface of the fractured area at the same time, so that one relies on visual control of only the external edges of the fractured pieces.

With the help of digital processes, the fragments are joined manually in simple cases by using visual control. It is not possible to use mechanical contact, since mechanical properties are not part of the digital objects in CAD/CAM methods. The transparency of the surface area can be changed instead, using the visualization properties of the digital objects, and so the otherwise hidden structures (i.e., the fractured areas of the fragments that need to be joined) are made visible (see Figure 9.9). This method allows the observation of internal structures and is similar in this regard to CT techniques. Using these visualization properties, it is possible to join two fragmented edges under visual control without visual obstruction caused by the fragment bodies (see Figure 9.10). The process of joining the fragments can be automated using additional software functions such as computations concerning optimization.

Once the fragments are joined, it is necessary to glue the two fractured surfaces together using the classical method, gravity being a major factor. This requires in addition the design and use of holding and supporting structures, since the glue needs to be applied and let dry for a certain time.

It is another advantage of the digitized procedure that gravity plays no role since the fragments are joined digitally. The absence of gravity has the advantage that the fractures do not need to be glued. This way, a number of working steps (e.g., selection of glue, application of glue, drying period) become unnecessary. A number of additional working steps, such as the construction of holding and support systems, are also rendered unnecessary, cutting down considerably the time needed for entire process of reconstruction.

The digitized method is especially useful if it comes to correcting the shape of the skull. Digital corrections are easy to perform, compared to the work that is required for dissolving and regluing joint fractured areas in order to correct the position of the fragments.

It is a time-consuming task to plan and perform the reconstruction of the skull. Using the classical method, the construction starts from the inside, progressing to the outside. It is important to follow this order, since the already joined areas would have to be opened if one was to add inner structures at a later point. It is easy to imagine the complications and additional working steps arising in such a case, increasing the amount of time spent on this process.

It thus becomes obvious that another advantage of the digitized process lies in the fact that the analyst determines the order in which the fractures are joined. The absence of mechanical contacts and gravity makes it possible to join the fragments in a free order. As a practical consequence, internal fragments can be added after completion of external parts without opening the reconstructed surface. The planning process that otherwise would be necessary regarding the order of the skull construction (from the inside to the outside) thus becomes unnecessary, simplifying the entire process of skull reconstruction.

9.3.3 METRIC CONTROL OF THE JOINT FRAGMENTS

In order to evaluate the quality of the joining process, certain measurement procedures are used. These measures allow an objective and quantitative comparison. The measuring techniques and possibilities applicable for the two different types of reconstruction methods differ greatly.

MEASUREMENTS OF LENGTH

The classic method uses tapes or dividers (determination of length by alignment with a ruler) for measuring the reconstructed skull. The flexible measuring tape is used to determine the curved length and the perimeter, the divider is employed to determine the linear distance between the two selected measurement points. For each measurement, it is necessary to have free access to the measurement points and curves. If the skull is already closed, no inner structures can be measured using the classical reconstruction method. These measures have to be taken during the joining process. It is only possible to measure the depth of the skull by drilling a hole in it, if the surface is already closed. Other problems arise regarding the geometry of the hole to be drilled. Gaining access to the selected measuring points on the inner structures is not an easy task.

It is an advantage of the digitized techniques that no mechanical contacts exist. This means that the digitized skull can be perforated without leaving any traces of destruction. The single fragments and thus the entire skull are made up of a multitude of points that can be used for different types of measurements. A number of metric functions that are part of the CAD program can be used for these measurements. Distance for example is measured in two steps. First, the two points whose distance is to be measured are manually selected. Second, their distance is calculated using the coordinate system and then displayed on the screen. The selection of points is completely free. This means that points lying on the outer or inner structures of the skull can be chosen for measurement. The digitized skull can be penetrated and thus allow for measurement of depth.

ANALYSIS OF THE PROFILE

In applying the classic process, it is not an easy task to determine the skull profile. Cutting across the skull in order to demonstrate the profile is not recommended since it results in the destruction of the skull and is also a work-intensive process. The skull being the basis for the modeled reconstruction of the face, one has to copy the constructed skull before its profile can be analyzed by bisecting the skull.

Again, the digitized procedure proves superior in that a multitude of cuts with different orientations can be performed on the digital skull without causing any damage. This way, different profiles of the skull are generated and analyzed metrically. The points of a profile are therefore combined by a traverse. The information regarding its length is accessible immediately after completion of the polygonization (using the properties of the polygon), not requiring manual measurements using the cursor.

PRECISION OF THE FIT

Joining the bone fragments as accurately as possible is crucial with regard to the addition of the remaining fragments and the shape of the whole skull. If mistakes have been made from the beginning, it is very likely that the entire skull is distorted, and the remaining fragments will not fit the gaps. It is possible to avoid these problems by controlling the precision of the fit during the joining of the bones.

In the classical method, the precision of the fit of the joined fragments can only be evaluated by looking at the outer edges of the fracture of two adjacent fragments and the shape of the surface in the area of the fracture. The possibilities to evaluate the precision of the fit are to measure the distance of the outer edges of the fracture between both fragments and to measure the curvature in the fracture area. Since we are dealing with the complex geometry of the skull, it is sometimes difficult to achieve these measurements.

The digitized process offers great advantages to determine the precision of the fit between two fracture surfaces. Since the fracture surfaces consist of a multitude of single points, the distance between the fracture edges can be determined using a distance calculation process between these points (see Figure 9.12). It is possible to determine it in one step for the entire fracture surface using the metric functions of the CAD programs. The result of the measuring process is demonstrated by a color code that has been applied to the fractured region. With only a small amount of time and effort invested, a direct result regarding the precision of the fit between the two fractures can be achieved (see Figure 9.13).

9.4 RESUMÉ AND PROSPECT

The method that has been presented is part of the process of the identification of unknown dead persons. Using this method, it is possible to develop a process that is completely digitized, from the reconstruction of the skull by joining the bone fragments up to the reconstruction of the surface of the face. This paper focuses on the digitized reconstruction of the skull (which could be looked at as a digitized 3D jigsaw puzzle), constituting the last missing component within the digitized process used for the identification of unknown dead persons. In order to support this new technology, a processing technique has been developed, based on the high-resolution 3D measurement of the fragments by SLT and using the functions of the CAD/CAM tools.

For the physical reconstruction of a skull, it is important to scrutinize the fractured pieces, to locate their matching parts, to test the matching parts using mechanical contact, and to verify the precision of the fit visually and metrically.

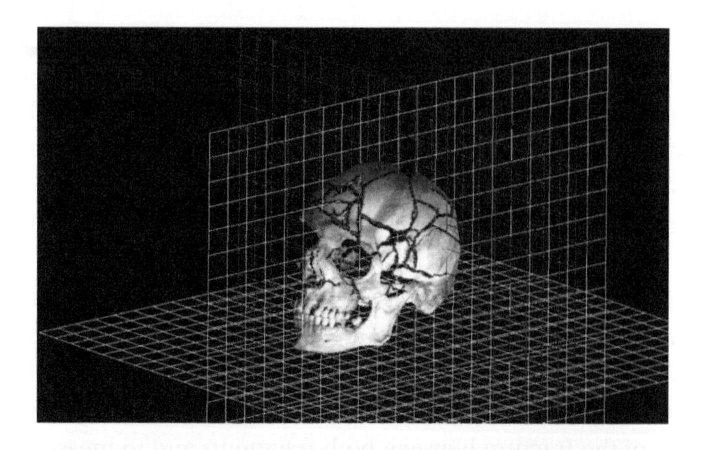

Figure 9.14

Digital skull for the facial reconstruction.

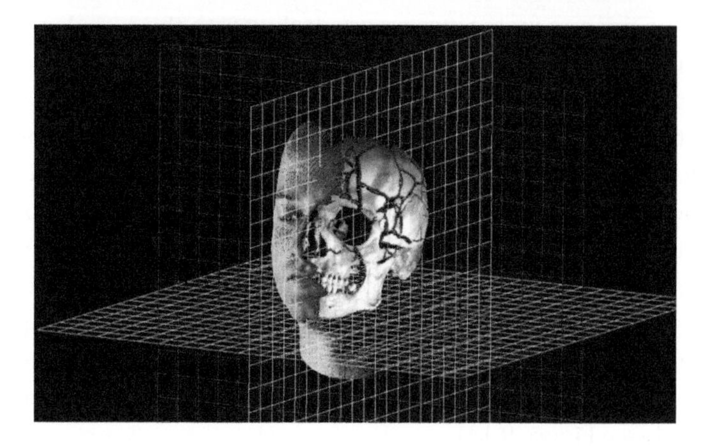

Figure 9.15

Facial reconstruction with skull and face shape.

All of these procedures are incorporated in the digitized processing techniques except for the mechanical contact. It is for this reason that techniques have been developed offering alternatives to this function. Apart from that, the digital processing technique offers an array of new functions that are not available using the classic procedure. The advantages of the digitized process are essentially due to the following factors:

- absence of gravity (no gluing, no holding and support systems)
- ability to penetrate the skull without causing destruction (joining the fragments in free order)
- transparency of the skull (view of inner structures)
- assembling of the fragments by direct visual control of the fracture surfaces
- nondestructive measurement (measurement of depth and skull profile)
- direct measurement of the precision of the fit using the fracture surfaces
- fast creation of copies (no repetition of all processing steps).

Furthermore it is possible to evaluate objectively the reconstructed skull using the metric CAD functions. Evaluation criteria can be developed in order to

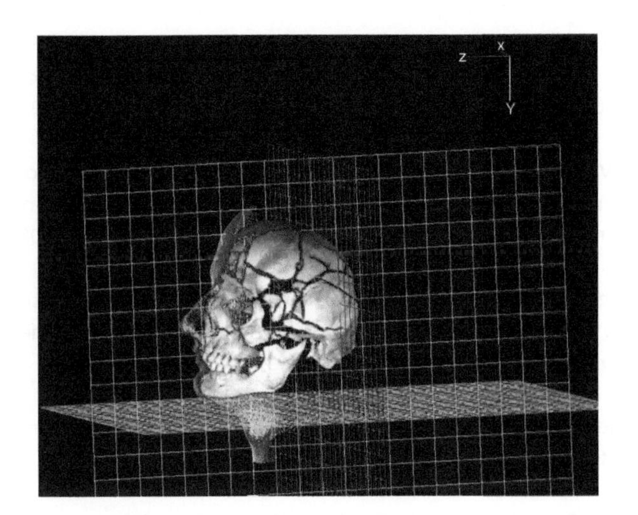

Figure 9.16
Facial reconstruction with skull and face shape from side.

apply an objective measure for the evaluation of differences resulting from the comparison between variants of the skull.

At the end of the presented method, the digital skull can be integrated into different facial reconstruction processes (Vanezis 1989, Nelson 1998, Quatrehomme *et al.* 1997, Blanz 2000) (see as an example for a facial reconstruction Figures 9.14–9.16).

Parts of this method are also applicable for the reconstruction of the face, leaving open the possibility to develop objective criteria for a scientific comparison, using for example a series of measurements, average figures, and deviations from the standard. Overall, this method has the potential to contribute considerably to the advancement of digital methods used for the identification of unknown dead persons.

REFERENCES

Blanz V. (2000) Automatische Rekonstruktion der dreidimensionalen Form von Gesichtern aus einem Einzelbild. Ph.D thesis, University of Tuebingen, Germany.

Helmer R. (1984) *Schädelidentifizierung durch elektronische Bildmischung: zugleich ein Beitrag zur Konstitutionsbiometrie und Dickenmessung der Gesichtsweichteile*. Heidelberg: Kriminalistik-Verl., 1984. - IX.

İşcan M. Y. and Helmer R. (eds.) (1993) *Forensic Analysis of the Skull: Craniofacial Analysis, Reconstruction, and Identification*. Wiley-Liss, New York.

Nelson L. A. and Michael S. D. (1998) "The Application of Volume Deformation to Three-Dimensional Facial Reconstruction: A Comparison with Previous Techniques", *Forensic Sci. Int.* 94, 167–181.

Quatrehomme G., Cotin S., Subsol G., Delingette H., Garidel Y., Grévin G., Fidrich M., Bailet P. and Ollier A. (1997) "A Fully Three-Dimensional Method for Facial Reconstruction Based on Deformable Models", *J. Forensic Sci.* 42(4), 649–652.

Sharom A. W., Vanezis P., Chapman R. C., Gonzales A., Blenkinsop C. and Rossi M. L. (1996) "Techniques in Facial Identification: Computer-Aided Facial Reconstruction Using a Laser Scanner and Video Superimposition", *Int. J. Legal Med.* 108, 194–200.

Subke J., Wehner H. D., Wehner F. and Szczepaniak S. (2000) "Streifenlichttopometrie (SLT). A New Method for a 3-dimensional Photorealistic Forensic Documentation in Color", *Forensic Sci. Int.* 113, 289–295.

Subke J., Wehner H. D., Wehner F. and Wolf H. (1998) "Wundtopographie mittels Streifenlichttopometrie", *Z. Rechtsmedizin Supplement 1* (8), A7.

Vanezis P., Blowes R. W., Linney A. D., Tan A. C., Richards R. and Neave R. (1989) "Application of 3-D Computer Graphics for Facial Reconstruction and Comparison with Sculpting Techniques", *Forensic Sci. Int.* 42, 69–84.

Wolf H. (1998) "Getting 3D Shape by Coded Light Approach in Combination with Phase Shifting", *Numerisation 3D/Human modelling, Salon et Congress sur la Numerisation 3D, Paris, 20.1.–21.1.1998.*

CHAPTER 10

FORENSIC FACIAL RECONSTRUCTION USING COMPUTER MODELING SOFTWARE

Stephanie L. Davy
Research Centre for Human Identification, School of Medicine, University of Sheffield, Beech Hill Rd, Sheffield S10 2RX, UK

Timothy Gilbert
Aims Solutions Ltd., Unit 3, Stoney St, Nottingham NG1 1LG, UK

Damian Schofield
School of Computer Science and IT, University of Nottingham, University Park, Nottingham NG7 2RD, UK

Martin P. Evison
Research Centre for Human Identification, School of Medicine, University of Sheffield, Beech Hill Rd, Sheffield S10 2RX, UK

10.1 INTRODUCTION

Currently, there is no single answer to the many challenges facing forensic facial reconstruction. The process of completing a three-dimensional (3D) clay reconstruction can take several days to complete. With the advent of user-friendly computer software and methods, the time taken to produce a facial reconstruction process could potentially be reduced to mere hours. As computer technology progresses and develops, computer-generated facial reconstruction techniques will improve. These developments could save both time and money, as well as increasing the reliability of the technique.

Existing technologies such as 3D scanners and digital cameras can be utilized to capture the geometry of a skull, but the technologies to reconstruct the skull have yet to obtain similar speed and efficiency improvements. The digital capture of a skull has several benefits. Firstly, the need for casting of a skull is eliminated, reducing the opportunity for damage to an original specimen,

Computer-Graphic Facial Reconstruction
John G. Clement and Murray K. Marks, Editors

as well as the cost of materials and time spent in a laboratory. As with most similar computer technology, computer-generated reconstructions can be more easily altered than can a clay version. With keystrokes or mouse clicks, features may be altered, added, or removed altogether. When working on a physical skull, there is no "undo" button.

Another benefit of computerized forensic facial reconstructions is that of reproducibility. If twenty practitioners were given the same face to manually reconstruct from the same skull, twenty different reconstructions are likely to result. This point was illustrated in the Green River serial-killer cases, in which multiple facial reconstructions of several victims were created. The results were highly variable from practitioner to practitioner and met with little success (Haglund and Reay 1991). However, with a computerized method using the same data and the same techniques, each practitioner should produce the same basic reconstruction. Ideally, the process would work for confirming a practitioner's use of tissue depths and facial features much in the same way as the FORDISC software package (Ousley and Jantz 1996) works for confirming (rather than determining) sex and ancestral affiliation. The software would suggest appropriate depths and features, but the practitioner would have the ability to override them or adjust them to accommodate for case-specific needs. Computer verification increases the accuracy and objectivity of a reconstruction. In most cases, the only variations between practitioners would be in the details that have not yet been fully scientifically established, such as ear shape or lip shape (however, there are recognized formulae which provide guidelines).

Since the time involved in completing a reconstruction will be greatly reduced with a satisfactory method of computerization, so will the costs. Billable hours can be reduced, and the only capital investment would be in the price of the software, which would run on an ordinary (existing) desktop computer system. This would make the practice more accessible and available to places that need the service most for cases of unidentifiable victims (i.e., typically underfunded police departments and medical examiners' offices). It is, however, recommended that such departments enlist the aid of a forensic anthropologist or otherwise qualified consultant to increase the chances of successful identification.

Additionally, computerized facial reconstructions could be implemented in situations where traditional facial reconstructions cannot. Typically, forensic facial reconstruction has not been employed in cases of mass graves or mass disasters due to time and cost constraints associated with Plasticine methods; computer-generated facial reconstructions could eliminate both of these constraints. Forensic facial reconstruction could be a very powerful tool in future mass human identification scenarios.

10.2 CURRENT LIMITATIONS

There are several limitations, both in currently available computer technology and in reliable data, which prevent the development of a workable automated software product for computerized facial reconstruction. While computer technology is advancing at an astounding rate, there are still several avenues that prevent realistic-looking reconstructions from being easily and rapidly produced. One of the problems is that the tissue-depth data upon which reconstructions are based are seen as unreliable, and are the subject of ongoing research.

At present, realistic skin and hair modeling within 3D-modeling software packages is very time-consuming and far from ideal. Using programs such as FaceGen (Singular Inversions Inc. 2002) one can use fairly realistic-looking skin textures, but such a texture loses its realism once stretched over a different skull. Issues associated with skin textures will be discussed further later in this chapter.

Other limitations to skin modeling include age-related features, such as wrinkles. Appropriate wrinkle modeling relies upon an interface of several disciplines, including computer programing as well as human biology and psychology. It is important that not only do wrinkles appear realistic in an aesthetic sense, but also that they are anatomically appropriate. Individuals age at different rates as well as by developing wrinkles in different areas. Such considerations must be made in order to ensure that the reconstructed individual is perceived to be of a suitable age by potential identifying witnesses. Several studies have been conducted regarding the perception of age in faces (Evison 2001). This has important implications for future work in computerized facial reconstruction. Burt and Perrett (1995) also found that shape and color may have an impact upon the interpretation of age.

10.3 WORK WITH 3D MODELING SOFTWARE

In a joint project between the University of Sheffield Forensic Anthropology teams and Aims Solutions Ltd., a University of Nottingham spin-out company, the authors have been able to develop new techniques for computerized facial reconstruction and create several reconstructions. The authors were able to undertake this project due to a generous grant from the Higher Education Innovation Fund (HEIF).

3ds max™ version 5 (Discreet™ 2002) is a program designed for computer modeling and animation. It provides a high level of flexibility and a substantial number of varied functions from which to choose. This seemed an ideal program for a project of this type, particularly since the development team had extensive experience of using this software. Since this small research project was experimental, it was possible to easily change the approach as the methodology was developed.

The Egyptology Department at the Bolton Museum (United Kingdom) enlisted the authors to attempt the computerized reconstruction of the face of a mummy using only radiographs. The mummy was an unknown male, aged between 20 and 35 years. He had been placed in the coffin of a female mummy, apparently because grave robbers prefer to sell mummies and sarcophagi in sets. Although the identity of the mummy is unknown, it was known that the body was found in an area used for the burial of priests and royalty.

This facial reconstruction was successfully completed and is described in this chapter. Two additional cases (one archaeological and one forensic) were also completed using the techniques developed during this project.

10.3.1 CAPTURING THE SKULL

In a "normal" facial reconstruction, the practitioner generally has the skull (or fragments thereof) in his/her physical possession. However, in this particular project, only frontal and lateral radiographs were available for use. The authors decided that the most efficient solution to this problem was to use an existing skull from the lab that was of a similar sex/age/ethnic affiliation and "morph" it to match the given radiographs. The skull was scanned using a Cyberware 3030 color laser scanner, Echo software was then used to create a polygonal model.

The skull model was converted into an editable mesh, which converts the surface into editable polygons (Figure 10.1). Then, the radiographs were imported into the software as images and set up as textures on solid 3D geometry so

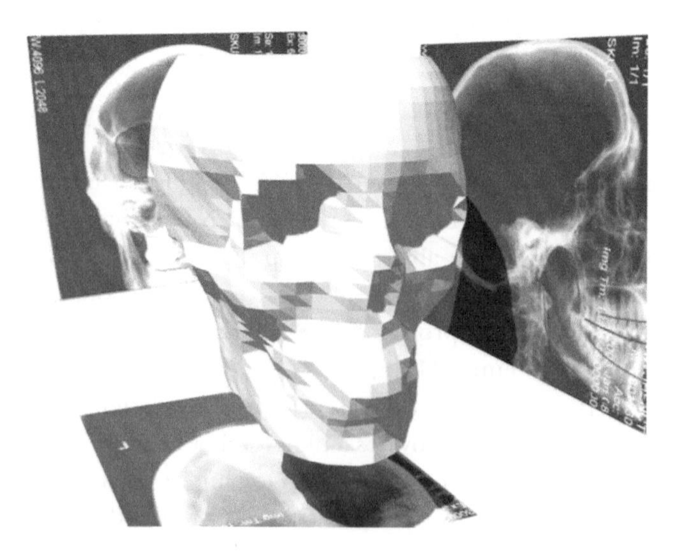

Figure 10.1

The laser-scanned skull with x-rays.

that they were visible in the lateral and frontal views. The skull was then lined up with the radiographs, and the polygons were manipulated to match the shape of the radiograph in perpendicular views (Figure 10.2). 3ds max™ allows the viewer to see the "world" in which she or he is working from multiple angles and in layers, which enabled the authors to easily ensure that all vertices making up the virtual skull were correctly located. Forensic cases are often more straightforward because the actual skull is usually available, and the geometry produced by the 3D scanner can be directly imported into the 3ds max™ software.

10.3.2 PLACING THE LANDMARKS

Small pyramids were used to represent the traditional tissue-depth markers utilized in clay reconstructions (Figure 10.3). The square bases were placed perpendicularly to the bone surface at the appropriate craniometric points on the skull. The height of the pyramids was input in millimeters to the measurements specified in the literature (Rhine and Campbell 1980). For clarity, each pyramid was individually renamed for the point it represented (i.e., nasion-right or glabella-left). For the regions in which tissue-depth data were lacking, additional pyramids were created in a second color (for differentiation purposes) at mathematically calculated intermediary points.

To calculate the size of the interpolated points, the spaces between the existing landmarks were broken down into a "grid" covering the entire surface, and the mid-point of any two locations on the same line of this grid added as a marker of an averaged height. For example, the gonions and the mental eminence were deemed to be on the same horizontal contour as each other. Hence, an interpolated point was added on the bottom edge of the

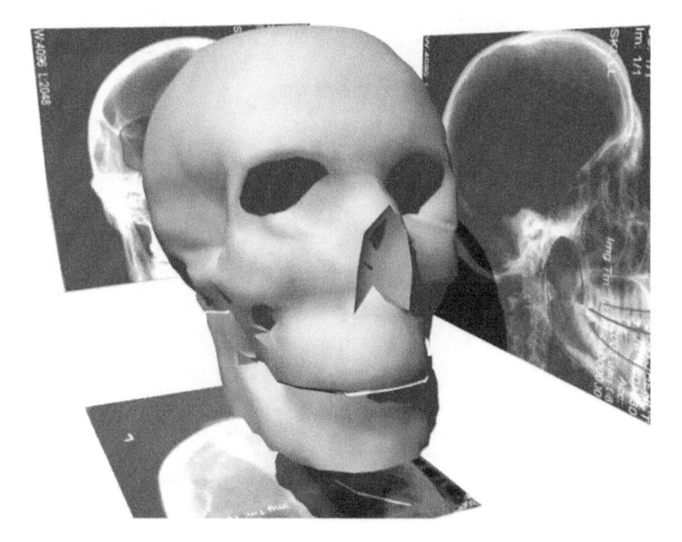

Figure 10.2
The skull after smoothing.

mandible halfway between the two points, and the height taken as an average of the two. As this distance was relatively large in comparison to others, additional points were added between this new point and the gonion, and between the point and the mental eminence. Again, averaging the points on either side provided the heights.

Although this method gives approximate values, the authors believe that it is of comparable accuracy to the existing method of adding clay strips to join the landmarks together. It could be postulated that the accuracy may be improved by taking into account the heights from more of the surrounding landmarks. There are a variety of mathematical methods that have been used to interpolate the size of intermediary landmark sites for craniofacial reconstruction (Albrecht *et al.* 2003, Attardi *et al.* 2001, Cairns 1999). However, the authors believe that the discrepancy between the different point heights calculated using these different mathematical techniques is minimal in comparison with the assumptions made during the reconstruction process. Figure 10.3 shows the final result of this process, complete with landmarks for the eyes, nose, and mouth. The creation of these parts is discussed later.

Initially, the computer work was a time-consuming process. Development of a suitable technique for the placement of the landmarks took several days for the animator to accomplish under the guidance of the forensic anthropologist. However, the time taken for this process was greatly reduced in subsequent

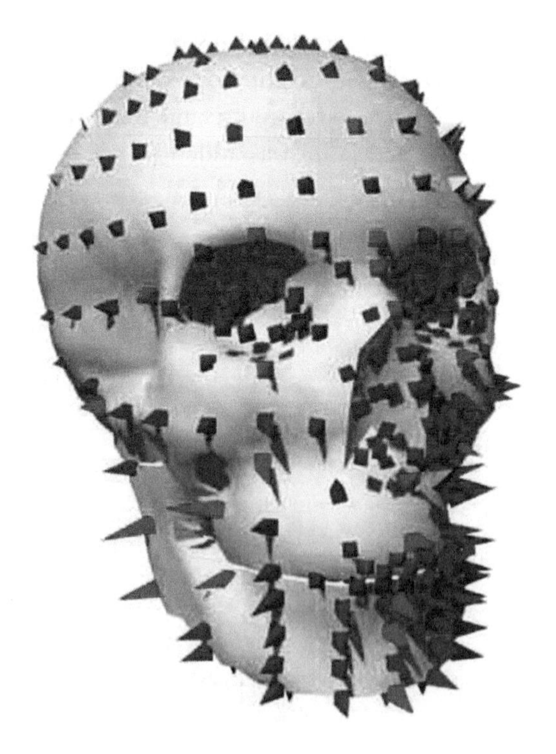

Figure 10.3

The skull with landmarks. Red denotes a height taken from literature, whereas blue denotes an interpolated value.

cases because the pyramids could be saved independently of the skull. Each group of landmark data, such as Caucasian females or Negroid males, was saved individually with the appropriate measurements. These can now be imported into future cases as a "cloud" of craniometric landmark points that are in the approximately correct location, but already have the correct height data applied. These can then be spatially adjusted until they are in the correct craniometric positions.

10.3.3 CREATING THE EYES

Creating the eyeballs was possibly one of the simplest of the reconstruction tasks. Two spheres were created to the dimensions recommended in the literature. Using a polygonal wire-frame view, portions of the spheres could be selected and appropriately colored using the materials editor function of 3ds max™ to create convincing textures for the pupils and irises. The whites of the eyes were slightly more difficult because they are not a true white in living subjects, so a gradient texture was used to redden the eyes towards the lids and corners. The eyeballs were then positioned in the sockets using the data detailed in research by Stephan (2002). The protrusion was carefully measured using the tape-measure feature provided in 3ds max™.

10.3.4 FORMING THE NOSE

The size of the nose was determined by using calculations based on Macho's (1986) research. The software dimensioning features were then used to create the proper dimensions, and depth markers were placed in the appropriate areas. Previously created generic nose geometry was merged into the scene and nonuniformly scaled to match the calculated sizes, and appropriate landmarks. This method was also used for the other facial features.

10.3.5 FORMING THE TISSUE

SPLINES AND SURFACE MODIFIERS

In the early stages of the project, the authors decided to utilize splines to connect the tissue-depth markers. Splines are curves that can be interpolated and smoothly fitted to their neighbors. They were used to provide a base surface over which a skin layer could be fitted. A number of techniques were attempted to construct the "spline cage", but this proved frustrating on several fronts. First, the process was very time-consuming and labor-intensive, requiring each spline to be connected continuously over the tissue-depth markers. The final curvature of the face was ultimately dependent upon the layout of the splines; the process became tedious as sections of the head were built and rebuilt to find the most effective structure. After the skin layer was applied using the 3ds max™ surface modifier function (a tool used to patch together a 3D polygonal surface based on the contours of a spline network), it was evident that the number of interpolated points used led to a face that had a relatively low polygon count. The resulting reconstruction was deemed jagged and rough, especially in the cheek regions.

In this case the problem was solved by smoothing the skin by applying the mesh-smoothing modifier tool in 3ds max™. In the future this problem could be overcome by adding more interpolated points, thereby creating a more detailed network of splines. This would obviously lengthen an already time-consuming process if carried out by hand, but the development of a semi-automated system to create the soft tissue could alleviate this. The development of such a system is seen by the authors as a nontrivial problem, since the way the landmark sites are linked can alter the look and feel of a reconstruction.

ANATOMICAL RECONSTRUCTION AND NURBS

The authors were interested in creating a more advanced method for reconstruction that incorporated the anatomically based method favored by many physical reconstructionists (Gerasimov 1971, Prag and Neave 1997). This method particularly wanted to examine the use of the underlying facial musculature in the modeling of the skin on the facial model. This was accomplished by the application of NURBS (Nonuniform rational B-splines). NURBS CV curves (control-vertex curves) are similar to splines in that they are curves that can be manipulated, but in this case each section of the curve is the average line between three weighted control points (Figure 10.4), whereas a spline is fitted to vertices that are positioned on the curve itself with individual orientations and weightings. The lofted surfaces generated from NURBS CV curves are generally smoother than the spline networks used earlier and have the added advantage that they can be manipulated quickly by altering the position of the CV curves. This makes the creation of complex shapes relatively simple to achieve, and the resulting muscles can be transferred to new skulls and fitted with a minimum of effort.

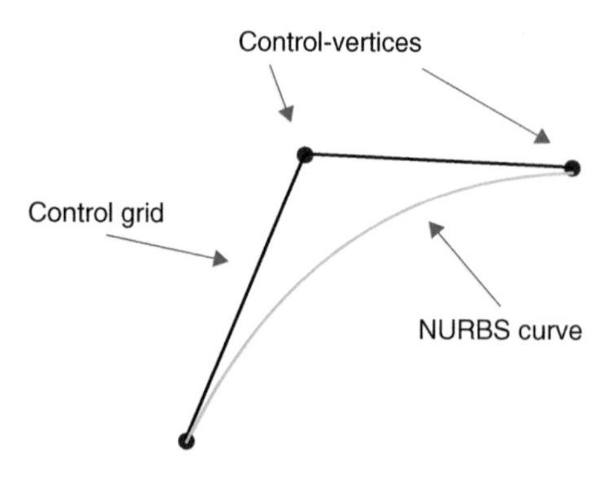

Figure 10.4

The basic construction of a NURBS CV curve.

NURBS CV curves were used to create elliptical cross sections, which were then lofted into surfaces replicating the gross musculature of the head (Figure 10.5). The cross sections were correlated with established diagrams of craniofacial muscles, along with the tissue-depth landmarks, to indicate the depth of the soft tissue over the surface of the skull.

The contours of the face were then built using more CV curves, following the shape of the underlying muscular tissue structure, then lofted into an approximate reconstruction of the subject's face. The resulting mesh (Figure 10.6) was carefully altered to provide added definition to details such as the eyes and the lips, and any imperfections in the surface corrected. This method undoubtedly created a more contoured and aesthetically pleasing face, although it was more time-consuming than the earlier methods developed. While the muscle "texture" was irrelevant to the final reconstruction, a pinkish color and striated texture was added to the muscles to give them a more realistic appearance.

TEXTURING THE FACE

One advantage that computer-generated facial reconstruction has over traditional methods is its ability to texture the faces realistically. In 3D computer modeling, texturing is a process akin to applying wallpaper to a flat surface, where a pattern or image is draped over the solid object. A similar technique

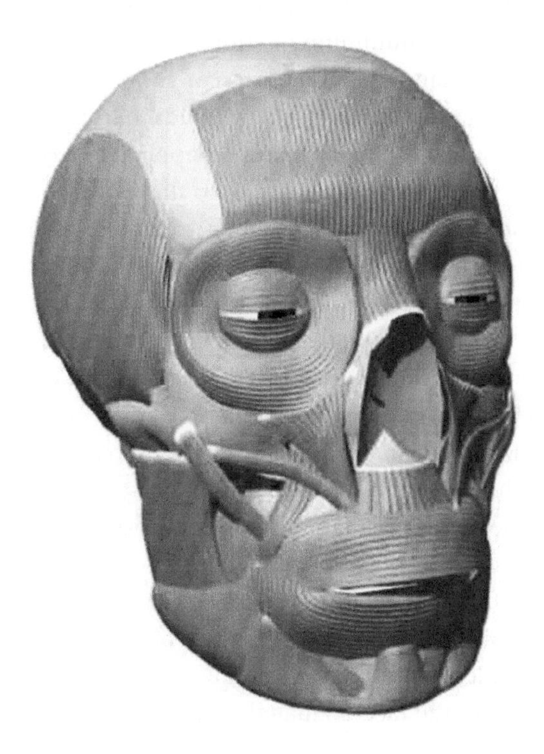

Figure 10.5
The skull with NURBS muscles.

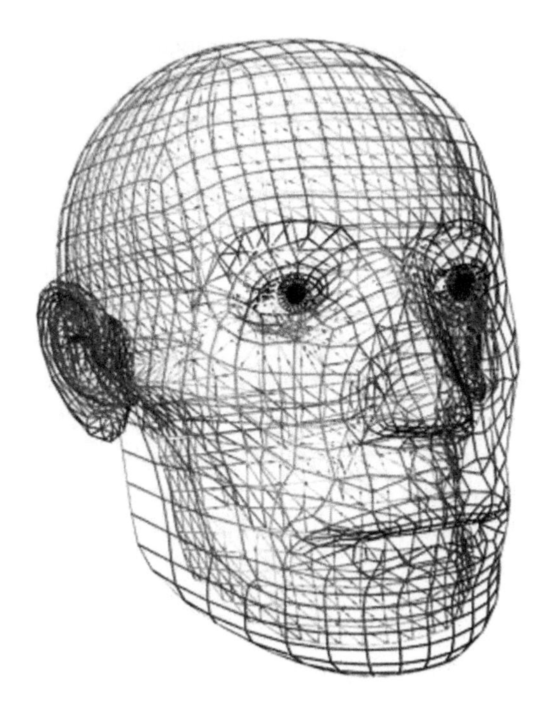

Figure 10.6

Wire-frame rendering of the face (including the skin, skull, eyes, and landmark sites).

was also possible with a clay head, but it required a fine-artist to paint directly onto the model. With 3ds max™ it is possible to drag-and-drop a texture onto the generated face with a minimum of effort.

In addition to the standard XYZ Cartesian coordinates, each vertex also has a UVW coordinate vector, which corresponds to its texture as opposed to its position in virtual space. Once a texture is applied to a mesh, a UVW wrap modifier is added to roughly fit the face onto the mesh (for example, applying the UVW wrap in the form of a cylinder would be similar to stretching a rubber tube with the face painted on over a clay head; the features might not align properly, but it gives a starting point for finer adjustment).

Once the face is visible on the head model, it can then be fine-tuned using the UVW Unwrap modifier feature in 3ds max™. This gives a two-dimensional representation of the UVW coordinates overlaid onto the face texture. The vertices can be moved in these two dimensions to fit the texture onto the head correctly. This stage can again be quite time-consuming—especially if the head is complex and has a large number of vertices. However, once the process is complete, the software remembers the individual UVW coordinates, and new textures can be quickly applied onto the head. This is of great value when examining the effects of aging and ethnicity on a face. A texture designed to look older or darker, for example, can be quickly applied and its effect on the "look" of the face evaluated.

For the face shown throughout this chapter, a texture generated by the FaceGen Modeller software package in 3ds max™ was used, as this software was already in use in other areas and provides good-quality textures manipulated by the adjustment of a range of facial variables and parameters. The texture could be produced using a wide variety of methods, including digital photographs of a real face or hand-painted artwork. The exact approach taken would depend upon the scenario, but it was felt that the FaceGen software could speed up this part of the process considerably and was suitable for use in this case.

10.4 RESULTS AND FUTURE WORK

The face of the Egyptian mummy generated using this technique is shown in Figure 10.7. As can be seen in the figure, there is a pronounced overbite on the upper lip. Initially, it was thought that this could be due to the lower mandible having sunk into the skull over the ages. However, this hypothesis was refuted by a forensic odontologist who confirmed that the position of the mandible was correct. This overbite on the upper lip particularly excited the Egyptologists, as the royal family of the pharaoh dynasty from the time the mummy originated are renowned for their pronounced overbite.

The reconstructions produced during this project were fairly impressive; however, there is still work that needs to be done to make the process simpler and more automated and the final images more lifelike. The reconstructed visages look computer-generated and are often evocative of video-game characters, but this can be rectified over time with the use of better skin textures and increased model complexity (an increased number of polygons). Also, the gradual increase in automation will allow the artist to produce models to a much higher level of detail than currently possible in a reasonable timeframe, which will only improve the realism of the reconstructed faces. Additionally, we hope to incorporate ongoing work in fields such as realistic hair modeling to improve the appearance of the heads, as well as the appearance of complicated skin features like the fine tissues around the eyes.

The processes discussed here were adapted from the existing physical methods. There were several advantages of using a digital medium, such as the ability to work from x-ray data, the improved use of musculature in the reconstruction, and the application of different textures. However, the main areas in which computerization is expected to improve reconstruction techniques (automation, for example) still require improvement. This is not to say that this study was not valuable: attempting to implement the traditional methods using modeling software has given the authors an insight into the unique

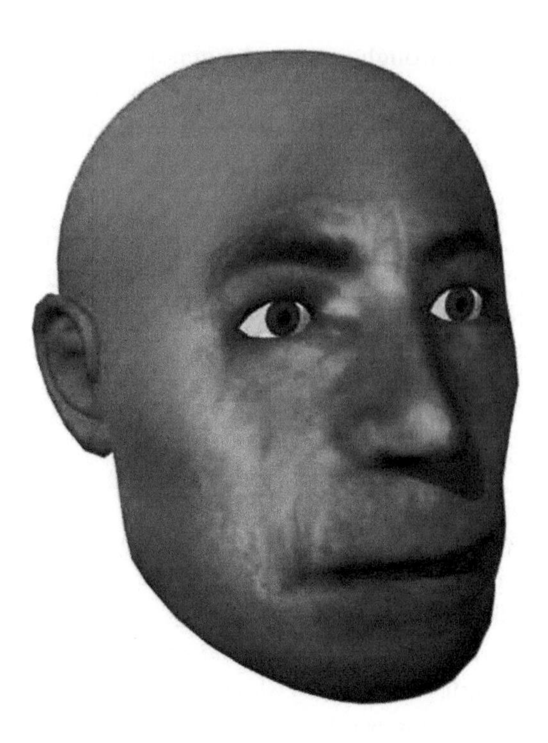

Figure 10.7
The completed face after mesh smoothing.

advantages and disadvantages of working with a virtual medium. It has also generated ideas of ways to improve and semiautomate the process. The authors believe that this can be accomplished without falling into the trap of using "generic" faces that fail to convey the individual characteristics of a face.

As for what automation can achieve, it is felt that the process of manually placing the landmark sites is something that will (for the foreseeable future at least) need to be carried out by hand. It may be possible to use a script to generate the interpolated points. The actual building of the face, spline by spline, is something that currently is best accomplished through human intervention. In the future, a process in which a prebuilt virtual wire frame is snapped onto landmarks, which are then placed by hand may provide a rapid solution. The authors believe that the manual positioning of the points would ensure that the nuances of the skull are taken into account, but the automated "cage" would save time.

3ds max™ has many advanced features which may yet be applied to this process. As the process is developed further, it is our hope to create a range of tissue-depth templates that can be adjusted to fit individual cases. Also, the flexibility of the software allows a continued update of the data as more research is conducted in areas of craniofacial identification such as tissue depths and relationships between the soft tissue and bony features.

10.5 COMPARISON WITH OTHER COMPUTERIZATION METHODS

Other researchers within the field of facial reconstruction have been working to create methods of computerized facial reconstruction for some years. The method discussed in this chapter, will hopefully be a cost-effective and less time-consuming alternative when finalized. Rather than to simply recreate all of the steps of a clay reconstruction, using a computer, it is the intent of the authors to create the most reliable, speedy, and accurate reconstructions possible with the available technology.

We have opted not to use photographic facial templates or donor faces and morph them directly onto the skull (Jones 2001, Tu *et al.* 2000, Vanezis *et al.* 2000) in favor of a developing method that can potentially compensate for a fuller range of individual features. In using facial templates, there is a potential to produce reconstructions that look more like the donor face(s) than the deceased's actual premortem face. The resulting image is often a composite of the donor faces. The work discussed in this chapter attempts to avoid this pitfall by using the skull to dictate facial appearance, rather than existing face templates being anchored to the skull. While some may argue that the use of computer graphics may sacrifice realism, a counterargument is that often a caricature of a person is more easily recognizable than an image that may resemble a generic, albeit realistic, template-based face. Additionally, there is no reason to assume that a computer reconstruction should be any less accurate or realistic than a clay model when similar techniques are used. Discrepancies in realism between clay and computerized reconstructions will continue to be an issue while the fields of forensic facial reconstruction and computer graphics are regarded as separate. As reconstruction experts gain experience with graphics packages, and graphics experts gain experience with reconstruction, the quality of the end products can only improve.

10.6 THE FUTURE

It is the intention of the authors to continue work using 3ds max™ and other 3D computer modeling software to incorporate further research on tissue and feature information as it becomes available. Future plans include the reconstruction of test cases using forensic cases with accompanying premortem photographs. These cases will be reconstructed blindly, meaning that the practitioners will not have access to the premortem information. This will test the reliability of the method as well as to lend information about techniques that may be improved upon in the future.

REFERENCES

Albrecht L., Haber J. and Seidel H. P. (2003) "Construction and Animation of Anatomically Based Human Hand Models", *Proc. ACM SIGGRAPH Symposium on Computer Animation (SCA) 2003.*

Attardi G., Betrò M., Forte M., Gori R., Guidazzoli A., Imboden S. and Mallegni F. (1999) "3D Facial Reconstruction and Visualization of Ancient Egyptian Mummies Using Spiral CT Data", *ACM SIGGRAPH 99, Sketches and Applications.*

Burt D. M. and Perrett D. I. (1995) "Perception of Age in Adult Caucasian Male Faces: Computer Graphic Manipulation of Shape and Colour Information", *Proc. R. Soc. Lond.* 259, 137–143.

Cairns M. (1999) "An Investigation Into The Use of 3D Computer Graphics For Forensic Facial Reconstruction", First Year Ph.D. Internal Report, Department of Computer Science, University of Glasgow.

Discreet Software (2002) 3ds max™. CD-ROM [June, 2003].

Evison M. P. (2001) "Modeling Age, Obesity and Ethnicity in a Computerized 3-D Facial Reconstruction", *Forensic Science Communications* 3(2).

George R. M. (1993) "Anatomical and Artistic Guidelines for Forensic Facial Reconstruction", in: *Forensic Analysis of the Skull* (M. Y. İşcan and R. P. Helmer, eds.). Wiley-Liss, New York, pp. 215–227.

Gerasimov M. M. (1971) *The Face Finder.* Hutchinson & Co, London.

Haglund W. D. and Reay D. T. (1991) "Use of Facial Approximation Techniques in Identification of Green River Serial Murder Victims", *Am. J. Forensic Medicine and Pathology* 12(2), 132–142.

Macho G. A. (1986) "An Appraisal of Plastic Reconstruction of the Nose", *J. Forensic Sci.* 31(4), 1391–1403.

Ousley S. D. and Jantz R. L. (1996) *FORDISC 2.0 Personal Computer Forensic Discriminant Functions.* University of Tennessee, Knoxville.

Prag J. and Neave R. (1997) *Making Faces Using Forensic and Archaeological Evidence.* Texas A&M University Press, College Station.

Rhine and Campbell (1980) "Thickness of Facial Tissues in American Blacks", *J. Forensic Sci.* 25(4), 847–858.

Singular Inversions, Inc. (2002) FaceGen Modeller CD-ROM [June 2003].

Stephan C. N. (2002) "Facial Approximation: Globe Projection Guideline Falsified by Exophthalmometry Literature", *J. Forensic Sci.* 47(4), 730–735.

PART III

PERCEPTION, RECOGNITION, AND IDENTITY

CHAPTER 11

CEILING RECOGNITION LIMITS OF TWO-DIMENSIONAL FACIAL APPROXIMATIONS CONSTRUCTED USING AVERAGES*

Carl N. Stephan
Department of Anatomical Sciences, University of Adelaide, Australia, 5005 and School of Dental Science, University of Melbourne, Victoria 3010, Australia

Ian S. Penton-Voak
Department of Experimental Psychology, University of Bristol BS8 1TN, UK

John G. Clement
School of Dental Science, University of Melbourne, Victoria 3010, Australia

Maciej Henneberg
Department of Anatomical Sciences, University of Adelaide, Australia, 5005

Portions of this work have been previously presented at the 54th Annual Meeting of the American Academy of Forensic Sciences 2002. Atlanta, Georgia.

11.1 INTRODUCTION

The process of constructing faces from skulls is known as facial approximation, among other names (e.g., facial reconstruction, facial reproduction). Since the aim of forensic facial approximation is to build a face from a skull that can be specifically and purposefully recognized as the person to whom the skull belongs (Neave and Prag 1997, Taylor 2001), accurate facial approximations are those that can be easily recognized correctly as the target individual (individual to whom the skull belongs) (Stephan 2002a). True success in facial approximation depends, therefore, on purposeful facial recognition and is distinct from forensic case success where correct matching may result from factors other than purposeful recognition of the facial approximation. Such factors include: contextual information, e.g., belongings of individuals found at the crime scene along with the skeleton (Haglund and Reay 1991), and chance (Henneberg and Stephan 2001), but also other factors like the eagerness of people who know a missing person to gain emotional closure through the identification of a loved one. Here facial-approximation success will be used to refer to true success (purposeful true positive recognition) unless stated otherwise.

Computer-Graphic Facial Reconstruction
John G. Clement and Murray K. Marks, Editors

Facial-approximation accuracy and success is controversial. The debate has been taking place at least since the publication of a critical paper in 1913 by von Eggeling. Since then many more authors have advocated doubt that facial approximation can reliably achieve its aim (e.g., Brues 1958, George 1993, Haglund 1998, Haglund and Reay 1991, Maat 1998–99, Montagu 1947, Henneberg and Stephan 2001, Stephan 2002b, 2003, Stewart 1979a, Suk 1935). However, many forensic practitioners continue to claim that method aims are achieved (e.g., Neave and Prag 1997, Taylor 2001). The controversy surrounding facial-approximation accuracy is perhaps not surprising because the task—the *complete* construction of a face from a bare skull—would appear to be extraordinarily difficult. This seems especially true since few specific relationships between hard and soft tissue are known, and much of the facial-approximation process is subjective and untested at this time, as has been the case in the past (Haglund 1998, Haglund and Reay 1991, Montagu 1947, Henneberg and Stephan 2001, Stephan 2002b, 2003, Suk 1935, von Eggeling 1913). Even if facial-approximation methods were entirely composed of systematically determined soft-tissue prediction rules, errors would still exist for each prediction method. Since the face is a complex structure and may require many soft-tissue prediction guidelines to be used, the accumulative error may be large. Thus, even if empirically tested guidelines were used, the accurate anatomical construction of the face would probably still be extremely difficult to achieve.

Most claims that facial-approximation techniques are accurate and successful have rested upon the flawed belief that forensic case success indicates accuracy. For example, Prag and Neave (1997, p. 10) state that "the fact that the majority of the forensic reconstructions are recognized and identified demonstrates beyond a doubt that the technique works". Certainly facial approximations have been successful in generating leads or tentative identifications in at least some forensic cases. Published examples are Cherry and Angel (1977), Farrar (1977), Gatliff and Snow (1979), Perper *et al.* (1988), Phillips *et al.* (1996), Prag and Neave (1997), Rathbun (1984), Stoney and Koelmeyer (1999), and Suzuki (1973). There is little doubt that these facial approximations have been correctly matched to their respective target individuals (person to whom the skull belongs) and have hence been successfully identified in the forensic sense. However, correct forensic matching does not necessarily indicate that the facial approximation has been purposefully recognized since there are often other confounding factors in forensic cases as highlighted above. It is also worth noting here that there are cases where facial approximations are not purposefully recognized (e.g., Haglund and Reay 1991), and it seems likely that many unsuccessful cases go unreported, resulting in a biased account of facial-approximation success when examining published case reports (Henneberg and Stephan 2001).

Reported success by practitioners also appears to be used by some authors to indicate facial-approximation accuracy. Some facial-approximation practitioners claim high facial-approximation success rates; for example, Gerasimov (1971) claims 100% success, Bender (Rubin 1998) 85%, Wilkinson (Wilkinson and Whittaker 2002) 75%, Gatliff (Gatliff and Snow 1979) 70%. Others claim more conservative but still high rates; for example, Neave (Neave and Prag 1997) claims 50–60%. In addition to the limitations described above for forensic case success (upon which practitioner success is based) reported practitioner success may further be an unreliable measure of facial-approximation accuracy because practitioners are often very enthusiastic about their work. Some success rates appear to have escalated without published method changes. For example, the reported success of R. Neave's method which is often described as either the "British" or "Manchester" method has increased from ~55% (Neave and Prag 1997) to 75% (Whittaker and Wilkinson 2002) without published method changes over this five-year period. Reports of practitioner success also appear to be plastic depending on who is quoting them. For example, although Gatliff has claimed a 70% recognition rate (Gatliff and Snow 1979), Wilkinson—who uses the Neave method—indicates that the American method as practiced by Gatliff only achieves a 65% success rate, while the British method as used by Neave is 75% successful (Whittaker and Wilkinson 2002), even though Neave himself reports that Gatliff has 72% success (Neave and Prag 1997, p.18) and that the success rate of the "British" (or "Manchester") method is between 50 and 60% (Neave and Prag 1997, p. 33). The lack of frequent quotation of actual case numbers as evidence for the success rates reported in the literature indicates that these success rates should be approached with caution, for without this evidence one cannot tell if these numbers were empirically derived using systematic methods.

Facial-approximation accuracy and success is also often supported with citations to the similarities or resemblances between the facial approximation and the target individual (see e.g., Gerasimov 1971, Helmer *et al.* 1993, Krogman 1946, Prag and Neave 1997, Suzuki 1973, Taylor, 2001). However, similarity may not necessitate recognition, upon which facial-approximation accuracy ideally depends (Stephan 2002a, Stewart 1979b). Most people familiar with facial-approximation techniques will be aware of cases where dissimilar facial approximations appear to have been recognized correctly while similar ones (identified through other means) have not been. Evidence that humans can recognize faces that are not exactly representative of their target individuals is demonstrated by our ability to recognize images of pixilated faces, cartoon faces, caricatured faces and other facial distortions (see, e.g., Benson and Perrett 1991, Rhodes *et al.* 1987). Furthermore, direct comparisons of similarity between facial approximations and their respective target individuals fails to take into account the nontarget individuals who may actually be more representative of the facial approximation than the target individual and may hence be recognized instead. This suspicion has been confirmed by a study demonstrating that correctly recognized facial approximations are not judged as any more similar to the person identified than facial approximations that are incorrectly recognized (Stephan 2002a).

Rather than using the approaches outlined above, facial-approximation accuracy can be better evaluated by laboratory testing, where confounding variables can be controlled and the actual numbers of correct recognitions for independent facial approximations can be counted. Such studies have been conducted, and some facial approximations have been correctly recognized at above-chance rates in such tests (Snow *et al.* 1970, Henneberg and Stephan 2001, van Rensburg 1993). Snow *et al.* (1970) found two facial approximations to be identified with above-chance rates, indicating that facial approximation may work. More recent tests following published facial-approximation methods have indicated that facial approximations are sometimes correctly recognized above chance, but that these instances are rare (Henneberg and Stephan 2001). Even when facial approximations are recognized above chance in these studies, the recognition rates generated are generally low, being much less than 54% above chance and on average about 25% (Snow *et al.* 1970, Henneberg and Stephan 2001, van Rensburg 1993). These rates seem to be well below the 70% recognition rate reported in studies where the same individual is identified from images taken at different times even if the view point and expression are constant (Hancock *et al.* 2000). Additionally it appears to be worth noting that, in many of these facial-approximation recognition studies, a large number of incorrect identifications are made, some at rates significantly above chance levels.

Systematic evaluations of facial approximations under laboratory conditions suffer from one major drawback. Usually people unfamiliar with the target individual are called upon to make an identification in these tests, whereas in forensic casework it is individuals who are familiar with the target individual who usually make the identification. Research has shown that there are differences between these two scenarios. In familiar recognition, "internal" facial features (e.g., eyes, nose, mouth, etc.) seem to play the most significant role in face identification, while in unfamiliar identification the "external" features (e.g., jaw line, hairline, etc.) are relied upon more (Ellis *et al.* 1979, Hancock *et al.* 2000). Additionally, in familiar recognition, structural codes may be relied upon more than in pictorial codes, which form the basis for unfamiliar recognition (Bruce and Young 1986). Thus, the results of laboratory tests of facial-approximation recognition using unfamiliar scenarios may not be representative of results of familiar identification scenarios, which are representative of actual casework.

Current facial-approximation techniques rely mostly upon predicting face dimensions and shapes from the skull, while little attention is usually given to specific face colors and textures, since these features are deemed not to be determinable from the skull (at least at the present time). Facial-approximation techniques also rely heavily on general trends (often averages) for predicting soft-tissue characters, especially those with little association with the skull (see Evenhouse *et al.* 1990, and Chapter 6). The question of facial-approximation accuracy can, therefore, be addressed not by assessing the accuracy or success of traditional methods but by determining the ability for faces with exact dimensions and shapes, but average color and texture, to be recognized (best-case-scenario facial approximations). Such a test would determine the ceiling recognition rates for facial-approximation methods, as features considered to be *potentially* determinable from the skull with "close" accuracy (i.e., face shape) would be exactly represented while information regarded as not readily determinable from the skull could be objectively represented as averages (i.e., face color and texture information). Recognition tests of these best-case-scenario facial approximations would then indicate the maximum true positive recognition rates that any facial approximation could generally be expected to achieve, because these facial approximations are constructed objectively (using mathematical face averages) and replicate exact face shapes, something which cannot be achieved in current practice using traditional facial-approximation methods.

Facial approximations displaying exact face shapes but nonspecific color and texture information can be easily constructed using computer-graphic techniques. Here, computer-graphic methods of Perrett *et al.* (Benson and Perrett 1992, Penton-Voak *et al.* 1999, Perrett *et al.* 1994, Perrett *et al.* 1998, Perrett and Rowland 1995, Tiddeman *et al.* 2001) were adapted to construct two-dimensional (2D) facial approximations with exact frontal face shapes but with average color and texture information. These facial approximations were then tested for their "recognizability" in familiar and unfamiliar identification scenarios. This investigation is expected to indicate the ceiling-level recognition rates for 2D facial approximations, since exact face shapes cannot be represented in real practice and features not determinable from the skull (face color and texture) are objectively represented as averages rather than being subjectively determined. Since face shapes of living individuals were replicated here, skulls were not used in the construction of these facial approximations.

This study highlights an alternative role for computer-graphic techniques in facial approximation, in contrast to their commonly identified role for producing digital faces from skulls using soft-tissue prediction methods simulated on computers. The use of computer-graphic methods for constructing facial approximations nontraditionally (without skulls) to assess method accuracy and success holds advantages because "facial approximations" can be made for, and compared to, living subjects. This allows for antemortem images (here photographs) to be easily obtained for as many target individuals as necessary and under the exact conditions desired. Furthermore, it enables the constructed faces to be manipulated, under controlled conditions, relative to known target faces. Additionally, these computer-graphic methods enable some ethical concerns common to traditional research tests to be avoided—for example, the exposure of individuals who knew the deceased to further emotional trauma associated with additional visual identification procedures. Yet, these methods still enable tests of familiar identification to be conducted because living people are used. This latter aspect is significant because in forensic casework it is people familiar with the target individual who usually recognize the facial approximation. These aspects cannot be so easily achieved using recognition tests of facial approximations constructed from skulls.

11.1.1 GENERATION OF THE AVERAGE FACE

We used 130 standardized face photographs of females self-reporting the socially perceived group membership of "European" (mean age 22.3, sd 4.0 years), to generate average faces used here to represent the face color and texture of the constructed facial approximations. This average face was generated using the refined methods described in Chapter 6. The average female "European" face is presented below with its respective delineation map (Figure 11.1).

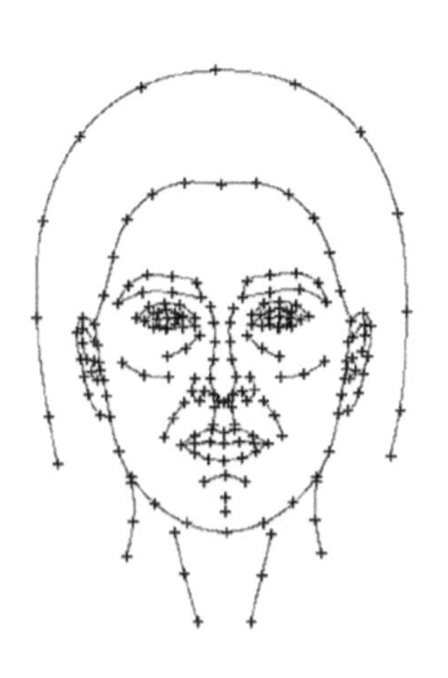

(a)

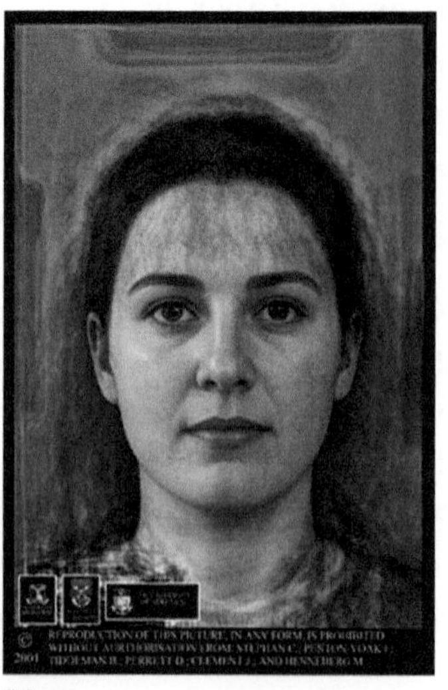

(b)

Figure 11.1

The average socially perceived European female face generated from 130 individuals. (a) The calculated average face shape to which individual face shapes are warped and color information blended. (b) The final average face after 130 face photographs of individuals had been warped and blended together.

WARPING OF THE AVERAGE FACE

Three female individuals (not included in the average), self-identifying as Europeans, from Melbourne Australia, were photographed and delineated as described in Chapter 6. The average face was then warped to the exact same frontal face shape for each of these three individuals using the averaging software developed by Perrett and colleagues (Benson and Perrett 1992, Penton-Voak *et al.* 1999, Perrett *et al.* 1994, Perrett *et al.* 1998, Perrett and Rowland 1995, Tiddeman *et al.* 2001); see Figure 11.2(b). Figures 11.2(a, c) show the original and the warped average faces (best-case-scenario facial approximations) for each target individual respectively. Two more facial approximations were generated according to methods described above using face photographs of two other individuals to test for false positives. These individuals were also from Melbourne, Australia. Thus, five best-case-scenario facial approximations were generated in total, including three whose target individuals were used to test for true positive recognitions and two whose target individual faces were used to test for false positive recognitions.

Two recognition tests were conducted. One was an unfamiliar scenario: the assessors did not know any of the individuals used in the study and tried to correctly identify the facial approximations by choosing individuals from a face pool (simultaneous face array or lineup). The other recognition test was a familiar scenario: the assessors knew the target individuals used in the study and attempted to identify the facial approximations from memory.

11.2 TRIALS OF UNFAMILIAR RECOGNITION

Forty-three assessors (27 females, mean age 22 years, sd 8 years; 16 males, mean age 30 years, sd 14 years) from Adelaide, Australia, who were unfamiliar with all faces—that is, they did not know any of the people whose faces were used in the experiment—took part in five recognition trials (one for each facial approximation). Assessors attempted to identify from a face pool the target individual whom the facial approximation represented. The face pool included six individuals from Melbourne, Australia (three target individuals and three nontarget individuals, Figure 11.3). The face pool was printed in color on Epson® Photo Quality Ink Jet Paper (matt) using an Epson® Stylus® 890 printer. Each face image measured 100 by 67 mm.

Since the experiment was primarily run during a University open day, trials were conducted, one at a time, in a set random order (facial approximation 1 first, then 2, then 3, etc., as indicated in Figure 11.2). This removed the need to randomly shuffle pictures, and increased the speed of participant throughput. Time was therefore traded for possible trial order effects,

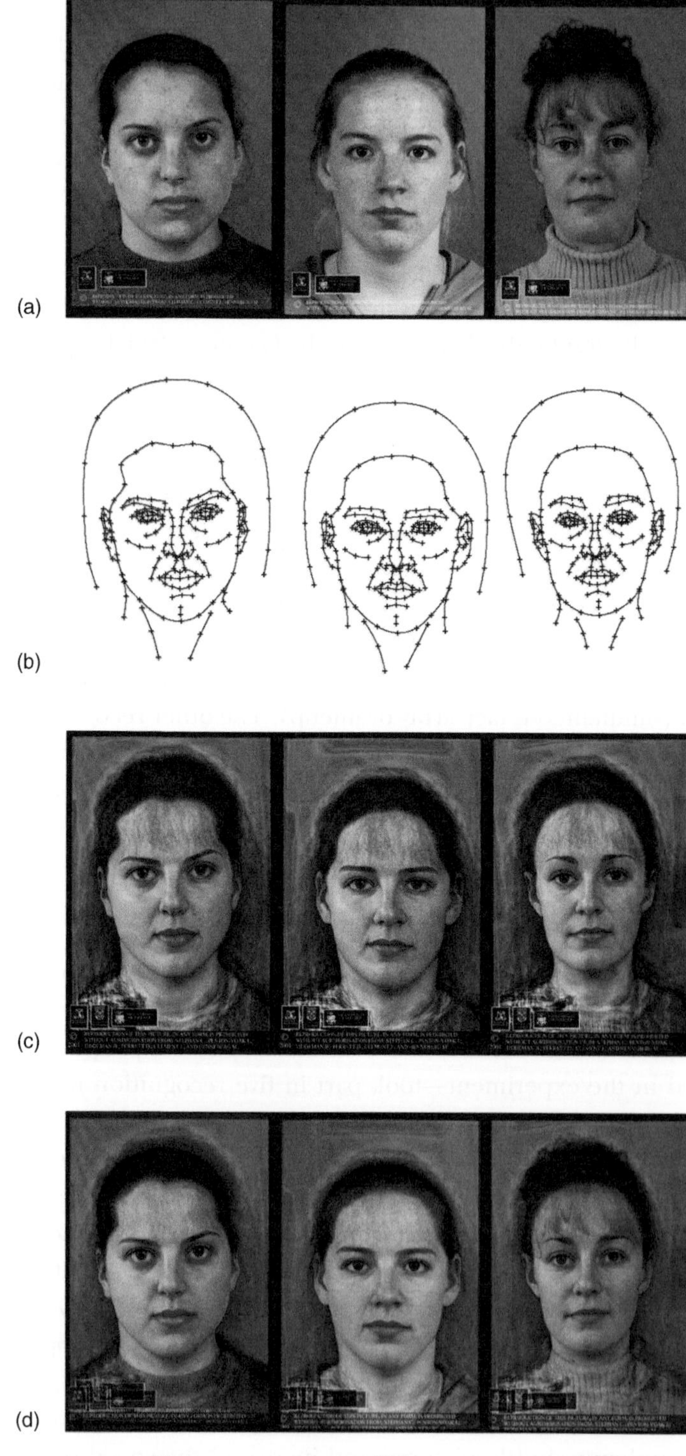

Figure 11.2

Generation of the best-case-scenario facial approximations whose target individuals were used for true positive recognition tests. (a) Actual photographs of the target individuals. (b) The delineations of face shapes for each individual. (c) The final facial approximations made by warping the color and texture information of the average face (Figure 11.1) to each individual's face shape. (d) The superimposition of the facial approximation with the original target face to demonstrate the exact replication of target individual face shapes.

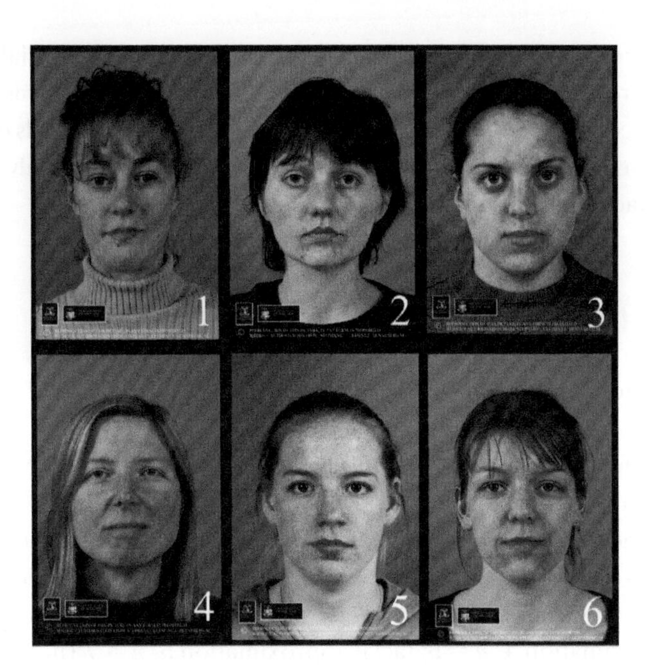

Figure 11.3

The face pool used in the tests of unfamiliar identification.

although such effects may be reduced since only five trials were conducted and no participant appeared to express fatigue. The three facial approximations with corresponding target individuals displayed in the face pool were numbers 1, 4, and 5, while the two "nontarget" facial approximations presented to test for false positives were numbers 2 and 3. Assessors were asked to examine a warped average face, compare it to the face pool, and attempt to make a correct identification, or indicate if they thought the target face was not present in the face pool. Assessors therefore had a 50% chance indicating if the "target" face was/was not present and an 8.3% chance of choosing any face in the face pool (50% chance that the face was there and a 16.7% (1/6) chance of choosing any one face from the six displayed: 50% × 16.7% = 8.3%).

A common face pool was used across recognition trials, so that the experimental procedure was simple, easily achieved by participants without constant investigator supervision, and so assessor throughput was rapid. This protocol is weaker than using new face pools for each trial, however, assessors were aware that facial-approximation methods include prediction error and that it was possible for two facial approximations that looked different to be of the same person or visa versa (i.e., two facial approximations while looking the same were of different people). Also, participants were unaware of how many different facial approximations (average facial warps) there were and if their respective target individual was, or was not, present in the face pool. Hence, each participant was forced to treat each trial independently. Results were evaluated to determine if assessors were choosing, on some occasions, the same face/s as those chosen in previous trials—an indication that facial approximations were actually being treated independently. This was the case in some instances (see results), apparently confirming the validity of protocols employed. Data were collated in the JMP® 4.0 statistical package and analyzed using Fisher's exact and Chi-squared tests ($p < 0.05$).

11.2.1 TRIALS OF FAMILIAR RECOGNITION

Ten assessors (mean age 22 years, sd 3 years) who personally knew *at least* one of target individuals included in the face pool for the trials of unfamiliar recognition also completed the 5 recognition trials. These trials differed from those for unfamiliar recognition since face pools were not used. Assessors were presented with each facial approximation and asked if they recognized whom the facial approximation characterized. A correct identification required participants to correctly name the person whom the facial approximation represented. Sample sizes of familiar assessors were: facial approximation 1, $n = 4$; facial approximation 4, $n = 5$; facial approximation 5, $n = 7$ (note that some individuals are included in more than one facial-approximation sample).

Nine assessors (mean age 30 years, sd 10 years) who knew at least one of the nontarget individuals included in the face pool used in the unfamiliar tests—namely the "distractor" faces (face pool photo 2, $n = 2$; face pool photo 4, $n = 7$; face pool photo 6, $n = 1$)—also completed the familiar recognition trials to help test for false-positive recognitions. All assessors indicated how long they had known the person in question and their relationship with that person.

11.3 RESULTS

11.3.1 UNFAMILIAR RECOGNITION

A considerable proportion (40%) of assessors identified the same face on one or more occasions for different facial approximations indicating that assessors did not necessarily discount a previously selected face for later trials even though the same face pool was used in all trials. This suggests that chance recognition rates were valid for later trials. Overall, there were 21 instances of repeated face selection, accounting for 42 identification responses, in a total of 215 recognition trials. Face-pool photo 1 (FPP1) was identified twice by twelve assessors; FPP2 twice by one assessor; FPP3 twice by three assessors; FPP4 twice by one assessor; FPP5 twice by one assessor; and FPP6 twice by three assessors. Facial approximations 3 and 5 (Figure 11.4) were the most frequently identified as representing the same face pool photo (FPP1; $n = 8$).

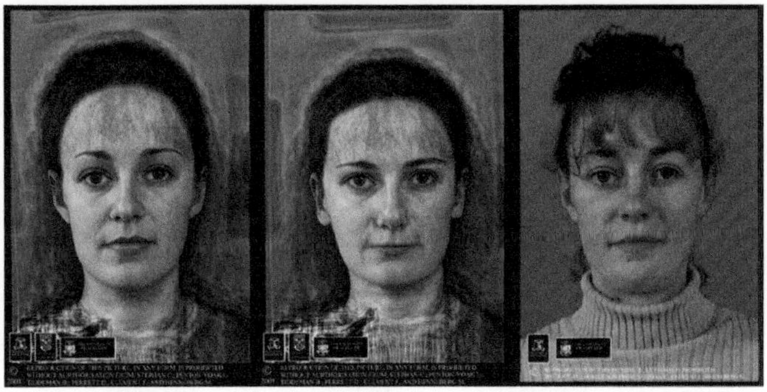

FA1 FA3 Target of FA5 (FPP1)

Figure 11.4
The facial approximations most frequently identified as the same target individual in unfamiliar identification.

Table 11.1 Summary table of recognition responses for each facial approximation in the trials of unfamiliar identification. Italicized rows indicate those facial approximations without target faces in the face pool. "NI" stands for "no identification response".

	No. assessors	% correct responses	% incorrect responses
FA1	43	44	56
FA2	*43*	*56(NI)*	*44*
FA3	*43*	*42(NI)*	*58*
FA4	43	28	72
FA5	43	56	44

Of the 129 identifications made when the target face was present in the face pool, 55 (43%) were true positive (correct) identifications, 36 (28%) were false positive (incorrect) identifications and the remainder consisted of 38 instances (29%) where no identification was (incorrectly) made (Table 11.1). Two of the three target faces were correctly identified above chance rates, $p < 0.05$ (Figure 11.5), the other being close to chance: $p < 0.07$. Facial approximation no. 5 (FA5) was identified the most accurately, with identification rates of 56%, which were statistically above chance rates (Fisher's exact test, $p < 0.001$). FA1 was correctly identified 44% of the time, which was also statistically above chance rates (Fisher's exact test, $p < 0.001$). FA4 was identified the least accurately, with identification rates of 28% (Fisher's exact test, $p < 0.07$). These results indicate that facial approximations displaying exact face shapes but average color and texture information may be correctly identified by unfamiliar assessors, but true positive recognition rates were not very high (average of ~43%), even though most were statistically significant.

In the two instances where target faces were not present (FA2 & FA3), identifications of the target face as not being present in the face pool were not significantly different from chance rates (Chi-squared test, $p > 0.05$, Figure 11.6). This indicates that, even though participants could correctly identify target individuals when present, they could not tell when target individuals were not present.

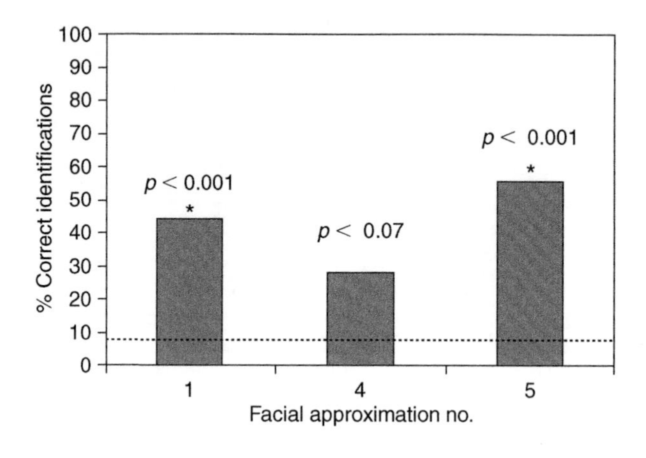

Figure 11.5

*True positive identification rates of facial approximations with target individuals: ········· indicates chance rate; * indicates statistical significance.*

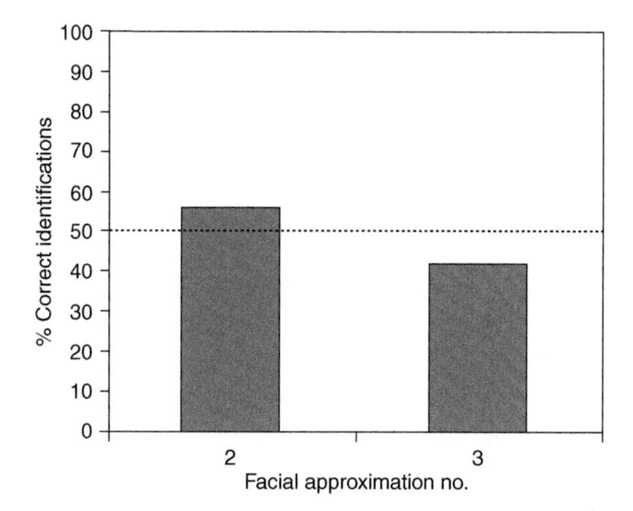

Figure 11.6

False positive identification rates of facial approximations without target individuals: ········· indicates chance rate.

FAMILIAR RECOGNITION

Of the three facial approximations represented by target individuals in the face pool for the unfamiliar trials, two were correctly identified (Table 11.2). Of the seven people familiar with the person represented by FA5, six made correct identifications (86%). Most of these assessors were colleagues of the target who had known her for three years. Of the five people familiar with the person represented by FA1, two made correct identifications (40%). Most of these assessors were friends of the target and had known her for about four years. It is worth noting that a sibling of the target who had known her for almost 20 years did not make a correct identification. Of the four people familiar with the person represented by FA4, none made correct identifications (0%). Most of these assessors had known the target for about two years but again a sibling who had known the target for almost 20 years did not make

Table 11.2 Summary table of recognition responses for people familiar with individuals included in the face pool. Italicized rows indicate responses by people familiar with individuals who were included in the face pool, but who were not used to construct facial approximations. "NI" stands for "no identification response". Note that a total of 10 individuals were used overall for familiar tests; some individuals knew more than one individual included in the face pool; one individual correctly identified a facial approximation not represented by a face in the face pool; and two individuals made incorrect identifications of facial approximations not represented by their respective faces in the face pool.

People familiar with...	No. assessors	No. correct responses	No. incorrect responses
FPP1 (corresponds to FA5)	7	6	1
FPP2	*6*	*6 (NI)*	*0*
FPP3 (corresponds to FA1)	5	2	3
FPP4	*7*	*7 (NI)*	*0*
FPP5 (corresponds to FA4)	4	0	4
FPP6	*1*	*1 (NI)*	*0*

	Unfamiliar	Familiar
FA1	44 (43)	40 (5)
FA4	28 (43)	0 (4)
FA5	56 (43)	86 (7)

Table 11.3 Summary table of the percentage correct in recognition responses for facial approximations with corresponding target faces in the face pool. Numbers in parentheses indicate total sample sizes.

a correct identification. No individuals familiar with the nontarget faces present in the face pool incorrectly identified any of the facial approximations.

Only two (2%) false positive identifications were made out of a total of 95 familiar responses. One assessor in the familiar testing scenario also correctly identified one of the "nontarget" facial approximations (a facial approximation not represented by a target face in the face pool used for unfamiliar testing).

COMPARISON BETWEEN TESTING SCENARIOS

Identification rates in the unfamiliar and familiar trials followed similar trends; however, the magnitude of the relative responses differed (Table 11.3). For example, in both familiar and unfamiliar scenarios, FA5 was correctly recognized the most, followed by FA1 and then FA4. However, FA5 was recognized considerably more reliably in the familiar identification (86%, total sample size 7) compared to the unfamiliar identification scenario (56%, total sample size 43). FA1 was recognized at similar rates in both scenarios: 40% (total sample size 5) in familiar compared to 44% (total sample size 43) in unfamiliar scenarios. FA4 was recognized much less in familiar scenarios (0%, total sample size 4) than in unfamiliar scenarios (28%, total sample size 43). Average recognition rates were similar between testing scenarios, being 42% for familiar and 43% for unfamiliar.

11.4 DISCUSSION

The results from the trials of unfamiliar and familiar recognition both generally indicate that best-case-scenario facial approximations (those displaying exact face shapes and dimensions but nonspecific face color and texture) promote facial recognition of the majority of target individuals, however, recognition rates are generally low: an average of 43%. The results also demonstrated that a large range of recognition success exists for individual facial approximations: some being recognized well and others hardly at all. However, the effect of testing conditions (familiar or unfamiliar) does not seem to be all that large generally: both conditions follow similar trends. Despite findings that many assessors repeated identifications for the same faces in the face pools used in the unfamiliar scenario, possible trial order effects for this group must be acknowledged. Therefore, it seems that the results of the familiar tests are more robust and perhaps should be given higher interpretative weighting.

Since exact face shapes constructed here using computer-graphic methods cannot be represented in casework facial approximation, the recognition rates observed are expected to be *dramatically* higher than those that would be obtained in general facial-approximation practice. This expectation seems to be supported by the literature, since systematic tests of traditional methods (Snow *et al.* 1970, Stephan and Henneberg 2001, van Rensburg 1993) generally report rates that are less than 48% above chance (the highest rate obtained in this study using tests of unfamiliar recognition). We also suspect that the average success rate of 43% found in this study for both familiar and unfamiliar scenarios may be skewed by the results of FA5, which appears to be a distinctive face (Figure 11.7). Greater ease of recognition when faces are distinctive is a well-recognized phenomenon in the literature (Benson and Perrett 1991, Bruce and Young 1998, Rhodes *et al.* 1987). In the tests of familiar identification, FA5 was identified at a recognition level twice that above the next-highest facial approximation. Since most people tend toward average face characters rather than toward extreme ends of variation, it appears that high recognition rates observed for distinctive faces may be less frequent in larger samples, that is, distinctive faces in smaller samples are likely to inflate recognition results. Consequently, the recognition rates of traditionally constructed facial approximations may be even less than that indicated by the results of this study.

Although the reliability of the facial-approximation method to achieve true positive recognitions in this study was rather high—that is, facial approximations were correctly recognized at least once in five out of six trials—the reliability in practice for traditional methods is probably much less. Even though true positive recognitions were generated in this experiment, recognition rates were close to 50% above chance on average. This indicates that, if one

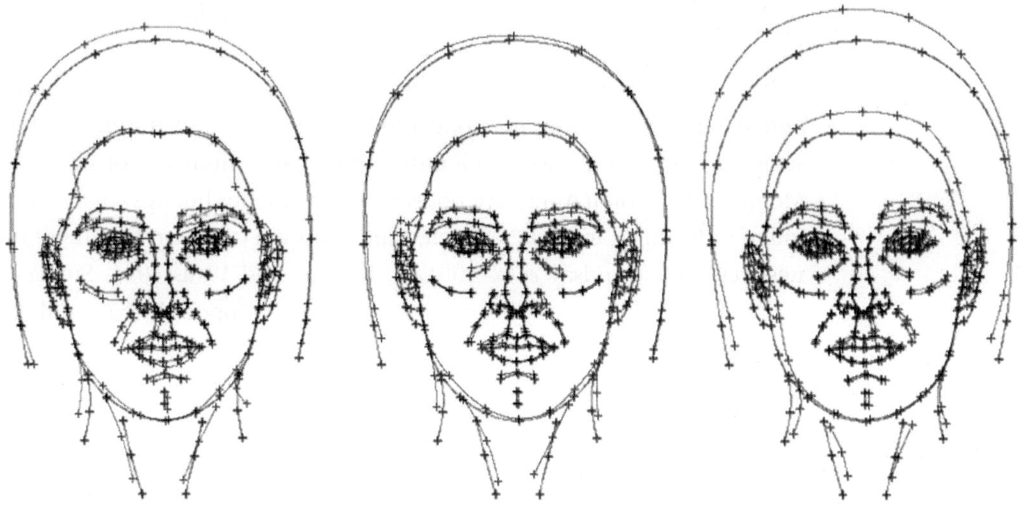

FA1 FA4 FA5

Figure 11.7 Superimpositions of the delineation maps of the target individuals (red) over the average (blue) to demonstrate distinctiveness. The average template has been rescaled according to interpupillary distance for each target individual. Images have been superimposed and aligned on the eyes. FA1 and FA4 show the least deviation from the average, while FA5 shows a relatively greater amount of deviation away from the average (compare hairlines, eyebrows, ears, jaw line, and neck lines).

person said that they recognized the facial approximation, then no reliable conclusion could be made if they were right or wrong. However, all facial approximations were identified at least once, except FA4 in the familiar tests, indicating that most had the potential to be identified in a forensic environment even if this result was due to chance alone. It should also be noted that successful recognition in the laboratory does not necessarily mean that the facial approximation will be recognized in the field, since laboratory tests exclude additional variables like the broadness of media coverage and who sees the media reports etc. (Haglund 1998).

Trends seen in the trials of unfamiliar recognition were also generally followed for familiar recognition, despite apparent differences in recognition or matching strategies employed (see the Introduction). The similar results obtained between the two testing scenarios conducted here suggest that unfamiliar individuals are useful in evaluating facial-approximation accuracy even though facial approximations are usually recognized by familiar individuals. This is significant for laboratory tests of traditional manual facial approximations since testing of familiar individuals can be problematic.

A limitation of testing unfamiliar subjects, indicated by this study, is that false positive identifications appear to be significantly increased in comparison with tests of familiar ones, at least when using face-pool protocols. Therefore, the previous suggestion that small but significant recognition rates by unfamiliar subjects of facial approximations (e.g., 8%) may not prove to be useful in real life, because many false positive identifications may be generated (Henneberg and Stephan 2001), does not appear to be true since familiar individuals rarely seem to make false positive identifications. Large numbers of false positive identifications when using face pools (or simultaneous lineups) in tests of unfamiliar individuals are to be expected since this is a common finding of eyewitness research (Lindsay *et al.* 1991a,b, Lindsay and Wells 1985, Steblay *et al.* 2001). Using sequential presentation methods as opposed to a simultaneous method may reduce false positive identifications, since assessors are forced to rely on more absolute criteria (i.e., is this the target individual or not?) rather than the relative criteria (which face looks most like the facial approximation?); see Lindsay *et al.* 1991a,b, Lindsay and Wells 1985, Steblay *et al.* 2001. However, it may be that facial approximations constructed using current methods are too ambiguous for assessors to choose a face in a sequential lineup: the facial approximations may not look similar enough to any of the faces to be identified. Such an effect would clearly indicate that facial-approximation techniques are not very accurate, but would also demonstrate the limited use of assessing facial-approximation accuracy using sequential lineup methods, even if this approach reduces false positive identifications. Further research in this area is needed with respect to facial approximation.

Using average face color to construct facial approximations in two dimensions is somewhat limited because some face shapes are not well represented from the skull in particular views. For example, in front views, the prominence of the cheekbones and nasal bridge are encoded mainly in the luminance information ("shape-from-shading": Cavanagh and Leclerc 1989), and is essentially rendered as average when average faces are stretched to fit a frontal-view shape, no matter how prominent the underlying zygomatic bones may be. Artistic representation may be more accurate in producing luminance values that reflect shapes indicative of the underlying bony structure, and hence accuracy and recognition may be higher if these subjective methods are used. However, it needs to be noted that such subjective interpretation is unlikely to be exact and may even be further away from reality than objective representation of these shapes using averages. Irrespectively, good approximation of the shape-from-shading information of the target individual appears to be produced here by using averages (see Figure 11.2). It also seems worth noting that, in traditional 2D facial approximations, the inclusion of soft-tissue depths that are not perpendicular to the line of view (e.g., those that project anteriorly in frontal views) are of little use in predicting face shape since the actual soft-tissue depths cannot be seen and subjective interpretation is needed to represent the shape from shading. Thus, any rendering of face contours by shading over these depths is entirely subjective, and the inclusion of these soft-tissue depth markers gives misleading impressions of methodological accuracy and rigor.

11.5 SUMMARY

Computer-graphic methods can be applied to facial approximation, not just for constructing facial approximations from skulls in digital formats, but also for constructing faces of living individuals that enable research of the usefulness of the facial-approximation method itself. Here we described a 2D approach that enables the determination of the highest recognition rates that objectively constructed 2D facial approximations can be expected to ever reasonably achieve, given the limits of current methods. By warping average face color and texture to exact frontal face shapes, we artificially created the most objective and exact facial approximations possible for several individuals, as exact face shapes cannot be replicated in normal facial approximation practice. Recognition tests (unfamiliar and familiar scenarios) of these best-case-scenario facial approximations reveal a broad range of recognition success, but on average such facial approximations were recognized correctly about 43% of the time. Two-dimensional facial approximations constructed manually, using traditional soft-tissue prediction methods are therefore expected to be recognized at *much* lower rates, since exact face shapes cannot be replicated in real casework. We also suspect that one of the target individuals approximated here possessed a rather distinctive face, which given the small sample of the study, may have skewed the results toward higher rates of recognition. Therefore, the recognition success of traditionally constructed facial approximations may be even less than that expected from results described here. Irrespectively, the recognition rates of facial approximations displaying exact 2D frontal face shapes were generally low. The lack of above-chance recognition of some approximations does not augur well for facial approximations constructed using traditional methods where exact face shapes of target individuals are unknown.

ACKNOWLEDGEMENTS

Special thanks go to those participants who consented to the display of their photographs in this chapter.

REFERENCES

Benson P. and Perrett D. (1992) "Face to Face With the Perfect Image", *New Scientist,* 22nd February, 26–29.

Benson P. J. and Perrett D. I. (1991) "Perception and Recognition of Photographic Quality Facial Caricatures: Implications for the Recognition of Natural Images", *Eur. J. Cognitive Psychol.* 3, 105–135.

Bruce V. and Young A. (1986) "Understanding Face Recognition", *Br. J. Psychol.* 77, 305–327.

Bruce V. and Young A. (1998) *In the Eye of the Beholder*. Oxford University Press, New York.

Brues A. M. (1958) "Identification of Skeletal Remains", *J. Criminal Law Criminology Police Science* 48, 551–556.

Cavanagh P. and Leclerc Y. G. (1989) "Shape from Shadows", *J. Exp. Psychol. Hum. Percept. Perform.* 15, 3–27.

Cherry D. G. and Angel J. L. (1977) "Personality Reconstruction from Unidentified Remains", *FBI Law Enforcement Bull.* 46, 12–15.

Ellis H. D., Shepherd J. W. and Davies G. M. (1979) "Identification of Familiar and Unfamiliar Faces from Internal and External Features: Some Implications for Theories of Face Recognition", *Perception* 8, 431–439.

Evenhouse R., Rasmussen M., and Sadler L. (1990) "Computer Aided Forensic Facial Approximation", *Biostereometric Technology and Applications* 1380, 147–156.

Farrar F. (1977) "From Skull to Visage: A Forensics Technique for Facial Restoration", *The Police Chief* 44, 78–80.

Gatliff B. P. and Snow C. C. (1979) "From Skull to Visage", *J. Biocommun.* 6, 27–30.

George R. M. (1993) "Anatomical and Artistic Guidelines for Forensic Facial Reconstruction", in: *Forensic Analysis of the Skull* (M. Y. İşcan and R. P. Helmer, eds.). Wiley-Liss, New York, pp. 215–227.

Gerasimov M. (1971) *The Face Finder* (A. H. Brodrick, Trans.). Hutchinson & Co, London.

Haglund W. D. (1998) "Forensic 'Art' in Human Identification", in: *Craniofacial Identification in Forensic Medicine* (J. G. Clement and D. L. Ranson, eds.). Arnold, London, pp. 235–243.

Haglund W. D. and Reay D. T. (1991) "Use of Facial Approximation Techniques in Identification of Green River Serial Murder Victims", *Am. J. Forensic Med. Pathol.* 12, 132–142.

Hancock P. J. B., Bruce V. and Burton A. M. (2000) "Recognition of Unfamiliar Faces", *Trends in Cognitive Sciences* 4, 330–337.

Helmer R. P., Rohricht S., Petersen D. and Mohr F. (1993) "Assessment of the Reliability of Facial Reconstruction", in: *Forensic Analysis of the Skull* (M. Y. İşcan and R. P. Helmer, eds.). Wiley-Liss, New York, pp. 229–246.

Krogman W. M. (1946) "The Reconstruction of the Living Head from the Skull", *FBI Law Enforcement Bull.* 17, 11–17.

Lindsay R. C. L., Lea J. A. and Fulford J. A. (1991a) "Sequential Lineup Presentation: Technique Matters", *J. Appl. Psychol.* 76, 741–745.

Lindsay R. C. L., Lea J. A., Nosworthy G. J., Fulford J. A., Hector J., LeVan V. and Seabrook C. (1991b) "Biased Lineups: Sequential Presentation Reduces the Problem", *J. Appl. Psychol.* 76, 796–802.

Lindsay R. C. L. and Wells G. L. (1985) "Improving Eyewitness Identifications from Lineups: Simultaneous Versus Sequential Lineup Presentation", *J. Appl. Psychol.* 70, 556–564.

Maat G. J. R. (1998–1999) "Facial Reconstruction: A Review and Comment", *TALANTA* 30–31, 247–253.

Montagu M. F. A. (1947) "A Study of Man Embracing Error", *Technology Review* 49, 345–347.

Penton-Voak I. S., Perrett D. I., Castles D. L., Kobayashi T., Burt D. M., Murray L. K. and Minamisawa R. (1999) "Menstral Cycle Alters Face Preference", *Nature* 399, 741–742.

Perper J. A., Patterson G. T. and Backner J. S. (1988) "Face Imaging Reconstructive Morphography: A New Method for Physiognomic Reconstruction", *Am. J. Forensic Med. Pathol.* 9, 126–138.

Perrett D. I., Lee K. J., Penton-Voak I., Rowland D., Yoshikawa S., Burt D. M., Henzill S. P., Castles D. L. and Akamatsu S. (1998) "Effects of Sexual Dimorphism on Facial Attractiveness", *Nature* 394, 884–887.

Perrett D. I., May K. A. and Yoshikawa S. (1994) "Facial Shape and Judgements of Female Attractiveness", *Nature* 368, 239–242.

Phillips V. M., Rosendorff S. and Scholtz H. J. (1996) "Identification of a Suicide Victim by Facial Reconstruction", *J. Forensic Sci.* 14, 34–38.

Prag J. and Neave R. (1997) *Making Faces: Using Forensic and Archaeological Evidence.* British Museum Press, London.

Rathbun T. A. (1984) "Personal Identification: Facial Reproductions", in: *Human Identification: Case Studies in Forensic Anthropology* (T. Rathbun and J. Buikstra, eds.). Charles C. Thomas, Springfield, IL, pp. 347–362.

Rhodes G., Brennan S. and Carey S. (1987) "Identification and Ratings of Caricatures: Implications for Mental Representations of Faces", *Cog. Psychol.* 19, 473–497.

Rowland D. A. and Perrett D. I. (1995) "Manipulating Facial Appearance Through Shape and Color", *IEEE* 15, 70–76.

Rubin S. (1998) "Murder, he Sculpted", *Reader's Digest* 62–67.

Snow C. C., Gatliff B. P. and McWilliams K. R. (1970) "Reconstruction of Facial Features from the Skull: An Evaluation of its Usefulness in Forensic Anthropology", *Am. J. Phys. Anthropol.* 33, 221–228.

Steblay N., Dysart J., Fulero S. and Lindsay R. C. L. (2001) "Eyewitness Accuracy Rates in Sequential and Simultaneous Lineup Presentations: A Meta-analytic Comparison", *Law and Human Behavior* 25, 459–473.

Stephan C. and Henneberg M. (2001) "Building Faces from Dry Skulls: Are They Recognized Above Chance Rates?", *J. Forensic Sci.* 46, 432–440.

Stephan C. (2002a) "Do Resemblance Ratings Measure the Accuracy of Facial Approximations?", *J. Forensic Sci.* 47, 239–243.

Stephan C. N. (2002b) "Facial Approximation: Falsification of Globe Projection Guideline by Exophthalmometry Literature", *J. Forensic Sci.* 47, 1–6.

Stephan C. N. (2003) "Facial Approximation: An Evaluation of Mouth-Width Determination", *Am. J. Phys. Anthropol.* 121, 48–57.

Stewart T. D. (1979a) *Essentials of Forensic Anthropology: Especially as Developed in the United States.* Charles C. Thomas, Springfield, IL.

Stewart T. D. (1979b) "Reconstruction of the Facial Soft Parts", in: *Essentials of Forensic Anthropology* (T. D. Stewart, ed.). Charles C. Thomas, Springfield, IL, pp. 255–274.

Stoney M. B. and Koelmeyer T. D. (1999) "Facial Reconstruction: A Case Report and Review of Development of Techniques", *Med. Sci. Law* 39, 49–60.

Suk V. (1935) "Fallacies of Anthropological Identifications", *Publications de la Facultae des Sciences de l'Universitae Masaryk* 207, 3–18.

Suzuki T. (1973) "Reconstitution of a Skull", *International Criminal Police Review* 264, 76–80.

Taylor K. T. (2001) *Forensic Art and Illustration*. CRC Press, Boca Raton.

Tiddeman B., Burt M. and Perrett D. (2001) "Prototyping and Transforming Facial Textures for Perception Research", *IEEE Computer Graphics and Applications* 21, 42–50.

van Rensburg J. (1993) "Accuracy of Recognition of 3-dimensional Plastic Reconstruction of Faces from Skulls", in: *Anatomical Society of Southern Africa*, p. 20. Game Reserve, Krugersdorp.

von Eggeling H. (1913) "Die Leistungsfahigkeit Physiognomischer Rekonbstruktionsversuche auf Grundlage des Schadels", *Archiv für Anthropologie* 12, 44–47.

Wilkinson C. M. and Whittaker D. K. (2002) "Juvenile Forensic Facial Reconstruction – A Detailed Accuracy Study". Paper presented at *the 10th Biennial* Scientific *Meeting of the International Association for Craniofacial Identification, Bari.*

CHAPTER 12

UTILIZATION OF 3D CEPHALOMETRIC FINITE-ELEMENT MODELING FOR MEASURING HUMAN FACIAL SOFT-TISSUE THICKNESS

B. Kusnoto and C. A. Evans

Department of Orthodontics, University of Illinois at Chicago, Chicago, Illinois 60612, USA

S. Poernomo and P. Sahelangi

Department of Forensic Science, Medical and Dental Division of Bhayangkara Police Headquarters, Ujung Pandang, Indonesia

12.1 INTRODUCTION

Sophisticated methods in mapping both facial soft tissue and skeletal structures have been developed for different purposes in computerized craniofacial analysis. Mapping of human craniofacial soft tissues and skeletal structures has been developed using various methods such as laser scanning, stereophotogrammetry, photographic systems, light digitizers, spatial digitizers, optoelectronic devices, and computerized tomography. These methods have been used to derive 3D measurements and modeling of hard and soft tissues of the human head.

A noninvasive, economical, yet reliable method for measuring human facial skeletal structure has been developed in the past. Recently attempts to correlate the underlying skeletal structure with the facial soft tissue by means of 3D computer modeling has been developed and packaged in computer software: 3DCeph.NET™ (Kusnoto *et al.* 2000).

Recently, utilization of laser surface scanners has become popular. By triangulating distances on the path of a laser beam reflected from the scanned surface, the surface laser scanner is able to detect not only the length and width of an object but also its depth. Its ease of use has opened various possibilities in laboratory research as well as clinical investigation. Assessment of the reliability of generating 3D object reconstructions by utilizing the Minolta Vivid700 3D surface laser scanner was done. Accuracy and reproducibility were tested for facial, dental, and skeletal scanning. Tests were conducted at varying distances between the object and the scanner. (Telcordia Technologies 2002). Starting in the late 1990s, companies have shown interest in developing 3D digital simulations of dental casts as an aid in orthodontic treatment and to replace plaster casts for ease of storage. Companies such as OrthoCAD™, GeoDigm™, SureSmile™, and Invisalign™ have made significant progress in developing computer algorithms to allow orthodontists to manipulate 3D digital data of the dentition in a more precise manner. Yet work still has to be done in perfecting the integration between 3D digital data of skeletal, facial, and dental modeling, as well as incorporating finite-element data on soft-tissue characteristics, muscle tension, and load under function in order to build a more complete simulation of the patient's facial characteristics.

With the rapid development of Internet information technology (IIT), Internet connectivity between research centers, institutions, private companies, and individuals has become more transparent. In August 2002, 75 000 000 hosts along with 171 000 000 users were found in the United States alone, with 174 199 million hosts and 840 695 million users worldwide. Most physicians connect to the Internet on a daily basis, and 42% work in practices that have Web sites, according to current research. IIT has become very popular in the medical and dental professions as a result of the introduction of new information technologies for browsing in journals and scientific literature, ordering equipment from suppliers, performing online consultations, accessing association Web sites, and communicating with other professionals. Physicians and dentists increasingly depend on computerization and the Internet (Kusnoto and Evans 2002).

Most cephalometric diagnostic systems currently on the market are based on client–server networking or just in a stand-alone computer. The software application will be installed in each terminal, whereas data can be either stored in terminals or in the server (main computer). On the contrary, the model described in this article (3DCeph.NET™) is based on the "metaframe". In this client–server model, both the software application and data reside in the main computer (server). An office administrator has full control of maintaining and securing the data, which complies with HIPAA regulation (Health Insurance Portability and Accountability Act of 1996) in which patient data can only be accessed by authorized personnel. The management office system described in this article was modeled after ASP (Application Service Provider) which enables the management office application and software and its data to be kept in a secure system, but at the same time allows authorized access from any computer terminal linked to an intranet or the Internet system. The ASP office management system allows every authorized terminal in the system to access the 3DCeph.NET software application and the database without installing anything in the terminal itself. This feature reduces installation time while effectively setting up the application in each terminal in the network.

The advantage of having the system easily adapted to intranet or Internet protocol allows full integration of the orthodontic practice or office. It can grow and yet easily be managed with increased security by adopting an integrated online ASP system facilitated by intranet or Internet technology (Kusnoto 2002).

12.2 MATERIALS AND METHOD

The purpose of this study is to develop a noninvasive, economical, and reliable method for measuring human facial soft-tissue thickness using 3D finite-element modeling. Custom computer software (3DCeph™ 2000, Department of Orthodontics, University of Illinois, Chicago, Illinois) using a stereophotogrammetry algorithm has been found to be accurate to 1.5 mm for linear measurements.

From 38 hard-tissue main landmarks and 36 soft-tissue main landmarks, 97 hard-tissue vectors, and 159 soft-tissue vectors were constructed (see Table 12.1). Soft-tissue thicknesses were calculated in fifteen places: orbit (2 places), forehead, zygoma (2 places), temporal region (2 places), cheek (2 places), nose, maxillary complex, upper lip, mandibulary complex, lower lip, and chin (see Table 12.2).

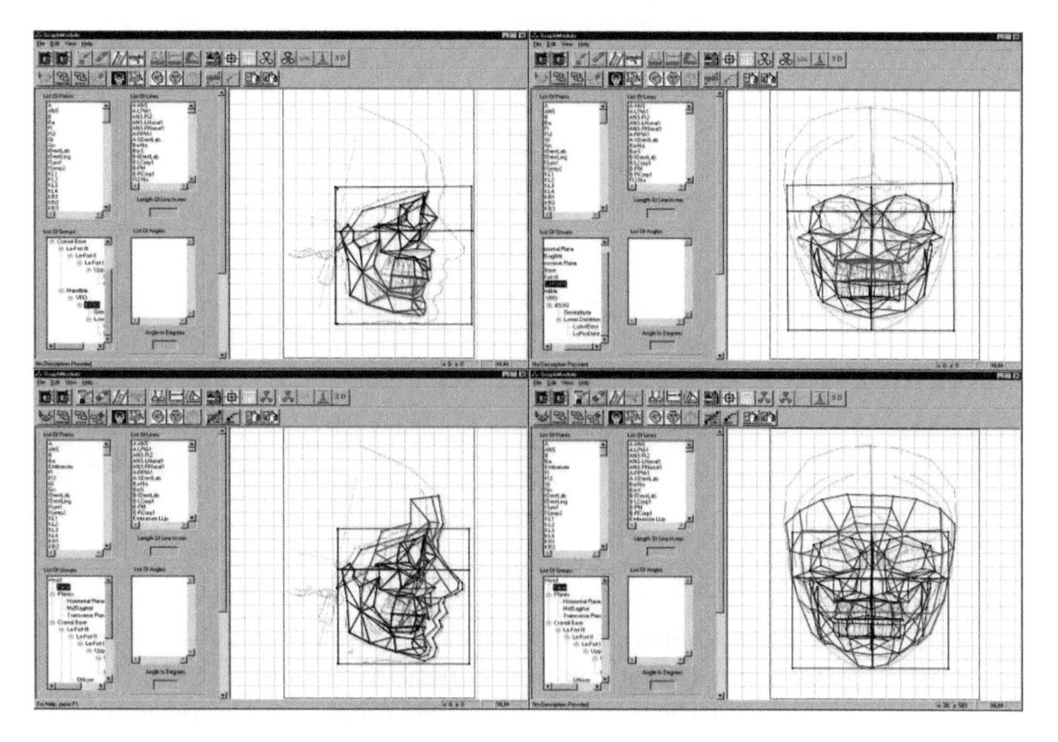

Figure 12.1 3DCeph.2000/3DCeph.NET™ integration module.

Table 12.1

List of 38 hard-tissue and 36 soft-tissue landmarks used to generate a 3D wire frame.

1. Right supraorbitale at the level of soft-tissue glabella
2. Soft-tissue glabella
3. Left supraorbitale at the level of soft-tissue glabella
4. Nasal tip
5. Nasal base
6. Upper lip
7. Lower lip
8. Soft-tissue B
9. Soft-tissue pogonion
10. Right maxillary points located on the cheek one-fourth of the distance between the right and left alar and right and left tragus, respectively
11. Right cheek point located on the cheek one-quarter of the distance between the right and left commissure and right and left tragus points
12. Left maxillary points located on the cheek one-fourth of the distance between the right and left alar and right and left tragus
13. Left cheek point located on the cheek one-quarter of the distance between the right and left commissure and right and left tragus points
14. Left tragus
15. Right tragus
16. Left commissure of the mouth
17. Right commissure of the mouth
18. Left alar
19. Right alar
20. Right gonion angle
21. Left gonion angle
22. Right antigonial notch
23. Left antigonial notch
24. Soft-tissue A point
25. Soft-tissue B point
26. Soft-tissue menton
27. Soft-tissue gnathion
28. Soft-tissue nasion
29. Soft-tissue R infraorbitale
30. Soft-tissue L infraorbitale
31. Soft-tissue R supraorbitale
32. Soft-tissue L supraorbitale
33. Inner R canthus
34. Inner L canthus
35. Outer R canthus
36. Outer L canthus
37. Upper incisor tip
38. Lower incisor tip

Hard tissue has the same number of basic/main landmarks as the soft tissue but with the addition of upper and lower central incisor tips (as projected to upper and lower lips).

Table 12.2

List of regions constructed from a 3D wire frame.

Region no.	Abbreviation	Description
1	FH1	Forehead 1
2	FH2	Forehead 2
*3	FH3	Forehead 3
*4	TM	Temple
5	NB	Nasal bridge
6	EB	Eyebrow
7	EL	Eyelid
8	CN	Canthus
*9	OR	Orbit
*10	ZG	Zygomatic
*11	CK	Cheek
12	NS	Nasal saddle
*13	TN	Tip of the nose
14	AC	Acanthion
*15	CL	Columella
*16	UL	Upper lip
*17	LL	Lower lip
*18	LJ	Lower jaw and angle of the mouth
19	CH	Chin
20	NK	Neck

* Measured for reliability and accuracy.

Eleven proportions between hard- and soft-tissue measurements were also used, including the ratio between nasal base aperture to cheilion, interpupillary distance to cheilion, and left and right margin of orbital rim to ectocanthion–endocanthion distance.

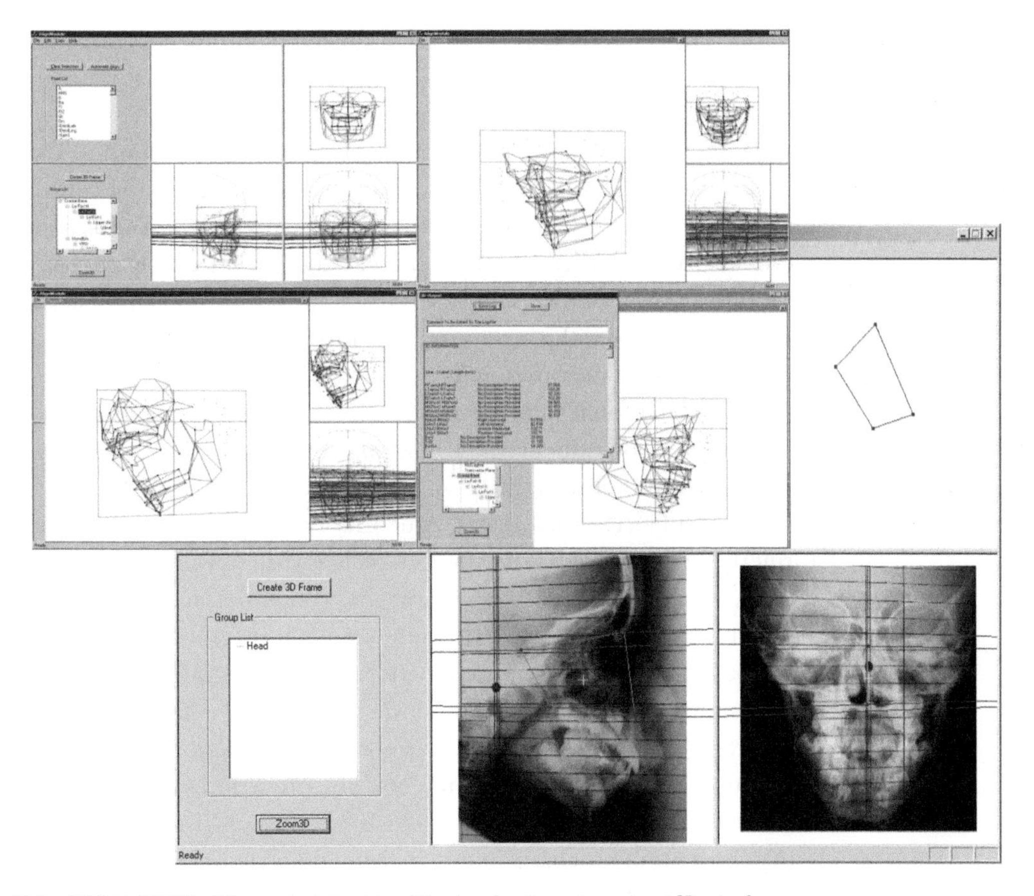

Figure 12.2 3DCeph.NET™ utilizes vector intercept and landmarks aligner to construct 3D wire frame.

Frontal and profile photographs of a subject's face labeled with six radiopaque markers made of lead foil were taken at a standardized distance. Two markers (round) were placed on the midsagittal line (glabella and pogonion), two markers (triangle) were placed on the right side of the face (supraorbitale and gonion angle), and the other two markers (square) were placed on the left side of the face (supraorbitale and gonion angle). At the same visit, lateral and anteroposterior cephalometric radiographs were taken with all radiopaque markers still in place. Radiographs and photographs were scanned into the computer.

Commercial computer-graphic software (Adobe Photoshop™) was used to scale the radiographs and photographs to the same magnification and superimpose one image on top of the other. Then, 3DCeph™ 2000 computer software loaded on a standard PC was used to digitize and correlate landmarks seen from different perspectives or projections and convert the 2D location of each landmark into its 3D spatial coordinates (x, y, z). (see Figure 12.2).

From those landmarks and their spatial coordinates, 3D wire-frame meshes can be established by connecting the landmarks in a triangular fashion to create a surface composed of multiple units. Finite-element modeling can be obtained following the creation of the wire-frame meshes. Using the six radiopaque markers, small errors due to head positioning can be minimized as the precision of corresponding hard-to-soft-tissue structures is increased, because these markers can be adjusted separately in their spatial locations. Lastly, soft-tissue thickness from any hard-tissue landmarks can be precisely measured within an accuracy of 1.5–2.0 mm, similar to computerized-tomography (CT) measurements.

Three-dimensional imaging has progressed from the Bolton–Broadbent cephalometer (Broadbent 1931) and 3D cephalometric computer software to the advanced CT-scan, MRI, and ultrasound 3D imaging. To fully reproduce the subject's anatomical structure three-dimensionally, technology formerly thought of as science fiction, such as virtual reality, holographic projection, and stereolithography now has potential in daily application. Radiography has been used to study craniofacial growth, but radiation is potentially harmful. CT scans are better for acquiring 3D information about the craniofacial complex, but the level of radiation is too high for routine use. Other 3D devices such as ultrasonic machines and 3D cameras require calibration and additional attachments. The procedures can become quite a challenge in clinical trials.

Assessments of facial asymmetry in living individuals have been performed two-dimensionally, resulting in lost data because complex 3D structures were projected onto flat 2D surfaces. Improvements on classic anthropometric linear and angular measurements include the use of optoelectronic systems, Moiré stripes, stereophotogrammetry, and laser scanners; these enable us to analyze 3D data involving surface area with mathematical methods such as Fourier series, euclidean distance matrix, and Ferrario's asymmetry vector (Ferrario *et al.* 2001). Three-dimensional facial landmarks used by Ferrario *et al.* (2001) and Weeden *et al.* (2001) include supraciliary points above the most superior aspect of the eyebrow, the midnose point located on the midline of the nasal bridge, middle interciliary point, nasal tip, commissure point, cheek point, and chin point. Data can be gained for studying asymmetrical facial structures, functional and facial soft-tissue movements and also differential facial growth. Berkowitz (1999) and Ishikawa (1999) studied the development of a repair to cleft lip and palate, via a 3D approach. They utilized a scanning device that analyzes movement of the cleft segments in space.

The Minolta Vivid700 3D Laser Surface Scanner operates by using a Class II laser, with $\lambda = 685$ nm at 25 mW, beam spread angle (2λ) of 21° horizontally and 0.1° vertically, object-to-scanner distance from 0.6 m to 2.5 m with the field of view 70 mm to 1100 mm, and scanning time of 0.6 seconds. The scanner utilized a half-inch frame transfer CCD, 380 000 pixels for its 3D data, and similar specification for the color CCD data. The scanner's output data are 200 × 200 × 256 for 3D and 400 × 400 for the color data. The total weight of the device is 9 kg (Minolta 2000). Spatial linear measurements were taken manually, using a caliper accurate to 0.5 mm. Each measurement was conducted twice at two different times, two days apart, and the average value was used.

12.2.1 TESTING THE METHOD

TESTING OF THE CALIBRATED GEOMETRICAL CYLINDER

A calibrated geometrical cylinder with the height of 141 mm and width of 46 mm was used and tested at two different times (T1 and T2) at exactly the same distance between the object and capture lens of the scanner (90 cm at zoom level 4, or a 25-mm lens). At each time point, data were obtained from 10 trials, and average values were calculated. At T3, the object was zoomed at zoom level 5 (46-mm lens) and 10 trials were obtained. At T4, the object was zoomed at zoom level 4 (25-mm lens) with a 70-cm distance from object to capture lens.

TESTING ON A DENTAL STUDY CAST

A dental study cast was scanned at two different times and two different object-to-scanner distances (T1 at 70 cm and T2 at 90 cm) both with the zoom level 4 (25-mm) lens. The intermolar width was measured from the intersection of the upper first molar palatal groove and the palatal gingival margin (point iL and iR for left and right side respectively), and was repeated 10 times for both T1 and T2. Palatal vault depth was measured as a perpendicular distance from midpoint between iL and iR to the midpalatal raphe (mr). For each time, T1 and T2, the measurement was repeated 10 times. Black markers were placed in point iL, iR, and mr to eliminate landmark identification error of the measured distances. For every scanning, we dismantled the scanning setting and recreated it again to be able to measure the error in the whole method, thus providing us with overall accuracy of the method. For each exposure, three different angulations (−45°, 0°, and 45°) relative to the occlusal surface were taken in order to overcome the undercut surface. Vivid700 3D software was then used to merge the three views and produce full 3D data of the model (see Figure 12.3).

TESTING ON A SILICONE FACIAL MODEL

A silicone model was made by using forensic technique on a human dried skull (see Figure 12.4). The model was also used to assess the reliability of 3DCeph2000™ software to assess the 3D soft-tissue thickness in order to relate

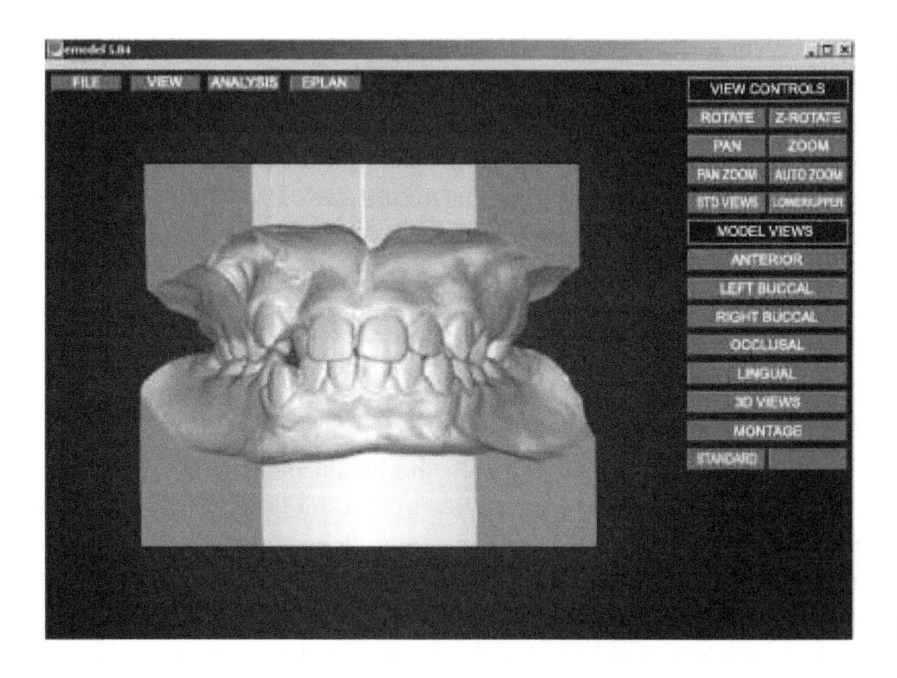

Figure 12.3

Sample of three-dimensional dental model (Courtesy of GeoDigm Corp).

the soft tissue to the hard tissue in space. Fifteen soft-tissue landmarks (A–O) were used. In each landmark, 15-mm-long nails were implanted, representing the normal surface line 10 mm above each corresponding landmark. Those landmarks are: (A) right supraorbitale at the level of soft-tissue glabella; (B) soft-tissue glabella; (C) left supraorbitale at the level of soft-tissue glabella; (D) nasal tip; (E) upper lip; (F) lower lip; (G) soft-tissue B; (H) soft-tissue pogonion; (I) right maxillary points located on the cheek one-fourth of the distance from between the right and left alar and right and left TMJ, respectively; (J) right cheek point located on the cheek one-quarter of the distance from between the right and left commissure and right and left TMJ points; (K) left maxillary points located on the cheek one-fourth of the distance from between the right and left alar and right and left TMJ; (L) left cheek point located on the cheek one-quarter of the distance from between the right and left commissure and right and left TMJ points; (M) left temple area; (N) right temple area; (O) chin. The facial model was also scanned from three different views ($-45°$, $0°$, and $45°$) to eliminate undercuts and merged with Vivid700 3D software (see Figure 12.5).

ACCURACY OF THE METHOD

All data were processed statistically for average value, standard deviation, maximum and minimum distortion, and differences. Differences were assessed by paired t tests with $p = 0.05$. The computer software using stereophotogrammetry (Grayson *et al.* 1988, 1991) with a vector intercept

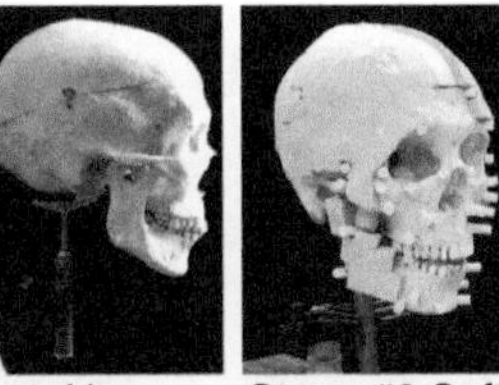
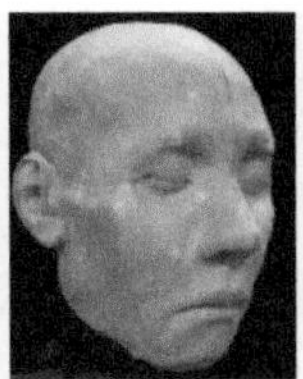
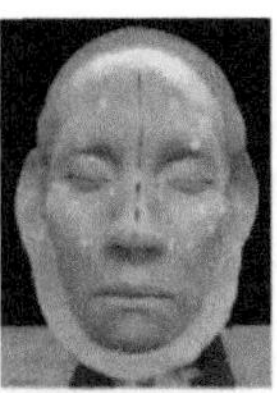

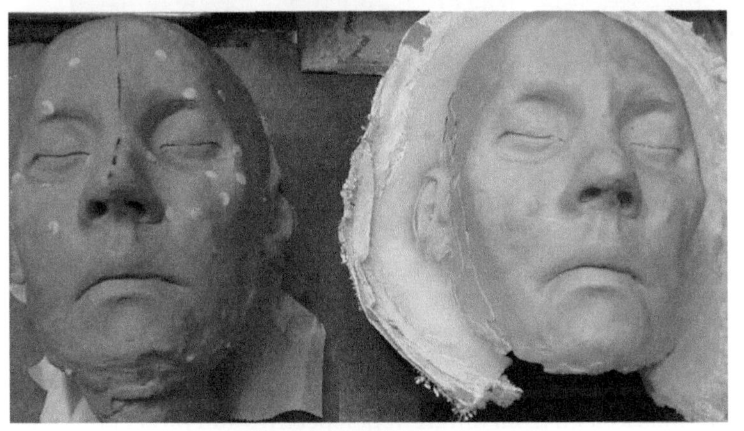

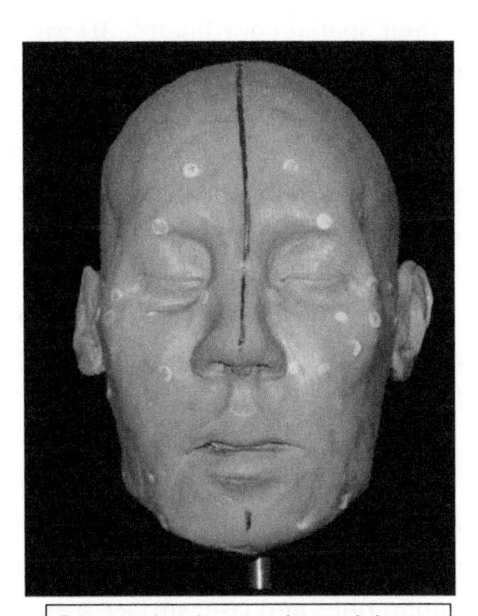

Figure 12.4
3D silicone model with embedded markers.

algorithm (Brown and Abbott 1989) was found to be accurate to better than 1.0 mm for linear measurements (Kusnoto *et al.* 1999). Fifty-one hard-tissue and sixty soft-tissue landmarks were used in our previous study. From those landmarks, 97 vectors in hard tissue and 159 vectors in soft tissue were

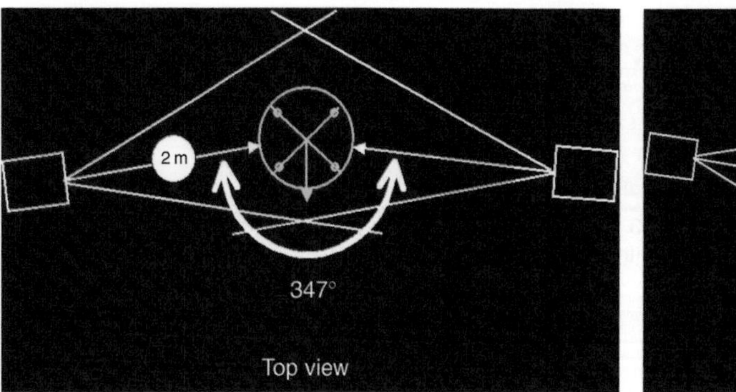

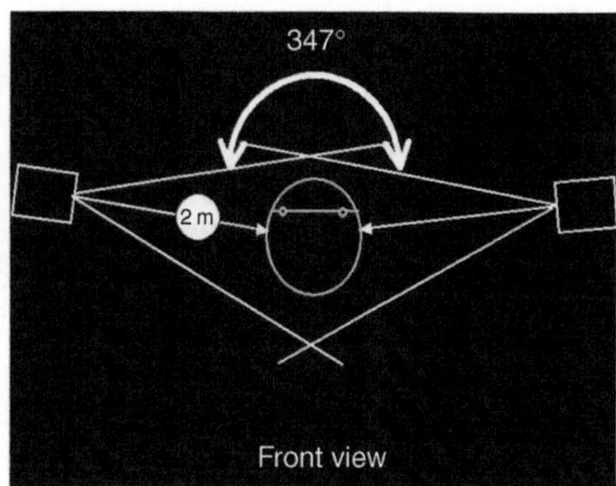

Figure 12.5 Coverage area on the facial laser surface scanning.

derived, and the accuracy was determined to be better than 1.0 mm in measuring soft-tissue thickness (Kusnoto *et al.* 2000) (see Figure 12.6).

12.2.2 DEVELOPMENT OF THE METHOD

The 3DCeph™ computer software running on a standard PC was able to correlate digitized landmarks seen from different perspectives and projections and convert the 2D location of each landmark into its 3D spatial coordinates (x, y, z). From those landmarks and their spatial coordinates, 3D wire-frame meshes can be established by connecting those landmarks in triangular fashion, creating multiple-unit surfaces. Finite-element modeling can be obtained following the creation of the wire-frame meshes (see Figure 12.7).

Soft-tissue thickness can be measured from any hard-tissue landmark to the corresponding soft-tissue landmark within 1.0-mm accuracy, comparable to CT-scan measurements. Unlike CT scans, which require at least 50–60 slices of x-ray projections, 3DCeph™ is able to aid in generating a 3D wire-frame model of a human skull with sufficient accuracy by utilizing two standard x-ray projections (lateral and PA). The automatic computerized landmark alignment module of 3DCeph™ enables the software to improve precision in locating any cephalometric landmarks and thus improve the overall accuracy of the 3D computer modeling.

Computerized stereophotogrammetry utilizing 3DCeph™ in combination with good radiographic, photographic, and laser surface-scanning techniques can be used as a noninvasive and economical, yet reliable, technique in determining soft-tissue thickness. Based on the model applied in 3DCeph™, the development of 3DCeph.NET™ was started to fully integrate with both 3D dental-cast and 3D facial-surface scanning as a noninvasive method of generating a "3D virtual patient" for improved accuracy in diagnosis and treatment planning. Furthermore, it utilizes the current Microsoft.NET technology,

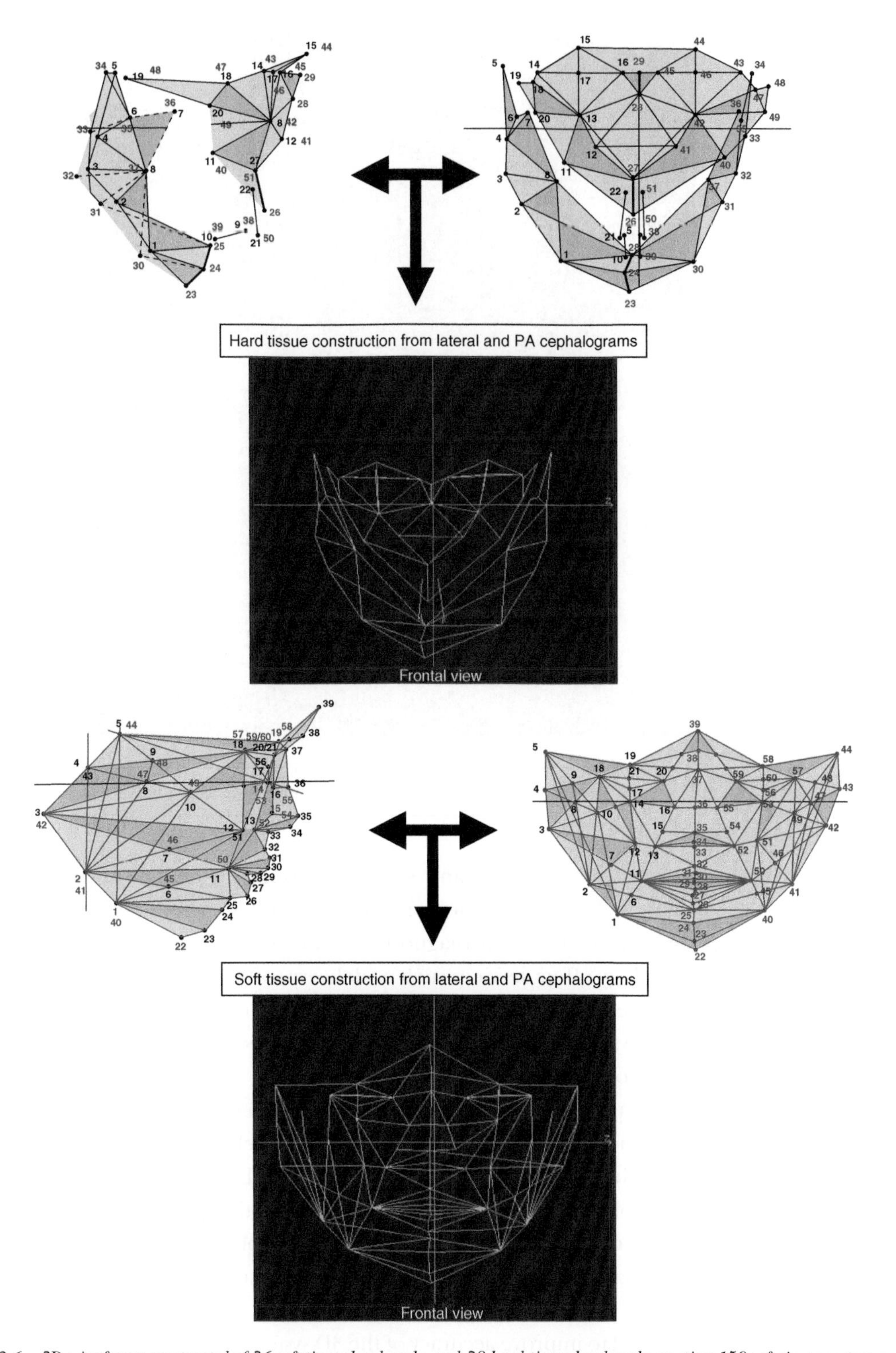

Figure 12.6 3D wire frame constructed of 36 soft tissue landmarks and 38 hard tissue landmarks creating 159 soft tissue vectors and 97 hard tissue vectors.

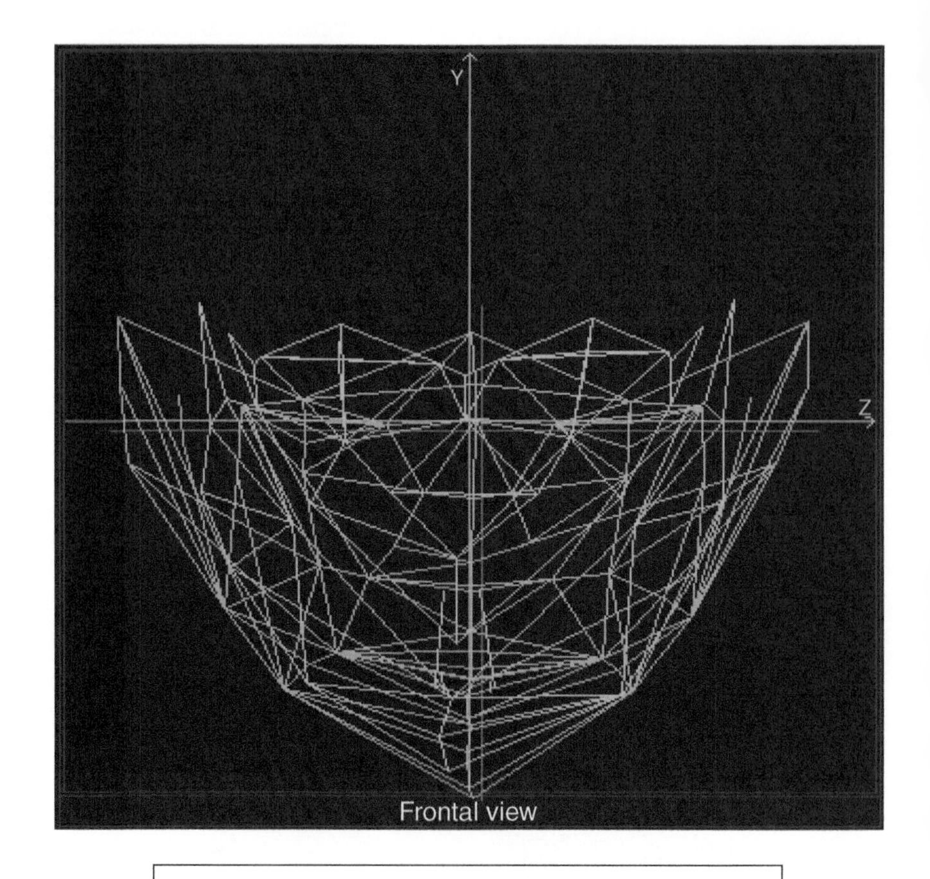

Figure 12.7

Merging hard tissue and soft tissue 3D wire frame model constructing 15 tissue depth landmarks of 11 surface regions.

allowing easy, reliable, and secure transmission of data through Internet channels. The combination of 3DCeph™ and Microsoft.NET technology will extend the orthodontic diagnosis ability over the Internet channel. The .NET technology offers services such as delivery software on the Web, a framework for universal services, and a server-centric computing model. It will run on any browser or any platform, and .NET is based on the newest Web standards (Kusnoto 2002, Microsoft.NET).

In conjunction with the software development, a headband equipped with electronic magnetic sensors will also be developed to ensure proper head positioning and standard calibration for all 3D images involved in this study (cephalometric radiographs, 3D scanning of the face, and dental cast). The calibrated headband will act as a registration plane based on these landmarks while changing the projection of the x-rays, as well as merging 3D scans of multiple planes of a subject. The predecessor of this headband, the facebow, was found to improve accuracy of the 3D system, but proved to be cumbersome in clinical application. By integrating an electronic magnetic sensor into the

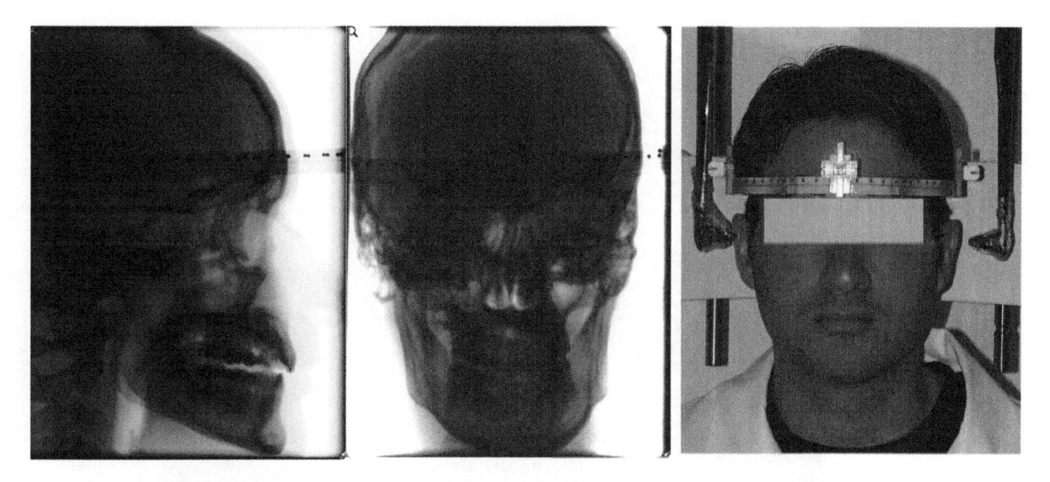

Figure 12.8 3DCeph™ head aligner with cephalostat adapter.

specially designed headband, one can ensure proper head positioning when the subject needs to be moved from one position (lateral) to another (PA). Thus head positioning error can be minimized. The built-in electronic magnetic sensor can be linked directly to the x-ray machine to trigger the exposure when the three points represented by three magnetic sensors placed on the left and right sides and frontal part of the headband are aligned with the sensor (see Figure 12.8).

This device was designed to increase accuracy in repositioning the subject after moving the head between taking one projection (i.e., lateral) and another projection (i.e., PA) to get an orthogonal (biplanar) projection pair, as described in previous research on stereophotogrammetry. In addition, this device will also provide registration points and planes while integrating multiple 3D data obtained from the subject by utilizing a 3D laser surface scanner. The limited scanning field of the scanner obliged users to take multiple sections of scanning (at least two) to be able to produce a full 3D facial or head structure. The proposed device can also be utilized to provide registration points and planes when integrating 3D facial scanning to a 3D wire-frame underlying skeletal structure, which later can give registration points for the 3D scanning of the dental cast (see Figure 12.9).

12.3 DISCUSSION

The laser surface scanner generates accurate 3D data. The availability of a lightweight user-friendly surface laser scanner in the field of orthodontics makes it possible to analyze growth, soft-tissue changes, treatment simulation, appliance designs, and treatment effects in three dimensions. Three-dimensional

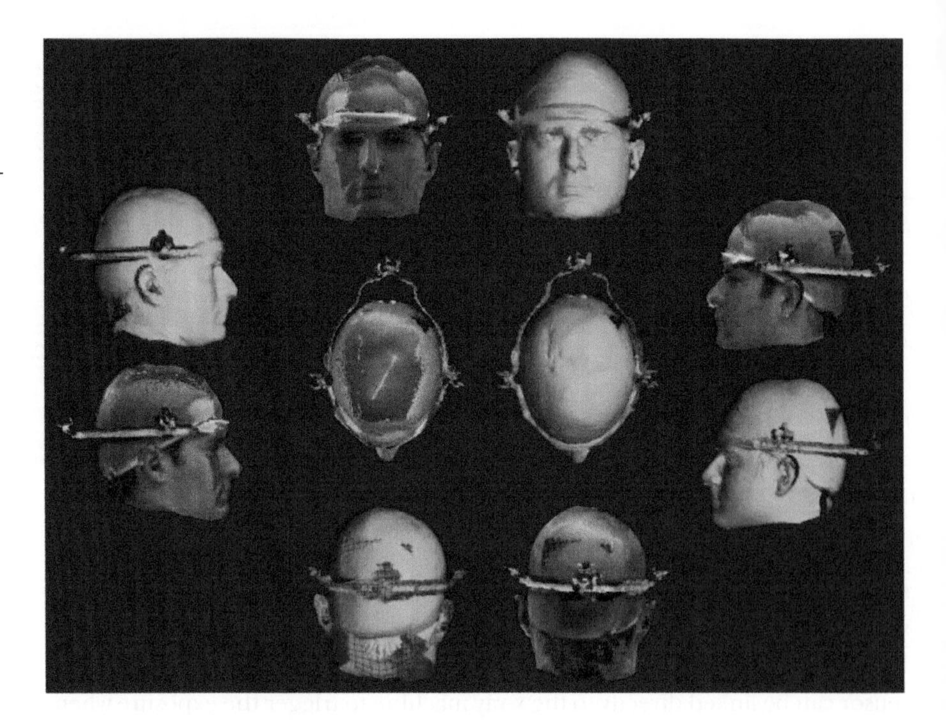

Figure 12.9

Sample of three-dimensional head model taken from multiple views to eliminate undercuts using special head-band to ensure precise integration of the segments.

computerized data derived from a laser scanner can also be transformed by utilizing computer-aided manufacturing (CAM) and stereolithography techniques to produce orthodontic appliances such as splints, computerized wire bending, e-models, and surgical simulation models. The self-correcting mechanism of the laser scanner in adjusting for image distortion gives flexibility for clinical research. The software can be utilized to merge images taken from different perspectives, thus eliminating undercuts. Interestingly, due to the nature of the laser beam spread, it was found that the smaller the object the more accurate the measurements.

Studies involving dental casts can be performed with ease since computerized 3D wire-frame diagrams allow models to be cut, superimposed, and measured in the computer. Measuring changes in area as well as length of curved parts gives more insight for many data sets. In the area of craniofacial anomalies, various studies could be made of cleft-lip repair, asymmetrical facial growth, change of head shape, and nasal molding procedures. It was found that, in all cases, the scanner produced more accurate measurements in height (x) and width (y) but less accurate in depth (z). In measuring intermolar width, the scanner tends to produce smaller values than the manual measurement; on the other hand, it produces bigger values when measuring palatal depth. The increase accuracy in measuring height (x) and width (y) is due to the horizontal laser-beam source that was used in the unit. The depth (z) was accumulated while the horizontal laser beam moved from top to bottom of the scanned objects, and so a time discrepancy occurs in the interval from the emission of the laser beam to its registration on the photosensitive sensor while scanning through the object's depth, which causes a slight increase in the *z* coordinate.

The need for 3D reconstruction as a diagnostic tool led to the development of sophisticated technology such as computerized tomography (CT). Despite the many applications of CT and its versatility, it has disadvantages. The cost of performing a 3D CT-scan reconstruction is far greater than that of several ordinary cephalograms. The radiation exposure from a CT survey is also much higher than the total radiation from several ordinary cephalograms. Moreover, with new developments in digital x-ray film, the amount of radiation exposure from cephalograms can even be reduced further by 90%. The use of special aligner in this study will facilitate the employment of 3D modeling to increase accuracy. The user does not need to have a special research cephalometric radiography unit with two perpendicular x-ray sources installed. The facebow enables the operator to use an ordinary single x-ray source unit with good precision. However, when available, an x-ray unit with two x-ray sources is preferable for ease of use, speed of procedure, and further lowering the risk of head positioning error. Even though it was not assessed in this study, it is possible to apply the aligner to produce an integrated 3D model embodying of a 3D wire-frame representation of the skeletal structure generated by stereophotogrammetry, and using 3D laser facial scanning and 3D scanning of the dental cast for greater detail and accuracy of the dentition. The prototype computer program used in this study, 3DCeph.NET™, provides a feature which enables the user to generate 3D modeling using any combination of lateral, frontal, and basilar projections. This does not mean that all cases will need all three cephalograms routinely. Selected cases—such as surgical cases, cases with significant posterior or anterior crossbites, or syndrome cases having significant asymmetry (both dental and/or skeletal)—will definitely benefit when assessed in three dimensions. Even in such cases, not all of them will need three projections (lateral, frontal, and basilar). Most cases can be reconstructed in 3D with adequate accuracy by using lateral and frontal projections. But, when any surgical simulation involves asymmetric movement, the use of basilar projection will be very helpful. For example, it is possible to locate the new mandibular dental and skeletal midlines in a hemifacial microsomia patient, because lengthening one side of the mandibular ramus will affect the other side as the whole mandible is repositioned.

Longitudinal evaluation of human craniofacial growth and development will definitely benefit from using 3DCeph.NET™, not only because it is inexpensive but also because less radiation exposure is needed for the individual participating in the study. A further benefit is its ability to integrate other

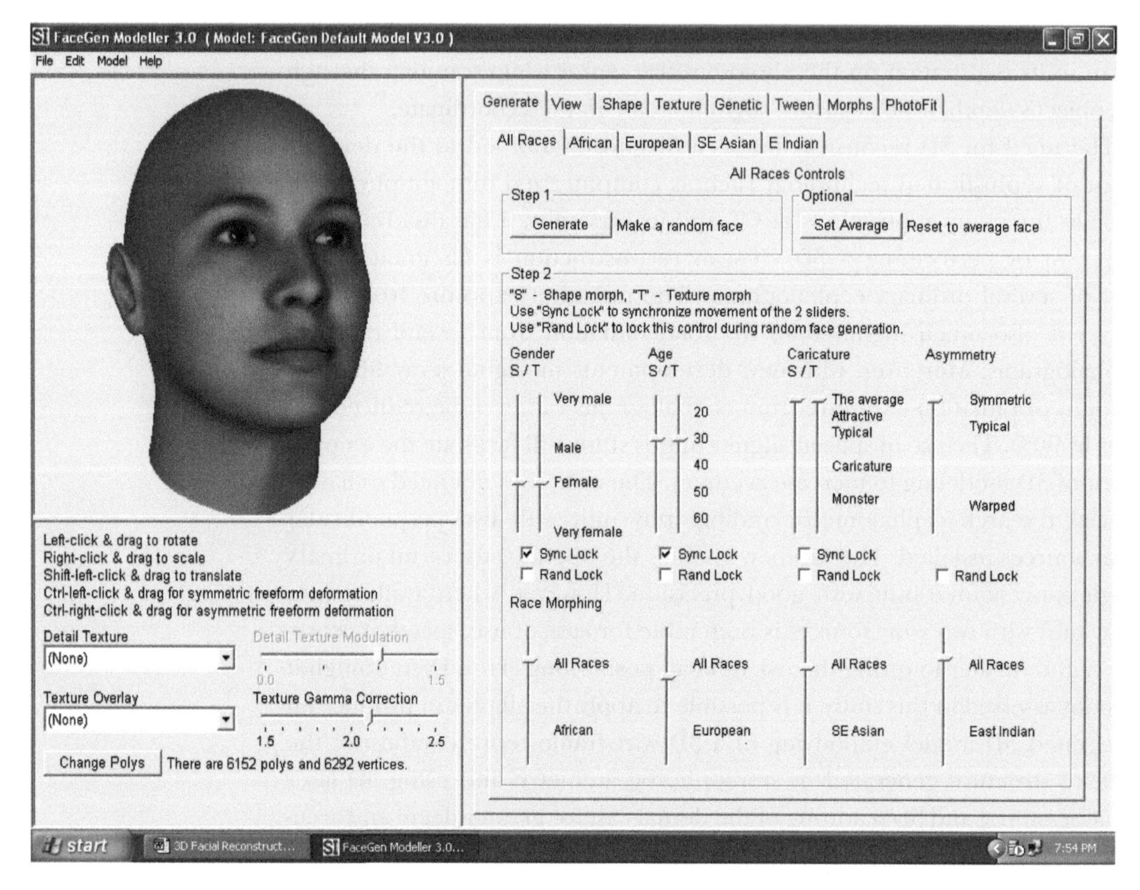

Figure 12.10 FaceGen™ by singular inversions © 2003. Adding facial expression, gender, racial, aging features and animation to static 3D facial scanning.

kinds of digital 3D data and its "Web-enabled" facility. By integrating such 3D modeling with surface-texturing and morphing capability, such as found in FaceGen™ (FaceGen 2003), not only can a static 3D model be generated but also an animated model with facial expressions and various skin textures mimicking aging, racial, and gender features can be added and simulated, thus increasing the accuracy of predicting soft-tissue shape based on hard-tissue evidence in the case of forensic application (see Figure 12.10).

12.4 CONCLUSIONS

Computerized stereophotogrammetry using 3DCeph™ 2000 in combination with good radiographic and photographic techniques can be used as a non-invasive, economical, and reliable method for determining soft-tissue thickness. The method can be adapted for analyzing forensic samples gathered in locations where only limited resources are available, such as in underdeveloped countries and rural areas.

It was anticipated that, in the near future, the data gathered from the 3DCeph.NET™ collectively from the authorized online users can be used to record any 3D growth norms and patterns in 3D and be incorporated with 3D CT data. In longitudinal studies, researchers will only need to take initial and final 3D CT data, whereas annual growth rates can be derived mathematically using data from biplanar radiographs analyzed by 3DCeph. Bone surface contours can be derived from a CT study and morphed to different sizes as growth occurs, and be recorded annually by the 3DCeph.

Combined with 3D cephalometry techniques and software packages, a complete 3D simulation can be obtained which gives both the orthodontist and surgeon better control in designing a treatment plan for the patient. Its application intraorally can also be valuable for clinical research, not only for saving time but also for patient comfort.

REFERENCES

Berkowitz S. (1999) "3D Study of SCUCL/P and CBCL/P for Treatment Evaluation", *Cleft Palate Craniofac. J.* 36, 450–456.

Broadbent B. H. (1931) "A New x-ray Technique and its Application to Orthodontia", *Angle Orthod.* 1, 45–66.

Brown T. and Abbott A. A. (1989) "Computer Assisted Location of Reference Points in Three Dimensions for Radiographic Cephalometry", *Am. J. Orthod. Dentofac. Orthop.* 95, 490–498.

FaceGen™. Singular Inversions © 2003. Vancouver, British Columbia, Canada.

Ferrario V. F., Sforza C., Ciusa V., Dellavia C. and Tartaglia G. M. (2001). "The Effect of Sex and Age on Facial Asymmetry in Healthy Subjects: A Cross-Sectional Study from Adolescence to Mid-Adulthood", *J. Oral Maxillofac. Surg.* 59, 382–388.

Grayson B. H., Cutting C., Bookstein F. L., Kim H. and McCarthy J. G. (1988) "The Three-Dimensional Cephalogram: Theory, Technique, and Clinical Application", *Am. J. Orthod. Dentofac. Orthop.* 94, 327–337.

Grayson B. H., Cutting C., Bookstein F. L., Kim H. and McCarthy J. G. (1991) "Landmarks in Three Dimensions: Reconstruction from Cephalograms Versus Direct Observation", *Am. J. Orthod. Dentofac. Orthop.* 100, 133–140.

Ishikawa H., Iwasaki H., Tsukada H., Chu S., Nakamura S. and Yamamoto K. (1999) "Dentoalveolar Growth Inhibition Induced by Bone Denudation on Palate", *Cleft Palate Craniofac. J.* 36, 450–456.

Kusnoto B. (2002) "Implementing Enterprise Resource Planning in Orthodontic Practice Management: The Way to Orthodontic e-Practice", *Craniofacial Growth Series. Moyers Symposium 2002.*

Kusnoto B. and Evans C. A. (2002) "The Reliability of Vivid700 3D Surface Laser Scanner: A Journey to Three-Dimensional Approach in Orthodontic Diagnosis, Research and Clinical Application", *Am. J. Orthod. Dentofac. Orthop.*

Kusnoto B., Evans C. A., BeGole E. A. and deRijk W. (1999) "Assessment of 3-Dimensional Computer Generated Cephalometric Measurements", *Am. J. Orthod. Dentofacial Orthop*. 116, 390–399.

Kusnoto B., Evans C. A., Poernomo S. and Sahelangi P. (2000) "Utilization of 3D Cephalometric Finite Elements Modeling for Measuring Human Facial Soft Tissue Thickness", *Forensic Science Communications* 2 (4, Part 2).

Microsoft .NET technology. http://www.w3schools.com/ngws/ngws_intro.asp

Minolta Vivid3D Laser Surface Scanner Technical Manual 2000.

Telcordia Technologies. NetSizer: Internet Growth Forecasting Tools. http://www.netsizer.com (Updated 09/03/02).

Weeden J. C., Trotman C. and Faraway J. J. (2001) "Three Dimensional Analysis of Facial Movement in Normal Adults: Influence of Sex and Facial Shape", *Angle Orthod*. 71, 132–140.

CHAPTER 13

COMPUTER-AIDED DENTAL IDENTIFICATION: DEVELOPING OBJECTIVE CRITERIA FOR COMPARISONS OF OROFACIAL SKELETAL CHARACTERISTICS TO PROVE HUMAN IDENTITY

David R. Senn and Paula Brumit

Center for Education and Research in Forensics, University of Texas Health Science Center at San Antonio Dental School, 7703 Floyd Curl Drive – Mail Code 7919, San Antonio, Texas 78229-3900, USA

13.1 INTRODUCTION

Traditional manual and visual techniques used in clinical patient treatment have been applied by forensic dentists to cases that require them to compare antemortem and postmortem radiographs. Most forensic dentists are skilled observers and readily make positive identifications or correctly recognize nonidentity when distinctive anatomical, pathological, or restorative features are present. When these features are less distinctive or absent, the radiographs are of inferior quality, or the radiographs were made from significantly different projection geometries, identification is sometimes difficult or impossible, even though the radiographs may be from the same person. This chapter will describe the traditional methods and detail two computer methods intended to optimize results and increase objectivity.

13.2 TRADITIONAL VISUAL RADIOGRAPH COMPARISON (SUBJECTIVE)

Forensic dentists have assisted medical examiners and coroners in unidentified-body cases for many years. In the United States, two cases are cited as the beginning of American forensic odontology: the 1776 identification by the silversmith and dentist Paul Revere of Major General Joseph Warren after his death at the Battle of Bunker (Breed's) Hill, and the evidence given by Dr. Nathan Cooley Keep in a scandalous homicide case at Harvard Medical School in 1850. These are generally considered to be the seminal cases for American forensic dental identification (Luntz and Luntz 1973, Cottone *et al.* 1982).

These early cases did not involve radiography but subjective recognition of dental restorations or prostheses fabricated by the dentists involved. Dental radiography did not become widespread until the middle 20th century but has now become the standard of care in North America and in most of the developed world. Dentists use radiographs to diagnose pathologic and developmental problems, to aid in treatment procedures, and to confirm both appropriate treatment and good dental health. Consequently, experienced dentists develop skill at recognizing both biologic and restorative features in those images. This recognition is the basis for most dental identifications and is adequate for the majority of the cases seen.

The improvement of dental health care has happily resulted in a healthier population. This dental health improvement combined with the inability to recover all dental structures in some decomposed and skeletonized bodies has a limiting effect on dental identifications that rely on anatomical and restorative features. Additionally, dental practitioners and their assistants expose radiographs from different projection geometries requiring modification of postmortem radiographic technique in an effort to emulate the antemortem radiograph parameters. In some cases, the antemortem radiographs are received long after the original postmortem records are made, and the variations in projection geometry require repeating the postmortem radiographic examination.

Changes in the judicial interpretation of expert-witness requirements and evidence based upon scientific knowledge for acceptance in courts of law, combined with the limitations mentioned above, made it clear that dental identification must move from an activity supported by only the skill, care, and judgement of individuals to a more demonstrably objective activity. This new legal requirement and the limitations of the side-by-side comparison of dental radiographs in difficult cases signal the need for more scientific approaches.

In *Daubert v. Merrell Dow Pharmaceuticals*, 509 U.S. 579 (1993), the Supreme Court stated that, when expert evidence based upon "scientific knowledge" is offered at trial, the judge, upon a proper challenge of the admissibility of the testimony, should act as a gatekeeper and determine whether the proffered evidence is "reliable" and can be trusted to be scientifically valid. The Court applied the following tests: (1) whether the expert's technique or theory can be or has been tested, that is, whether the expert's theory can be challenged in some objective sense, or whether it is instead simply a subjective approach that cannot reasonably be assessed for reliability; (2) whether the technique or theory has been subject to peer review and publication; (3) the known or potential rate of error of the technique or theory when applied; (4) the existence and maintenance of standards and controls; and (5) whether the technique or theory has been generally accepted in the scientific community.

13.3 COMPUTER-AIDED RADIOGRAPH COMPARISON (LESS SUBJECTIVE)

Digital radiographs may be acquired using any of the commercially available intraoral digital sensors or scanned from film radiographs using a flatbed scanner with transparency-scanning adaptors. Digital or digitized film antemortem and postmortem radiographs are then opened in Adobe Photoshop. Because the actual size of an image on radiographic film varies with the distance the film is from the teeth, it is necessary to resize images to ensure that comparisons are made on images that are the same size. Using landmarks in restorations or anatomical features of the teeth, the embedded measure tool in Photoshop, and using the Help>Resize Image or Image>Image Size commands from the toolbar it is possible to ensure that features to be compared in both images are compatible in size.

13.3.1 TECHNIQUE 1: HOLLOW-VOLUME OVERLAY COMPARISON

Using the Image>Adjust> commands and the Magic Wand tool, individual restorations in the postmortem image are depicted as either solid-volume or hollow-volume images. Those images are transferred to the antemortem image. Using the Edit>Transform>Rotate commands and the Move tool, the postmortem image can be aligned in the same orientation as the antemortem and the direct comparison accomplished (see Figure 13.1).

13.3.2 TECHNIQUE 2: TRANSPARENCY OVERLAY COMPARISON

This technique allows overlaying transparent images of postmortem radiographs over nontransparent antemortem images. The transparency factor can be adjusted to allow a fade-in–fade-out comparison. The transparent image can be moved onto or away from the underlying antemortem image. Figure 13.1 illustrates a nondynamic print version of the technique showing that distinctive features such as metal restorations seen in antemortem radiographs (AM) and postmortem radiographs (PM) can be helpful in comparisons. The hollow-volume outline (HV) of the restoration from either image

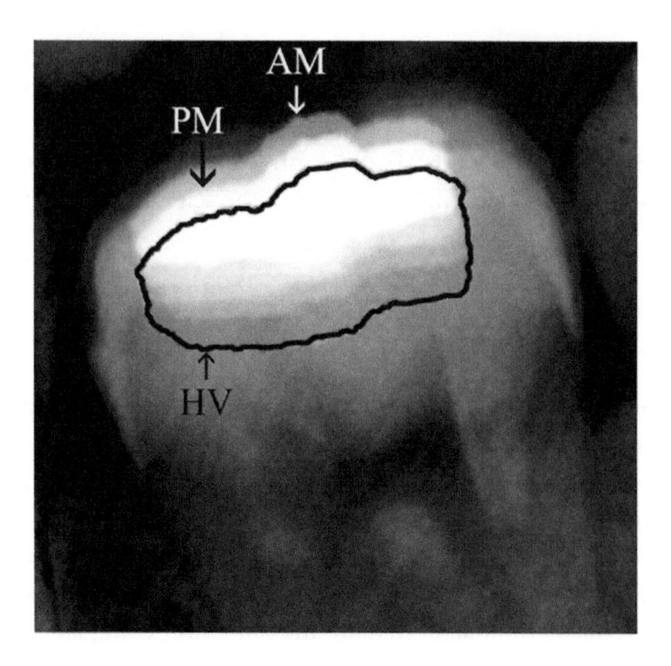

Figure 13.1
Hollow-volume overlay.

can be moved from AM to PM or vice versa to demonstrate degree of similarity (see Figure 13.1).

As in earlier nondigital methods, exposing the postmortem radiographs in the same or similar orientations as used in the antemortem generates similar images of the same restorations with little or no difference caused by changes in projection geometry. This is not always possible in casework. Modification of the shape of one or the other image may be needed to form the best basis for an opinion on identity. This method and similar methods described by Bowers and Johanson (2000) require training and practice to generate consistent results. Cases with metal restorations are best suited to the hollow-volume technique. The transparency-overlay method works well with cases with or without restorations. Both methods seem complicated when described but become intuitive when practiced.

Direct computer comparison of antemortem and postmortem digital or digitized radiographs allows for direct and less-subjective comparisons. Indirect or side-by-side comparisons are subjective. The direct techniques allow the investigator to illustrate comparisons that are more scientifically reproducible, and they are utilized as teaching techniques for postdoctoral forensic odontology students. They facilitate dental identification demonstrations to medical examiners and coroners and may be useful tools in the courtroom to illustrate identifications to judges and juries and help to verify identity in disputed identity cases.

13.4 DIGITAL RADIOGRAPHIC COMPARISON USING COMPUTER SOFTWARE (OBJECTIVE)

13.4.1 CURRENT POSTMORTEM RADIOGRAPHIC COMPARISON PROBLEMS

As previously stated, traditional visual radiographic identification is subjective in nature. Often these radiographs include restorations or prostheses that facilitate comparisons. When there are no restorations or other man-made aids, it is often possible to make identifications from distinctive anatomical features such as the morphology of tooth roots, tooth crowns, maxillary sinuses, and frontal sinuses as well as bone trabeculation features, the path of nerve canals, and the location and features of foramina.

There are many challenges in applying this method of comparison when no restorations or distinctive anatomical features are present. They include the varying projection geometries and fluctuating densities of even well-made radiographs and problems from underexposed or overexposed antemortem films. These confounding factors bring the accuracy of subjective identification into question. Additionally, in the post-Daubert world, questions about the degree of certainty and threshold of probability may cause examiners to hesitate in making positive identifications without objective background support data.

Examiners prefer to objectively compare radiographs. Earlier attempts at objective comparisons using subtraction radiography have proved unsatisfactory, primarily because of the lack of robust technology. One early examiner stated "Although the difference was statistically highly significant, the distribution of gray shades in the two groups overlapped. Thus, the gray shades in the subtraction image cannot per se unequivocally establish the identity of a victim, but may add to the subjective comparison of two radiographs in victim identification" (Wenzel and Anderson 1994).

With the aid of computer automation and mathematical algorithms, objective identification may now be possible. The resulting statistical data may allow a level of certainty heretofore not supportable under the new rules of evidence.

13.4.2 COMPUTER SOFTWARE SOLUTIONS

In the ten years since subtraction radiography was only an aid to subjective analysis, much work has been accomplished. There are now reportedly no fewer than 38 computer applications suitable for comparing radiographs using applications of algorithms (Lehmann *et al.* 2000). An algorithm is a finite series of clearly defined logical steps to solving a problem. In this application, mathematically specific techniques are used to implement image-processing

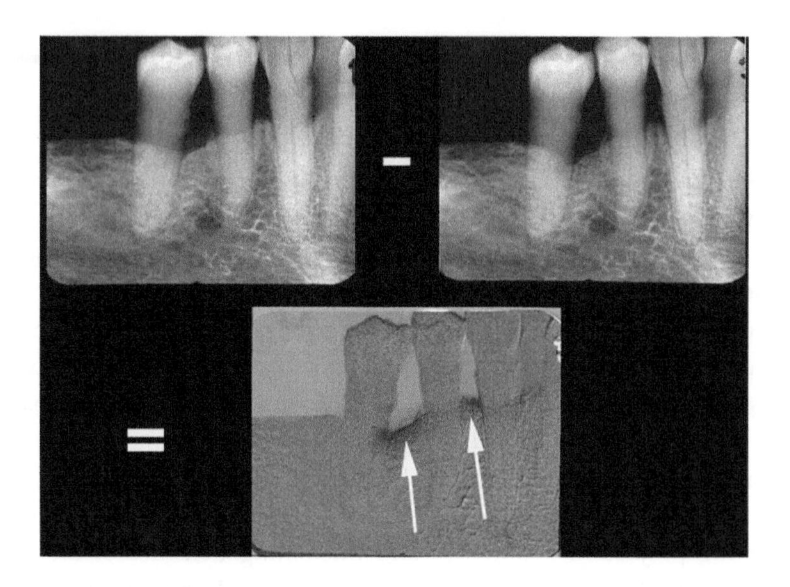

Figure 13.2

The white arrows indicate areas of barely discernible bone loss seen in the later of two radiographs taken eight months apart.

or analysis operations that rely on data derived from an additional advancement in dental radiography.

13.4.3 DIGITAL SUBTRACTION RADIOGRAPHY

The comparison of antemortem and postmortem radiographs for identification using this new method is derived from a well-known but not clinically widely used technique: digital subtraction radiography. In applying this technique, similar structures in two images are de-emphasized, dissimilar structures are enhanced, and a quantitative measure of similarity can be determined. The image difference or similarity can be seen visually and can be measured, quantified, and statistically compared and reported (see Figure 13.2).

13.4.4 IMAGE REGISTRATION

Recently developed computer software can "register" images. Registration is the process of determining a relationship between the content of two images, including the projection of one image onto the geometry of the other by interpolation (Lehmann *et al.* 2000). This implies that, by applying mathematical transformation algorithms, the software may be able to adjust and correct for the effects of different projection geometries and different grayscale densities originally recorded. The images may then be aligned and superimposed once the registration is performed. These two images then may be compared pixel by pixel or in their entirety, and the resulting similarities and differences quantified. The software used in the experiments discussed in this chapter is UTHSCSA ImageTool©, freeware developed by S. Brent Dove, DDS, MS at the University of Texas Health Science Center in San Antonio.

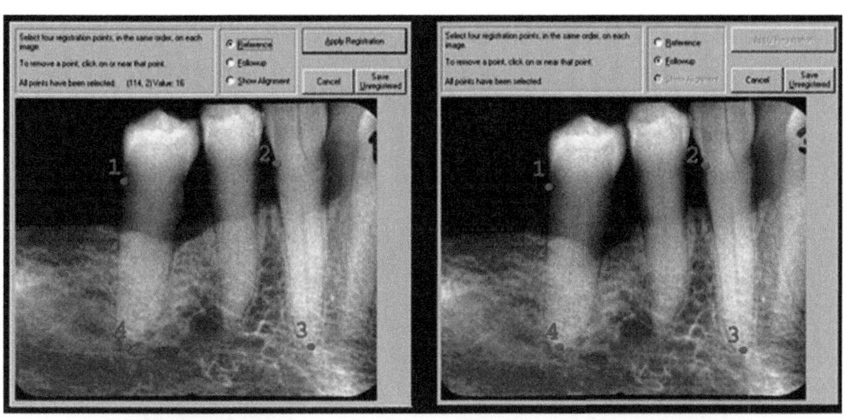

Figure 13.3

Reference image and follow-up image.

In the second and subsequent phases, Image Tool's plug-in companion for forensic dental applications, UT-ID, was also used.

Operators initiate registration of images by selecting four analogous anatomical points on two radiographs that may or may not be images of the same individual (see Figure 13.3). The selected points in each radiograph must be coplanar and not co-linear, and the points chosen must be the same anatomical points in both radiographs. Common points chosen have been readily visible anatomical features that meet the requirements such as root apices and the interproximal cementoenamel junction (CEJ). Other possible points could include the interradicular junction of roots of molars and interproximal margins of crowns.

13.5 UTHSCSA IMAGETOOL© AND UT-ID TECHNIQUE

13.5.1 REGISTRATION OF IMAGES

The software uses a reference image and a follow-up image for image registration. These images are analogous to antemortem and postmortem images in forensic identification cases. Using the appropriate tool, the anatomical points are selected in the same order in both images. The points define the area of interest (AOI) that the software will analyze (see Figure 13.3). After registering and overlaying the two images, the software de-emphasizes similar pixels and enhances dissimilar pixels, resulting in a modified image that will be very similar, if from the same individual, and different if from different individuals (see Figure 13.4).

Figure 13.5 shows the same exercise on a different individual. These are research images taken on the same specimen from the same parameters.

Figure 13.4

Close up of the registered images seen in Figure 2. Differences in bone density enhanced. (Bone loss from periodontitis.)

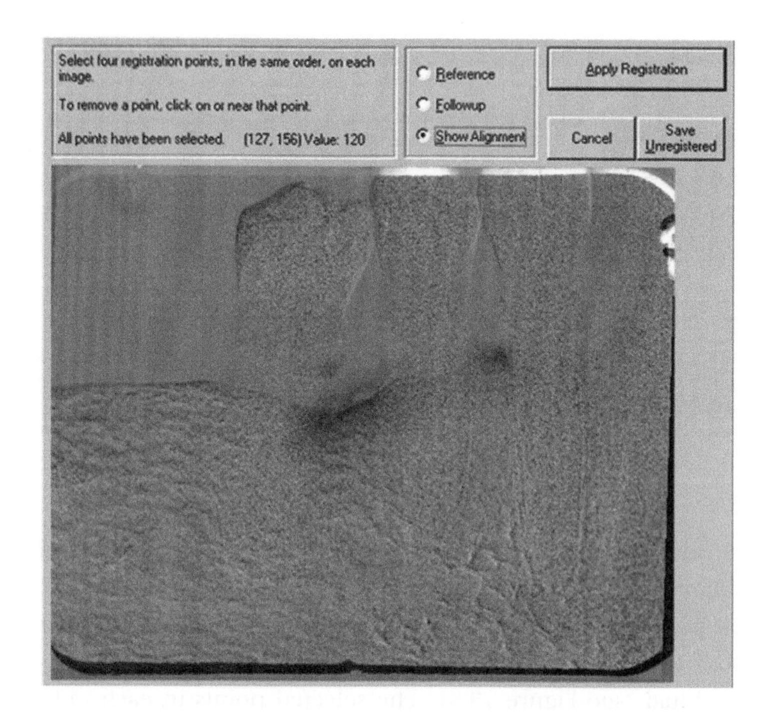

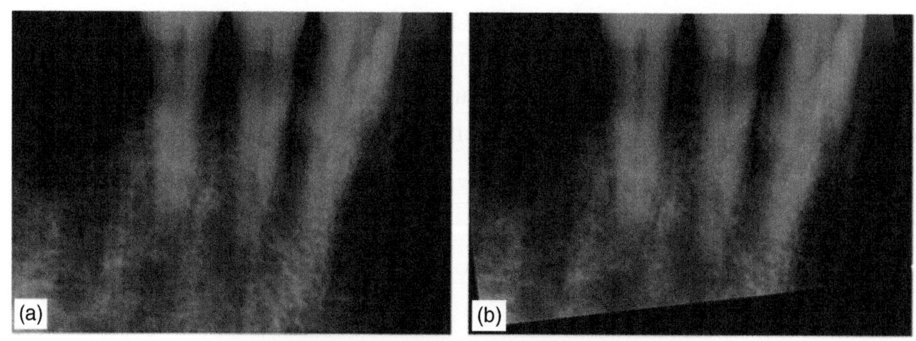

Images (a) and (b) are registered

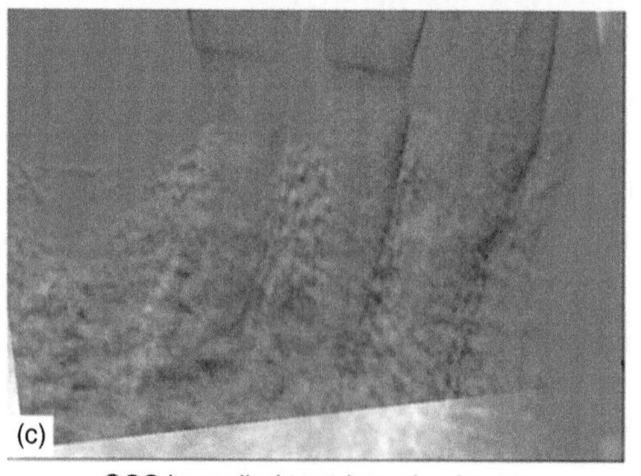

CCC is applied to subtraction image

Figure 13.5 *Images (a) and (b) are registered and (c) CCC is applied to subtraction image.*

The images may not be 100% similar even under these controlled conditions, due partly to system noise in digital imaging (see Figure 13.5).

13.5.2 MEASURES OF IMAGE SIMILARITY

The traditional method of measuring image similarity is *subjective* as it is determined by visual interpretation based on points of concordance. This new method of measuring image similarity is *objective* and based on digital comparison of elements of registered images. The reporting modality for the statistical analysis of image similarity is the "cross covariance coefficient" (CCC). According to the study by Lehmann *et al.* (1997), the cross covariance coefficient is an appropriate measure of image similarity. The CCC and another application of the coefficient were explored in studies explained in the following pages.

13.6 PHASE I: PILOT STUDY

To test the application of Image Tool software to this new method of objective identification, a pilot study was performed. Ten anatomically similar human jaw specimens were harvested from human mandibular premolar areas. The segments all contained cuspids, first premolars, and second premolars. All were clinically similar in morphology. The specimens were serially mounted on an optical bench by a threaded bolt cemented into each specimen (see Figure 13.6).

Fifteen digital radiographic images were exposed for each specimen. The first two images were made from the same projection parameters as a control. The ensuing thirteen images were made by rotating the orientation of the

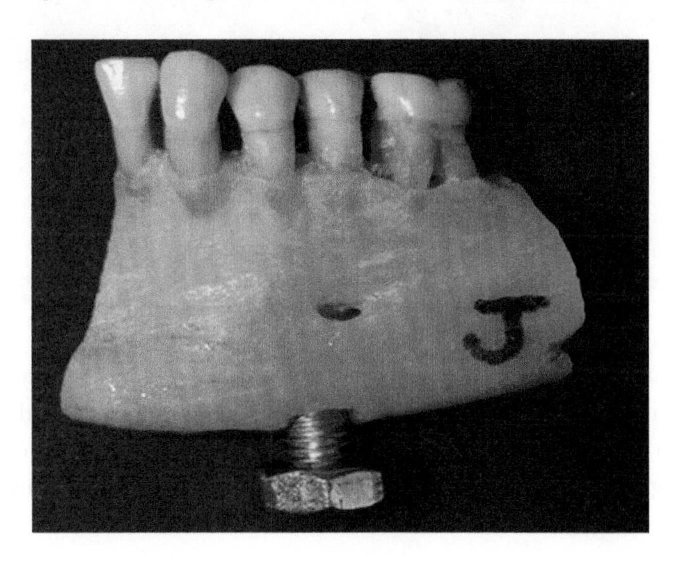

Figure 13.6

Example J (one of 10 mounted specimens).

Figure 13.7

Optical bench mounted source-specimen-sensor.

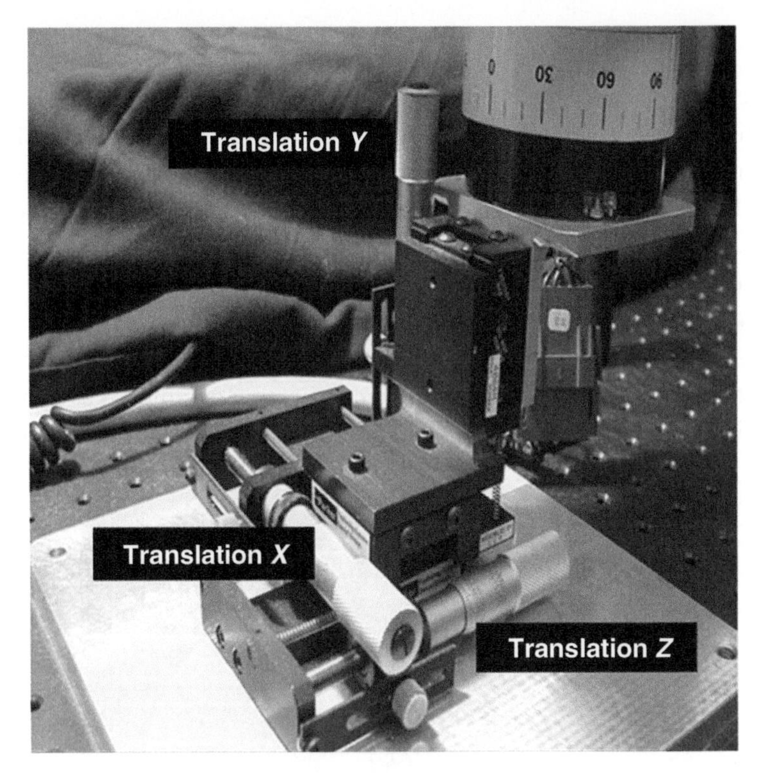

Figure 13.8

Source vernier adjustments.

target sensor around all three axes (*X*, *Y*, and *Z*). The x-ray source was also variably translated along the *X*, *Y*, and *Z* axes and included varying the source distance to target and sensor. All of these adjustments were designed to simulate the varying projection geometries and distances used in clinical dental examinations (see Figures 13.7, 13.8, and 13.9). Excessive rotation of the radiation

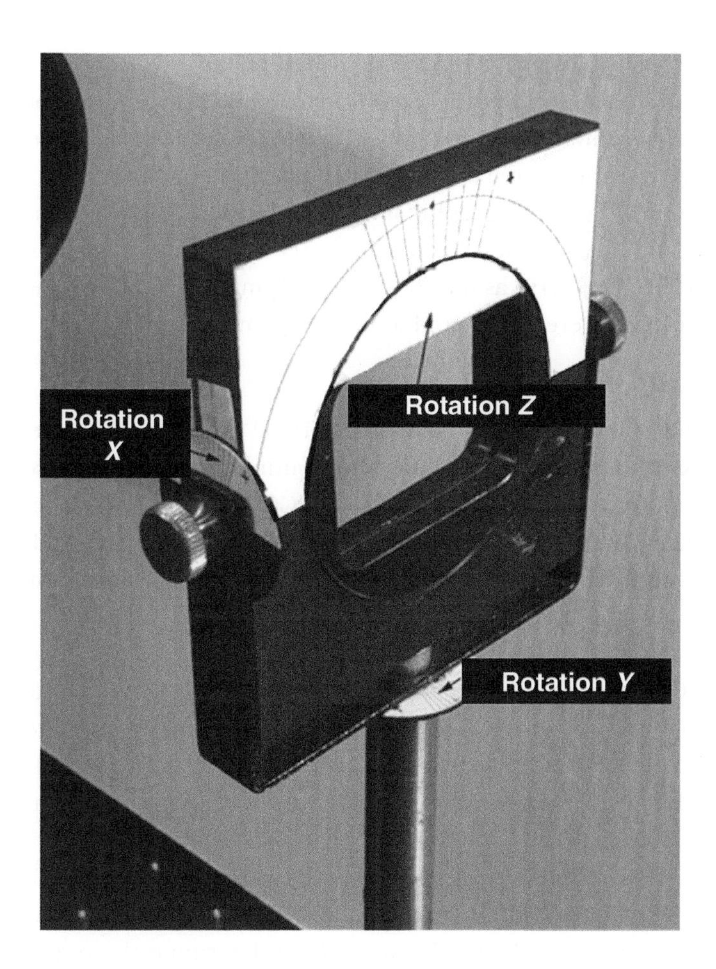

Figure 13.9
Sensor positioner.

source would have prevented the rays from finding the sensor. The initial source-to-object distance was 40 cm, and the initial source-to-detector distance was 41.5 cm. The radiographic sensor used was the Schick CDR sensor.

13.6.1 IMAGE SIMILARITY

The index of similarity, the CCC was calculated by the Image Tool software. The comparative analysis was performed on each reference image to itself and to all of the other images. The unregistered images, those at different projection geometries that were not corrected or aligned were analyzed, as were the registered images. The selected image was compared to itself and to all the other images.

13.6.2 IMPORTANCE OF REGISTRATION

Unregistered images are unsuitable for comparison in forensic identification. Unregistered images taken at different times show a low degree of similarity even if they are images of the same specimen or individual. In the Student t test, the difference is significant at $p < 0.0001$. While registration improves the similarity of most images, if they are not images of the same specimen or the same individual, the degree of similarity should not be high.

Ten sets of fifteen radiographic images, one set for each specimen, were created by the methods described in the preceding paragraphs. One specimen was selected to serve as the "postmortem" image. All of the images from all ten specimens were considered to be "antemortem" images.

13.6.3 PILOT STUDY RESULTS

The postmortem images were compared with all other possible antemortem images. Examiners were blinded as to the identity of the images chosen as the postmortem. Consequently, registration and CCC analysis could be evaluated as an objective means of forensic identification. An initial threshold of identity was established, and the software was able to select the correct specimen and make a positive identification 100% of the time.

The mean CCC for images that were from the same individual was 0.974 and the CCC range for those images was 0.877 to 0.995 with a standard deviation of 0.018. The mean CCC for comparisons between different individuals was 0.471, the range 0.133 to 0.829, and the standard deviation 0.145. There were no false positives and no false negatives and of course no overlapping of the ranges of the CCC.

Results of the pilot study were encouraging and indicated that general-population studies would be appropriate. A large-scale clinical study using actual clinical dental radiographs would help determine the practicality of the technique and facilitate refinement of the CCC numerical threshold for identification that should lie somewhere between 0.829 and 0.877 based on the pilot study.

13.7 PHASE II: COMPUTER-BASED IMAGE ANALYSIS FOR POSTMORTEM IDENTIFICATION

13.7.1 EXPANDED CLINICAL STUDY

A larger-scale clinical study ($N = 47$) followed to assess the practical application of this technique. The pilot study had shown that computer automation and mathematical algorithms worked in theory. Could the method work when comparing clinical radiographs taken years before to a clinical radiograph taken years later by different operators using different equipment at—more likely than not—different projection angles? The analysis of data for this phase took advantage of the newly developed plug-in for Image Tool: UT-ID. Both are freeware developed at the University of Texas Health

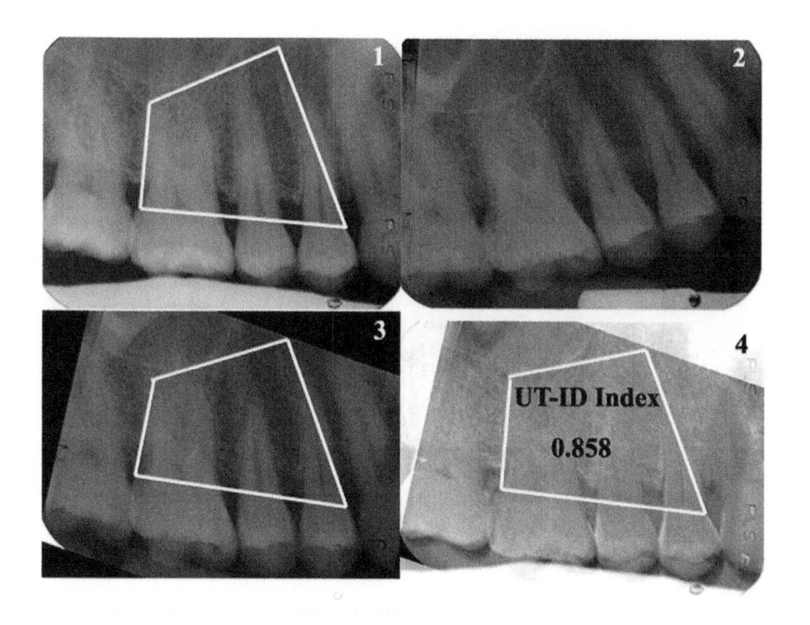

Figure 13.10

1. 2001 Radiograph (AOI selected). 2. 1987 Radiograph. 3. 1987 Radiograph (AOI selected). 4. Images registered.

Science Center at San Antonio. UT-ID streamlined and automated many of the repetitive tasks involved in the collection and analysis of data.

Phase II required the examination of dental radiographic film images, so all radiographic images were digitized by scanning. Various sites in both the maxillary and mandibular arch were selected for study. Then, as in the pilot study, all images are registered to themselves and to all other images from the same sites (see Figure 13.10). The CCC, now styled the UT-ID Index, was calculated to give a numerical index of image similarity for each comparison. The evolving threshold for identification was applied, and the resulting UT-ID Index of each comparison was analyzed for *identity* or *nonidentity*. Based on the statistical analysis from the pilot study, it was estimated that a CCC or UT-ID Index of 0.855+ would indicate positive identification. The comparison shown in Figure 13.10 had a UT-ID Index of 0.858 and was in fact a valid *positive identification.*

NONIDENTITY

Figure 13.11 shows an analysis example with a UT-ID Index of 0.733 indicating nonidentity. These are in fact radiographs of two different individuals.

13.7.2 RESULTS OF THE PHASE II EXPANDED STUDY

The phase II study demonstrated that the method is robust and valid in conditions similar to those seen in forensic cases. There is, however, work yet to be done. Comparison of radiographs using this technique in actual forensic cases is still pending. The anticipated problems with comparing images from

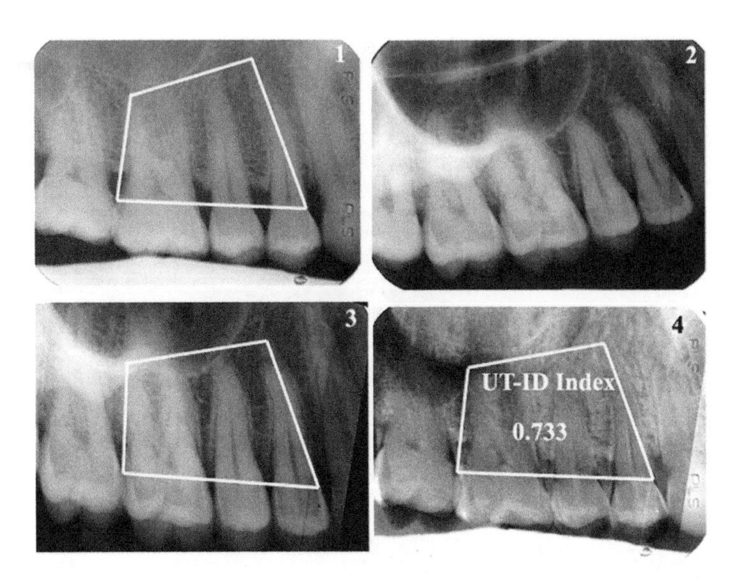

Figure 13.11

1. 2002 Radiograph (AOI selected). 2. 1997 Radiograph. 3. 1997 Radiograph (AOI selected). 4. Registered and subtracted.

decomposed or skeletonized cases with antemortem images have not yet been addressed.

There were false positives and negatives in the clinical comparisons. The mean UT-ID Index for identity (those cases that were in fact the same individual) was 0.931 and the range was 0.825 (a false negative) to 1.000 with a standard deviation of 0.055. The mean index for nonidentity was 0.505 with a range of 0.006 to 0.865 (a false positive) and a standard deviation of 0.206. The statistical summary is as follows:

Threshold UT-ID Index = 0.855	Sensitivity = 0.920
Accuracy = 99.582%	Specificity = 0.998
Error rate = 0.418%	Positive predictive value = 0.920

The Federal rules of evidence and the court's decisions in *Daubert vs. Merrell Dow Pharmaceuticals* have changed the rules for scientific evidence in federal courts. Many states have followed suit and adopted similar rules of evidence for testimony in state courts. Not only must the method be generally accepted by the scientific community, as before under the Frye rule, but it also must be deemed to be scientifically valid by the judges acting as gatekeepers for forensic and expert testimony. The guidelines followed by judges consider: (1) whether the method is testable and if it has been tested, (2) whether the technique has a known error rate, (3) if there are standards for applying the technique, (4) if the method or technique has been published and peer reviewed, and finally (5) whether the technique has general acceptance in the scientific community.

The UT-ID technique has met, or is very close to meeting, each of the first four requirements. The studies currently underway and others planned for the near future should fulfill those requirements soon. The fifth must await additional testing, practical application, and experience.

The purpose for the development of this technique and for this chapter is to advance the tasks involved with dental identification toward objective, accurate, and robust methods for use with cases involving those unfortunate persons who have not only died but are in peril of being lost and unidentified. Relatives of victims have told us that the latter is often much worse than the former. Those victims, their families, and the legal system deserve our best efforts.

REFERENCES

Bowers J. M. and Johanson R. (2000) "Digital Analysis of Bite Marks using Adobe Photoshop". Forensic Imaging Inst.

Cottone J. A. *et al.* (1982) *Outline of Forensic Dentistry.* Year Book Medical Publishers, pp. 20–23.

Daubert v. Merrell Dow Pharmaceuticals (1993) 509 U.S. 579.

Lehmann T. M., Grondahl H. G. and Benn D. K. (2000) "Computer-Based Registration for Digital Subtraction in Dental Radiology", *Dentomaxillofacial Radiology* 29, 323–346.

Lehmann T. M., Kaser A. and Repges R. (1997) "A Comparison of Mathematical Similarity Measures for Digital Subtraction Radiography", *Computers in Biology and Medicine* 27(2), 151–167.

Luntz L. L. and Luntz P. (1973) *Handbook for Dental Identification.* Lippincott, pp. 1–15.

Wenzel A. and Anderson L. (1994) "A Quantitative Analysis of Subtraction Images Based on Bite-Wing Radiographs for Simulated Victim Identification in Forensic Dentistry", *J. Forensic Odontostomatology* 12(1), 1–5.

CHAPTER 14

TWO METHODOLOGIES OF MEMORY RESEARCH: "EXPLANATION-TESTING" AND "RECONSTRUCTION"

Sam S. Rakover
Department of Psychology, Haifa University, Haifa 31905, Israel

14.1 INTRODUCTION

For the last six years I have been reflecting on the methodological and the philosophical implications of the "catch model" for reconstruction (identification) of a face previously seen (the target face), which was developed by myself and Baruch Cahlon (e.g., Rakover and Cahlon 1989, 1999, 2001). For example, in Rakover (2001) I discussed the explanatory properties of the model, and in Rakover (2002b) I argued that the model can be viewed as a counterinstance to the following well-accepted major and natural methodological requirement. Accordingly, one confirms a theory if the prediction–observation (p–o) gap is small (e.g., zero), and one disconfirms a theory if the p–o gap is big—namely, the prediction does not correspond to the observation. In contrast to the demand that the p–o gap *decrease,* I argued that success in reconstructing the target face requires, within a certain limits, an *increase* in the p–o gap.

Continuing this line of thought, I propose in the present chapter that research in human memory involves two types of methodology. The "explanation-testing" methodology, which is well-accepted in the natural sciences and in psychology, offers proficient procedures for providing sound explanations—namely, theories that provide efficient explanations, and empirical testing of these theories. The "reconstruction" methodology, which is new, proposes procedures for accurate reconstruction of past events (e.g., the target face) from memory, and for explaining a successful reconstruction.

The present chapter is arranged as follows. In Section 14.2, entitled "memory research has two different goals", I present the major ideas for the proposed two methodologies of memory research. In the next sections, I elaborate these ideas. In Section 14.3, which gives a brief summary of the catch model, I present the basic theoretical and empirical elements of this model as an example (actually the only example I am aware of) for reconstructing of past events—the target

Computer-Graphic Facial Reconstruction
John G. Clement and Murray K. Marks, Editors

face—from memory. In Section 14.4, titled "the D-R method: three conditions for reconstruction of past events", I discuss the three conditions of the deductive-reconstruction (D-R) method whose fulfillment will ensure successful reconstruction of the target face. In Section 14.5, concerning substantiation of the D-R method by the catch model, I demonstrate that indeed this model corroborates the D-R method's three conditions. Hence, the model has the capability to reconstruct the target face successfully. In Section 14.6, which asks if we need the reconstruction methodology to achieve reconstruction of past events, I defend the proposal that, while the reconstruction methodology leads to successful reconstruction of the target face, the usual explanation-testing methodology fails to achieve this goal. And in Section 14.7, the discussion, I write briefly about the relation between the new methodology and four relevant topics in the philosophy of science.

14.2 MEMORY RESEARCH HAS TWO DIFFERENT GOALS

Since the early 1980s, an expanding line of research in errors and distortions of memory has emerged (for a critical review see Koriat, Goldsmith & Pansky, 2000), encompassing the following eleven research areas: Gestalt approach to changes in memory over time, spatial memory and distortion, memory for gist versus detail, schema-based effects on memory accuracy, source monitoring, illusions stemming from fluency misattribution, false recall and recognition, misleading postevent information, real-life false memories and their creation, eyewitness memory, and autobiographical memory.

Most of these research areas were aimed at providing (1) a memory theory that explains why and how memory becomes changed and distorted over time, and (2) an empirical test of a given memory theory. However, several other research areas such as real-life false memories, eyewitness testimony, and autobiographical memory, have dealt with the problem of how to reconstruct past events (PEs) accurately from memory. For example, a debate has been ongoing in the area of real-life false memories over the authenticity of recovered memories of childhood sexual abuse. In contrast to clinical psychologists, who believe that these are genuine repressed memories, cognitive researchers have suggested that these recovered PEs are actually generated by the psychotherapeutic process itself. And in the area of eyewitness memory, there is an acute and disturbing problem: generally, the police reconstruction of the culprit's face from the witness's memory is not accurate (for review see Rakover & Cahlon 2001). As distinct from the foregoing research areas, the latter two instances exemplify research that is not aimed at testing explanations of memory, but at rebuilding PEs accurately from memory.

Given these research examples, which are associated with two different methodological goals (explanation-testing vs reconstruction), the following important question arises. Does the research area of PE reconstruction from memory require a research methodology different from the one employed in research aimed at testing explanations of memory? My answer is in the affirmative. To support this answer, the terms *methodology* and *method* need to be clarified first. In philosophy, *methodology* refers to the study of scientific principles, methods, theories, and models of obtaining knowledge in general and in specific disciplines (for a thorough historical review and discussion, see Nola and Sankey 2000). A methodology has a prescriptive characteristic: it argues for and tells one what are the best or most efficient procedures for achieving the goal of acquiring knowledge in a research domain. For example, while the methodology of cognitive psychology recommends that explanation of behavior should be based on the appeal to cognitive representations and the rules that operate on them, the methodology of radical behaviorism recommends avoiding this concept of explanation and concentrating on the observable stimulus–response relationship (e.g., Skinner 1977).

Accordingly, I use *methodology* to refer to a general scientific approach, which consists of a group of procedures, methods, and models by which one obtains knowledge in the research area of memory. I argue for two methodologies: one focuses on explaining a memory phenomenon and on testing a memory theory empirically, and the other focuses on how to reconstruct PEs successfully from memory and on explaining a successful reconstruction.

A *method* is a procedure for achieving a particular scientific goal. For example, Mill's inductive methods are well-known procedures for reaching a causal conclusion based on a group of observations; the hypothetico-deductive (H-D) method is a well-known procedure for testing a scientific theory empirically; and the deductive-reconstruction (D-R) method is my proposed procedure for successfully reconstructing PEs from memory (Rakover 2001, 2002b). Given these delineations, I propose to distinguish two methodologies of research in memory: explanation-testing and reconstruction.

The *explanation-testing* methodology handles the following general empirical relation: remembering is a function of both PEs and a "memory theory", where "remembering" signifies the information remembered as measured by a memory task, such as a yes–no recognition test, two-alternative forced choice, or similarity judgement; "PEs" signify past events: the information presented by certain laboratory procedures or the information occurring in the everyday context (such as faces, objects, landscapes); and "memory theory" signifies a theory (model) aiming at providing an explanation of the remembered information. This methodology has two major goals. It aims to provide an *explanation* (why and how we remember and forget) by employing certain explanation models such as those used by cognitive psychology (either by manipulation of symbols or by networks of neuron-like units); and it aims to *test* a memory theory by employing certain procedures of empirical testing such as the well-known hypothetico-deductive (H-D) method (e.g., Glymour 1980, Kuhn 1970, Popper 1972, Rakover 1990, Salmon 1984).

According to this methodology we *explain* remembering by an appeal to the experimental situation (the manipulation of the independent variable, i.e., the presentation of PEs, such as words, sentences, or pictures of faces) and a memory theory or model, currently based on an analogy with the computer. To do so, we deduce from PEs in conjunction with a memory theory a prediction (a description of the phenomenon under study). If the prediction corresponds to the phenomenon observed, then the phenomenon is explained in terms of the memory theory. This procedure of explanation follows the well-known deductive-nomological (D-N) and the deductive-statistical (D-S) models of explanation (see Hempel 1965) with the following major difference. While the Hempelian models employ laws of nature (deterministic or statistical), the cognitive-psychology explanation employs a cognitive memory theory. As mentioned above, a cognitive explanation requires specification of the cognitive mechanism that causally mediates between input and output. This mechanism has to answer the following two major questions: How is the world represented in a cognitive system? How are representations manipulated or processed? (For a discussion of models of explanations, see Hempel 1965, Rakover 1990, 1997, and Salmon 1984, 1989. For discussion of the requirements of cognitive psychology see Palmer and Kimchi 1986, Rakover and Cahlon 2001, and Thagard 1996.) According to the explanation-testing methodology, we *test* a memory theory by deducing a prediction from a memory theory in conjunction with the experimental situation. If the observed phenomenon matches the prediction, then the memory theory is confirmed—and if not, the theory is refuted. (As mentioned above, this description follows the well-known H-D method. In fact, this method is more complicated than described here and also includes in addition auxiliary hypotheses, or background theory, which finally determines the acceptance or rejection of a theory. See discussions on these issues by Kuhn 1970, Popper 1972, Glymour 1980, Rakover 1990, Salmon 1984.)

Although there is a similarity between the procedures of *explanation* and of *testing* in their logical structure, these two procedures differ in the following major respect. In explaining a given phenomenon, we assume that the theory is correct (or more accurately, we assume that the theory is well-grounded theoretically and empirically), so that the explanation of a given phenomenon is not provided by a false theory. In contrast, when we test a given theory, the status of that theory is at stake: we examine whether the theory is supported by the empirical results.

As an example of the use of the explanation-testing methodology, let us consider two attempts to explain the "facial inversion effect". This effect relates to the finding that recognition of inverted faces (chin above, hair below) is less accurate (by about 25%) than recognition of upright faces. Furthermore, inversion impairs recognition of faces more than of objects such as houses and landscapes (e.g., Diamond and Carey 1986, Rakover and Teucher 1997, Valentine 1988). Diamond and Carey (1986) proposed a memory theory that explains this effect. Accordingly, recognition of upright faces is based on both featural and configurational information (where featural information is about individual features and configurational information is about the spatial relations among the features: see Rakover 2002a). By contrast, recognition of an inverted face is based mainly on featural information. Hence, this theory explains the facial inversion effect by proposing that presenting faces upside-down impairs the configurational information, which in turn decreases face recognition. Rakover and Teucher (1997) tested Diamond and Carey's theory by deducing a prediction from it, namely that inversion cannot impair recognition of isolated facial features such as eyes, nose, and mouth. The results disconfirmed this theory: inversion did impair recognition of isolated features. Hence, configurational information is not a condition for the inversion effect. The results were explained by an alternative theory, which I call the "facial schemas", and which does predict the impairment of recognition of inverted isolated facial features.

Many other experiments also exemplify the use of the explanation-testing methodology. For example, top-down schema-based processes explain changes and distortions in PEs, and certain retroactive cognitive processes account for the effects of misleading postevent information (see Koriat *et al.* 2000). We test the retroactive theory by deducing, for instance, one prediction from that theory and another prediction from an alternative theory (learning, proactive, or decay theories), and by deciding empirically which prediction is confirmed or refuted by the experimental results.

The *Reconstruction* methodology handles the following general empirical relation: PEs are a function of performance and a "reconstruction theory", where "PEs" signify past events, the information that was presented in the past and that is to be reconstructed accurately from memory; "performance" signifies the results obtained in a memory task (the task's output); and a "reconstruction theory" (model) signifies the special theory aiming at an accurate reconstruction of PEs.

The reconstruction theory consists of two rules: (1) a "performance rule", which determines how a memory task should be performed, and (2) an "analysis rule", which determines how the results of that memory task (the task's output) should be analyzed. The aim of these two rules is to guarantee an accurate PE reconstruction.

The memory task is executed by both the performance rule and by the participant. The former tells us how the memory task *should be executed in order to achieve successful PE reconstruction,* whereas the latter tells us how the same memory task *has been actually performed by the participant.* Both these outputs (that of the performance rule and that of the participant) are analyzed by the same analysis rule. These procedural differences, as we shall see immediately, are very important for achieving an accurate reconstruction of PEs.

The reconstruction methodology has two major goals. It aims to *reconstruct* PEs from memory by employing the deductive-reconstruction (D-R) method developed by Rakover (2001, 2002b), which consists of three conditions whose fulfillment guarantees an accurate reconstruction of PEs from memory; and it aims to provide an *explanation* of a successfully reconstruction of PEs from memory by employing a special kind of explanation: a successful reconstruction of PEs is dependent on the fulfillment of the D-R method's three conditions (for details see Section 14.7, the discussion, below).

The D-R method consists of two kinds of conditions: theoretical and empirical. The fulfillment of the *theoretical condition* guarantees that an accurate reconstruction will be derived mathematically from the reconstruction theory or model. As mentioned above, this theory or model determines by a performance rule how the memory task should be performed and by an analysis rule how the performance rule's output should be analyzed. These two rules are designed in such a way that together they will result mathematically in an accurate reconstruction of PEs (e.g., the target face).

Fulfillment of the *empirical conditions* guarantees that an actual reconstruction of PEs from a participant's memory will be accurate. How is this done? It is done through the fulfillment of the following "matching" condition: a match is required between the participant's performance and the performance rule's output. If the participant's performance in a memory task matches the output of the performance rule in that task, and if we apply to the participant's performance the same analysis rule (which was applied to the performance rule's output), then PEs will be accurately reconstructed from the participant's memory.

The logic behind this conclusion is simple: if a PE is derived from A (performance rule's output) and B (analysis rule), then it is derived also from C (participant's performance) and B, since A = C. That is, the PE is reconstructed from memory. (Note that another empirical condition of the D-R method, which will be discussed below, handles the situation in which the matching between the performance rule's output and the participant's performance is not complete.)

Furthermore, the matching between the participant's performance and the performance rule's output can be viewed as empirical support for the hypothesis that the performance rule describes the participant's cognitive processes. Finally, note that the reconstruction methodology does not deal with the following questions. How does one remember one's own past memories, PEs? Is one's memory correct, distorted, or fabricated? These questions are handled by the explanation-testing methodology, which proposes a memory theory that explains why and how errors occurred. That is, the retrieval of one's own memories is an interesting behavior, which we, the researchers, attempt to understand by employing the explanation-testing methodology. By contrast, the reconstruction methodology deals with a different question: how can we, the researchers, be assured that we can accurately reconstruct PEs from one's memory? My answer is: by employing reconstruction methodology.

14.3 A BRIEF SUMMARY OF THE CATCH MODEL: AN EXAMPLE OF AN ACCURATE RECONSTRUCTION OF PAST EVENTS FROM MEMORY

Research on the widely applied Photofit and the Identikit techniques, used by police for reconstructing, and identifying, faces previously seen, has shown that their facial composites bear little resemblance to these faces (e.g., Bruce 1988, Davies 1981, 1986, Kovera *et al.* 1997, Rakover and Cahlon 2001). Furthermore, it was found that computer-driven systems such as the E-fit, which are based on the computerization of the mechanical systems such as the Photofit and the Identikit, did not result in better reconstruction of the target face from memory than the mechanical systems (e.g., Davies *et al.* 2000). These can be attributed to three main factors.

First, the process of facial-composite production starts with a verbal description of the remembered target face. Several experiments have shown that verbal description impairs face recognition (e.g., Dodson *et al.* 1997, Finger and Pezdek 1999, Schooler and Englster-Schooler 1990).

Second, while a witness has perceived and processed a face as a whole, Identikit and Photofit, as well as computer-driven systems, try to reconstruct the target face by using isolated facial values such as narrow/round eyes and long/short/wide noses. For example, out of many exemplars of the eyes, the eyewitness attempts to find the one most similar to the remembered eyes of the target face. I do believe that the human brain is able to decompose the memory of a whole face into its parts, but this process is achieved at the considerable price of memory errors, since such decomposition destroys the configurational-holistic information of a face. Many experiments stressed the extreme importance of this type of information in perception and in memory of faces. The configurational theory suggests that configurational information (the spatial relations among facial features) is more important than featural information (e.g., Diamond and Carey 1986). The effects of configurational changes, such as changing the distance between the eyes, nose, and mouth or local inversion of the eyes and mouth (a manipulation that creates the "Thatcher illusion", Thompson 1980), disappear when the face is inverted. However, inversion does not have such effects when the changes in a face are featural, such as thickening of the eyebrows (e.g., Bartlett and Searcy 1993, Bartlett *et al.* 2003, Leder and Bruce 2000, Rhodes *et al.* 1993, Searcy and Bartlett 1996). The Holistic theory suggests that featural and configurational information is perceived as a whole unit, one Gestalt. Recognition of isolated features is impaired, and perception and memory of the whole is better than perception and memory of its parts (e.g., Farah *et al.* 1995, Tanaka and Farah 1993, 2003, Tanaka and Sengco 1997). Furthermore, the accepted differentiation between perception of faces and perception of other objects suggests that, whereas perception of faces is based on holistic information processing, object perception is based on decomposition of the whole into its parts (e.g., Biederman and Kalocsai 1998, McKone *et al.* 2003, Rakover and Cahlon 2001, Tanaka and Farah 2003).

Third, the use of many samples of facial values (such as small nose and round chin) to locate the specific facial value most similar to the target face causes serious interference in the process of retrieving information from the witness's memory (e.g., Farah 1992, Rakover and Cahlon 1989, 1999, 2001, Tanaka and Farah 1993). For example, Rakover and Cahlon (2001) divided the face into five facial dimensions (hair & forehead, eyes, nose, mouth, and chin) with n facial values per dimension (e.g., round eyes, long mouth). This division allowed them to generate multiple facial composites. They found that, as the number of facial values (n) increased (e.g., from 2 different eyes to 9 different eyes), the accuracy in the reconstruction of a face previously seen decreased.

Given these considerations, we (Rakover and Cahlon) decided to develop a new model and experimental procedure for reconstructing the target face by using recognition memory of a whole face. The *catch* model is a mathematical model designed to reconstruct the target face from its features (e.g., hair & forehead, eyes, nose, mouth, and chin). These features are identified *after* a participant decides which of two whole test faces is more similar to the remembered target face, as part of a two-stage experiment. In the first stage, the study stage, the participant is presented with a picture of a face—the target face—for about twenty seconds. In the test stage the participant is required to perform a similarity-judgement task: she or he is presented with a series of pairs of test faces: one on the left and one on the right. Neither of the test faces is the target. In each trial, the participant is presented with one test pair, and she is

A. Hair and forehead	B. Eyes	C. Noses	D. Mouths	E. Chins
(a_1) completely bald	(b_1) slanting	(c_1) long	(d_1) wide	(e_1) pointed
(a_2) medium	(b_2) narrow	(c_2) medium	(d_2) medium	(e_2) rounded
(a_3) with hair	(b_3) round	(c_3) short	(d_3) small	(e_3) squared

Table 14.1

Example of a face division into five dimensions and three values per dimension.

required to choose the face that most resembles the remembered target face. The participant's choices are then analyzed by what I call the "analysis rule", which leads to the reconstruction of the target face.

A face is defined as a vector of facial values (e.g., small *mouth*, blue *eyes*), where each value belongs to a different facial dimension (e.g., *mouth*, *eyes*). In the examples in parentheses, the italicized words stand for facial dimensions, which in conjunction with their adjectives represent their values. An illustration of a division of a face into five dimensions and three values per dimension is depicted in Table 14.1.

In this example, there are $3^5 = 243$ possible faces. There are five dimensions, each having three different values: $a_i b_j c_k d_m e_n$ ($i, j, k, m, n = 1, 2, 3$). Only one of the 243 facial composites is the target face (F_t) and the rest are test faces (F). An example of a target face is: F_t: a_1 b_1 c_1 d_1 e_1, or for the sake of brevity, F_t: 1 1 1 1 1 (e.g., F_t: completely bald, slanting eyes, long nose, wide mouth, and pointed chin); and an example of a test pair consisting of two test faces is F_L: 1 1 1 2 3 and F_R: 1 2 3 3 3 (where L stands for the left side of a test pair and R for the right side).

We assume that F_t is represented in memory as a gestalt, together with background stimulation and the knowledge of when and where F_t was perceived. This information is processed mainly automatically, and can also be partially processed in various ways, depending on the participant's intentions and goals, and the requirements of the memory task. We further assume that F is identified as F_t in terms of cognitive memory processes involving similarity judgements. The values of F are compared with the values of F_t represented in memory, and the level of similarity between F and F_t is determined in terms of the number of their common values. If the similarity is maximal, then F is identified as F_t. This assumption led to the model's *performance rule*, which determines how the similarity-judgement task should be performed:

(a) Each F is compared with F_t to see if it has the same values as F_t.

(b) For each F the number of "matches", that is, the number of values common to both F_t and a test face F, is determined. We denote the number of matches by $\mu(W_F)$, where W_F is the vector associated with F as follows:

$$(W_F)_i = \begin{Bmatrix} 1 \text{ if } (F_t)_i = (F)_i \\ 0 \text{ otherwise} \end{Bmatrix}, \quad \text{and} \quad \mu(W_F) = \sum_{i=1}^{k} (W_F)_i.$$

($\mu(W_F)$ constitutes an index of similarity between a test face and F_t.)

(c) The F with the highest number of "matches" or $\mu(W_F)$ is selected.

For example, if the target face is F_t: 1 1 1 1 1, and a test pair is F_L: 1 1 2 3 1, F_R: 2 3 2 1 3, then the catch model will select F_L, since $\mu(W_{F_L}) = 3 > \mu(W_{F_R}) = 1$. The performance rule described here is typical of many similarity rules reported in the literature (e.g., Estes 1994, Medin and Schaffer 1978, Nosofsky 1984, Tversky 1977. For reviews and discussions see, e.g., Melara 1992, Nosofsky 1992). Of all these similarity rules, the one developed in Tversky's (1977) contrast model is the most relevant for the present case. Despite many differences between the catch model and Tversky's contrast model, under certain conditions it can be shown that the present perfomance rule is a particular case of the contrast model. (Note that the development of the present performance rule occurred before Rakover and Cahlon became aware of Tversky's important work.)

Given the choice data, F_t is identified by means of the *analysis rule*, which determines how to analyze the data:

(a) For each test pair, the values that appear in the chosen F, and do not appear in the nonchosen F, are recorded. We shall call these values the *differentiating values*. For example, if the test pair is F_L: 1 1 1 2 3 and F_R: 1 2 3 3 3, and F_L is chosen, then the differentiating values are: $-$1 1 2$-$, where a dash signifies values that do not differentiate between F_L and F_R;

(b) For each facial dimension, across several choice trials, the one differentiating value chosen most frequently by the participant (i.e., the one associated with the highest *frequency of choice*) is selected. Consider, for example, facial dimension (A). If a_1 is associated with the frequency of choice of 100, a_2 with 75, and a_3 with 25, then a_1 is selected as the expected F_t value; and

(c) F_t is reconstructed by using the values selected in (b).

In most of our experiments we used Penry's (1971a,b) Photofit kit to compose various faces. Facial composites were made of $k = 5$ facial dimensions and $n = 2, 3, 6, 9$ facial values per dimension. A special computer program was developed to present these composites on a PC screen.

The research program of the catch model deals with many interesting problems, such as the following:

1 The *equal pairs* problem: The model cannot make a similarity decision in cases where the number of matches between values of the left test face and F_t is equal to the number of matches between values of the right test face and F_t (e.g., F_t: 11111; test pair: F_L: 11323 and F_R: 21331). We call these pairs "equal pairs". (Note that "unequal pairs" are those pairs for which the model can make a similarity decision.) We solve this problem by showing that the target face can be reconstructed despite the occurrence of equal pairs, and by solving the "saliency" problem.

2 The *Saliency* problem: The catch model assigns the same weight (one point) to each facial dimension—a situation that generates the equal-pairs problem and does not correspond to reality. Rakover and Cahlon (1999) propose a solution to this problem by ascribing different weights to different dimensions of the target face. For example, since the eyes draw more attention than the nose, the eyes dimension was ascribed greater weight than the nose dimension.

3 The problem of the *number of values* (n) *per dimension*: As mentioned above, we used Penry's (1971a,b) Photofit kit in our experiments. Composites were made of 5 facial dimensions and with $n = 2, 3, 6$, and 9 facial values per dimension. We found that as n increased, correct reconstruction of the target face tended to *decrease*. This decrease is due to a retroactive process, since the test faces were composed of a greater number of facial values. We dealt with this interference effect in a number of ways. For example, we expanded the analysis rule to include the non chosen test faces; and we categorized the facial values in terms of their shared visual similarity, using a multi-dimensional scaling technique. As a result, we obtained several similarity categories per dimension. (This categorization was done independently and before the reconstruction of F_t.) Using these similarity categories, we were able successfully to reconstruct a group of faces very similar to F_t (i.e., a set of facial vectors similar to the vector of F_t).

All this required continuous experimentation and the development of special computer programs for generation of target faces, test pairs, and the sampling of a small number of test pairs from all possible pairs (see Rakover and Cahlon 2001).

14.4 THE D-R METHOD: THREE CONDITIONS FOR RECONSTRUCTION OF PAST EVENTS

Having described the catch model, I shall now describe the D-R method's three conditions whose fulfillment ensures successful reconstruction of a PE (i.e., the target face) from memory. The D-R method provides essential conditions for judging whether a given performance rule and an analysis rule will result in reconstruction of the PE from memory. The method is a procedural schema, in which one inserts a particular performance rule (such as the similarity judgement used in the catch model) and an analysis rule (such as the one used in the catch model), to determine whether reconstruction of the PE (such as F_t) from memory can be successful. To facilitate understanding of the D-R method, the three conditions are next described as they apply to the specific case of the catch model. Following this description, I shall present the D-R method in a general form.

1 The *provability* condition. This is a mathematical proof that shows that the reconstruction of the target face is deduced from the performance rule, which determines how the similarity-judgement task has to be performed, and an

analysis rule, which determines how the choice data (the output of the similarity-judgement task) should be analyzed. This proof guarantees that the target face is indeed reconstructed. More specifically, the performance rule determines for the similarity-judgement task which of the two test faces most resembles the remembered target face. The analysis rule analyzes the chosen faces into their differentiating values in a way that leads to the reconstruction of the target face. Given these two rules, it has been proven that the target face is reconstructed successfully.

2 The *matching* condition. Given the provability condition, if the participant's choices in the similarity-judgement task match the choices made by the catch model's performance rule, and if the participant's choices are analyzed by the model's analysis rule, then past events will be successfully reconstructed from the participant's memory. If the participant's choices are identical to the choices produced by the performance rule, then the same target face will also be reconstructed from the participant's memory. According to the provability condition, replacing the performance rule's choices with the subject's choices will render the same final result: reconstruction of the target face.

3 The *error-robustness* condition. What if the participant's choices do not match the performance rule's choices completely? If a full and complete match between the participant's choices and the performance rule's choices is required, then the reconstruction of the target will fail. Hence, one must ask the following crucial question: to achieve the reconstruction of the target, how many of the participant's choices have to match the choices made by the performance rule? How many errors can the participant make and *still achieve reconstruction of the target face?* (An error is defined in terms of the performance rule: e.g., if the performance rule determines that the left test face of a test pair is more similar to the target than is the right test face, then an error is defined as the choice of the right test face.) Given this, one would like the reconstruction theory to be *error-robust*: that is, reconstruction of the target succeeds despite the participant's multiple errors. In other words, one would like the theory to withstand a maximum number of errors and still be able to reconstruct the target face. The greater the number of errors sustained, the higher the method's error-robustness in achieving reconstruction of the target. I call this number of errors the "maximum errors allowable" (MEA), where allowable refers to the maximal number of errors that the model can sustain and still achieve successful reconstruction of the target face. Hence, when a participant's errors exceed the MEA, the reconstruction cannot be achieved: namely, the target face cannot be reconstructed from memory.

The error-robustness condition can be apprehended by an analogy to the qualities of a tool such as a wrench. To achieve its goal, a wrench has to have certain qualities such as size and hardness—one cannot turn a 3-cm screw made of steel with a 5-mm wrench made of cardboard. Similarly, a reconstruction theory, which is conceived of as a tool designed to achieve the goal of a successful reconstruction of a face from memory, has to have certain qualities. According to the D-R method, the MEA is the quality required from the reconstruction theory in order to achieve its goal: it has to withstand many errors: it has to be error-robust.

I shall now present the D-R method in its general form. Accordingly, the target face belongs to the general category of past events (PEs); the similarity-judgement task belongs to a memory task; the similarity choice between two test faces belongs to a performance rule; the reconstruction of the target face from the differentiating values belongs to an analysis rule; and MEA refers to "maximum errors allowable" appropriate to a given performance rule.

1 The *provability* condition. Past events have to be deduced from the performance rule, which determines how a memory task should be performed, and the analysis rule, which determines how to analyze the performance rule's output.
2 The *matching* condition. If a participant's performance in the memory task matches the output produced by the performance rule, and if the participant's choices are analyzed by the analysis rule, then the PE will actually be reconstructed from the participant's memory.
3 The *error-robustness* condition. The reconstruction of a PE from memory is successful if the number of errors is not higher than the MEA.

As can be seen, the provability condition constitutes the theoretical part of the D-R method, whereas the matching condition constitutes the empirical part, and the error-robustness condition constitutes the empirical as well as the theoretical part of the method. If the provability condition is met, then the PE is reconstructed successfully in theory. If the matching condition is met, the reconstruction is made from the participant's memory. Hence, this condition makes a connection between theory and observation. Finally, the error-robustness condition theoretically stipulates the limit for the theory–observation linkage. It calculates the MEA in theory (e.g., the maximum percentage of errors that still allows successful reconstruction as determined by the catch model), as well as the observed percentage of errors made by the participant. If the latter percentage is too large, complete reconstruction of the PE cannot be attained. Given the D-R method's conditions, does the catch model indeed substantiate the D-R method?

14.5 SUBSTANTIATION OF THE D-R METHOD BY THE CATCH MODEL

Given the catch model described above, we were able to prove mathematically the following major conclusions (see Rakover and Cahlon 1989, 2001):

1 The chosen test face contains a larger number of differentiating values that belong to the target face than does the rejected face.

2 Given a facial dimension, the differentiating value with the highest frequency of choice is the value belonging to the target face. Namely, the catch model identifies the target face theoretically. *Hence, the catch model satisfies the provability condition.*

3 Even if the sample of test pairs, which is randomly drawn from all possible test pairs, contains only a small number of pairs, it is possible to reconstruct the target face. As the number of test pairs in the sample increases, so does the likelihood of accurately reconstructing the target face.

4 As the number of participants (or eyewitnesses) increases, so does the likelihood of reconstructing the target face.

5 Even if errors are made in the choice of the test faces, namely when the choice of test face is not the choice determined by the model (e.g., if F_t is 11111, and a test pair: F_L is 11231 and F_R is 23312, then an error will be made when F_R is chosen, and not F_L), the target face is reconstructed. [The calculation of MEA is dependent on k, n, type of test pairs (unequal, equal), and sample size of the test pairs. For example, MEA = 31.7% for all unequal test pairs constructed from $k = 4$ dimensions with $n = 2$ values per dimension.] *Hence, the catch model satisfies the error-robustness condition.*

As conclusions 1–5 indicate, *the catch model satisfies both the provability condition and the error-robustness condition.* Furthermore, the catch model has also proved empirically successful. In several laboratory experiments using a small and random sampling of test pairs, we were able in many cases to reconstruct the target face or the group of faces most similar to the target face. Moreover, strong experimental support was found for all the predictions derived from our mathematical propositions and corollaries of the catch model. In these experiments, the percentage of errors that still allowed identification of F_t reached about 35%. This may suggest that the performance rule describes the cognitive process involved in the participant's performing the similarity-judgement task: the participant's choices correspond to the choices made by the catch model's performance rule (for details see Rakover and Cahlon 1989, 1999, 2001). *Hence, the catch model succeeded in satisfying the matching condition and the error-robustness condition.*

In view of this, it is safe to conclude that the catch model fulfills the above three conditions and therefore substantiates the D-R method. Hence, the application of the reconstruction methodology to the research area of eye-witness memory results in a successful reconstruction of the target face.

14.6 DO WE NEED THE RECONSTRUCTION METHODOLOGY TO ACHIEVE A RECONSTRUCTION OF PE?

Having described the explanation-testing methodology and the reconstruction methodology, the following questions arise. Is the reconstruction methodology necessary for reconstruction of a PE? Is it not possible to use the explanation-testing methodology instead of the reconstruction methodology, and reach the goal of the latter?

These questions are based on what I call the "memory limit of reconstruction" (MLR) argument. If reconstruction is dependent on memory, and if what one remembers (the remembered PE) is erroneous, different from the actual PE, then the reconstruction of the PE cannot be better than what is remembered. If this is true, then the remembered PE sets the limit of reconstruction. Hence, (a) the reconstruction methodology cannot surpass what one remembers, and (b) what one remembers is handled by the explanation-testing methodology. My answer to the MLR argument is as follows.

The fact that one remembers, for example, 70% of the PE's information by using one method of memory testing does not mean that there are no other methods of testing that improve accuracy of memory to a great extent. In fact, research in memory shows over and over again that remembering is improved by use of better methods of memory testing. As examples, compare recall versus recognition or cued recall; consider the improvements in remembering due to the principle of encoding specificity (see Tulving 1983), due to the cognitive interview in eyewitness's situation (see Fisher *et al.* 1989), and due to the catch model, which overcomes many problems in face reconstruction (such as verbal description of the target face and decomposition of the whole face into isolated features). These problems have been encountered by other methods of face reconstruction such as the Photofit and the Identikit (see Rakover and Cahlon 2001). Hence, it is safe to suggest that what one remembers is not the maximum that one can, and accordingly, improvement in memory means improvement in reconstruction of the PE.

Still, the very fact that memory can be improved by means of better memory tests, does not justify the employment of the reconstruction methodology. My answer is that there are two important reasons for employing this methodology.

14.6.1 CONDITIONS THAT ENSURE PE RECONSTRUCTION

To the best of my knowledge, there is no memory theory that ensures accurate reconstruction of PEs. Rather, although there are a very few instances where remembering is free of errors, in general a memory theory is designed to deal with the phenomena of forgetting, errors and distortions of memory, and false memories. Given this and the fact that the explanation-testing methodology is aimed at evaluating whether a memory theory succeeds in explaining the phenomena of memory decrease over time, it follows that explanation-testing methodology does not provide an assurance of PE reconstruction. By contrast, the reconstruction methodology does provide this assurance by fulfilling the D-R method's three conditions. If it is proven mathematically, as in the case with the catch model, that a performance rule and an analysis rule result in PE reconstruction, and if the participant's behavior in the memory task corresponds to the performance rule's output (i.e., it is less than the appropriate MEA), then the reconstruction of PE from the participant's memory is guaranteed. Hence, the D-R method provides a sufficient condition for PE reconstruction: the fulfillment of the method's conditions. While the reconstruction methodology is equipped with the required method for assuring PE reconstruction, the explanation-testing methodology is not. And vice versa: while the explanation-testing method is equipped with the required methods for explanation of memory impairment and testing of a memory theory, the reconstruction method is not.

14.6.2 APPLICATION OF EXPLANATION-TESTING METHODOLOGY TO THE CATCH MODEL

Here I will show that the application of the explanation-testing methodology to the experimental situation of the catch model can lead to self-contradiction and failure to reconstruct the target face. I assume two hypothetical situations and two performance rules: primary and alternative. While the primary rule does lead to a successful reconstruction of the target face, the alternative rule does not.

Situation A: The correspondence between the primary performance rule and the participant's choices is 60%. However, the target face is successfully reconstructed from the participant's memory, since the participant's percentage of errors (40%) is not higher than the MEA = 40% (the percentage of errors that still allows a successful reconstruction).

Situation B: Correspondence between the alternative performance rule and the participant's choices is 90%. However, since the correspondence between the alternative rule and the primary rule is 50%, the alternative rule's percentage of error is higher than the MEA, and therefore the alternative rule cannot lead to a successful reconstruction of the target face.

As a simple example that illustrates these two situations consider Table 14.2. There are 10 test pairs. The primary performance rule (primary rule) determines that all the choices have to be the right test face. The analysis rule shows that these choices result in a successful reconstruction of the target face. The participant's choices are as follows: the first four choices are left and the other six choices are right. The participant's percent of error is 40% (not higher than the MEA), and therefore the PE is reconstructed from memory. The alternative performance rule (alternative rule) determines that the first five choices are left and the rest of the choices are right. The alternative rule's percentage of errors with regard to the participant's choices is only 10% (i.e., the correspondence between the alternative rule and the participant's choices is 90%),

Source of choices	Ten test pairs	Results
Primary rule used by D-R method	R R R R R R R R R R	Target face is reconstructed
Participant's choices	L L L L R R R R R R	Target face is reconstructed, since MEA = 40%.
Primary rule used by the explanation-testing methodology	R R R R R R R R R R	Primary rule is rejected, since only 60% of the participant's choices are predicted; target face is recon structed, since MEA = 40%
Alternative rule used by the explanation-testing methodology	L L L L L R R R R R	Alternative rule is accepted, since 90% of the participant's choices are predicted; target face cannot be reconstructed, since percent error (50%) > MEA = 40%

Table 14.2

An example of the two situations: A and B (see text).

whereas the alternative rule's percentage of errors with regard to the primary rule is 50%, which is above the MEA. Thus, the target face cannot be reconstructed by the alternative rule.

Let us examine now each of the two situations from the point of views of our two methodologies. In both situations A and B there is a contradiction between the two methodologies.

SITUATION A

While the target face can be reconstructed from the participant's memory, since a 40% error rate (with regard to the primary rule) is not higher than the MEA, the explanation-testing methodology rejects this very rule as a bad theory, since it generates a high percentage of errors (with respect to the participant's choices): the prediction does not correspond to the observation. Hence, the explanation-testing methodology rejects a theory that leads to a successful reconstruction of the target face. This would place the explanation-testing methodology in a self-contradicting situation. On the one hand, the primary performance rule has to be rejected, since its predictive power of the participant's choices is low; on the other hand the very same rule has to be accepted, since the rule leads to a successful reconstruction.

SITUATION B

While the target face cannot be reconstructed by the alternative rule, since a 50% error rate (with regard to the primary rule) is higher than the MEA, the explanation-testing methodology accepts this very rule as a good theory, since it generates a very low percentage of errors (with respect to the participant's choices). Hence, the explanation-testing methodology accepts a theory that cannot lead to a successful reconstruction of the target face. This also places the explanation-testing methodology in a self-contradictory situation. On the one hand, the alternative performance rule has to be accepted, since its predictive power of the participant's choices is very high; and on the other hand the very same rule has to be rejected, since this very rule fails to reconstruct the target face.

Furthermore, in a comparison of the primary and alternative rules, the explanation-testing methodology is put in an unsolvable situation—a dilemma. On the one hand it has to reject the primary rule and prefer the alternative rule, since the latter rule generates higher correspondence with the participant's choices. But on the other hand it has to reject the alternative rule and prefer the primary rule, since the latter rule is the one that leads to the reconstruction of the target face.

Note that this dilemma does not occur for the reconstruction methodology, since the primary performance rule is conceived of by this methodology as means to achieve a successful reconstruction of the target face. Hence, any performance rule, as well as any participant's responding, is evaluated in terms of the D-R method's error-robustness condition, namely whether the percentage of errors is less than the MEA. If it is, then the target face is reconstructed. That is, while the reconstruction methodology provides us with a sufficient condition (fulfillment of the D-R method's three requirements) for a successful PE reconstruction (e.g., the target face), the explanation-testing methodology (the H-D method) does not.

One possible critique of the above example of the primary-alternative rules is that the acceptance or rejection of a rule is dependent on the result of a statistical test (which is part of the methods employed by the explanation-testing methodology). Accordingly, let us assume that the primary rule's prediction, 60%, is above the chance level. In this case, the explanation-testing methodology accepts the primary rule, which leads to the target-face reconstruction. Does this mean that the application of the explanation-testing methodology to the experimental situation of the catch model is smooth and successful? My answer is no. Consider the alternative rule, which predicts 90% of the participant's choices. Clearly, the alternative rule is accepted by the explanation-testing methodology as a very good theory, a better theory, since 90% is above the chance level and since this methodology prefers the alternative rule, which predicts a higher percentage of the participant's choices than the primary rule (90% vs. 60%). But the alternative rule fails to reconstruct the target face.

The above discussion shows that there are many cases where the explanation-testing methodology (1) accepts bad rules, which cannot lead to the target face reconstruction, and rejects good rules, which do lead to reconstruction, and (2) encounters a self-contradiction of acceptance and rejection of the same performance rule, and a dilemma of acceptance and rejection of two performance rules, one rule which leads to reconstruction and one which does not.

14.7 DISCUSSION

Having presented sound arguments for the reconstruction methodology, I shall now discuss four issues: first, the question whether this methodology is merely a technique developed under the umbrella of the explanation-testing methodology; second, the question of explanation provided by the D-R method; third, the question of the methodology's scope, and finally the question of the unity of science.

14.7.1 TECHNOLOGY

Despite the above arguments, one may propose that the differences between the reconstruction and the explanation-testing methodologies are not particularly significant. In the final analysis the success of the former methodology depends on its ability to produce a good reconstruction, which is evaluated routinely by the explanation-testing methodology. Hence, it is possible to propose that the reconstruction methodology is subordinate to the explanation-testing methodology, and can be viewed as an efficient technique whose development is inspired by the latter methodology. My answer to this critique is as follows. It is true that the reconstruction methodology depends on an empirical test: the production of a good reconstruction. In this respect the two methodologies are similar. However, there is a major difference between them, which shows that it is impossible to accept this critique. As has been shown above, the application of the explanation-testing methodology (the H-D method) to the reconstruction research domain leads to acceptance of bad rules that cannot produce successful reconstruction, rejection of good rules, and creation of inner contradictions. By comparison, the reconstruction methodology avoids all these problems and produces a successful reconstruction. Since a successful technology cannot be built on faulty methodology, this proposal is unsound: it is wrong to view the reconstruction methodology as a mere technological improvement rooted in the explanation-testing methodology.

Note also that the concept of technology does not correspond to the concepts of methodology and method as delineated in the introduction. Briefly, without entering the debate regarding the complex relationships between science and technology, it is safe to suggest that a large part of modern technology is based on scientific theoretical knowledge. Hence, I shall delineate technology as a practical realization of scientific theories and models (where the process of practical realization involves creativity, knowledge of how to do, and skill). For example, a radio is a realization of Maxwell's electromagnetic theory (together with other auxiliary theories and practical knowledge); and the catch model, together with the aid of the D-R method, *can lead* to the development of a practical system, which may improve the process of identifying—reconstructing the suspect's face. However, this technical improvement is different from a methodology or a method in its goal and structure, e.g., it does not have explanatory and normative qualities, whereas methodology and method do.

14.7.2 EXPLANATION

What kind of an explanation is provided by the reconstruction methodology for a successful reconstruction of PE from memory? I will answer the question with regard to the example of the catch model. A successful reconstruction of the target face is explained in terms of the fulfillment of the D-R method's three conditions: provability, matching, and error-robustness. If the method's requirements are fulfilled, then the PE is reconstructe from memory. This explanation can be conceived of from the perspectives of the following two models of explanation: the teleological model and Hempel's (1965) deductive-nomological (D-N) model. From the former model's point of view, it may be argued that the D-R method provides a teleological kind of explanation, since the performance rule and the analysis rule of the catch model can be regarded as means, tools, to achieve the goal of a successful reconstruction.

From the latter model's point of view, it may be argued that the explanation provided by the D-R method is similar to the D-N model, since it is based on deduction. (Note that a teleological explanation is based on "practical syllogisms" and not on deduction. For a discussion, see Rakover 1997.) To make the latter point of view plain, I shall first describe Hempel's D-N model schematically:

Premises: (a) Laws

(b) Antecedent or initial conditions

Conclusion: A description of the phenomenon to be explained.

The description of the phenomenon to be explained is logically deduced from the initial conditions in conjunction with at least one law. For example, one explains why a stone falls about 4.9 m in 1 second, by using the law of free falling bodies: $s = \frac{1}{2} gt^2$, where s signifies distance, t time, and g the acceleration caused by gravity, and by plugging the initial condition of $t = 1$ sec into this law. Hence, this model provides us with a general schema for explanation for answering why-questions, by showing that the phenomenon deduced is an example of a law.

Now I shall formulate the D-R method along with the catch model so as to fit into the deductive structure of Hempel's model of explanation:

STAGE 1: CATCH MODEL

Premises 1: (a) Test pairs

(b) Performance rule (similarity judgement)

(c) Choices

(d) Analysis rule

Conclusion 1: Accurate reconstruction of the target face

STAGE 2: PARTICIPANT

Premises 2: (a) Test pairs

(b) Choices fulfill matching and error-robustness conditions

(c) Analysis rule

Conclusion 2: Accurate reconstruction of the target face from memory

In stage 1, the catch model successfully reconstructs the target face theoretically. An accurate image of the target face is deduced mathematically through the employment of the performance and the analysis rules. Thus, the model fulfills the provability condition. In stage 2, a successful reconstruction of the target face is deduced from the participant's memory, since his/her similarity choices fulfill the matching and error-robustness conditions. The participant's choices displace the model's choices, and in conjunction with the analysis-rule results, as in stage 1, lead to an accurate reconstruction of the target face.

This structure of the D-R method can be further abstracted and simplified into the following basic logical form:

Stage 1: F_t is deduced from the performance rule's choices and the analysis rule

Stage 2: the participant's choices are identical to the performance rule's choices;

Conclusion: F_t is deduced from the participant's choices and the analysis rule (i.e., F_t is successfully reconstructed from memory).

Does this structure of the D-R method fulfill the requirements of the D-N model? The answer is no. Except for the fact that both the D-R method and the D-N model are based on logic and on empirical observations, the D-R method differs from the D-N model in all respects. The major difference is that the D-R method does not employ a law. It is hard to see the performance rule and the analysis rule as universal laws. Even the performance rule by itself cannot be conceived of as a law in the sense similar to the concept of a law (e.g., the law of free-falling bodies). At most it can be put forward as a hypothesis suggesting that one's similarity judgements follow this rule. However, as mentioned above, there are several alternative similarity rules, which attempt to capture at least part of the cognitive processes involved in similarity judgements (e.g., Melara 1992, Nosofsky 1992). Furthermore, as Rakover and Cahlon (2001) have shown, there are several rules (performance and analysis) that can lead to a successful reconstruction of F_t. Unlike a universal law, here we have several ways by which one can reach the goal of reconstruction. In contrast to the D-N model, the D-R method does not demand that the performance rule and the analysis rule will be true. Given a certain memory task, all that is required is that these rules will lead deductively to a successful reconstruction of F_t. Hence, given a new memory task, it is possible that new rules will have to be invented to achieve the goal of accurate reconstruction of the PE.

So, in view of these arguments, the following question arises: what kind of an explanation is provided by the D-R method? In my view, a successful reconstruction of a particular F_t is explained as an example deduced from the fulfillment of the D-R method's three conditions. Stage 1 is completed by fulfilling the provability condition. Stage 2 is done when the matching and the error-robustness conditions are fulfilled. Given these, a successful reconstruction of a particular F_t is explained deductively by appeal to the fulfillment of the D-R method's conditions, and a failure to achieve reconstruction is explained by appeal to the failure to realize these conditions (e.g., when the participant's percentage of errors is higher than the MEA). In other words, one may conceive of the explanation provided by the D-R method as a teleological explanation (as means to achieve a successful reconstruction of PE from memory) molded into a deductive structure.

14.7.3 SCOPE

To the best of my knowledge, the catch model is the only research program that substantiates the D-R method theoretically and empirically. Nevertheless, the following points should be emphasized. First, Rakover and Cahlon (1999, 2001) have shown that there are several performance rules and analysis rules that can lead to target-face reconstruction. Second, as mentioned in Section 14.2 above, many research areas, such as eyewitness memory, autobiographical memory, and traumatic childhood sexual abuse (e.g., Koriat *et al.* 2000), are aimed at reconstructing PEs from memory. These research areas, although sharing the goal of the reconstruction methodology, still cannot fulfill the D-R method's conditions as the catch model has done. In a way similar to the catch model, for each research area one has to develop the appropriate set of stimuli and the specific reconstruction theory (performance and analysis rules). Here it should be noted that several attempts to validate memories (PE) by employing the explanation-testing methodology have failed. It appears difficult to discriminate between true and false memories (e.g., Loftus 1997, Ross 1997).

In view of the foregoing, one apparently cannot apply the reconstruction methodology to a phenomenon lacking memory. That is why I propose that any physical phenomenon that does not have a mechanism similar to human memory cannot be investigated by means of the reconstruction methodology, but it can by the explanation-testing methodology.

In physics, the explanation-testing methodology is applied to both types of situation: *predicting* a phenomenon by appeal to a theory and the initial conditions, and *retrodicting* (reconstructing) the initial conditions by an appeal to a theory and the phenomenon. For example, on the one hand we can predict the distance of fall from the law of free-falling bodies and time (i.e., the initial conditions); on the other hand we can use this very same law and the distance to retrodict time. That is, in physics there is "time symmetry": one can empirically test the same theory by comparing the predicted observation with the actual observation, and by comparing the retrodicted initial conditions with the actual initial conditions.

Given this, the following question arises. Why in physics does the explanation-testing methodology suit all kinds of research, whereas in memory research the explanation-testing methodology does not efficiently suit all kinds of research (i.e., it does not suit the reconstruction area of research)? My answer is based on the fact that memory generates errors and that errors are treated differently in the natural sciences and in psychology (especially in the reconstruction area).

In the natural sciences, errors are attributed not to the phenomenon to be explained, but to theories and experimental methods (e.g., errors of sampling and measurement; for a discussion of types of experimental errors see Hon 1989). For example, a free-falling body does not make an error, and nature does not say "Sorry, I made a mistake, a mutation. This hen with three legs should not have been born". Nature does not have normative rules by which it judges what is correct and what is an error. It is we, human beings, who have postulated normative rules for evaluating what is right and what is wrong. Only we can judge a three-legged hen as an astonishing deviation, a mutation. In contrast to physics, psychology is immersed in all kinds of normative rules, and therefore assumes that participants in experiments do make mistakes and that these are an important part of the behavior to be evaluated and explained. For example, the debate on the inversion of faces, mentioned above, is about errors in recognition of upright versus upside-down faces, where an error is viewed as a deviation from the full information presented in the past. Hence, psychology handles two types of error: methodological (theories or experimental methods) and behavioral. The methodological error is treated in psychology by means of statistical tools that assume that errors are randomly distributed around a true value, whereas the behavioral errors are the subject matter to be accounted for by a psychological theory.

Considering this distinction, I suggest now that these two conceptions of an error lead to the employment of two types of methodology in psychology.

When one deals with the area of memory change over time (e.g., errors and distortions), one uses the explanation-testing methodology in a way similar to its use in the natural sciences. However, when one deals with the reconstruction of PEs from memory, I recommend using the reconstruction methodology. In the former situation, one tests a theory, which predicts errors of memory in a given situation, by using statistics based on random error distribution (e.g., one asks such questions as: is the experimental group's average of memory error significantly higher than that of the control group?). In the latter situation one treats errors (i.e., deviations from the performance rule's predictions) in a different way: as a behavioral criterion for achieving reconstruction of PE from memory. According to the D-R method, if the participant's number of errors is not higher than the maximum error allowable (MEA), then past events can be reconstructed from memory.

14.7.4 UNITY OF SCIENCE

The above discussion regarding the scope of the reconstruction methodology may suggest that there is a methodological distinction between psychology and the natural sciences: errors are treated differently. This may be conceived of as a case against the program of scientific unity. The general idea behind this program is that scientific knowledge of all branches of science has to be integrated and unified. There are several proposals how this could be done. For example, the positivists proposed to reduce all kinds of theoretical terms to observations in all scientific branches. This proposal failed, since it has been convincingly argued that, even in the natural sciences, observational terms are theory-laden (see Rakover 1990). Another proposal, which is still hotly debated, concerns theory reduction. Accordingly, a reduced law (theory), such as a psychological law, is deduced from a reducing law (theory), such as a neurophysiological law, in conjunction with a correspondence rule, which identifies the appropriate concepts in the reducing and the reduced laws (theories). This proposal of psychoneurophysiological reduction has been criticized by many scientists and philosophers, who point out that phenomenological terms, which refer to conscious private experiences, cannot be reduced to neurophysiology. From an ontological point of view, it is hard to see, to explain, how consciousness emerges from the material stuff of the brain. As a result, some researchers have turned to another avenue of unification, and have suggested the possibility of integrating sciences on the basis of methodology (e.g., Faye 2002). If science is distinguished by its methodology, it is possible to argue that all branches of science employ the same basic methodological principles and methods. This approach unifies science methodologically and leaves each scientific branch ontologically autonomous. One does not have to reduce psychology to physiology, and physiology to chemistry and physics, in order to achieve scientific unification. This is achieved methodologically. While scientific knowledge may be of different kinds, it is attained by employing the same methodology.

The above distinction between two memory methodologies argues against this proposal. While one can raise the hypothesis that the explanation-testing methodology, which has been developed in the realm of natural sciences, is also employed in psychology (e.g., Rakover 1990, 2003), one cannot raise a similar hypothesis with regard to the reconstruction methodology. This methodology is unique to the area of memory, human memory, for achieving the goal of rebuilding PEs. The two methodologies cannot be viewed as harmonious, since they may lead to contradictory results. Furthermore, they treat errors in different ways. In the natural sciences, errors are attributed only to theory and experimental methods. In the social and the behavioral sciences, such as psychology, errors are viewed also as the phenomena to be explained. While the explanation-testing methodology treats errors as the behavior to be explained by comparing them with the statistical distribution of errors, the reconstruction methodology treats errors as a behavioral threshold for attaining an accurate reconstruction of PEs from memory. Hence, it is hard to see how one can establish unity of science on the basis of mutual methodology. I propose that even in psychology itself there are two different methodologies for research in memory.

REFERENCES

Bartlett J. C. and Searcy J. H. (1993) "Inversion and Configuration of Faces", *Cog. Psychol.* 25, 281–316.

Bartlett J. C., Searcy J. H. and Abdi H. (2003) "What are the routes to face recognition?", in: *Perception of Faces, Objects, and Scenes: Analytic and Holistic Processes* (M. A. Peterson and G. Rhodes, eds.). Oxford University Press, Oxford.

Biederman I. and Kalocsai P. (1998) "Neural and Psychophysical Analysis of Object and Face Recognition", in: *Face Recognition: From Theory to Application* (H. Wechsler, P. J. Phillips, V. Bruce, F. F. Soulie and T. S. Huang, eds.). Berlin: NATO Scientific Affairs Division: Springer.

Bruce V. (1988) *Recognizing Faces.* LEA, New Jersey.

Davies G. (1981) "Free Recall Systems", in: *Perceiving and Remembering Faces* (G. Davies, H. Ellis and J. Shepherd, eds.). Academic Press, New York.

Davies G. (1986) "The Recall and Reconstruction of Faces: Implications for Theory and Practice", in: *Aspects of Face Processing* (H. D. Ellis, M. A. Jeeves, F. Newcombe and A. Young, eds.). Martinus Nijhof, Boston.

Davies G., van der Willik P. and Morrison L. J. (2000) "Facial Composite Production: A Comparison of Mechanical and Computer-Driven Systems", *J. Appl. Psychol.* 85, 119–124.

Diamond R. and Carey S. (1986) "Why Faces Are and Are Not Special: An Effect of Expertise", *J. Exp. Psychol: General* 115, 107–117.

Dodson C. S., Johnson M. K. and Schooler J. W. (1997) "The Verbal Overshadowing Effect: Why Descriptions Impair Face Recognition?", *Memory & Cognition* 25, 129–139.

Estes W. K. (1994) *Classification and Cognition.* Oxford University Press, New York.

Farah M. J. (1992) "Is an Object an Object an Object? Cognitive and Neuropsychological Investigation of Domain Specificity in Visual Object Recognition", *Current Directions in Psychological Science* 1, 164–169.

Farah M. J., Tanaka J. W. and Drain H. M. (1995) "What Causes the Face Inversion Effect?", *Journal of Experimental Psychology: Human Perception and Performance* 21, 628–634.

Faye J. (2002) *Rethinking Science: A Philosophical Introduction to the Unity of Science.* Ashgate, Hampshire.

Finger K. and Pezdek K. (1999) "The Effect of the Cognitive Interview on Face Identification Accuracy: Release from Overshadowing", *J. Appl. Psychol.* 84, 340–348.

Fisher R. P., Geiselman R. E. and Amador M. (1989) "Field Test of the Cognitive Interview: Enhancing the Recollection of Actual Victims and Witnesses of Crime", *J. Appl. Psychol.* 74, 722–727.

Glymour C. (1980) *Theory and Evidence*. Princeton University Press, Princeton, NJ.

Hempel C. G. (1965) *Aspects of Scientific Explanation and Other Essays in the Philosophy of Science.* The Free Press, New York.

Hon G. (1989) "Toward a Typology of Experimental Errors: An Epistemological View", *Studies in History and Philosophy of Science* 20, 469–504.

Koriat A., Goldsmith M. and Pansky A. (2000) "Toward a Psychology of Memory Accuracy", *Ann. Rev. Psychol.* 51, 481–537.

Kovera M. B., Penrod S. D., Pappas C. and Thill D. L. (1997) "Identification of Computer-Generated Facial Composites", *J. Appl. Psychol.* 82, 235–246.

Kuhn T. S. (1970) *The Structure of Scientific Revolutions.* University of Chicago Press, Chicago.

Leder H. and Bruce V. (2000) "When Inverted Faces are Recognized: The Role of Configural Information in Face Recognition", *Q. J. Exp. Psychol.* 53A, 513–536.

Loftus E. F. (1997) "Creating False Memories", *Scientific American* 227, 51–55.

McKone E., Martini P. and Nakayama K. (2003) "Isolating Holistic Processing in Faces (and Perhaps Objects)", in: *Perception of Faces, Objects, and Scenes: Analytic and Holistic Processes* (M. A. Peterson and G. Rhodes, eds.). Oxford University Press, Oxford.

Medin D. L. and Schaffer M. M. (1978) "Context Theory of Classification Learning", *Psychol. Rev.* 85, 207–234.

Melara R. D. (1992) "The Concept of Perceptual Similarity: From Psychophysics to Cognitive Psychology", in: *Psychophysics Approaches to Cognition* (D. Algom, ed.). Elsevier, New York.

Nola R. and Sankey H. (2000) "A Selective Survey of Theories of Scientific Method", in: *After Popper, Kuhn and Feyerabend: Recent Issues in Theories of Scientific Method* (R. Nola and H. Sankey, eds.). Kluwer Academic Publishers, Dordrecht, pp. 1–65.

Nosofsky R. M. (1984) "Choice, Similarity and Context Theory of Classification", *Journal of Experimental Psychology: Learning, Memory and Cognition* 10, 104–114.

Nosofsky R. M. (1992) "Similarity Scaling and Cognitive Process Models", *Ann. Rev. Psychol.* 43, 25–53.

Palmer S. E. and Kimchi R. (1986) "The Information Processing Approach to Cognition", in: *Approaches to Cognition: Contrasts and Controversies* (T. J. Knapp and L. C. Robertson, eds.). LEA, New Jersey.

Penry J. (1971a) *Looking at Faces and Remembering Them: A Guide to Facial Identification.* Blek Books, London.

Penry J. (1971b) *Photofit Kit.* John Wadington of Kirkstall, Leeds.

Popper K. R. (1972) *The Logic of Scientific Discovery.* Wiley, New York.

Rakover S. S. (1990) *Metapsychology: Missing Links in Behavior, Mind, and Science.* Paragon/Solomon, New York.

Rakover S. S. (1997) "Can Psychology Provide a Coherent Account of Human Behavior? A Proposed Multiexplanation-Model Theory", *Behavior and Philosophy* 25, 43–76.

Rakover S. S. (2001) "The Deductive-Reconstruction Method and the Catch Model: Methodological and Explanatory Features", in: *Explanation: Theoretical Approaches and Applications* (G. Hon and S. S. Rakover, eds.). Kluwer Academic Press, Dordrecht, pp. 185–205.

Rakover S. S. (2002a) "Featural vs. Configurational Information in Faces: A Conceptual and Empirical Analysis", *Br. J. Psychol.* 93, 1–30.

Rakover S. S. (2002b) "Reconstruction of Past Events from Memory: An Alternative to the Hypothetico-Deductive (H-D) Method", *Behavior and Philosophy* 30, 101–122.

Rakover S. S. (2003) "Experimental Psychology and Duhem's Problem", *J. Theory of Social Behaviour* 33, 45–66.

Rakover S. S. and Cahlon B. (1989) "To Catch a Thief with Recognition Test: The Model and some Empirical Results", *Cog. Psychol.* 21, 423–468.

Rakover S. S. and Cahlon B. (1999) "The Catch Model: A Solution to the Problem of Saliency in Facial Features", *Spatial Vision* 12, 73–81.

Rakover S. S. and Cahlon B. (2001) *Face Recognition: Cognitive and Computational Processes.* John Benjamins, Amsterdam/Philadelphia.

Rakover S. S. and Teucher B. (1997) "Facial Inversion Effects: Parts and Whole Relationship", *Perception & Psychophysics* 59, 752–761.

Rhodes G., Brake K. and Atkinson A. (1993) "What's Lost in Inverted Faces?", *Cognition* 47, 25–57.

Ross M. (1997) "Validating Memories", in: *Memory for Everyday and Emotional Events* (N. L. Stein, P. A. Ornstein, B. Tversky and C. Brainerd, eds.). LEA, New Jersey.

Salmon W. C. (1984) *Scientific Explanation and the Causal Structure of the World.* Princeton University Press, Princeton, New Jersey.

Salmon W. C. (1989) *Four Decades of Scientific Explanation.* University of Minnesota Press, Minneapolis, MN.

Schooler J. W. and Englster-Schooler T. Y. (1990) "Verbal Overshadowing of Visual Memories: Some Things are Better Left Unsaid", *Cog. Psychol.* 22, 36–71.

Searcy J. H. and Bartlett J. C. (1996) "Inversion and Processing of Component and Spatial-Relational Information in Faces", *J. Exp. Psychol.: Human Perception and Performance* 22, 904–915.

Skinner B. F. (1977) "Why I am not a Cognitive Psychologist", *Behaviorism* 5, 1–10.

Tanaka J. W. and Farah M. J. (1993) "Parts and Wholes in Face Recognition", *Q. J. Exp. Psychol.* 46A, 225–245.

Tanaka J. W. and Farah M. J. (2003) "The Holistic Representation of Faces", in: *Perception of Faces, Objects, and Scenes: Analytic and Holistic Processes* (M. A. Peterson and G. Rhodes, eds.). Oxford University Press, Oxford.

Tanaka J. W. and Sengco J. (1997) "Features and Their Configuration in Face Recognition", *Memory and Cognition* 25, 583–592.

Thagard P. (1996) *Mind: Introduction to Cognitive Science.* MIT Press, Cambridge, MA.

Thompson P. (1980) "Margaret Thatcher: A New Illusion", *Perception* 9, 483–484.

Tversky A. (1977) "Features of Similarity", *Psychol. Rev.* 84, 327–352.

Tulving E. (1983) *Elements of Episodic Memory.* Oxford University Press, London.

Valentine T. (1988) "Upside-Down Faces: A Review of the Effect of Inversion upon Face Recognition", *Br. J. Psychol.* 79, 471–491.

CHAPTER 15

USING LASER SCANS TO STUDY FACE PERCEPTION

Harold Hill
ATR Human Information Science Labs, Keihanna Science City, Kyoto 619-0288, Japan

15.1 INTRODUCTION

This chapter will review a selection of the psychological experiments that, in the fifteen or so years since their invention (Linney 1992, Watanabe and Suenaga 1991), have made use of three-dimensional (3D) facial reconstructions based on laser range data, so-called "laser scans", to study human-face perception. In many cases the technology has suggested to psychologists new ways of asking theoretically important empirical questions, many of which would not have been possible otherwise. Previously almost all research on face perception, particularly face recognition, made use of photographs. The advent of laser scans has allowed us to go beyond what is possible with photographs, particularly in asking questions about two key areas: the perception of 3D face shape, and the perception of the movement of the face. In both these areas, laser scans have allowed the generation of controlled stimuli with clearly defined properties. These stimuli can then be shown to observers, and performance on different tasks measured as a function of the information available in the stimulus using standard psychophysical paradigms.

The chapter is divided into two main sections, the first dealing with the perception of 3D shape and the second dealing with the perception of motion.

15.2 THE PERCEPTION OF SHAPE

Faces are 3D surfaces, and perhaps the classic problem in visual perception is how we see a 3D world on the basis of 2D retinal images. Perhaps the most compelling evidence for the importance of 3D shape for face perception comes from the hollow-face illusion (Gregory 1970)—please see Figure 15.1—which is no doubt familiar to anyone who has worked with 3D facial reconstructions. When a thin-shell model of a face (with no back to the head) is

Computer-Graphic Facial Reconstruction
John G. Clement and Murray K. Marks, Editors

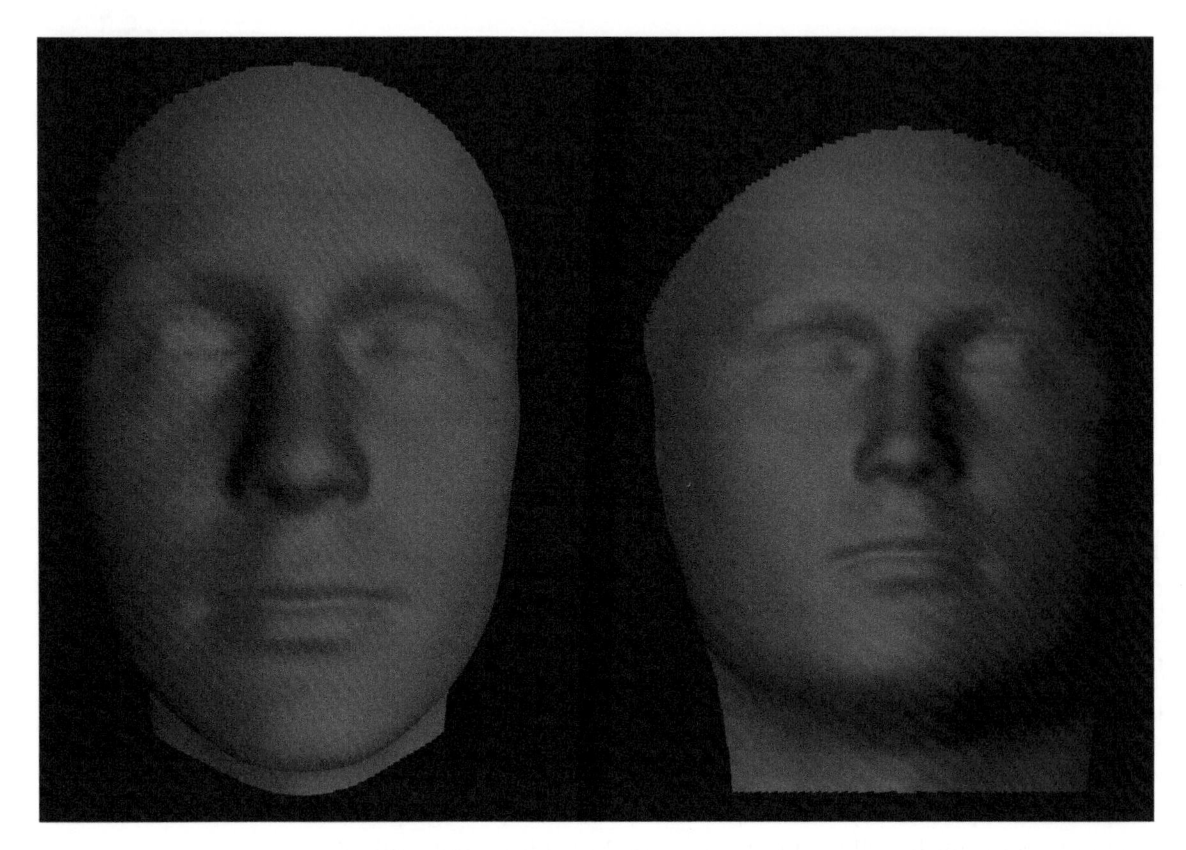

Figure 15.1 The hollow-face illusion. The figure shows the same 3D laser scan viewed from in front (left) and from behind (right). In order to make the images the 3D model was rotated 180° about its central vertical axis, leaving lighting and viewpoint unchanged. Although differences due to perspective are clearly visible—for the hollow version on the right, the nose is smaller because it is further away, while the contour is larger because it is now nearer—both images look like normal convex faces, though with opposite apparent lighting directions. The change in lighting direction, and indeed the illusion itself, reflects the ambiguity of patterns of shading, which are always consistent with two possible solutions: a convex surface lit from one direction or a concave surface lit from the opposite direction (Horn 1977).

rotated, both front and rear views will appear as normal faces with the nose facing towards the observer. This illusion predates computerized facial reconstructions and, even more remarkably, works with a real object under natural viewing conditions. The point to be made here is that the information about 3D surface shape captured by computerized facial reconstructions and rendered using shading, appears to have such an important role in human facial perception that it can override other, unambiguous and powerful, cues to depth and the knowledge that the surface is in fact hollow, to produce a compelling illusory percept. The average head used to make this and other illustrations in this chapter was provided by Nikolaus Troje, and comes from the database he assembled at the Max Planck Institute of Biological Cybernetics in Tübingen, Germany (Vetter and Blanz 1999, Vetter and Troje 1997).

The input for face perception, the retinal image(s), is a function of the 3D shape of the face, its reflectance properties and the viewing conditions. A central problem for both human and machine visual systems is recovering object-specific properties despite differences in viewing conditions. Different faces seen under the same viewing conditions will produce more similar images than the same face seen under different viewing conditions (Moses *et al.* 1994). Extracting 3D shape may be critical in solving this task, though it should be said most current successful computational models of face recognition in no way make the convexity or concavity of the underlying surface explicit (e.g., Biederman and Kalocsai 1997). A review of the current debates between view-based and object-based theories of object recognition is beyond the scope of this chapter, and discussion here is limited to evidence about recognition across changes in viewpoint provided by experiments using laser scans.

Two major determinants of viewing conditions that have profound effects on the retinal image are lighting and viewpoint. The availability of 3D laser scanners has allowed these to be precisely controlled when making stimuli, although this is also possible to an extent with photographs. Laser scans have the advantage that the resolution of viewing and lighting angle can be chosen at will and implemented immediately. Also, as the laser scan remains constant, the experimenter can be sure that viewing conditions can be varied independently of any change in the face itself. As well as information about facial shape, laser scans also provide information about surface reflectance in the form of a video-based RGB texture captured at the same time as the range data. This allows control over another primary determinant of the retinal image: surface reflectance. This separation of 3D shape and reflectance is not possible with photographs (though see separations of 2D shape and texture using photographs: Craw and Cameron 1991, Hancock *et al.* 1996).

Experiments using laser scans to look at the effects of viewpoint and lighting on human perception of facial shape are reviewed below, together with experiments investigating how the addition of information about surface reflectance affects patterns of performance. Lastly, adaptation experiments relating to whether and how differences in the 3D shape of faces are encoded will be summarized.

15.2.1 VIEWPOINT

SHAPE ALONE

The viewpoint is critical to the perception of any 3D object. It will determine many properties of the image including what surfaces are visible, the external and self-occluding contours, and the 2D distances between features. Although not perfect, we are remarkably good at being able to recognize people across changes in viewpoint despite the large image differences introduced. Understanding how this is accomplished is of interest not only to those interested in understanding the brain, but also to people attempting to build machine vision systems capable of the same tasks. Two central questions that have been addressed using laser scans are whether any particular view is "best" and whether face recognition is view-dependent.

In face-to-face communication we are most familiar with the "full-face" or frontal view, usually defined as having 0° rotation (please see Figure 15.2). This is also the view where the approximate bilateral symmetry of the face is most apparent. However the "three-quarter" angled view, normally defined as a 45° rotation in depth around the vertical axis of the head, is commonly used in photography and portraiture and may constitute a canonical view for faces (e.g., Bruce *et al.* 1987). Lastly there is evidence that the profile or 90° view, although it may be one of the views that cells are commonly tuned to (Perrett *et al.* 1985), may be particularly bad for some tasks.

Experiments using laser scans based on shape information alone—that is, rendered with a uniform matte albedo—are broadly consistent with this

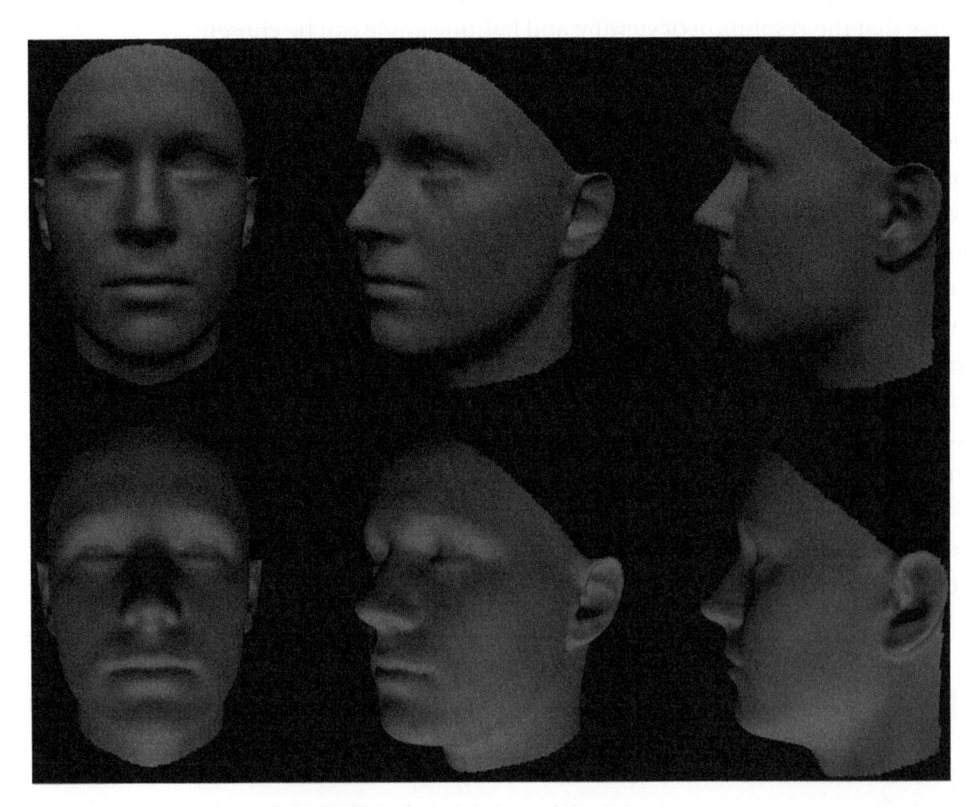

Figure 15.2 The figure shows the same average 3D laser scan in three different orientations: From left to right full-face (0°), three-quarter (45°), and profile (90°) view, rendered with a directional light source from 45° above (top row), and 45° below (bottom row).

picture. When any advantage is reported, it appears to be associated with the three-quarter or similarly angled view. For example, there appears to be a slight advantage for recognizing familiar people from three-quarter views, as compared with full-face views (for male faces), with a decrement for profile views (Bruce *et al.* 1991, Hill and Bruce 1996). For matching previously unfamiliar faces, the view presented first, the learned view, appears to be more important than the test view (Hill *et al.* 1997, O'Toole *et al.* 1998, Troje and Bülthoff 1996). Again, if any advantage is shown, an angled view appears to be the best view for learning on the basis of shape information.

Even when there is no absolute difference between different views, the pattern of generalization depends on the viewpoint and on an interaction between learned and tested view (Hill *et al.* 1997, O'Toole *et al.* 1998, Troje and Bülthoff 1996). In general, performance falls off with viewing angle, as might be expected, but this is mediated by the effect of the symmetry of the face with, for example, the three-quarter view generalizing well to its symmetric pair. This effect works for other angled views but not always for profile. However, differences in the effects on profile may reflect a limitation of the laser-scan technology which does not capture hair well, meaning that the back of the head has to be removed before rendering.

Another novel use of laser scans to study viewpoint has been in testing how temporal association may be important in associating different view-based representations of an object. The results showed that temporal association in the context of a rotating view can be strong enough to cause views of different faces to become associated with a single identity (Wallis and Bülthoff 2001).

ADDING TEXTURE

When surface texture, in the form of a cylindrical projection of RGB values, is added to the shape, the rendered stimuli more closely resemble photographs. The addition of texture also makes it possible to compare texture-mapped shape with shape only, while keeping other aspects of experimental design unchanged.

The first finding with respect to viewpoint is that the addition of texture improves performance, often to 100%. In order to produce similar levels of performance and reveal differences between conditions, presentation time is normally reduced for textured images (Hill *et al.* 1997, Troje and Bülthoff 1996). This is probably because surface texture provides a number of cues, such as skin color, that are invariant with respect to viewpoint and that can support matching between views. Even with reduced viewing time, the addition of texture tends to reduce the effect of changing the viewpoint. For the three-quarter view, the effect of changing the viewpoint is eliminated. This view can also produce the best generalization for textured images, whereas a slightly more angled view can be better for shape-only stimuli. Overall the patterns of results with shaded and textured stimuli are similar—generalization depends on learned view and falls off with increasing angle of rotation once the effect of symmetry has been taken into account—consistent with the idea that the primary determinant of the effects of viewpoint is the 3D shape captured by laser scans.

Another approach to investigating the relative contributions of shape and texture has involved normalizing shape and texture separately (O'Toole *et al.* 1999). Results showed that both sources of identity-specific information corresponded significantly to recognition across changes in viewpoint. There was an interesting interaction with the sex of the face, with shape more important for male faces. This is consistent with previous results, male faces appear to be better recognized than female faces when viewed as shape-only representations (Bruce *et al.* 1991, Hill and Bruce 1996).

As well as presenting shape and texture separately and together, it is also possible to present inconsistent shape and texture information (Hill *et al.* 1995). When presented in isolation, shape information appears to be more useful for making the distinction between Japanese and Caucasian faces (88%) than between male and female faces (72%), and this is independent of view. With texture presented as a cylindrical projection, performance is better overall, and sex judgements (97%) are more accurate than "race" judgements (90%). When contradictory shape and texture information is presented, decisions appear to be based primarily on texture information. However, for the "race" decision, shape is more important, particularly as the angle of view increases.

SUMMARY

In summary, laser scans have provided a powerful tool for investigating recognition in relation to viewpoint, particularly by allowing the effect of underlying shape to be investigated independently from the effect of texture. Results show that shape alone provides useful information for many tasks including recognition. An angled view provides the best access to shape information. Generalization between views on the basis of shape and that generalization depends primarily on the learned view, with symmetry playing an important part. The addition of texture improves generalization, but the underlying effects of shape on viewpoint generalization remain. Both texture and shape affect decisions, but their relative contribution depends on both task and viewpoint.

15.2.2 LIGHTING

Another important determinant of the image available for recognition is lighting. Indeed lighting is analogous to viewpoint in some ways: both determine which surfaces are visible and, for example, attached shadow boundaries for a particular lighting direction correspond to the occluding contour for that viewpoint. The importance attached to lighting faces in photography, film, the theater, and computer graphics attests to the importance of this factor in the perception of faces.

As for viewpoint, shaded laser scans give control over lighting direction while keeping other factors constant. Again we can ask whether any particular lighting direction is "best" and whether recognition performance generalizes over changes in lighting.

One particularly dramatic effect of lighting, which is detrimental to recognition, is lighting the face from below (Johnston *et al.* 1992). This has been explored in detail using laser scans, confirming that lighting from below is detrimental when only shape information is available (Hill and Bruce 1996; please see Figure 15.2). This is consistent with an important role for shape-from-shading in face perception (Bruce 1988), though the familiar pattern of shading (e.g., shadowed eyes but well lit nose and forehead) may also play a part. There is much work to be done exploring experimentally which lighting direction or combination of directions is most effective for recognition and other tasks, and the effects of different lighting models.

There is also accumulating evidence, mainly from experiments using laser scans, that there are decrements associated with matching between lighting directions (Braje 2003, Braje *et al.* 1998, Hill and Bruce 1996, Liu *et al.* 1999). When view is constant, there is a decrement associated with changing lighting direction between above and below, but also often between two directions of top or, to an even greater extent, bottom lighting. This has been shown both with matching tasks and a learning task, though in both cases learning is from a single image, which may induce more image-dependent performance than more natural learning conditions.

Again the use of laser scans has allowed experiments not possible with photographs. For example, it is possible to compare matching across lighting directions with and without cast shadows (Braje *et al.* 1998). This experiment showed that the decrements associated with matching between lighting directions were not dependent on the presence of shadows. Cast shadows result in an additional increase in response time for matching though not for learning.

The separation of the effects of shading from those of different pigmentation carried by the texture map has also been used to investigate the well known detrimental effect of photographic negation on face recognition (Bruce and Langton 1994, Liu *et al.* 1999). It has been observed that photographic negatives resemble bottom-lit faces in some ways (Johnston *et al.* 1992). However, the effects of bottom lighting and negation on pigmented areas are clearly different. Although the effects of negation on surface pigmentation may be of primary importance, matching negated images of rendered laser scans without texture has shown detrimental effects of negation of top-lit faces even when pigmentation is not present. This is dependent on light being from above a certain angle, which leads to the particular pattern of light and dark areas associated with both top lighting and photographic negation. The detrimental effect of photographic negation can be reversed when the original images are lit from below, consistent with the two effects canceling each other out.

A direct comparison of matching across lighting with or without texture has not been carried out, though effects of lighting have been reported both with (Braje *et al.* 1998) and without (Hill and Bruce 1996) texture present. Direct comparison between laser scans and photographs showed the pattern of effects of lighting and view with effects of lighting that were at least as large.

15.2.3 VIEWPOINT AND LIGHTING

Many of the experiments covered so far have involved changes in both view and lighting, and this has interesting relationships between the effects. Firstly, for recognition, there is some evidence that lighting may be more important for less angled views, particularly the full-face view, than for more angled views, particularly the profile (Hill and Bruce 1996). This probably reflects the increased salience of lighting-invariant occluding contour information in the angled views.

In the case of matching between views, there are two main reasons for a change in viewpoint: movement of the head itself and movement of the observer. These have different implications for what happens to the lighting with respect to the face being viewed. If it is the observer that moves then, normally, the light will stay constant with respect to the viewed face (that is unless the light is in some way connected to the observer, as with a flashlight or car headlights). This means that the patterns of shading on the face remain the same, and the problem of generalizing across viewpoint is the same as for differently pigmented areas. In this case, performance is probably determined by the degree of overlap of visible surfaces (taking into account the effects of symmetry). However, in the case of movement of the viewed face, the spatial relationship of the face to both the light source and the observer changes. This results in different patterns of shading on the face as well as different surfaces being visible. In both these there is a significant effect of changing view—for example, "moving observer" (Liu *et al.* 1999) or moving head (Hill and Bruce 1996, Troje and Bülthoff 1996, Troje and Bülthoff 1998).

For a matching task using upright faces, there is no additional effect of changing viewpoint if lighting is changed. This is although, in these experiments, the particular directions of lighting used involved a change in both lighting and head orientation relative to the observer, and the combined effects were not equivalent to any possible observer or head movement. For inverted faces and unfamiliar nonfacial objects there was usually an additional effect of changing view. Matching between views of upright heads is more accurate when lighting is from above than from below (Hill and Bruce 1996, Liu *et al.* 1999). Given that images including contour differences are no different, this is consistent with the importance of a light-from-above assumption for establishing a view-point-insensitive surface-based representation. This advantage applies even when "above" is actually a photographic negative of a face lit from below. These results also show that performance is not just based on matching patterns of intensity, as similarities in intensities are unaffected by photographic negation.

Lastly, a change in lighting direction can induce a shift in the apparent orientation of the head (Troje and Siebeck 1998). This effect can be explained in terms of a simple model based on the relative amount of light on the different sides of the face. Again this effect remains even when texture is added to the faces.

15.2.4 FACE SPACE

The idea that faces are represented as points within a multi-dimensional face space (Valentine 1991) has been investigated using the data from laser scans. The 3D positions of corresponding points on a population of faces can be represented as a vector and submitted to principal-components analysis (PCA) to reduce the dimensionality (Vetter and Blanz 1999, Vignali *et al.* 2003). It is also possible to use linear discriminant analysis and similar techniques to extract meaningful and perceptually valid dimensions within this space related to, for example, sex and ethnicity. Thus the space spanned by the principal components (PC space) provides a workable face space, and a number of experiments have been undertaken to test predictions within this framework.

If faces are represented within a face space relative to a mean or norm face, it should be possible to caricature them by exaggerating the differences of individual faces from the norm (Rhodes 1996). However, caricatures of laser scans had the unexpected effect of increasing the apparent age of the faces (O'Toole *et al.* 1997). This is of interest in its own right and reflects the laser scan's ability to capture wrinkling, jowls, and the boniness of the face which, when exaggerated, all increase the perceived age. A number of experiments have looked at anticaricatures, that is interpolations of the individual face towards the average, and even antifaces, which extrapolate the original face onto the other side of the mean (Blanz *et al.* 2000). While nearness in PC space often corresponds well to perceived similarity, there appears to be a perceptual discontinuity across the average. This is consistent with a special role for the average in the encoding of faces. Further evidence for this view comes from experiments using antifaces for adaptation. Adaptation effects, from the simplest retinal aftereffects, can inform about how the brain encodes information, and have been referred to as the psychologist's micro-electrode (Frisby 1979). Adapting to an antiface can improve recognition of the corresponding face and cause the average face to take on the corresponding face's identity (Leopold *et al.* 2001). Recently several labs have been investigating and found that adaptation effects appear to generalize across changes in view. This would be consistent with the possibility of view-independent shape-based internal representations.

In summary, statistical analysis of face shape based on laser scans can be used to create a face space which appears to capture perceived differences between faces. This may reflect encoding by humans and has practical uses in terms of the analysis and synthesis of faces.

15.3 MOTION

A recent active area in the study of facial perception is concerned with the perception of facial movement. Movement is clearly central to many tasks involving faces, in particular both verbal and nonverbal communication, as the tragic effects of a lack of facial movement characteristic of Moebius syndrome demonstrate. However most initial research on face perception involved photographs, and these clearly provide sufficient information for a large number of tasks. This has been a problem empirically, as it is difficult to show effects of motion when performance is already at ceiling with static images. The animation of laser scans with motion-capture data has provided one way of overcoming this difficulty, while at the same time opening up new experimental possibilities.

Key questions concerning the perception of facial motion are:

- Does motion facilitate face recognition and other tasks?
- If so, how?
- How is facial motion encoded by the brain?
- How is the perception of motion related to the perception of shape?

Experiments involving laser scans have allowed all these questions to be addressed in novel ways not possible with other sorts of stimuli. The basic methods will be described, followed by a summary of experiments and results and the conclusions that they have led to.

15.3.1 METHODS

These experiments combine laser scans with motion-capture data to create "performance-driven" animations (please see Figure 15.3). Motion capture involves tracking the position of 2D or 3D markers from, in this case, the face.

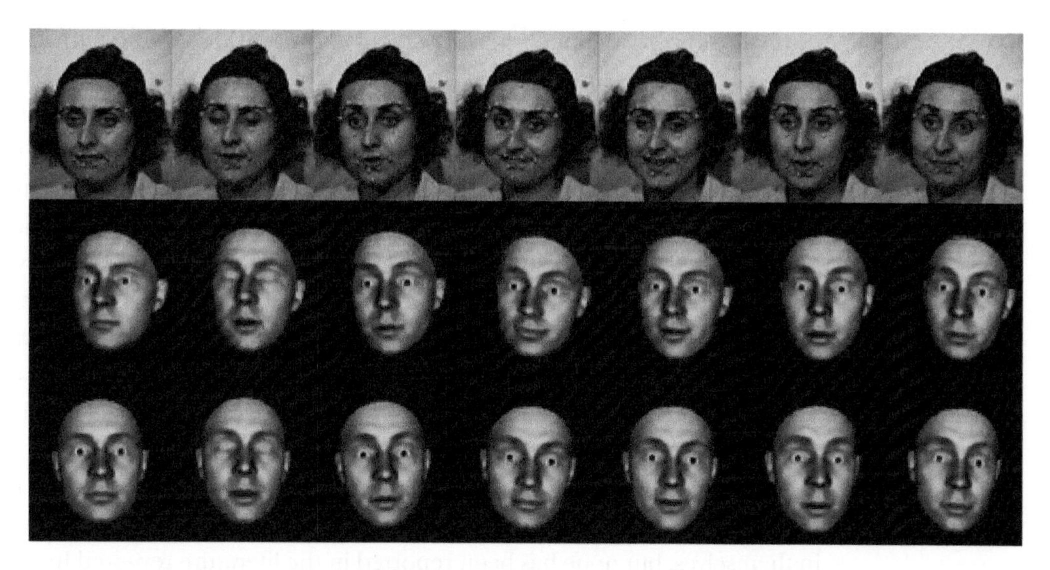

Figure 15.3 The figure shows corresponding frames for the original video and two viewpoints of the animated version. As detailed in the text, the movement captured from the video is mapped onto an average laser scan using a fixed weighting function (figure taken from Hill and Johnston 2001).

In addition, the rigid motion of the whole head is sometimes tracked (whole-body motion capture is of course common in the animation industry and has been used to study the perception of biological motion; see Troje 2002). The output of this process is in the form of *x*, *y*, *z*, *t* data for the markers used. This data are numerically manipulable for experimental purposes and can be presented as simple point-light-type displays (Hill *et al.* 2003). It is normal to estimate the rigid motion of the whole head (if present) from the absolute position of the rigid markers used. Head motion can then be represented as three translations and three rotations. The nonrigid motion of the face is then encoded relative to the head-centered coordinate system.

Rigid motion can then be straightforwardly applied to move the laser scan. Applying nonrigid motion is more complex. A perfect solution is not possible if the shape of the surface being animated is different from that of the original surface as, by definition, nonrigid motion implies that all points move independently to an extent. One of the advantages of this technique, both for experiments and for entertainment, is that it allows the same motion to be applied to any shape, but the resulting motion will also reflect the particular mapping used.

There are two main techniques for mapping motion to shape: weight maps or the weighting of blend shapes from the motion data. A system using weighted blend shapes is described by Kuratate in this volume. The experiments discussed here mainly used weight maps. In this case, the movement of each marker is associated with a particular point on the laser scan, which normally moves with one hundred percent of the marker's motion. In addition to this, an area of influence is painted on the surface associated with that marker's movement, but with the percentage of the movement falling off as a function of distance from the marker. The fall-off function can take any form, with linear and polynomial functions often used. These regions of influence may overlap, in which case an appropriate way of combining their influences has to be defined. While the mapping function is to an extent arbitrary, it is designed so that the motion of the animation matches the original movement as closely as possible. In order to avoid the mapping function becoming a confounding variable, this function is normally kept constant for all the animations in an experiment. This contrasts with normal practice in the animation industry, where functions will be tweaked for each combination of actor and model to create the desired effect. The effect of the mapping function on performance for tasks involving the perception of facial movement would be of interest in themselves, but none has been reported in the literature reviewed here. The shape animated in these studies is either kept constant or systematically varied.

15.3.2 EXPERIMENTS

The aim of the experiments using animated laser scans is to examine the effects of motion-based information. The first experiments considered here concentrated on recognition on the basis of motion information. Evidence that motion may be useful for recognition has come from studies using degraded video (for a review, see O'Toole *et al.* 2002). However these stimuli often contain residual spatial clues (although experimental designs are used to control for this). With animated laser scans, it is possible to be sure that all the available information is derived from motion, though the motion always has spatial consequences. The other advantage of this method is that it allows different components of the motion to be separated, particularly rigid and nonrigid motion.

One problem with both laser scans and motion capture is the lack of readily available data for faces of famous, or even personally familiar, people. As with studies of shape, this has again led to the widespread use of matching, discrimination, and learning experimental paradigms. For recognition, we can show that motion provides sufficient information to discriminate between different individuals. For example, if observers are presented with sixteen animations of the same laser scan driven by four different examples of four people speaking similar material, observers are able to group the animations according to identity significantly better that chance (Hill and Johnston 2001). Rigid motion appears particularly useful for this task, perhaps because people have characteristic head movements, while much of their facial movement is determined by what they are saying and thus, in this experiment, is common to different individuals. Discrimination performance was also tested using an odd-one-out procedure. For this task, three animations are shown, two of which are animated with different examples of movement from person A and one with movement from person B. Observers have to identify which of the animations is animated with motion B. Again underlying structural information is kept constant through use of an average laser scan. The results again showed that motion provides useful information for discriminating on the basis of identity. Additionally, turning the animations upside-down reduced performance, showing that the motion is encoded better as meaningful motion of an upright face than as simple low-level orientation-independent image motion. This implies that the observer's prior experience with upright faces is adding to their performance.

In order to investigate whether the animated motion related to observers' existing knowledge of facial motion, we tested people's ability to categorize sex on the basis of motion alone. Again motion provided useful information for this task. As no feedback was given, this result also shows that the animated motion is sufficient to access stored knowledge about differences in how males and females move their faces. For this task nonrigid motion appeared more useful than rigid motion, suggesting that there are task-related differences, and these are not simply because rigid motion is easier to animate than nonrigid motion. For sex judgements, there were detrimental effects both of presenting stimuli inverted and of playing them backwards. The latter manipulation leaves much motion information and all frame-based static information unchanged and suggests that the direction-dependent pattern of movement is critical. There was no effect of playing animation backwards for the discrimination task, but this may have been because no access to prior representation encoded forwards was required.

The use of motion for recognition, together with its relationship to shape information, has been further explored using laser scans (Knappmeyer *et al.* 2003). In this research, laser scans were used not only to separate the effects of form and motion, but also to systematically vary the form information available through 3D morphing. In the experiments, observers learned two faces, each associated with a particular predefined set of expressive and chewing movements while carrying out an unrelated task. They were then tested on intermediate morphs of the two faces, animated with either one of the learned motions. The results showed that, even when subjects were instructed to base their judgements on form information, motion systematically biased their decisions. Adding identity-specific texture information reduced, but did not eliminate, the effect of motion. The effects generalized to novel faces sharing a "family resemblance" to the learned faces (they were 50% morphs of a new individual with the learned individual). Although performance was worse overall, the effect of motion also generalized across a change in image orientation, upright to inverted, between study and test. This suggests that at least some of the useful properties of facial motion for recognition are orientation-invariant.

Inverting orientation can be seen as an extreme example of generalization across viewpoint, and laser scans have also been used to investigate the generalization of motion across the changes in view associated with rotations in depth (Watson *et al.* 2002). In contrast to the difficulties already discussed in recognizing identity from shape across changes in viewpoint, performance is often at ceiling when discriminating motion. When performance is reduced below ceiling by presenting only a subset of the learning stimulus at test, differences between conditions become apparent. For example it appears that the perception of rigid head movements may be more dependent on view than those of nonrigid movements. The latter may be encoded in terms of a face-centered coordinate system.

Additional evidence about how motion is encoded comes from studies that have exaggerated motion. The premise for these studies, which was taken from studies of two-dimensional facial caricatures (Brennan 1985, Rhodes 1996, Rhodes *et al.* 1987), is that effective exaggerations will reflect the encoding of motion. Results show that exaggerating spatial position frame-by-frame relative to the average can enhance the perception of the nonlinguistic differences associated with saying the same sentence in different ways (Hill *et al.* 2002). This finding highlights the fact that motion and spatial information cannot be truly separated—even when the same head is animated, different motions will result in different spatial configurations: so-called "motion-induced spatial information" (Knappmeyer *et al.* 2003). The effect of exaggeration suggests that this information is critical for some tasks, and that some motion-dependent information may be encoded spatially. Animated laser scans using methods described by Kuratate (this volume) have also been used to study the perception of facial speech (Munhall *et al.* 2004). This research has shown the usefulness of rigid, as well as nonrigid, motion for this task.

In summary, the combination of laser scans with motion-capture data has shown that motion provides useful information in a variety of tasks. The experiments have been particularly useful in providing evidence that motion itself provides supplementary information, in addition to enhancing the encoding of three-dimensional shape.

15.4 CONCLUSION

In conclusion, laser scans have provided a powerful tool for investigating many aspects of the visual perception of faces. The 3D structure and surface reflectance of the face captured by laser scans, together with lighting and viewpoint, are the key determinants of the 2D retinal images on which subsequent processing has to be based. Additionally, the use of motion capture and performance-driven animation allows the effects of motion to be examined.

Laser scans have been valuable in investigating how viewing conditions affect access to the constant cues to identity provided by differences in underlying shape. Results show that human performance is sensitive to changes in both lighting and viewpoint. Performance is better when faces are presented upright, showing the importance of existing knowledge about facial structure that observers bring to the experiments. One aspect of face structure that may be particularly important in this context is symmetry, though image symmetry as well as object symmetry appears critical. Angled views, including the three-quarter view, facilitate the perception of shape. Recognition of familiar faces and matching between either viewpoint or lighting condition, appears to be better when lighting is from above. The presence of cast shadows can produce additional decrements, probably because shadows, like occlusions of viewpoint, hide useful features and also introduce additional contours. The pattern of effects of both viewpoint and lighting cannot all be explained in terms of image differences (though these are an important determinant of performance, particularly for matching tasks), and may reflect the construction of a 3D, if view-dependent, representation of the face. Adaptation experiments suggest that 3D shape may be represented within a face space, with reference to a central tendency.

The addition of texture, either by texture-mapping laser scans or through the use of photographs, improves generalization across viewing conditions but does not change the underlying pattern of effects. This is consistent with shape being the primary determinant of the effect of viewing condition but texture providing additional cues to identity independent of the viewing condition. When shape and texture are directly contrasted, surface texture appears to be the more important cue for many tasks. Texture is relatively more important in frontal views and shape in angled views.

Laser scans, combined with motion capture, have also provided a way to look at the effects of face and head motion while controlling for facial shape. Results have shown that motion provides useful information for a number of tasks, including recognition. The use of a constant underlying facial structure has explicitly provided evidence for the importance of motion in its own right, rather than just as an additional cue to shape, for these tasks. Consistent with this, motion can provide useful information even when associated with a highly abstracted face structure. However, motion has also been shown to influence categorizations even when shape is present and explicitly attended to.

Although a valuable tool, there are some limitations of the use of laser scans. The absence of hair or a back to the head may have important effects on patterns of results, as may presenting disembodied heads. The lack of availability of laser scans of faces of famous or personally familiar people has also hampered research and led to overreliance on matching and learning paradigms. This is especially frustrating, since underlying shape may be particularly important for familiar faces, as it remains constant. Matching tasks will always tend to emphasize image properties. There are also mentions of specific difficulties in the perception of laser scans of females. One limitation of the texture information available with laser scans is that it is itself in part dependent on the lighting conditions when it is recorded, and not just on the lighting setup used for rendering. Lastly, with all working involving computer graphics and particular animated movement, there is the danger of falling into the "uncanny valley" (Mori 1982), whereby graphics that are close to, but not exactly like, real faces seem to be less acceptable to observers than more abstract representations that do not even attempt to be realistic.

However, in summary, the advantages of laser scans for research both in giving control over viewing conditions and in allowing the separate contributions of different determinants of the facial image to be assessed far outweigh the disadvantages. Work reported elsewhere in this volume shows many of these problems may be solved, as well as suggesting many possibilities for future work.

ACKNOWLEDGEMENT

Some of this research was conducted as part of "Research on Human Communication" with funding from the National Institute of Information and Communications Technology of Japan.

REFERENCES

Biederman I. and Kalocsai P. (1997) "Neural and Psychophysical Analysis of Object and Face Recognition", *Face Recognition: From Theory to Applications*. Springer, Stirling, Scotland.

Blanz V., O'Toole A. J., Vetter T. and Wild H. A. (2000) "On the Other Side of the Mean: the Perception of Discriminability in Human Faces", *Perception* 29, 885–891.

Braje W. L. (2003) "Illumination Encoding in Face Recognition: Effect of Position Shift", *J. Vision* 3(2), 161–170.

Braje W. L., Kersten D., Tarr M. J. and Troje N. F. (1998) "Illumination Effects in Face Recognition", *Psychobiol.* 26(4), 371–380.

Brennan S. E. (1985) "The Caricature Generator", *Leonardo* 18, 170–178.

Bruce V. (1988) *Recognizing Faces*. Lawrence Erlbaum Associates, London.

Bruce V., Healey P., Burton A. M., Doyle A., Coombes A., and Linney A. (1991) "Recognising Facial Surfaces", *Perception* 20, 755–769.

Bruce V. and Langton S. (1994) "The Use of Pigmentation and Shading Information in Recognising the Sex and Identities of Faces", *Perception* 23, 803–822.

Bruce V., Valentine T. and Baddeley A. (1987) "The Basis of the 3/4 View Advantage in Face Recognition", *App. Cog. Psychol.* 1, 109–120.

Craw I. and Cameron P. (1991) "Parameterizing Faces for Recognition and Reconstruction", *Proceedings of the British Machine Vision Conference* (P. Mowforth, ed.). Springer Verlag, Berlin.

Frisby J. (1979) *Seeing: Illusion, Brain, and Mind*. Oxford University Press, Oxford.

Gregory R. L. (ed.) (1970) *The Intelligent Eye*. Weidenfeld and Nicolson, London.

Hancock P. J. B., Burton A. M. and Bruce V. (1996) "Face Processing: Human Perception and Principal Components Analysis", *Memory and Cognition* 24(1), 26–40.

Hill H. and Bruce V. (1996) "Effects of Lighting on the Perception of Facial Surfaces", *J. Exp. Psychol. Hum. Percept. Perform.* 22(4), 986–1004.

Hill H., Bruce V. and Akamatsu S. (1995) "Perceiving the Sex and Race of Faces: the Role of Shape and Colour", *Proc. R. Soc. Lond. B. Biol. Sci.* 261(1362), 367–373.

Hill H., Jinno Y. and Johnston A. (2003) "Comparing Solid-Body with Point-Light Animations", *Perception* 32(5), 561–566.

Hill H. and Johnston A. (2001) "Categorizing Sex and Identity from the Biological Motion of Faces", *Current Biol.* 11(11), 880–885.

Hill H., Pollick F. E., Kamachi M. Watson T. L. and Johnston A. (2002) "Using the Principles of Facial Caricature to Exaggerate Human Motion", *Perception* 31(Supplement), 60–61.

Hill H., Schyns P. G. and Akamatsu S. (1997) "Information and viewpoint dependence in face recognition", *Cognition* 62(2), 201–222.

Horn B. K. P. (1977) "Understanding Image Intensities", *Artificial Intelligence* 8, 201–231.

Johnston A., Hill H. and Carman N. (1992) "Recognising Faces: Effects of Lighting Direction, Inversion, and Brightness Reversal", *Perception* 21(3), 365–375.

Knappmeyer B., Thornton I. M. and Bülthoff H. H. (2003) "The Use of Facial Motion and Facial Form During the Processing of Identity", *Vision Research* 43, 1921–1936.

Leopold D. A., O'Toole A. J., Vetter T. and Blanz V. (2001) "Prototype-Referenced Shape Encoding Revealed by High-Level Aftereffects", *Nature Neuroscience* 4(1), 89–94.

Linney A. (1992) The Use of 3-D Graphics for the Simulation and Prediction of Surgery. *Processing Images of Faces* (V. B. A. Burton, ed.). NJ, Ablex, Norwood, pp. 149–178.

Liu C. H., Colin C. A., Burton A. M. and Chaudhuri A. (1999) "Lighting Direction Affects Recognition of Untextured Faces in Photographic Positive and Negative", *Vision Research* 39(24), 4003–4009.

Mori M. (1982) *The Buddah in the Robot*. Charles E. Tuttle Co.

Moses Y. and Adini Y. *et al.* (1994) "Face Recognition: the Problem of Compensating for Changes in Illumination Direction". *European Conference on Computer Vision*.

Munhall K., Jones J. A., Callan D. E., Kuratate T. and Vatikiotis-Bateson E. (2004) "Visual Prosody and Speech Intelligibility", *Psychol. Sci.* 15(2), 133–137.

O'Toole A. J., Edelman S. and Bülthoff H. H. (1998) "Stimulus-Specific Effects in Face Recognition over Changes in Viewpoint", *Vision Research* 38(15–16), 2351–2363.

O'Toole A. J., Roark D. and Abdi H. (2002) "Recognizing Moving Faces: A Psychological and Neural Synthesis", *Trends in Cognitive Science* 6, 261–266.

O'Toole A. J., Vetter T. and Blanz V. (1999) "Three-Dimensional Shape and Two-Dimensional Surface Reflectance Contributions to Face Recognition: an Application of Three-Dimensional Morphing", *Vision Research* 39(18), 3145–3155.

O'Toole A. J., Vetter T., Volz H. and Salter E. M. (1997) "Three-Dimensional Caricatures of Human Heads: Distinctiveness and the Perception of Facial Age", *Perception* 26(6), 719–732.

Perrett D. I., Smith P. A. J., Potter D. D., Mistlin A. J., Head A. S., Milner A. D. and Jeeves M. A. (1985) "Visual Cells in the Temporal Cortex Sensitive to Face View and Gaze Direction", *Proceedings of the Royal Society of London* Series B 233, 293–317.

Rhodes G. (1996) *Superportraits*. Psychology Press, Hove, East Sussex.

Rhodes G., Brennan S. E. and Carey S. (1987) "Identification and Ratings of Caricatures: Implications for Mental Representations of Faces", *Cog. Psychol.* 19, 473–497.

Troje N. F. (2002) "Decomposing Biological Motion: A Framework for Analysis and Synthesis of Human Gait Patterns", *J. Vision* 2, 371–387.

Troje N. F. and Bülthoff H. H. (1996) "Face Recognition Under Varying Poses: the Role of Texture and Shape", *Vision Res.* 36(12), 1761–1771.

Troje N. F. and Bülthoff H. H. (1998) "How is Bilateral Symmetry of Human Faces Used for Recognition of Novel Views?", *Vision Res.* 38(1), 79–89.

Troje N. F. and Siebeck U. (1998) "Illumination-Induced Apparent Shift in Orientation of Human Heads", *Perception* 27, 671–680.

Valentine T. (1991) "A Unified Account of the Effects of Distinctiveness, Inversion and Race in Face Recognition", *Q. J. Exp. Psychol.* 44A, 161–204.

Vetter T. and Blanz V. (1999) "A Morphable Model for the Synthesis of 3D Faces", *SIGGRAPH.* Addison Wesley, Los Angeles.

Vetter T. and Troje N. F. (1997) "Separation of Texture and Shape in Images of Faces for Image Coding and Synthesis", *J. Optical Society of America A – Optics, Image Science and Vision* 14, 2152–2161.

Vignali G., Hill H. and Vatikiotis-Bateson E. (2003) "Linking the Structure and Perception of 3D Faces: Gender, Ethnicity and Expressive Posture", *Audio-Visual Speech Processing (AVSP), St Jorioz, France.* Institut de la Communication Parlee, INP Grenoble.

Wallis G. and Bülthoff H. H. (2001) "Role of Temporal Association in Establishing Recognition Memory", *Proceedings of the National Academy of Science* 98(8), 4800–4804.

Watanabe Y. and Suenaga Y. (1991) "Synchronized Acquisition of Three-Dimensional Range and Color Data and Its Applications", in: *Scientific Visualization of Physical Phenomena* (M. Patrikalsis, ed.). Springer-Verlag, Tokyo.

Watson T. L., Johnston A., Hill H. and Troje N. F. (2002) "Differential Processing of Facial Motion", in: *Dynamic Perception* (R. P. Wurt and M. Lappe, eds.). Aka Press, Berlin, pp. 271–275.

PART IV

APPLICATIONS OF COMPUTER-GRAPHIC FACIAL RECONSTRUCTION

INVESTIGATION OF ETHNIC DIFFERENCES IN FACIAL MORPHOLOGY BY THREE-DIMENSIONAL AVERAGING

Ashraf I. Shaweesh*, C. David L. Thomas, and John G. Clement
School of Dental Science, University of Melbourne, Victoria 3010, Australia

*Jordan University of Science and Technology, Jordan

16.1 INTRODUCTION

Although an individual's identity is revealed by the general physical look of the body, including behavioral characteristics and gait, the face still plays a major role in recognition. It also holds anthropological information about age, sex, and population of origin. The process of facial comparison has not only found applications in forensic medicine through the identification of criminals and the deceased, but also in genetics in the diagnosis of craniofacial anomalies with distinctive faces.

It is believed that the human face has ethnically specific characteristics. Studies of the facial differences between ethnically different populations have previously been accomplished by comparing average values of measurements of single variables and proportions (Farkas 1994). Such measurements were either done directly on the face using simple calipers and tapes, indirectly from two-dimensional (2D) photographs—with the inherent limitations of dealing with a 2D representation of a three-dimensional (3D) object—or interactively from 2D digital images. A more advanced approach utilizes these individual dimensions from 3D facial scans. However, in all of the above approaches, the amount of information gained through comparing these linear dimensions is limited. Measurements that describe the location of individual anatomical landmarks do not describe the whole face; there is still a lot of shape information present between these single measurements which may have great significance to the process of recognition and proof of identity.

The knowledge that a great deal of potentially very important information was being ignored prompted the authors to consider other approaches to achieving more comprehensive comparisons between faces. One method

Computer-Graphic Facial Reconstruction
John G. Clement and Murray K. Marks, Editors

that has proved successful is a computer-assisted system of facial averaging. Comparison is done between the facial averages of specific ethnic groups rather than by averaging individual dimensions. This provides a more holistic comparison by including the shape information hidden between landmarks and previously left unmeasured.

Face averaging has been an important approach for investigations in the field of psychology particularly in studies of facial attractiveness with relation to mate/partner preference (Little 2001, Little 2002, Penton-Voak 2001). It has been established that averaging, as well as increases in symmetry, make western faces more attractive (Halberstadt 2003). This in turn has prompted researchers to apply this technique to faces of people from nonwestern cultures (Rhodes 2001) and even nonhuman subjects (Halberstadt 2003). However, although there is an extensive literature about face averaging in relation to attractiveness and mate or partner preference, there is little published about interethnic morphological differences. In one study (Rhodes 2001), mixed-race averages were created, but for the purpose of studying attractiveness, not the interethnic differences.

Existing work on face averaging was carried out from 2D digital images using computer software (e.g., Gryphon's Morph™: Rhodes, 1999). Averages were created by selecting a set of landmark points and generating the average location (*x* and *y* coordinates) of each landmark. Each image was then warped into those average configurations. Averaging the gray-level or color values of each corresponding pixel produced an average texture image. Some techniques applied additional modifications to amplify the edges and to preserve textural details (Stephan 2003).

Such a 2D facial average has two main disadvantages: Firstly it is a 2D representation of the 3D face, thus ignoring the considerable amount of information present in the third dimension. Secondly, before making the composite face, each face was warped into the average-landmark configuration, a procedure that makes the average face inaccurate in areas distant from the averaged landmarks.

It was clear from the above that 3D facial averaging was worth developing. The previous literature about 3D averaging is very limited in scope. Nute (2000) used an optical surface laser scanner to study 3D growth in children and how it differs between sexes. They developed a facial averaging system to generate and compare 3D average faces for children of the same age and sex. This allowed for studying growth changes in both sexes. However, similar to the 2D averaging, the average was created by a set of landmark points whose 3D coordinates (*x*, *y*, and *z*) were averaged to give the average scan. Whilst this provided a 3D representation of the 3D face, it held the same problem of inaccuracy in the areas of the face distant from the averaged landmarks. Ideally, a 3D averaging system should consider all parts of the face evenly; that is, it should average the whole face.

In the study described in this chapter, a new facial averaging system was developed. The facial average represents the average of the *z* dimension pixel coordinates of the facial images. A commercial 3D surface digitizer (NEC "Fiore") was used to generate the 3D images. Sex-specific facial averages were created and compared between two ethnic groups: Japanese and European.

16.2 MATERIALS AND METHOD

16.2.1 PARTICIPANTS

The three-dimensional facial images for this experiment were from two ethnic cohorts: Japanese and European. The eighty Japanese faces were of young and middle-aged adult males. Dr Mineo Yoshino and his staff collected these scans at the National Research Institute of Police Science (NRIPS) in Japan as part of a collaborative program of research with the University of Melbourne School of Dental Science. As there were originally no females in this cohort, we had to recruit a number of young adult Japanese females into our study and also to include some South Korean faces. The number of females in this group was twelve in total. The inclusion of non-Japanese faces is not ideal but it is believed that Japanese and Korean faces have sufficiently similar facial morphology to make our comparisons meaningful.

The second group consisted of Australians of European origin: seventy males and thirty females. The males were of a spread of ages similar to that of the Japanese males. With two or three exceptions, the European females were young adults. In all cases, people at the extremes of body type were excluded.

16.2.2 THE NEC "FIORE" 3D FACIAL SCANNER AND ASSOCIATED SOFTWARE

NEC in Japan developed the Fiore 3D digitizer (Figure 16.1), with the collaboration of NRIPS, for forensic and medical research. Fiore has been utilized by NRIPS as a computer-assisted system for the identification of suspects by the matching of a suspect's three-dimensional image with a video image of an offender taken by a surveillance camera (Yoshino 2000). The results of such investigations have been accepted in the Japanese courts as a "proof of identity". In addition to Fiore and its control software, the 3D-Rugle3 program (Medic Engineering, Kyoto, Japan) is used for performing the facial measurements and comparisons.

Fiore comprises a pair of cameras and projectors that measure each side of the face, and in combination the two 3D images provide coverage from the

Figure 16.1 The Fiore 3D digitizer with two digital CCD cameras (top) and two light projectors (bottom).

lateral border of one ear to the other (with occasional exceptions where one or both ears were missed due to operator error). Images are obtained within a set volume of 300 × 400 × 200 mm, an angular width of 220°, and a resolution of 480 × 640 pixels, and the capture process takes about two seconds. The output files have *x,y,z* triplets and RGB color information for each data point, and the measurement error in depth is estimated to be less than 0.16 mm.

3D-Rugle3 has facilities for performing comparison between two 3D images, adjusting their relative positions, sizes, and orientation, and for measuring the distance between them. Rugle also has the ability to show section profiles in the vertical and horizontal planes. By selecting three or more points on each of two images and aligning them, the images can be brought into matching locations and orientations.

16.2.3 FACE DEFINITION

In order for the results of averaging to be meaningful, standardization of the location and orientation of the faces was necessary. In the raw scans, there was variability from one facial image to another in the extent of the surface acquired, with most of the faces including the ears while a few did not. This was a particular problem where the subject had very full cheeks or heavy sideburns.

Some faces had much of the forehead obscured by long hair, which spoiled the quality of the surface scan in that area. To overcome these problems it was necessary to process the facial scans and, in order to do this in a reproducible manner, a standardized definition was needed of what the "face" was.

For the purposes of this experiment the face was defined relative to a coronal plane located 50 mm posterior to the subnasale. Only the part of the face anterior to that plane was included in the analysis. This definition included the eyes, the nose, the cheeks, the mouth and much of the lateral parts of the face but excluded the ears and the areas just in front of them.

The upper boundary of the face was defined by choosing the point in the midline of the face 10 mm superior to the left superciliare landmark. From this point, two straight lines were drawn to both sides passing through the superciliare landmark of the same side and continuing until the outer edge of the face. The part of the face above those two lines was deleted.

16.2.4 FACE ALIGNMENT AND SUPERIMPOSITION

The first image of each of the four groups was aligned to bring the Frankfort plane* approximately horizontal. The other images in the group were opened in turn and brought into alignment with the first one. In carrying out the superimposition, the subnasale was chosen to be the reference point, and each image translated in x, y, and z to bring this landmark into alignment with the same point in the first image. The nasion points in all images were then brought to the same x and z values but not necessarily the same y value of nasion in the reference image. This aligned the second image with the facial midline parallel to that of the reference image. This process was facilitated by the ability of 3D-Rugle3 to display the vertical and the horizontal profiles during the superimposition. At the end of this process of image alignment, which used all the facilities of 3D-Rugle3 but was otherwise entirely manual, there were four sets of anatomically aligned facial scans. At this stage, no attempt was made to adjust the faces to a common scale.

**A standard craniometric reference plane passing through the right and left porion and the left orbitale; drawn on the profile radiograph or photograph from the superior margin of the acoustic meatus to the orbitale.*

16.2.5 FACE AS A MICROSOFT EXCEL SHEET

3D-Rugle3 provides a facility for the export of facial scans to a comma-separated-value (.csv) file that can be imported into a Microsoft Excel spreadsheet. The inherent limitation of Excel for this purpose is that there are a maximum of 256 columns in a spreadsheet and thus exported images must be reduced in size by a scale factor of 0.5. After all images had been aligned they were saved as 256 × 256 arrays in Excel sheets, the number in each cell being the z value of the surface at the (x, y) location represented by the cell coordinates.

16.2.6 FACE AVERAGING

Initial attempts at generating facial averages used the Excel spreadsheets directly, but this process proved to be very time-consuming, and memory limitations in the PC restricted the number of faces in any one set to about twenty. To address this problem, one of the authors (CDLT) developed software using Matlab V6.5 that opens the .csv files directly and allows a user to calculate the average z value of up to eighty faces. The associated standard deviation can also be recorded and the output exported as images or .csv files. The averages, or standard deviations, of the facial images are exported in a format that can be imported into 3D-Rugle3, displayed in 3D, and manipulated and compared in the same manner as any 3D surface scan. A significant current limitation of this method is that it forms its output using only the z data and ignores the color information in the original scans. It is hoped that this deficiency will soon be rectified, and we shall then be able to generate the average 3D topographic faces with averaged color and texture information too.

16.3 EXPERIMENTS

In *experiment 1*, four 3D face averages were created:

- Japanese male average from 70 Japanese faces
- European male average from 70 European faces
- Japanese female average from 12 Japanese faces
- Two European female averages from 30 and 12 European faces.

Each pair of same-sex averages were matched, and the details of racial difference studied.

In *experiment 2*, the threshold number for averages was estimated. This threshold is the minimum number of faces from which the average face is created that is very similar in 3D topography to any other average face created from the same number of *different* scans. The original male groups consisted of 70 faces each and were subdivided into 3 groups (a, b, and c) containing 23 faces each after excluding the face number 70. In each subgroup 22 averages were created from a descending number of contributing faces each time (average from 23, average from 22, ... , average from 2).

In *experiment 3*, a modified Japanese female average face was created from 12 faces after correcting for size differences. All of the 12 faces were rescaled by standardizing the 3D *midline* distance from the interpupillary line to the most forward-projecting point on the anterior surface of the chin (pogonion). The modified face average was then created and compared with the original average.

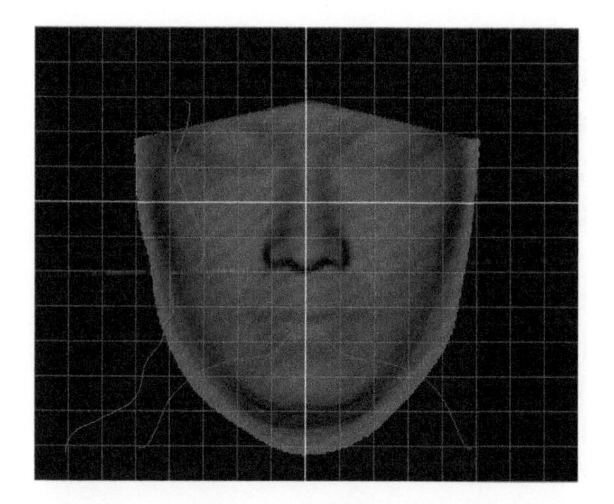

Figure 16.2

Japanese male average from 70 faces.

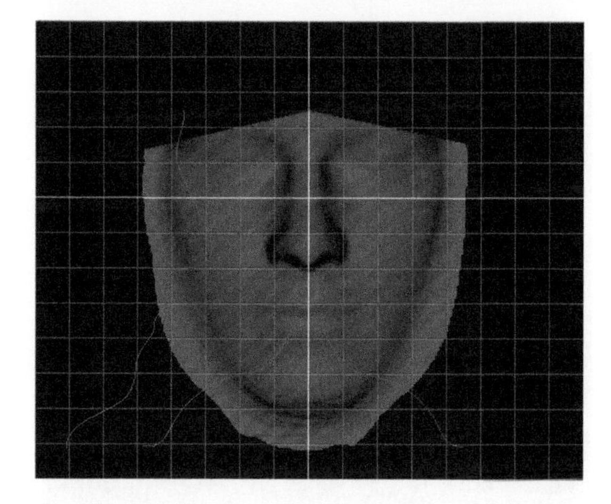

Figure 16.3

European male average from 70 faces.

16.4 RESULTS AND DISCUSSION

16.4.1 EXPERIMENT 1

Figures 16.2 and 16.3 show two average faces created from 70 different Japanese and 70 different European male 3D facial images, respectively. Figure 16.4 shows the average European female face created from 30 faces, and Figure 16.5 shows the average Japanese female face from 12 faces. All average faces are exhibited in the frontal view with a vertical and a horizontal profile.

The color of the output display of the average face surfaces was pink, as this is the color by default of any imported 3D data. For better contrast, the color can be changed to gray. However, the average face is still monochromatic because the average facial data do not contain any color information.

By matching the two ethnically-variant male averages (Figure 16.6) to study the differences in facial morphology (Figure 16.7), it can be clearly seen that the two averages are different. The matching value is 10.4 mm. The *matching*

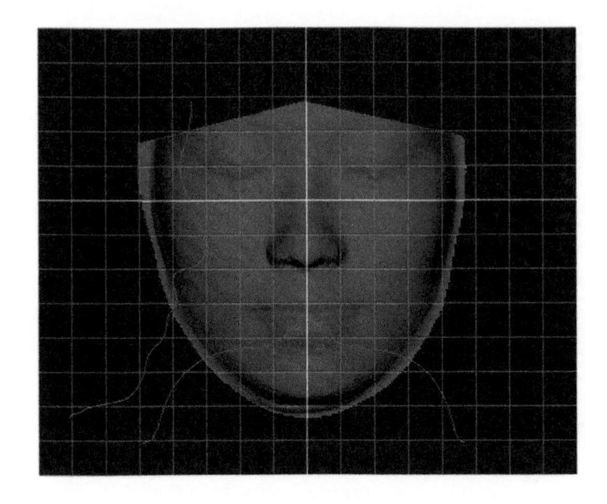

Figure 16.4

Japanese female average from 12 faces.

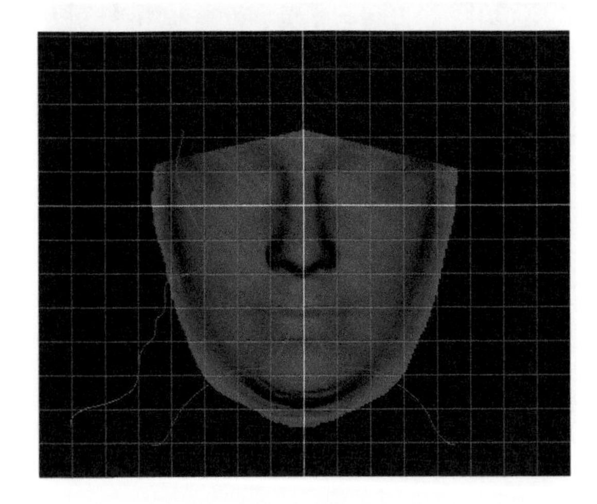

Figure 16.5

European female average from 30 faces.

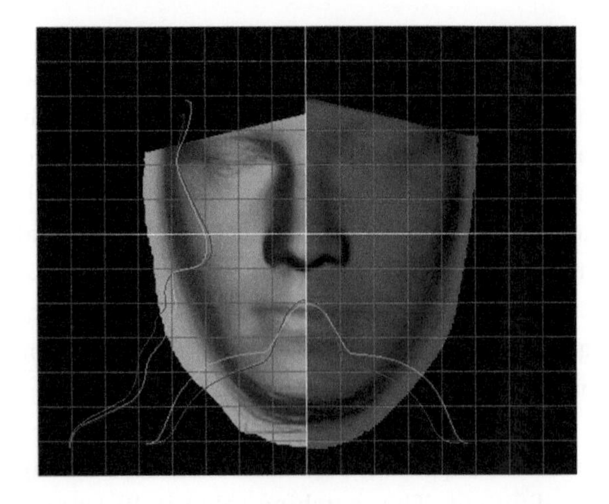

Figure 16.6

European male average from 70 faces (gray with red profile line) versus Japanese male average from 70 faces (pink with green profile line).

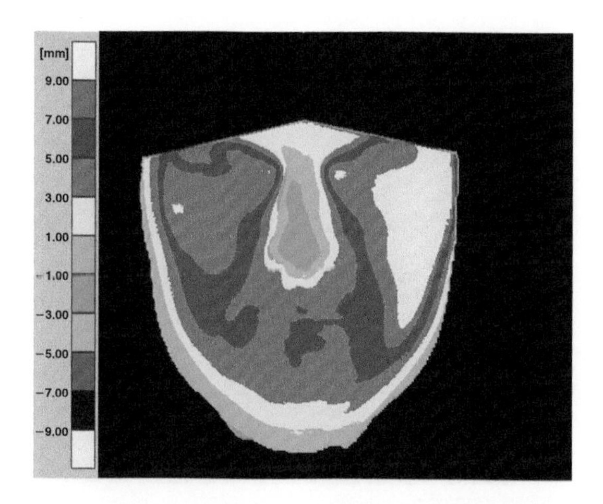

Figure 16.7

Amount of depth (z value) difference between the two averages in Figure 16.5.

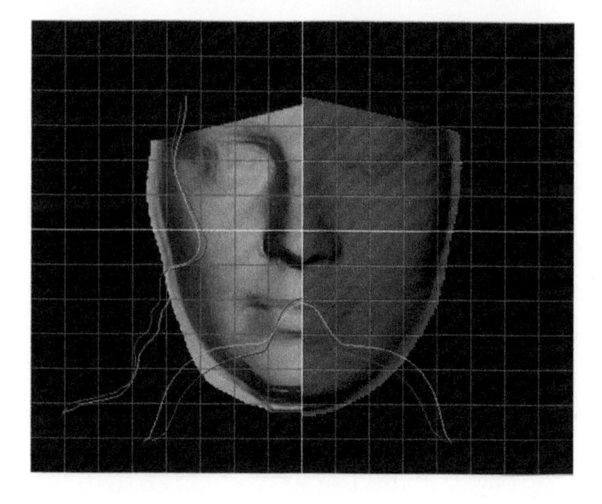

Figure 16.8

European female average from 12 faces (gray with red profile line) versus Japanese female average from 12 faces (pink with green profile line).

value represents the average absolute normal distance between each two corresponding pixels. *Normal* distance (Medic Engineering 2002) is the distance from each pixel of image 1 to the corresponding pixel of image 2 in the direction of the normal vector at the pixel of image 1.

Because the numbers of faces in the two female racial groups are different, a European female average face from random 12 faces was created and matched with the Japanese female average face from 12 faces (Figures 16.8 and 16.9). Similarly, the two averages are different with a matching value of 12.7 mm.

JAPANESE MALE AVERAGE VERSUS EUROPEAN MALE AVERAGE

The distances to be considered as significant here are those above 3 mm. Most of the major differences between the two male averages were in the orbital and the cheek areas and to a lesser extent the jaw area. This is because the Japanese male face is in general flatter than the European male face. The Japanese face

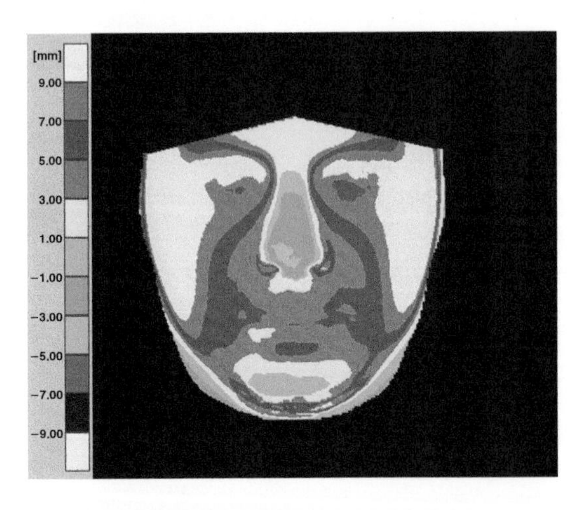

Figure 16.9

Amount of depth (z value) difference between the two averages in Figure 16.8.

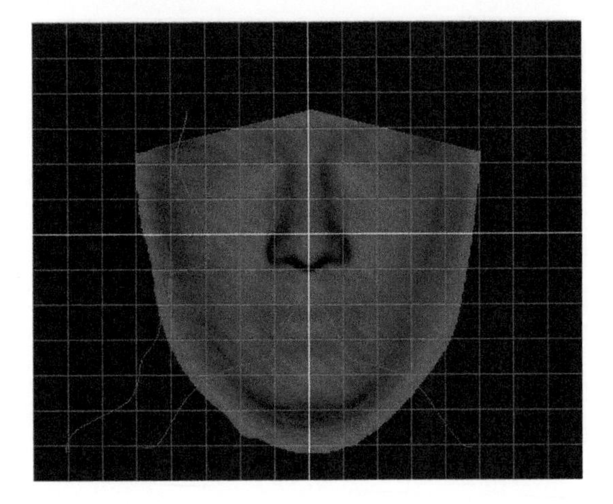

Figure 16.10

Hybrid male average from 140 faces: 70 European and 70 Japanese faces.

has a more protruding glabella-forehead area and also upper and lower jaw area when compared to the European male face. Although this might be well known, the Japanese male nose is shown to be shorter and broader than the European male nose.

JAPANESE FEMALE AVERAGE VERSUS EUROPEAN FEMALE AVERAGE

Although the differences here are slightly more marked, they share the same areas of difference as found in the male groups. There is one exception in the chin area, which shows much less difference than in the male groups. However, because the numbers of faces contributed to these two averages were only 12 compared to 70 in the male groups, results cannot be as reliable.

HYBRID MALE FACE AVERAGE

Figure 16.10 shows an average male "hybrid" face created by 140 faces: 70 European and 70 Japanese faces. The hybrid face was matched with the two

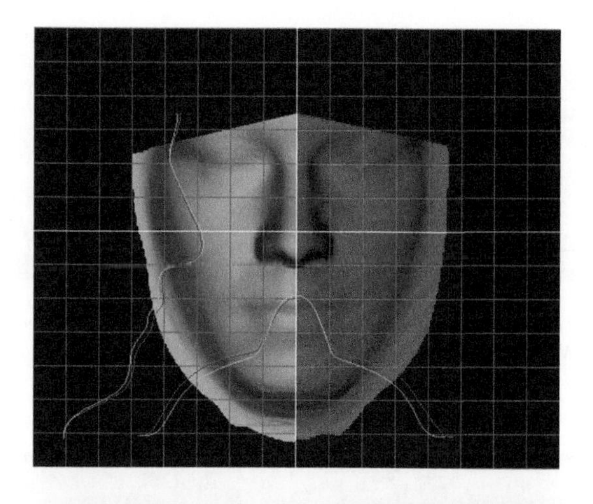

Figure 16.11

Hybrid male average from 140 faces (gray with red profile line) versus European male average from 70 faces (pink with green profile line).

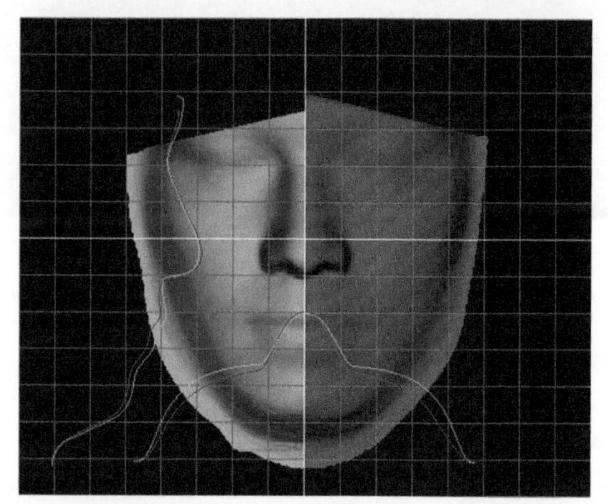

Figure 16.12

Hybrid male average from 140 faces (gray with red profile line) versus Japanese male average from 70 faces (pink with green profile line).

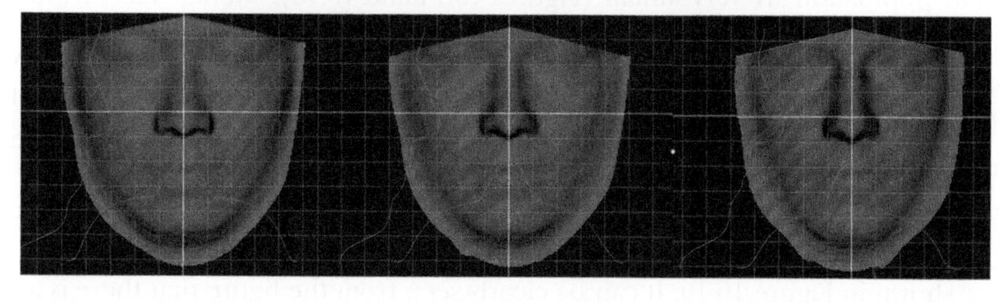

Figure 16.13 Left to right: Japanese male average (70 faces), hybrid male average (140 faces), European male average (70 faces).

averages that created it (Figures 16.11 and 16.12). The matching value between the hybrid average face and the Japanese male average was 6.3 mm. A nearly similar value of 6.5 mm was found between the hybrid face and the European male average. Figure 16.13 shows the three male averages together.

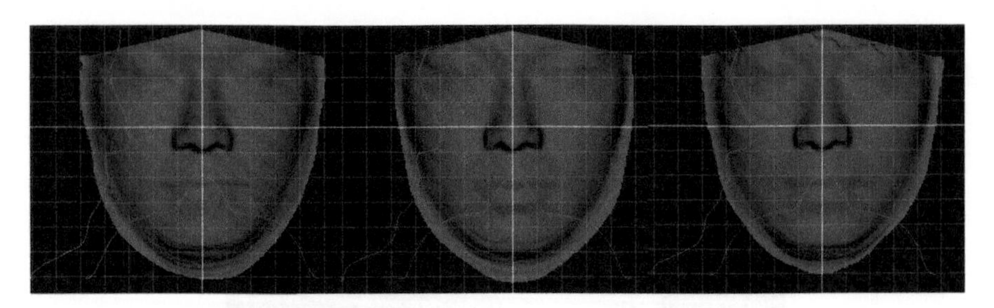

Figure 16.14 Three Japanese male average faces created from completely different cohorts of Japanese male faces, 23 faces each. Matching values between 1 and 2 = 1.5 mm, 2 and 3 = 1.9 mm, and between 2 and 3 = 1.4 mm.

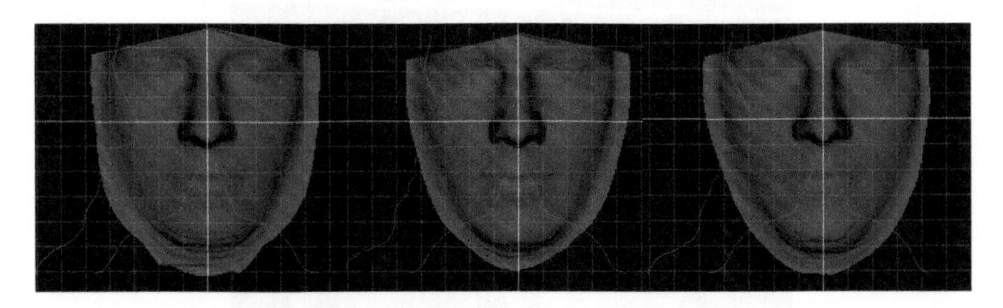

Figure 16.15 Three European male average faces created from completely different cohorts of European male faces, 23 faces each. Matching values between 1 and 2 = 1.9 mm, 2 and 3 = 1.4 mm, and between 2 and 3 = 1.6 mm.

16.4.2 EXPERIMENT 2

It was found out that average faces created from different cohorts of faces of the same population are very similar (Figures 16.14 and 16.15). Average faces from different subgroups of the same ethnic group were matched. Matching was done between each two averages with the same number of contributing faces (e.g., a Japanese male average in the first subgroup created from 20 faces was matched with another Japanese average created from 20 faces but in the second or third subgroup and so on). Tables 16.1 and 16.2 show the results.

Plots of the matching values resulting from each of two matched subgroups are shown in Figure 16.16. It can be clearly seen from the figure that there is a plateau starting from around 12 faces. This means that, in any subgroup, the average face created by 12 faces is similar to that created from 23 or even more—because, when the average face created by 12 is matched and compared with a corresponding one of another subgroup, the matching value would not be that different from that when the corresponding averages created by 23 faces were matched. From this plot it can be estimated that the average threshold lies somewhere between 12 and 15 faces. When averaging the six plots in Figure 16.13 (Figure 16.17) it can be concluded that the average threshold is around 14 faces.

Table 16.1 E = European, M = male, av = average, Match v = Matching value in millimeters.

Subgroup-1	Match v	Subgroup-2	Match v	Subgroup-3	Match v	Subgroup-1
EM1-av-23	1.919	EM2-av-23	1.422	EM3-av-23	1.583	EM1-av-23
EM1-av-22	1.894	EM2-av-22	1.432	EM3-av-22	1.591	EM1-av-22
EM1-av-21	1.999	EM2-av-21	1.489	EM3-av-21	1.635	EM1-av-21
EM1-av-20	1.611	EM2-av-20	1.291	EM3-av-20	1.449	EM1-av-20
EM1-av-19	1.551	EM2-av-19	1.287	EM3-av-19	1.329	EM1-av-19
EM1-av-18	1.751	EM2-av-18	1.284	EM3-av-18	1.389	EM1-av-18
EM1-av-17	1.781	EM2-av-17	1.421	EM3-av-17	1.227	EM1-av-17
EM1-av-16	1.776	EM2-av-16	1.326	EM3-av-16	1.348	EM1-av-16
EM1-av-15	1.591	EM2-av-15	1.149	EM3-av-15	1.262	EM1-av-15
EM1-av-14	1.5	EM2-av-14	1.295	EM3-av-14	1.391	EM1-av-14
EM1-av-13	1.807	EM2-av-13	1.484	EM3-av-13	1.403	EM1-av-13
EM1-av-12	2.024	EM2-av-12	1.594	EM3-av-12	1.449	EM1-av-12
EM1-av-11	2.019	EM2-av-11	1.794	EM3-av-11	1.475	EM1-av-11
EM1-av-10	2.025	EM2-av-10	1.812	EM3-av-10	1.635	EM1-av-10
EM1-av-9	1.93	EM2-av-9	1.886	EM3-av-9	1.694	EM1-av-9
EM1-av-8	1.96	EM2-av-8	2.083	EM3-av-8	1.613	EM1-av-8
EM1-av-7	2.015	EM2-av-7	2.269	EM3-av-7	1.635	EM1-av-7
EM1-av-6	1.88	EM2-av-6	2.726	EM3-av-6	2.185	EM1-av-6
EM1-av-5	2.14	EM2-av-5	3.484	EM3-av-5	2.899	EM1-av-5
EM1-av-4	3.375	EM2-av-4	3.589	EM3-av-4	2.091	EM1-av-4
EM1-av-3	4.457	EM2-av-3	4.296	EM3-av-3	2.315	EM1-av-3
EM1-av-2	4.329	EM2-av-2	5.251	EM3-av-2	3.076	EM1-av-2

Table 16.2 J = Japanese, M = male, av = average, Match v = Matching value in millimeters.

Subgroup-1	Match v	Subgroup-2	Match v	Subgroup-3	Match v	Subgroup-1
JM1-av-23	1.491	JM2-av-23	1.921	JM3-av-23	1.362	JM1-av-23
JM1-av-22	1.651	JM2-av-22	2.175	JM3-av-22	1.458	JM1-av-22
JM1-av-21	1.525	JM2-av-21	1.81	JM3-av-21	1.442	JM1-av-21
JM1-av-20	1.324	JM2-av-20	1.666	JM3-av-20	1.481	JM1-av-20
JM1-av-19	1.305	JM2-av-19	1.887	JM3-av-19	1.493	JM1-av-19
JM1-av-18	1.39	JM2-av-18	2.292	JM3-av-18	1.665	JM1-av-18
JM1-av-17	1.227	JM2-av-17	2.36	JM3-av-17	1.781	JM1-av-17
JM1-av-16	1.298	JM2-av-16	2.404	JM3-av-16	2.043	JM1-av-16
JM1-av-15	1.433	JM2-av-15	2.263	JM3-av-15	2.047	JM1-av-15
JM1-av-14	1.558	JM2-av-14	2.205	JM3-av-14	1.716	JM1-av-14
JM1-av-13	1.514	JM2-av-13	2.136	JM3-av-13	1.934	JM1-av-13
JM1-av-12	1.612	JM2-av-12	2.237	JM3-av-12	1.895	JM1-av-12
JM1-av-11	1.939	JM2-av-11	2.322	JM3-av-11	1.753	JM1-av-11
JM1-av-10	1.744	JM2-av-10	2.442	JM3-av-10	1.754	JM1-av-10
JM1-av-9	2.372	JM2-av-9	2.515	JM3-av-9	1.583	JM1-av-9
JM1-av-8	2.573	JM2-av-8	2.75	JM3-av-8	1.67	JM1-av-8
JM1-av-7	2.603	JM2-av-7	2.971	JM3-av-7	1.66	JM1-av-7
JM1-av-6	2.394	JM2-av-6	2.922	JM3-av-6	2.106	JM1-av-6
JM1-av-5	2.524	JM2-av-5	2.901	JM3-av-5	2.177	JM1-av-5
JM1-av-4	2.661	JM2-av-4	3.156	JM3-av-4	2.323	JM1-av-4
JM1-av-3	2.578	JM2-av-3	2.81	JM3-av-3	2.413	JM1-av-3
JM1-av-2	4.781	JM2-av-2	4.828	JM3-av-2	5.799	JM1-av-2

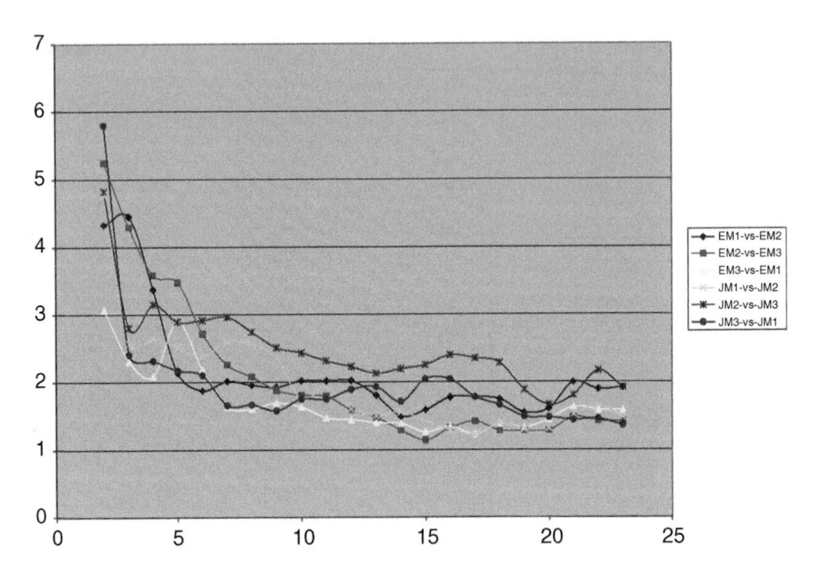

Figure 16.16 Table 1 plotted. Here Y is the matching value in millimeters and X is the number of faces in each average.

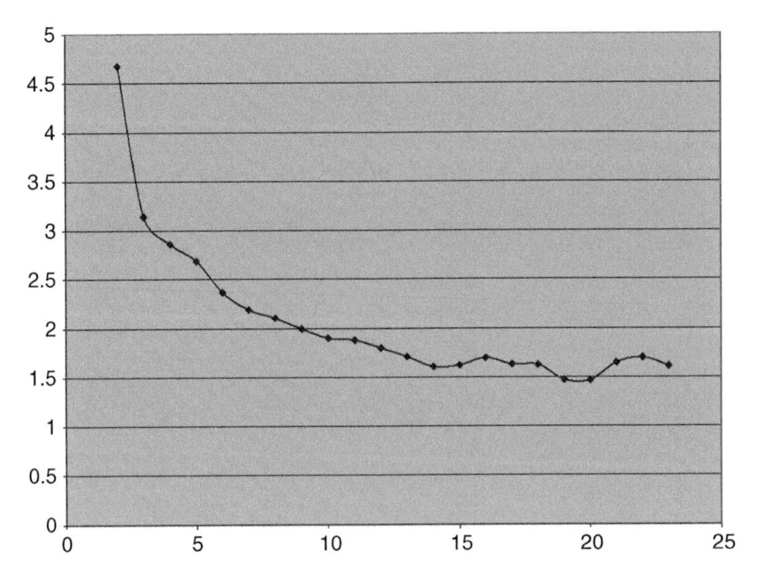

Figure 16.17 Average of the six plots in Figure 16.15. Here Y is the matching value in millimeters, and X is the number of faces in each average.

16.4.3 EXPERIMENT 3

Figure 16.18 shows a modified Japanese female average face created from 12 faces after correcting for size differences. It was matched with the unmodified average face (Figure 16.19) created from the same faces but without correcting for size. The two average faces are shown together in Figure 16.20.

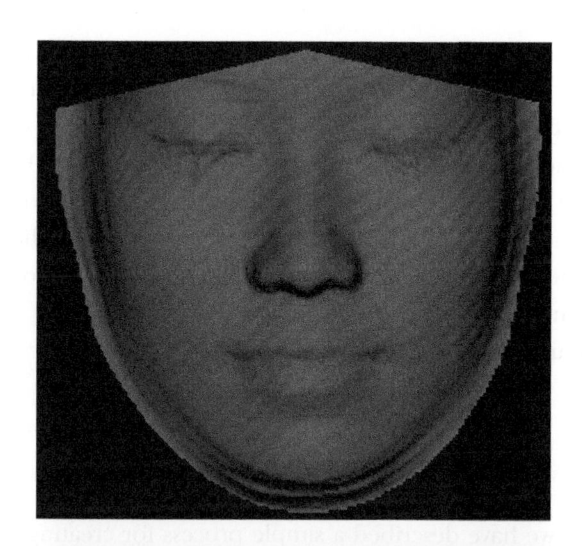

Figure 16.18

Modified Japanese female average face created from 12 faces after correcting for size.

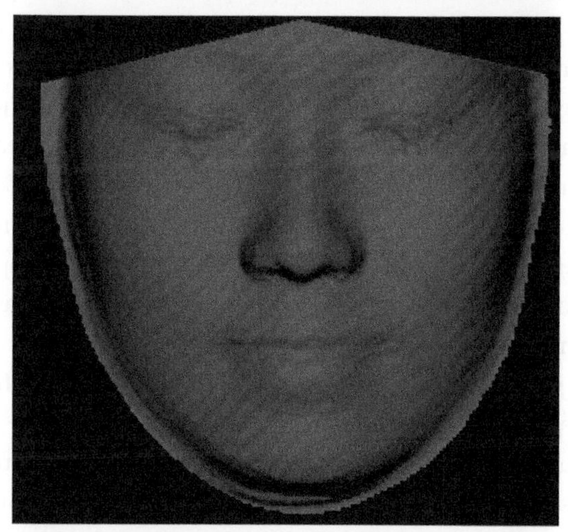

Figure 16.19

Unmodified Japanese female average face created from 12 faces without correcting for size.

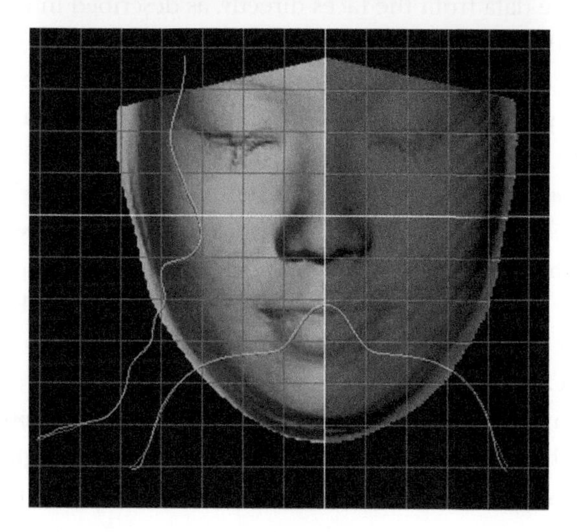

Figure 16.20

Modified Japanese female average from 12 faces after correcting for size (gray with red profile line) versus unmodified Japanese female average from the same 12 faces without correcting for size (pink with green profile line).

The matching value between the two averages was 1.00 mm. It can be inferred that correcting for size does not play a significant role in modifying the 3D morphology of the average face. It only corrects for the average outlines of the nose, mouth, and eyes. It is evident from Figures 16.18 and 16.19 that the facial features like the mouth, the nose, and the eyes are better and more cleanly outlined in the modified average when compared with those of the unmodified one. It is of interest that, in order to get such clean average outlines, more non-size-standardized faces are needed. When standardizing for size, averages are compared based on the shape factor as the size factor is excluded.

16.5 CONCLUSIONS

In this chapter, we have described a simple process for creating what we have called "average" faces. The principal aim of this work is to create what might be better called "archetypal" faces to represent the faces of distinctive groups of people. These groupings may be based on ethnicity or on the presence of genetic syndromes where the effects are expressed in the facial features of those affected. The process we have described involves averaging of the depth values on 3D surface scans of the faces after the scans have been aligned with each other using anatomical features. In the near future, this process will be extended to include the averaging of the color information associated with each location in the scans.

The process just described appears to capture the desired features of the faces but is certainly open to improvement, and the authors are currently considering the issues involved in, and alternative approaches to, the creation of archetypal faces. Methods for combining faces may be categorized as either using the surface data from the faces directly, as described in this chapter, or using some method for generating a parametric description of the faces. The derived parameters can then be processed—perhaps by averaging, but other approaches are possible—and then the resulting face can be constructed from the parameters.

Direct methods are limited by the lack of any links to the underlying anatomy; the methods treat the face as merely a set of coordinates and associated color information. This limits the method's applicability to faces of very similar size or requires the use of some method for size standardization. Even after correction for size, variations in facial proportions may result in the combining of features that are not quite the same anatomically.

Parametric methods require the identification of the desired features of the face, probably by hand, but some workers have made progress with automated methods. This process may just require the location of standard anatomical landmarks, or it may need an operator to draw in outlines of features such as the nose or mouth. Alternatively, landmarks may be used to define a set of parasagittal and transverse profiles that can be subjected to (for example) a Fourier shape analysis. With the features reduced to numerical form, the processing can take many forms depending upon the purpose of the exercise.

The success of any project must depend upon the match between the requirements and the method of analysis chosen; the requirement for the creation of average faces differing from those for archetypes or for the generation of faces intermediate between two extremes.

ACKNOWLEDGEMENTS

The work described in this chapter could not have been done without the considerable help and support of NEC Japan, the National Research Institute of Police Science (NRIPS), and Medic Engineering. NEC Japan provided the Fiore digitizer on loan. Dr Mineo Yoshino and his staff at NRIPS inspired the authors to start work on 3D facial imaging and collected the Japanese male faces. Mr Toyohisa Tanjiri of Medic Engineering provided the 3D-Rugle3 software and gave generous assistance with its use and by providing modifications at very short notice. Professor Clement and Mr Thomas have received financial support from the Australian Research Council via Discovery-Project Grant No. DP0208510.

REFERENCES

Farkas G. L. (1994) *Anthropometry of the Head and Face* (2nd edn.). Raven Press, pp. 243–351.

Halberstadt J. and Rhodes G. (2003) "It's Not Just Average Faces that are Attractive: Computer-Manipulated Averageness Makes Birds, Fish, and Automobiles Attractive", *Psychonomic Bulletin & Review* 10(1), 149–156.

Little A. C., Burt D. M., Penton-Voak I. S. and Perrett D. I. (2001) "Self-perceived Attractiveness Influences Human Female Preferences for Sexual Dimorphism and Symmetry in Male Faces", *Proceedings of the Royal Society of London – Series B: Biological Sciences* 268(1462), 39–44.

Little A. C., Jones B. C., Penton-Voak I. S., Burt D. M. and Perrett D. I. (2002) "Partnership Status and the Temporal Context of Relationships Influence Human Female Preferences for Sexual Dimorphism in Male Face Shape", *Proceedings of the Royal Society of London – Series B: Biological Sciences* 269(1496), 1095–2100.

Medic Engineering (2002) *3D-Rugle 3* software manual (Medic Engineering, Kyoto, Japan).

Nute S. J. and Moss J. P. (2000) "Three-dimensional Facial Growth Studied by Optical Surface Scanning", *J. Orthodontics* 27(1), 31–38.

Penton-Voak I. S., Jones B. C., Little A. C., Baker S., Tiddeman B., Burt D. M. and Perrett D. I. (2001) "Symmetry, Sexual Dimorphism in Facial Proportions and Male Facial Attractiveness", *Proceedings of the Royal Society of London – Series B: Biological Sciences* 268(1476), 1617–1623.

Rhodes G., Sumich A. and Byatt G. (1999) "Are Average Facial Configurations Attractive Only Because of their Symmetry?", *Psychol. Sci.* 10, 52–58.

Rhodes G., Yoshikawa S., Clark A., Lee K., McKay R. and Akamatsu S. (2001) "Attractiveness of Facial Averageness and Symmetry in Non-Western Cultures: In Search of Biologically Based Standards of Beauty", *Perception* 30(5), 611–625.

Stephan C. (2003) PhD Thesis, University of Adelaide.

Yoshino M., Matsuda H., Kubota S., Imaizumi K. and Miyasaka S. (2000) "Computer-assisted Facial Image Identification System using a 3-D Physiognomic Range Finder", *Forensic Sci. Int.* 109, 225–237.

CHAPTER 17

ESTIMATION AND ANIMATION OF FACES USING FACIAL MOTION MAPPING AND A 3D FACE DATABASE

Takaaki Kuratate
ATR Human Information Science Labs, Keihanna Science City, Kyoto 619-0288, Japan

Eric Vatikiotis-Bateson
Department of Linguistics, University of British Columbia, Vancouver, BC, Canada, and ATR Human Information Science Labs, Keihanna Science City, Kyoto 619-0288, Japan

Hani Camille Yehia
Department of Electronic Engineering, Universidade Federal de Minas Gerais, Belo Horizonte, Brazil

17.1 INTRODUCTION

Realistic facial animation remains one of the major challenges in computer graphics. The first step in such animation is to acquire a realistic face model. Expensive scanning devices such as laser range finders are convenient for capturing realistic face models. However, as presented by Blanz and Vetter (1999), Blanz *et al.* (2001), and Hwang *et al.* (2000), a 3D face database is quite useful for creating models from existing face characteristics in the database. Once a database is established, almost any 3D face can be created from features extracted from photographs.

With the face model in hand, it seems easy to create movement for a talking head. However, accurate movement poses another major challenge: if the created face motion is not accurate or does not correspond to speech, perception may be altered. In certain cases, movement can induce incorrect speech perception, as with the well-known McGurk effect (McGurk and MacDonald 1976), which has been demonstrated on computer-generated face models (Massaro, UCSC website). Additionally, incorrect movement often garners harsh reactions from people viewing the animation: after animations reach a certain point of realism, people begin to object to any deviations from true human behavior.

Face deformation during speech production is an important motion problem. Every person has unique facial deformation characteristics corresponding to their speech production that are determined by geometrical configurations of the skull and jaw, facial muscle structures, and skin thickness and stiffness properties. For this reason, using a muscle-based model is a good solution for creating face motion for speech (Waters 1987, Thalmann *et al.* 1988, Lee *et al.* 1995). However these models require the initialization of muscle structure for each new face model, and extensive computation to simulate muscle motion.

An algorithm that transfers face deformation from one subject to another using a neutral-face database was proposed by Blanz *et al.* (2003). However, this algorithm can only reference static facial aspects of the neutral faces comprising the database, and there is no guarantee that the transferred face deformation is reasonable for the target subjects.

In this chapter, we describe our method for creating and transferring face motion for talking heads based on statistical analysis of deformation properties of over 200 subjects in our 3D face database, each with the same set of face postures. We also discuss methods for creating textured 3D faces and face postures from two photographs using this database. First we describe how our 3D face database is created and analyzed by principal-component analysis (PCA). Then we show how we estimate a 3D face from feature points extracted from two photographs of an unknown subject. Starting with the estimated 3D model, face postures are then estimated from similar faces in the database. Finally, using a similarity measure for deformation characteristics of individual faces obtained by another PCA, we show that face motion from motion-capture data can be easily transferred to the estimated face or to other faces in the database to create animation using our facial motion mapping technique.

17.2 CREATING AND ANALYZING A 3D FACE DATABASE

To create our database, we scanned various subjects with Cyberware's 3D color digitizers (4020RGB/PS and 3030RGB/PS). These 3D digitizers employ a laser-scanning head mounted on an arm that rotates around a platform where a subject is seated. A single 360° scan takes 17 seconds and results in 3D range data and a surface-texture image of the subject's head. Nine postures per subject were scanned: neutral, mouth open, clenched, lip protrusion, the vowels /i/, /o/, and /u/, smile with mouth open, and smile with mouth closed. This set of postures was selected for its ability to represent the functional deformation of the face during speech while limiting the discomfort and scanning time for the subjects. Previously, we scanned up to 30 postures per subject,

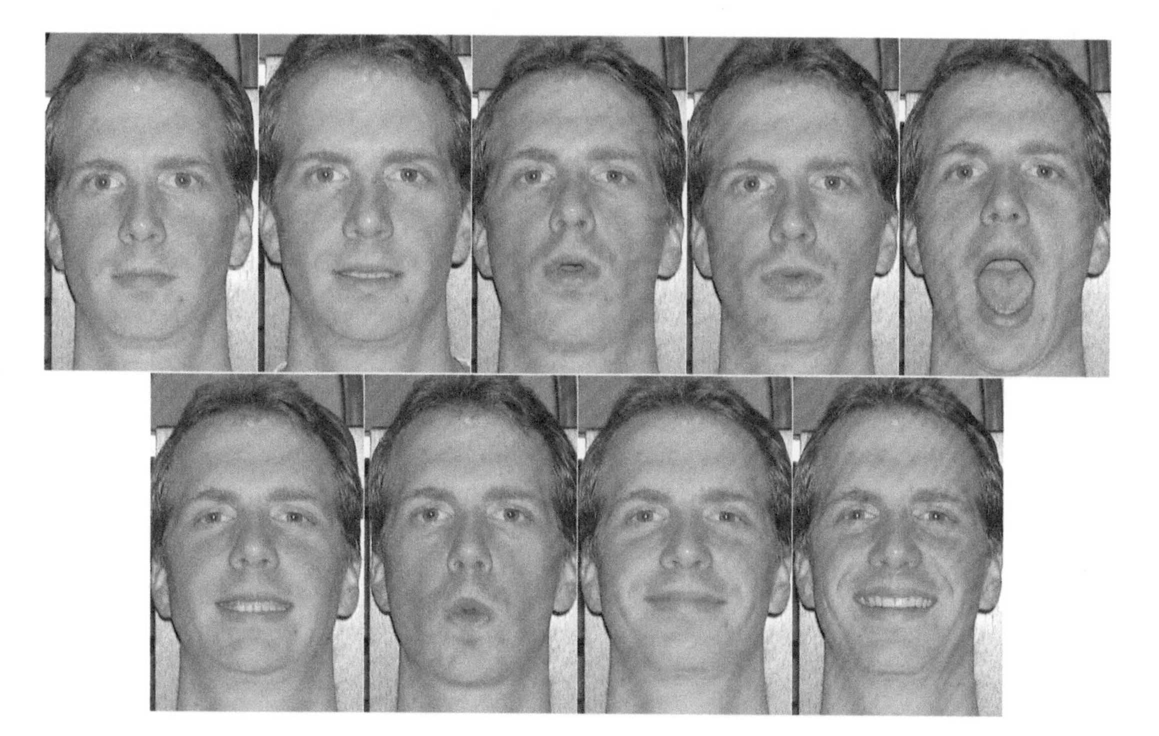

Figure 17.1 The nine basic face postures scanned for the 3D face database: in the top row are neutral, three vowels (/i/, /o/, /u/), and open mouth; in the bottom row are clenched, lip protrusion, and smiles with mouth closed and open.

which took over an hour and required extensive processing time. With fewer postures, scanning took less than 20 minutes per subject, and animation results have actually improved (for discussion, see Vatikiotis-Bateson *et al.* 1999). To date, more than 500 subjects have been scanned with this protocol, and over 200 subjects have been processed as described in the following subsection.

17.2.1 MAKING A LARGE-SCALE 3D FACE DATABASE

The raw range data are simple 3D scan-line data represented by cylindrical coordinates, and cannot be easily analyzed without further processing. Therefore, we adapt a predefined generic mesh to each scanned face and store the adapted mesh as an entry in the 3D face database. Figure 17.2 shows the current generic mesh model. To guide adaptation, basic feature lines are defined on the face by hand. They include eye boundaries, eyebrow boundaries, nose lines, lip contours, a jaw line, and a hair boundary. Then field morphing (Beier and Neely 1992) is used to smoothly transfer all nodes from the generic mesh onto the target range data. After adaptation of the scanned postures, all faces have the same mesh topology and can be more easily analyzed. Specific face regions can also be extracted for further analysis. Currently 200 subjects are represented by the generic mesh topology.

Figure 17.2 An example of a generic mesh (left) and its adaptation to 3D raw data based on feature lines. After the adaptation, specific regions can be extracted for further analysis.

For analysis, each adapted face mesh is expressed as a column vector f_i containing $3N$ mesh nodes, representing the x, y, z values for each 3D node:

$$f_i = [x_{i1}, x_{i2}, \ldots, x_{iN}; y_{i1}, y_{i2}, \ldots, y_{iN}; z_{i1}, z_{i2}, \ldots, z_{iN}]^{\mathrm{T}}. \tag{1}$$

After processing K faces, the ensemble of adapted mesh nodes is arranged in matrix form as

$$\boldsymbol{F} = [f_1 \quad f_2 \quad \ldots \quad f_K]. \tag{2}$$

The "mean face" $\boldsymbol{\mu}_{\mathrm{f}}$ is then defined as the vector formed by the average value of each row of F. It is then subtracted from each column of F, generating

$$\boldsymbol{F}_{\mathrm{M}} = [f_1 \quad f_2 \quad \ldots \quad f_K], \tag{3}$$

the matrix of facial deformations from the mean face. Any facial shape can now be expressed by the sum

$$f = f_{\mathrm{m}} + \boldsymbol{\mu}_{\mathrm{f}}. \tag{4}$$

17.2.2 FACIAL PCA

The principal components of $\boldsymbol{F}_{\mathrm{M}}$ can be found by applying singular-value decomposition (SVD) (Horn and Johnson 1985) to the covariance matrix

$$\boldsymbol{C}_{\mathrm{f}} = \boldsymbol{F}_{\mathrm{M}}\boldsymbol{F}_{\mathrm{M}}^{\mathrm{T}}, \tag{5}$$

yielding

$$\boldsymbol{C}_{\mathrm{f}} = \boldsymbol{U}\boldsymbol{S}\boldsymbol{U}^{\mathrm{T}}, \tag{6}$$

where $\boldsymbol{U}$ is a unitary matrix whose columns contain the $K - 1$ eigenvectors of $\boldsymbol{C}_{\mathrm{f}}$ normalized to unit length, and $\boldsymbol{S}$ is a diagonal matrix whose diagonal entries are the respective eigenvalues. Each eigenvalue of $\boldsymbol{S}$ denotes the variance accounted for by the respective eigenvector. Thus the sum of all eigenvalues is the total variance of the data.

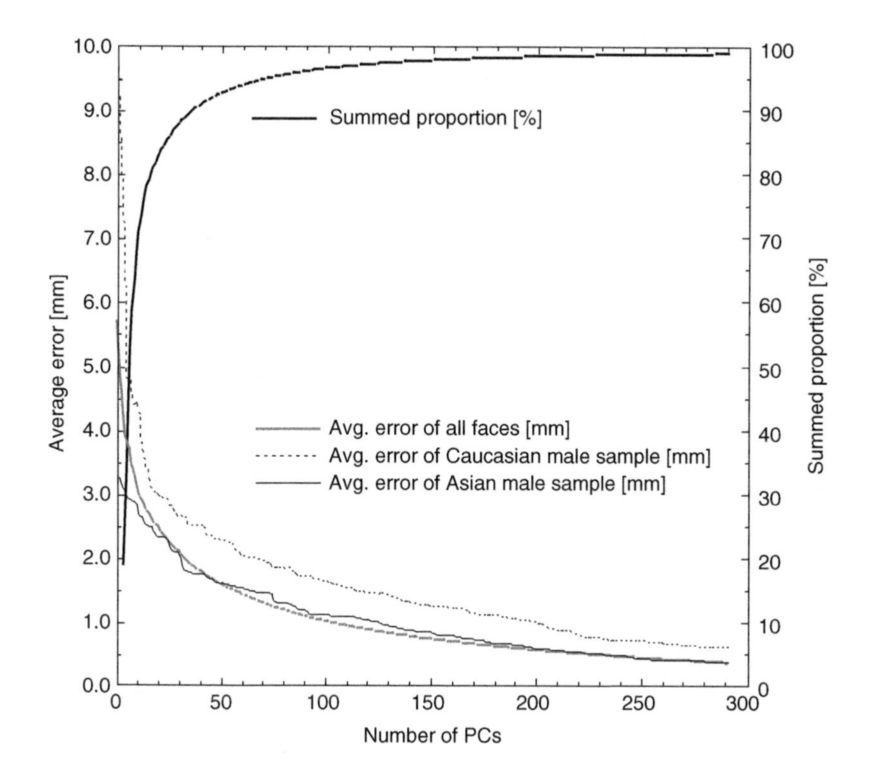

Figure 17.3

Cumulative proportion of total variance (darker thick line, scale on the right) and averaged distance errors between the original and reconstructed face for all faces in the database (gray thick line) are compared with errors for the faces used in Figure 17.4 (thin lines).

The principal components defined by the columns of $\boldsymbol{U}$ can be used to express any facial shape by the linear combination

$$f_{\mathrm{m}} = \boldsymbol{U}\boldsymbol{\alpha}, \tag{7}$$

where $\boldsymbol{\alpha}$ is the vector of principal component coefficients. Thus, for all K shapes used in this analysis, all face-representation coefficients are expressed as a matrix

$$\boldsymbol{A} = [\boldsymbol{\alpha}_1 \quad \boldsymbol{\alpha}_2 \quad \dots \quad \boldsymbol{\alpha}_K], \tag{8}$$

where each column vector $\boldsymbol{\alpha}$ is obtained by

$$\boldsymbol{\alpha} = \boldsymbol{U}^{\mathrm{T}} f_{\mathrm{m}}, \tag{9}$$

which is derived from Equation (7).

Figure 17.3 shows the cumulative proportion of total variance against the number of principal components under 291, where the eigenvalues are larger than 1.0. The figure also includes the average distance error per node between original faces and reconstructed faces discussed in the next section.

17.2.3 EVALUATION OF FACE RECONSTRUCTION

When we apply PCA to 200 subjects with nine face postures each, or 1800 faces, we see that the contribution of the lower principal components is relatively

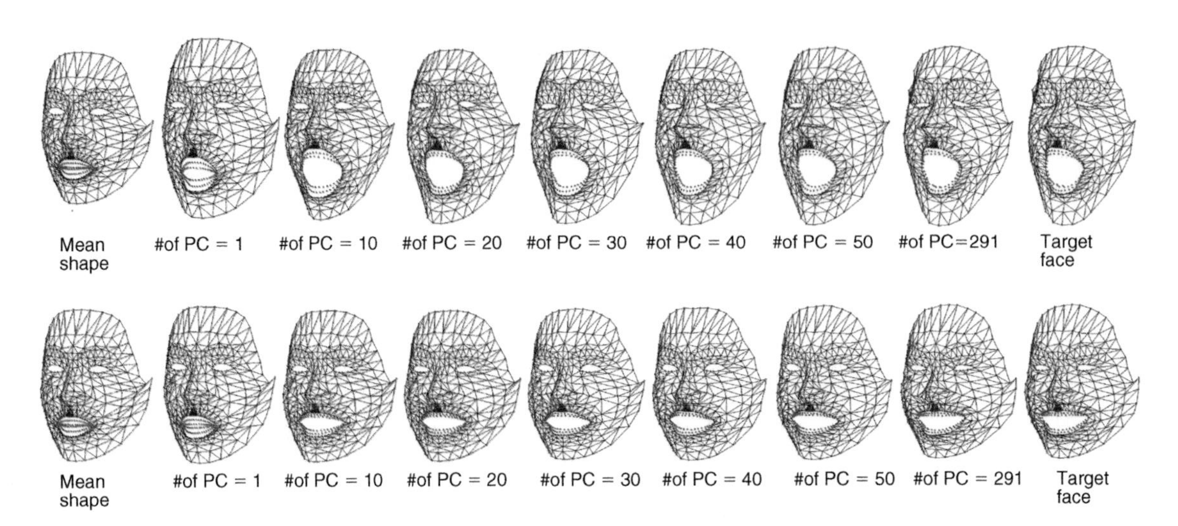

Figure 17.4 Effect of number of PCs on reconstructing the original face for a Caucasian male (top) and an Asian male (bottom) from the mean shape (far left) to the target face (far right). From left to right, the middle seven faces are reconstructed from 1, 10, 20, 30, 40, 50, and 291 PCs, respectively.

small when compared to the top components. Figure 17.4 shows an example of reconstructing a face using different numbers of PCs for a Caucasian male (top) and an Asian male (bottom). The face at the far left is the mean face obtained from analysis of $K = 1683$ faces. The middle seven faces are linear combinations of 1, 10, 20, 30, 40, 50, and 291 principal components, summed to the mean face. (Eigenvalues after 291 become smaller than one.) These can be compared to the original face on the far right, which shows a mouth-open posture for the Caucasian subject, and a smile with mouth open for the Asian subject. These examples demonstrate that increasing the number of PCs improves the accuracy of the reconstruction. The first 10 PCs result in a radical deformation from the mean face towards the target (original) face posture, but the difference from the target is still quite clear. Using 30 PCs, it is difficult to visually detect any difference, even when the reconstructed and original images are compared side by side. In fact, preliminary objective evaluation suggests that 30 to 50 PCs are enough to identify the subject and the face posture. In other words, one mean face and 30 to 50 control parameters or dimensions may be sufficient to differentiate 1800 faces in the database. This is a significant data reduction. Figure 17.3 shows the average distance error per node between original faces and faces reconstructed with different numbers of principal components for all faces, and errors for the two individual examples mentioned above. The database used for this particular analysis consists of $s = 187$ subjects, $K = 1683$ faces, with 79 Caucasians (45 males, 34 females), 105 Asians (69 males, 36 females), and 3 Africans (2 males, 1 female).

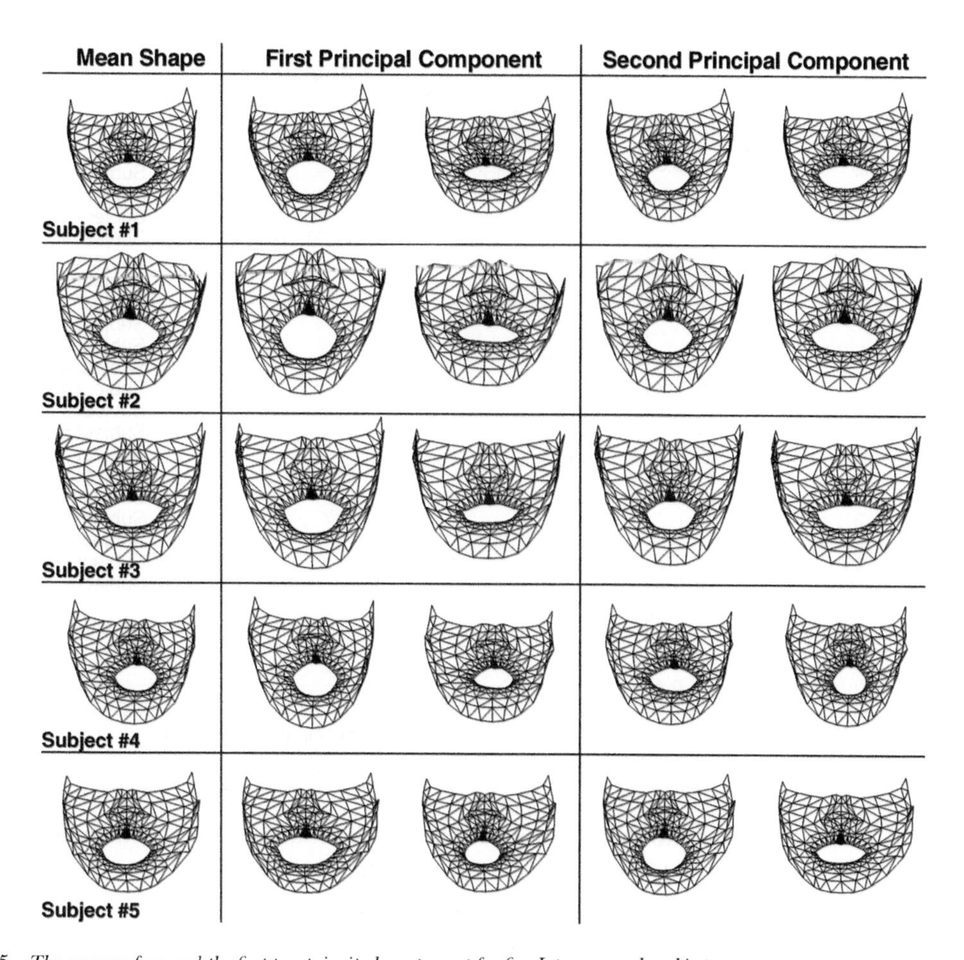

Figure 17.5 The average face and the first two principal component for five Japanese male subjects.

17.2.4 INDIVIDUAL FACIAL PCA

By applying facial PCA as described in Equations (1) through (7) to the nine postures for individual subjects, deformation characteristics of each subject are available. Even though personal deformation features exist for each subject, the extracted major components are quite similar across subjects because the scanned face postures are the same for each subject. The top two major components found for individuals in our database are jaw elevation deformation and lip rounding with protrusion (including, in the opposite direction, horizontal lip spreading). The findings are quite consistent across the database, although the order of the first two PCs is sometimes interchanged. Figure 17.5 shows the mean face and first principal component extracted from the lower face for five Japanese male subjects. Each row shows a different subject; the left column shows the mean face; the middle and right columns show the deformation from mean shape by one standard deviation (+/−). In this figure, we see that jaw elevation

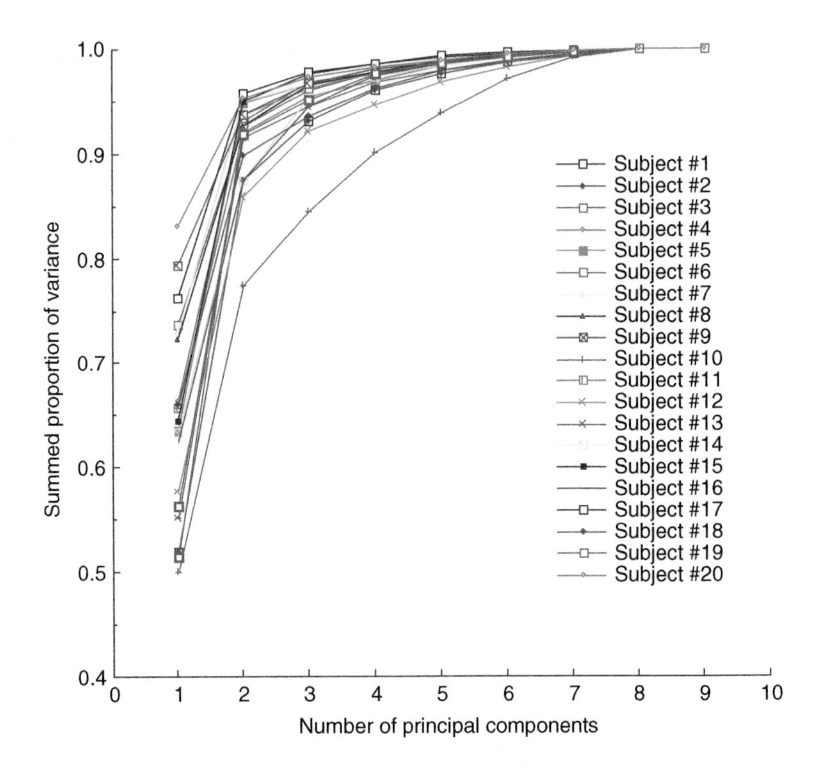

Figure 17.6
The cumulative proportion of variance versus the number of principal components for 20 individual subjects in the database.

is related to the first component, and lip rounding and protrusion is related to the second component for all but the bottom subject, whose components are the same but reversed in order. In both cases, the first component recovers 60–80% of the variance, and the top two components recover more than 90%. Most subjects show similar results. The third component, however, varies widely among subjects, showing many different deformation characteristics.

Figure 17.6 shows the summed proportion of total variance by the number of principal components for 20 individual subjects in the database. As shown in the figure, the patterning of components is essentially the same. Only one subject shows appreciably different characteristics in this example because this subject was less expressive than the other subjects.

17.2.5 FACE MOTION REPRESENTATION BY INDIVIDUAL PCS

Individual facial PCA results provide an efficient representation of facial motion for talking-head animation, allowing us to represent the motion by a small set of parameters in the principal component space (Kuratate *et al.* 1998). Suppose that all $K = 9$ faces of one subject have the same n mesh nodes which directly correspond to motion-capture data recorded from that subject. For each face scan, the $3n$ (n markers $\times$ 3 dimensions) positions are expressed by a column vector $\boldsymbol{p}_i$. Since the values in $\boldsymbol{p}_i$ are a subset of the values of the single adapted mesh f, they can be extracted and arranged in the matrix

$$\boldsymbol{P} = [\boldsymbol{p}_1 \quad \boldsymbol{p}_2 \quad \cdots \quad \boldsymbol{p}_K]. \tag{10}$$

Removing the mean position $\boldsymbol{\mu}_{\mathrm{pm}}$, the vector formed by the average of each row of $\boldsymbol{P}$ gives

$$\boldsymbol{P}_{\mathrm{M}} = [\boldsymbol{p}_{\mathrm{m}1} \quad \boldsymbol{p}_{\mathrm{m}2} \quad \cdots \quad \boldsymbol{p}_{\mathrm{m}K}]. \tag{11}$$

$\boldsymbol{P}_{\mathrm{M}}$ and $\boldsymbol{A}$, a matrix of linear combination values obtained from individual PCA results, are then used to determine a minimum-mean-squared-error (MMSE) estimator $\boldsymbol{E}_{\mathrm{m}}$:

$$\boldsymbol{A} \sim \boldsymbol{E}_{\mathrm{m}}\, \boldsymbol{P}_{\mathrm{M}}, \tag{12}$$

$$\boldsymbol{E}_{\mathrm{m}} = \boldsymbol{A}\boldsymbol{P}_{\mathrm{M}}^{\mathrm{T}}(P_{\mathrm{M}}P_{\mathrm{M}}^{\mathrm{T}})^{-1}. \tag{13}$$

Then $\boldsymbol{\alpha}$ for unknown input $\boldsymbol{p}_{\mathrm{u}}$ of a motion-capture frame can be estimated by the linear estimator $\boldsymbol{E}_{\mathrm{m}}$:

$$\boldsymbol{\alpha} \sim \boldsymbol{E}_{\mathrm{m}}\, \boldsymbol{p}_{\mathrm{mu}} = \boldsymbol{E}_{\mathrm{m}}(\boldsymbol{p}_{\mathrm{u}} - \boldsymbol{\mu}_{\mathrm{pm}}). \tag{14}$$

Therefore, input motion-capture data can be represented by a series of linear-combination values of individual PCs. Using $\boldsymbol{\alpha}$, a novel face in each frame is calculated by

$$f_{\mathrm{motion}} = \boldsymbol{\mu}_{\mathrm{s}} + \boldsymbol{U}_{\mathrm{s}}\, \boldsymbol{\alpha}, \tag{15}$$

where $\boldsymbol{\mu}_{\mathrm{s}}$ and $\boldsymbol{U}_{\mathrm{s}}$ represent respectively a mean face for this subject and individual principal components.

Figure 17.7 shows the variation of the components of $\boldsymbol{\alpha}$, jaw elevation, and the speech signal over time for an American male subject. As we can see, the time-dependent behavior of the second principal component for this subject is almost identical to vertical jaw motion. The basic cyclical structure is the same for all of the components, which is in agreement with the long-held belief in speech science that jaw motion determines the basic time course of speech behavior (Stetson 1905).

17.3 3D FACE ESTIMATION FROM PARTIAL FACE FEATURE INFORMATION

In this section, we describe a general approach to 3D face estimation using the 3D face database, and address the specific case of estimation from photographs. If partial information of a face is obtained, it can be used to estimate the entire face structure using a known relation between a subset of data points and the entire face.

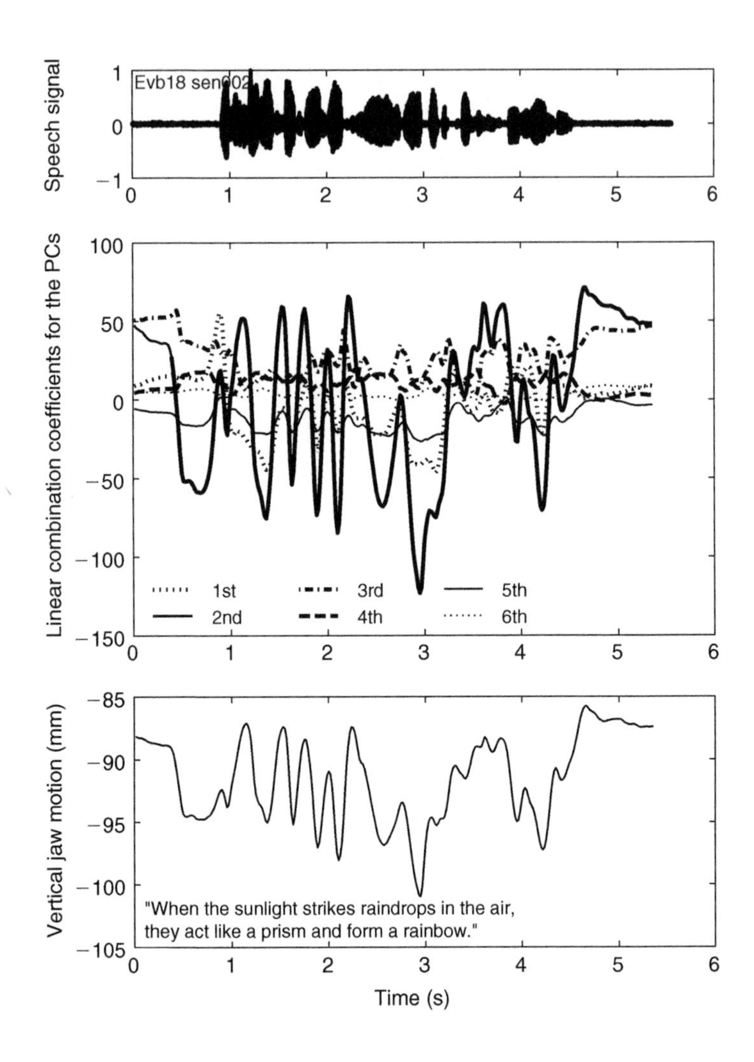

Figure 17.7

Time-series plots of the top six principal components used to synthesize the talking face after parametrization by the facial-marker positions at each time step. The behavior of the second component is almost identical to that of the jaw ($R = .95$).

17.3.1 LINEAR ESTIMATOR

Suppose that there is a subset of n points of the 3D face mesh used in this database. Then 3D coordinates of these n points can be represented by a single column vector $\boldsymbol{p}$:

$$\boldsymbol{p} = [x_1, x_2, \ldots, x_n; y_1, y_2, \ldots, y_n; z_1, z_2, \ldots, z_n]^{\mathrm{T}}. \tag{16}$$

If we apply PCA to this subset of points for all faces or for a subgroup of faces in the database, principal components $\boldsymbol{U}_{\mathrm{p}}$ and a linear-combination coefficient vector $\boldsymbol{\beta}$ can be obtained by using Equations (8) and (9) using $\boldsymbol{\mu}_{\mathrm{p}}$ and $\boldsymbol{p}_{\mathrm{m}}$, the mean shape of $\boldsymbol{p}$ and the difference of $\boldsymbol{p}$ from $\boldsymbol{\mu}_{\mathrm{p}}$ respectively, yielding the following relation:

$$\boldsymbol{\beta} = \boldsymbol{U}_{\mathrm{p}}^{\mathrm{T}} \boldsymbol{p}_{\mathrm{m}}. \tag{17}$$

Therefore, all linear combination matrices for the faces used for this PCA can be expressed by a single matrix

$$\boldsymbol{B} = [\boldsymbol{\beta}_1 \quad \boldsymbol{\beta}_2 \quad \dots \quad \boldsymbol{\beta}_K]. \tag{18}$$

Since the columns of $\boldsymbol{B}$ comprise a subset of the full set of face points given by $\boldsymbol{A}$, the linear estimator $\boldsymbol{E}$ can be defined by the following relation:

$$\boldsymbol{A} \cdot \boldsymbol{EB}. \tag{19}$$

Both $\boldsymbol{A}$ and $\boldsymbol{B}$ are known values for a certain face group, and thus the linear estimator $\boldsymbol{E}$ can be obtained by

$$\boldsymbol{E} \sim \boldsymbol{AB}^{\mathrm{T}}(\boldsymbol{BB}^{\mathrm{T}})^{-1}. \tag{20}$$

Using this linear estimator $\boldsymbol{E}$ makes it possible to estimate $\boldsymbol{\alpha}$, the linear-combination values of the principal components for an entire face, from $\boldsymbol{\beta}$, the other linear-combination values of the principal components for the subset points:

$$\boldsymbol{\alpha} \sim \boldsymbol{E\beta}. \tag{21}$$

Therefore, if we extract feature points $\boldsymbol{p}_{\mathrm{new}}$ for an unknown face corresponding to $\boldsymbol{p}$, the following equation will estimate an entire face $\boldsymbol{f}_{\mathrm{new}}$:

$$\boldsymbol{f}_{\mathrm{new}} = \boldsymbol{\mu}_{\mathrm{f}} + \boldsymbol{U\alpha}_{\mathrm{new}} \tag{22}$$

$$\sim \boldsymbol{\mu}_{\mathrm{f}} + \boldsymbol{UE\beta}_{\mathrm{new}} \tag{23}$$

$$\sim \boldsymbol{\mu}_{\mathrm{f}} + \boldsymbol{UEU}_{\mathrm{p}}^{\mathrm{T}}(\boldsymbol{p}_{\mathrm{new}} - \boldsymbol{\mu}_{\mathrm{p}}). \tag{24}$$

The examples shown in this chapter are estimated from the neutral-face subgroup of the database.

17.3.2 OBTAINING FEATURE POINTS FROM PHOTOGRAPHS

The linear estimation described above requires definition of a small number of 3D feature points in the generic mesh structure. Here we use a profile silhouette line and six additional feature points (outside eye corners, lip corners and jawline end-points at both ears) which can be easily and efficiently extracted from a side-view or a front-view photograph, noting that:

- A profile silhouette line is easily extracted from a side-view photograph, and requires no special 2D-to-3D translation
- The six feature points are relatively easy to extract from a front-view photograph
- Corresponding points for the silhouette and three of the additional features easily map to the other photograph
- Both views enable us to obtain 3D feature coordinates using a simple parallel projection.

Photographs are adjusted to the same scale and approximate horizontal angle as needed. Figure 17.8 shows an example of a pair of photographs used to acquire feature points, and Figure 17.9 shows manually extracted feature points. The silhouette line is represented with the same number of nodes as in the generic mesh side view; only the end points of the midsagittal line are defined in the front view. Three-dimensional coordinates in pixel scale can now be found for all feature points.

After scaling these 3D pixel coordinates to real-life measurements by rough estimation of a subject's face size, we can apply linear estimation. Figure 17.10 shows some results of 3D face estimation. All estimations in this section are based on a database consisting of $s = 200$ subjects and $K = 1800$ faces with 88 Caucasians (48 males, 40 females), 108 Asians (69 males, 39 females), and 4 Africans (2 males, 2 females).

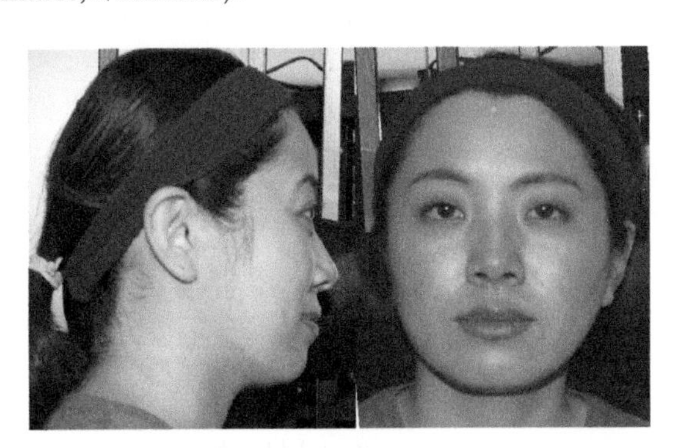

Figure 17.8
An example of photographs used to acquire feature points.

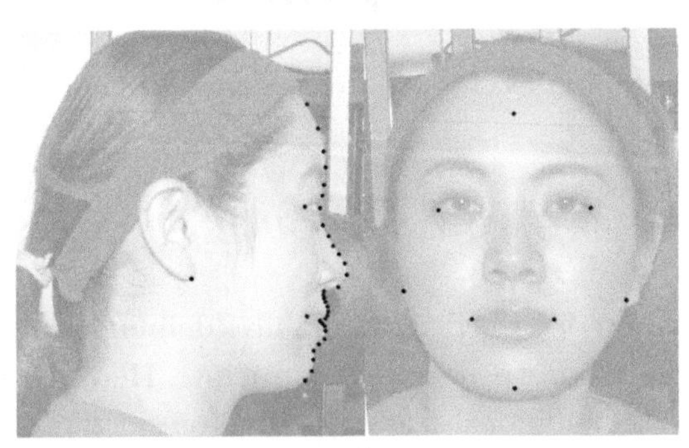

Figure 17.9
Extracted feature points.

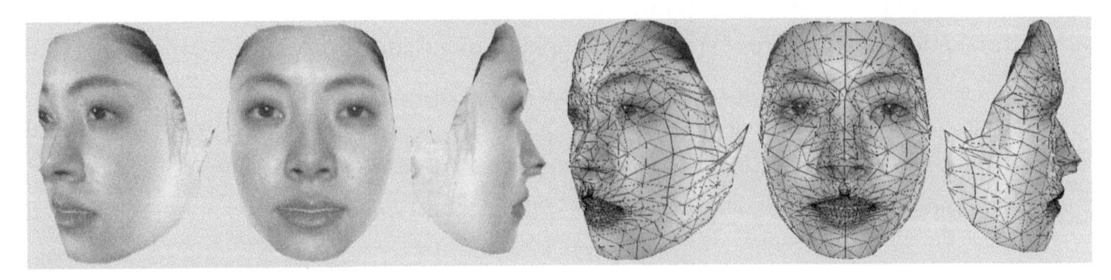

Figure 17.10 Neutral 3D face estimated from two photographs.

17.3.3 TEXTURE ACQUISITION

The texture image used in this figure is created from the two original photographs. After the 3D model is estimated, it can be rendered onto original 2D pixel coordinates using the relation between feature points on the photographs and the estimated model. This allows us to determine the correspondence between texture coordinates and image coordinates for an individual image. Next, we use these texture coordinates to map into the generic mesh coordinate space by exploiting the identical mesh topology of the projected models.

Figure 17.11 shows the results of mapping a side-view and a front-view image. As you can see, the better parts of each image complement the other. We exploit this by providing a blending mask—see Figure 17.12(a)—used to obtain an improved hybrid texture image as shown in Figure 17.12(b).

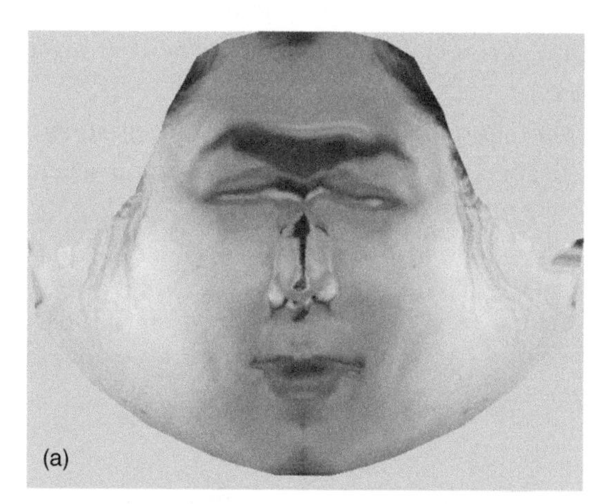

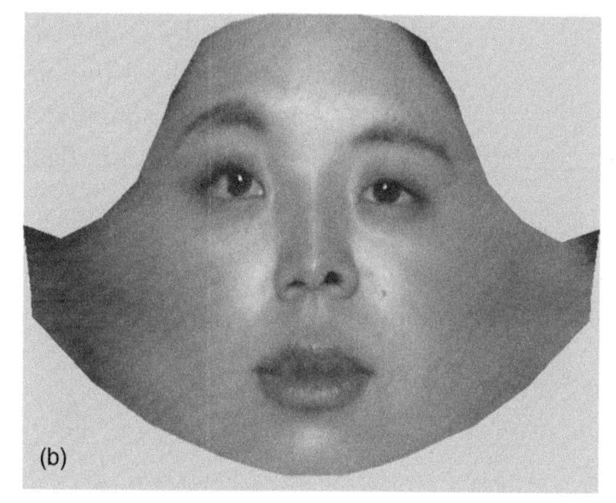

Figure 17.11 Texture images obtained from (a) a side-view photograph and (b) a front-view photograph.

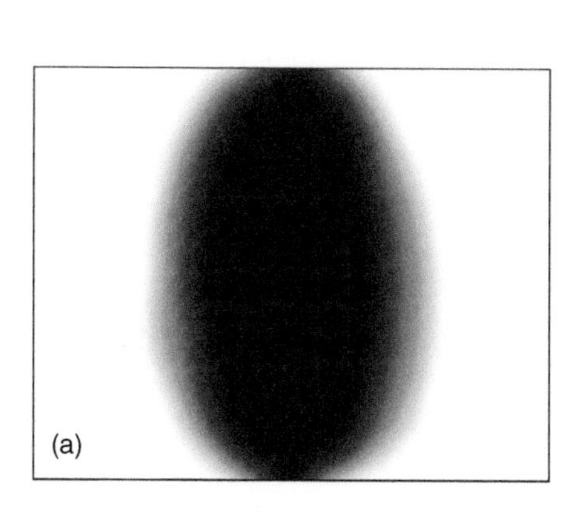

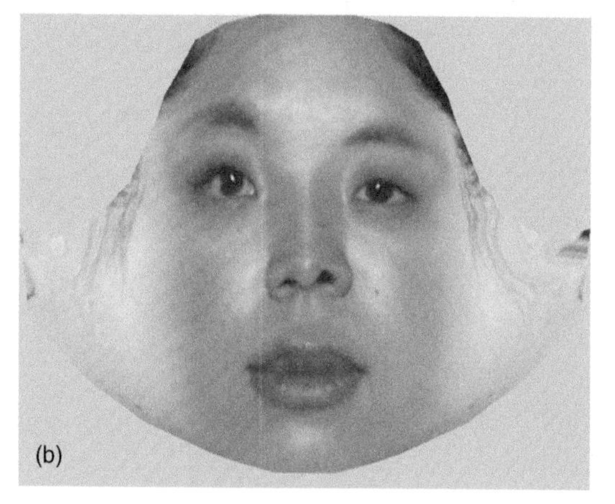

Figure 17.12 (a) A blending mask for the texture images and (b) a blended texture created from two individual textures.

17.4 ESTIMATION OF FACE POSTURES

Once a 3D face model and surface texture are acquired, we can employ the database to estimate other facial expressions. In the principal-component space obtained from analyzing all faces in the database, individual face postures form a cluster around the neutral face, as shown in Figure 17.13. By describing the unknown input face in this space, similar faces in the database can be found by simply measuring the distance between the input neutral face and any neutral face in the database.

Once all distances are examined, one or more faces can be selected as "similar face(s)" in this space. Then the face posture distribution of these candidate(s) can be used to estimate the deformations of the input face for postures in the database. In the following examples, we choose the top five candidates and create an expression vector from the neutral face with 50%, 25%, 10%, 10%, and 5% weightings respectively to obtain the new expression deformations for the target face.

The faces estimated from photographs were given the same mesh structure as faces in the database, deliberately simplifying the estimation scheme.

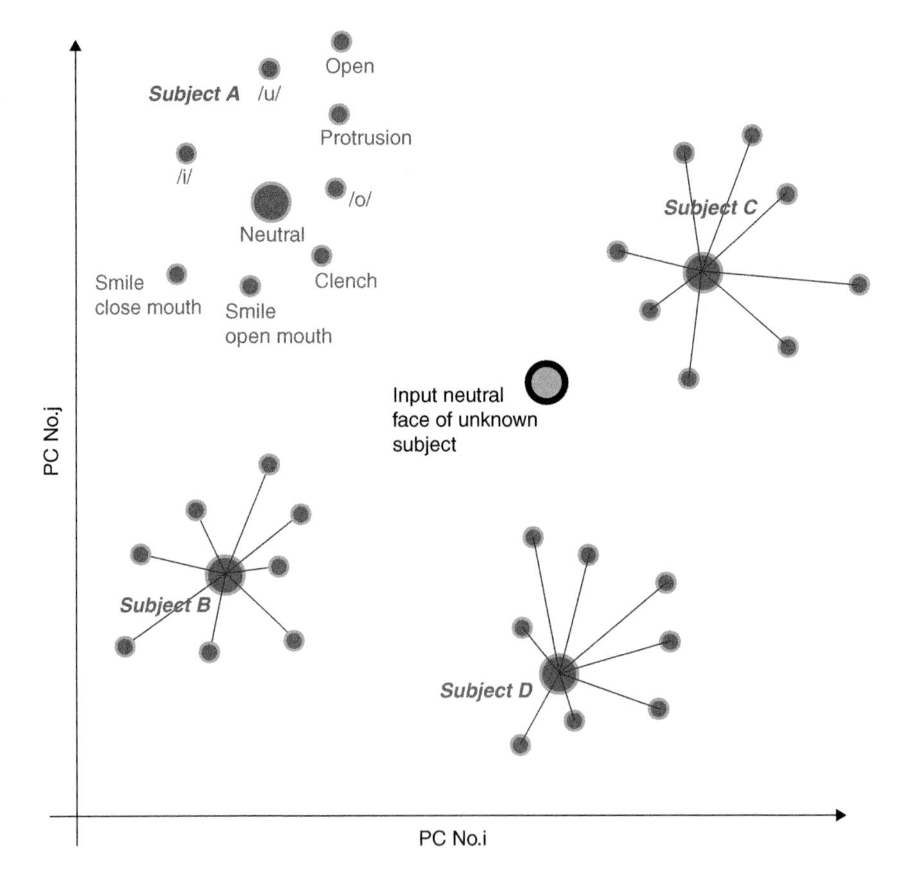

Figure 17.13

This conceptual figure shows the distribution of individual face postures in the principal-component space.

In addition to photographs, posture estimation is effective for estimating expressions for inanimate models, as illustrated in the next section.

17.4.1 EXPRESSION ESTIMATION RESULTS

Figure 17.14 shows estimation results for eight expression postures starting from the neutral face in Figure 17.8. We also applied this method to inanimate models, including a statue of Venus, which was scanned with the Cyberware scanner; see Figure 17.15(a), like the human subjects. Of course only one posture was available, and a generic mesh was adapted to the data, resulting in the 3D model shown in Figure 17.15(b). Expression estimation results

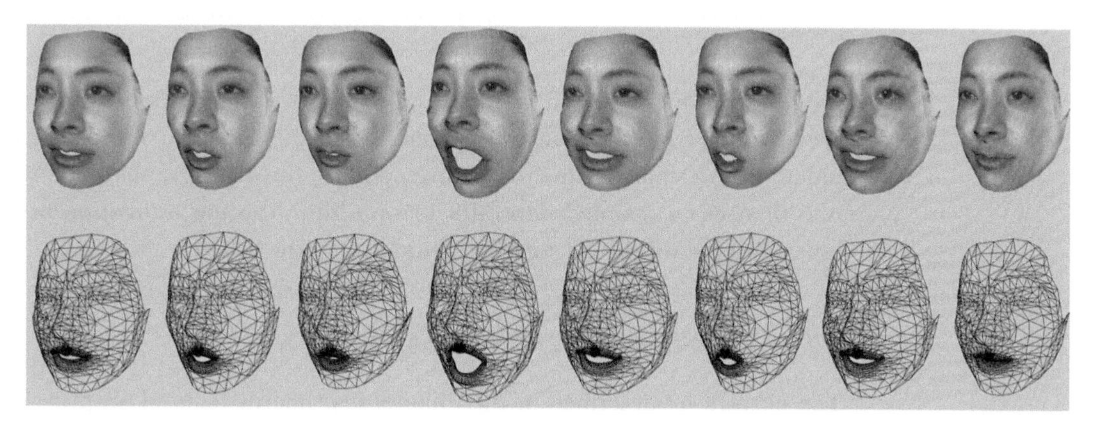

Figure 17.14 Eight postures estimated for the face model in Figure 17.1 (/i/,/o/,/u/, open, clench, lip protrusion, open-mouth smile, and closed-mouth smile).

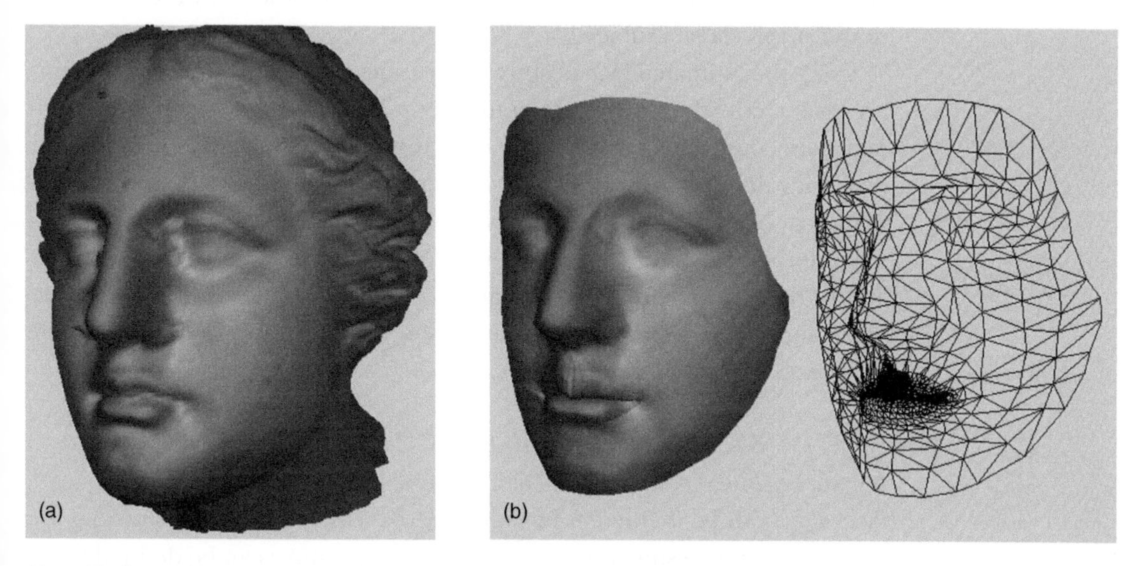

Figure 17.15 (a) The 3D model of a Venus statue scanned by a Cyberware 3030RGB scanner and (b) the generic mesh adaptation results (textured and wire-frame).

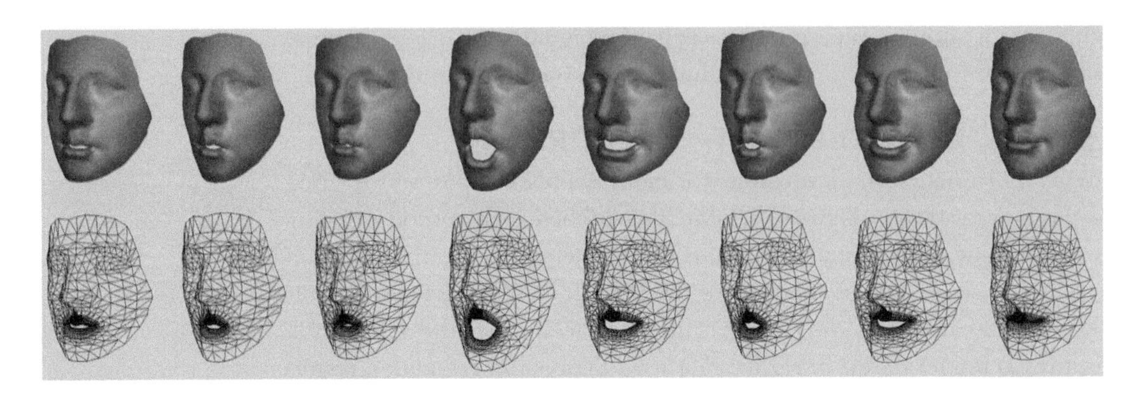

Figure 17.16 The eight estimated expressions for the Venus statue (/i/,/o/,/u/, open, clench, lip protrusion, open-mouth smile and closed-mouth smile).

are shown in Figure 17.16. As the results show, reasonable face expressions are obtained from the database estimation scheme. However, estimating the model from a small number of feature points in the photographs is less accurate than using scanned data with feature lines, causing estimation errors especially around the eye and lip boundaries of the faces.

17.5 FACIAL MOTION MAPPING

The posture set described in this chapter is primarily focused on providing sufficient information to synthesize and analyze talking heads for perceptible audiovisual speech. Given that we can estimate this set for inanimate 3D faces and for models created from photographs, we can now easily create animations for this class of subjects.

Using the estimated face postures, we extract individual deformation characteristics by further PCA on the nine faces. The major two principal components are consistent across the set, even though the individual faces deform in slightly different ways. As noted earlier, the order of the first two components may be switched, but in most cases the first component reflects jaw elevation information, and the second corresponds to lip rounding with protrusion and horizontal lip spreading (Kuratate *et al.* 2001). Using this similarity, we can transfer face motion from one person to other models quite easily by *facial motion mapping* (Kuratate *et al.* 2003).

17.5.1 BASIC MAPPING ALGORITHM

A matrix of linear combination coefficients of the source face $\boldsymbol{A}_{\text{source}}$ and target face $\boldsymbol{A}_{\text{target}}$ can be defined as in Equation (8). Using the face posture set for both faces, linear estimation for mapping face postures can be defined by

$$\boldsymbol{A}_{\text{target}} \sim \boldsymbol{E}_{\text{mapping}} \boldsymbol{A}_{\text{source}}. \tag{25}$$

Both $\boldsymbol{A}_{\text{source}}$ and $\boldsymbol{A}_{\text{target}}$ are already known, so $\boldsymbol{E}_{\text{mapping}}$ can be determined by

$$\boldsymbol{E}_{\text{mapping}} = \boldsymbol{A}_{\text{target}} \boldsymbol{A}_{\text{source}}^{\mathsf{T}} (\boldsymbol{A}_{\text{source}} \boldsymbol{A}_{\text{source}}^{\mathsf{T}})^{-1}. \quad (26)$$

Thus $\boldsymbol{\alpha}_{\text{target}}$ for the new face is estimated from any $\boldsymbol{\alpha}$ of the source face:

$$\boldsymbol{\alpha}_{\text{target}} \sim \boldsymbol{E}_{\text{mapping}}\, \boldsymbol{\alpha}. \quad (27)$$

When the order of the major components differs between source and target, $\boldsymbol{A}_{\text{source}}$ is multiplied by an exchange matrix $\boldsymbol{X}$ before determining $\boldsymbol{E}_{\text{mapping}}$ in Equation (26):

$$\boldsymbol{A}' = \boldsymbol{X}\boldsymbol{A}_{\text{source}}. \quad (28)$$

This exchange matrix is also used when components differ in sign, and, when used, should also be applied to $\boldsymbol{\alpha}$.

17.5.2 ANIMATION RESULTS

Figure 17.17 shows selected frames of sample animation. The top row shows video images of the original speaker's face during a motion-capture session using the OPTOTRAK (Northern Digital Inc., Canada) system. This motion-capture data drives the original speaker's face model (second row) by the individual PCA-based technique discussed in Sections 17.2.4 and 17.2.5 (Kuratate *et al.* 1998). Then the linear-combination values $\boldsymbol{\alpha}$ of this model are mapped to a face model generated from photographs (third row), and to the Venus model (bottom row) by facial motion mapping in each frame. The resulting animation is quite natural, with the speech deformations being estimated from a real person's data and mapped as described to the new faces.

Other examples of facial motion mapping are shown in the last five rows of Figure 17.18. The first row shows original video frames captured simultaneously during an OPTOTRAK motion-capture session for an American male subject. The second row shows OPTOTRAK markers overlaid on the original video frames. The third and fourth rows show a synthesized talking-head animation of the original speaker, which is transparently overlaid on the original video frames in the third row. The fifth to seventh rows show the result of facial motion mapping to other 3D models: a Japanese male subject, a 3D male character, and a 3D dog model. The last two rows show facial motion mapping to 2D models: a human-like cartoon face and a cartoon deer. In these examples, the original head orientation parameters were directly applied to the target models.

In the dog's case, although preliminary animation lacks any sort of lip structure, jaw synchronization is excellent. The main deficiency is lack of detailed facial information for the target animal. Once such information is obtained we are confident that this technique can easily create realistic talking creatures.

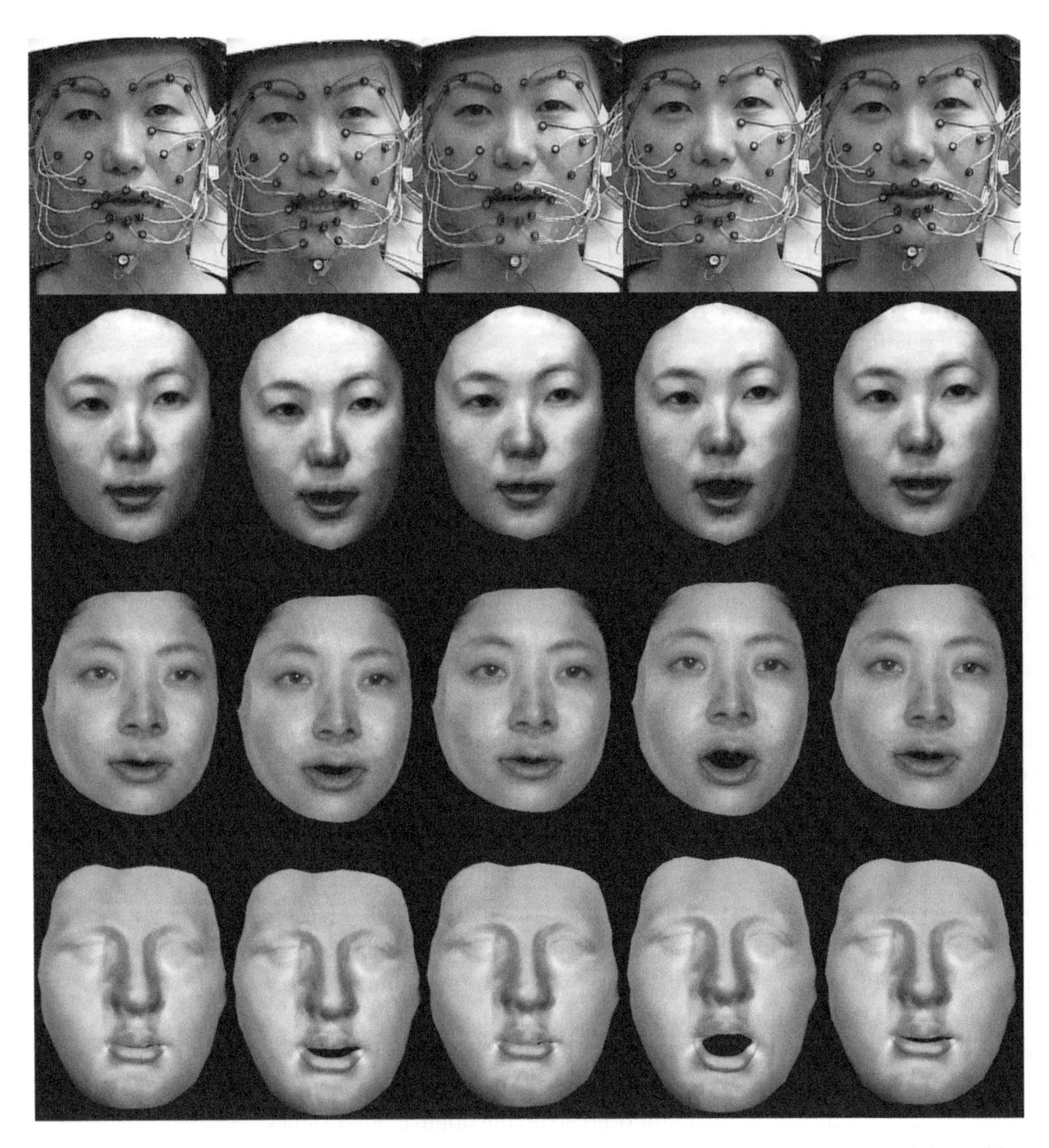

Figure 17.17 Selected frames from an animation sequence mapped from motion-capture data (top) to the original speaker's face model (second row), to a face model created from photographs (third row), and to the Venus model (bottom).

17.5.3 EVALUATION OF MAPPED MOTION

Though the resulting animation looks promising, we would like to verify that the mapped face motion is valid for the target subjects. Theoretically, the best way to evaluate the mapped motion is to have the target subject speak exactly the same sentence in the same manner as the source subject, measure the face motion, and compare it with the mapped motion. However, it is almost

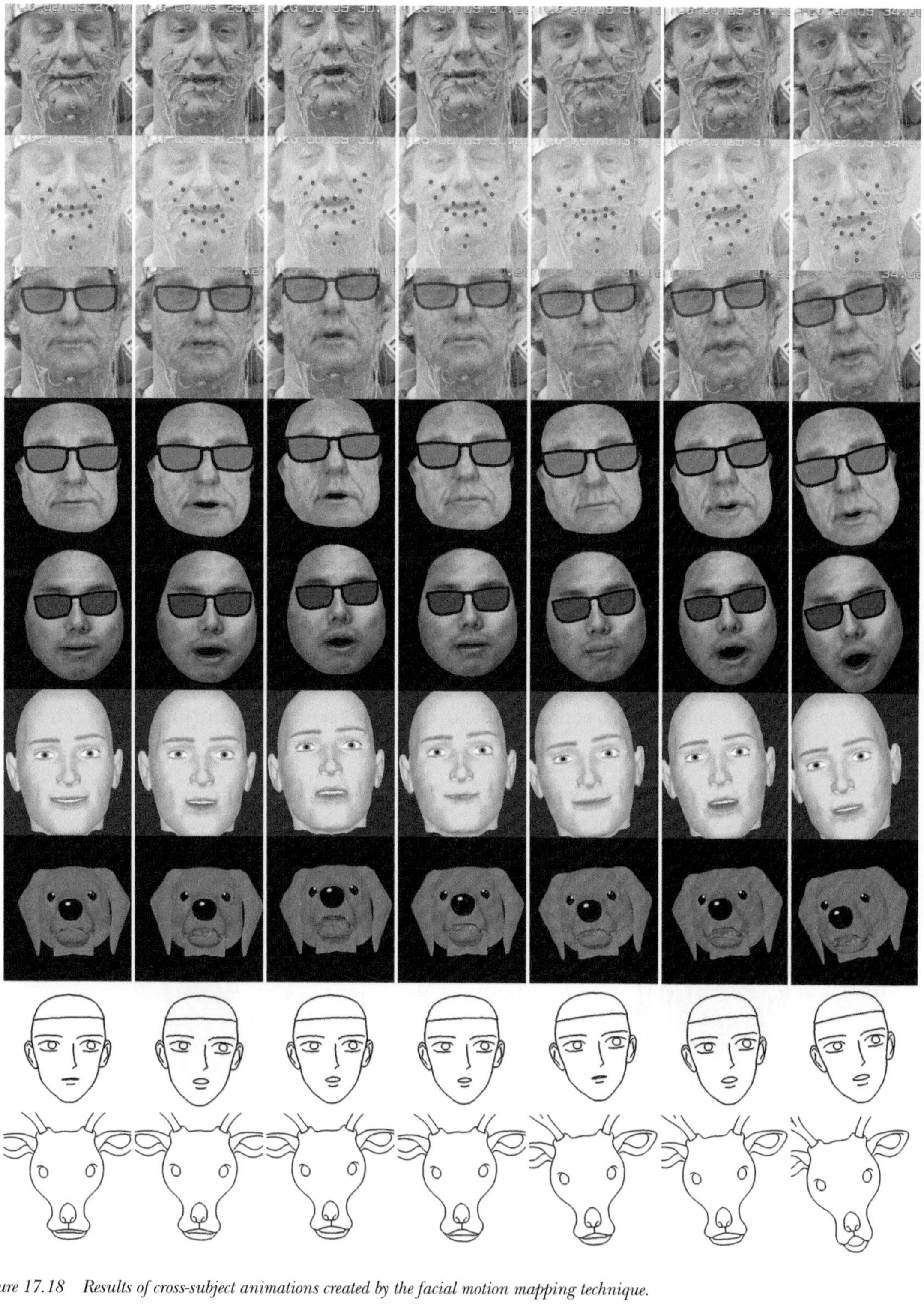

Figure 17.18 Results of cross-subject animations created by the facial motion mapping technique.

impossible to speak in exactly the same way as another person. Therefore we evaluate our results by comparing the time-dependent properties of the first two major principal components, noting that these components cover more than 90% of the total variance, and that their deformation effects are much more notable than the other components.

The American male subject and the Japanese male target shown in Figure 17.18 were chosen for this evaluation. First we selected four English sentences spoken by the American subject for transfer to the Japanese subject, and eight Japanese sentences spoken by the Japanese subject for comparison. We then extracted linear-combination values of these speakers to reconstruct talking-face animations with their individual face models.

The continuous lines in Figure 17.19(a) show changes in the first and second principal components during vocalization of all sentences. The gray lines in the left figure represent the Japanese subject's trajectory, and the black lines represent the American subject's trajectory. This figure tells us that the American subject's linear-combination values cannot be applied to the target subject because the distribution and direction of the trajectories are quite different.

The distribution of the trajectories denotes the range over which that face will change during speech with respect to the two major principal components. If one trajectory is outside the major area of the other trajectory, mapping will result in an unusual face for the target subject. Additionally, trajectory direction denotes how the face will deform using the first two components. Different directions indicate different face motion during speech. Therefore

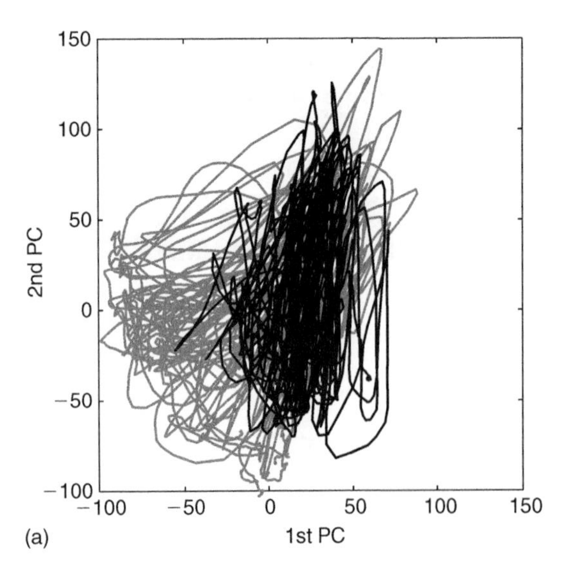

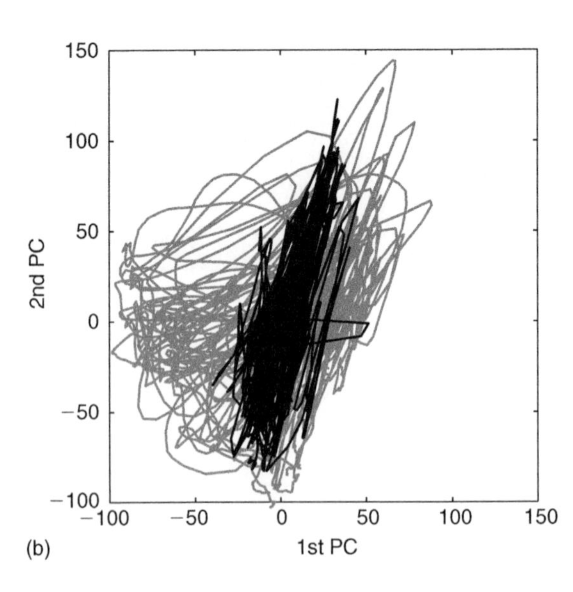

Figure 17.19 The trajectory of the first two PCs during speech for a source subject (black): (a) before and (b) after applying facial motion mapping; and the trajectory of the target subject (gray).

Figure 17.19(a) says that using the American subject's linear combination values for the target subject's face model will result in some unusual face postures, and the target face will move differently than that of the original subject.

In Figure 17.19(b) the Japanese subject's trajectory is again shown in gray, but the motion originating from the American subject (in black) now results from facial motion mapping. When compared to the left figure, we see that the area of the black trajectory is now almost entirely included in the area of the gray trajectory, and the direction of the black trajectory matches one of the direction groups of the gray lines. This implies that the face motion transferred by facial motion mapping is in the possible range of the target's original face motion.

17.6 SUMMARY

In this chapter, we discussed an original method for creating 3D facial expression postures from front and side photographs using PCA results of a 3D face database containing at present 500 subjects, each with the same set of face postures. The estimated face postures have deformation characteristics similar to subjects registered in the database which are implicitly embedded in the estimated face postures when predicting face deformation from similar faces. This similarity allows us to apply a PCA-based facial motion mapping technique to create a talking-head animation driven by an arbitrary speaker's face motion. In this way we move closer to realizing realistic and perceptibly valid animations of talking heads, still a difficult challenge for the animation community. These methods are important for auditory-visual speech research and applications in natural user-interface design, 3D face modeling, entertainment, and education.

ACKNOWLEDGEMENTS

The research reported here was supported in part by a contract with the National Institute of Information and Communications Technology of Japan entitled "Research on Human Communication".

REFERENCES

Beier T. and Neely S. (1992) "Feature-Based Image Metamorphosis", *Computer Graphics* 26, 35–42.

Blanz V., Basso C., Poggio T. and Vetter T. (2003) "Reanimating Faces in Images and Video", *Proceedings of Eurographics 2003*, 22(3).

Blanz V. and Vetter T. (1999) "A Morphable Model for the Synthesis of 3d Faces", in: *Computer Graphics Proceedings, Annual Conference Series* ACM SIGGRAPH, Los Angeles, August 8–13, pp. 187–194.

Blanz V. and Vetter T. (2001) "Reconstructing the Complete 3d Shape of Faces from Partial Information", *Computer Graphics Technical Report University of Freiburg* (1).

Horn R. and Johnson C. (1985) *Matrix Analysis*. Cambridge.

Hwang B. W., Blanz V., Vetter T. and Lee S.-W. (2000) "Face Reconstruction from a Small Number of Feature Points", *International Conference on Pattern Recognition (ICPR2000)*, pp. 842–845.

Kuratate T., Masuda S. and Vatikiotis-Bateson E. (2001) "What Perceptible Information Can Be Implemented in Talking Head Animations", *IEEE International Workshop on Robot and Human Interactive Communication* (*ROMAN2001*), pp. 430–435.

Kuratate T., Vatikiotis-Bateson E. and Yehia H. (2003) "Cross-Subject Face Animation Driven by Facial Motion Mapping", *Proceedings of 10th ISPE International Conference on Concurrent Engineering (CE2003): Advanced Design, Production and Management Systems*, pp. 971–979.

Kuratate T., Yehia H. and Vatikiotis-Bateson E. (1998) "Kinematics-Based Synthesis of Realistic Talking Faces", *Proceedings of AVSP'98—International Conference on Auditory-Visual Speech Processing*, pp. 185–190.

Lee Y., Terzopoulos D. and Waters K. (1995) "Realistic Modeling for Facial Animation", *Proceedings of SIGGRAPH95*, pp. 55–62.

Massaro D. W. UCSC Perceptural Science Lab. *http://mambo.ucsc.edu/.*

McGurk H. and MacDonald J. (1976) "Hearing Lips and Seeing Voices", *Nature,* 746–748.

Stetson R. H. (1905) "A Motor Theory of Rhythm and Discrete Succession ii", *Psychol. Rev.* 12, 293–350.

Thalmann N. M., Primeau E. and Thalmann D. (1988) "Abstract Muscle Action Procedures for Human Face Animation", *The Visual Computer* 3, 290–297.

Vatikiotis-Bateson E., Kuratate T., Kamachi M. and Yehia H. C. (1999) "Facial Deformation Parameters for Audiovisual Synthesis", in: *Proceedings of AVSP'99* (*Auditory-Visual Speech Processing*), Santa Cruz, CA (D. W. Massaro, ed.), pp. 118–122.

Waters K. (1987) "A Muscle Model for Animating Three-Dimensional Facial Expression", *Computer Graphics* 21, 17–24.

CHAPTER 18

FACIAL IMAGE IDENTIFICATION SYSTEM BASED ON 3D PHYSIOGNOMIC DATA

Mineo Yoshino

First Forensic Science Division, National Research Institute of Police Science, 6-3-1, Kashiwanoha, Kashiwa, Chiba 277-0882, Japan

18.1 INTRODUCTION

Facial images are important and information-rich records of anthropological characteristics. They have been used as valuable components of human-identification systems since the 19th century, when Bertillon introduced the first formal system for the identification of criminals. Recently, facial image identification has become increasingly important in criminal cases due to the widespread use of surveillance cameras. At the National Research Institute of Police Science, in Japan, 220 case reports involving facial image identification were written between 1988 and 1999. The crimes submitted for examination were in the categories: robbery and theft (38.2%), illegal immigration (17.7%), violation of road-traffic law (16.8%), forgery and fraud (14.5%), bodily injury and homicide (8.2%), arson and destruction of structures (3.6%), and others (1.0%). Clearly the reliability of the identifications made from facial images is becoming a serious concern in forensic anthropology.

In general, facial image identification is approached using three methods: morphological comparison of facial features, facial image anthropometry, and face-to-face superimposition. Morphological comparison of facial images is based on the morphological classification of facial components such as facial types, eyebrows, eyes, nose, lips, and ears (İşcan 1993, Vanezis *et al.* 1996, Miyasaka *et al.* 1997). Facial image anthropometry involves quantitative analysis based on indices that are calculated from measurements of facial dimensions (Catterick 1992, Miyasaka *et al.* 1995, Kubota *et al.* 1997). In order to assess directly the degree of matching between two facial images, the technique of video superimposition has been applied (Majumder and Shinha 1989, Maples and Austin 1992, Vanezis and Brierley 1996). However, this latter technique requires that all the facial images of suspects be taken in exactly

Computer-Graphic Facial Reconstruction
John G. Clement and Murray K. Marks, Editors

the same orientation as the facial image at the crime scene. Maples and Austin (1992) reported that the face-to-face video superimposition technique was useful in cases where the suspect could be photographed by laboratory personnel in the correct position relative to the camera. Vanezis and Brierley (1996) applied the video superimposition technique to identify the facial images of suspects in 46 criminal cases. They stated that direct comparisons could be made in 36 cases, including 20 cases where there was a major discrepancy in view point. In our 220 actual cases, the face-to-face superimposition method could be applied to only 9. As described above, the comparison of facial images taken with a surveillance camera and mug shots of suspects often is a difficult task, because surveillance cameras usually look down upon the scene whereas mug shots are frontal and lateral or oblique images. To solve this problem, the authors (1996) developed a face-to-face video superimposition system using 3D physiognomic analysis. This system was a useful tool for facial image identification because the video superimposition of two facial images could be performed under the same facial orientation. Subsequent work using this method has demonstrated that comparison with 3D facial images can play a useful role in the identification of criminals (Kubota *et al.* 1997, Linney and Coombes 1998, Proesmans and Van Gool 1998, Yoshino *et al.* 1996). Despite this demonstrated usefulness, several problems such as operation time and issues with the anthropometrical analysis arose in the system. With these problems in mind, the author and co-workers (Yoshino *et al.* 2000a,b) attempted to build a new computer-assisted facial image identification system using a 3D physiognomic range finder (Ishiyama *et al.* 1999). The new system enabled morphological comparison, anthropometrical analysis, and reciprocal-point matching to be carried out on the face-to-face superimposition images.

18.2 EQUIPMENT

This system consists of two main pieces of equipment: a 3D physiognomic range finder for acquiring 3D morphological data of the face, and a computer-assisted facial image superimposition unit for comparing the 3D facial image with the 2D facial image (Figure 18.1). The physiognomic range finder (NEC Fiore, Japan) has two projectors with sinusoidal gratings that can be moved to provide phase shift, and two CCD cameras positioned at the left and right sides of the apparatus (Figure 18.2). The projector brightness and grating position are controlled by a computer (NEC Mate NX MA45D, 384-MB memory, 16.8-GB hard disk), and interface boards in the same machine acquire the digital images from the cameras. The measurement volume of

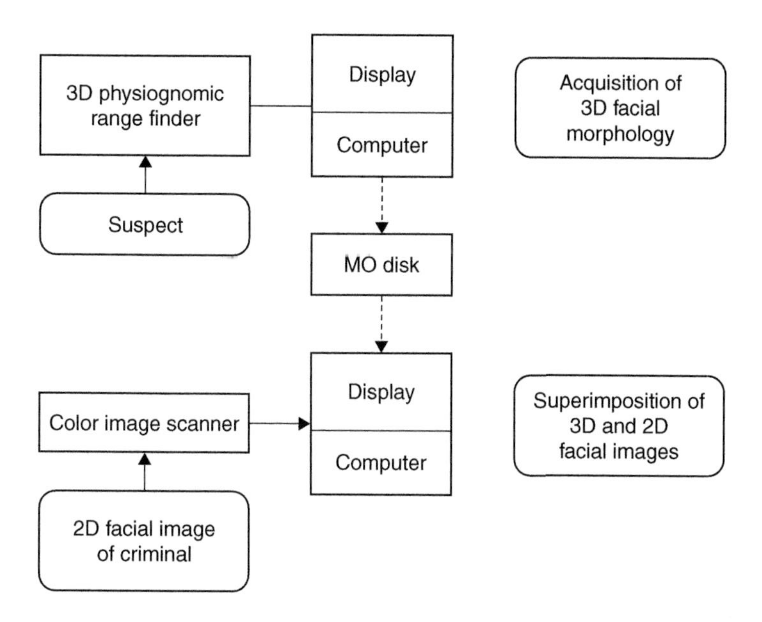

Figure 18.1

Schema of the computer-assisted facial image identification system.

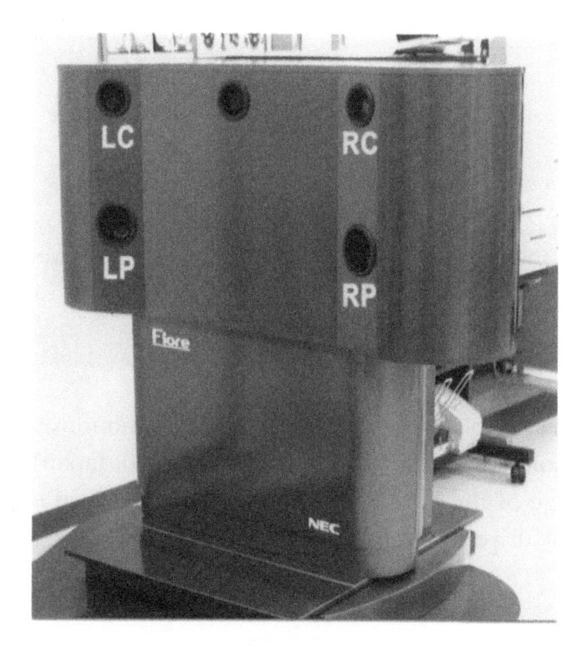

Figure 18.2

3D physiognomic range finder (Fiore). The range finder has two sinusoidal-grating projection devices (LP, RP) and two CCD cameras (LC, RC) for the left and right sides of the face.

the 3D range finder is 300 × 400 mm with a depth of plus and minus 100 mm. The angular coverage of the head taken with two CCD cameras is 220°, giving a sufficiently large measurement range to enable data for the ear shape to be included (Figure 18.3). The computer-assisted facial image superimposition unit comprises a host computer (NEC Mate NX MA45D, 128-MB memory, 16.8-GB hard disk) including proprietary software (MEDIC Engineering,

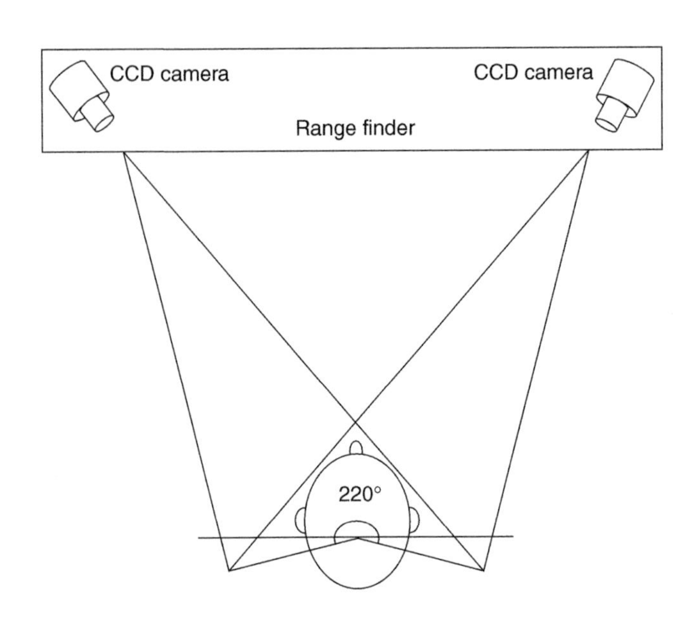

Figure 18.3

Illustration showing the region of a face used for measurement by the 3D physiognomic range finder. A wide field of facials view can be covered with two CCD cameras.

Figure 18.4

Computer-assisted facial image superimposition unit. (A) host computer, (B) flat surface color display, (C) color image scanner.

Japan), a flat surface color display (MITSUBISHI Diamondtron Flat RDF19X, Japan), and a color image scanner (EPSON GT-9600, Japan) for inputting a 2D facial image of the criminal (Figure 18.4). To record data, a 640-MB 3.5-inch MO disk drive is attached to this system.

18.3 OPERATION METHODS

18.3.1 3D PHYSIOGNOMIC RANGE FINDER

At first, color images of the face are taken with the two CCD cameras (Figure 18.5). In the same facial position, the fringes produced by the sinusoidal grating projection device are projected onto the face (Figure 18.6), and the CCD camera then captures the four grating images of the face. The resolution is 480 $\times$ 640 pixels, and the whole process is completed in 2.3 seconds. The

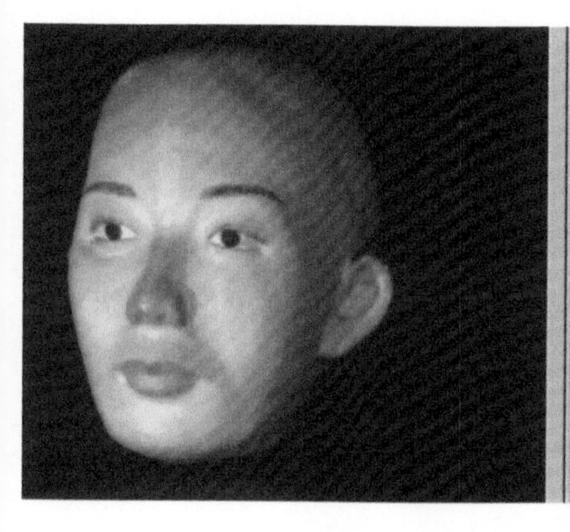
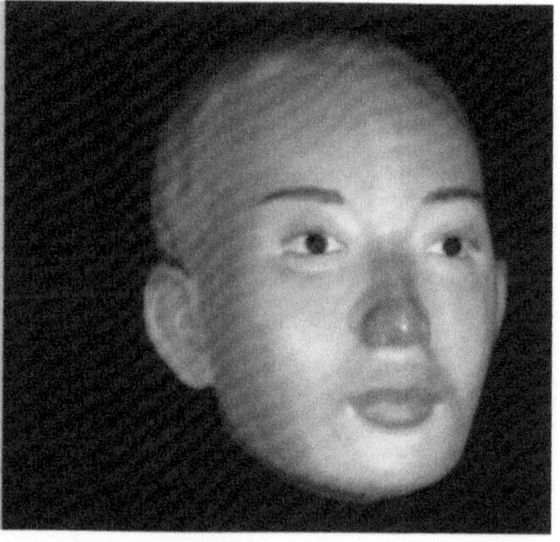

Figure 18.5

The texture image of the right and left side of a face.

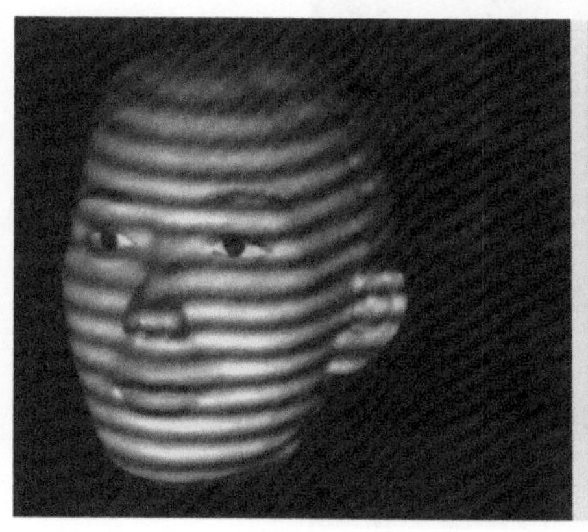
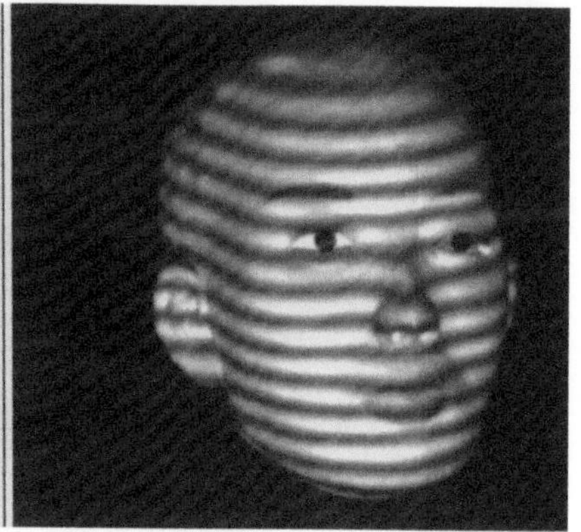

Figure 18.6

The grating image of the right and left side of a face.

brightness value at time t of each pixel (with pixel coordinates x, y) on the facial surface is described by:

$$I(t, x, y) = A(x, y) + B(x, y) \cos[\phi(x, y) + t],$$

where $A(x, y)$, $B(x, y)$, and $\phi(x, y)$ are the bias, amplitude, and phase at $t = 0$, respectively. The phase reveals the depth data on the point of the facial surface. When the four grating images of the face are measured at $t = 0, \pi/2, \pi, 3\pi/2$, the phase of each point of the facial surface is calculated from brightness values with

$$\phi(x, y) = \tan^{-1} \frac{I_{3\pi/2}(x, y) - I_{\pi/2}(x, y)}{I_0(x, y) - I_\pi(x, y)}.$$

The absolute range measurement and phase unwrapping stability are obtained by the three-points-of-view method, using one grating projection and two cameras, and *vice versa*, respectively (Figure 18.7). The phase-unwrapping value is transformed to the 3D coordinates, which reveals the 3D

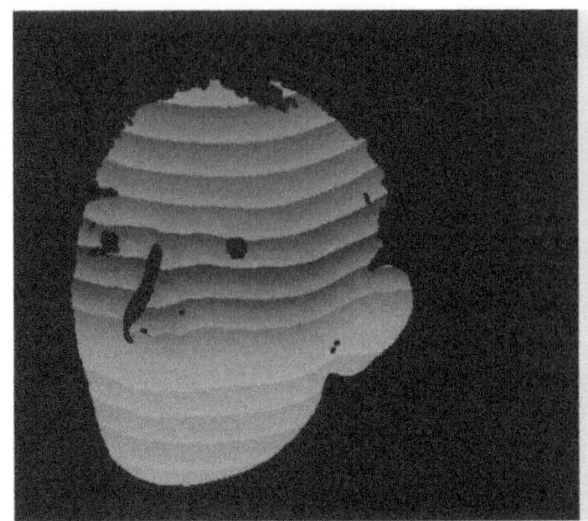
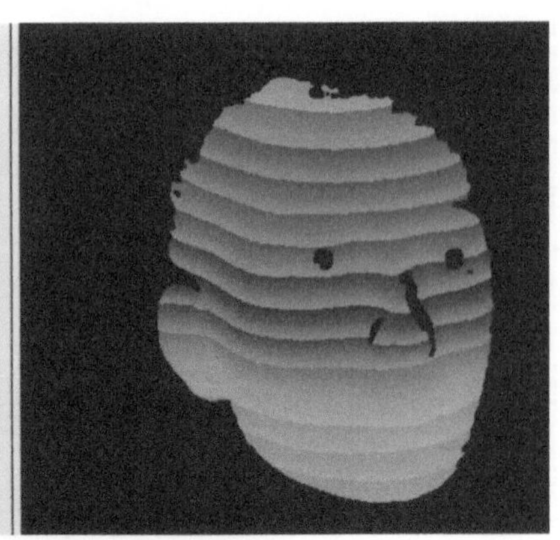

Figure 18.7
The phase-unwrapping image of the right and left side of a face.

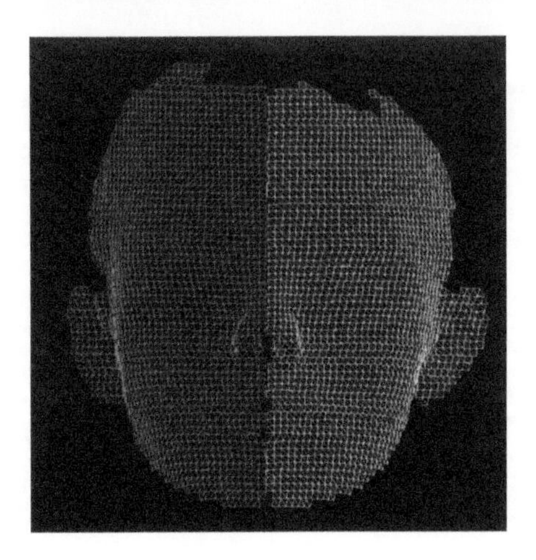

Figure 18.8
The 3D framework image of the face generated from the phase-unwrapping image in Figure 18.7.

morphological data of face. The RGB value is computed from the bias $A(x, y)$ by the following equation:

$$A(x, y) = \sum_{t=0,\ \pi/2,\ \pi,\ 3\pi/2} I(t, x, y).$$

The 3D facial image is composited from the 3D morphological data of the left and right side of the face and checked under both the framework and texture modes (Figure 18.8). The 3D facial image data is stored in the MO disk or directly transferred to the facial image superimposition system through the network (Figure 18.9). The data size per person is about 23 MB for the total facial image data including the grating image, and about 6 MB for only the 3D facial image data, respectively.

18.3.2 COMPUTER-ASSISTED FACIAL IMAGE SUPERIMPOSITION

To make the comparison between a 3D facial image of a suspect and a 2D facial image taken at the scene of a crime, the 3D facial image is first reproduced on

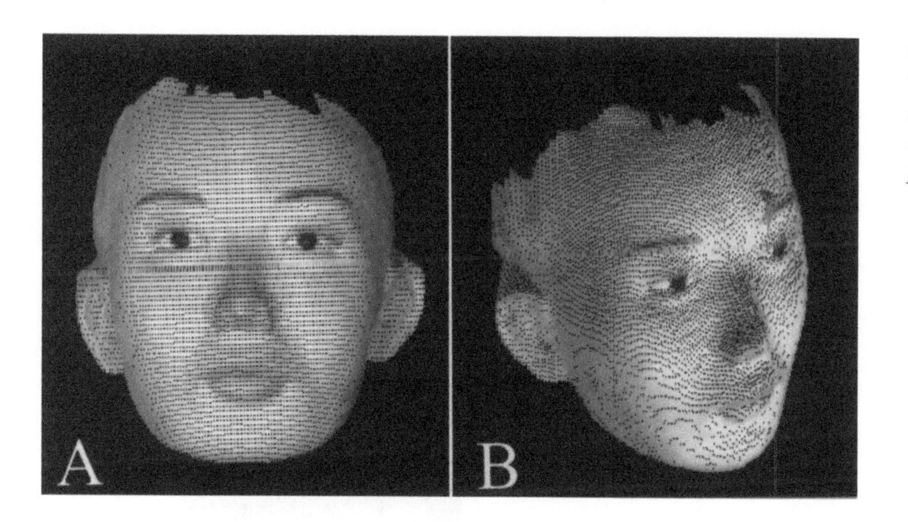

Figure 18.9

The fine framework images reproduced from the 3D data shown in Figure 18.8. (A) frontal view, (B) oblique view.

the display of the host computer from the MO disk and then the 2D facial image is taken with the color image scanner and stored within the computer. Scaling of the facial image is performed by converting the original 3D measurement data according to the number of pixels on the display. In this system, any perspective distortion of the 3D facial image can be electronically corrected by inputting the distance between a surveillance camera and a face of a criminal. The 3D facial image is able to move in any direction under the fine-framework mode (Figure 18.9).

For the superimposition of the 3D and 2D facial images, the preliminary adjustment of the orientation of the 3D facial image to that of the 2D facial image is automatically carried out based on the matching of seven anthropometric points, that is, the left and right pupils, nasion, pronasale, stomion, and the left and right subaurale on both images. Then, the 3D facial image is exactly adjusted to match the orientation and size of the 2D facial image using the fine-framework mode. After the determination of the orientation and size of both images, the fine-framework mode of the 3D facial image is converted to the fine-texture image. The shape and positional relationships of facial components between the 3D and 2D facial images are examined by the fade-out or wipe-image mode (Figure 18.10).

In this system, fifteen anthropometric points are plotted on the 3D and 2D facial images using the mouse, and the relative locations of these points are used for evaluating the measurement data and the fit between the anthropometric points on the two images (Figure 18.11). If more points (for example those with special characteristics such as a mole or fleck) are required for the assessment of match, three optional points can be marked on both images. Depending on the orientation of the 2D facial image, up to 18 anthropometric points

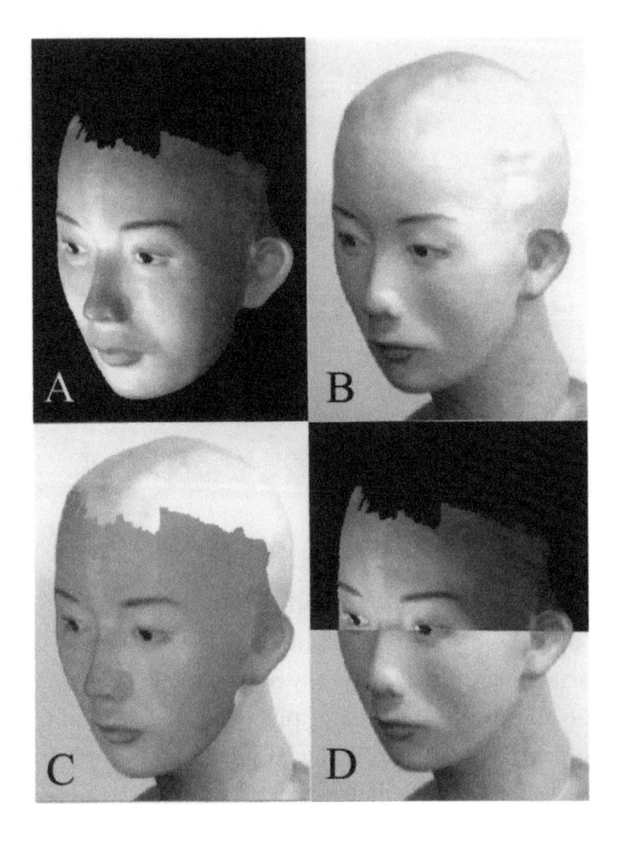

Figure 18.10

Face-to-face superimposition. (A) 3D facial image, (B) 2D facial image, (C) total mixing image of A and B, (D) horizontal wipe image. These superimposition images reveal a good match of the outline of the face, and of the shape and position of facial components such as the eyebrows, eyes, nose, lips, and ears.

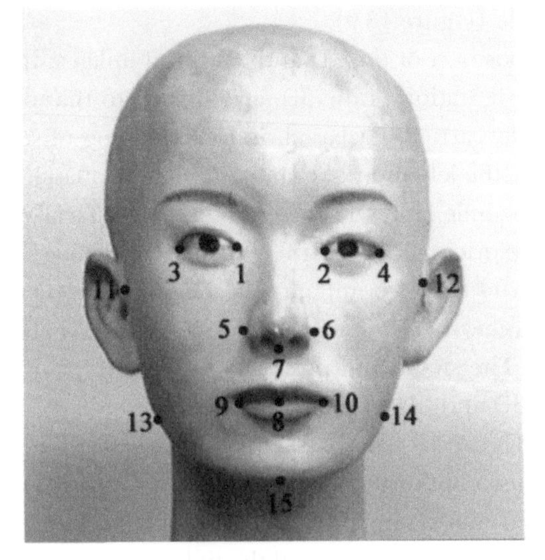

Figure 18.11

Fifteen anthropometric points used in this system. (1) right entocanthion, r-en; (2) left entocanthion, l-en; (3) right ectocanthion, r-ex; (4) left ectocanthion, l-ex; (5) right alare, r-al; (6) left alare, l-al; (7) subnasale, sn; (8) stomion, sto; (9) right cheilion, r-ch; (10) left cheilion, l-ch; (11) right zygion, r-zy; (12) left zygion, l-zy; (13) right gonion, r-go; (14) left gonion, l-go; (15) gnathion, gn.

can be selected. In Figure 18.12, sixteen anthropometric points, including three optional points (i.e., the left superaurale, subaurale, and tragion) are marked on the 3D and 2D facial images. The color of the selected points is yellow in the 3D facial image and red in the 2D one. The distance between

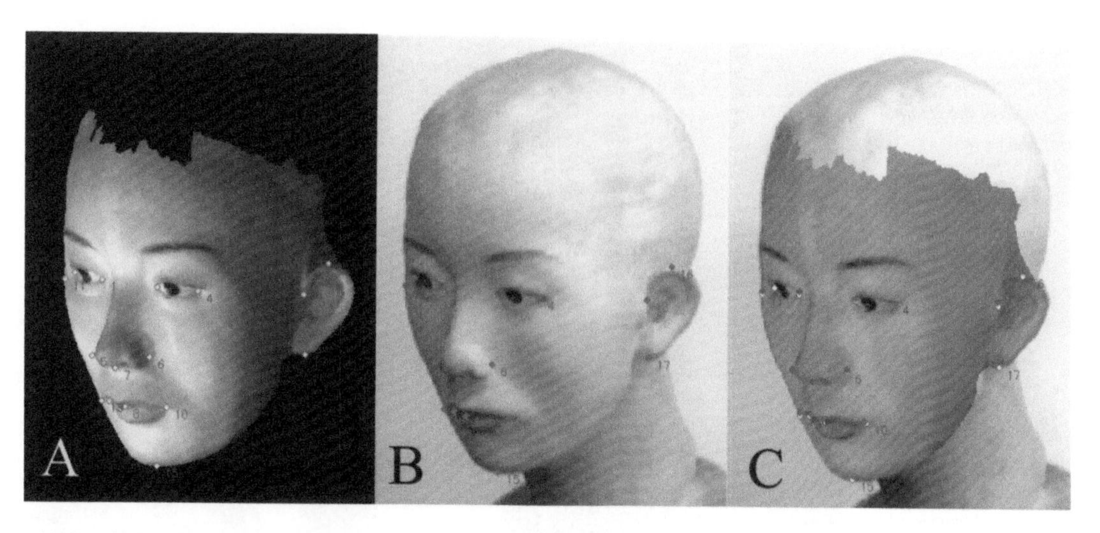

Figure 18.12 Anthropometric points on the 3D (A) and 2D (B) facial images. C shows the superimposition image of the selected points on the 3D and 2D facial images. Sixteen points including a standard point (sn) are very nearly consistent each other. (16) left superaurale, (17) left subaurale (18) left tragion.

Table 18.1

Anthropometric data for the 3D and 2D facial images in Figure 18.12.

Measurement		Distance (mm)		Measurement		Angle (degrees)	
Item	(No.)	3D	2D	Item	(No.)	3D	2D
en-en	(1-2)	32.0	32.0	en-sn-en	(1-7-2)	37.4	37.0
ex-ex	(3-4)	69.9	71.2	ex-sn-ex	(3-7-4)	71.1	71.4
al-al	(5-6)	30.9	30.4	al-sn-al	(5-7-6)	127.8	127.1
ch-ch	(9-10)	31.3	30.1	ch-sn-ch	(9-7-10)	59.2	62.8
sn-gn	(7-15)	57.6	55.7	ex-gn-ex	(3-15-4)	37.6	38.4
sto-gn	(8-15)	35.4	34.9	ch-gn-ch	(9-15-10)	46.6	46.4
sa-sba	(16–17)	52.0	51.7	zy-gn-sba	(11-15-17)	79.2	78.8

the selected two points and angle among the selected three points in both images are automatically measured (Table 18.1). The selected points on the 3D and 2D facial images are superimposed based on a standard point (stomion), and the reciprocal point-to-point differences between images are compared (Figure 18.12). The distance between the corresponding anthropometric points on both images is calculated from the coordinate values (Table 18.2). The image of each superimposition step and the measurement data shown on the display are recorded within the MO disk, and output using a color digital printer (PICTROGRAPHY 3000, Fujix, Japan).

18.4 EXPERIMENTAL STUDY

18.4.1 MATERIALS AND METHODS

The 3D facial data of 25 Japanese male examinees were obtained using the 3D physiognomic range finder. The 2D left oblique facial images of the examinees

Table 18.2

Reciprocal point-to-point difference between the 3D and 2D facial images in Figure 18.12.

Point	No.	Distance (mm)	Point	No.	Distance (mm)
r-en	1	1.8	r-ch	9	1.4
l-en	2	1.2	l-ch	10	1.4
r-ex	3	3.1	r-zy	11	1.8
l-ex	4	0	r-go	13	1.8
r-al	5	0.6	gn	15	1.9
l-al	6	1.2	l-sa	16	4.5
sn	7 (standard)	0	l-sba	17	4.3
sto	8	1.8	l-t	18	2.5
Mean: 1.8	SD: 1.2	Min: 0	Max: 4.5		

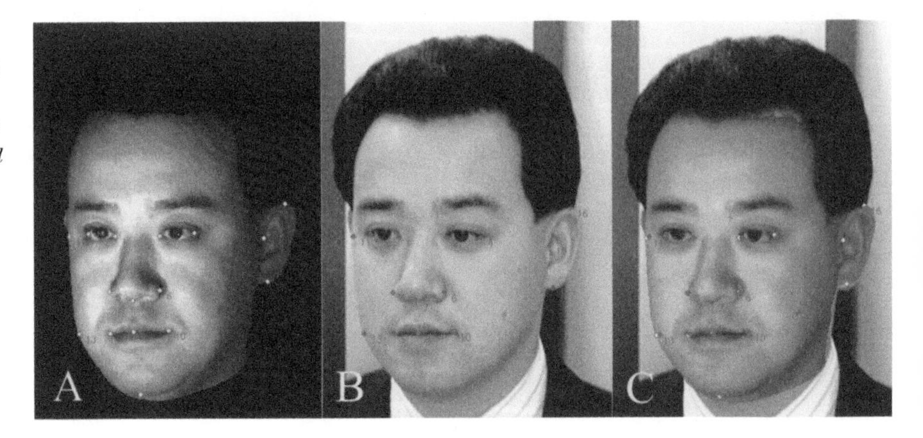

Figure 18.13

Superimposition of the selected anthropometric points on the 3D and 2D facial images. (A) 3D facial image, (B) 2D facial image, (C) superimposition image of A and B.

were taken with a digital still camera (Nikon® DS-505A, 50 mm F1.4) from a distance of about 2 meters.

For evaluating the match of the 3D and 2D facial images of the same person, the 3D facial image of each examinee was compared to the 2D facial image ten times, yielding 250 superimpositions. When comparing different people, the 3D facial images of 25 examinees were each compared to the 2D facial images of the other 24 examinees, yielding 600 superimpositions. As shown in Figure 18.13, altogether sixteen anthropometric points were used in this experimental study. The selected points were the original thirteen points with the exception of the right zygion and gonion and the optional three points in the left ear. The average distance obtained from sixteen reciprocal point-to-point differences between both images was used as a matching criterion.

18.4.2 RESULTS

The descriptive statistics for the average distance of the matching points between the 3D and 2D facial images of the same person in 25 examinees are shown in Table 18.3. The data showed that the measurements of the reciprocal point-to-point differences, including the errors introduced by the determination of the anthropometric points, were reproducible and reliable. Table 18.4

Examinee	*n*	Mean	SD	Min	Max (mm)	Examinee	*n*	Mean	SD	Min	Max (mm)
1	10	2.0	0.3	1.5	2.6	14	10	2.4	0.2	2.0	2.8
2	10	2.1	0.3	1.9	2.6	15	10	2.6	0.2	2.3	2.8
3	10	2.5	0.2	2.2	3.0	16	10	2.3	0.3	1.8	2.7
4	10	2.4	0.3	1.7	3.0	17	10	2.5	0.2	2.3	2.9
5	10	2.6	0.3	1.9	3.0	18	10	2.2	0.3	1.5	2.6
6	10	2.2	0.2	2.0	2.6	19	10	2.5	0.3	1.9	3.0
7	10	2.1	0.3	1.7	2.8	20	10	2.6	0.3	2.2	3.1
8	10	2.6	0.3	2.3	3.3	21	10	2.2	0.2	1.9	2.4
9	10	2.3	0.2	1.8	2.6	22	10	2.1	0.2	1.8	2.5
10	10	2.1	0.3	1.5	2.4	23	10	2.4	0.2	1.9	2.7
11	10	2.7	0.2	2.2	3.0	24	10	2.4	0.3	2.0	2.8
12	10	2.3	0.5	1.7	3.2	25	10	1.9	0.3	1.4	2.3
13	10	2.5	0.5	1.7	3.1						

Table 18.3

Descriptive statistics for the average distance of the reciprocal points between the 3D and 2D facial images of the same person in 25 examinees.

Superimposition image	*n*	Mean	SD	Min	Max (mm)
Same person	250	2.3	0.4	1.4	3.3
Different person	600	4.7	1.0	2.6	7.0

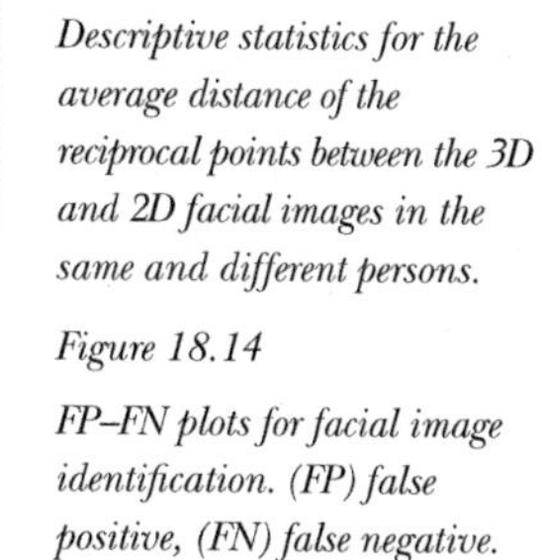

Table 18.4

Descriptive statistics for the average distance of the reciprocal points between the 3D and 2D facial images in the same and different persons.

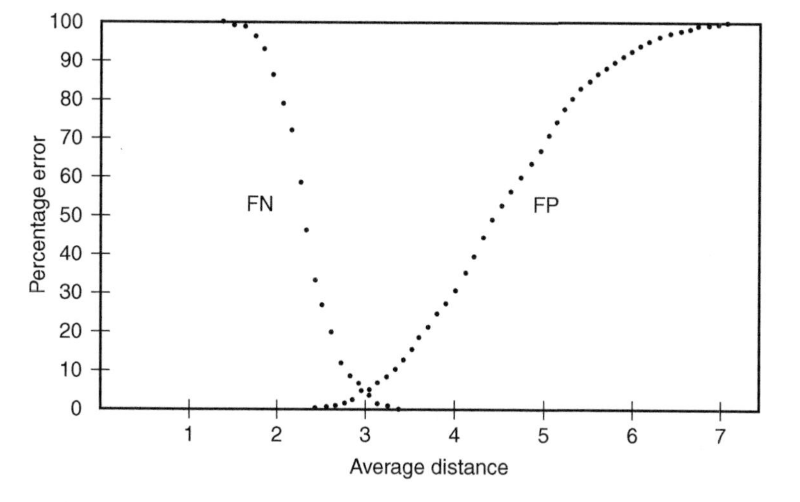

Figure 18.14

FP–FN plots for facial image identification. (FP) false positive, (FN) false negative. The average distance and percentage error at the FP–FN crossover point are 3.1 mm and 4.2%.

showed the descriptive statistics for the average distance in the superimposition of both the same and different persons. The average distance in the superimposition of the same person ranged from 1.4 to 3.3 mm, while the range of the average distance in superimposition of different persons was 2.6 to 7.0 mm. The mean value of the average distance was 2.3 mm for the same person and 4.7 mm for different persons, respectively. The difference of means between both cases was significant at the 0.001 level of confidence ($t = 37.8$, df $= 848$).

Plots of false positive (FP) and false negative (FN) identifications for the 3D and 2D facial images, based on the average distance, are shown in Figure 18.14.

Figure 18.15
The 2D facial image of the target person (No. 2 examinee).

Table 18.5
Assessment of the propriety of the threshold for identifying the 2D and 3D facial images (Target person: No. 2 examinee).

Examinee	Average distance	Examinee	Average distance
1	3.6	14	5.8
2	2.2	15	4.5
3	4.1	16	4.3
4	4.6	17	4.6
5	3.1	18	3.7
6	3.6	19	3.0
7	4.2	20	3.6
8	5.0	21	4.3
9	5.8	22	3.6
10	4.0	23	4.3
11	4.2	24	4.5
12	4.1	25	3.9
13	4.1		

The average distance and percentage error at the FP–FN crossover point were 3.1 mm and 4.2%. In this experimental study, false positives were not found where the average distance was 2.5 mm or less. Thus, in order to eliminate false identifications, the threshold of the average distance for a true positive match must be reduced to 2.5 mm.

18.4.3 MODEL CASE

To assess the validity of the threshold for true positives, a model case in which the 2D image of one examinee was identified from the 3D facial images of 25 examinees was experimentally investigated. An oblique facial image of No. 2 examinee, which was taken with the digital still camera at a distance of 5 meters, was used as the target person (Figure 18.15). The quality of the 2D facial image was average, to match the quality of images that have been submitted in actual cases. Table 18.5 shows the average distance in the superimposition image in

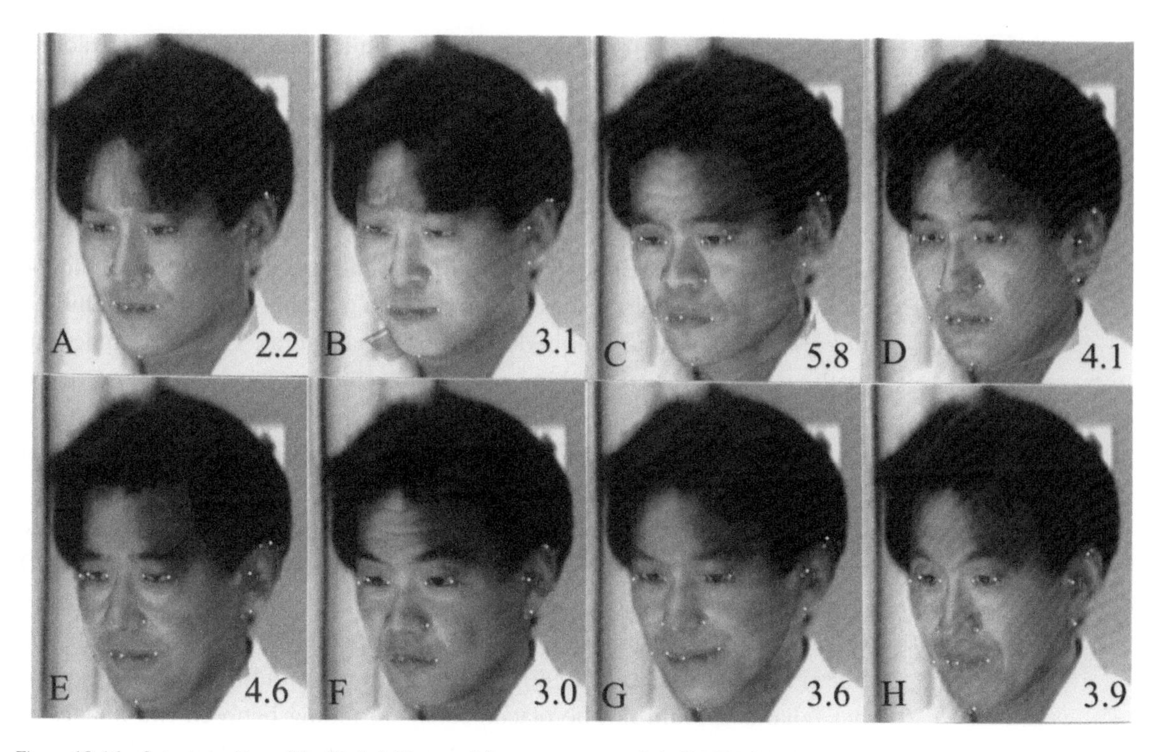

Figure 18.16 Superimposition of the 2D facial image of the target person and the 3D facial images of examinees. The average distance is shown in the lower right corner of each facial image. (A) No. 2, (B) No. 5, (C) No. 9, (D) No. 12, (E) No. 17, (F) No. 19, (G) No. 22, (H) No. 25.

25 examinees. Although three examinees (No. 2, No. 5, and No. 19), were included under the FP–FN crossover point, No. 2 examinee showed the average distance under the threshold for true positive (Table 18.5, Figure 18.16). Consequently, the 2D facial image of the target person was identified as No. 2 examinee with scientific certainty.

18.5 DISCUSSION

Facial image identification is carried out to determine whether or not a facial image at the scene of a crime is that of a suspect. Although morphological comparison of facial components is mainly used for identifying facial images in case work, the orientation of the criminal's facial image is different from that of the suspect's in almost all cases. Therefore, the examiner should consider any discrepancy in angulation when deciding whether the dissimilarity between facial components is real, or due to differences in orientation. In the latter case, the indices based on facial measurements cannot strictly be used as the indicator for comparing both images. The computer-assisted facial image identification system using the 3D physiognomic range finder was developed to solve the problems described above (Yoshino *et al.* 2000a). In this 3D range finder, the sinusoidal grating projection with the phase-shift method was incorporated into the measurement of the 3D morphology of faces (Ishiyama *et al.* 1999). The operation time for obtaining 3D physiognomic data was reduced by one quarter compared with that of the old system (Yoshino *et al.* 1996). Thus, it was suggested that the 3D physiognomic range finder could be applied to the suspect. In this 3D range finder, a wide facial view, including the ears, could be accomplished with two CCD cameras. This is advantageous for the comparison of facial images, because the ear is generally considered to be an important component for personal identification. Vanezis and Brierley (1996) also reported that the ear was a significant feature in 6 out of 11 positive identification cases in their casework.

Using the fade-out mechanism under the fine-framework mode of this system, the 3D facial image could be easily adjusted to the orientation of the 2D facial image. This process may be more precise and practical when compared with the video superimposition system developed by Majumudar and Shinha (1989) and Yoshino *et al.* (1996). However, Vanezis and Brierley (1996) stated that reliance should not be placed solely on fading between two images to assess a morphological match, because of the well-established observation that the human eye may be led from one image to another, blending the two together, and thus be left with the impression that there is a good match. As shown in the superimposition technique, the wipe mode was more suitable for detailed examinations for matching between two facial images because the components of each image could be clearly observed at the leading edge of the wipe. Moreover, in this system, the superimposition image of the anthropometric points on the 3D and 2D facial images could be expressed by computer-assisted processing. This finding, as well as the total mixing and wipe images, can be easily interpreted for lay people.

In this 3D range finder, the absolute range measurement could be obtained by the geometrical criteria between two cameras and one projector, giving the anthropometric analysis (Ishiyama *et al.* 1999). As shown in Table 18.1, the anthropological measurement of the 3D and 2D facial images could be quickly performed on the display with the mouse in operation, and their data was compared with each other. Catterick (1992) applied an image-processing system to recognize facial photographs using two indices calculated from three facial measurements of the midline of the face. He stated that the measurement data would objectively support morphological findings, although the discriminating power based on facial measurements would be limited. The anthropometric analysis would improve the reliability of facial identification in cases where the facial components such as eyes and eyebrows were hidden by sunglasses.

Bajnoczky and Kiralyfalvi (1995) used the difference between the coordinate values of 8–12 pairs of anthropometric points in both the skull and face for judging the match between the skull and facial images by the superimposition technique. They mentioned that their method is suitable for filtering out false positive identifications. In the present study, the average distance obtained from sixteen matching-point differences between the 3D and 2D facial images was used as the matching criterion. The average distance and percentage error at the FP–FN crossover point were 3.1 mm and 4.2%. Although it is a fundamental requirement of forensic science that an identification method yields extremely high true positive and true negative decisions it is also important that the method does not produce a high proportion of false positive identifications. As shown in the model case, two examinees were identified as false positive if the average distance at the FP–FN crossover point was used as the threshold. Considering this result and the above concept, the threshold of the average distance must be set under 2.5 mm to avoid false positive identifications. It was suggested that the facial image comparison using reciprocal-points matching was reliable when the threshold of the average distance was 2.5 mm.

In conclusion, this facial image identification system involving morphological comparison, anthropometric analysis, and reciprocal-points matching will provide accurate and reliable identification. In future, if several combined mathematical judgements including this matching criterion were introduced to facial image identification, then automatic retrieval and verification for the 3D facial image database of suspects could be performed effectively.

REFERENCES

Bajnoczky I. and Kiralyfalvi L. (1995) "A New Approach to Computer-Aided Comparison of Skull and Photograph", *Int. J. Legal Medicine* 108, 157–161.

Catterick T. (1992) "Facial Measurements as an Aid to Recognition", *Forensic Sci. Int.* 56, 23–27.

İşcan M. Y. (1993) "Introduction to Techniques for Photographic Comparison: Potential and Problems", Chapter 5 in: *Forensic Analysis of The Skull* (M. Y. İşcan and R. P. Helmer, eds.). Wiley-Liss, NY.

Ishiyama R., Sakamoto S., Kitano Y., Tong W. and Tajima J. (1999) "A Range Finder for Human Face Measurement", *Technical Report of Institute of Electronics, Information and Communication Engineers* PRMU99–24, 35–42 (in Japanese).

Kubota S., Matsuda H., Imaizumi K., Miyasaka S. and Yoshino M. (1997) "Anthropometric Measurement and Superimposition Technique for Facial Image Comparison Using

3D Morphologic Analysis", *Report of National Research Institute of Police Science* 50, 88–95 (in Japanese).

Linney A. and Coombes A. M. (1998) "Computer Modelling of Facial Form", Chapter 15 in: *Craniofacial Identification in Forensic Medicine* (J. G. Clement and D. L. Ranson, eds.). Arnold, London.

Majumudar T. and Shinha P. (1987) "Photographs of the Human Face and Broken Projective Symmetry", *J. Forensic Sci. Soc.* 29, 387–395.

Maples W. R. and Austin D. E. (1992) "Photo/Video Superimposition in Individual Identification of the Living", Presented at the *44th Annual Meeting of the American Academy of Forensic Sciences, New Orleans, Louisiana, February 17–22, 1992*.

Miyasaka S., Kubota S., Matsuda H., Imaizumi K., Yoshino M. and Seta S. (1995) "Anatomical Correlation Between Face Types and Facial Components, I. Anthropometrical Findings in Japanese Adult Males", *Report of National Research Institute of Police Science* 48, 159–170 (in Japanese).

Miyasaka S., Kubota S., Matsuda H., Imaizumi K. and Yoshino M. (1997) "Anatomical Correlation between Face Types and Facial Components, II. Morphological Findings in Japanese Adult Males", *Report of National Research Institute of Police Science* 50, 96–108 (in Japanese).

Proesmans M. and Van Gool L. (1998) "Getting Facial Features and Gestures in 3D", in: *Face Recognition* (H. Wechsler *et al.*, eds.). Springer, Berlin, pp. 288–309.

Vanezis P. and Brierley C. (1996) "Facial Image Comparison of Crime Suspects Using Video Superimposition", *Science and Justice* 36, 27–33.

Vanezis P., Lu D., Cockburn J., Gonzalez A., McCombe G., Trujillo O. and Vanezis M. (1996) "Morphological Classification of Facial Features in Adult Caucasian Males Based on an Assessment of Photographs of 50 Subjects", *J. Forensic Sci.* 41, 786–791.

Yoshino M., Kubota S., Matsuda H., Imaizumi K., Miyasaka S. and Seta S. (1996) "Face-to-Face Video Superimposition Using Three Dimensional Physiognomic Analysis", *Japanese J. Science and Technology for Identification* 1, 11–20.

Yoshino M., Matsuda H., Kubota S., Imaizumi K. and Miyasaka S. (2000a) "Computer-Assisted Facial Image Identification System Using a 3D Physiognomic Range Finder", *Forensic Sci. Int.* 109, 225–237.

Yoshino M., Matsuda H., Kubota S., Imaizumi K. and Miyasaka S. (2000b) "Assessment of Computer-Assisted Comparison between 3D and 2D Facial Images", *Japanese J. Science and Technology for Identification* 5, 9–15.

CHAPTER 19

A NEW RETRIEVAL SYSTEM USING A 3D FACIAL IMAGE DATABASE

Mineo Yoshino
First Forensic Science Division, National Research Institute of Police Science, 6-3-1, Kashiwanoha, Kashiwa, Chiba 277-0882, Japan

19.1 INTRODUCTION

Recently, a facial image identification system using both a 3D facial range finder "Fiore" (NEC Engineering, Japan) and a 2D/3D facial image superimposition method was developed (Yoshino *et al.* 2000). This system has proven to be a useful tool for facial image identification, because the superimposition of two facial images can be performed under the same facial orientation by rotating the 3D facial image, and the shape and positional relationships of their facial components can be compared to each other in the same condition. Furthermore, this system enabled morphometric matching using facial outlines and anatomical landmarks, giving objective results based on numerical data (Fraser *et al.* 2003, Yoshino *et al.* 2001, Yoshino *et al.* 2002). This facial identification system was set up for one-to-one comparison, not for one-to-many comparison. For one-to-many comparison, facial recognition systems have been developed and commercially released. These facial recognition systems are based on several different mathematical approaches such as statistical information methods (Howell 1999a, Moghaddan and Pentland 1998, Peacock *et al.* 2004, Poluton 1998, Zhao *et al.* 1998), graph matching (Howell 1999a, Wiskott *et al.* 1999, Wurts 1999), and neural networks (Gutta and Wechsler 1998, Howell 1999a,b, Pandya and Szabo 1999, Sinha 1998). Commercially available software packages are designed to verify a facial image of a known person belonging to a relatively small database of facial images, and are restricted to comparison of nearly frontal images of the face under the 2D image mode. Thus, it seems that these programs are not adequate for police investigation, because the facial image taken at the crime scene is not, in most cases, a frontal view. A possible exception to this is the use of passport photographs in illegal immigration cases. If a robust system for identifying facial images taken from severely disadvantageous angles is developed, the

3D facial images could be effectively used as a database. In this chapter, the author would like to propose a new database retrieval system using 3D facial images as a pilot study.

19.2 SOFTWARE PACKAGES

Two software packages were used for the new retrieval system for a database of 3D facial images. An essential prerequisite for matching a 2D facial image of a criminal taken at the scene of a crime to the 3D facial images in the database acquired by the police is that the orientation of the 3D facial images of all suspects can be adjusted to match that of the 2D facial image of the criminal. As the first step, a software package "3D-Rugle3 for Face-To-Face" (Medic Engineering, Kyoto, Japan) was designed for automatically adjusting the orientation of all 3D facial images in the database (Yoshino *et al.* 2003). Using this software, each 3D facial image taken with Fiore was approximately normalized in its orientation to the Frankfort horizontal plane, and then 14 anatomical landmarks were plotted on the 3D facial image (Figure 19.1). These images were stored in a host computer (Dell Precision 340, USA) as the 3D facial image database of model suspects. For the 2D facial image of the target person, the corresponding anatomical landmarks to the 3D facial image were also plotted (Figure 19.2). Some parameters such as rotation angle and facial size were calculated from the anatomical landmarks between the 2D and 3D facial images. According to the parameters, the facial orientation of each 3D facial image in the database was automatically adjusted to that of the

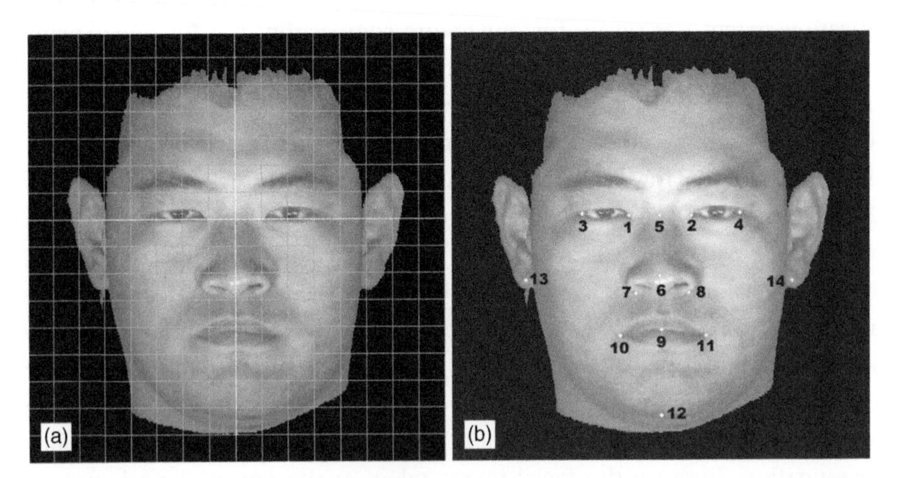

Figure 19.1 The normalized 3D facial image of (a) a model suspect and (b) 14 anatomical landmarks. (1) right entocanthion, (2) left entocanthion, (3) right ectocanthion, (4) left ectocanthion, (5) mid-point of both entocanthion, (6) pronasale, (7) lower point of right alare, (8) lower point of left alare, (9) stomion, (10) right cheilion, (11) left cheilion, (12) gnathion, (13) right ear lobe, (14) left ear lobe.

2D facial image of the target person. After the adjustment of the orientation of 3D facial images to common axes, superimpositions of single 2D (target person) to multiple 3D images (model suspects) from the database were made in batches of eight on the monitor (Figure 19.3). These images could be scrolled and converted to show the 3D image only (Figure 19.4). From the results of a total of 5000 superimpositions of the 2D facial images of 50 subjects that were compared automatically with the 3D facial images of 100 subjects, it is suggested that the software designed would be of practical application for the automatic adjustment of facial orientation in the 3D facial image database (Yoshino *et al.* 2003).

In the retrieval step, commercially available software "FaceList" (OMRON Co., Japan) was improved in its robustness against changes in facial orientation, and used to identify the facial image of the target person from the adjusted 3D facial images in the database. The adjusted 3D facial image is

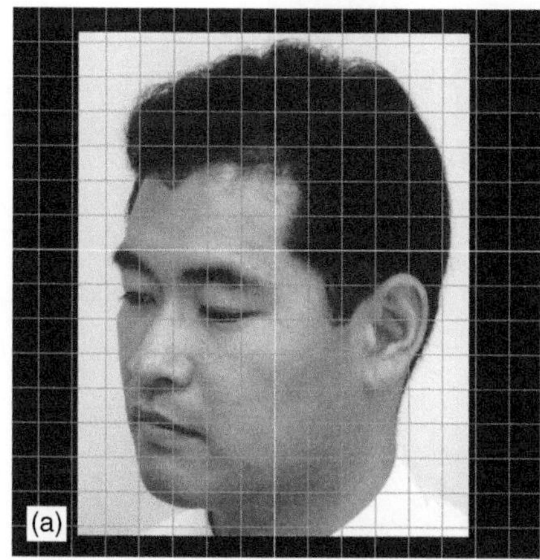

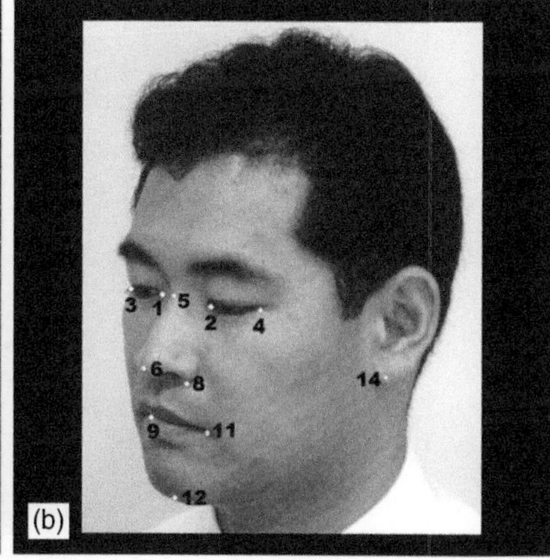

Figure 19.2

The 2D oblique image of (a) a target person and (b) the corresponding 11 visible anatomical landmarks to the 3D facial image.

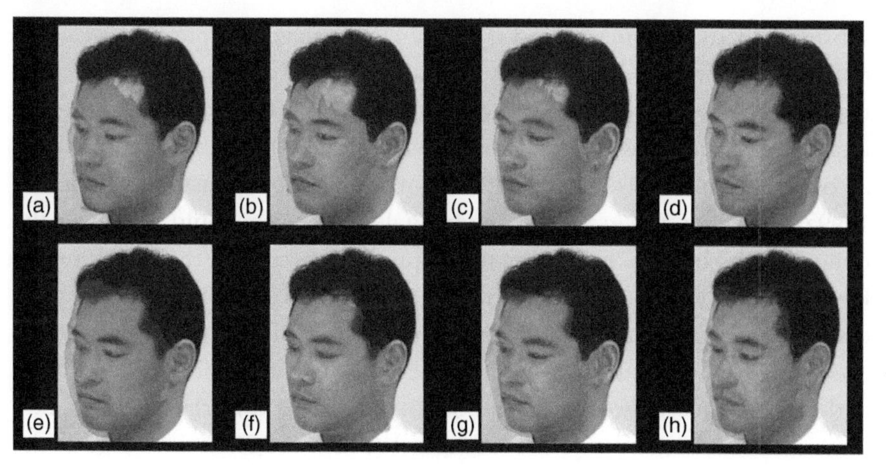

Figure 19.3

Superimposition images of the 2D facial image of the target person (subject No. 64) and adjusted 3D facial images of the database. (a) subject No. 61, (b) subject No. 62, (c) subject No. 63, (d) subject No. 64, (e) subject No. 65, (f) subject No. 66, (g) subject No. 67, (h) subject No. 68.

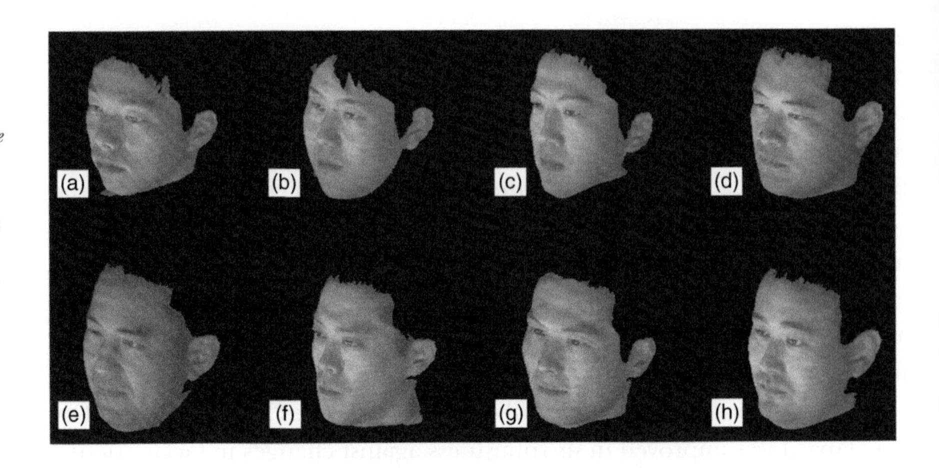

Figure 19.4

The 3D facial images of the database converted from Figure 19.3. These images are used for retrieving the database. (a) subject No. 61, (b) subject No. 62, (c) subject No. 63, (d) subject No. 64, (e) subject No. 65, (f) subject No. 66, (g) subject No. 67, (h) subject No. 68.

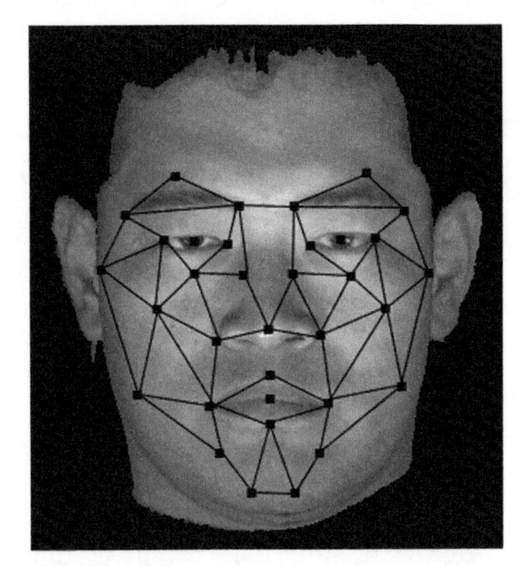

Figure 19.5

A scheme of the graph for detecting facial characteristics. The graph is composed of 50 nodes.

substantially the 2D image, and thus the facial image comparison is carried out in the 2D image mode. This software is based on the graph-matching method as shown in Figure 19.5. A coarse match of the graph onto the test image is firstly made with fixed parameters, followed by finer matching using a cost function to offset graph distortion against object distortion (Howell 1999a). However, the graph for the frontal facial image could not cover the oblique facial images. For correctly adapting the graph to the facial images taken from various angles, five different graphs for frontal, left oblique, right oblique, upward, and downward were set up. A suitable graph is selected according to the facial orientation of the subject. The graph has fifty nodes, and the distance between each node and the light and dark information around the node determine the similarity between the 2D facial image of the

Figure 19.6

The anatomical three points on the 2D facial image for correctly detecting the 3D facial images of the database.

criminal and adjusted 3D facial images of the database. In this software, in order to correctly detect the 3D facial images of the database, three anatomical points—that is, the left pupil, right pupil, and stomion—can be plotted on the 2D facial image of the criminal (Figure 19.6).

19.3 EVALUATION OF THE RETRIEVAL SYSTEM FOR THE 3D FACIAL IMAGE DATABASE

19.3.1 FACIAL IMAGE DATABASE SETS

As model suspects, the 3D facial data of 132 Japanese male adult subjects were obtained using "Fiore" and stored in the host computer. In order to test identification performance of the improved software FaceList, the 2D facial images which showed various angles were made from the 3D facial image of subject No. 64 by 3D-Rugle3 for Face-To-Face. The right oblique 2D images were obtained at every 10 degrees (10, 20, 30, 40, 50, 60 degrees) from the 3D facial image at the horizontal position (Figure 19.7). The downward 2D images were also obtained at every 10 degrees (10, 20, 30, 40, 50 degrees) from the 3D facial image at the frontal position (Figure 19.8). A total of 11 database sets, which consist of the adjusted 3D facial images of 132 subjects, were made by 3D-Rugle3 for Face-To-Face.

As ordinary 2D facial images of the target persons, a total of 110 2D facial images including the frontal (29 subjects), left oblique (60 subjects), and right

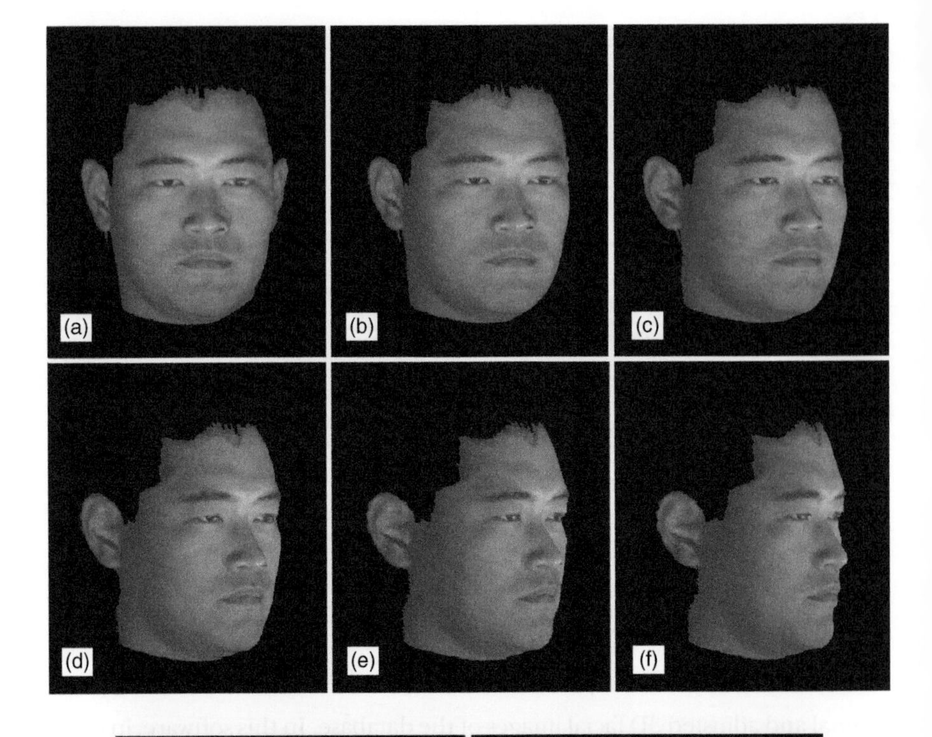

Figure 19.7

The right oblique 2D images obtained from the 3D facial image of subject No. 64. (a) 10°, (b) 20°, (c) 30°, (d) 40°, (e) 50°, (f) 60°.

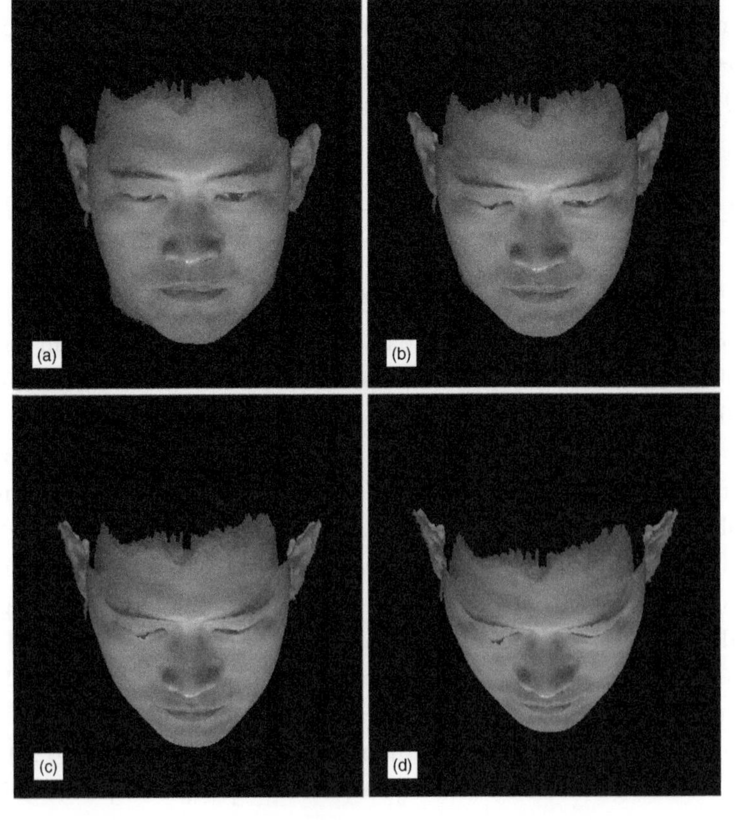

Figure 19.8

The downward 2D images obtained from the 3D facial image of subject No. 64. (a) 20°, (b) 30°, (c) 40°, (d) 50°.

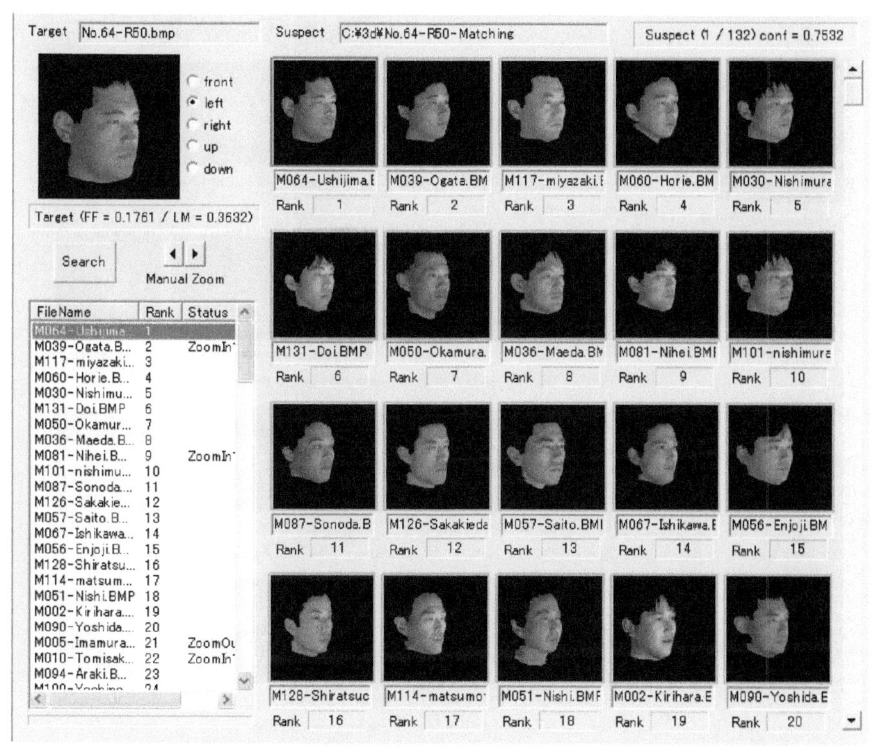

Figure 19.9

The 2D right oblique image with 50° of the target person—see Figure 19.7(e), the upper left corner—and the 3D facial images of the database. The 3D facial image of the target person is selected at the first rank in the database.

oblique (21 subjects) images were taken with a digital still camera (DSC-S70, SONY, Japan) from the 132 subjects under uncontrolled lighting conditions. A total of 110 database sets were made by 3D-Rugle3 for Face-To-Face and stored in the host computer (Yoshino *et al.* 2005).

19.3.2 COMPARING FACIAL IMAGES

Each 2D facial image obtained from the 3D facial image of subject No. 64 was compared to the adjusted 3D facial images of 132 subjects in each database set by FaceList. As shown in Figure 19.9, the 2D facial image of the target person is shown in the upper left corner of the retrieval result image. The 3D facial images of the database were ranked in batches of twenty and could be scrolled (Figure 19.9). The file name, rank, and status are shown in the lower left corner of the retrieval result image (Figure 19.9). In the right oblique images of subject No. 64, the 3D facial image of the target person could be selected at the first rank in the database at up to a 50° angle (Figure 19.9). However, in the right oblique image with 60° angle of subject No. 64, the 3D facial image of the target person ranked thirty-fourth in the database (Figure 19.10). In the downward images of subject No. 64, the 3D facial image of the target person ranked first in the database up to 40° angle (Figure 19.11).

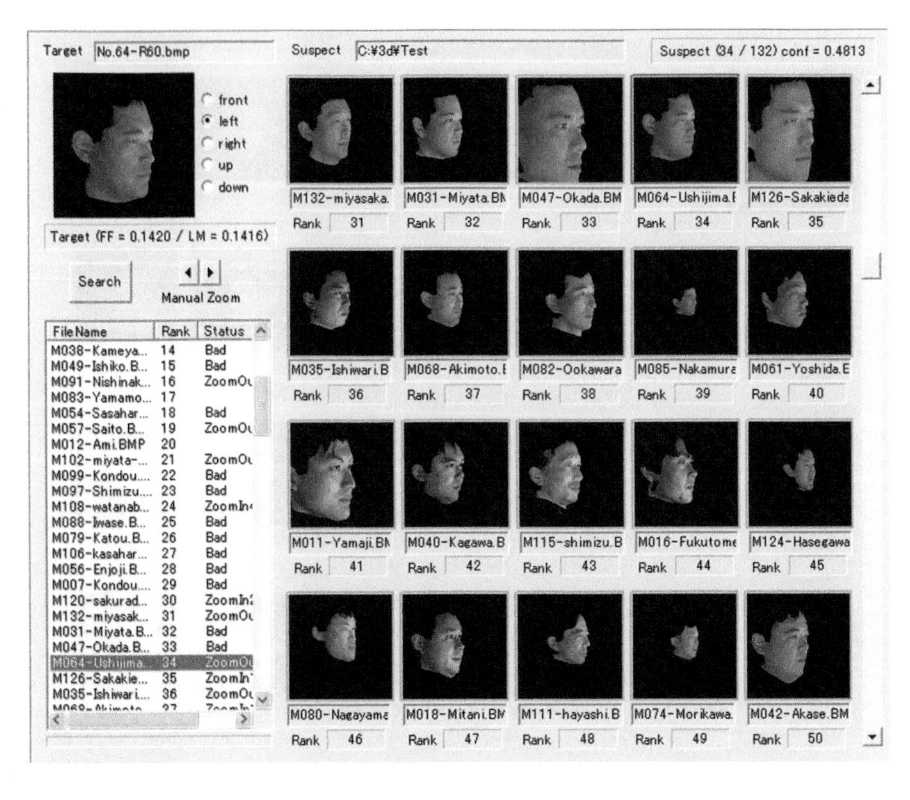

Figure 19.10

The 2D right oblique image with 60° of the target person—see Figure19.7(f), the upper left corner—and the 3D facial images of the database. The 3D facial image of the target person ranked thirty-fourth in the database.

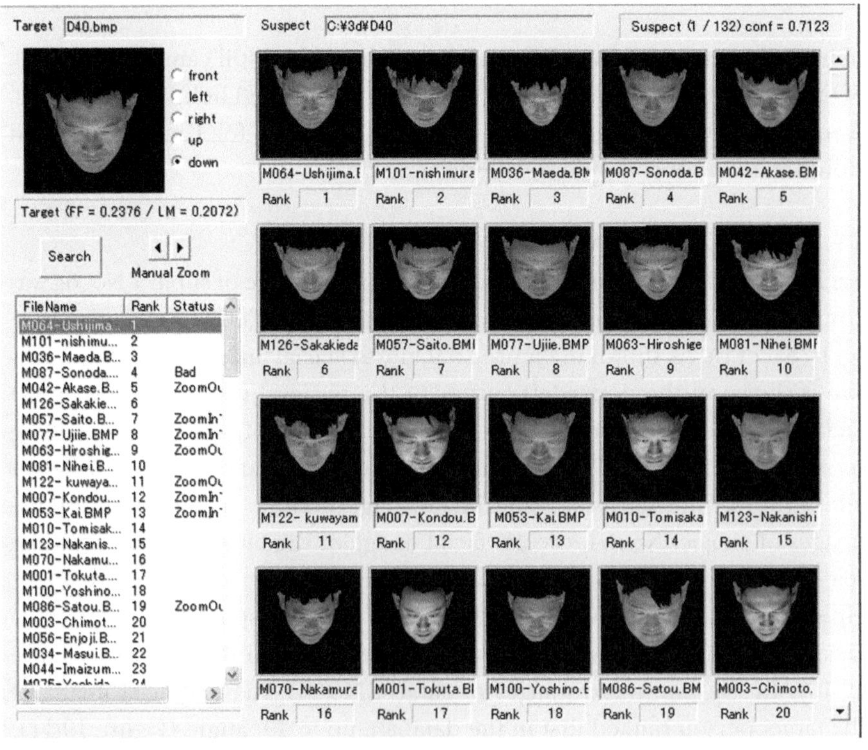

Figure 19.11

The 2D downward image with 40° of the target person—see Figure19.8(c), the upper left corner—and the 3D facial images of the database. The 3D facial image of the target person ranked first in the database.

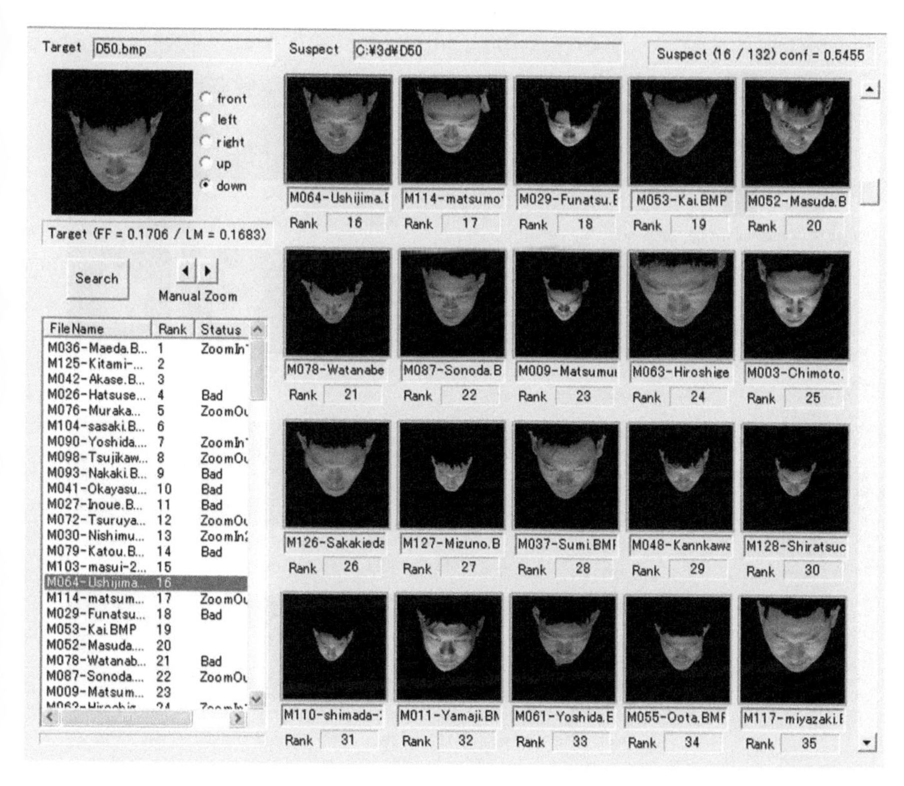

Figure 19.12

The 2D right oblique image with 50° of the target person—see Figure 19.8(d), the upper left corner—and the 3D facial images of the database. The 3D facial image of the target person ranked sixteenth in the database.

In contrast, in the downward image with 50° angle of subject No. 64, the 3D facial image of the target person ranked sixteenth in the database (Figure 19.12). As shown in Figures 19.10 and 19.12, the 3D facial images showing poor matching status increased in number at such severe angles. This result revealed that, with 60° of horizontal rotation and 50° angle of downward rotation, the graph did not suitably fit on the adjusted 3D facial image. According to the New York Times, 18 Oct. 1998, the local feature analysis which is a derivative of the eigenface method (principal-component analysis) could recognize an individual facing up to 35° away from the camera. Peacock (2004) mentioned that "Optasia" (Image Metrics plc, UK) based on a statistical information method could recognize an individual within 20° of a front-facing aspect. Considering these facts, it is suggested that FaceList has robustness against differences in facial image orientation. In particular, the robustness against the downward image is clear, and this software can be used effectively for identifying facial images of suspects because the surveillance cameras typically look down upon the scene.

Two examples of retrieval results image are shown in Figures 19.13 and 19.14. The facial images of the target person (subject No. 64) in these cases were taken with the digital still camera. In the frontal and left oblique images of the target person, the 3D facial image of subject No. 64 ranked first in the

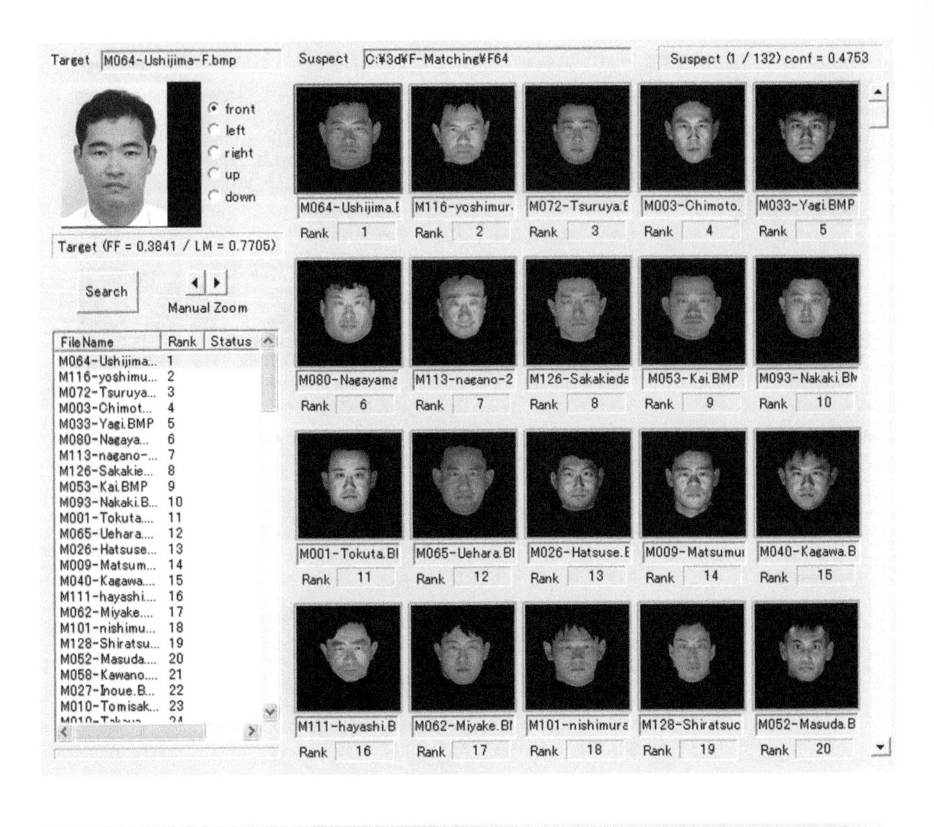

Figure 19.13

The 2D frontal image of the target person taken with the digital still camera (subject No. 64, the upper left corner) and the 3D facial images of the database. The 3D facial image of subject No. 64 ranked first in the database.

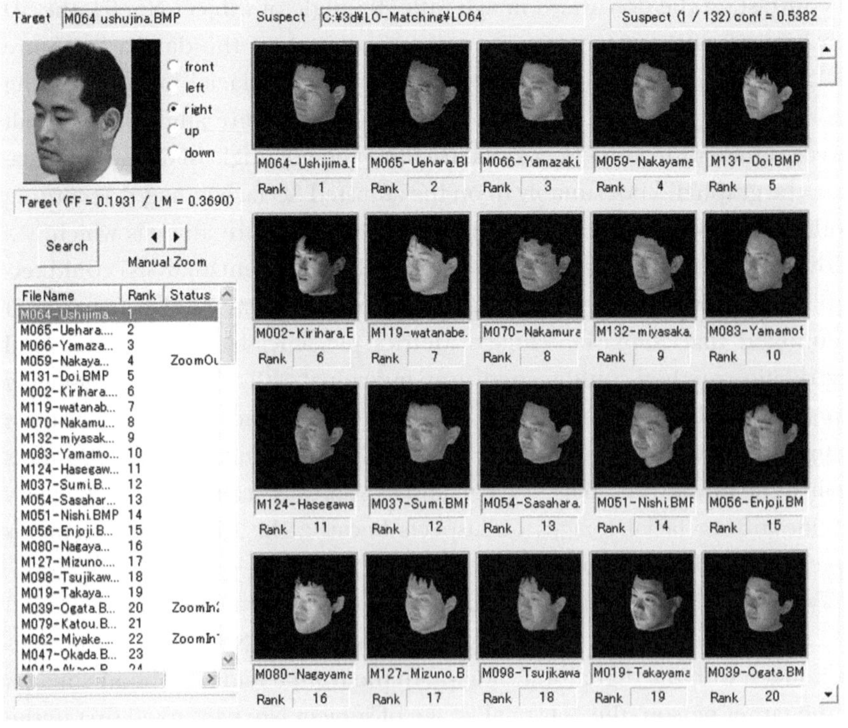

Figure 19.14

The 2D left oblique image of the target person taken with the digital still camera (subject No. 64, the upper left corner) and the 3D facial images of the database. The 3D facial image of subject No. 64 ranked first in the database.

database of 132 subjects. In our experimental study (Yoshino *et al.* 2005), the 3D facial image of the target person was selected as the first of the database in 28 out of 110 database sets (25.5%). The percentage of the first rank is 24.1% for frontal images, 26.7% for left oblique images, and 23.8% for right oblique images respectively. Wiskott *et al.* (1999) experimentally tested the performance of the graph-matching method for the facial image orientation. According to those workers, the first-rank recognition rates were 94% for 11° angle (108 Bochum database), 88% for 22° (108 Bochum database), and 18% for 45° (250 FERET database), respectively. They described that their basic system compensates for rotation in depth only in that matching is done with a bunch graph of the new view, and correspondences are defined between fiducial points of the new view and fiducial points of the standard view for which the model graphs are available. Our results might be caused by differences of the light and shade information around the node between the 2D facial image taken with the digital still camera and the 3D facial image taken with the facial range finder. Peacock *et al.* (2004) described that the key reason for the disappointing performance in automatic face recognition systems is that such systems are unable to handle adequately the various factors such as facial orientation, expression, lighting condition, image quality, and so on. From the results of feasibility tests, they mentioned that the recognition performance was most strongly affected by lighting conditions. In 75 out of 110 database sets (68.2%), the 3D facial image of the target person was ranked in the top 10 of the database (Yoshino *et al.* 2005). The percentage within the top 10 of the database was 75.9% for frontal images, 65.0% for the left oblique images, and 66.7% for the right oblique images, showing that the ranking performance in the frontal images was better than that in both oblique images. These results suggest that this system is inadequate for the identification level, but may be feasible as a screening method in a small database. Despite the performance of the new image retrieval system being less than the authors had anticipated, this pilot study has clearly shown that, with future development, it has the potential to become a useful technique for law enforcement and forensic science. In order to apply this system in a database to screen facial images of suspects, the ranking performance for the target person needs to be improved, and the technical problem with its application to the large database needs to be solved.

19.4 CONCLUSIONS

A new retrieval system for a 3D facial image database was proposed as a pilot study. This system has two steps, firstly to automatically adjust the orientation of all 3D facial images in a database to that of the 2D facial image of a target person, and then to identify the facial image of the target person from the adjusted 3D facial images in the database using a graph-matching method. From the experimental study, it was concluded that the software developed for the first step is applicable to the automatic adjustment of facial orientation in the 3D facial image database, and the modified software for the second step improved the robustness against the facial image taken with severely disadvantageous angles. The percentage within the top 10 of the database was about 70%, suggesting that this system may be feasible for screening methods in a small database. In this system, it is necessary to make the data set of adjusted 3D facial images for the 2D facial image of the target person prior to comparing the target person and each image of the database. In future, the 2D facial image of the target person will be directly compared to each 3D facial image of the database.

REFERENCES

Fraser N. L., Yoshino M., Imaizumi K., Blackwell S. A., Thomas C. D. L. and Clement J. G. (2003) "A Japanese Computer-Assisted Facial Identification System Successfully Identifies non-Japanese Faces", *Forensic Sci. Int.* 135, 122–128.

Gutta S. and Wechsler H. (1998) "Modular Forensic Architectures", in: *Face Recognition* (H. Wechsler *et al.*, eds.). Springer, Berlin, pp. 327–347.

Howell A. J. (1999a) "Introduction to Face Recognition", in: *Intelligent Biometric Techniques in Fingerprint and Face Recognition* (L. C. Jain *et al.*, eds.). CRC Press, Boca Raton, pp. 217–283.

Howell A. J. (1999b) "Face Unit Radial Basis Function Networks", in: *Intelligent Biometric Techniques in Fingerprint and Face Recognition* (L. C. Jain *et al.*, eds.). CRC Press, Boca Raton, pp. 317–334.

Moghaddan B. and Pentland A. (1998) "Beyond Linear Eigenspaces: Bayesian Matching for Face Recognition", in: *Face Recognition* (H. Wechsler *et al.*, eds.). Springer, Berlin, pp. 230–243.

Pandya A. S. and Szabo R. R. (1999) "Neural Networks for Face Recognition", in: *Intelligent Biometric Techniques in Fingerprint and Face Recognition* (L. C. Jain *et al.*, eds.). CRC Press, Boca Raton, pp. 287–314.

Peacock C., Goode A. and Brett A. (2004) "Automatic Forensic Face Recognition from Digital Images", *Science & Justice* 44, 29–34.

Poulton G. T. (1998) "Face Recognition Research at CSIRO", in: *Face Recognition* (H. Wechsler *et al.*, eds.). Springer, Berlin, pp. 599–609.

Sinha P. (1998) "A Symmetry Perceiving Adaptive Neural Network and Facial Image Recognition", *Forensic Sci. Int.* 98, 67–89.

Wiskott L., Fellous J. M., Kruger N. and von der Malsburg C. (1999) "Face Recognition by Elastic Bunch Graph Matching", in: *Intelligent Biometric Techniques in Fingerprint and Face Recognition* (L. C. Jain *et al.*, eds.). CRC Press, Boca Raton, pp. 355–396.

Wurts R. P. (1999) "Face Recognition from Correspondence Maps", in: *Intelligent Biometric Techniques in Fingerprint and Face Recognition* (L. C. Jain *et al.*, eds.). CRC Press, Boca Raton, pp. 337–353.

Yoshino M., Imaizumi K., Tanijiri T. and Clement J. G. (2003) "Automatic Adjustment of Facial Orientation in 3D Face Image Database", *Japanese J. Science and Technology for Identification* 8, 41–47.

Yoshino M., Matsuda H., Kubota S., Imaizumi K. and Miyasaka S. (2000) "Computer-Assisted Facial Image Identification System Using a 3-D Physiognomic Range Finder", *Forensic Sci. Int.* 109, 225–237.

Yoshino M., Noguchi K., Atsuchi M., Kubota S., Imaizumi K., Thomas C. D. L. and Clement J. C. (2001) "Evaluation of Morphometrical Matching in Face-to-Face Superimposition" *Program – The 7th Indo-Pacific Congress on Legal Medicine and Forensic Sciences*, Melbourne, September 2001. P. 206.

Yoshino M., Noguchi K., Atsuchi M., Kubota S., Imaizumi K., Thomas C. D. L. and Clement J. G. (2002) "Individual Identification of Disguised Faces by Morphometrical Matching", *Forensic Sci. Int.* 127, 97–103.

Yoshino M., Taniguchi M., Imaizumi K., Miyasaka S., Tanijiri T., Yano H., Thomas C. D. L. and Clement J. G. (2005) "A New Retrieval System for a Database of 3D Facial Images", *Forensic Sci. Int.* 148, 113–120.

Zhao W., Krishnaswamy A., Chellappa R., Swets D. L. and Weng J. (1998) "Discriminant Analysis of Principal Components for Face Recognition", in: *Face Recognition* (H. Wechsler *et al.*, eds.). Springer, Berlin, pp. 73–85.

AUTHOR INDEX

Page numbers for figures have suffix **f**, those for tables have suffix **t**

Printed and bound by CPI Group (UK) Ltd, Croydon, CR0 4YY

08/05/2025

01865022-0006